2019

苏州统计年鉴

SUZHOU STATISTICAL YEARBOOK

苏州市统计局
SUZHOU STATISTICS BUREAU
国家统计局苏州调查队 编
STATE STATISTICS BUREAU SUZHOU
INVESTIGATION TEAM

总期31期 NO:31

中国统计出版社
China Statistics Press

图书在版编目（ＣＩＰ）数据

苏州统计年鉴. 2019 / 苏州市统计局, 国家统计局苏州调查队编. -- 北京 : 中国统计出版社, 2019.9
ISBN 978-7-5037-8946-5

Ⅰ. ①苏… Ⅱ. ①苏… ②国… Ⅲ. ①统计资料－苏州－2019－年鉴 Ⅳ. ①C832.533-54

中国版本图书馆CIP数据核字(2019)第183089号

苏州统计年鉴-2019

作　　者 / 苏州市统计局 国家统计局苏州调查队
责任编辑 / 钟　钰
装帧设计 / 苏州市新彩视广告印务有限公司
出版发行 / 中国统计出版社有限公司
地　　址 / 北京市丰台区西三环南路甲6号
邮政编码 / 100073
电　　话 / 邮购（010）63376909 书店（010）68783171
网　　址 / http://csp.stats.gov.cn
印　　刷 / 苏州印刷总厂有限公司
经　　销 / 新华书店
开　　本 / 890mm×1240mm 1/16
字　　数 / 1400千字
印　　张 / 48印张
版　　别 / 2019年9月第1版
版　　次 / 2019年9月第1次印刷
定　　价 / 350.00元

本书附同版本CD-ROM一张，光盘内容以书面文字为准。
如有印装差错，由本社发行部调换。

《苏州统计年鉴—2019》编委会

《苏州统计年鉴—2019》编辑部

编　辑：苏州市统计局　国家统计局苏州调查队

出　版：中国统计出版社

印　刷：苏州印刷总厂有限公司

EDITORIAL BOARD

EDITORIAL DEPARTMENT

Edited By: Suzhou Statistics Bureau State Statistics Bureau Suzhou Investigation Team

Published By: China Statistics Press

Printed By: Suzhou General Printing House Co.,Ltd.

2018年的苏州 >>>

1072.17
年末常住总人口（万人）
Year-end Total Population
(10000 persons)

703.55
年末户籍总人口（万人）
Year-end Population
(10000 persons)

18597.47
地区生产总值（亿元）
Gross Domestic Product
(100 million yuan)

9450.20
第三产业增加值（亿元）
Added Value of Tertiary Industry
(100 million yuan)

33354.01
规模以上工业总产值（亿元）
Gross Industrial Output Value Above Designated Size (100 million yuan)

2119.99
一般公共预算收入（亿元）
General Public Budget Revenue
(100 million yuan)

4555.70
固定资产投资额（亿元）
Total Value of Investment In Fixed Assets
(100 million yuan)

5746.90
社会消费品零售总额（亿元）
Total Retail Sales of Consumer Goods
(100 million yuan)

3541.14
进出口总额（亿美元）
Total Exports and Imports
(USD 100 million)

2068.31
出口总额（亿美元）
Exports (USD 100 million)

45.25
实际使用外资（亿美元）
Amount of Foreign Capital Actually Used (USD 100 million)

28560.45
金融机构人民币存款余额（亿元）
Deposit Balance of Financial Institutions by Year End(100 million yuan)

26546.23
金融机构人民币贷款余额（亿元）
Loans Balance of Financial Institutions by Year End
(100 million yuan)

63481
城镇居民人均可支配收入（元）
Per Capita Disposable Income of Urban Households (yuan)

32420
农村居民人均可支配收入（元）
Per Capita Net Income of Rural Residents (yuan)

102.6
居民消费价格指数（以上年价格为100）
General Consumer Price Index of Urban Residents
(Preceding year is taken as 100)

经济发展 >>>

地区生产总值 (亿元)
Gross Domestic Product (100 millon yuan)

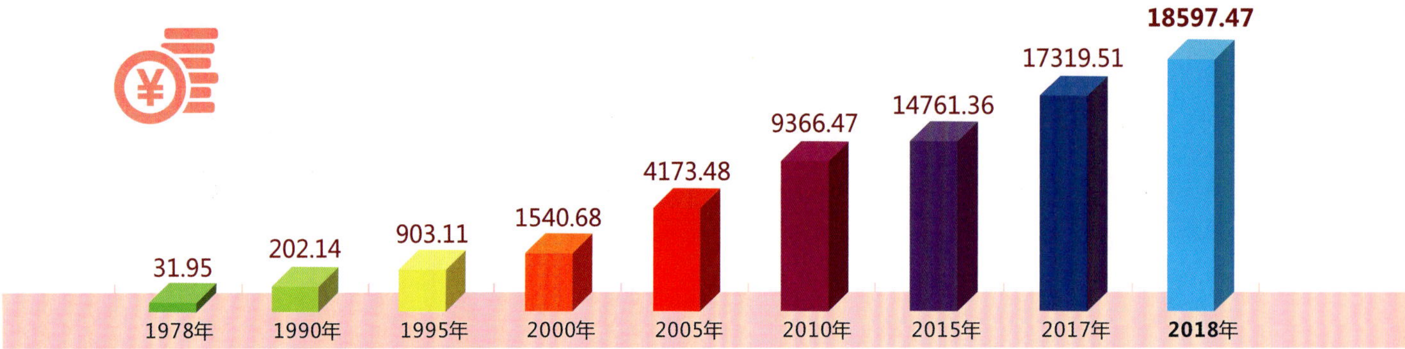

规模以上工业总产值 (亿元)
Gross Industrial Output Value Above Designated Size (100 millon yuan)

社会消费品零售总额 (亿元)
Total Retail Sales of Consumer Goods
(100 million yuan)

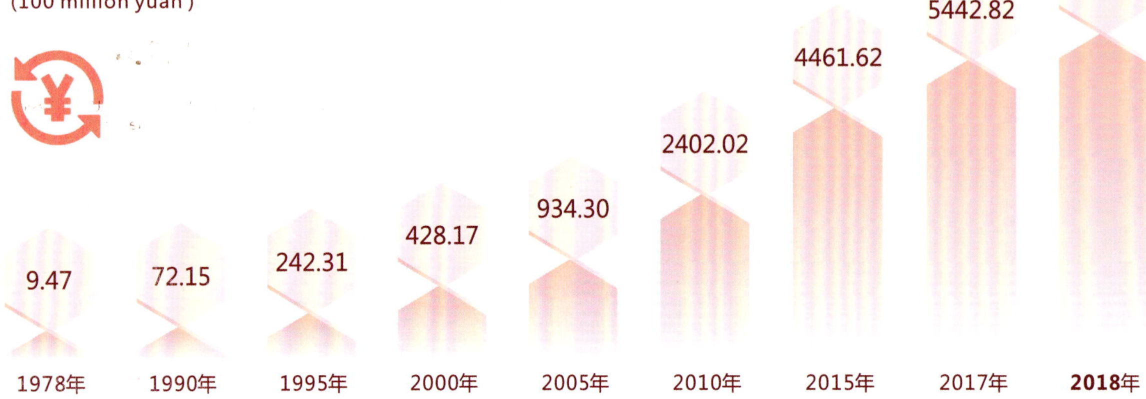

进出口总额（亿美元）
Total Imports and Exports (USD 100 millon)

	进出口总额
1990年	1.88
1995年	45.92
2000年	200.70
2005年	1405.89
2010年	2740.76
2015年	3053.50
2017年	3160.79
2018年	**3541.14**

出口总额（亿美元）
Exports (USD 100 millon)

	出口总额
1990年	1.55
1995年	23.35
2000年	104.81
2005年	727.75
2010年	1531.08
2015年	1814.59
2017年	1871.61
2018年	**2068.31**

一般公共预算收入（亿元）
General Public Budget Revenue (100 million yuan)

1998年	45.07
2000年	80.39
2005年	316.78
2010年	900.55
2015年	1560.76
2016年	1730.04
2017年	1908.10
2018年	**2119.99**

一般公共预算支出（亿元）
General Public Budget Expenditure (100 million yuan)

1998年	45.99
2000年	78.11
2005年	335.28
2010年	825.67
2015年	1527.17
2016年	1617.11
2017年	1771.47
2018年	**1952.71**

产业结构 >>>

地区生产总值构成（%）
Proportions in Gross Domestic Product (%)

100
地区生产总值
Gross Domestic Product

	1978年	1990年	2000年	2010年	2017年	**2018年**
第一产业 Primary Industry	28.1	17.3	5.9	1.5	1.2	**1.2**
第二产业 Secondary Industry	55.7	61.0	56.5	57.4	47.6	**48.0**
第三产业 Tertiary Industry	16.2	21.7	37.6	41.1	51.2	**50.8**

就业人口构成（%）
Composition of Employment Population (%)

100
就业人口
Employment Population

	1978年	1990年	2000年	2010年	2017年	**2018年**
第一产业 Primary Industry	62.3	29.7	21.0	3.8	3.3	**3.1**
第二产业 Secondary Industry	27.1	51.3	49.8	62.2	59.1	**58.6**
第三产业 Tertiary Industry	10.6	19.0	29.2	34.0	37.6	**38.3**

	2014年	2015年	2016年	2017年	**2018年**
新兴产业产值占规模以上工业总产值比重（%）The Proportion of the Emerging Industries in the Gross Output Value of the Industrial Above Designated Size (%)	47.5	48.7	49.8	50.8	**52.4**
高端装备制造业产值占规模以上工业总产值比重（%）The Proportion of High-end Equipment Manufacturing Industrial in the Gross Output Value of the Industries Above Designated Size (%)	10.2	10.6	11.2	11.1	**11.8**

服务业投资占固定资产投资比重（%）

The Percentage of the Service Industry Investment in the Fixed Assets Investment (%)

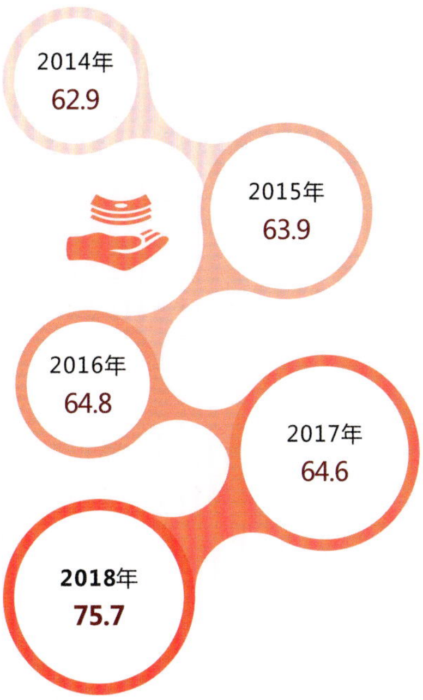

民间投资占固定资产投资比重（%）

The Percentage of the Private Investment in the Fixed Assets Investment (%)

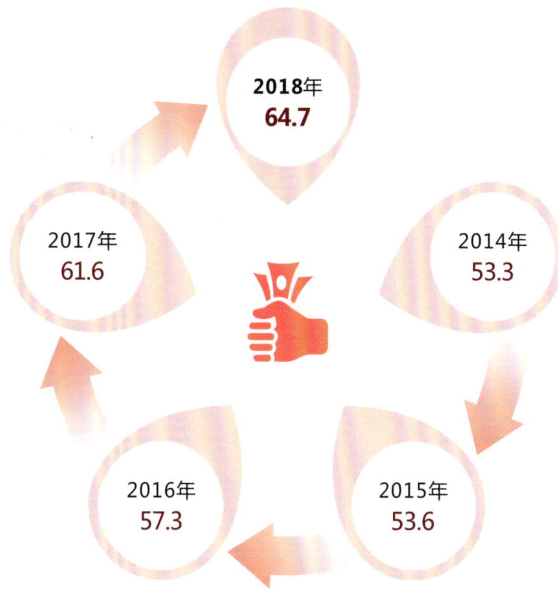

高新技术产业投资占工业投资比重（%）

The Percentage of Hi-Tech Manufacturing Industry Investment in the Industrial Investment (%)

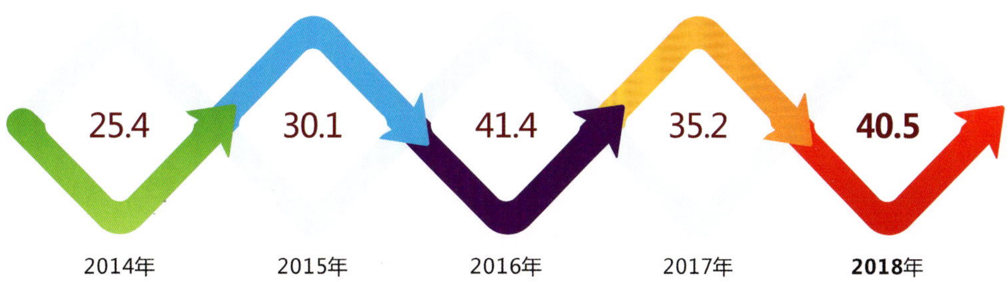

创新驱动 >>>

年份	发明专利申请量（件） Applications Examined of Inventions (unit)	发明专利授权量（件） Applications Granted of Inventions (unit)
1995年	47	41
2000年	224	32
2005年	988	148
2010年	12935	1370
2015年	43241	10488
2017年	45768	11618
2018年	**50116**	**10845**

年末万人有效发明专利拥有量（件）

Effective Invention Patent Ownership Per 10000 Persons by Yeay End (unit)

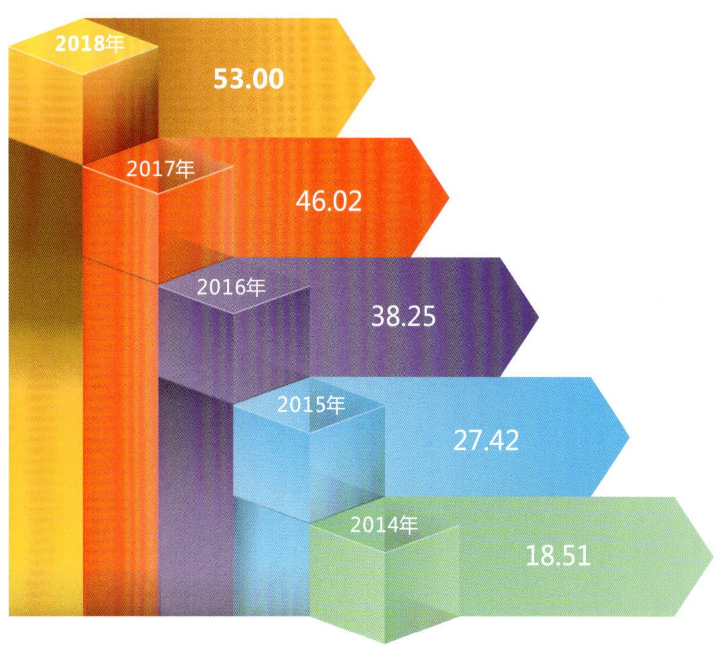

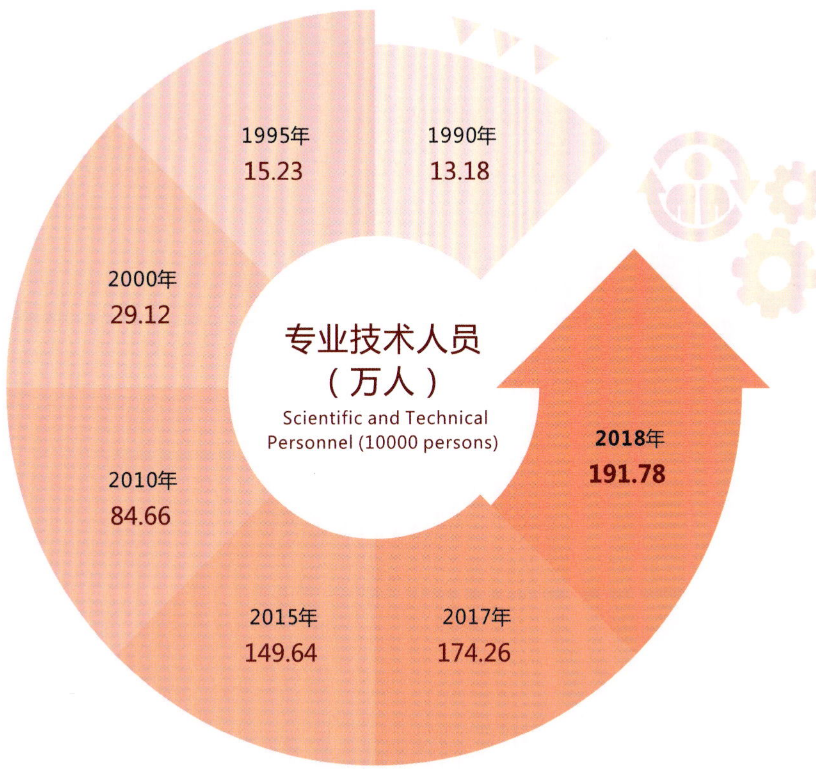

人才数量（人）
Number of Talents (person)

	2014年	2015年	2016年	2017年	**2018年**
国家级重大人才引进工程人才数 Number of Talents in the National Level Talent Introduction Project	157	187	219	237	**250**
省"双创人才"人数 Talents of the Introduction of High-level Innovation and Entrepreneurship Program of Jiangsu Province	501	579	683	782	**873**
市"姑苏领军人才计划"人才数 Talents of the City of Suzhou Leading Talent Plan	606	741	866	1012	**1206**

创新驱动 >>>

科技进步贡献率（%）

The Contribution Rate of Scientific and Technological Progress (%)

2014年 61.1

2015年 62.0

2016年 62.9

2017年 63.7

2018年 64.5

规模以上工业企业研发经费投入（亿元）

Expenditures on Research and Development of Above-Scale Industrial Enterprises (100 million yuan)

2014年 318.02

2015年 336.83

2016年 361.50

2017年 393.43

2018年 518.05

每万劳动力中高技能人才（人）
Highly Skilled Talents Per 10000 Labor Forces (person)

2014年	2015年	2016年	2017年	**2018年**
672	711	758	793	**833**

指标	2014年末	2015年末	2016年末	2017年末	**2018年末**
人才总量（万人） Total Talents (10000 persons)	212.04	228.13	244.21	260.01	**276.48**
高层次人才（万人） High-level Talents (10000 persons)	15.53	17.80	20.05	22.30	**24.49**
高技能人才（万人） Highly Skilled (10000 persons)	46.63	49.19	52.43	54.87	**57.68**
省级以上工程技术研究中心（家） Engineering Technology Centers at or above The Provincial Level (unit)	524	585	625	677	**732**
省级以上企业技术中心（家） Enterprise Technology Centers at or above The Provincial Level (unit)	285	327	381	447	**505**
省级以上工程中心（实验室）（家） Engineering Centers (Laboratories) at or above The Provincial Level (unit)	47	57	68	79	**90**

民生发展 >>>

普通高等学校在校学生数（万人）
Number of Students in Regular Higher Education Institutions (10000 persons)

2013年	2014年	2015年	2016年	2017年	**2018年**
20.19	20.95	21.48	21.93	22.28	**23.56**

	2018年
各类学校数（所） Number of Schools of Various Types (unit)	**799**
在校学生数（万人） Number of Students Enrollment (10000 persons)	**146.42**
高等教育毛入学率（%） Gross Eurollment Rate of Higher Education (%)	**69.1**

	2014年	2015年	2016年	2017年	**2018年**
每千人拥有卫生机构床位数（张） Number of Beds in Health Institutions Per 1000 Persons (unit)	5.21	5.59	5.94	6.24	**6.43**
每千人拥有医院床位数（张） Number of Hospital Beds Per 1000 Persons (unit)	4.61	4.97	5.32	5.25	**5.41**
每千人拥有医生数（人） Number of Doctors Per 1000 Persons (person)	2.39	2.47	2.60	2.83	**3.06**
每千人拥有注册护士数（人） Number of Professional Nurses Per 1000 Persons (person)	2.39	2.66	2.88	3.23	**3.51**

2018年

市民体质监测合格率（%）
Qualification Rate of Citizens' Physical Fitness Monitoring (%)
95.7

75.9
城乡公共服务支出占一般公共预算支出的比重（%）
The Percentage of the Urban and Rural Public Service Expenditures in the General Public Budget Expenditures (%)

职工最低工资标准（元/月）
Minimum Wage Standard for Emplyees (yuan/month)
2020

945
城乡居民最低生活保障标准（元/月）
Standards of Subsistence Allowances for Urban and Rural Residents (yuan/month)

2018年

2018年
17.55
新增就业（万人）
New Employment (10000 persons)

城镇登记失业率（%）
Urban Registered Unemployment Rate (%)
2018年
1.78

2018年
98.70
苏州籍应届高校毕业生就业率（%）
Employment Rate of New Colloge Graduates with Suzhou as Their Native Place (%)

民生发展 >>>

2018年

城镇常住居民人均可支配收入(元)
Per Capita Disposable Income of the Urban Residents (yuan)

63481 总平均 Average

20%低收入户 Low Income House-holds	28819
20%中低收入户 Lower Middle Income House-holds	43587
20%中等收入户 Middle Income House-holds	55486
20%中高收入户 Upper Middle Income House-holds	72843
20%高收入户 High Income House-holds	139797

农村常住居民人均可支配收入(元)
Per Capita Disposable Income of the Rural Residents (yuan)

32420 总平均 Average

20%低收入户 Low Income House-holds	14543
20%中低收入户 Lower Middle Income House-holds	21973
20%中等收入户 Middle Income House-holds	27800
20%中高收入户 Upper Middle Income House-holds	35867
20%高收入户 High Income House-holds	66728

37403

城镇常住居民人均生活消费支出（元）
Per Capita Consumer Spending of the Urban Residents (yuan)

项目	城镇	农村
食品烟酒 Food, Alcoholic Drinks and Tobacco	9406	5443
衣着 Clothing	2120	1169
居住 Residence	9306	5258
生活用品及服务 Daily Necessities and Services	1965	1229
交通通信 Transportation and Communication	6153	3870
教育文化娱乐 Education, Culture and Entertainment	5703	2589
医疗保健 Healthcare	1776	1500
其他用品及服务 Other Supplies and Services	975	528

21587

农村常住居民人均生活消费支出（元）
Per Capita Consumer Spending of the Rural Residents (yuan)

57.87
节能环保支出
Energy Saving and Environmental Protection Spending
108.10
农林水支出
Agricultural, Forestry and Water Affairs Spending
112.89
医疗卫生与计划生育支出
Expenditure for Medicine and Public Health
185.46
社会保障和就业支出
Social Security and Employment
152.28
科学技术支出
Science and Technology Spending
48.88
文化体育与传媒支出
Culture, Sports and the Media
312.95
教育支出
Expenditure for Operating Expenses of Education
64.96
交通运输支出
Transportation Spending
2018年一般公共预算支出
1952.71亿元
General Public Budget Expenditure (100 million yuan)

民生发展 >>>

	1985年	1990年	1995年	2000年	2005年	2010年	2015年	2017年	**2018年**
城镇居民人均可支配收入（元） Per Capita Disposable Income of Urban Households (yuan)	918	2150	5790	9274	16276	29219	50390	58806	**63481**
城乡收入比（农村=1） Income Ratio Between Urban and Rural Areas (rural=1)	1.24	1.29	1.30	1.70	1.94	1.99	1.97	1.96	**1.96**
农村居民人均可支配收入（元） Per Capita Disposable Income of Rural Residents (yuan)	739	1664	4444	5462	8393	14657	25580	29977	**32420**

在岗职工平均工资（元）
Average Wages of Staff and Workers (yuan)

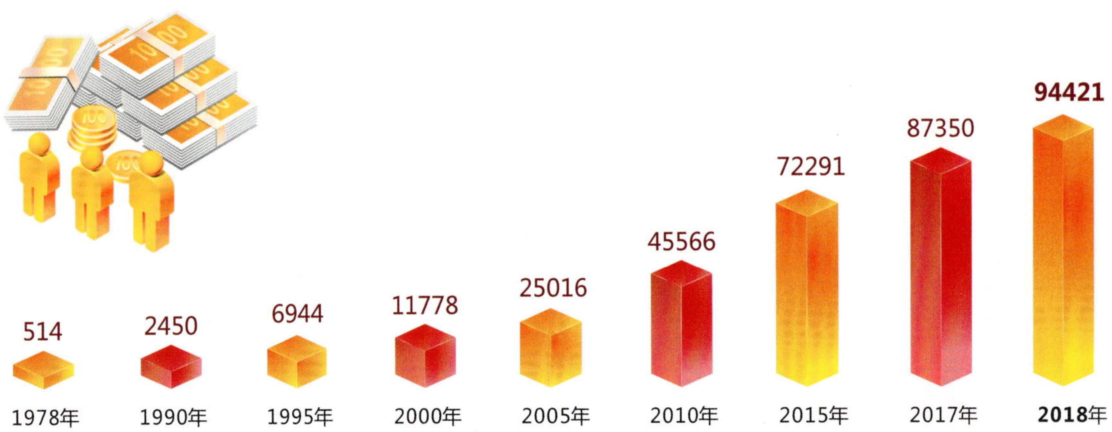

市区居民消费价格总指数（以上年价格为100）
General Consumer Price Index of Urban Residents (Preceding Year is Taken as 100)

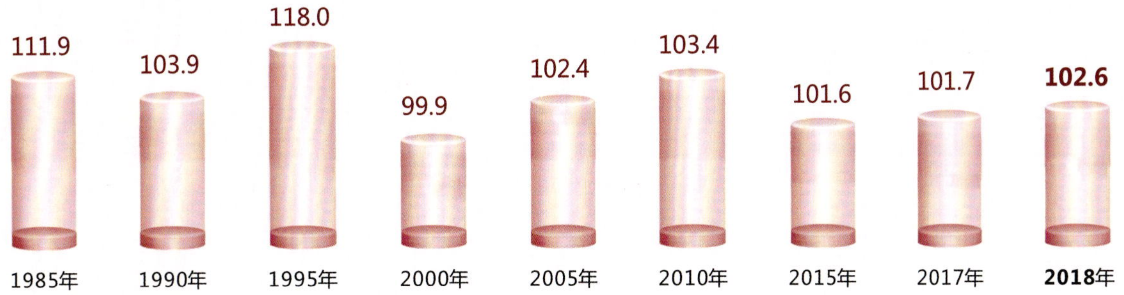

参加社会保险人数（万人）
Number of People Covered by Social Insurance (10000 persons)

	2014年	2015年	2016年	2017年	**2018年**
基本养老保险参保人数 Number of People Covered by Endowment Insurance	506.06	511.57	520.68	548.63	**575.83**
基本医疗保险参保人数 Number of People Covered by Medical Insurance	593.94	611.72	635.09	688.31	**737.08**
失业保险参保人数 Number of People Covered by Unemployment Insurance	400.93	423.54	446.62	464.57	**505.02**
工伤保险参保人数 Number of People Covered by Work Injury Insurance	418.88	426.25	439.30	473.26	**512.23**
生育保险参保人数 Number of People Covered by Childbirth Insurance	431.99	437.26	450.76	490.35	**529.13**

环境保护 >>>

	2014年	2015年	2016年	2017年	2018年
城镇污水处理率（%） Treatment Rate of Sewage in town (%)	95.03	95.26	95.08	95.45	**95.79**
生活垃圾无害化处理量 (万吨) Volume of No Harm Disposal of Garbage (10000 tons)	355.90	383.82	427.41	481.18	**325.56**
建成区绿化覆盖率（%） Coverage Rate of Green Areas in Developed Areas (%)	42.93	43.08	42.66	42.15	**42.27**
人均公园绿地面积(平方米) Per Capita Park Green Areas (sq.m)	15.36	15.31	15.01	14.40	**13.72**
单位GDP化学需氧量排放强度(千克/万元) Chemical Oxygen Demand Emission Intensity Per GDP (kg/10000 yuan)	0.57	0.47	0.42	0.36	**0.34**
单位GDP二氧化硫排放强度(千克/万元) Sulfur Dioxide Emission Intensity Per GDP (kg/10000 yuan)	1.25	1.04	0.87	0.71	**0.65**
单位GDP氨氮排放强度(千克/万元) Ammonia Nitrogen Emission Intensity Per GDP (kg/10000 yuan)	0.11	0.10	0.09	0.07	**0.07**
单位GDP氮氧化物排放强度(千克/万元) Nitrogen Oxide Emission Intensity Per GDP (kg/10000 yuan)	1.73	1.37	1.21	1.05	**0.92**
市区空气质量优良天数比例(%) In the Urban Areas the Proportion of Days With Good Air Quality (%)	63.6	66.9	69.0	71.5	**73.7**

规模以上工业六大高能耗行业
Six High Energy Consumption Industry Above Designated Size

六大高能耗行业综合能耗占规模以上工业企业综合能耗比重（%）
The Proportion of Comprehensive Energy Consumption of Six High Energy Consumption Industry Accounted for Industry Above Designated Size （%）

行业 Industry	2014年	2015年	2016年	2017年	**2018年**
非金属矿物制品业 Nonmetal Mineral Products	2.6	2.1	1.5	1.5	**1.7**
黑色金属冶炼和压延加工业 Smelting and Pressing of Ferrous Metals	33.2	34.1	33.9	34.6	**33.8**
电力、热力生产和供应业 Production and Supply of Electricity and Thermal Power	29.3	28.6	28.7	27.9	**29.4**
纺织业 Textile Industry	5.8	5.8	5.8	5.5	**5.3**
造纸和纸制品业 Papermaking and Paper Products	5.3	5.3	5.3	5.1	**4.9**
化学原料和化学制品制造业 Raw Chemical Materials and Chemical Products	6.7	6.9	7.6	7.8	**7.0**

六大高能耗行业综合能耗占规模以上工业企业综合能耗比重（%）
The Proportion of Comprehensive Energy Consumption of Six High Energy Consumption ndustry Accounted for Industry Above Designated Size （%）

2014年	2015年	2016年	2017年	**2018年**
82.9	82.8	82.8	82.4	82.0

市政建设 >>>

	2014年末	2015年末	2016年末	2017年末	**2018年末**
建成区面积（平方公里） Build Up Area (sq.km)	735.15	747.84	733.39	751.23	**756.20**
城市实有道路长度（公里） Length of Roads of Urban Civil (km)	5977	6109	9373	10263	**9994**

	2014年末	2015年末	2016年末	2017年末	**2018年末**
公共汽车营运车辆（辆） Operating Bus Routes (coach)	6948	7355	7710	8303	**8780**
公共汽车营运线路总长度（公里） Length of Bus Routes (km)	12187	12561	13002	14444	**14658**

	2014年	2015年	2016年	2017年	**2018年**
公共汽车客运总量（万人次） Number of Passengers Carried By Bus (10000 person-times)	95708	95717	87698	89180	**85420**

公共自行车租赁点(个)
Public Bicycle Rental Point (unit)

2014年	2015年	2016年	2017年	**2018年**
2794	3227	3691	4306	**4999**

公共自行车累计投入车辆（辆）
Total Number of Public Bicycle (coach)

2014年	2015年	2016年	2017年	**2018年**
68525	75985	89686	100662	**122712**

出租车运营车辆（辆）
Operating Vehicles (coach)

2014年	2015年	2016年	2017年	**2018年**
8988	9018	9018	9018	**9018**

出租车客运总量（万人次）
Number of Passengers Carried by Taxi (10000 person-times)

2014年	2015年	2016年	2017年	**2018年**
23992	22814	19256	16271	**13541**

市政建设 >>>

	2014年	2015年	2016年	2017年	**2018年**
供水总量（万立方米） Total Volume of Water Supply (10000 cu.m)	105978	108649	112829	107861	**114613**
天然气供气总量（万立方米） Total Natural Gas Supply (10000 cu.m)	284811	273861	279408	283181	**292732**

		2015年	2016年	2017年	**2018年**
运营车辆（辆） The Number of Operating Vehicles(coach)	地铁 Metro	215	320	592	**608**
	有轨电车 Tram	90	90	90	**207**
营运线路总长度 (公里) Total Length of Light Rail Transit Operating Routes (km)	地铁 Metro	52.3	67.9	120.7	**120.7**
	有轨电车 Tram	17.8	17.8	17.8	**28.9**
客运量 (万人次) Number of Passengers Carried By Light Rail (10000 person-times)	地铁 Metro	13633	14851	24570	**32414**
	有轨电车 Tram	148	206	272	**391**

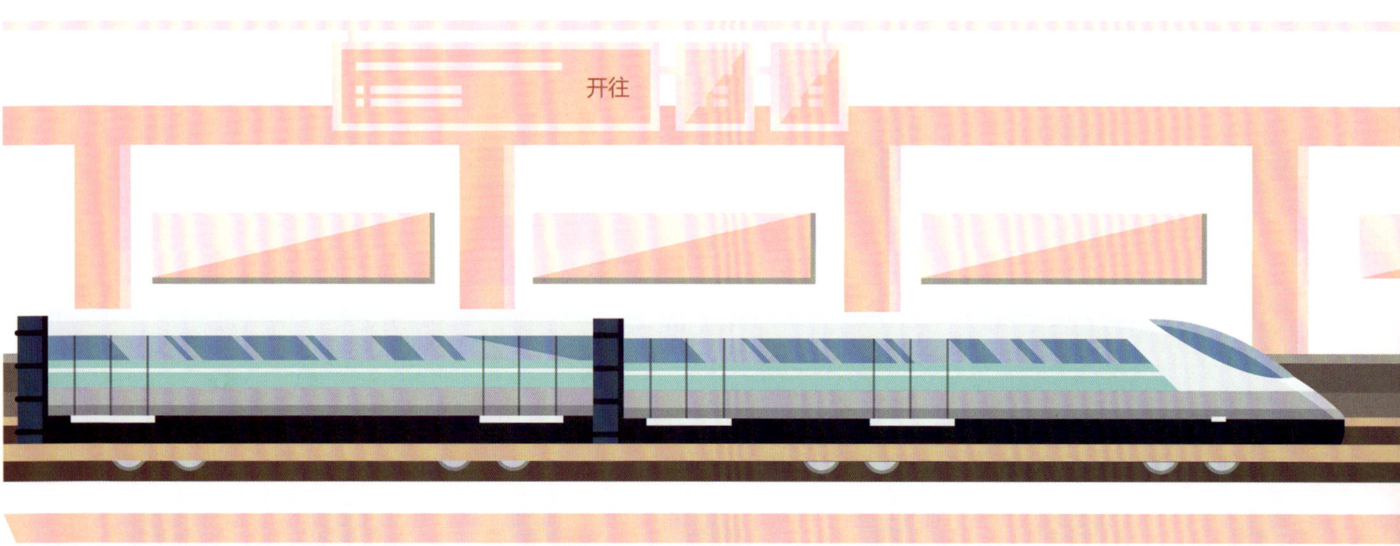

编 者 说 明

1.《苏州统计年鉴-2019》以大量统计数据，全面、系统地反映2018年苏州经济、社会各方面的发展情况。

2.本年鉴内容包括：发展成果图，综合，人口、劳动力，农业，工业，建筑业，运输、邮电业，贸易餐饮业，对外经济、国际旅游，服务业，能源消费，固定资产投资，企业调查，财政、金融、保险，物价指数，人民生活，科技，教育、文化，卫生、体育，民政、司法，城市建设、环境保护，城市比较等二十二个部分。

3.本年鉴辑入的统计数据以2018年为主，主要指标还列示了建国以来主要历史年份的统计数据。资料主要来自苏州市统计局、国家统计局苏州调查队的各项定期统计报表和抽样调查资料，部分资料来自苏州各主管部门。

4. 根据国家统计制度的变化，部分历史数据作相应的调整，读者在使用历史资料时，凡以往年鉴与本年鉴有出入的，均以本年鉴为准。

5.2012年9月吴江撤市设区，原沧浪区、平江区、金阊区合并设立姑苏区。本年鉴表内全市数据包括姑苏区，吴中区，相城区，虎丘区、高新区，工业园区，吴江区，常熟市，张家港市，昆山市，太仓市，市区中包含吴江区数据（气象、水文、物价指数除外）。

6. 本年鉴中的符号说明：

"…"　　表示数据不足本表最小单位数；

"空格"　表示该项统计数据不详；

"－"　　表示无该项统计数据；

"#"　　表示其中数。

《苏州统计年鉴》公开出版以来，受到社会各界的关注和支持，不少读者对年鉴的内容和编辑工作提出了许多宝贵的意见，对此，我们深表感谢。欢迎读者一如既往地对年鉴的不足之处批评指正，帮助我们进一步提高编辑水平。

Complier's Note

Ⅰ.***Suzhou Statistical Yearbook 2019*** is a publication which provides comprehensive and systematic data covering the economic and social development in Suzhou Municipality in 2018.

Ⅱ.This yearbook is comprised of 22 parts including Achievement Graphs and Charts, General Survey, Population and Labor Force, Agriculture, Industry, Construction, Transportation, Post and Telecommunication, Wholesale, Retail Sales and Catering Business, Export-Oriented Economy and International Tourism, Services, Consumption of Energy, Investment in Fixed Assets, Enterprises Survey, Finance, Banking and Insurance, Price Indices, People's Livelihood, Science and Technology, Education and Culture, Public Health and Sports, Civil Administration, Judiciary and Other Items, Urban Construction and Environmental Protection, Cities Compare.

Ⅲ. The statistics in the yearbook are mainly the statistics in 2018, and the main indicators also list the statistical data in the key years since the founding of the People's Republic of China. The data mainly comes from the periodic statistical reports and sample survey data of Suzhou Municipal Bureau of Statistics and Suzhou Investigation Team of National Bureau of Statistics, and some of the information comes from administrative departments of Suzhou municipal government.

Ⅳ. According to the changes of the national statistical system, some historical data is adjusted accordingly, and in the use of historical data, when the data in previous yearbooks is different from that in this yearbook, the data in this yearbook is to be used.

Ⅴ. In September, 2012 Wujiang City was changed into Wujiang District, and the original Changlang District、Pingjiang Dictrict and Jinchang District were merged to become Gusu District. The whole city's data in the yearbook includes the data of Gusu District, Wuzhong District, Xiangcheng District, Huqiu District、 Suzhou New District, Suzhou Industrial Park, Wujiang District, Changshu City, Zhangjiagang City, Kunshan City and Taicang city, and the data of the central city includes that of Wujiang District (except the data of meteorology, hydrology and price).

Ⅵ. Explanations on symbols used in this yearbook:

"…" indicates that the data are not large enough to be rounded into the minimal unit,

"space" indicates that the data is unknown and indicates the data not available,

" – " indicates the data not available,

" # " indicates the component items.

Here we'd like to express our sincere thanks to the readers who have provided us so many invaluable suggestions on content selection and compilation of the yearbook. Our thanks also go to those friends in all circles of society who have shown their support and care to the publication of the yearbook. We welcome any suggestions and comments from readers at large so as to help us to further improve our work of compilation.

目 录
CONTENTS

二、人口、劳动力

POPULATION AND LABOR FORCE

三、农　业

AGRICULTURE

四、工　业
INDUSTRY

五、建 筑 业

CONSTRUCTION

六、运输、邮电业

TRANSPORTATION , POST AND TELECOMMUNICATION

七、贸易餐饮业

TRADE AND CATERING BUSINESS

八、对外经济、国际旅游

FOREIGN TRADE ECONOMY AND INTERNATIONAL TOURISM

九、服务业

SERVICES

十、能源消费

CONSUMPTION OF ENERGY

十一、固定资产投资

INVESTMENT IN FIXED ASSETS

十二、企业调查

ENTERPRISES SURVEY

十三、财政、金融、保险

FINANCE, BANKING AND INSURANCE

十四、物价指数

PRICE INDICES

十五、人民生活

PEOPLE'S LIVELIHOOD

十六、科　　技

SCIENCE AND TECHNOLOGY

十八、卫生、体育

PUBLIC HEALTH AND SPORTS

十九、民政、司法
CIVIL ADMINISTRATION, JUDICIARY

二十、城市建设、环境保护

URBAN CONSTRUCTION AND ENVIRONMENTAL PROTECTION

二十一、城市比较
CITIES COMPARE

2018年苏州市国民经济和社会发展概况

2018年，面对错综复杂的宏观环境，全市上下坚持以习近平新时代中国特色社会主义思想为指导，全面贯彻党的十九大精神，紧紧围绕“六个高质量”发展目标，坚持稳中求进工作总基调，自觉践行新发展理念，扎实推进供给侧结构性改革，大力实施十二项“三年行动计划”，全市经济运行总体平稳，创新驱动、改革开放、城乡建设、生态保护、民生事业等各项工作取得新进展，高质量发展取得新成效。

一、综合

经济运行稳中有进。全市实现地区生产总值1.86万亿元，按可比价计算比上年增长6.8%。全年实现一般公共预算收入2119.99亿元，比上年增长11.1%。其中税收收入1929.5亿元，增长15.3%，占一般公共预算收入的比重达91%。全年一般公共预算支出1952.7亿元，比上年增长10.2%。其中城乡公共服务支出1484.4亿元，占一般公共预算支出的比重达76%。

经济结构不断优化。全市服务业增加值占地区生产总值比重达到50.8%。实现制造业新兴产业产值占规模以上工业总产值比重达52.4%，比上年提高1.6个百分点。先导产业加快发展。新一代信息技术、生物医药、纳米技术、人工智能四大先导产业产值占规模以上工业总产值的比重达15.7%。成为首批国家服务型制造示范城市。

改革开放纵深迈进。苏州工业园区、张家港市、昆山经济技术开发区获评江苏改革开放40周年先进集体，6人获评先进个人。商事制度改革、事中事后监管等举措获国务院通报表彰。全年新增私营企业9.9万家，注册资本4302亿元；新增个体户17.6万家，注册资金219亿元。国资国企改革稳步实施，新设混合所有制企业21家，完成企业公司制改革4家。在全国率先启动推广“互联网+不动产抵押登记”模式。供给侧结构性改革取得实效。关停淘汰落后低效企业1757家。降低企业负担399亿元，“补短板”项目完成投资259.7亿元。

二、农业和农村建设

农业生产调整优化。全市实现农林牧渔业总产值410.09亿元。推广耕地轮作休耕，提升耕地质量。全年夏粮总产量23.85万吨，比上年下降9.6%；秋粮总产量64.07万吨，比上年下降3.0%。夏粮、秋粮亩产分别比上年提高3.5%和1.3%。畜禽养殖环境整治力度加大,全年猪牛羊禽肉产量3.85万吨，比上年下降49.7%；禽蛋产量0.92万吨，比上年下降58.9%；水产品产量19.56万吨，比上年下降16.4%。

现代农业稳步发展。全年新增高标准农田7.37万亩，新增现代农业园区面积5.38万亩。年末全市农业机械化水平达89.3%。全市农业龙头企业实现销售收入1390亿元，比上年增长6.1%。产业融合发展加快推进。新型农业经营主体不断壮大，全市组建农业产业化联合体46个，认定新型职业农民1562名。年末全市各类农民合作社3747家，集体合作农场217家。农村集体经济总资产1970亿元，村均年稳定性收入850万元，分别比上年增长7.1%和4.3%。

三、工业和建筑业

工业经济增量提质。全市实现规模以上工业总产值3.34万亿元，比上年增长6.1%。其中民营工业企业实现产值1.20万亿元，比上年增长8.5%；外商及港澳台工业企业实现产值2.05万亿元，比上年增长4.6%。35个行业大类中有26个行业保持增长，行业增长面达74.3%。10个行业大类产值超一千亿元，其中前六大行业实现产值2.16万亿元，比上年增长5.7%。高端产品产量较快增长。新能源汽车产量比上年增长83%，3D打印设备产量增长51.4%，工业机器人产量增长32.2%。新增国家智能制造新模式和试点示范项目5个，新增省级示范智能车间144个，累计达262个。

建筑业稳步发展。全市完成建筑业总产值2412亿元，比上年增长23.4%，其中建筑安装工程产值2393亿元，比上年增长23.2%。竣工产值1707亿元，比上年增长10.6%，竣工率70.8%。全市资质以上建筑业企业房屋施工面积10419万平方米，比上年增长11.5%，其中新开工面积4073万平方米，比上年增长19.4%。年末拥有总承包和专业承包资质建筑企业1345家，实现利税162亿元，比上年增长15.2%。建筑业全员劳动生产率39.2万元/人，比上年增长18.8%。建筑业企业在外省完成建筑业产值740亿元，比上年增长31.9%。

四、固定资产投资和房地产开发

投资需求保持稳定。全市完成固定资产投资4556亿元，同口径增长4.5%。其中工业投资1102亿元，同口径持平；服务业投资3450亿元，增长6.1%；民间投资2949亿元，增长14%。投资结构继续优化调整。服务业投资占固定资产投资的比重达75.7%，比上年提高1.1个百分点；工业技术改造投资和高新技术产业投资占工业投资比重分别达77.5%和40.5%。民间投资主体地位稳固，占固定资产投资比重达64.7%。

房地产市场平稳发展。全年完成房地产开发投资2558亿元，比上年增长10.9%。全市房屋新开工面积2801万平方米，比上年增长9.2%；房屋施工面积11659万平方米，比上年下降2.0%；房屋竣工面积1507万平方米，比上年下降29.7%；商品房销售面积1994万平方米，比上年增长3%，其中住宅销售面积1788万平方米，比上年增长5.9%。

五、国内贸易和旅游

市场消费保持稳定。全年实现社会消费品零售总额5746.9亿元，比上年增长7.4%。其中批发和零售业零售额5034.6亿元，比上年增长7.1%；住宿和餐饮业零售额712.3亿元，比上年增长9%。生活类商品增势较好。限额以上批发和零售业粮油食品类、日用品类、家具类商品零售额分别比上年增长12.8%、15.3%和19%。新型商业模式较快发展。全年电子商务网络零售交易额超2000亿元。限额以上批发和零售业实现互联网零售额495亿元，比上年增长14.8%。

旅游市场健康发展。全市实现旅游总收入2601亿元，比上年增长11.8%，其中旅游外汇收入25.22亿美元。全年接待入境过夜游客182.78万人次，接待国内游客12848万人次，分别比上年增长4.1%和6.7%。年末全市共有5A级景区6家（11个点）、4A级景区35家、五星级饭店28家。高等级景区、星级酒店、旅游度假区、乡村旅游点数量继续保持全省领先。

六、开放型经济

对外贸易迎难而上。全年实现进出口总额3541.1亿美元，比上年增长12%。其中出口突破2000亿美元，达2068.3亿美元，增长10.5%；进口1472.8亿美元，增长14.2%。分注册类型看，外商及港澳台商投资企业实现进出口2558.9亿美元，比上年增长7.8%，占全市进出口总额比重达72.3%；民营企业和国有企业进出口分别增长19.9%和41.2%。从贸易市场看，对美国出口578.3亿美元，比上年增长8.3%；对欧盟、东盟出口分别增长8.6%和15.7%；对“一带一路”沿线国家和地区出口425.9亿美元，增长11.3%。贸易方式积极转变。全市实现一般贸易出口688.7亿美元，比上年增长13.6%。一般贸易出口占全市出口比重达33.3%，较上年提高0.9个百分点。

服务贸易创新发展。全年服务贸易进出口247.1亿美元，比上年增长11.2%。获批国家深化服务贸易创新发展试点。服务外包平稳发展。全市服务外包接包合同额117.9亿美元，服务外包离岸执行额48.26亿美元。

“引进来”与“走出去”同步发展。全年新设外商投资项目1013个，实际使用外资45.25亿美元，其中服务业实际使用外资占比达43.7%，新兴产业和高技术项目使用外资占比达51.5%。年末全市具有地区总部特征或共享功能的外资企业超300家。全年新批境外投资项目中方协议投资额26.8亿美元。对外投资扩面增量。在“一带一路”沿线国家和地区新增投资项目64个，中方协议投资额9.11亿美元。

七、交通运输和邮政

交通运输健康发展。年末全市公路总里程12173公里，其中高速公路598公里。全市公路、水路客运量2.98亿人次，客运周转量121.19亿人公里；全市公路、水路货运量1.62亿吨，货物周转量267.82亿吨公里，分别比上年增长8.2%和7.3%；苏州港集装箱吞吐量635.51万标箱，比上年增长8.2%。

汽车保有量稳步增长。年末拥有汽车391万辆，其中私家客车328万辆，分别比上年增长9.9%和9.2%。

邮政业务快速发展。全年邮政业务收入181.57亿元，比上年增长14.7%。全年发送快递12.5亿件，增长20.1%；实现快递业务收入156.21亿元，增长17.8%。

八、金融

金融运行保持稳定。年末全市金融机构总数859家，年末全市金融机构人民币存款余额28560.45亿元，比年初增加2092.85亿元，比年初增长7.9%；金融机构人民币贷款余额26546.23亿元，比年初增加2555.08亿元，比年初增长10.7%。

保险业务保持平稳。全年新增保险公司4家，年末达86家，保险公司分支机构916家。全年保费收入629.7亿元，比上年下降2.8%；保险赔付支出181.3亿元，比上年增长10.9%。

资本市场稳步发展。全年新增上市公司8家，年末上市公司总数达135家，累计募集资金2777亿元。其中境内A股上市公司107家，数量列全国第五、全省第一，累计募集资金2563亿元。全年新增债券融资1184亿元。年末全市证券机构托管市值总额5075亿元，全年证券营业部证券交易总额4万亿元。

九、科技和教育

科技创新加快推进。全市财政性科技投入152亿元，占一般公共预算支出的7.8%。张家港、常熟、昆山入围国家首批创新型县（市）建设名单。高新技术产业产值占规模以上工业总产值的比重达到47.7%。全市新增高新技术企业952家，累计达5416家。新增省级以上工程技术研究中心73家，累计达732家；新增省级以上企业技术中心58家，累计达505家；新增省级以上工程中心（实验室）11家，累计达90家；年末省级以上公共技术服务平台60家，其中国家级15家。

创新载体加快培育。启动建设市产业技术研究院，与中科院、南京大学、牛津大学等一批国内外大院大所合作共建的重大创新载体落户苏州。年末全市省级以上科技孵化器112家，孵化面积395万平方米。年末共有国家级众创空间52家，省级众创空间190家。服务的创业团队近4000个,初创企业近5000家。

创新实力不断增强。年末全市各类人才总量276.48万人，其中高层次人才24.49万人。全市拥有高技能人才57.68万人。新增国家级人才引进工程入选者13人，累计达250人，其中创业类人才131人。新增省“双创人才”91人，累计达873人。专利工作成效显著。中国（苏州）知识产权保护中心获批建设。新增国家知识产权示范企业16家。年末万人有效发明专利拥有量达53件，比上年增加6.98件。

教育公共服务水平不断提升。新建中小学、幼儿园52所，改扩建17所，新增学位6.8万个。年末全市拥有各类学校799所，在校学生146.42万人，毕业生28.61万人，专任教师9.25万人。其中普通高等院校26所，普通高等学校在校学生23.56万人，毕业生5.91万人。高等教育毛入学率69.1%。推动教育均衡优质发展。推进集团化办学，增加普通高中教育资源供给，统筹全市名优教师，打造免费线上教育平台。

十、文化、卫生和体育

文化事业繁荣兴盛。全年文化产业实现主营业务收入5720亿元，比上年增长9%。苏州第二图书馆如期建成，苏州湾文化中心主体结构封顶，苏州博物馆西馆、吴文化博物馆等项目建设顺利推进。完成705个村（社区）综合性文化服务中心标准化建设。成功举办世界遗产城市组织第三届亚太区大会、中国昆剧艺术节、中国苏州评弹艺术节、苏州国际设计周等重大活动。获评全球首个“世界遗产典范城市”。

健康苏州建设扎实推进。苏大附二院浒关院区建成运行，市疾控中心迁建，苏大附一院二期项目开工建设。引进高水平临床医学专家团队26个，年末累计达到53个。新建、改扩建基层医疗卫生机构24家。年末全市拥有各类医疗卫生机构3380个，其中医院206个，社区卫生服务中心、卫生院172个。卫生机构床位数6.89万张，其中医院病床5.80万张；拥有卫生技术人员8.52万人，其中执业医师和执业助理医师3.29万人。

体育事业稳步发展。全民健身工程提档升级。新增健身步道252公里。苏州奥林匹克体育中心、东园体育休闲公园建成投用。成功举办2018年国际田联世界竞走团体锦标赛、2018冰壶世界杯苏州站等高规格体育赛事。在第十九届省运会上取得历史最好成绩。体育彩票销售首次突破50亿元。

十一、人口和就业

人口总量保持稳定。年末全市常住人口1072.17万人，其中城镇人口815.39万人。全市户籍人口703.55万人，户籍人口出生率9.82‰，户籍人口自然增长率2.79‰。

就业创业形势良好。全市新增就业17.55万人，开发公益性岗位8941个，城乡就业困难人员实现就业3.75万人。城镇登记失业率1.78%。苏州籍应届高校毕业生就业率达98.7%。全力推进大众创业。全年支持成功自主创业人数19441人，其中引领大学生创业2344人，扶持农村劳动力自主创业2467人。

十二、人民生活和社会保障

居民收入稳步提高。根据抽样调查，全市城镇常住居民人均可支配收入6.35万元，比上年增长8%；农村常住居民人均可支配收入3.24万元，比上年增长8.1%。

物价水平温和上涨。市区居民消费价格总水平比上年上涨2.6%。其中食品烟酒类价格上涨2.2%；衣着类价格上涨5.0%；居住类价格上涨2.9%；生活用品及服务类价格上涨3.5%；交通和通信类价格上涨1.6%；教育文化和娱乐类价格上涨3.1%；医疗保健类价格上涨0.8%；其他用品和服务类价格上涨2.5%。

社会保障水平进一步提高。全市最低工资标准上调至2020元/月。年末全市基本养老保险参保人数575.83万人，比上年增加27.20万人。城镇职工基本医疗保险参保人数737.08万人，失业保险参保人数505.02万人，工伤保险参保人数512.23万人，生育保险参保人数529.13万人，分别比上年增加48.76、40.45、38.97和38.77万人。全年新增缴存公积金职工81.64万人，年末缴存住房公积金职工数达307.15万人，全年职工提取公积金319.7亿元。

城乡最低生活保障标准提高至每人每月945元。年末全市1.43万户、共计2.15万人享受低保，全年发放低保金2.17亿元。全市新增日间照料中心110个、助浴点20个。开工建设保障性住房21205套，基本建成27196套，新增租赁补贴发放2604户。

强化食品药品安全监管。全年累计抽检各类食品7.26万批次，每千人抽检率6.8批次，动态合格率98.22%。全年查办食品药品违法案件6198件，比上年增长32%。在省内率先启动食品药品生产经营严重失信联合惩戒机制，出台评定严重失信者管理办法。

十三、城市建设和公用事业

全年完成基础设施投资488.5亿元。沪通铁路苏州段一期工程开展铺轨作业，江苏南沿江城际铁路苏州段、通苏嘉甬纳入盐通铁路先行实施段开工建设。524国道相城段改扩建、桐泾路北延、独墅湖第二通道等重点道路交通项目开工建设。轨道交通3号线主体完工，5号线加快推进，6号线、S1线开工建设，有轨电车1号线延伸线、2号线开通试运营。1000千伏淮上线苏通管廊过江隧道全线贯通。智慧城管大数据平台（二期）建成投用。5G通信试点稳步推进。

全年全社会用电量1562.5亿千瓦时，比上年增长3.9%。其中工业用电量1227.8亿千瓦时，增长2.1%；城乡居民生活用电量136.6亿千瓦时，增长9.7%。市区管道天然气供气总量10.33亿立方米。全市拥有区域供水厂25座，总供水能力722.5万立方米/日，其中市区自来水供水能力达到350万立方米/日。全市生活污水处理能力达到375万立方米/日，城镇生活污水处理率95.8%。

年末城市轨道交通（含有轨电车）运营线路总长149.6公里，全年运营总里程1676万列公里，线网客流总量32805万人次。市区新辟、优化调整公交线路63条，年末市区公交线路总数达446条，全年营运里程3.31亿公里，总客运量5.56亿人次。古城区（环护城河内）实现纯电动、插电式混合动力、氢能公交车100%全覆盖。

十四、环境保护和节能降耗

生态保护得到加强。全年环保投入664亿元。太仓、吴江、吴中建成首批省级生态文明建设示范县区。市区$PM_{2.5}$平均浓度42微克/立方米，市区空气质量优良天数比例为73.7%，比上年提高2.2个百分点。国考、省考断面水质优III比例分别为68.8%和76%，通江支流优III比例达到97.6%。市区新增及改造绿地面积350万平方米。山水林田湖生态保护带日益完善。全年完成森林抚育5.03万亩，年末全市陆地森林覆盖率达29.9%。

节能减排稳步推进。全年劝退、拒批不符合环保要求建设项目358个，涉及投资额32.9亿元。完成大气污染防治工程治理项目1256项。淘汰低端落后化工企业260家，整治“散乱污”企业（作坊）35425家，完成省下达的煤炭消费总量削减任务。

2018年，苏州经济社会发展取得了来之不易的成绩，经济运行保持在合理区间，新旧动能加快转换，质量效益改善提升，经济社会发展协调性可持续性不断增强，但经济社会发展仍面临不少困难和问题，经济下行压力增大，产业转型任务艰巨，自主创新能力和经济发展质量有待进一步提高，生态环境保护、节能减排和污染防治任务依然繁重。2019年，全市上下要继续以习近平新时代中国特色社会主义思想为指导，继续坚持稳中求进工作总基调，坚持新发展理念，坚持推进高质量发展，以供给侧结构性改革为主线，深化市场化改革，扩大高水平开放，加快建设现代化经济体系，继续打好三大攻坚战，以持续推进十二项“三年行动计划”为抓手，进一步稳就业、稳金融、稳外贸、稳外资、稳投资、稳预期，确保全市经济平稳增长，继续推动苏州高质量发展走在最前列，以优异成绩庆祝中华人民共和国成立70周年。

AN OVERVIEW OF THE 2018 ECONOMIC AND SOCIAL DEVELOPMENT OF SUZHOU MUNICIPALITY

In 2018, in the face of the complicated macro environment, the whole city adhered to the guidance of Xi Jinping's thought of socialism with Chinese characteristics in the new era, fully implemented the spirit of the 19th National Congress of the Communist Party of China, closely focused on the development goal of "six high qualities", persisted in seeking progress in stability as the overall tone of work, consciously practiced the new development concept, solidly promoted the supply-side structural reform, and vigorously implemented the 12 projects of the "three-year action plan", and as a result, the city's economic operation was generally stable, new progress made in such aspects of work as innovation as a driving force, reform and opening up, urban and rural construction, ecological protection and the people's livelihood, and new achievements made in high-quality development.

1. General survey

The economic operation was stable with progress. The city achieved a regional GDP of 1.86 trillion yuan, an increase of 6.8% over the previous year calculated by comparable price. The year's general public budget revenue was 211.999 billion yuan, an increase of 11.1% over the previous year. Of it, the tax revenue was 192.95 billion yuan, an increase of 15.3% and accounting for 91% of the general public budget revenue. The year's general public budget expenditure was 195.28 billion yuan, an increase of 10.2% over the previous year. Of it, the urban and rural public service expenditure was 148.44 billion yuan, accounting for 76% of the general public budget expenditure.

The economic structure was continuously optimized. The added value of the city's service industry accounted for 50.8% of the regional GDP. The output value of the emerging industries in the manufacturing industry was 1.73 trillion yuan, accounting for 52.4% of the total output value of the industries above designated size and an increase of 1.6 percentage points over the previous year. The pilot industries were accelerating their development. The output value of the four leading industries of information technology, biomedicine, nanotechnology and artificial intelligence accounted for 15.7% of the total output value of the industries above designated size. Suzhou became one of the first-batch national service-oriented manufacturing demonstration cities.

Reform and opening up were progressing in depth. Suzhou Industrial Park, Zhangjiagang City and Kunshan Economic and Technological Development Zone were awarded advanced collectives of the 40th anniversary of Jiangsu's reform and opening up, and 6 people evaluated as advanced individuals. The reform of the commercial system, the in-process and post-event supervision and other measures were commended by the State Council. In the year there were 99,000 newly-started private enterprises with a registered capital of 430.2 billion yuan; 176,000 newly-started self-employed households with a registered capital of 21.9 billion yuan. The reform of the state-owned enterprises was steadily implemented, 21 mixed-ownership enterprises newly established and four state-owned enterprises successfully transformed into corporations. Suzhou was the first in the country to launch the "Internet + real estate mortgage registration" model. The reform of the supply-side structure achieved practical results. 1,757 backward and inefficient enterprises were shut down or eliminated. 39.9 billion yuan of burden was reduced from the enterprises, and an investment of 25.97 billion yuan in the "filling the short board" projects completed.

2. Agriculture and rural construction

Agricultural production was adjusted and optimized. The city's total output value of agriculture, forestry, animal husbandry and fishery was 41.009 billion yuan. The rotation of cultivated land for fallow was promoted and the quality of cultivated land improved. In the year the total output of summer grain was 238,500 tons, down 9.6% from the previous year; the total output of autumn grain was 640,700 tons, down 3.0% from the previous year. The per mu yield of the summer grain and that of the autumn grain increased by 3.5% and 1.3% respectively over the previous year. The efforts to remediate the livestock and poultry farming environment increased. In the year the output of pork, beef, lamb and poultry was 38,500 tons, down 49.7% from the previous year; the output of eggs was 9,200 tons, down 58.9% from the previous year; the output of aquatic products was 195,600 tons, down 16.4% from the previous year.

Modern agriculture was developing steadily. In the year there was 73,700 mu of newly-built high-standard farmland and 53,800 mu of newly-built modern agricultural parks. At the end of the year the level of agricultural mechanization in the city reached 89.3%. The city's leading agricultural enterprises achieved sales revenue of 139 billion yuan, an increase of 6.1% over the previous year. The development of industrial integration was accelerating. The main bodies of new agricultural management were growing steadily, and in the city 46 agricultural industrialization complexes were established and 1,562 new professional farmers identified. At the end of the year there were 3,747 farmers' cooperatives of various types in the city. There were 217 collective cooperative farms. The total assets of the rural collective economy were 197 billion yuan, and the average annual stable income of the villages 8.5 million yuan, an increase of 7.1% and 4.3% respectively over the previous year.

3. Industries and construction industry

The production of industrial economy was increased and its quality improved. The city's total output value of the industries above designated size was 3.34 trillion yuan, an increase of 6.1% over the previous year. Of it, the private industrial enterprises realized an output value of 1.20 trillion yuan, an increase of 8.5% over the previous year; the foreign companies, and Hong Kong, Macao and Taiwan industrial enterprises realized an output value of 2.05 trillion yuan, an increase of 4.6% over the previous year. Twenty-six of the 35 major industries maintained growth, with industry growth reaching 74.3%. The output value of 10 major industries exceeded 100 billion yuan, of which the top six industries achieved an output value of 2.17 trillion yuan, an increase of 5.7% over the previous year. The output of high-end products was growing rapidly. The output of new-energy vehicles increased by 83% over the previous year, that of 3D printing equipment by 51.4%, and that of industrial robots by 32.2%. There were 5 newly-built national intelligent manufacturing new model and pilot demonstration projects, and 144 newly-built provincial-level demonstration intelligent workshops, with a total of 262 ones.

The construction industry was developing steadily. The city's total construction output value reached 241.2 billion yuan, an increase of 23.4% over the previous year, of which the output value of the construction and installation projects was 239.3 billion yuan, an increase of 23.2% over the previous year. The output value of the completed projects was 170.7 billion yuan, an increase of 10.6% over the previous year, and the completion rate was 70.8%. The construction area by the city's construction enterprises above the qualifications was 104.19 million square meters, an increase of 11.5% over the previous year, of which the newly-started construction area was 40.73 million square meters, an increase of 19.4% over the previous year. At the end of the year there were 1,345 general contracting companies and professional contractor qualification construction companies, which achieved profits and taxes of 16.2 billion yuan, an increase of 15.2% over the previous year. The total labor productivity of the construction industry was 392,000 yuan / person, an increase of 18.8% over the previous year. The output value of the construction projects completed by the city's construction enterprises in other provinces was 74.0 billion yuan, an increase of 31.9% over the previous year.

4. Fixed asset investment and real estate development

Investment demand remained stable. The city's investment in the fixed assets was 455.6 billion yuan, an increase of 4.5% over the previous year. Of it the industrial investment was 110.2 billion yuan, the same as the previous year; the service industry investment 345 billion yuan, an increase of 6.1%; the private investment 294.9 billion yuan, an increase of 14%. The investment structure continued to be optimized and adjusted. The service industry investment accounted for 75.7% of the fixed asset investment, an increase of 1.1 percentage points over the previous year; the industrial technology transformation investment and the high-tech industry investment accounted for 77.5% and 40.5% of the industrial investment respectively. The main status of the private investment was solid, accounting for 64.7% of the fixed asset investment.

The real estate market was developing steadily. In the year the investment in real estate development was 255.8 billion yuan, an increase of 10.9% over the previous year. The newly-started construction areas of the city's housing were 28.01 million square meters, an increase of 9.2% over the previous year; the construction areas of housing 116.59 million square meters, down 2.0% from the previous year; the completed construction areas of housing 15.07 million square meters, down 29.7% from the previous year. 3%; the sales areas of commercial housing 19.94 million square meters, an increase of 3% over the previous year, of which the sales areas of residential housing 17.88 million square meters, an increase of 5.9% over the previous year.

5. Domestic trade and tourism

Market consumption remained stable. The year's total retail sales of social consumer goods reached 574.69 billion yuan, an increase of 7.4% over the previous year. Of them the retail sales of the wholesale and retail enterprises were 503.46 billion yuan, an increase of 7.1% over the previous year; the retail sales of the accommodation and catering industry 71.23 billion yuan, an increase of 9% over the previous year. Goods for livelihood were growing better. The retail sales of grain, oil and food, daily necessities, and furniture in the wholesale and retail enterprises above designated size increased by 12.8%, 15.3% and 19% respectively over the previous year. The new business model was developing faster. In the year the e-commerce network retail transaction volume exceeded 200 billion yuan. The Internet retail sales of the wholesale and retail enterprises above designated size reached 49.5 billion yuan, an increase of 14.8% over the previous year.

The tourism market was developing healthily. The city's total tourism revenue was 260.1 billion yuan, an increase of 11.8% over the previous year, of which the tourism foreign exchange revenue was 2.522 billion US dollars. In the year 1,827,800 inbound overnight visitors and 128.48 million domestic tourists were received, an increase of 4.1% and 6.7% respectively over the previous year. At the end of the year there were 6 5A-level scenic spots (11 points), 35 4A-level scenic spots and 28 five-star hotels in the city. The number of high-level scenic spots, star-rated hotels, tourist resorts and rural tourist spots continued to lead the province.

6. Open economy

Foreign trade was on the rise. The total volume of imports and exports in the year reached 354.11 billion US dollars, an increase of 12% over the previous year. Of it the exports exceeded 200 billion US dollars and reached 206.83 billion US dollars, an increase of 10.5%; the imports reached 147.28 billion US dollars, an increase of 14.2%. According to the type of registration, the volume of imports and exports of the foreign companies, and Hong Kong, Macao and Taiwan enterprises was 255.89 billion US dollars, an increase of 7.8% over the previous year and accounting for 72.3% of the total import and export volume of the city; the volume of imports and exports of the private enterprises and that of the state-owned enterprises increased by 19.9% and 41.2% respectively. From the perspective of the trade market, the volume of exports to the United States was 57.83 billion US dollars, an increase of 8.3% over the previous year; the volume of exports to the EU and ASEAN increased by 8.6% and 15.7% respectively; the volume of exports to countries and regions along the "Belt and Road" was 42.59 billion US dollars, an increase of 11.3%. The trade pattern was changing positively. The volume of city's general trade exports was 68.87 billion US dollars, an increase of 13.6% over the previous year. The volume of the general trade exports accounted for 33.3% of the city's exports, an increase of 0.9 percentage points over the previous year.

Service trade was developing innovatively. In the year the volume of the imports and exports of the service trade was 24.71 billion US dollars, an increase of 11.2% over the previous year. Suzhou was approved by the state as a pilot city to deepen the service trade innovative development. Service outsourcing was developing steadily. The city's service outsourcing contracted contracts amounted to 11.79 billion US dollars, and the service outsourcing offshore execution was 4.826 billion US dollars.

"Introducing into" and "going out" were developing simultaneously. In the year 1,013 foreign investment projects were newly established, and the foreign capital actually used was 4.525 billion US dollars, of which the foreign capital actually used in the service industry accounted for 43.7%, and the foreign capital used in the emerging industries and high-tech projects 51.5%. At the end of the year there were over 300 foreign-funded enterprises with regional headquarters characteristics or shared functions. In the year the amount of the Chinese agreement investment in the newly-approved overseas investment projects was 2.68 billion US dollars. The areas of overseas investment were expanded and the quantity increased. There were 64 newly-approved investment projects in the countries and regions along the "Belt and Road", and the amount of the Chinese agreement investment was 911 million US dollars.

7. Transportation, post and telecommunications

Transportation was developing healthily. At the end of the year the total length of the city's highways was 12,173 kilometers, including 598 kilometers of expressways. The city's highway and waterway passenger traffic was 298 million passengers, and the passenger traffic turnover 12.119 billion person-kilometers; the city's road and waterway freight volume was 162 million tons, and the cargo turnover 26.782 billion tons, up 8.2% and 7.3% respectively over the previous year; the container throughput of Suzhou Port was 6,355,100 TEUs, an increase of 8.2% over the previous year.

Car ownership was growing steadily. At the end of the year there were 3.91 million vehicles in the city, including 3.28 million private cars, an increase of 9.9% and 9.2% respectively over the previous year.

The postal business was developing rapidly. In the year the postal business income was 18.157 billion yuan, an increase of 14.7% over the previous year. In the year 1.25 billion pieces were sent by express delivery, an increase of 20.1%; the express delivery business income was 15.621 billion yuan, an increase of 17.8%.

8. Finance

Financial operations remained stable. At the end of the year the total number of financial institutions in the city was 859 ones. At the end of the year the RMB deposit balance in the city's financial institutions was 2,856.045 billion yuan, an increase of 209.285 billion yuan compared with the beginning of the year, an increase of 7.9% over the beginning of the year; the RMB loan balance in the city's financial institutions was 2,654.623 billion yuan, an increase of 255.508 billion yuan compared with the beginning of the year, an increase of 10.7% over the beginning of the year.

The insurance business remained stable. In the year there were four newly-established insurance companies, with a total of 86 insurance companies and 916 branches of insurance companies in the city at the end of the year. In the year the insurance premium income was 62.97 billion yuan, down 2.8% from the previous year; the insurance claims expenditure was 18.13 billion yuan, an increase of 10.9% over the previous year.

The capital market was developing steadily. In the year there were 8 newly-listed companies, with a total of 135 listed companies and a total raised capital of 277.7 billion yuan at the end of the year. Of them there were 107 domestic A-share listed companies, ranking the fifth in the country and the first in the province and with a total raised capital of 256.3 billion yuan. In the year 118.4 billion yuan of bond financing was newly raised. At the end of the year the total market value of the securities institutions in the city was 507.5 billion yuan. The year's total securities transaction of the securities business department was 4 trillion yuan .

9. Science, technology and education

Technological innovation was accelerating. In the city the fiscal investment in science and technology was 15.2 billion yuan, accounting for 7.8% of the general public budget expenditure. Zhangjiagang, Changshu and Kunshan were shortlisted for the construction of the first batch of innovative counties (cities) in the country. The output value of the high-tech industries accounted for 47.7% of the total output value of the industries above designated size. There were 952 newly-started high-tech enterprises in the city, with a total of 5,416 ones. There were 73 newly-started engineering technology research centers at or above the provincial level, with a total of 732 ones; there were 58 newly-started enterprise technology centers at or above the provincial level, with a total of 505 ones; there were 11 newly-started engineering centers (labs) at or above the provincial level, with a total of 90 ones; at the end of the year there were 60 public technical service platforms at or above the provincial level, of which 15 ones were at the national level.

The cultivation of innovative carriers was accelerated. The construction of the city's Industrial Technology Research Institute was launched, and the major innovation carriers co-built with a number of domestic and foreign universities and institutions such as the Chinese Academy of Sciences, Nanjing University and Oxford University settled in Suzhou. At the end of the year there were 112 technology incubators at or above the provincial level in the city, with an incubation area of 3.95 million square meters. At the end of the year there were 52 national mass creation spaces and 190 provincial-level ones. There were nearly 4,000 entrepreneurial teams supplied with service, and nearly 5,000 startup enterprises.

The strength of innovation was constantly increasing. At the end of the year the total number of talents in the city was 2,764,800 people, of whom 244,900 people were high-level talents. There were 576,800 highly-skilled personnel in the city. 13 people were newly selected into the national talent introduction projects, with a total of 250 people, of whom 131 people were entrepreneurial talents. 91 people were newly selected into the provincial "double-creative talents", with a total of 873 people. The patent work achieved remarkable results. China (Suzhou) Intellectual Property Protection Center was approved for construction.

There were 16 new national intellectual property model enterprises. At the end of the year the number of effective invention patents of 10,000 people reached 53.00, an increase of 6.98 patents over the previous year.

The level of public service in education continued to increase. There were 52 primary and middle schools and kindergartens newly built and 17 ones rebuilt or expanded, with 68,000 new student places. At the end of the year there were 799 schools of all types, 1,464,200 students, 286,100 school graduates, and 92,500 full-time teachers in the city. Of them there were 26 general institutions of higher learning, 235,600 college students and 59,100 college graduates. The gross enrollment rate for higher education was 69.1%. A balanced and quality development of education was promoted. The group-based education was promoted, the supply of ordinary high school education resources increased, the city's famous excellent teachers coordinated, and a free online education platform created.

10. Culture, health and sports

The cultural undertakings were flourishing. In the year the main business income of the cultural industry was 572 billion yuan, an increase of 9% over the previous year. Suzhou Second Library was completed as scheduled, the main structure of Suzhou Bay Cultural Center capped, and the construction of the West Pavilion of Suzhou Museum, the Wu Culture Museum and other projects was smoothly advanced. The standardization construction of 705 village (community) comprehensive cultural service centers was completed. The 3rd Asia Pacific Conference of the World Heritage City Organization, China Kunqu Opera Art Festival, China Suzhou Pingtan Art Festival, Suzhou International Design Week and other major events were successfully held. Suzhou was awarded the world's first "World Heritage Model City".

The healthy Suzhou construction was solidly advanced. The Xuguan Branch of the Second Affiliated Hospital of Soochow University was completed and put into operation, the Municipal Disease Control Centre relocated and built, and the construction of the project of the second phase of the First Affiliated Hospital of Soochow University started. 26 high-level clinical medical expert teams were introduced from elsewhere, with a total of 53 ones at the end of the year. 24 primary health care institutions were newly established, or rebuilt and expanded. At the end of the year there were 3,380 medical and health institutions of various kinds in the city, including 206 hospitals and 172 community health service centers and hospitals. There were 68,900 beds in the health institutions, including 58,000 hospital beds; there were 85,200 health technicians, including 32,900 practicing physicians and practicing assistant physicians.

The sports industry was developing steadily. The national fitness project was upgraded. There were 252 kilometers of newly-built fitness trails. Suzhou Olympic Sports Center and Dongyuan Sports and Leisure Park were completed and put into use. 2018 IAAF World Walking Team Championships, 2018 Curling World Cup Suzhou Station and other high-profile sports events were successfully held. The best results in history were achieved at the 19th Provincial Games. The sports lottery sales exceeded 5 billion yuan for the first time.

11. Population and employment

The total population remained stable. At the end of the year there were 10,721,700 permanent residents in the city, including 8,153,900 urban ones. The registered population of the city was 7,035,500 people, the birth rate of the registered population 9.82‰, and the natural growth rate of the registered population 2.79‰.

The employment and entrepreneurship situation was good. In the city 175,500 people were newly offered jobs, 8,941 public welfare posts developed, and 37,500 people with employment difficulties in urban and rural areas employed. The urban registered unemployment rate was 1.78%. The employment rate of the recent college graduates of Suzhou nationality reached 98.7%. Mass entrepreneurship was fully promoted. In the year 19,441 people were supported to be successfully self-employed, of whom 2,344 college students were led to start businesses and 2,467 rural laborers supported to start their own businesses.

12. People's livelihood and social security

The residents' income was increasing steadily. According to the sample survey, the per capita disposable income of the urban permanent residents in the city was 63,500 yuan, an increase of 8% over the previous year; the per capita disposable income of the rural permanent residents was 32,400 yuan, an increase of 8.1% over the previous year.

The price level was rising modestly. The overall level of consumer prices in the urban areas rose by 2.6% over the previous year. Of them the prices of food, tobacco and alcohol rose by 2.2%; those of clothing by 5.0%; those of housing by 2.9%; those of daily necessities and services by 3.5%; those of transportation and communications by 1.6%; those of education, culture and entertainment by 3.1%; those of medical treatment and health care by 0.8%; those of other supplies and services by 2.5%.

The level of social security was further improved. The city's minimum wage standard was raised to 2020 yuan / month. At the end of the year the number of People Covered by Endowment Insurance was 5,758,300 people, an increase of 272,000 people over the previous year. The number of urban workers participating in basic medical insurance was 7,370,800 people, that in unemployment insurance 5,050,200 people, that in work-related injury insurance 5,122,300 people, and that in maternity insurance 5,291,300 people, an increase of 487,600 people, 404,500 people, 389,700 people and 387,700 people. In the year there were 816,400 new employees depositing housing fund, at the end of the year the number of employees depositing housing fund reached 3,071,500, and in the year the provident fund withdrawn by employees amounted to 31.97 billion yuan.

The minimum living standard for urban and rural residents was raised to 945 yuan per person per month. At the end of the year there were 14,300 households with a total of 21,500 people enjoying minimum living allowances in the city, and in the year of 217 million yuan of minimum living allowances was issued. In the city there were 110 newly-established day-care centers and 20 help-bathing points. The construction of 21,205 sets of affordable housing was started, 27,196 sets basically completed, and 2,604 new households issued lease subsidies.

The food and drug safety supervision was strengthened. In the year a total of 72,600 batches of various types of food were sampled, and the sampling rate per thousand persons 6.8 batches and the dynamic pass rate 98.22%. In the year 6,198 illegal food and drug cases were investigated and handled, an increase of 32% over the previous year. In the province Suzhou took the lead in launching a joint disciplinary mechanism for seriously untrustworthy food and drug production and management, and introduced management measures for assessing seriously untrustworthy persons.

13. Urban construction and public utilities

In the year the infrastructure investment was 48.85 billion yuan. The track laying was started in the first phase of the Suzhou section of the Hutong Railway, and the construction of the Suzhou section of the intercity railway along the Yangtze River in southern Jiangsu and that of the first implementation section of the Tongsujiayong Railway incorporated into the Yantong Railway were started. The construction of the rebuilding and expansion of the Xiangcheng section of National Highway 524, the north extension of Tongjing Road, the second underground passage of the Dushu Lake and other key road traffic projects was started. The main body of Rail Transit Line 3 was completed, the building of Line 5 accelerated, and the building of Line 6 and Line S1 started, and the extension line of Tram Line 1 and Line 2 opened for trial operation. The river tunnel of the Sutong pipe gallery of the 1,000-kilovolt Huaishang line was dug through. The big data platform (phase II) for the smart city management was completed and put into use. The 5G communication pilot was steadily advancing.

In the year the electricity consumption of the whole society was 156.25 billion kilowatt hours, an increase of 3.9% over the previous year. Of it the industrial electricity consumption was 122.78 billion kilowatt hours, an increase of 2.1%; the urban and rural residents' electricity consumption was 13.66 billion kilowatt hours, an increase of 9.7%. The total gas supply of the pipeline natural gas in the urban areas was 1033 million cubic meters. In the city there were 25 regional water supply plants, the total water supply capacity was 7.225 million cu.m / day, of which the urban tap water supply capacity reached 3.5 million cu.m / day. The city's domestic sewage treatment capacity reached 3.75 million cu.m / day and the urban domestic sewage treatment rate was 95.8%.

At the end of the year the total length of the operating line of the urban rail transit (including trams) was 149.6 kilometers, and in the year the total operating mileage 16.76 million kilometers and the total line network passenger flow 328.05 million passengers. In the urban areas 63 bus lines were newly opened to operation, or optimized and adjusted. At the end of the year there were 446 public transport lines in the urban areas, and in the year the operating mileage was 331 million kilometers and the total passenger traffic was 556 million passengers. 100% full coverage of pure electric, plug-in hybrid or hydrogen energy buses was realized in the ancient city (within the moat).

14. Environmental protection and energy saving and reducing energy consumption

Ecological protection was strengthened. In the year 66.4 billion yuan was invested in environmental protection. Taicang, Wujiang and Wuzhong were built into the first batch of provincial-level ecological civilization construction demonstration counties or districts. In the urban areas the $PM_{2.5}$ average concentration was 42 micrograms / cubic meter, and the proportion of the days of excellent or good air quality 73.7%, an increase of 2.2 percentage points over the previous year. The proportion of water quality III in the national and provincial examination sections was 68.8% and 76% respectively, and the proportion of water quality III in the tributaries into the Yangtze River reached 97.6%. In the urban areas 3.5 million square meters of green areas were newly built or rebuilt. The ecological protection zones of mountains, water, forests, fields, lakes were becoming more and more perfect. In the year the cultivation of 50,300 mu of forests was completed, and at the end of the year the city's land forest coverage rate reached 29.9%.

Energy saving and emission reduction were progressing steadily. In the year 358 construction projects that did not meet environmental requirements were dismissed or disapproved and involved an investment of 3.29 billion yuan. 1,256 management projects of the air pollution prevention and control project were completed. 260 low-end backward chemical enterprises were eliminated, and 35,425 "scattered, chaotic or polluting" enterprises (workshops) rectified, and the task of reducing the total coal consumption given by the provincial government completed.

In 2018, Suzhou's economic and social development achieved hard-won results, the economic operation remained within a reasonable range, the conversion of the old and new kinetic energies was accelerated, the quality and efficiency were improved, and the coordination and sustainability of the economic and social development were continuously enhanced, but the economic and social development was still facing many difficulties and problems, the downward pressure on the economy was increasing, the task of industrial transformation was arduous, the capacity for independent innovation and the quality of economic development needed to be further improved, and the tasks of ecological environmental protection, energy saving and emission reduction and pollution prevention were still arduous. In 2019, the whole city should continue to follow Xi Jinping's thought of socialism with Chinese characteristics in the new era as the guide, continue to persist in seeking progress in stability as the overall tone of work, adhere to the new development concept, adhere to the promotion of high-quality development, treat the supply-side structural reform as the main line, deepen market-oriented reforms, expand high-level openness, accelerate the construction of a modern economic system, continue to fight the three major battles, continue to promote the twelve projects of the "three-year action plans" as a starting point, further stabilize employment, finance, foreign trade, foreign investments, investments and expectations, ensure the steady growth of the city's economy, continue to promote the high-quality development of Suzhou at the forefront, and celebrate the 70th anniversary of the founding of the People's Republic of China with outstanding achievements.

一、综　合

CHAPTER 1
GENERAL SURVEY

综 合
GENERAL SURVEY

从统计数字看2018年的苏州
SUZHOU IN STATISTICS OF 2018

苏州在全国的地位
POSITION OF SUZHOU IN THE COUNTRY

地区生产总值	Gross Domestic Product	居全国第 7 位	7th Place in the Country
一般公共预算收入	General Public Budget Revenue	居全国第 5 位	5th Place in the Country
进出口总额	Total Imports and Exports	居全国第 4 位	4th Place in the Country

苏州在全省的地位
POSITION OF SUZHOU IN JIANGSU PROVINCE

地区生产总值	Gross Domestic Product	居全省第 1 位	First Place in Jiangsu
一般公共预算收入	General Public Budget Revenue	居全省第 1 位	First Place in Jiangsu
进出口总额	Total Imports and Exports	居全省第 1 位	First Place in Jiangsu

苏州的人口
POPULATION OF SUZHOU

年末户籍总人口	Year-end Registered Population	703.55	万人	10 000 persons
年末户籍总户数	Year-end Registered Households	230.92	万户	10 000 households
户籍人口密度	Density of Registered Population	813	人/平方公里	person/sq.km
年末常住人口	Year-end Permanent Population	1 072.17	万人	10 000 persons
常住人口密度	Density of Permanent Population	1 238	人/平方公里	person/sq.km

苏州的经济发展
ECONOMIC DEVELOPMENT OF SUZHOU

		2018年	1979-2018年平均增长(%) Average Growth Rate
地区生产总值 (亿元)	Gross Domestic Product (100 million yuan)	18 597.47	13.1
# 第三产业	Tertiary Industry	9 450.20	14.6
规模以上工业总产值	Gross Industrial Output Value Above Designated Size	33 354.01	–
固定资产投资	Investment in Fixed Assets	4 555.70	23.2
社会消费品零售总额	Total Retail Sales of Consumer Goods	5 746.90	17.4
进出口总额 (亿美元)	Total Exports and Imports (USD 100 million)	3 541.14	–
实际使用外资	Actual Utilization of Foreign Capital	45.25	–

苏州的人均水平
PER CAPITA LEVEL OF SUZHOU

地区生产总值	Gross Domestic Product	173 765	元	yuan
社会消费品零售总额	Total Retail Sales of Consumer Goods	53 696		
一般公共预算收入	General Public Budget Revenue	19 808		
城镇非私营单位在岗职工平均工资	Average Wage of Staff and Works	94 421		
全体常住居民可支配收入	Disposable Income of All the Residents	55 476		
城镇常住居民可支配收入	Disposable Income of Urban Residents	63 481		
农村常住居民可支配收入	Disposable Income of Rural Residents	32 420		
市区拥有道路面积	Per Capita Area of Roads of Urban Residents	31.49	平方米	sp. m
每万人拥有医生数	Number of Doctors Serving Per 10000 Persons	30.64	人	person

苏州的一天
ONE DAY IN SUZHOU

地区生产总值	Gross Domestic Product	509 520	万元	10 000 yuan
一般公共预算收入	General Public Budget Revenue	58 082		
规模以上工业总产值	Gross Industrial Output Value Above Designated Size	913 808		
固定资产投资额	Investment in Fixed Assets	124 814		
社会消费品零售总额	Total Retail Sales of Consumer Goods	157 449		
进出口总额	Total Imports and Exports	97 018	万美元	USD 10 000
# 出　口	Exports	56 666		
实际使用外资	Actual Utilization of Foreign Capital	1 240		

行政区划及自然概况

行政区划

苏州简称苏。下辖4个县级市：常熟市，张家港市，昆山市，太仓市；6个区：姑苏区，吴中区，相城区，高新区、虎丘区，工业园区和吴江区。2018年末，全市共有镇52个、街道41个、行政村1025个、居委会1180个。

位　置

苏州位于长江三角洲中部，在北纬30度47分至32度零2分，东经119度55分至121度20分之间，东邻上海，南连浙江省嘉兴、湖州两市，西傍太湖，与无锡相接，北枕长江。

苏州地理位置优越。京沪高速铁路、沪宁铁路、沪宁和沿江高速公路贯穿东西，京杭大运河和常台高速公路连接南北，境内河港密布，公路四通八达。横卧北侧的长江是重要水运干道。位于长江下游南岸的苏州港是国家一类口岸。

地　势

苏州地处太湖为中心的浅碟形平原的底部，地形以平原为主，全市地势低平，一般高程为海拔3.5至5米。东南部地势低洼，最低点低洼地在海拔2米以下。西南部多小山丘，穹窿山主峰“箬帽峰”，海拔341.7米，有“吴中之巅”之称。

面　积

苏州全市总面积8657.32平方公里。河流、湖泊、滩涂面积占全市土地面积的36.6%。2018年末市区建成区面积为475.88平方公里。

河　流

苏州是著名的江南水乡，拥有各级河道2万多条，大小湖泊300多个，著名的有太湖、阳澄湖、长江、京杭运河等。

气　候

苏州属亚热带湿润性季风海洋性气候，四季分明，气候温和，雨量充沛。2018年市区平均气温17.8摄氏度，降水量1369.2毫米。

ADMINISTRATIVE DIVISIONS & NATURAL CONDITIONS

Administrative Divisions

Suzhou is called Su in short. It includes four county-level cities: Changshu city, Zhangjiagang city, Kunshan city and Taicang city, and six districts: Gusu District, Wuzhong District,Xiangcheng District, New & Hi-tech, Huqiu District , Industrial Park and Wujiang District. There are 52 totally towns, 41 sub-districts, 1025 villages and 1180 neighborhood committees in Suzhou.

Location

Suzhou lies in the center of Yangtse River Delta, between 30°47′—32°02′E and 119°55′—121°20′N. It borders on Shanghai on the east, Jiaxing and Huzhou of Zhejiang on the south, Taihu Lake and Wuxi on the west and Yangtse on the north.

Suzhou enjoys strategic geographical location. Hu-Ning Railway, Hu-Ning Expressway and the riparian highway runs from east to west; Beijing-Hangzhou Grand Canal and Chang-Tai expressway connect south and north. Suzhou abounds in waterways and highways. Yangtse Rive that lies on the north of the city is a key waterway artery. Suzhou Port on the south bank of the lower reaches

Typography

Suzhou, at the bottom of a shallow saucer-shaped plain with Lake Tai at its center, is low and even. Average height is 3.5m-5m above sea level. The southeast part is relatively lower, with the lowest point 2m below sea level. The southwest is a hilly area, with the highest point, the peak of Qionglong Hill, 341.7m above sea level.

Area

The total area of Suzhou is 8657.32 sq.km, the river, lake, beach area accounted for 36.6% of the city's land area. At the end of 2018, Built-up Urban Area covers 475.88 sq.km.

Rivers & Lakes

Suzhou is a famous water country region to the south of Yangtse River. It has over 20 000 rivers and over 300 lakes of various size. Famous among them are Taihu Lake, Yangcheng Lake, Yangtse River & Beijing-Hongzhou Canal, etc.

Climate

Suzhou's climate belongs to monsoon of subtropical moist marine climate zone, with distinct four seasons, Suzhou has a mild climate with plenty rainfall. Average temperature of the year is 17.8℃ and annual precipitation is 1369.2 S millimeter in 2018.

表1-1

行政区划和土地面积(2018年末)
ADMINISTRATIVE DIVISION AND LAND AREA (END OF 2018)

单位：个　　(unit)

地　区	Region	镇 Town	村 Village	街　道 Subdistrict	居委会 Neighborhood Committee	土地面积(平方公里) Area of Land (sq.km)
全　市	**Whole Municipality**	**52**	**1 025**	**41**	**1 180**	**8 657.32**
市　区	**Urban Area**	**20**	**436**	**34**	**626**	**4 652.84**
姑苏区	Gusu District	–	4	8	169	83.42
吴中区	Wuzhong District	7	84	7	104	2 231.46
相城区	Xiangcheng District	4	68	7	76	489.96
高新区、虎丘区	New & Hi-tech Zone, Huqiu District	2	31	4	58	332.37
工业园区	Industrial Park	–	–	4	148	278.19
吴江区	Wujiang District	7	249	4	71	1 237.44
县级市	**Cities at County Level**	**32**	**589**	**7**	**554**	**4 004.48**
常　熟	Changshu	8	214	6	118	1 276.32
张家港	Zhangjiagang	8	153	–	144	986.73
昆　山	Kunshan	10	149	–	210	931.51
太　仓	Taicang	6	73	1	82	809.93

注：全市土地面积根据第二次全国土地调查结果调整，土地面积中含太湖、阳澄湖、淀山湖等大型湖泊水域面积。河流、湖泊、滩涂面积占全市土地面积的36.6%。

Note:The land area of the whole municipality is adjusted according to the result of the second national land survey, includes water area of Taihu Lake, Yangcheng Lake, Dianshan Lake and so on. The river, lake, beach area accounted for 36.6% of the city's land area.

表1-2

市区分月气象情况 (2018年)
MONTHLY CLIMATE CONDITIONS OF URBAN AREA (2018)

月 份	Month	平均气温 (摄氏度) Average Temperature (℃)	降水量 (毫米) Precipitation (mm)	日照时数 (小时) Sunshine Hours (hours)	平均相对湿度 (%) Average Relative Humidity (%)	平均风力 (米/秒) Average Wind Force (m/second)
全 年	**Annual Total**	**17.8**	**1 369.2**	**1 668.4**	**73**	**2.7**
1月	Jan.	3.7	98.3	78.5	76	2.7
2月	Feb.	5.4	64.1	115.6	68	2.4
3月	Mar.	12.5	61.7	139.6	74	2.6
4月	Apr.	18.3	106.3	173.8	65	2.8
5月	May	22.9	123.0	126.1	73	2.7
6月	Jun.	25.8	76.6	149.1	71	2.7
7月	Jul.	29.6	166.8	205.3	76	3.2
8月	Aug.	29.7	233.1	207.1	76	3.5
9月	Sept.	25.8	206.9	136.6	75	2.3
10月	Oct.	18.7	18.7	162.2	66	2.3
11月	Nov.	13.9	79.5	102.1	81	2.3
12月	Dec.	7.4	134.2	72.4	78	2.7

注:本表数据不含吴江区。 Note: The data in this table does not include Wujiang.

表1-3

分地区气象、水文情况 (2018年)
CLIMATE AND HYDROLOGIC CONDITIONS BY REGION (2018)

地 区	Region	年平均气温(摄氏度) Annual Average Temperature (℃)	年极端最高气温(摄氏度) Highest Temperature of the Year (℃)	年极端最低气温(摄氏度) Lowest Temperature of the Year (℃)	年降水量(毫米) Annual Precipitation (mm)	年降水日(天) Raining Days of the Year (day)	年平均气压(百帕) Annual Average Pressure (hPa)
市 区	Urban Area	17.8	37.9	-4.7	1 369.2	161	1 015.2
吴江区	Wujiang District	17.9	37.5	-6.0	1 247.0	140	1 015.6
常 熟	Changshu	17.6	37.8	-5.8	1 571.8	138	1 015.9
张家港	Zhangjiagang	17.3	37.4	-5.3	1 363.3	130	1 014.9
昆 山	Kunshan	17.8	37.9	-5.5	1 176.0	144	1 015.7
太 仓	Taicang	17.1	38.0	-7.6	1 615.8	134	1 015.6

表1-3 续表 Continued

地 区	Region	年无霜期(天) Annual Frost-free Period (day)	年日照时间(小时) Annual Sunshine Hours (hours)	年平均相对湿度(%) Annual Average Relative Humidity (%)	年平均风力(米/秒) Annual Average Wind-force (meter /second)	最高水位(米) Highest Water Level (m)	最低水位(米) Lowest Water Level (m)
市 区	Urban Area	265	1 668.4	73	2.7	4.11	3.03
吴江区	Wujiang District	275	1 852.4	73	1.9	3.77	2.87
常 熟	Changshu	276	1 826.6	76	2.1	4.12	2.93
张家港	Zhangjiagang	265	1 935.0	73	2.1	4.59	2.99
昆 山	Kunshan	278	1 762.1	74	2.0	3.63	2.79
太 仓	Taicang	277	2 068.0	78	2.3	3.69	2.72

注:本表市区数据不含吴江区。 Note: The data in this table does not include Wujiang.

表1-4

重要年份国民经济主要指标

指　标		Item		1952年	1978年
人　口		**Population**			
年末户籍总人口	(万人)	Year-end Population	(10 000 persons)	352.32	506.27
年末户籍总户数	(万户)	Total Number of Households (year-end)	(10 000 households)	88.33	137.42
劳动力		**Labor Force**			
年末从业人员	(万人)	Employed Persons (year-end)	(10 000 persons)	158.87	301.15
地区生产总值	(亿元)	**Gross Domestic Product**	(100 million yuan)	4.38	31.95
# 第三产业		Tertiary Industry		1.29	5.18
农　业		**Agriculture**			
1.农林牧渔业总产值		Gross Output Value of Farming, Forestry, Animal Husbandry and Fishery			18.75
2.主要农产品产量		Output of Major Farm Products			
粮　食	(万吨)	Grain	(10 000 tons)	133.41	294.26
油　料		Oil-bearing Crops		2.50	9.13
蚕　茧	(吨)	Silkworm Cocoons	(ton)	3 047	3 325
水产品	(万吨)	Aquatic Products	(10 000 tons)	2.15	8.22
猪出栏数	(万头)	Slaughtered Fattened Hogs	(10 000 heads)	22.16	185.66
猪年末存栏数		Hogs in Stock at Year–end		37.98	264.31
工　业		**Industry**			
1.规模以上工业总产值	(亿元)	Gross Industrial Output Value Above Designated Size	(100 million yuan)		
2.规模以上工业企业主要经济指标		The main index of Above Designated Size			
资产总计		Total Assets			
负债合计		Total Liabilities			
主营业务收入		Major Business Revenue			
利税总额		Total Taxes and Profits			
利润总额		Total Profits			
运输邮电		**Transportation and Postal**			
1.全社会公路水运货运量	(万吨)	Total Freight Traffic of Highways and Waterways	(10 000 tons)	209	2 195
2.全社会公路水运客运量	(万人次)	Total Passenger Traffic of Highways and Waterways	(10 000 person-times)	383	3 296
3.邮电业务总收入	(万元)	Postal and Telecommunications Business Volume	(10 000 yuan)	402	1 774
4.函　件(邮政系统)	(万件)	Letters Delivered (post system)	(10 000 pcs)	781	1 732
5.报刊杂志累计数	(万份)	Number of Newspapers and Magazines Circulation	(10 000 copies)	941	7 234

注：1. 2010年起，从业人员计算口径调整。
2. 地区生产总值从2004年起根据研发支出核算方法进行了相关修订。
3. 公路客运量自2013年起不包括公交车和出租车的运输量；公路货运量自2013年起不包含农用车和拖拉机的运输量。
4. 2013年起，邮政业务总收入中包含规模以上快递公司快递业务收入。

MAJOR NATIONAL ECONOMICAL INDICATORS OF IMPORTANT YEARS

1980年	1990年	2000年	2010年	2014年	2015年	2016年	2017年	2018年
518.62	561.02	578.17	637.66	661.08	667.01	678.20	691.07	703.55
142.33	173.36	198.18	211.79	217.46	219.23	222.44	226.58	230.92
317.17	346.74	313.89	687.50	693.40	691.40	691.30	691.60	692.30
40.68	202.14	1 540.68	9 366.47	13 994.42	14 761.36	15 748.58	17 319.51	18 597.47
6.80	43.90	579.62	3 852.94	6 693.79	7 275.32	8 064.22	8 861.65	9 450.20
11.42	58.12	169.30	271.29	392.49	415.17	424.67	424.69	410.09
254.31	283.50	193.95	114.43	110.46	108.22	96.35	92.40	87.92
8.16	14.01	12.61	3.45	2.04	1.57	1.34	1.18	0.59
4 784	9 785	7 291	638	357	295	237	199	193
8.71	21.73	34.51	27.70	26.70	26.21	25.49	23.41	19.56
310.14	193.54	198.50	117.70	103.46	94.89	84.46	69.45	35.63
250.34	154.62	104.75	83.51	76.69	66.44	60.34	29.54	13.66
		2 396.51	24 651.67	30 322.17	30 249.25	30 713.99	31 468.77	33 354.01
		2 346.98	19 351.14	26 108.97	26 895.74	28 356.50	30 203.70	32 223.44
		1 422.37	11 143.67	14 400.82	14 268.20	14 838.02	15 875.99	16 923.09
		2 245.72	24 577.51	30 397.27	29 768.65	30 380.18	32 005.86	34 108.40
		184.09	1 988.28	2 074.08	2 075.15	2 388.24	2 589.28	2 821.51
		97.16	1 507.06	1 460.13	1 529.04	1 772.74	2 002.15	2 094.05
2 712	3 211	7 816	13 417	12 953	13 005	13 508	14 937	16 159
4 813	6 764	18 559	56 475	39 958	34 645	32 130	31 903	29 762
2 300	12 818	441 910	1 726 867	2 752 456	2 937 920	3 267 824	3 541 523	3 979 385
2 245	3 051	5 476	27 841	25 449	23 258	13 814	11 222	9 441
9 977	16 246	30 461	30 438	30 832	29 367	27 128	28 220	26 792

Note: 1.In 2010,employed person use the new caliber.

2.Since 2004 the regional GDP has been revised according to the R&D expenditure accounting method.

3.The highway passenger transport volume in 2013 did not include that of buses and taxis; The highway freight transport volume in 2013 did not include that of agricultural vehicles and tractors.

4.In 2013 the total postal revenues began to include the business income of above-scale express courier companies.

表1-4 续表 1

指标	Item	1952年	1978年
国内贸易	**Domestic Trade**		
社会消费品零售总额 (亿元)	Total Retail Sales of Consumer Goods (100 million yuan)	3.12	9.47
对外经济和国际旅游	**Foreign Trade Economy and International Tourism**		
1.进出口总额 (亿美元)	Total Exports and Imports (USD 100 million)	–	–
出口总额	Exports	–	–
进口总额	Imports	–	–
2.使用外资	Utilization of Foreign Capital		
新设外资项目数 (个)	Number of Projects of Signed Contracts (unit)	–	–
新增注册外资金额 (亿美元)	Newly Added Value of Foreign Capital Signed (USD 100 million)	–	–
实际使用外资	Amount of Foreign Capital Actually Used	–	–
# 第三产业	Tertiary Industry	–	–
3.国际旅游	International Tourism		
接待境外游客 (万人次)	Number of Foreign Tourists (10 000 person-times)	–	–
电 力	**Electricity**		
全社会用电量 (亿千瓦时)	Electricity Consumption of the Whole Society (100 million kwh)	0.45	13.88
# 工业用电量	Industrial Consumption of Electricity		
固定资产投资	**Investment in Fixed Assets**		
固定资产投资 (亿元)	Investment in Fixed Assets (100 million yuan)		1.40
# 房地产开发投资	Value of Investment in Real Estate Development		
财 政	**Public Finance**		
一般公共预算收入 (亿元)	General Public Budget Revenue (100 million yuan)		
一般公共预算支出	General Public Budget Expenditure		
金 融	**Finance**		
金融机构人民币存款余额(亿元)	Deposit Balance of Financial Institutions (100 million yuan)	0.26	7.37
金融机构人民币贷款余额	Loans Balance of Financial Institutions	0.11	15.45

注：1.2013年起接待境外旅游者人数为公安登记统计口径。
2.2018年国家固定资产投资统计方法制度改革，统计方法口径有调整，总量、增速与以往年度不具可比性。

Continued 1

1980年	1990年	2000年	2010年	2014年	2015年	2016年	2017年	2018年
15.67	72.15	428.17	2 402.02	4 099.83	4 461.62	4 936.79	5 442.82	5 746.90
–	1.88	200.70	2 740.76	3 113.06	3 053.50	2 737.58	3 160.79	3 541.14
–	1.55	104.81	1 531.08	1 811.78	1 814.59	1 639.41	1 871.61	2 068.31
–	0.33	95.89	1 209.68	1 301.28	1 238.90	1 098.18	1 289.18	1 472.83
–	164	943	1 537	905	860	784	985	1 013
–	1.44	46.78	169.20	85.79	89.39	57.25	89.54	107.71
–	0.70	28.83	85.35	81.20	60.00	48.49	45.04	45.25
–	–	2.15	23.23	30.54	26.74	20.79	15.33	19.78
8.37	27.84	71.41	265.15	190.24	197.20	209.98	227.25	240.76
20.53	50.77	190.04	1 024.10	1 268.12	1 311.72	1 382.58	1 503.53	1 562.49
	38.14	153.17	855.25	1 044.14	1 074.20	1 116.30	1 202.04	1 227.77
2.87	55.37	516.43	3 617.82	6 230.67	6 124.43	5 648.49	5 629.59	4 555.70
	1.65	61.18	935.80	1 764.44	1 864.95	2 163.24	2 305.82	2 557.91
		80.39	900.55	1 443.82	1 560.76	1 730.04	1 908.10	2 119.99
		78.11	825.67	1 304.83	1 527.17	1 617.11	1 771.47	1 952.71
15.68	132.20	1 477.01	13 570.35	21 755.17	23 659.10	25 864.26	26 467.59	28 560.45
21.19	134.10	970.60	10 133.15	17 247.94	19 200.10	21 924.44	23 986.62	26 546.23

Note: 1.In 2013 the number of foreign tourists began to be the public security registration statistics caliber.

2.In 2018, the national statistical system for fixed assets investment was reformed, the statistical methods adjusted, and the total amount and growth rate not comparable to those of previous years.

表1-4 续表 2

指 标	Item	1952年	1978年
物价指数(以上年价格为100)	**Price Indices** (The Price of Preceding Year is Taken as 100)		
市区居民消费价格总指数	General Consumer Price Index of Urban Residents		
市区商品零售价格总指数	General Retail Price Index of Urban Area		
人民生活	**People's Livelihood**		
城镇非私营单位在岗职工平均工资 (元)	Average Wages of Urban Non-private Units (yuan)	455	514
农村居民人均可支配收入	Per Capita Net Income of Rural Residents		226
农村居民人均消费支出	Per Capita Living Expenditure of Rural Residents		212
城镇居民人均可支配收入	Per Capita Disposable Income of Urban Households		
城镇居民人均消费支出	Per Capita Living Expenditure of Urban Residents		
住户存款余额 (亿元)	Amount of Household Deposits (100 million yuan)		1.77
教 育	**Education**		
1.专任教师数 (人)	Number of Full-time Teachers (person)	10 573	40 127
2.在校学生数 (万人)	Students Enrollment (10 000 persons)	33.93	96.81
#普通高等学校 (人)	Institutions of Higher Education (person)	2 349	6 502
中等职业教育学校	Secondary Vocational Education Schools		2 748
技工学校	Skilled Workers' Schools		1 181
普通中学 (万人)	Regular Secondary Schools (10 000 persons)	3.40	32.76
小 学	Primary Schools	29.42	62.96
3.毕业生数	Graduates	2.20	26.27
卫 生	**Health Care**		
卫生机构数 (所)	Number of Health Institutions (unit)	238	971
#医院、卫生院	Hospitals	16	204
床位数 (张)	Number of Beds (bed)	1 372	14 470
#医院、卫生院	Hospitals		13 209
卫生技术人员 (人)	Number of Medical Personnel (person)	3 256	12 902
#医 生	Doctors	2 363	5 434

注：2014年起，教育相关指标包含外来工子弟学校数据，城乡居民人民币储蓄存款余额口径调整为住户存款口径。2013年起在岗职工平均工资调整为城镇非私营单位口径。

Continued 2

1980年	1990年	2000年	2010年	2014年	2015年	2016年	2017年	2018年
	103.9	99.9	103.4	102.1	101.6	102.7	101.7	102.60
104.2	103.2	98.5	103.1	101.7	100.4	100.5	101.5	102.50
687	2 450	11 778	45 566	66 956	72 291	79 870	87 350	94 421
271	1 664	5 462	14 657	23 560	25 580	27 691	29 977	32 420
296	1 415	4 073	10 397	15 390	16 761	18 820	20 298	21 587
	2 150	9 274	29 219	46 677	50 390	54 341	58 806	63 481
	1 805	7 027	17 879	28 973	31 136	33 305	35 104	37 403
3.64	73.33	803.70	4 655.56	7 022.63	7 358.04	7 913.85	8 166.44	9 168.45
35 978	40 145	47 908	65 174	76 340	79 114	82 015	86 054	92 496
81.28	71.13	87.69	95.85	117.98	124.37	131.04	137.56	146.42
8 819	16 280	47 701	187 829	209 479	214 816	219 347	222 838	235 649
5 231	25 293	60 185	74 828	57 606	59 227	61 202	61 061	58 880
1 757	5 866	12 346	32 158	24 173	23 743	23 593	23 861	26 381
22.86	21.73	30.47	27.25	27.96	29.25	30.98	33.44	36.05
56.79	44.56	44.84	38.84	60.63	65.07	69.37	73.06	78.13
18.44	14.15	19.26	24.19	22.97	25.03	26.86	29.03	28.61
1 125	1 537	1 319	2 675	3 063	3 121	3 175	3 160	3 380
207	207	197	216	263	271	283	286	302
13 720	18 424	19 504	39 204	55 218	59 304	63 241	66 640	68 921
12 385	16 223	17 582	36 839	52 887	56 894	60 847	64 417	66 626
14 514	22 253	24 881	46 507	64 281	68 179	72 166	79 623	85 188
6 316	10 895	11 594	18 156	25 352	26 197	27 667	30 259	32 852

Note: Starting from 2014, the relevant indicators of education include data from schools for children of migrant workers.Amount of saving deposits in urban and rural areas was adjusted to the scope of the household deposits caliber. In 2013 the average wages of the workers in the post were adjusted to the scope of the urban non-private units caliber.

表1-5 重要年份国民经济主要指标发展速度

指　标	Item	2018年为	
		1952年	1978年
人　口	**Population**		
年末户籍总人口	Year-end Population	199.7	139.0
年末户籍总户数	Total Number of Households (year–end)	261.4	168.0
劳动力	**Labor Force**		
年末从业人员	Employed Persons (year–end)	185.3	175.9
地区生产总值	**Gross Domestic Product**	1 077.8倍	139.4倍
# 第三产业	Tertiary Industry		236.5倍
农　业	**Agriculture**		
1.农林牧渔业总产值	Gross Output Value of Farming, Forestry, Animal Husbandry and Fishery		377.7
2.主要农产品产量	Output of Major Farm Products		
粮　食	Grain	65.9	29.9
油　料	Oil–bearing Crops	23.8	6.5
蚕　茧	Silkworm Cocoons	6.3	5.8
水产品	Aquatic Products	910.0	238.0
猪出栏数	Slaughtered Fattened Hogs	160.8	19.2
猪年末存栏数	Hogs in Stock at Year–end	36.0	5.2
工　业	**Industry**		
1.规模以上工业总产值	Gross Industrial Output Value Above Designated Size		
2.规模以上工业企业主要经济指标	The main index of Above Designated Size		
资产总计	Total Assets		
负债合计	Total Liabilities		
主营业务收入	Major Business Revenue		
利税总额	Total Taxes and Profits		
利润总额	Total Profits		
运输邮电	**Transportation and Postal**		
1.全社会公路水运货运量	Total Freight Traffic of Highways and Waterways	144.7倍	13.8倍
2.全社会公路水运客运量	Total Passenger Traffic of Highways and Waterways	175.6倍	20.4倍
3.邮电业务总收入	Postal and Telecommunications Business Volume	8 766.3倍	1 986.5倍
4.函　件	Letters Delivered	12.1倍	545.1
5.报刊杂志累计数	Number of Newspapers and Magazines Circulation	28.5倍	370.4

注：地区生产总值、农林牧渔业总产值的发展速度按可比价格计算。

GROWTH RATES OF MAJOR NATIONAL ECONOMICAL INDICATORS OF IMPORTANT YEARS

以下各年的%	% of the Following Years							1979-2018年 平均增长% Average Growth Rate %
1980年	1990年	2000年	2010年	2014年	2015年	2016年	2017年	
135.7	125.4	121.7	110.3	106.4	105.5	103.7	101.8	0.8
162.2	133.2	116.5	109.0	106.2	105.3	103.8	101.9	1.3
175.9	160.9	177.8	100.7	99.9	100.2	100.2	100.1	1.6
117.1倍	34.8倍	765.3	193.5	132.2	123.0	114.4	106.8	13.1
193.4倍	58.9倍	944.1	228.3	142.4	128.5	117.0	108.1	14.6
381.5	233.8	132.2	112.3	97.9	94.6	96.0	95.6	3.4
34.6	31.0	45.3	76.8	79.6	81.2	91.2	95.1	-3.0
7.3	4.2	4.7	17.2	29.2	37.9	44.4	50.5	-6.6
4.0	2.0	2.6	30.3	54.1	65.4	81.4	97.0	-6.9
224.6	90.0	56.7	70.6	73.3	74.6	76.8	83.6	2.2
11.5	18.4	17.9	30.3	34.4	37.5	42.2	51.3	-4.0
5.5	8.8	13.0	16.4	17.8	20.6	22.6	46.2	-7.1
		12.5倍	123.9	118.7	118.4	117.1	106.1	
		794.4	171.2	127.5	122.6	115.5	106.2	
		676.9	155.2	120.8	119.7	114.7	106.0	
		12.0倍	151.1	120.0	121.9	119.8	106.6	
		11.1倍	157.0	139.4	134.5	120.3	101.5	
		16.3倍	153.7	149.3	143.1	125.4	101.4	
11.2倍	941.8	386.9	189.1	124.8	124.3	119.6	108.2	6.8
14.0倍	994.5	362.4	95.6	74.5	85.9	92.6	93.3	7.8
1 532.2倍	274.9倍	797.5	204.1	144.5	135.4	121.8	112.4	20.9
420.5	309.4	172.4	33.9	37.1	40.6	68.3	84.1	4.3
268.5	164.9	88.0	88.0	86.9	91.2	98.8	94.9	3.3

Note: The regional GDP and the total output value of agriculture, forestry, animal husbandry and fishery are all calculated at comparable prices.

表1-5 续表 1

指　标	Item	2018年为	
		1952年	1978年
国内贸易	**Domestic Trade**		
社会消费品零售总额	Total Retail Sales of Consumer Goods	1 877.0倍	618.0倍
对外经济和国际旅游	**Foreign Trade Economy and International Tourism**		
1.进出口总额	Total Exports and Imports		
出口总额	Exports		
进口总额	Imports		
2.使用外资	Utilization of Foreign Capital		
新设外资项目数	Number of Projects of Signed Contracts		
新增注册外资金额	Newly Added Value of Foreign Capital Signed		
实际使用外资	Amount of Foreign Capital Actually Used		
# 第三产业	Tertiary Industry		
3.国际旅游	International Tourism		
接待境外旅游者人数	Number of Foreign Tourists		
电　力	**Electricity**		
全社会用电量	Electricity Consumption of the Whole Society	3 472.2倍	112.6倍
# 工业用电量	Industrial Consumption of Electricity		
固定资产投资	**Investment in Fixed Assets**		
固定资产投资	Investment in Fixed Assets		4 191.6倍
# 房地产开发投资	Value of Investment in Real Estate Development		
财　政	**Public Finance**		
一般公共预算收入	General Public Budget Revenue		
一般公共预算支出	General Public Budget Expenditure		
金　融	**Finance**		
金融机构人民币存款余额	Deposit Balance of Financial Institutions	11.0万倍	3 875.2倍
金融机构人民币贷款余额	Loans Balance of Financial Institutions	24.1万倍	1 718.2倍

Continued 1

以下各年的%	% of the Following Years							1979-2018年平均增长% Average Growth Rate %
1980年	1990年	2000年	2010年	2014年	2015年	2016年	2017年	
373.6倍	81.1倍	13.7倍	243.8	142.8	131.0	118.4	107.4	17.4
	1 883.6倍	17.6倍	129.2	113.8	116.0	129.4	112.0	
	1 334.4倍	19.7倍	135.1	114.2	114.0	126.2	110.5	
	4 463.1倍	15.4倍	121.8	113.2	118.9	134.1	114.2	
	617.7	107.4	65.9	111.9	117.8	129.2	102.8	
	74.8倍	230.2	63.7	125.6	120.5	188.1	120.3	
	173.0倍	417.3	62.0	65.2	75.4	93.3	100.5	
		920.2	85.2	64.8	74.0	95.2	129.1	
45.5倍	13.7倍	533.1	143.6	126.6	122.1	114.7	105.9	
76.1倍	30.8倍	822.2	152.6	123.2	119.1	113.0	103.9	12.5
	32.2倍	801.6	143.6	117.6	114.3	110.0	102.1	
2 047.4倍	106.2倍	11.4倍	162.6	94.4	96.1	104.2	104.5	23.2
	1 550.2倍	41.8倍	273.3	145.0	137.2	118.2	110.9	
		26.4倍	235.4	146.8	135.8	122.5	111.1	
		25.0倍	236.5	149.7	127.9	120.8	110.2	
1 821.5倍	216.0倍	19.3倍	210.5	131.3	120.7	110.4	107.9	22.9
1 252.8倍	198.0倍	27.4倍	262.0	153.9	138.3	121.1	110.7	20.5

表1-5 续表 2

指 标	Item	2018年为	
		1952年	1978年
物价指数	**Price Indices**		
市区居民消费价格总指数	General Consumer Price Index of Urban Residents		
市区商品零售价格总指数	General Retail Price Index of Urban Area		548.7
人民生活	**People's Livelihood**		
城镇非私营单位在岗职工平均工资	Average Wages of Urban Non-private Units	213.8倍	189.2倍
农村居民人均可支配收入	Per Capita Net Income of Rural Residents		144.5倍
农村居民人均消费支出	Per Capita Living Expenditure of Rural Residents		118.9倍
城镇居民人均可支配收入	Per Capita Disposable Income of Urban Households		
城镇居民人均消费支出	Per Capita Living Expenditure of Urban Residents		
住户存款余额	Amount of Household Deposits		4 995.5倍
教 育	**Education**		
1.专任教师数	Number of Full-time Teachers	830.8	218.9
2.在校学生数	Students Enrollment	395.7	138.7
# 普通高等学校	Institutions of Higher Education	100.3倍	36.2倍
中等职业教育学校	Secondary Vocational Education Schools		21.4倍
技工学校	Skilled Workers' Schools		22.3倍
普通中学	Regular Secondary Schools	10.4倍	107.6
小 学	Primary Schools	224.2	104.8
3.毕业生数	Graduates	12.3倍	103.3
卫 生	**Health Care**		
卫生机构数	Number of Health Institutions	14.2倍	348.1
# 医院、卫生院	Hospitals	18.9倍	148.0
床位数	Number of Beds	50.2倍	476.3
# 医院、卫生院	Hospitals		504.4
卫生技术人员	Number of Medical Personnel	26.2倍	660.3
# 医 生	Doctors	13.9倍	604.6

Continued 2

以下各年的%	% of the Following Years							1979-2018年平均增长% Average Growth Rate %
1980年	1990年	2000年	2010年	2014年	2015年	2016年	2017年	
	357.6	152.6	122.6	108.9	107.2	104.4	102.6	
515.7	241.9	126.8	115.4	105.1	104.6	104.1	102.5	
141.6倍	39.7倍	825.9	213.5	141.0	130.6	118.2	108.1	14.0
120.5倍	19.6倍	598.0	222.8	137.6	126.7	117.1	108.1	13.2
85.2倍	17.8倍	619.0	242.5	140.3	128.8	114.7	106.4	12.7
	30.8倍	715.1	208.0	136.0	126.0	116.8	108.0	
	19.4倍	497.6	195.6	129.1	120.1	112.3	106.5	
2 420.9倍	120.2倍	11.0倍	189.4	130.6	124.6	115.9	112.3	23.7
244.1	218.8	183.3	134.8	121.2	116.9	112.8	107.5	2.0
165.2	188.7	153.1	140.1	124.1	117.7	111.7	106.4	0.8
26.7倍	14.5倍	494.0	125.5	112.5	109.7	107.4	105.7	9.4
11.3倍	232.8	97.8	78.7	102.2	99.4	96.2	96.4	8.0
15.0倍	449.7	213.7	82.0	109.1	111.1	111.8	110.6	8.1
154.2	162.2	115.7	129.3	128.9	123.2	116.4	107.8	0.2
116.2	148.1	147.2	169.9	128.9	120.1	112.6	106.9	0.1
147.2	191.8	140.9	112.2	124.6	114.3	106.5	98.6	0.1
300.4	219.9	256.3	126.4	110.3	108.3	106.5	107.0	3.2
145.9	145.9	153.3	139.8	114.8	111.4	106.7	105.6	1.0
502.3	374.1	353.4	175.8	124.8	116.2	109.0	103.4	4.0
538.0	410.7	378.9	180.9	126.0	117.1	109.5	103.4	4.1
586.9	382.8	342.4	183.2	132.5	124.9	118.0	107.0	4.8
520.1	301.5	283.4	180.9	129.6	125.4	118.7	108.6	4.6

表1-6

部分年份国民经济主要比例关系
MAJOR PROPORTIONS IN NATIONAL ECONOMY OF PARTIAL YEARS

单位：% (%)

指　标	Item	2014年	2015年	2016年	2017年	2018年
常住人口城乡比例	**Ratio of Urban Population and Rural Population in Total Resident Population by Type of Industry**					
城镇人口	Urban Population	74.0	74.9	75.5	75.8	76.1
乡村人口	Rural Population	26.0	25.1	24.5	24.2	23.9
常住人口从业人员三次产业比例	**Ratio of Total Resident Population by Type of Industry**					
第一产业	Primary Industry	3.5	3.4	3.4	3.3	3.1
第二产业	Secondary Industry	60.5	60.0	59.6	59.1	58.6
第三产业	Tertiary Industry	36.0	36.6	37.0	37.6	38.3
地区生产总值中三次产业比例	**Ratio of GDP by Type of Industry**					
第一产业	Primary Industry	1.5	1.4	1.4	1.2	1.2
第二产业	Secondary Industry	50.7	49.3	47.4	47.6	48.0
第三产业	Tertiary Industry	47.8	49.3	51.2	51.2	50.8
农林牧渔业总产值中各业比例	**Ratio in Total Output of Farming, Forestry, Animal Husbandry and Fishery**					
农　业	Agriculture	41.2	41.6	42.1	42.7	43.3
林　业	Forestry	6.2	6.2	5.8	5.9	6.0
牧　业	Animal Husbandry	9.9	9.3	8.8	7.5	5.9
渔　业	Fishery	31.2	31.2	32.1	32.5	32.8
农林牧渔服务业	Farming, Forestry, Animal Husbandry, Fishery and Service Industry	11.5	11.7	11.2	11.4	12.0
规模以上工业轻重工业产值比例	**Ratio of Light and Heavy Industries in Total Industrial Output Above Designated Size**					
轻工业	Light Industry	25.8	25.2	25.1	23.9	22.8
重工业	Heavy Industry	74.2	74.8	74.9	76.1	77.2

表1-6 续表 Continued

单位：% (%)

指 标	Item	2014年	2015年	2016年	2017年	2018年
建筑业总产值比例	**Ratio of Gross Output Value of Construction**					
# 建筑工程	Construction	92.0	92.1	91.8	91.5	91.1
安装工程	Installation	7.2	7.2	7.5	7.9	8.1
社会消费品零售总额比例	**Ratio of Total Retail Sales of Consumer Goods**					
# 批发和零售业	Wholesale and Retail Sale Trades	87.3	87.9	88.0	88.0	87.6
住宿和餐饮业	Accommodation and Catering Trade	11.7	12.1	12.0	12.0	12.4
进出口比例	**Ratio of Imports and Exports**					
出口额	Exports	58.2	59.4	59.9	59.2	58.4
进口额	Imports	41.8	40.6	40.1	40.8	41.6
实际使用外资中三次产业比例	**Ratio of Amount of Foreign Capital Actually Utilized of Foreign Funded Enterprises by Type of Industry**					
第一产业	Primary Industry	0.1	0.1	0.1	…	…
第二产业	Secondary Industry	62.3	61.8	57.0	66.0	56.3
第三产业	Tertiary Industry	37.6	38.1	42.9	34.0	43.7
专利授权量比例	**Ratio of Number of Patent Applications Granted**					
发 明	Inventions	9.6	16.8	24.8	21.8	14.3
实用新型	Utility Models	58.5	57.7	64.7	68.7	76.8
外 观	Designs	31.9	25.5	10.5	9.5	8.9
税收收入占一般公共预算收入比例	**Proportion of General Public Budget Revenue that Tax Revenue Accounting For**	**86.2**	**85.8**	**87.0**	**87.7**	**91.0**

表1-7

部分年份国民经济主要指标日均水平
MAJOR DAILY INDICATORS OF NATIONAL ECONOMY OF PARTIAL YEARS

指　标	Item	2014年	2015年	2016年	2017年	2018年
地区生产总值 (万元)	Gross Domestic Product (10 000 yuan)	377 011	397 372	423 975	474 507	509 520
农林牧渔业总产值	Gross Output Value of Farming, Forestry, Animal Husbandry and Fishery	10 753	11 375	11 635	11 635	11 235
规模以上工业总产值	Gross Industrial Output Value Above Designated Size	830 744	828 746	841 479	862 158	913 808
一般公共预算收入	General Public Budget Revenue	39 557	42 761	47 398	52 277	58 082
粮食产量 (吨)	Yield of Grain Crops (ton)	3 026	2 965	2 640	2 531	2 409
水产品产量	Output of Aquatic Products	732	718	698	641	536
生铁产量	Pig Iron	75 228	74 651	71 913	73 377	72 881
钢材产量	Steel Products	109 966	114 609	109 150	116 303	125 826
笔记本计算机产量 (万台)	Laptop Computer (10 000 unit)	16.78	13.41	11.11	11.32	11.09
发电量 (万千瓦时)	Power Generation (10 000 kwh)	271 22	26 963	27 943	28 758	29 860
社会消费品零售总额 (万元)	Total Retail Sales of Consumer Goods (10 000 yuan)	112 324	122 236	135 254	149 118	157 449
固定资产投资额	Investment in Fixed Assets	170 703	167 793	154 753	154 235	124 814
竣工住宅建筑面积 (平方米)	Floor Space of Residential Buildings Completed (sq.m)	39 541	40 862	40 596	49 445	27 641
进出口总额 (万美元)	Total Exports and Imports (USD 10 000)	85 289	83 658	75 002	86 597	97 018
# 出　口	Exports	49 638	49 715	44 915	51 277	56 666
市区公共汽车客运总量(万人次)	Passenger Traffic of Buses in Urban Area (10 000 person-times)	189.90	183.81	169.64	160.46	152.26
市区家庭天然气用量 (万立方米)	Household Natural Gas Consumption in Urban Area (10 000 cu.m)	50.07	63.63	66.26	47.30	56.09
汽车上牌数 (辆)	Number of Vehicles Registration (coach)	1 026	1 122	1 354	1358	1 243
快　递 (万件)	Number of Express (10 000 pcs)	101.21	154.47	233.13	285.08	342.30
出生人数 (人)	Birth Population (person)	211	180	206	225	188
死亡人数	Death Population	121	125	117	135	134
结　婚 (对)	Marriages (couple)	159	153	132	126	126
离　婚	Divorces	54	55	59	68	71

注：此表日均指标按每年365天计算。

Note：The major daily indicators in this table are calculated by 365 days per year.

表1-8

部分年份国民经济主要指标人均水平
MAJOR PER CAPITA INDICATORS OF NATIONAL ECONOMY OF PARTIAL YEARS

指标	Item	2014年	2015年	2016年	2017年	2018年
地区生产总值 (元)	Gross Domestic Product (yuan)	129 925	136 702	145 556	162 388	173 765
农林牧渔业总产值	Gross Output Value of Farming, Forestry, Animal Husbandry and Fishery	3 706	3 913	3 994	3 982	3 832
规模以上工业总产值	Gross Industrial Output Value Above Designated Size	286 292	285 101	288 891	295 052	311 643
一般公共预算收入	General Public Budget Revenue	13 632	14 710	16 272	17 890	19 808
一般公共预算支出	General Public Budget Expenditure	12 320	14 394	15 210	16 609	18 245
粮食产量 (公斤)	Grain (kg)	104	102	91	87	82
水产品产量	Aquatic Products	25	25	24	22	18
生铁产量	Pig Iron	2 593	2 568	2 469	2 511	2 486
钢材产量	Steel Products	3 790	3 943	3 747	3 980	4 291
笔记本计算机产量 (台)	Laptop Computer (unit)	5.78	4.61	3.82	3.87	3.78
发电量 (千瓦时)	Power Generation (kwh)	9 347	9 276	9 593	9 842	10 183
社会消费品零售总额 (元)	Total Retail Sales of Consumer Goods (yuan)	38 709	42 051	46 435	51 032	53 696
固定资产投资额	Investment in Fixed Assets	58 828	57 723	53 129	52 783	42 566
进出口总额 (美元)	Total Exports and Imports (USD)	29 392	28 779	25 749	29 636	33 087
# 出口	Exports	17 106	17 103	15 420	17 548	19 325
卫生机构床位数 (张/万人)	Number of Beds in Health Institutions (unit/10 000 persons)	52.07	55.86	59.48	62.38	64.28
卫生技术人员 (人/万人)	Number of Medical Technical Personnel (person/10 000 persons)	60.62	64.22	67.88	74.53	79.45
# 医生	Doctors	23.91	24.68	25.98	28.32	30.64
全体常住居民可支配收入(元)	Disposable Income of the Resident Population (yuan)	39 780	42 987	46 595	51 208	55 476
全体常住居民消费支出	Consumer Spending of the Resident Population	24 920	26 847	28 983	31 202	33 327
城镇常住居民可支配收入	Disposable Income of the Urban Residents	46 677	50 390	54 341	58 806	63 481
城镇常住居民消费支出	Consumer Spending of the Urban Residents	28 973	31 136	33 305	35 104	37 403
农村常住居民可支配收入	Disposable Income of the Rural Residents	23 560	25 580	27 691	29 977	32 420
农村常住居民消费支出	Consumer Spending of the Rural Residents	15 390	16 761	18 820	20 298	21 587
住户存款余额	Deposits of Households at Year-end	66 151	69 311	74 436	76 439	85 513

注：此表人均指标按常住人口计算。居民收支为抽样调查数据。

Note：The per capita indicators in this table are calculated by the resident population. The income and expenditure of the residents were the survey data.

表1-9

苏州市国民经济主要指标在全省的地位 (2018年)
POSITION OF SUZHOU'S MAJOR NATIONAL ECONOMICAL INDICATORS IN THE PROVINCE (2018)

指　　标	Item	苏　州 Suzhou City	江　苏 Jiangsu Province	苏州占江苏的比重(%) Percentage of Suzhou in Jiangsu
年末户籍总人口　（万人）	Total Population (year-end)　(10 000 persons)	703.55	7 831.86	9.0
年末常住总人口	Resident Population (year-end)	1 072.17	8 050.70	13.3
# 城镇人口	Urban Population	815.39	5 604.09	14.5
地区生产总值　（亿元）	Gross Domestic Product　(100 million yuan)	18 597.47	92 595.40	20.1
第一产业	Primary Industry	213.99	4 141.72	5.2
第二产业	Secondary Industry	8 933.28	41 248.52	21.7
第三产业	Tertiary Industry	9 450.20	47 205.16	20.0
农林牧渔业总产值	Gross Output Value of Farming, Forestry, Animal Husbandry and Fishery	410.09	7 192.46	5.7
主要农产品产量	Output of Major Farm Products			
粮　食　（万吨）	Grain　(10 000 tons)	87.92	3 660.28	2.4
油　料	Oil-bearing Crops	0.59	86.04	0.7
水产品	Aquatic Products	19.56	494.80	4.0
牛　奶	Cow Milk	7.16	50.03	14.3
规模以上工业企业主要产品产量	Output of Major Industrial Products Above Designated Size			
发电量　（亿千瓦时）	Electricity　(100 million kwh)	1 089.88	4 933.54	22.1
钢　材　（万吨）	Steel Products　(10 000 tons)	4 592.66	12 146.72	37.8
粗　钢	Raw Steel	3 743.23	10 426.16	35.9
农用氮、磷、钾化学肥料总计(折纯)	Agricultural Chemical Fertilizers (Pure)	51.73	165.93	31.2
纱	Yarn	55.50	303.20	18.3
布　（亿米）	Cloth　(100 million meters)	6.92	69.40	10.0
全社会用电量　（亿千瓦时）	Electricity Consumption　(100 million kwh)	1 562.49	6 128.27	25.5
# 工业用电量	Industry	1 227.77	4 396.06	27.9
社会消费品零售总额　（亿元）	Total Retail Sales of Consumer Goods　(100 million yuan)	5 746.90	33 230.35	17.3

表1-9 续表 Continued

指 标	Item	苏 州 Suzhou City	江 苏 Jiangsu Province	苏州占江苏的比重(%) Percentage of Suzhou in Jiangsu
进出口总额 (亿美元)	Total Exports and Imports (USD 100 million)	3 541.14	6 640.43	53.3
出口总额	Total Exports	2 068.31	4 040.44	51.2
进口总额	Total Imports	1 472.83	2 599.99	56.6
新增注册外资金额	Newly Added Value of Foreign Capital Signed	107.71	605.22	17.8
实际使用外资	Amount of Foreign Capital Actually Used	45.25	255.92	17.7
一般公共预算收入 (亿元)	General Public Budget Revenue (100 million yuan)	2 119.99	8 630.16	24.6
一般公共预算支出	General Public Budget Expenditure	1 952.71	11 658.22	16.7
金融机构人民币存款余额	Deposit Balance of Financial Institutions at Year-end	28 560.45	139 717.98	20.4
金融机构人民币贷款余额	Loans Balance of Financial Institutions at Year-end	26 546.23	115 719.00	22.9
普通高等学校在校学生 (万人)	Students Enrollment of Institutions of Higher Education (10 000 persons)	23.56	200.09	11.8
普通中学在校学生	Students Enrollment of Regular Secondary Schools	36.05	323.84	11.1
小学在校学生	Students Enrollment of Primary Schools	78.13	560.44	13.9
卫生机构 (所)	Health Institutions (unit)	3 380	33 254	10.2
# 医 院	Hospitals	206	1 853	11.1
卫生机构床位数 (万张)	Number of Beds in Health Institutions (10 000 units)	6.89	49.08	14.0
卫生技术人员 (万人)	Number of Medical Personnel (10 000 persons)	8.52	59.00	14.4
# 医 生	Doctors	3.29	23.34	14.1
注册护士	Professional Nurse	3.76	26.03	14.4
全体常住居民人均可支配收入(元)	Per Capita Disposable Income of the Resident Population (yuan)	55 476	38 096	–
城镇常住居民人均可支配收入	Per Capita Disposable Income of the Urban Residents	63 481	47 200	–
农村常住居民人均可支配收入	Per Capita Disposable Income of the Rural Residents	32 420	20 845	–

表1-10

历年地区生产总值
GROSS DOMESTIC PRODUCT OVER THE YEARS

单位：亿元 (100 million yuan)

年 份 Year	地区生产总值 Gross Domestic Product	第一产业 Primary Industry	第二产业 Secondary Industry	第三产业 Tertiary Industry	总计中：工业 In Total: Industry	人均地区生产总值（元） Per Capita GDP (yuan)	人均地区生产总值（美元） Per Capita GDP (USD)
1952	4.38	2.01	1.09	1.29	1.06	126	
1965	10.78	4.95	3.74	2.10	3.56	254	
1970	15.03	6.26	6.16	2.62	5.61	325	
1975	23.32	8.18	10.98	4.15	10.08	471	
1978	31.95	8.97	17.79	5.18	16.69	634	
1980	40.68	10.03	23.85	6.80	22.61	787	
1985	91.91	18.07	56.67	17.17	52.59	1 714	584
1990	202.14	35.00	123.24	43.90	112.52	3 617	756
1995	903.11	80.37	543.41	279.33	499.12	15 784	1 890
2000	1 540.68	90.96	870.10	579.62	790.83	26 692	3 224
2001	1 760.28	91.41	999.89	668.98	912.11	30 384	3 671
2002	2 080.37	91.72	1 211.52	777.13	1 106.87	35 733	4 317
2003	2 801.56	75.75	1 771.86	953.95	1 586.61	47 693	5 762
2004	3 365.94	78.60	2 235.13	1 052.21	2 088.97	46 619	5 633
2005	4 173.48	82.08	2 712.03	1 379.37	2 550.74	56 142	6 854
2006	4 948.07	94.80	3 193.04	1 660.23	3 019.45	63 131	7 919
2007	5 914.31	105.26	3 687.52	2 121.53	3 497.55	69 910	9 194
2008	7 163.40	121.17	4 331.65	2 710.58	4 098.86	79 825	11 494
2009	7 851.01	129.01	4 642.92	3 079.08	4 361.02	84 894	12 427
2010	9 366.47	140.80	5 372.73	3 852.94	5 035.10	94 430	13 949
2011	10 885.92	161.02	6 103.77	4 621.13	5 700.99	103 739	16 061
2012	12 207.81	176.53	6 672.74	5 358.54	6 225.26	115 891	18 359
2013	13 191.33	193.29	6 955.11	6 042.93	6 462.84	124 872	20 165
2014	13 994.42	203.98	7 096.65	6 693.79	6 563.23	132 131	21 510
2015	14 761.36	215.71	7 270.33	7 275.32	6 715.07	139 127	22 337
2016	15 748.58	221.81	7 462.55	8 064.22	6 894.16	148 129	22 300
2017	17 319.51	221.98	8 235.88	8 861.65	7 606.45	162 388	24 052
2018	18 597.47	213.99	8 933.28	9 450.20	8 240.37	173 765	26 259

注：1.2004年起人均地区生产总值按常住人口计算，下同。
2.地区生产总值从2004年起根据研发支出核算方法进行了相关修订，下同。

Note: 1. In 2004, per capita GDP began to be calculated according to the resident population, the same below.
2. Since 2004 the regional GDP has been revised according to the R&D expenditure accounting method，the same below.

表1-11

历年地区生产总值构成
PROPORTIONS IN GROSS DOMESTIC PRODUCT OVER THE YEARS

单位：%　(%)

年份 Year	地区生产总值 Gross Domestic Product	第一产业 Primary Industry	第二产业 Secondary Industry	第三产业 Tertiary Industry	总计中：工业 In Total: Industry
1952	100.0	45.9	24.8	29.3	24.2
1965	100.0	45.9	34.6	19.5	33.0
1970	100.0	41.6	41.0	17.4	37.3
1975	100.0	35.1	47.1	17.8	43.2
1978	100.0	28.1	55.7	16.2	52.2
1980	100.0	24.7	58.6	16.7	55.6
1985	100.0	19.7	61.6	18.7	57.2
1990	100.0	17.3	61.0	21.7	55.7
1995	100.0	8.9	60.2	30.9	55.3
2000	100.0	5.9	56.5	37.6	51.3
2001	100.0	5.2	56.8	38.0	51.8
2002	100.0	4.4	58.2	37.4	53.2
2003	100.0	2.7	63.2	34.1	56.6
2004	100.0	2.3	66.4	31.3	62.1
2005	100.0	1.9	65.0	33.1	61.1
2006	100.0	1.9	64.5	33.6	61.0
2007	100.0	1.8	62.3	35.9	59.1
2008	100.0	1.7	60.5	37.8	57.2
2009	100.0	1.7	59.1	39.2	55.5
2010	100.0	1.5	57.4	41.1	53.8
2011	100.0	1.4	56.1	42.5	52.4
2012	100.0	1.4	54.7	43.9	51.0
2013	100.0	1.5	52.7	45.8	49.0
2014	100.0	1.5	50.7	47.8	46.9
2015	100.0	1.4	49.3	49.3	45.5
2016	100.0	1.4	47.4	51.2	43.8
2017	100.0	1.2	47.6	51.2	43.9
2018	100.0	1.2	48.0	50.8	44.3

表1-12

历年地区生产总值指数

INDICES OF GROSS DOMESTIC PRODUCT OVER THE YEARS

(以上年为100，按可比价格计算 Takes Preceding Year as 100, Calculated at Comparable Price)

单位：% (%)

年 份 Year	地区生产总值 Gross Domestic Product	第一产业 Primary Industry	第二产业 Secondary Industry	第三产业 Tertiary Industry	总计中：工业 In Total: Industry	人均地区生产总值 Per Capita GDP
1979	104.0	86.2	107.0	124.1	106.6	102.6
1980	114.5	103.9	124.1	98.5	126.1	113.2
1981	107.5	94.7	110.5	112.7	109.9	106.4
1982	107.5	115.6	106.8	101.6	105.9	106.3
1983	111.2	95.6	113.0	123.1	112.2	110.5
1984	126.3	135.3	126.5	117.4	126.0	126.1
1985	130.0	96.3	138.8	132.9	139.4	129.6
1986	108.1	111.1	106.5	112.2	105.0	107.2
1987	116.4	100.1	120.4	114.2	118.1	115.2
1988	116.8	99.4	121.7	109.3	120.2	115.7
1989	95.5	96.4	94.0	101.7	95.7	94.6
1990	113.5	108.6	116.3	104.9	117.7	112.5
1995	114.8	111.8	114.5	116.5	114.9	114.4
2000	112.6	104.1	112.7	113.8	113.1	112.3
2001	112.3	101.2	112.6	113.6	112.9	111.9
2002	114.5	101.1	116.3	113.8	116.3	114.0
2003	118.0	94.5	121.7	115.0	120.3	117.0
2004	117.6	99.5	120.4	114.5	122.5	116.1
2005	115.3	100.7	115.2	116.5	115.5	112.0
2006	115.8	105.1	115.7	116.8	116.2	109.8
2007	116.1	104.6	115.6	117.8	116.0	107.6
2008	113.2	103.5	112.1	116.3	112.6	106.7
2009	111.5	103.9	110.0	114.6	109.5	108.2
2010	113.3	103.9	113.3	113.7	113.3	105.6
2011	112.0	104.4	111.5	112.9	111.8	105.9
2012	110.1	104.1	107.8	113.4	107.5	109.7
2013	109.6	102.7	107.5	112.6	107.6	109.3
2014	108.3	100.0	106.2	111.2	106.2	108.0
2015	107.5	103.3	104.8	110.8	104.3	107.3
2016	107.5	99.0	105.3	109.9	105.4	107.3
2017	107.1	100.8	106.0	108.2	106.7	106.7
2018	106.8	95.4	105.6	108.1	106.0	106.4

表1-13

全市生产总值
GROSS DOMESTIC PRODUCT IN THE WHOLE CITY

项　　目	Item	2017年	2018年	增长%(可比价) Increased (%) (at comparable prize)
全市生产总值 (亿元)	**Gross Domestic Product** (100 million yuan)	**17 319.51**	**18 597.47**	**6.8**
按产业分	**Grouped by Industry**			
第一产业	Primary Industry	221.98	213.99	-4.6
第二产业	Secondary Industry	8 235.88	8 933.28	5.6
第三产业	Tertiary Industry	8 861.65	9 450.20	8.1
按行业分	**Grouped by Sector**			
农林牧渔业	Farming, Forestry, Animal Husbandry and Fishery	247.55	240.01	-3.9
工　业	Industry	7 606.45	8 240.37	6.0
建筑业	Construction	630.95	694.56	0.4
交通运输、仓储和邮政业	Transportation, Logistics and Postal	518.44	545.34	4.3
批发和零售业	Wholesale and Retail Trade Services	2 233.74	2 341.88	4.3
# 零售业	Retail Trade Services	456.64	478.98	3.4
住宿和餐饮业	Accommodation and Catering Services	475.88	511.06	4.6
# 餐饮业	Catering Services	414.51	445.75	4.6
金融业	Financial Industries	1 421.24	1 520.59	6.1
房地产业	Real Estate	1 066.86	1 133.57	4.4
其他服务业	Other Service Industries	3 118.40	3 370.09	14.3
营利性服务业	Profitable Service Industries	1 599.85	1 761.95	19.3
非营利性服务业	Non-profit Service Industries	1 518.55	1 608.14	8.8
人均地区生产总值(户籍人口) (元)	**Per Capita GDP** (Household Register Population) (yuan)	**252 975**	**266 704**	**4.8**
人均地区生产总值(常住人口)	**Per Capita GDP** (the Resident Population)	**162 388**	**173 765**	**6.4**

表1-14 分地区生产总值 (2018年)

项　目	Item	姑苏区 Gusu District	吴中区 Wuzhong District
绝对值 (亿元)	**Absolute Value** (100 million yuan)		
地区生产总值	**Gross Domestic Product**	**709.35**	**1 124.73**
第一产业	Primary Industry	–	22.15
第二产业	Secondary Industry	66.67	525.89
第三产业	Tertiary Industry	642.68	576.69
总计中：工业	In Total:Industry	13.22	473.11
人均地区生产总值(户籍人口) (元)	Per Capita GDP (Household Register Population) (yuan)	96 633	166 680
人均地区生产总值(常住人口)	Per Capita GDP (The Resident Population)	74 222	99 126
构　成 (%)	**Composition** (%)		
地区生产总值	**Gross Domestic Product**	**100.0**	**100.0**
第一产业	Primary Industry	–	1.9
第二产业	Secondary Industry	9.4	46.8
第三产业	Tertiary Industry	90.6	51.3
总计中：工业	In Total:Industry	1.9	42.1
比上年增长 (可比价) (%)	**Increase Over Last Year** (at comparable prize) (%)		
地区生产总值	**Gross Domestic Product**	**6.0**	**6.7**
第一产业	Primary Industry	–	-2.3
第二产业	Secondary Industry	1.6	4.2
第三产业	Tertiary Industry	6.6	9.4
总计中：工业	In Total:Industry	5.3	4.5
人均地区生产总值(户籍人口)	Per Capita GDP (Household Register Population)	5.8	3.9
人均地区生产总值(常住人口)	Per Capita GDP (The Resident Population)	5.8	6.0

GROSS DOMESTIC PRODUCT BY REGION (2018)

相城区 Xiangcheng District	高新区、虎丘区 New & Hi-tech Zone, Huqiu District	工业园区 Industrial Park	吴江区 Wujiang District	常 熟 Changshu	张家港 Zhangjiagang	昆 山 Kunshan	太 仓 Taicang
771.06	**1 256.27**	**2 570.27**	**1 925.03**	**2 400.23**	**2 720.18**	**3 832.06**	**1 330.72**
8.51	1.85	1.26	43.10	39.90	30.63	31.62	34.98
380.10	758.82	1 432.95	986.79	1 230.01	1 423.68	2 074.53	675.47
382.45	495.60	1 136.06	895.14	1 130.32	1 265.87	1 725.91	620.27
301.39	707.19	1 345.93	924.33	1 161.97	1 352.35	1 951.17	631.33
179 448	315 154	486 785	230 059	224 631	292 737	433 995	271 329
104 888	210 187	315 054	147 302	158 334	216 023	230 270	185 465
100.0	**100.0**	**100.0**	**100.0**	**100.0**	**100.0**	**100.0**	**100.0**
1.1	0.1	0.0	2.2	1.7	1.2	0.9	2.6
49.3	60.4	55.8	51.3	51.2	52.3	54.1	50.8
49.6	39.5	44.2	46.5	47.1	46.5	45.0	46.6
39.1	56.3	52.4	48.0	48.4	49.7	50.9	47.4
6.7	**7.0**	**7.1**	**7.0**	**6.8**	**6.7**	**7.2**	**6.8**
-26.9	-24.6	-0.9	-2.8	-5.8	-3.1	1.8	-3.6
5.7	7.0	5.0	6.0	6.7	3.3	5.4	6.4
8.7	7.1	9.7	8.5	7.2	10.5	9.3	7.7
7.0	7.4	5.2	6.3	7.1	3.5	5.7	6.8
4.0	2.7	1.7	6.0	6.8	6.5	2.3	5.6
6.5	6.5	6.4	6.6	6.6	6.4	6.9	6.2

表1-15

私营企业户数 (2018年末)

单位：户

项　目	Item	全 市 Whole Municipality
私营企业	**Private Enterprises**	**603 205**
农、林、牧、渔业	Farming , Forestry ,Animal Husbandry and Fishery	2 673
采矿业	Mining and Quarrying	19
制造业	Manufacturing	125 117
电力、热力、燃气及水生产和供应业	Electricity, Heat, Gas and Water Production and Supply Industries	355
建筑业	Construction	42 077
批发和零售业	Wholesale and Retail Trade Services	212 729
交通运输、仓储和邮政业	Transportation, Logistics and Postal	15 566
住宿和餐饮业	Accommodation and Catering Services	4 427
信息传输、软件和信息技术服务业	Information Transmission, Software and Information Technology Services	20 597
金融业	Financial Industries	1 821
房地产业	Real Estate	16 705
租赁和商务服务业	Leasing and Business Services	70 746
科学研究和技术服务业	Scientific Research and Technical Services	66 611
水利、环境和公共设施管理业	Water Conservancy, Environment and Public Facilities Management	1 608
居民服务、修理和其他服务业	Resident Services, Repairs and Other Services	9 886
教　育	Education	2 309
卫生和社会工作	Health and Social Work	964
文化、体育和娱乐业	Culture, Sports and Entertainment	8 986
其他行业	Others	9

NUMBER OF PRIVATE ENTERPRISES (END OF 2018)

(household)

市 区 Urban Area	# 吴江区 Wujiang District	常 熟 Changshu	张家港 Zhangjiagang	昆 山 Kunshan	太 仓 Taicang	本年开业 Opened in This Year	本年注销 Cancelled in This Year
351 873	**64 810**	**52 633**	**50 548**	**117 806**	**30 345**	**99 180**	**16 676**
1 806	517	276	203	252	136	230	73
16	2	–	3	–	–	4	–
62 143	19 735	14 432	14 487	24 931	9 124	10 789	1 829
184	73	59	43	43	26	50	32
25 283	3 929	2 165	2 677	9 691	2 261	7 581	1 038
116 686	24 621	23 440	19 988	44 744	7 871	31 233	5 993
8 230	1 307	1 227	1 854	2 666	1 589	2 443	394
2 838	403	319	157	947	166	816	213
15 781	1 157	971	537	2 762	546	4 006	921
1 403	166	134	66	152	66	200	70
9 284	1 590	1 219	690	4 358	1 154	3 203	571
49 116	4 995	3 696	3 440	11 717	2 777	14 141	2 927
43 578	3 841	2 682	4 979	11 861	3 511	19 171	1 847
856	172	220	94	365	73	178	44
6 347	1 077	978	684	1 380	497	1 577	369
1 260	244	195	241	521	92	671	51
418	83	160	78	240	68	264	27
6 638	895	459	327	1 174	388	2 620	277
6	3	1	–	2	–	3	–

表1-16

私营企业从业人员 (2018年末)

单位：人

项　目	Item	全　市 Whole Municipality
私营企业	**Private Enterprises**	**4 814 840**
农、林、牧、渔业	Farming , Forestry ,Animal Husbandry and Fishery	19 150
采矿业	Mining and Quarrying	172
制造业	Manufacturing	1 868 664
电力、热力、燃气及水生产和供应业	Electricity, Heat, Gas and Water Production and Supply Industries	3 628
建筑业	Construction	358 523
批发和零售业	Wholesale and Retail Trade Services	1 110 365
交通运输、仓储和邮政业	Transportation, Logistics and Postal	111 265
住宿和餐饮业	Accommodation and Catering Services	46 687
信息传输、软件和信息技术服务业	Information Transmission, Software and Information Technology Services	111 830
金融业	Financial Industries	15 595
房地产业	Real Estate	135 382
租赁和商务服务业	Leasing and Business Services	439 692
科学研究和技术服务业	Scientific Research and Technical Services	426 399
水利、环境和公共设施管理业	Water Conservancy, Environment and Public Facilities Management	17 844
居民服务、修理和其他服务业	Resident Services, Repairs and Other Services	79 260
教　育	Education	12 981
卫生和社会工作	Health and Social Work	12 376
文化、体育和娱乐业	Culture, Sports and Entertainment	44 941
其他行业	Others	86

EMPLOYMENT OF PRIVATE ENTERPRISES (END OF 2018)

(person)

市 区 Urban Area	# 吴江区 Wujiang District	常 熟 Changshu	张家港 Zhangjiagang	昆 山 Kunshan	太 仓 Taicang	附：注册资金 (万元) Registered Capital (10 000 yuan)
2 500 424	**517 263**	**551 944**	**639 484**	**819 367**	**303 621**	**361 415 989**
11 307	2 816	2 538	1 845	1 909	1 551	946 890
101	13	–	71	–	–	56 003
826 269	272 468	319 333	310 103	279 346	133 613	59 793 138
1 281	524	670	1 015	278	384	695 835
184 664	27 764	27 988	37 494	86 715	21 662	25 544 849
579 993	120 361	107 449	153 353	216 356	53 214	55 420 034
51 882	7 228	8 352	20 452	16 414	14 165	7 342 084
28 816	4 103	5 116	2 323	8 287	2 145	1 239 220
82 634	5 621	5 030	4 192	15 648	4 326	7 838 875
11 853	1 069	1 680	784	920	358	23 950 857
77 099	11 411	11 319	6 984	29 421	10 559	15 226 519
292 422	27 586	24 126	31 991	70 177	20 976	113 518 192
254 298	21 688	21 110	51 421	67 864	31 706	41 613 573
9 073	1 203	2 614	1 199	4 091	867	1 723 677
43 570	6 667	9 888	10 024	11 576	4 202	2 449 339
7 003	1 102	969	1 967	2 458	584	387 661
5 768	1 120	1 121	2 005	2 403	1 079	369 691
32 357	4 498	2 591	2 261	5 502	2 230	3 298 492
34	21	50	–	2	–	1 060

表1-17

个体劳动者户数 (2018年末)

单位：户

项　　目	Item	全　市 Whole Municipality
个体劳动者	**Self-employed Individuals**	**886 664**
农、林、牧、渔业	Farming , Forestry ,Animal Husbandry and Fishery	3 464
采矿业	Mining and Quarrying	9
制造业	Manufacturing	95 266
电力、热力、燃气及水生产和供应业	Electricity, Heat, Gas and Water Production and Supply Industries	62
建筑业	Construction	14 197
批发和零售业	Wholesale and Retail Trade Services	512 470
交通运输、仓储和邮政业	Transportation, Logistics and Postal	21 833
住宿和餐饮业	Accommodation and Catering Services	101 584
信息传输、软件和信息技术服务业	Information Transmission, Software and Information Technology Services	2 290
金融业	Financial Industries	10
房地产业	Real Estate	3 264
租赁和商务服务业	Leasing and Business Services	38 009
科学研究和技术服务业	Scientific Research and Technical Services	5 026
水利、环境和公共设施管理业	Water Conservancy, Environment and Public Facilities Management	539
居民服务、修理和其他服务业	Resident Services, Repairs and Other Services	80 007
教　育	Education	2 379
卫生和社会工作	Health and Social Work	682
文化、体育和娱乐业	Culture, Sports and Entertainment	5 355
其他行业	Others	218

NUMBER OF SELF-EMPLOYED INDIVIDUALS (END OF 2018)

(household)

市 区 Urban Area	# 吴江区 Wujiang District	常 熟 Changshu	张家港 Zhangjiagang	昆 山 Kunshan	太 仓 Taicang	本年开业 Opened in This Year	本年注销 Cancelled in This Year
413 957	**97 808**	**124 633**	**97 098**	**187 131**	**63 845**	**175 805**	**48 896**
1 449	609	692	539	391	393	589	74
3	1	–	2	4	–	1	1
35 573	8 090	17 436	12 797	21 067	8 393	13 874	4 859
16	6	23	10	8	5	–	5
2 952	660	2 719	1 985	4 413	2 128	5 331	422
254 961	61 679	76 071	47 489	98 223	35 726	78 964	25 407
4 064	2 633	4 205	8 363	3 394	1 807	3 938	428
52 126	11 118	10 846	9 986	21 546	7 080	28 511	10 963
829	121	158	552	598	153	751	275
2	1	–	2	5	1	5	2
1 063	29	169	459	1 149	424	499	178
10 948	2 795	1 504	2 756	21 353	1 448	23 417	1 188
2 939	323	379	325	1 068	315	1 532	245
200	23	84	60	107	88	140	12
42 289	8 886	9 586	10 731	12 009	5 392	16 279	4 325
811	170	156	405	908	99	531	117
396	136	24	101	111	50	92	22
3 334	528	581	536	562	342	1 135	373
2	–	–	–	215	1	216	–

表1-18

个体劳动者从业人员 (2018年末)

单位：人

项　　目	Item	全　市 Whole Municipality
个体劳动者	**Self-employed Individuals**	**1 715 925**
农、林、牧、渔业	Farming , Forestry ,Animal Husbandry and Fishery	8 145
采矿业	Mining and Quarrying	14
制造业	Manufacturing	303 914
电力、热力、燃气及水生产和供应业	Electricity, Heat, Gas and Water Production and Supply Industries	123
建筑业	Construction	35 678
批发和零售业	Wholesale and Retail Trade Services	799 063
交通运输、仓储和邮政业	Transportation, Logistics and Postal	27 248
住宿和餐饮业	Accommodation and Catering Services	258 529
信息传输、软件和信息技术服务业	Information Transmission, Software and Information Technology Services	3 969
金融业	Financial Industries	19
房地产业	Real Estate	7 115
租赁和商务服务业	Leasing and Business Services	54 817
科学研究和技术服务业	Scientific Research and Technical Services	10 137
水利、环境和公共设施管理业	Water Conservancy, Environment and Public Facilities Management	1 379
居民服务、修理和其他服务业	Resident Services, Repairs and Other Services	182 031
教　育	Education	6 591
卫生和社会工作	Health and Social Work	1 747
文化、体育和娱乐业	Culture, Sports and Entertainment	15 398
其他行业	Others	8

EMPLOYMENT OF SELF-EMPLOYED INDIVIDUALS (END OF 2018)

(person)

市 区 Urban Area	# 吴江区 Wujiang District	常 熟 Changshu	张家港 Zhangjiagang	昆 山 Kunshan	太 仓 Taicang	附：注册资金 (万元) Registered Capital (10 000 yuan)
886 071	**177 087**	**232 256**	**169 623**	**344 632**	**83 343**	**8 000 352**
4 068	1 569	1 589	1 056	854	578	106 403
6	1	–	1	7	–	68
132 131	24 056	63 254	40 990	50 046	17 493	1 127 188
40	10	36	19	20	8	580
8 752	1 414	8 165	6 925	8 642	3 194	202 644
434 953	93 165	99 522	59 175	165 632	39 781	4 049 936
7 242	3 443	4 931	8 042	5 057	1 976	174 038
153 051	26 539	24 383	22 348	48 812	9 935	1 207 398
1 542	186	222	936	1 106	163	15 419
8	2	–	2	8	1	51
2 023	38	261	1 165	3 191	475	24 145
20 626	4 331	2 648	3 979	25 805	1 759	207 823
6 245	675	741	705	2 008	438	42 445
544	75	223	248	233	131	7 484
101 854	19 301	24 081	20 824	28 567	6 705	711 729
2 597	487	282	1 125	2 449	138	28 554
1 196	450	43	167	255	86	9 096
9 190	1 345	1 875	1 916	1 937	480	85 329
3	–	–	–	3	2	20

主要统计指标解释

行政区划 指国家对行政区域的划分。根据有关法规规定，我国的行政区域划分如下：(1)全国分为省、自治区、直辖市；(2)省、自治区分为自治州、地区、自治县、市；(3)自治州分为县、自治县、市；(4)县、自治县分为乡、民族乡、镇；(5)直辖市和较大的市分为区、县；(6)国家在必要时设立的特别行政区。

气温 指空气的温度，我国一般以摄氏度为单位表示。气象观测的温度表是放在离地面约1.5米处通风良好的百叶箱里测量的，因此，通常说的气温指的是离地面1.5米处百叶箱中的温度。

相对湿度 指空气中实际水气压与当时气温下的饱和水气压之比。

降水量 指从天空降落到地面的液态或固态(经融化后)水，未经蒸发、渗透、流失而在地面上积聚的深度。

日照时数 指太阳实际照射地面的时数。

国内（地区）生产总值（GDP） 指一个国家或地区的所有常住单位在一定时期内所生产的全部最终产品和服务的价值总和，是反映经济总体状况最重要的指标。

GDP核算有三种方法，即生产法、收入法和支出法，三种方法从不同的角度反映国民经济生产活动成果。生产法是从生产过程中创造的货物和服务价值中，剔除生产过程中投入的中间货物和服务价值，得到增加值的一种方法。国民经济各行业生产法增加值计算公式如下：增加值＝总产出－中间投入。将国民经济各行业生产法增加值相加，得到生产法国内生产总值。收入法是从生产过程形成收入的角度，对生产活动成果进行核算。按照这种计算方法，增加值由劳动者报酬、生产税净额、固定资产折旧和营业盈余四个部分组成。计算公式为：增加值＝劳动者报酬＋生产税净额＋固定资产折旧＋营业盈余。国民经济各行业收入法增加值之和等于收入法国内生产总值。支出法是从生产活动成果最终使用的角度计算国内生产总值的一种方法。最终使用包括最终消费支出、资本形成总额及货物和服务净出口三部分。

三次产业 三次产业的划分是世界上较为常用的产业结构分类，根据《国民经济行业分类》（GB/T 4754—2017），三次产业划分是：

第一产业是指农、林、牧、渔业（不含农、林、牧、渔专业及辅助性活动）；

第二产业是指采矿业（不含开采专业及辅助性活动），制造业（不含金属制品、机械和设备修理业），电力、热力、燃气及水生产和供应业，建筑业；

第三产业是指除第一产业、第二产业以外的其他行业。

EXPLANATORY NOTES ON MAIN STATISTICAL INDICATORS

Divisions of Administrative Areas refers to the division of administrative areas by the State. The relative laws stipulate that 1) the whole country is divided into provinces, autonomous regions and municipalities directly under the Central Government; 2) provinces and autonomous regions are further divided into autonomous prefectures, counties, autonomous counties and cities; 3) autonomous prefectures are further divided into counties, autonomous counties and cities; 4) counties and autonomous counties are further divided into townships, ethnic townships and towns; 5) municipalities and large cities are divided into districts and counties, 6) the State shall, when necessary, establish special administrative regions.

Temperature refers to the air temperature. China uses centigrade as the unit. The thermometry used for weather observation is put in a breezy shutter, which is 1.5 meters high from the ground. Therefore, the commonly used temperature refers to the temperature in the breezy shutter 1.5 meters away from the ground.

Relative Humidity refers to the ratio of actual water vapour pressure to the saturation water vapour density under the current temperature.

Volume of Precipitation refers to the deepness of liquid state or solid state (thawed) water falling from the sky to the ground that has not been evaporated, infiltrated or run off.

Sunshine Hours refer to the actual hours of sun irradiating the earth, usually expressed in hours.

Gross Domestic (Regional) Product (GDP) refers to the sum of the total value of all final products and services produced by all resident units of a country or region for a certain period of time, and is the most important indicator reflecting the overall state of the economy.

There are three methods for GDP accounting, namely the production method, the income method and the expenditure method, and the three methods reflect the results of national economic production activities from different angles. The production method is a method of obtaining the added value from the value of goods and services created in the production process, eliminating the value of intermediate goods and services invested in the production process. The formula for calculating the added value of the production method in various industries of the national economy is as follows: added value = total output -- intermediate input. When the added values of the production method of various industries in the national economy are added, the gross domestic product of the production method is obtained. The income method is to calculate the results of production activities from the perspective of income from the production process. According to this calculation method, the added value consists of four parts: labor compensation, net production tax, depreciation of fixed assets and operating surplus. The calculation formula is: added value = labor compensation + net production tax + depreciation of fixed assets + operating surplus. The sum of the added values of the income method in all sectors of the national economy is equal to the gross domestic product of the income method. The expenditure method is a method of calculating gross domestic product from the perspective of the final use of production activities. The final use includes three parts: final consumption expenditure, total capital formation, and net exports of goods and services.

Three Industries The division of three industries is a more common classification of industrial structure in the world. According to the "Industry Classification of the National Economy" (GB/T 4754--2017), the three industries are divided into:

The primary industry refers to the industries of agriculture, forestry, animal husbandry and fishery (excluding the professions of agriculture, forestry, animal husbandry and fishery, and auxiliary activities);

The secondary industry refers to the mining industry (excluding the mining profession and auxiliary activities), manufacturing (excluding metal products, machinery and equipment repair), electricity, heat, gas and water production and supply, construction;

The tertiary industry refers to other industries except the primary industry and the secondary industry.

二、人口 劳动力

CHAPTER 2 POPULATION AND LABOR FORCE

2 人口　劳动力 POPULATION AND LABOR FORCE

主要统计指标 MAJOR STATISTICAL INDICATORS

2018年末常住人口	Resident Population	1 072.17	万人	10 000 persons
城镇人口比重	Proportion of Urban Population	76.1	%	
2018年末户籍总户数	Total Households	230.92	万户	10 000 households
比上年增长	Increase Over Last Year	1.9	%	
2018年末户籍总人口	Total Household Population	703.55	万人	10 000 persons
比上年增长	Increase Over Last Year	1.8	%	
2018年末户籍人口中:	In the Household Population			
出生人数	Birth Population	68 487	人	persons
出生率	Birth Rate	9.82	‰	
死亡人数	Death Population	49 004	人	persons
死亡率	Death Rate	7.03	‰	
自然增长人数	Natural Growth Population	19 483	人	persons
自然增长率	Natural Growth Rate	2.79	‰	
2018年末就业人口	Employment Population	692.30	万人	10 000 persons
比上年增长	Increase Over Last Year	0.1	%	
2018年城镇非私营单位从业人员平均工资	Average Wages of Employees in Urban Non-private Units	94 124	元	yuan
比上年增长	Increase Over Last Year	7.7	%	

表2-1

全市人口普查主要数据
MAIN DATA OF THE PREVIOUS CENSUS

指　标		Item		1982年 "三普" The Third Census in 1982	1990年 "四普" The Fourth Census in 1990	2000年 "五普" The Fifth Census in 2000	2010年 "六普" The Sixth Census in 2010
常住人口	(万人)	**Resident Population**	(10 000 persons)	**527.53**	**564.36**	**679.22**	**1 045.99**
男		Male		264.87	282.77	336.41	533.45
女		Female		262.66	281.59	342.82	512.54
性别比(女性为100)		Sex Ratio (Female = 100)		100.84	100.42	98.13	104.08
家庭户规模	(人/户)	**Family Size**	(person/household)	**3.50**	**3.51**	**3.15**	**2.84**
各年龄组人口	(万人)	**Population by Age Group**	(10 000 persons)				
0-14岁		Aged 0—14		126.08	105.07	97.88	96.31
15-64岁		Aged 15—64		367.23	413.75	516.25	860.77
65岁及以上		Aged 65 and Over		34.22	45.54	65.09	88.91
劳动适龄人口	(万人)	**Working Age Population**	(10 000 persons)	**326.88**	**370.77**	**469.16**	**779.41**
男（16-59岁）		Male (Aged 16—59)		172.01	194.75	241.46	414.93
女（16-54岁）		Female (Aged 16—54)		154.87	176.02	227.70	364.48
民族人口	(万人)	**Population by Ethnicity**	(10 000 persons)				
汉　族		Han Nationality		527.25	563.79	677.56	1 038.70
占总人口比重	(%)	Proportion	(%)	99.94	99.89	99.76	99.30
少数民族		Minority Nationalities		0.28	0.57	1.66	7.29
占总人口比重	(%)	Proportion	(%)	0.06	0.11	0.24	0.70
各种受教育程度的人口	(万人)	**Population with Various Education Attainments**	(10 000 persons)	**342.56**	**411.63**	**596.41**	**975.11**
小　学		Primary School		191.98	199.25	219.89	226.64
初　中		Junior Secondary School		108.69	149.02	249.88	402.38
高中、中专		Senior Secondary School and Technical Secondary School		37.71	52.82	94.41	199.79
大专及以上		Junior College and Above		4.18	10.55	32.23	146.30
#大学专科		Junior College				20.32	88.49
大学本科		Undergraduate College				11.39	53.21
研究生		Graduate College				0.52	4.60
城乡人口	(万人)	**Population by Residence**	(10 000 persons)				
城镇人口		Urban Population		108.24	146.01	387.73	732.95
乡村人口		Rural Population		419.29	418.35	291.49	313.04

表2-2

分地区常住人口
RESIDENT POPULATION BY REGION

单位：万人 (10 000 persons)

地 区	Region	2017年末 End of 2017 常住人口 Total Population	2017年末 End of 2017 城镇人口比重 (%) Proportion of Urban Population (%)	2018年末 End of 2018 常住人口 Total Population	2018年末 End of 2018 城镇人口比重 (%) Proportion of Urban Population (%)
全 市	**Whole Municipality**	**1 068.36**	**75.80**	**1 072.17**	**76.05**
市 区	**Urban Area**	**553.15**	**81.64**	**556.02**	**81.84**
姑苏区	Gusu District	95.39	100.00	95.75	100.00
吴中区	Wuzhong District	112.95	71.95	113.98	72.20
相城区	Xiangcheng District	73.51	70.39	73.51	70.50
高新区、虎丘区	New & Hi-tech Zone , Huqiu District	59.61	87.92	59.93	88.29
工业园区	Industrial Park	81.30	99.71	81.87	99.76
吴江区	Wujiang District	130.39	68.81	130.98	69.16
县级市	**Cities at County Level**				
常 熟	Changshu	151.61	68.23	151.58	68.54
张家港	Zhangjiagang	125.78	68.13	126.06	68.44
昆 山	Kunshan	166.24	72.78	166.59	73.06
太 仓	Taicang	71.58	67.19	71.92	67.40

注：常住人口根据当年人口变动情况抽样调查数据推算。
Note:Resident population is calculated according to the change of the population sample survey data.

表2-3

历年年末户籍户数、人口数

单位：人

年　份 Year	全市总人口 Total Population of Whole Municipality	按地区分 By Region					
		市　区 Urban Area	# 吴江区 Wujiang District	常熟市 Changshu	张家港市 Zhangjiagang	昆山市 Kunshan	太仓市 Taicang
1949	3 386 027	1 613 652	468 631	681 358	484 098	304 813	302 106
1952	3 523 189	1 671 208	490 870	693 474	497 929	348 754	311 824
1957	3 851 040	1 839 466	539 483	750 452	538 305	382 491	340 326
1962	3 996 505	1 912 708	541 890	773 606	569 442	389 084	351 665
1965	4 295 134	2 057 262	585 879	820 204	618 233	427 467	371 968
1970	4 680 237	2 199 896	657 381	894 054	698 071	483 290	404 926
1975	4 926 040	2 319 193	693 119	939 340	735 534	509 228	422 745
1978	5 062 702	2 392 332	708 187	964 437	756 618	521 320	427 995
1980	5 186 167	2 490 995	716 057	980 263	762 715	523 532	428 662
1985	5 351 145	2 597 103	733 017	998 031	782 712	537 940	435 359
1990	5 610 165	2 732 375	764 187	1 032 888	834 070	564 610	446 222
1995	5 729 088	2 805 659	777 226	1 043 573	850 486	580 504	448 866
2000	5 781 689	2 843 674	771 822	1 039 064	854 953	594 592	449 406
2001	5 805 252	2 864 844	770 320	1 037 618	853 597	600 279	448 914
2002	5 838 599	2 893 397	769 423	1 036 229	852 718	606 936	449 319
2003	5 909 656	2 940 849	772 186	1 037 962	860 195	619 534	451 116
2004	5 988 510	2 985 027	777 509	1 043 132	868 640	637 157	454 554
2005	6 073 101	3 034 158	783 094	1 047 659	879 033	654 603	457 648
2006	6 160 814	3 089 935	788 438	1 054 825	887 804	666 809	461 441
2007	6 244 311	3 146 191	793 172	1 061 410	893 039	679 846	463 825
2008	6 297 530	3 177 364	795 254	1 065 018	898 430	690 435	466 283
2009	6 332 903	3 199 301	797 240	1 066 417	900 132	699 885	467 168
2010	6 376 558	3 224 328	799 569	1 066 908	905 085	711 333	468 904
2011	6 423 336	3 254 268	801 784	1 067 183	907 868	723 644	470 373
2012	6 478 054	3 289 922	804 868	1 067 798	910 208	737 565	472 561
2013	6 538 372	3 328 982	808 562	1 067 263	914 740	752 926	474 461
2014	6 610 766	3 374 960	814 370	1 068 844	919 816	769 746	477 400
2015	6 670 124	3 412 564	817 952	1 068 211	922 757	787 031	479 561
2016	6 781 957	3 480 163	824 518	1 068 666	926 592	823 547	482 989
2017	6 910 682	3 562 955	832 739	1 069 079	929 018	862 709	486 921
2018	7 035 490	3 640 885	840 768	1 067 968	929 429	903 238	493 970

YEAR-END HOUSEHOLDS AND POPULATION OVER THE YEARS

(person)

按性别分 By Sex		年平均人口 Average Person Per Year	总户数(户) Total Number of Households (household)	平均每户人口 Average Person	人口密度 (人/平方公里) Density of Population (person/sq.km)
男 Male	女 Female				
1 685 685	1 700 342	3 384 031	815 858	4.15	399
1 768 903	1 754 286	3 467 676	883 279	3.99	415
1 910 677	1 940 363	3 818 428	950 301	4.05	453
1 977 577	2 018 928	3 966 800	1 080 214	3.70	471
2 143 538	2 151 596	4 294 262	1 081 437	3.97	506
2 330 843	2 349 394	4 642 755	1 203 088	3.89	551
2 461 171	2 464 869	4 904 225	1 269 739	3.88	580
2 534 209	2 528 493	5 036 822	1 374 222	3.68	596
2 598 646	2 587 521	5 167 938	1 423 285	3.64	611
2 685 217	2 665 928	5 335 524	1 556 308	3.44	630
2 812 685	2 797 480	5 588 121	1 733 612	3.24	661
2 866 058	2 863 030	5 721 692	1 878 344	3.05	675
2 873 897	2 907 792	5 771 988	1 981 783	2.92	681
2 882 853	2 922 399	5 793 471	1 994 777	2.91	684
2 900 486	2 938 113	5 821 926	2 019 150	2.89	688
2 927 836	2 981 820	5 874 128	2 049 073	2.88	696
2 963 235	3 025 275	5 949 083	2 058 936	2.91	705
3 003 445	3 069 656	6 030 805	2 068 264	2.93	715
3 045 120	3 115 694	6 116 958	2 072 444	2.97	726
3 085 728	3 158 583	6 202 563	2 087 038	2.99	736
3 110 084	3 187 446	6 270 921	2 096 473	3.00	742
3 125 028	3 207 875	6 315 217	2 106 918	3.01	746
3 144 153	3 232 405	6 354 731	2 117 941	3.01	751
3 164 805	3 258 531	6 399 947	2 132 385	3.01	757
3 189 087	3 288 967	6 450 695	2 140 419	3.03	763
3 215 645	3 322 727	6 508 213	2 155 714	3.03	770
3 247 621	3 363 145	6 574 569	2 174 611	3.04	779
3 273 640	3 396 484	6 640 445	2 192 281	3.04	770
3 325 291	3 456 666	6 726 041	2 224 446	3.05	783
3 385 031	3 525 651	6 846 320	2 265 822	3.05	798
3 441 658	3 593 832	6 973 086	2 309 153	3.05	813

表2-4

历年户籍人口自然变动情况
NATURAL CHANGE OF POPULATION OVER THE YEARS

年 份 Year	出 生 Birth		死 亡 Death		自然增长 Natural Growth	
	人数(人) Population (person)	出生率(‰) Birth Rate (‰)	人数(人) Population (person)	死亡率(‰) Death Rate (‰)	人数(人) Population (person)	自然增长率(‰) Natural Growth Rate(‰)
1949	112 250	33.17	36 481	10.78	75 769	22.39
1952	128 700	37.11	32 286	9.31	96 414	27.80
1957	151 343	39.63	42 553	11.14	108 790	28.49
1962	123 893	31.23	45 428	11.45	78 465	19.78
1965	138 504	32.59	36 606	8.61	101 898	23.98
1970	119 799	25.80	31 297	6.74	88 502	19.06
1975	67 435	13.75	31 667	6.46	35 768	7.29
1978	73 308	14.55	32 800	6.51	40 508	8.04
1980	60 835	11.77	33 726	6.53	27 109	5.24
1985	55 305	10.37	36 219	6.79	19 086	3.58
1990	67 998	13.32	37 402	6.69	30 596	6.63
1995	48 803	8.53	40 073	7.00	8 730	1.53
2000	44 002	7.62	40 677	7.05	3 325	0.58
2001	36 694	6.33	38 930	6.72	-2 236	-0.39
2002	40 068	6.88	41 634	7.15	-1 566	-0.27
2003	42 786	7.28	42 308	7.20	478	0.08
2004	47 501	7.98	40 814	6.86	6 687	1.12
2005	48 477	8.04	41 385	6.86	7 092	1.18
2006	46 325	7.57	39 111	6.39	7 214	1.18
2007	48 552	7.83	40 503	6.53	8 049	1.30
2008	47 772	7.62	41 743	6.66	6 029	0.96
2009	49 663	7.86	41 427	6.56	8 236	1.30
2010	58 402	9.19	42 866	6.75	15 536	2.44
2011	58 732	9.18	41 956	6.56	16 776	2.62
2012	68 097	10.56	45 010	6.98	23 087	3.58
2013	67 396	10.36	44 478	6.84	22 918	3.52
2014	76 837	11.69	44 178	6.72	32 659	4.97
2015	65 846	9.92	45 691	6.88	20 155	3.04
2016	75 303	11.20	42 685	6.35	32 618	4.85
2017	82 241	12.01	49 334	7.20	32 907	4.81
2018	68 487	9.82	49 004	7.03	19 483	2.79

表2-5

分地区户籍户数与人口情况 (2018年末)
HOUSEHOLDS AND POPULATION BY REGION (END OF 2018)

地　　区	Region	总户数(户) Total Number of Households (household)	总人口(人) Total Population (person)	按性别分(人) By Sex (person)	
				男 Male	女 Female
全　　市	**Whole Municipality**	**2 309 153**	**7 035 490**	**3 441 658**	**3 593 832**
市　区	**Urban Area**	**1 196 124**	**3 640 885**	**1 787 728**	**1 853 157**
姑苏区	Gusu District	283 551	734 824	359 903	374 921
吴中区	Wuzhong District	207 128	682 917	333 935	348 982
相城区	Xiangcheng District	134 509	434 897	212 180	222 717
高新区、虎丘区	New & Hi-tech Zone , Huqiu District	126 514	407 023	201 221	205 802
工业园区	Industrial Park	180 126	540 456	267 192	273 264
吴江区	Wujiang District	264 296	840 768	413 297	427 471
县级市	**Cities at County Level**	**1 113 029**	**3 394 605**	**1 653 930**	**1 740 675**
常　熟	Changshu	322 476	1 067 968	517 583	550 385
张家港	Zhangjiagang	323 325	929 429	454 331	475 098
昆　山	Kunshan	309 217	903 238	443 585	459 653
太　仓	Taicang	158 011	493 970	238 431	255 539

表2-5 续表 1　Continued 1

地　　区	Region	年平均人口(人) Average Person Per Year (person)	平均预期寿命 e°x (岁) Average Life-span (age)		
			合　计 Total	男 Male	女 Female
全　　市	**Whole Municipality**	**6 973 086**	**83.54**	**81.23**	**85.87**
市　区	**Urban Area**	**3 601 920**	**83.72**	**81.50**	**86.00**
姑苏区	Gusu District	734 068	84.26	81.69	87.03
吴中区	Wuzhong District	674 784	83.52	81.45	85.56
相城区	Xiangcheng District	429 684	83.35	81.09	85.61
高新区、虎丘区	New & Hi-tech Zone , Huqiu District	398 621	83.76	81.19	86.34
工业园区	Industrial Park	528 010	83.58	81.65	85.50
吴江区	Wujiang District	836 754	83.38	81.23	85.60
县级市	**Cities at County Level**	**3 371 166**	**83.37**	**80.98**	**85.73**
常　熟	Changshu	1 068 524	82.95	80.49	85.34
张家港	Zhangjiagang	929 224	82.89	80.25	85.57
昆　山	Kunshan	882 974	84.05	81.96	86.15
太　仓	Taicang	490 446	84.27	81.98	86.50

表2-5 续表 2 Continued 2

地　　区	Region	出生人数（人）Birth Population (person)	出生率（‰）Birth Rate (‰)	死亡人数（人）Death Population (person)	死亡率（‰）Death Rate (‰)
全　市	**Whole Municipality**	**68 487**	**9.82**	**49 004**	**7.03**
市　区	**Urban Area**	**38 438**	**10.67**	**23 770**	**6.60**
姑苏区	Gusu District	5 182	7.06	6 059	8.25
吴中区	Wuzhong District	7 862	11.65	4 229	6.27
相城区	Xiangcheng District	5 132	11.94	2 805	6.53
高新区、虎丘区	New & Hi-tech Zone , Huqiu District	4 766	11.96	2 031	5.10
工业园区	Industrial Park	7 393	14.00	2 074	3.93
吴江区	Wujiang District	8 103	9.68	6 572	7.85
县级市	**Cities at County Level**	**30 049**	**8.91**	**25 234**	**7.49**
常　熟	Changshu	6 932	6.49	9 259	8.67
张家港	Zhangjiagang	7 077	7.62	7 047	7.58
昆　山	Kunshan	12 524	14.18	4 836	5.48
太　仓	Taicang	3 516	7.17	4 092	8.34

表2-5 续表 3 Continued 3

地　　区	Region	自然增长人数（人）Natural Growth Population (person)	自然增长率（‰）Natural Growth Rate (‰)	迁入人数（人）Number of the Transferred From Outside (person)	迁出人数（人）Number of the Transferred to Outside (person)
全　市	**Whole Municipality**	**19 483**	**2.79**	**124 776**	**19 326**
市　区	**Urban Area**	**14 668**	**4.07**	**74 975**	**11 348**
姑苏区	Gusu District	-877	-1.19	15 010	2 557
吴中区	Wuzhong District	3 633	5.38	15 375	1 540
相城区	Xiangcheng District	2 327	5.42	7 823	598
高新区、虎丘区	New & Hi-tech Zone , Huqiu District	2 735	6.86	12 008	1 885
工业园区	Industrial Park	5 319	10.07	18 432	3 495
吴江区	Wujiang District	1 531	1.83	6 327	1 273
县级市	**Cities at County Level**	**4 815**	**1.43**	**49 801**	**7 978**
常　熟	Changshu	-2 327	-2.18	3 233	1 503
张家港	Zhangjiagang	30	0.03	3 018	2 247
昆　山	Kunshan	7 688	8.71	34 532	3 173
太　仓	Taicang	-576	-1.17	9 018	1 055

表2-6

婚姻登记情况 (2018年)
CONDITIONS OF MARRIAGE REGISTRATION (2018)

地 区	Region	准予结婚登记(对) Marriage Legally Registered (couple)	女性晚婚率(%) Rate of Marriage at Mature Age for Female (%)	离婚(对) Divorced (couple)
全 市	**Whole Municipality**	**45 950**	**83.71**	**25 837**
市 区	**Urban Area**	**26 085**	**84.20**	**15 690**
姑苏区	Gusu District	5 747	79.41	3 468
吴中区	Wuzhong District	4 400	84.46	2 735
相城区	Xiangcheng District	3 142	80.88	1 807
高新区、虎丘区	New & Hi-tech Zone , Huqiu District	3 247	86.88	1 934
工业园区	Industrial Park	4 671	87.19	3 264
吴江区	Wujiang District	4 878	85.47	2 482
县级市	**Cities at County Level**	**19 865**	**82.79**	**10 147**
常 熟	Changshu	5 791	81.55	2 423
张家港	Zhangjiagang	5 893	88.08	2 722
昆 山	Kunshan	5 577	87.45	3 570
太 仓	Taicang	2 604	74.62	1 432

表2-7

生育情况 (2018年)
CONDITIONS OF BIRTH (2018)

地 区	Region	育龄妇女年末人数 (万人) Number of Woman of Child-bearing Age (10 000 persons)	总和生育率(%) Total Fertility Rate(%)
全 市	**Whole Municipality**	**152.11**	**1.12**
市 区	**Urban Area**	**78.70**	**1.16**
姑苏区	Gusu District	14.55	0.76
吴中区	Wuzhong District	14.64	1.34
相城区	Xiangcheng District	9.09	1.27
高新区、虎丘区	New & Hi-tech Zone , Huqiu District	8.76	1.23
工业园区	Industrial Park	13.25	0.92
吴江区	Wujiang District	18.41	1.24
县级市	**Cities at County Level**	**73.41**	**1.09**
常 熟	Changshu	21.91	0.99
张家港	Zhangjiagang	20.22	0.97
昆 山	Kunshan	20.32	1.38
太 仓	Taicang	10.95	0.92

表2-8

历年按三次产业划分的年末就业人口及构成
EMPLOYMENT POPULATION AND ITS COMPOSITION BY THREE INDUSTRIES OVER THE YEARS

年 份 Year	年末就业人口 (万人) Total Employed Persons (10 000 persons)	第一产业 Primary Industry	第二产业 Secondary Industry	第三产业 Tertiary Industry	构 成 (%) Composition (%)	第一产业 Primary Industry	第二产业 Secondary Industry	第三产业 Tertiary Industry
1952	158.87	128.58	13.55	16.74	100.0	80.9	8.5	10.6
1957	177.69	144.40	17.95	15.34	100.0	81.3	10.1	8.6
1970	260.61	213.62	30.40	16.59	100.0	81.9	11.7	6.4
1975	282.34	213.12	45.49	23.73	100.0	75.5	16.1	8.4
1978	301.15	187.70	81.57	31.88	100.0	62.3	27.1	10.6
1980	317.17	184.93	98.85	33.39	100.0	58.3	31.2	10.5
1985	349.44	128.37	168.49	52.58	100.0	36.7	48.2	15.1
1990	346.74	103.13	177.84	65.77	100.0	29.7	51.3	19.0
1995	324.45	65.08	178.98	80.39	100.0	20.0	55.2	24.8
2000	313.89	65.90	156.27	91.72	100.0	21.0	49.8	29.2
2001	321.96	66.29	158.98	96.69	100.0	20.6	49.4	30.0
2002	323.75	61.66	161.38	100.71	100.0	19.0	49.9	31.1
2003	346.19	55.02	195.31	95.86	100.0	15.9	56.4	27.7
2004	358.82	48.61	211.11	99.10	100.0	13.6	58.8	27.6
2005	393.72	43.38	231.68	118.66	100.0	11.0	58.9	30.1
2006	429.46	35.94	263.71	129.81	100.0	8.4	61.4	30.2
2007	483.40	33.64	307.23	142.53	100.0	7.0	63.5	29.5
2008	495.53	32.11	303.86	159.56	100.0	6.5	61.3	32.2
2009	518.66	29.45	311.04	178.17	100.0	5.7	60.0	34.3
2010	687.50	26.00	427.90	233.60	100.0	3.8	62.2	34.0
2011	691.00	25.60	427.10	238.30	100.0	3.7	61.8	34.5
2012	694.30	25.30	427.10	241.90	100.0	3.7	61.5	34.8
2013	695.20	25.10	425.90	244.20	100.0	3.6	61.3	35.1
2014	693.40	24.50	419.80	249.10	100.0	3.5	60.5	36.0
2015	691.40	23.80	414.50	253.10	100.0	3.4	60.0	36.6
2016	691.30	23.50	412.10	255.70	100.0	3.4	59.6	37.0
2017	691.60	22.70	409.00	259.90	100.0	3.3	59.1	37.6
2018	692.30	21.70	405.80	264.80	100.0	3.1	58.6	38.3

注:本表2009年及以前数据为城镇单位从业人员、城镇私营与个体从业人员、农村劳动者之和；2010年起数据口径为16周岁及以上常住人口中，从事一定社会劳动或经营活动，并取得劳动报酬或经营收入的人口。

Note: The data in the table in 2009 and before was the sum total of the employees of urban units, the urban private employees and individual self-employed and the rural workers.Since 2010 the data caliber has been the population of the permanent residents of 16 years of age and older who are engaged in certain social labor or business activities and obtain labor compensation or operating income.

表2-9

分地区就业人口及构成
EMPLOYMENT POPULATION AND ITS COMPOSITION BY REGION

地 区	Region	2017年末 End of 2017 就业人口(万人) Employment Population (10 000 persons)	第一产业 Primary Industry	第二产业 Secondary Industry	第三产业 Tertiary Industry	就业人口构成(%) Composition of Employment Population(%)	第一产业 Primary Industry	第二产业 Secondary Industry	第三产业 Tertiary Industry
全 市	**Whole Municipality**	**691.60**	**22.70**	**409.00**	**259.90**	**100.0**	**3.3**	**59.1**	**37.6**
市 区	**Urban Area**	**347.59**	**10.43**	**198.79**	**138.37**	**100.0**	**3.0**	**57.2**	**39.8**
姑苏区	Gusu District	47.71	0.02	16.13	31.56	100.0	0.1	33.8	66.1
吴中区	Wuzhong District	74.37	4.97	42.79	26.61	100.0	6.7	57.5	35.8
相城区	Xiangcheng District	49.30	0.97	30.69	17.64	100.0	2.0	62.2	35.8
高新区、虎丘区	New & Hi-tech Zone , Huqiu District	36.85	0.51	22.63	13.71	100.0	1.4	61.4	37.2
工业园区	Industrial Park	53.20	0.34	33.37	19.49	100.0	0.6	62.7	36.7
吴江区	Wujiang District	86.16	3.62	53.18	29.36	100.0	4.2	61.7	34.1
县级市	**Cities at County Level**	**344.01**	**12.27**	**210.21**	**121.53**	**100.0**	**3.6**	**61.1**	**35.3**
常 熟	Changshu	104.44	3.81	63.59	37.04	100.0	3.6	60.9	35.5
张家港	Zhangjiagang	77.19	4.26	46.09	26.84	100.0	5.5	59.7	34.8
昆 山	Kunshan	116.58	1.67	73.93	40.98	100.0	1.4	63.4	35.2
太 仓	Taicang	45.80	2.53	26.60	16.67	100.0	5.5	58.1	36.4

表2-9 续表 Continued

地 区	Region	2018年末 End of 2018 就业人口(万人) Employment Population (10 000 persons)	第一产业 Primary Industry	第二产业 Secondary Industry	第三产业 Tertiary Industry	就业人口构成(%) Composition of Employment Population(%)	第一产业 Primary Industry	第二产业 Secondary Industry	第三产业 Tertiary Industry
全 市	**Whole Municipality**	**692.30**	**21.70**	**405.80**	**264.80**	**100.0**	**3.1**	**58.6**	**38.3**
市 区	**Urban Area**	**348.01**	**9.96**	**197.21**	**140.84**	**100.0**	**2.9**	**56.6**	**40.5**
姑苏区	Gusu District	47.68	0.02	15.82	31.84	100.0	0.0	33.2	66.8
吴中区	Wuzhong District	74.40	4.75	42.49	27.16	100.0	6.4	57.1	36.5
相城区	Xiangcheng District	49.41	0.93	30.48	18.00	100.0	1.9	61.7	36.4
高新区、虎丘区	New & Hi-tech Zone , Huqiu District	36.95	0.49	22.47	13.99	100.0	1.3	60.8	37.9
工业园区	Industrial Park	53.38	0.32	33.14	19.92	100.0	0.6	62.1	37.3
吴江区	Wujiang District	86.19	3.45	52.81	29.93	100.0	4.0	61.3	34.7
县级市	**Cities at County Level**	**344.29**	**11.74**	**208.59**	**123.96**	**100.0**	**3.4**	**60.6**	**36.0**
常 熟	Changshu	104.42	3.64	63.06	37.72	100.0	3.5	60.4	36.1
张家港	Zhangjiagang	77.15	4.07	45.70	27.38	100.0	5.3	59.2	35.5
昆 山	Kunshan	116.90	1.59	73.42	41.89	100.0	1.4	62.8	35.8
太 仓	Taicang	45.82	2.44	26.41	16.97	100.0	5.3	57.7	37.0

表2-10 历年分地区城镇非私营单位从业人员及在岗职工人数

单位：万人

年 份 Year	全市从业人员 Employees of the Whole City	# 在岗职工 Fully Employed Staff and Workers	市区从业人员 Employees of the Urban Area	# 在岗职工 Fully Employed Staff and Workers	#吴江区从业人员 Employees of Wujiang District	# 在岗职工 Fully Employed Staff and Workers
1975		50.34		33.41		4.74
1978		60.91		40.90		5.56
1980		70.30		47.52		6.43
1985		85.84		56.78		8.60
1990		95.43		60.91		9.51
1995		96.62		58.05		8.88
1996		94.51		56.40		8.68
1997		93.69		55.33		8.12
1998		78.88		44.12		6.91
1999		76.24		42.42		6.31
2000		74.09		39.53		5.77
2001		73.45		38.90		7.14
2002		74.16		38.22		6.79
2003		81.09		42.92		7.54
2004		87.18		46.19		7.76
2005		100.44		54.35		8.37
2006		111.39		62.37		8.50
2007		122.97		68.73		9.13
2008		118.08		65.77		9.04
2009		115.80		65.28		9.14
2010		126.97		72.68		11.04
2011		129.83		71.92		11.36
2012		130.40		72.60		11.50
2013	293.40	285.47	150.23	145.90	25.84	25.22
2014	315.42	307.21	162.46	158.02	34.03	33.48
2015	303.93	295.79	157.59	153.41	33.46	32.99
2016	288.69	279.90	146.71	141.72	31.95	31.34
2017	290.97	282.52	150.77	146.30	32.73	32.24
2018	290.13	280.60	153.28	148.37	32.53	31.95

注：2012年及以前为城镇国有集体单位在岗职工期末人数，2013年起调整为城镇非私营单位从业人员期末人数和在岗职工期末人数。

EMPLOYEES AND EMPLOYEES ON THE JOB OF URBAN NON-PRIVATE UNITS BY REGION OVER THE YEARS

(10 000 persons)

常熟市从业人员 Employees of Changshu City	# 在岗职工 Fully Employed Staff and Workers	张家港市从业人员 Employees of Zhangjiagang City	# 在岗职工 Fully Employed Staff and Workers	昆山市从业人员 Employees of Kunshan City	# 在岗职工 Fully Employed Staff and Workers	太仓市从业人员 Employees of Taicang City	# 在岗职工 Fully Employed Staff and Workers
	5.96		4.80		2.97		3.20
	7.20		5.32		3.77		3.72
	8.22		5.88		4.27		4.41
	9.88		8.07		5.28		5.83
	11.98		9.50		6.21		6.83
	12.89		11.05		8.48		6.15
	12.70		10.33		8.90		6.18
	12.88		10.00		9.28		6.20
	11.31		8.82		9.04		5.59
	10.50		8.56		9.12		5.64
	10.34		8.17		10.65		5.40
	10.03		8.08		11.23		5.21
	9.66		8.12		12.67		5.49
	9.59		8.45		13.53		6.60
	9.70		9.33		14.16		7.80
	10.64		10.15		16.02		9.28
	10.42		11.57		16.89		10.14
	11.12		12.71		18.69		11.72
	10.92		12.45		17.34		11.60
	11.18		12.27		16.17		10.90
	11.62		13.07		18.32		11.28
	12.37		13.88		19.58		12.08
	12.22		14.47		19.21		11.90
21.06	20.72	29.27	28.71	79.88	77.92	12.96	12.22
25.90	25.17	29.39	28.78	82.64	81.04	15.03	14.19
25.64	25.03	28.33	27.29	78.03	76.37	14.34	13.69
26.59	25.90	26.96	26.05	74.09	72.46	14.34	13.77
24.47	23.91	25.51	24.62	75.35	73.46	14.87	14.22
25.26	24.65	26.03	25.11	71.04	68.61	14.52	13.86

Note: The number of employees of the state-owned and collective units in the urban areas at the end of the period in 2012 and before began to be adjusted in 2013 to the number of employees in the urban non-private units at the end of the period and the number of employees on the job at the end of the period.

表2-11

历年分地区城镇非私营单位从业人员及在岗职工平均工资

单位：元

年 份 Year	全市从业人员 Employees of the Whole City	# 在岗职工 Fully Employed Staff and Workers	市区从业人员 Employees of the Urban Area	# 在岗职工 Fully Employed Staff and Workers	#吴江区从业人员 Employees of Wujiang District	# 在岗职工 Fully Employed Staff and Workers
1975		489		505		452
1978		514		537		498
1980		687		704		643
1985		1 106		1 107		987
1990		2 450		2 512		2 393
1995		6 944		6 917		6 319
1996		7 742		7 681		7 006
1997		8 443		8 462		7 687
1998		9 616		9 947		8 613
1999		10 583		11 258		9 468
2000		11 778		12 898		10 324
2001		13 670		15 231		11 478
2002		15 924		17 902		13 605
2003		19 790		22 024		16 919
2004		22 510		24 991		19 157
2005		25 016		26 905		22 236
2006		28 010		29 775		25 911
2007		31 404		32 952		30 740
2008		36 090		37 826		35 440
2009		40 261		42 513		40 303
2010		45 566		47 780		44 393
2011		51 660		54 011		49 281
2012		57 622		59 692		55 949
2013	61 995	61 416	63 634	63 595	58 074	57 999
2014	67 381	66 956	68 603	68 378	61 022	60 974
2015	72 656	72 291	74 406	74 321	62 949	63 011
2016	80 187	79 870	83 392	83 293	68 206	68 004
2017	87 431	87 350	91 735	91 772	73 219	73 212
2018	94 124	94 421	98 775	99 169	78 505	78 498

注：2012年及以前为城镇国有集体单位在岗职工平均工资，2013年开始调整为城镇非私营单位从业人员平均工资和在岗职工平均工资。

AVERAGE WAGE OF STAFF AND WORKERS OF URBAN NON-PRIVATE UNITS BY REGION OVER THE YEARS

(yuan)

常熟市从业人员 Employees of Changshu City	# 在岗职工 Fully Employed Staff and Workers	张家港市从业人员 Employees of Zhangjiagang City	# 在岗职工 Fully Employed Staff and Workers	昆山市从业人员 Employees of Kunshan City	# 在岗职工 Fully Employed Staff and Workers	太仓市从业人员 Employees of Taicang City	# 在岗职工 Fully Employed Staff and Workers
	450		415		469		502
	472		443		496		522
	586		654		638		693
	1 156		1 079		1 068		1 100
	2 474		2 183		2 352		2 327
	7 196		7 163		6 818		6 452
	7 920		7 806		7 919		7 570
	8 472		8 214		8 598		8 353
	9 325		8 907		9 235		9 272
	9 801		9 436		9 591		10 211
	10 246		10 156		10 658		11 006
	11 500		11 777		12 271		12 114
	13 590		13 702		14 383		13 334
	18 063		17 081		17 602		16 084
	20 327		20 226		20 099		18 564
	22 994		23 330		22 928		22 078
	25 411		26 042		25 989		25 503
	28 732		29 089		29 704		30 111
	33 420		33 538		33 735		34 716
	37 095		36 597		37 394		38 718
	41 784		42 518		41 669		45 120
	47 917		50 041		46 749		51 045
	53 982		56 591		53 461		57 037
59 847	58 600	60 886	60 629	56 484	55 616	62 177	61 812
64 308	63 675	66 634	66 466	60 771	59 868	68 707	68 252
72 134	71 300	70 530	70 694	65 136	64 254	78 402	78 407
81 079	80 489	77 580	77 976	71 884	70 967	87 939	87 994
84 273	84 002	86 274	86 759	77 352	76 815	102 653	103 622
95 600	95 577	90 685	91 204	82 325	82 142	107 475	109 345

Note: . The average wage of employees and the average wage of employees on the job who began to be adjusted to the urban non-private units in 2013.

表2-12

分地区分行业城镇非私营单位从业人员(2018年末)
(县市部分)

单位：人

项　目	Item	全　市 Whole Municipality
总　　计	**Total**	**2 901 253**
一、按登记注册类型分	**Grouped by Registration Status**	
内资单位	Domestic Units	1 160 946
国有单位	State-owned Units	296 023
集体单位	Collective-owned Units	44 803
股份合作单位	Share-holding Cooperative Units	5 128
联营单位	Joint Ownership Units	401
有限责任公司	Limited Liability Corporations	554 351
股份有限公司	Share-holding Corporations Ltd.	245 731
其他单位	Other Enterprises	14 509
港澳台商投资单位	Units with Investment from HongKong, Macao and Taiwan	549 768
外商投资单位	Units with Foreign Investment	1 190 539
二、按行业分	**Grouped by Sector**	
农林牧渔业	Farming, Forestry, Animal Husbandry and Fishery	108
采矿业	Mining and Quarrying	416
制造业	Manufacturing	1 932 744
电力、燃气及水的生产和供应业	Power, Gas and Water Production and Supply	13 898
建筑业	Construction	126 216
批发和零售业	Wholesale and Retail Trade Services	120 487
交通运输、仓储和邮政业	Transportation, Logistics and Postal	86 347
住宿和餐饮业	Accommodation and Catering Services	42 624
信息传输、软件和信息技术服务业	Information Transmission, Software and Information Technology Services	41 084
金融业	Financial Industries	67 051
房地产业	Real Estate	62 476
租赁和商务服务业	Renting and Labor Services	45 570
科学研究和技术服务业	Scientific Research and Technical Services	31 575
水利、环境和公共设施管理业	Water Conservancy, Environment and Public Facilities Management	18 485
居民服务和其他服务业	Residents Service and Other Service Trades	9 671
教　育	Education	113 251
卫生和社会工作	Health Care and Social Work	72 591
文化、体育和娱乐业	Culture, Sports and Entertainment	8 948
公共管理和社会组织	Public Administration and Social Organizations	107 711

EMPLOYEES OF URBAN NON-PRIVATE UNITS BY SECTORS AND REGIONS (END OF 2018) (PARTS OF THE COUNTIES AND CITIES)

(person)

市 区 Urban Area	常 熟 Changshu	张家港 Zhangjiagang	昆 山 Kunshan	太 仓 Taicang
1 532 824	**252 552**	**260 265**	**710 428**	**145 184**
644 304	101 841	202 805	152 650	59 346
163 956	29 967	32 480	49 048	20 572
20 180	6 214	5 131	9 614	3 664
2 114	614	305	1 939	156
130	33	–	238	–
282 453	40 134	139 697	65 646	26 421
163 426	24 309	24 754	25 080	8 162
12 045	570	438	1 085	371
259 496	76 282	14 484	178 648	20 858
629 024	74 429	42 976	379 130	64 980
87	–	21	–	–
416	–	–	–	–
960 242	179 178	144 233	559 953	89 138
5 792	3 232	2 136	1 297	1 441
75 246	7 920	27 349	11 644	4 057
56 418	5 947	14 371	39 359	4 392
39 458	7 084	12 118	14 637	13 050
35 504	899	2 734	2 446	1 041
32 122	562	5 107	2 671	622
46 690	5 703	4 534	6 244	3 880
47 021	1 308	6 196	6 524	1 427
30 744	5 685	3 014	3 877	2 250
24 630	1 358	1 520	3 261	806
9 096	2 488	1 394	5 157	350
5 977	329	2 288	989	88
65 126	10 358	10 558	19 513	7 696
38 444	8 952	8 872	11 456	4 867
5 586	1 070	1 086	983	223
54 225	10 479	12 734	20 417	9 856

表2-13

分地区分行业城镇非私营单位从业人员(2018年末)(市区部分)

单位：人

项　目	Item	市　区 Urban Area
总　计	**Total**	**1 532 824**
一、按登记注册类型分	**Grouped by Registration Status**	
内资单位	Domestic Units	644 304
国有单位	State-owned Units	163 956
集体单位	Collective-owned Units	20 180
股份合作单位	Share-holding Cooperative Units	2 114
联营单位	Joint Ownership Units	130
有限责任公司	Limited Liability Corporations	282 453
股份有限公司	Share-holding Corporations Ltd.	163 426
其他单位	Other Enterprises	12 045
港澳台商投资单位	Units with Investment from HongKong, Macao and Taiwan	259 496
外商投资单位	Units with Foreign Investment	629 024
二、按行业分	**Grouped by Sector**	
农林牧渔业	Farming, Forestry, Animal Husbandry and Fishery	87
采矿业	Mining and Quarrying	416
制造业	Manufacturing	960 242
电力、燃气及水的生产和供应业	Power, Gas and Water Production and Supply	5 792
建筑业	Construction	75 246
批发和零售业	Wholesale and Retail Trade Services	56 418
交通运输、仓储和邮政业	Transportation, Logistics and Postal	39 458
住宿和餐饮业	Accommodation and Catering Services	35 504
信息传输、软件和信息技术服务业	Information Transmission, Software and Information Technology Services	32 122
金融业	Financial Industries	46 690
房地产业	Real Estate	47 021
租赁和商务服务业	Renting and Labor Services	30 744
科学研究和技术服务业	Scientific Research and Technical Services	24 630
水利、环境和公共设施管理业	Water Conservancy, Environment and Public Facilities Management	9 096
居民服务和其他服务业	Residents Service and Other Service Trades	5 977
教　育	Education	65 126
卫生和社会工作	Health Care and Social Work	38 444
文化、体育和娱乐业	Culture, Sports and Entertainment	5 586
公共管理和社会组织	Public Administration and Social Organizations	54 225

EMPLOYEES OF URBAN NON-PRIVATE UNITS BY SECTORS AND REGIONS (END OF 2018) (PARTS OF THE URBAN AREA)

(person)

姑苏区 Gusu District	吴中区 Wuzhong District	相城区 Xiangcheng District	高新区、虎丘区 New Hi-tech Zone & Huqiu District	工业园区 Industrial Park	吴江区 Wujiang District
150 465	**186 391**	**112 681**	**312 165**	**445 868**	**325 254**
142 640	93 969	68 042	86 962	127 374	125 317
51 050	25 593	27 376	11 610	17 159	31 168
1 759	4 174	7 247	2 269	1 364	3 367
911	273	–	135	–	795
16	42	–	45	–	27
58 316	45 001	21 980	46 569	54 843	55 744
27 742	18 456	11 259	23 767	48 141	34 061
2 846	430	180	2 567	5 867	155
2 220	21 650	15 271	54 639	66 906	98 810
5 605	70 772	29 368	170 564	251 588	101 127
–	51	–	–	–	36
–	–	–	416	–	–
803	113 546	59 213	223 782	301 480	261 418
1 029	869	233	732	923	2 006
17 231	11 261	16 265	9 590	14 383	6 516
14 198	7 056	1 619	5 617	23 988	3 940
20 736	3 629	1 443	4 353	4 901	4 396
5 061	3 562	1 796	18 606	4 492	1 987
7 678	33	294	8 714	14 881	522
10 586	464	18	6 700	25 479	3 443
10 866	7 982	2 795	9 292	12 151	3 935
10 237	4 422	140	2 230	11 426	2 289
5 003	3 928	415	5 542	8 792	950
1 782	1 587	545	1 866	493	2 823
3 260	1 075	35	313	891	403
14 477	12 189	7 713	7 632	9 747	13 368
14 393	6 249	3 664	3 740	3 153	7 245
3 149	574	217	724	757	165
9 976	7 914	16 276	2 316	7 931	9 812

表2-14 全市城镇非私营单位从业人员及平均工资 (2018年)

项　目	Item	从业人员（人） Number of Employed Persons (person)
总　计	**Total**	**2 901 253**
一、按地区分	**Grouped by Region**	
市　区	Urban Area	1 532 824
姑苏区	Gusu District	150 465
吴中区	Wuzhong District	186 391
相城区	Xiangcheng District	112 681
高新区、虎丘区	New & Hi-tech Zone, Huqiu District	312 165
工业园区	Industrial Park	445 868
吴江区	Wujiang District	325 254
常　熟	Changshu	252 552
张家港	Zhangjiagang	260 265
昆　山	Kunshan	710 428
太　仓	Taicang	145 184
二、按登记注册类型分	**Grouped by Registration Status**	
内资单位	Domestic Units	1 160 946
国有单位	State-owned Units	296 023
集体单位	Collective-owned Units	44 803
股份合作单位	Share-holding Cooperative Units	5 128
联营单位	Joint Ownership Units	401
有限责任公司	Limited Liability Corporations	554 351
股份有限公司	Share-holding Corporations Ltd.	245 731
其他单位	Other Enterprises	14 509

EMPLOYEES OF CITY'S URBAN NON-PRIVATE UNIES, AVERAGE WAGES AND MEDIAN WAGES (2018)

	从业人员平均工资 (元) Average Remuneration (yuan)		从业人员工资中位数 (元) Median of Wage (yuan)	
# 在岗职工 Fully Employed Staff and Workers		# 在岗职工 Fully Employed Staff and Workers		# 在岗职工 Fully Employed Staff and Workers
2 805 980	**94 124**	**94 421**	**78 466**	**78 630**
1 483 727	98 775	99 169	82 951	82 951
142 073	117 769	122 045	113 312	113 350
177 188	89 109	89 461	74 711	74 711
111 303	89 605	89 731	81 191	79 084
303 232	87 354	87 017	76 822	74 747
430 439	121 901	122 420	105 492	105 492
319 492	78 505	78 498	67 714	67 714
246 490	95 600	95 577	78 516	77 821
251 059	90 685	91 204	78 432	80 136
686 127	82 325	82 142	72 326	72 576
138 577	107 475	109 345	89 777	91 932
1 109 601	118 050	110 391	91 480	93 918
280 468	150 758	155 486	147 069	153 111
41 829	105 723	109 545	113 418	119 976
4 862	74 073	74 825	67 685	67 685
399	136 040	136 572	114 768	114 768
529 473	82 378	83 768	74 377	74 711
238 550	115 034	116 815	88 551	89 776
14 020	115 715	118 428	122 030	122 030

表 2-14 续表

项 目	Item	从业人员（人）Number of Employed Persons (person)
港澳台商投资单位	Units with Investment from HongKong, Macao and Taiwan	549 768
外商投资单位	Units with Foreign Investment	1 190 539
三、按行业分	**Grouped by Sector**	
农林牧渔业	Farming, Forestry, Animal Husbandry and Fishery	108
采矿业	Mining and Quarrying	416
制造业	Manufacturing	1 932 744
电力、燃气及水的生产和供应业	Power, Gas and Water Production and Supply	13 898
建筑业	Construction	126 216
批发和零售业	Wholesale and Retail Trade Services	120 487
交通运输、仓储和邮政业	Transportation, Logistics and Postal	86 347
住宿和餐饮业	Accommodation and Catering Services	42 624
信息传输、软件和信息技术服务业	Information Transmission, Software and Information Technology Services	41 084
金融业	Financial Industries	67 051
房地产业	Real Estate	62 476
租赁和商务服务业	Renting and Labor Services	45 570
科学研究和技术服务业	Scientific Research and Technical Services	31 575
水利、环境和公共设施管理业	Water Conservancy, Environment and Public Facilities Management	18 485
居民服务和其他服务业	Residents Service and Other Service Trades	9 671
教 育	Education	113 251
卫生和社会工作	Health Care and Social Work	72 591
文化、体育和娱乐业	Culture, Sports and Entertainment	8 948
公共管理和社会组织	Public Administration and Social Organizations	107 711

Continued

# 在岗职工 Fully Employed Staff and Workers	从业人员平均工资（元）Average Remuneration (yuan)	# 在岗职工 Fully Employed Staff and Workers	从业人员工资中位数（元）Median of Wage (yuan)	# 在岗职工 Fully Employed Staff and Workers
533 610	76 502	76 502	68 513	67 880
1 162 769	89 001	87 725	77 022	75 759
73	109 417	130 288	93 933	93 933
416	93 255	93 255	93 255	93 255
1 891 538	82 981	82 233	74 431	67 714
13 812	128 446	129 066	120 915	121 511
115 938	68 869	69 501	61 417	61 417
114 516	89 530	89 612	68 533	69 596
82 813	86 955	88 945	83 394	83 394
40 810	45 890	46 033	46 291	46 291
40 915	172 550	172 952	155 539	155 539
63 556	205 359	212 394	197 360	197 360
58 232	84 979	88 480	51 806	57 092
40 725	88 874	93 077	66 481	74 923
30 687	154 327	155 613	128 600	136 235
15 903	80 928	88 165	60 322	68 624
9 358	65 485	65 965	57 551	59 839
104 370	143 117	150 979	142 853	151 910
68 550	138 934	141 326	144 508	144 833
8 686	109 040	111 872	86 099	86 099
105 082	164 135	166 828	153 973	153 973

表2-15

市区城镇非私营单位从业人员平均工资（2018年）
AVERAGE WAGES OF EMPLOYEES OF NON-PRIVATE UNITS IN THE URBAN AREA (2018)

单位：元 (yuan)

项　目	Item	平均工资 Average Remuneration	# 在岗职工 Fully Employed Staff and Workers
总　计	**Total**	**98 775**	**99 169**
一、按登记注册类型分	**Grouped by Registration Status**		
内资单位	Domestic Units	111 820	114 109
国有单位	State-owned Units	147 188	149 949
集体单位	Collective-owned Units	87 036	88 199
股份合作单位	Share-holding Cooperative Units	71 990	73 919
联营单位	Joint Ownership Units	89 137	90 039
有限责任公司	Limited Liability Corporations	85 801	87 814
股份有限公司	Share-holding Corporations Ltd.	124 905	126 470
其他单位	Other Enterprises	122 848	124 554
港澳台商投资单位	Units with Investment from HongKong, Macao and Taiwan	78 023	77 880
外商投资单位	Units with Foreign Investment	94 457	93 408
二、按行业分	**Grouped by Sector**		
农林牧渔业	Farming, Forestry, Animal Husbandry and Fishery	102 552	127 231
采矿业	Mining and Quarrying	93 255	93 255
制造业	Manufacturing	86 956	86 342
电力、燃气及水的生产和供应业	Power, Gas and Water Production and Supply	122 510	122 988
建筑业	Construction	76 615	77 250
批发和零售业	Wholesale and Retail Trade Services	89 558	89 238
交通运输、仓储和邮政业	Transportation, Logistics and Postal	92 988	93 249
住宿和餐饮业	Accommodation and Catering Services	43 794	43 828
信息传输、软件和信息技术服务业	Information Transmission, Software and Information Technology Services	184 493	185 037
金融业	Financial Industries	213 144	214 406
房地产业	Real Estate	83 733	87 384
租赁和商务服务业	Renting and Labor Services	97 315	104 563
科学研究和技术服务业	Scientific Research and Technical Services	153 613	154 914
水利、环境和公共设施管理业	Water Conservancy, Environment and Public Facilities Management	89 800	92 840
居民服务和其他服务业	Residents Service and Other Service Trades	73 146	74 599
教　育	Education	136 528	140 893
卫生和社会工作	Health Care and Social Work	134 647	136 963
文化、体育和娱乐业	Culture, Sports and Entertainment	102 818	105 551
公共管理和社会组织	Public Administration and Social Organizations	162 850	163 919

主要统计指标解释

人口数　指一定时点、一定地区范围内有生命的个人总和。年度统计的年末人口数指每年12月31日24时的人口数。

出生率(又称粗出生率)　指在一定时期内(通常为一年)一定地区的出生人数与同期内平均人数(或期中人数)之比，用千分率表示。本资料中的出生率指年出生率，其计算公式为：

$$出生率=\frac{年出生人数}{年平均人数}\times1000‰$$

式中：出生人数指活产婴儿，即胎儿脱离母体时(不管怀孕月数)，有过呼吸或其他生命现象。年平均人数指年初、年底人口数的平均数，也可用年中人口数代替。

死亡率(又称粗死亡率)　指在一定时期内(通常为一年)一定地区的死亡人数与同期内平均人数(或期中人数)之比，用千分率表示。本资料中的死亡率指年死亡率，其计算公式为：

$$死亡率=\frac{年死亡人数}{年平均人数}\times1000‰$$

人口自然增长率　指在一定时期内(通常为一年)人口自然增加数(出生人数减死亡人数)与该时期内平均人数(或期中人数)之比，用千分率表示。计算公式为：

$$人口自然增长率=\frac{本年出生人数-本年死亡人数}{年平均人数}\times1000‰$$

$$=人口出生率-人口死亡率$$

就业人口　指在一定年龄以上，有劳动能力，为取得劳动报酬或经营收入而从事一定社会劳动的人员。具体指年满16周岁，为取得报酬或经营利润，在调查周内从事了1小时（含1小时）以上劳动的人员；或由于学习、休假等原因在调查周内暂时处于未工作状态，但有工作单位或场所的人员；或由于季节性歇业、单位不景气放假等原因在调查周内暂时处于未工作状态，但不满三个月的人员。

单位从业人员　指在各级国家机关、政党机关、社会团体及企业、事业单位中工作，取得工资或其他形式的劳动报酬的全部人员。包括在岗职工、再就业的离退休人员、民办教师以及在各单位中工作的外方人员和港澳台方人员、兼职人员、借用的外单位人员和第二职业者。不包括离开本单位仍保留劳动关系的职工。各单位的就业人员反映了各单位实际参加生产或工作的全部劳动力。

城镇非私营单位从业人员　指在城镇非私营单位工作，并由单位支付劳动报酬的人员，包括在岗职工和其他就业人员。城镇非私营单位是指城镇地区全部非私营法人单位，具体包括国有单位、城镇集体单位、联营经济、股份制经济、外商投资经济、港澳台投资经济等单位。

职工　指在国有、城镇集体、联营、股份制、外商和港、澳、台投资、其他单位及其附属机构工作，并由其支付工资的各类人员。不包括下列人员：(1)乡镇企业就业人员；(2)私营企业就业人员；(3)城镇个体劳动者；(4)离休、退休、退职人员；(5)再就业的离、退休人员；(6)民办教师；(7)在城镇单位中工作的外方及港、澳、台人员；(8)其他按有关规定不列入职工统计范围的人员。(1998年及以后的数据均为在岗职工数据，其他相关指标如职工工资总额，职工平均工资等指标也从1998年按此口径进行了相应调整)。

国有单位　指资产归国家所有的经济组织。包括按《中华人民共和国企业法人登记管理条例》规定登记注册的非公司制的经济组织，以及中央、地方各级国家机关、事业单位和社会团体。

集体单位 指生产资料归集体所有，并按《中华人民共和国企业法人登记管理条例》规定登记注册的经济组织。

其他单位 包括股份合作单位、联营单位、有限责任公司、股份有限公司、港澳台商投资单位以及外商投资单位等其他登记注册类型单位。

城镇非私营单位在岗职工 指在本城镇地区非私营单位工作，以及有工作岗位，但由于学习、病伤产假等原因暂未工作，仍由单位支付工资的人员。在岗职工还包括：应订立劳动合同而未订立劳动合同人员（如使用的农村户籍人员）；处于试用期人员；编制外招用的人员，如临时人员；派往外单位工作，但工资仍由本单位发放的人员（如挂职锻炼、外派工作等情况）；本单位使用的且由本单位支付工资的劳务派遣人员。

平均工资 指企业、事业、机关单位的职工在一定时期内平均每人所得的货币工资额。它表明一定时期职工工资收入的高低程度，是反映职工工资水平的主要指标。计算公式为:

$$\text{平均工资} = \frac{\text{报告期实际支付的全部职工工资总额}}{\text{报告期全部职工平均人数}}$$

中位数 是指将总体各单位标志值按大小顺序排列，处于中间位置的那个标志值。在许多不易计算平均值的情况下，可用中位数代表总体的一般水平。由于中位数的确定仅取决于它在数列中的位置，因此不受数列中极端标志值的影响。中位数的确定依据提供的具体资料不同而采取相应的方法。

EXPLANATORY NOTES ON MAIN STATISTICAL INDICATORS

Total Population refers to the total number of people alive at a certain point of time within a given area. The annual statistics on total population is taken at midnight, the 31st of December.

Birth Rate (or Crude Birth Rate) refers to the ratio of the number of births to the average population (or mid-period population) during a certain period of time (usually a year), expressed in ‰. Birth rate in the chapter refers to annual birth rate. The following formula is used:

$$\text{Birth Rate} = \frac{\text{Number of Births}}{\text{Annual Average Population}} \times 1000‰$$

Number of births in the formula refers to live births, i.e. when a baby has breathed or showed any vital phenomena regardless of the length of pregnancy.

Annual average population is the average of the number of population at the beginning of the year and that at the end of the year. Sometimes it is substituted by the mid-year population.

Death Rate (or Crude Death Rate) refers to the ratio of the number of deaths to the average population (or mid-period population) during a certain period of time (usually a year), expressed in ‰. Death rate in the chapter refers to annual death rate. The following formula is used:

$$\text{Death Rate} = \frac{\text{Number of Deaths}}{\text{Annual Average Population}} \times 1000‰$$

Natural Growth Rate of Population refers to the ratio of natural increase in population (number of births minus number of deaths) in a certain period of time (usually a year) to the average population (or mid-period population) of the same period, expressed in ‰. The following formula is applied:

$$\begin{array}{c}\text{Natural Growth}\\ \text{Rate of Population}\end{array} = \frac{\text{Number of Births - Number of Deaths}}{\text{Annual Average Population}} \times 1000‰$$

$$= \text{Birth Rate-Death Rate}$$

Employment Population refers to persons above a specified age who had labour capacity and performed some social work for compensation or business gains. Specifically, it refers to persons, aged 16 and over, who performed some work for compensation or business gains for one hour or more during the reference period; or persons who do not work for the reasons of study or on holiday, but had work units or sites during the reference period; or persons who do not work for the reasons of seasonal closing business, recession etc, but not exceeding three months during the reference period.

Persons Employed in Various Units refer to all the persons working in government agencies of various levels, political and party organizations, social organizations, enterprises and institutions, and receiving wages or other forms of payment. They include fully-employed staff and workers, re-employed retirees, teachers in the schools run by the local people, foreigners and Chinese compatriots from Hong Kong, Macao, and Taiwan working in various units, part-time employees, employees of other units working temporarily at current posts, and employees holding the second job, but do not include persons who have left their working units while keeping their labor contract (employment relation) unchanged. This indicator reflects the total number of laborers actually engaged in production or other operations in various units.

Urban non-private unit employees refer to people who work in urban non-private units and are paid by the units, including staff and workers and other employees. Urban non-private units refer to all non-private legal entities in urban areas, including state-owned units, urban collective units, associated economic units, share economic units, foreign invested economic units, and Hong Kong, Macao and Taiwan invested economic units.

Staff and Workers refer to persons working in, and receive payment from units of state ownership, collective ownership, joint ownership, share holding ownership, foreign ownership, and ownership by entrepreneurs from Hong Kong, Macao, and Taiwan, and other types of ownership and their affiliated units. They do not include 1) persons employed in township enterprises,

2) persons employed in private enterprises, 3) urban self-employed persons, 4) retirees, 5) re-employed retirees, 6) teachers in the schools run by the local people, 7) foreigners and persons from Hong Kong, Macao and Taiwan who work in urban units, and 8) other persons not to be included by relevant regulations. (Data since 1998 refer to fully employed staff and workers. Other related statistics indicators, such as total wage bill and average wage are adjusted since 1998 accordingly).

State-owned Units refer to economic units whose assets are owned by the state, including non-corporation units registered according to *Regulation of the People's Republic of China on the Registration of Enterprises and Corporations*, state organs, institutions and social organizations at the central-level and local levels.

Collective-owned Units refer to economic units registered according to *Regulation of the People's Republic of China on the Registration of Enterprises and Corporations* where the means of production are collectively owned.

Units of Other Types of Ownership refer to units registered with other types of ownership, including cooperative units, joint ownership units, limited liability corporations, share holding corporations, units funded by entrepreneurs from Hong Kong, Macao, and Taiwan, and foreign- funded units.

Urban Non-private Unit Staff and Workers refer to people who work in non-private units in urban areas, and people who have a post, but are temporarily not working because of learning, sick leave, injury leave or maternity leave and other reasons and are still paid by the units. Workers in the post also include people who should have but have not had a labor contract (such as rural workers employed); people who are in probation; people who are recruited outside the preparation of personnel staffing, such as temporary workers; people who are assigned to work outside the unit but are still paid by the unit (things such as training with the post suspended and work assignments outside the unit); and dispatched personnel who are used and paid by the unit.

Average Wage refers to the average wage in money terms per person during a certain period of time for staff and workers in enterprises, institutions, and government agencies, which reflects the general level of wage income during a certain period of time and is calculated as follows:

$$\text{Average Wage} = \frac{\text{Total Wage Bill of Staff and Workers at Reference Time}}{\text{Average Number of Staff and Workers at Reference Time}}$$

The Median refers to the symbol value which is in the middle position of the sequence that is in symbol values size order. In many cases that are not easy to calculate the average, the median of the available median represents the general level of the population. Because the median is determined only by its position in the sequence, so it is not affected by the extreme value of the sequence. The determination of the median is based on the specific information provided by the different ways to take the corresponding.

三、农　业

CHAPTER 3
AGRICULTURE

3 农 业
AGRICULTURE

主要统计指标
MAJOR STATISTICAL INDICATORS

2018年末乡村实有从业人员	Rural Real Employed persons	171.58	万人	10 000 persons
比上年增长	Increase Over Last Year	0.0	%	
2018年农作物播种面积	Sown Areas Of Farm Crops	217.79	千公顷	1 000 hectares
比上年增长	Increase Over Last Year	-3.5	%	
2018年农林牧渔业总产值(现价)	Gross Output Value of Farming, Forestry, Animal Husbandry and Fishery（Current Prices ）	410.09	亿元	100 million yuan
比上年增长	Increase Over Last Year	-3.4	%	
2018年农林牧渔业总产值(可比价格)	Gross Output Value of Farming, Forestry, Animal Husbandry and Fishery (at Comparable Price)	407.45	亿元	100 million yuan
比上年增长	Increase Over Last Year	-4.4	%	
2018年农林牧渔业增加值	Value Added of Farming, Forestry, Animal Husbandry and Fishery	240.01	亿元	100 million yuan
比上年增长	Increase Over Last Year	-3.1	%	
2018年粮食总产量	Total Yield of Grain Crops	87.92	万吨	10 000 tons
比上年增长	Increase Over Last Year	-4.9	%	

表3-1

部分年份农村基本情况
BASIC CONDITIONS OF COUNTRYSIDE OF PARTIAL YEARS

项　目	Item	2014年	2015年	2016年	2017年	2018年
农村组织 （个）	**Village Units** (unit)					
镇政府	Town Governments	55	55	55	53	52
村民委员会	Number of Villagers' Committees	1 041	1 039	1 034	1 026	1 025
村民小组	Villager Group	26 837	26 671	26 454	26 351	26 377
乡村户数、人口	**Households and Rural Population**					
乡村总户数 （万户）	Number of Households (10 000 households)	89.08	88.32	87.50	87.33	87.34
乡村总人口 （万人）	Rural Population (10 000 persons)	288.83	286.16	283.23	282.64	283.26
年末乡村实有从业人员	**Rural Employees of year-end**					
合　计	Total	174.76	173.30	171.89	171.54	171.58
1.按性别分	Grouped by Sex					
男劳动力	Male	89.81	89.19	88.65	88.05	88.62
女劳动力	Female	84.95	84.11	83.24	83.49	82.96
2.按行业分	Grouped by Sector					
农林牧渔业	Farming, Forestry, Animal Husbandry and Fishery	22.81	22.26	21.83	21.18	21.02
农　业	Farming	14.29	13.97	13.69	13.41	13.54
林牧渔业	Forestry, Animal Husbandry and Fishery	8.52	8.29	8.14	7.77	7.48
工　业	Industry	105.05	104.31	103.57	104.01	104.35
建筑业	Construction	9.88	10.02	9.66	9.74	9.65
交通运输、邮电业	Transportation, Postal and Telecommunications Services	5.51	5.51	5.48	5.31	5.45
信息传输、计算机服务和软件业	Information Transmission, Software and Information Technology Services	1.11	1.18	1.22	1.25	1.33
批发和零售业	Wholesale and Retail Trade Services	10.22	10.28	10.24	10.31	10.43
住宿和餐饮业	Accommodation and Catering Services	4.50	4.47	4.55	4.57	4.62
金融保险业	Banking and Insurance	0.86	0.88	0.94	0.98	1.04
房地产、社会服务业	Real Estate and Social Services	2.39	2.35	2.31	2.33	2.43
卫生、体育、社会福利业	Health Care, Sporting and Social Welfare	1.04	1.06	1.10	1.10	1.15
文、教、艺术和广播影视业	Culture, Education and Arts, Radio, Film and Television	0.96	0.97	0.97	1.00	1.06
科研和综合技术服务业	Scientific Research and Polytechnical Services	0.22	0.23	0.26	0.28	0.31
乡镇经济组织管理	Rural Economic Management	1.16	1.16	1.19	1.22	1.25
其　他	Others	9.05	8.62	8.57	8.26	7.49

表3-2

历年年末乡村实有从业人员

RURAL REAL EMPLOYED PERSONS OVER THE YEARS (YEAR-END)

单位：万人 (10 000 persons)

年 份 Year	全 市 Whole Municipality	市 区 Urban Area	# 吴江区 Wujiang District	常 熟 Changshu	张家港 Zhangjiagang	昆 山 Kunshan	太 仓 Taicang
1949	124.93	45.96	17.08	30.24	20.54	12.66	15.53
1952	130.35	48.80	17.87	30.47	20.79	14.74	15.55
1957	146.38	57.93	22.31	32.48	24.60	16.07	15.30
1962	150.22	60.28	20.73	33.87	23.51	15.72	16.84
1965	176.82	72.24	24.23	38.71	28.78	18.21	18.88
1970	222.22	92.13	32.71	48.02	36.45	23.91	21.71
1975	233.63	97.64	34.39	49.47	36.77	25.55	24.20
1978	244.55	98.51	34.76	52.83	41.78	26.30	25.13
1980	250.74	103.00	36.76	54.20	40.94	26.83	25.77
1985	269.24	112.57	39.61	57.10	44.62	30.19	24.76
1990	260.51	113.95	40.59	57.44	37.52	29.69	21.91
1995	230.96	101.07	37.77	50.02	32.96	26.29	20.62
2000	213.75	95.34	33.22	49.76	30.17	22.16	16.32
2001	212.22	95.50	32.13	49.47	30.16	21.52	15.57
2002	210.55	94.36	31.85	49.37	30.20	21.29	15.33
2003	209.42	92.50	30.88	49.96	30.35	21.33	15.28
2004	207.60	90.48	32.04	49.24	30.60	22.30	14.98
2005	207.20	89.88	31.99	48.83	30.54	23.14	14.81
2006	206.90	88.59	32.36	48.52	30.92	22.73	16.14
2007	205.49	89.90	32.81	44.63	31.14	22.96	16.86
2008	205.94	89.76	32.40	43.87	33.10	22.60	16.61
2009	199.99	84.68	32.25	42.92	33.49	22.47	16.43
2010	190.42	74.88	31.98	42.42	33.68	22.50	16.94
2011	184.77	73.31	32.67	40.89	32.55	21.39	16.63
2012	179.54	70.82	31.71	39.74	31.61	21.21	16.16
2013	176.85	69.71	31.24	39.16	31.16	20.90	15.92
2014	174.76	68.70	30.78	38.78	30.70	20.85	15.73
2015	173.30	67.76	30.32	38.76	30.45	20.80	15.53
2016	171.89	66.75	29.87	38.42	30.42	20.78	15.52
2017	171.54	66.57	29.83	38.41	30.36	20.91	15.29
2018	171.58	65.32	29.81	38.38	31.77	20.92	15.19

表3-3

历年农林牧渔业总产值
GROSS OUTPUT VALUE OF FARMING, FORESTRY, ANIMAL HUSBANDRY AND FISHERY OVER THE YEARS

单位：万元 (10 000 yuan)

年 份 Year	总产值 Gross Output Value	农 业 Farming	# 种植业 Planting	林 业 Forestry	牧 业 Animal Husbandry	渔 业 Fishery	农林牧渔服务业 Farming,Forestry,Animal Husbandry,Fishery and Service Industry
1978	187 469	163 707	163 015	557	18 837	4 368	
1979	193 422	162 903	162 044	582	25 343	4 594	
1980	114 163	83 915	82 812	720	23 600	5 928	
1985	274 220	171 637	148 084	3 091	62 215	37 277	
1990	581 222	349 554	290 067	5 025	119 400	107 243	
1995	1 416 173	918 417	697 111	9 834	233 110	254 812	
1996	1 625 939	1 077 094	779 714	6 725	242 010	300 110	
1997	1 650 915	1 071 369	751 572	9 011	231 268	339 267	
1998	1 654 137	1 047 069	693 739	8 789	239 493	358 786	
1999	1 647 033	1 012 489	630 165	11 583	224 721	398 240	
2000	1 692 982	1 001 634	610 779	11 740	231 251	448 357	
2001	1 734 596	962 669	562 869	27 485	247 416	497 026	
2002	1 744 598	901 031	516 749	43 046	245 472	555 049	
2003	1 562 657	561 773	561 773	38 031	232 988	547 683	182 182
2004	1 639 627	589 162	589 162	50 311	249 959	562 791	187 404
2005	1 628 655	577 417	577 417	63 554	217 068	594 059	176 557
2006	1 721 844	663 120	663 120	72 351	214 312	601 890	170 171
2007	1 810 817	663 883	663 883	86 189	274 583	609 590	176 572
2008	2 334 155	878 179	878 179	126 262	330 251	727 964	271 499
2009	2 489 315	940 627	940 627	147 646	347 466	785 044	268 532
2010	2 712 943	1 052 848	1 052 848	161 828	357 452	853 943	286 872
2011	3 098 576	1 210 220	1 210 220	179 825	411 440	978 319	318 772
2012	3 377 237	1 350 458	1 350 458	204 834	402 031	1 066 347	353 567
2013	3 698 219	1 507 763	1 507 763	231 267	400 479	1 156 898	401 812
2014	3 924 922	1 614 539	1 614 539	244 711	388 226	1 226 420	451 026
2015	4 151 748	1 728 527	1 728 527	258 763	387 641	1 293 042	483 775
2016	4 246 673	1 788 110	1 788 110	247 639	373 939	1 360 760	476 225
2017	4 246 938	1 811 431	1 811 431	251 247	319 855	1 381 075	483 330
2018	4 100 858	1 776 435	1 776 435	245 678	240 964	1 344 111	493 670

注：2008年数据根据第二次农业普查、第二次经济普查已作调整。
Note:The 2008 data were adjusted according to the second agricultural census and the second economic census.

表3-4

历年粮食、棉花、油料播种面积
SOWN AREAS OF GRAIN CROPS, COTTON AND OIL-BEARING CROPS OVER THE YEARS

单位：千公顷 (1 000 hectares)

年 份 Year	粮 食 Grain Crops	夏 粮 Summer Grain	秋 粮 Autumn Grain	棉 花 Cotton	油 料 Oil-bearing Crops	# 油菜籽 Rapeseeds
1949	527.02	193.56	333.46	44.58	39.95	39.25
1952	562.96	220.65	342.31	61.73	46.19	45.57
1957	593.95	238.15	355.80	46.05	45.46	44.81
1962	505.48	199.85	305.63	41.46	34.31	33.49
1965	499.19	188.97	310.22	47.56	37.92	37.41
1970	598.12	185.07	413.05	46.50	41.72	41.59
1975	644.58	181.05	463.53	48.30	46.23	46.19
1978	636.61	179.59	457.02	47.76	47.89	47.77
1980	600.83	178.75	422.08	47.39	51.46	51.38
1985	500.49	197.12	303.37	44.50	90.11	89.95
1990	471.29	197.89	273.40	33.21	74.23	74.05
1995	398.73	159.41	239.32	25.40	67.17	66.84
2000	290.33	105.93	184.40	11.29	61.56	60.82
2001	234.05	76.29	157.76	11.92	58.49	57.70
2002	219.07	75.52	143.55	7.63	52.43	51.69
2003	173.56	60.72	112.84	6.58	39.42	38.85
2004	167.61	51.21	116.40	6.35	31.64	31.12
2005	169.85	54.28	115.57	4.46	33.22	32.67
2006	163.26	58.63	104.63	2.97	27.86	27.41
2007	153.45	59.71	93.74	2.39	28.02	27.62
2008	161.24	64.19	97.05	2.37	17.70	17.11
2009	159.09	64.81	94.28	2.02	19.49	18.90
2010	157.90	66.99	90.91	1.59	14.47	13.95
2011	157.07	67.93	89.14	1.39	11.65	11.04
2012	157.20	70.02	87.18	1.18	10.09	9.53
2013	151.13	68.40	82.73	0.96	9.26	8.77
2014	149.08	68.52	80.56	0.80	7.82	7.33
2015	145.57	66.50	79.07	0.60	6.03	5.60
2016	143.24	64.28	78.96	0.45	5.40	5.01
2017	135.15	59.43	75.72	0.21	2.87	2.59
2018	124.47	51.94	72.53	0.13	2.37	2.05

注：2007年起数据根据第三次全国农业普查已作调整，下同。

Note: Since 2007 data were adjusted according to the second agricultural census , same below.

表3-5

历年粮食、棉花、油料总产量
TOTAL YIELD OF GRAIN CROPS, COTTON AND OIL-BEARING CROPS OVER THE YEARS

年 份 Year	粮 食 (万吨) Grain Crops (10 000 tons)	夏 粮 Summer Grain	秋 粮 Autumn Grain	棉 花 (吨) Cotton (ton)	油 料 (吨) Oil-bearing Crops (ton)	# 油菜籽 Rapeseeds
1949	84.01	8.98	75.03	4 450	14 420	14 130
1952	133.41	16.81	116.60	14 810	24 950	24 080
1957	135.69	20.73	114.96	16 490	26 410	25 430
1962	152.32	31.09	121.23	14 560	17 250	16 660
1965	210.32	40.55	169.77	40 820	41 120	39 360
1970	223.62	38.27	185.35	35 880	57 060	56 300
1975	241.87	42.96	198.91	37 350	55 780	55 460
1978	294.26	66.70	227.56	36 330	91 320	90 610
1980	254.31	75.64	178.67	35 180	81 620	81 120
1985	238.49	59.02	179.47	42 600	141 020	140 480
1990	283.50	75.74	207.76	36 932	140 129	139 760
1995	265.67	66.26	199.41	40 210	145 608	144 798
2000	193.95	40.61	153.34	11 722	126 066	123 917
2001	159.48	23.93	135.55	12 976	102 529	100 106
2002	146.42	22.30	124.12	7 527	78 093	75 896
2003	112.77	17.90	94.87	6 816	62 418	60 347
2004	117.71	20.44	97.27	7 450	69 234	67 387
2005	110.76	22.76	88.00	4 605	69 593	68 143
2006	111.21	24.38	86.83	3 117	63 019	61 779
2007	94.13	24.66	69.47	2 459	64 107	62 980
2008	112.56	30.89	81.67	2 525	42 571	40 884
2009	112.38	30.49	81.89	2 135	46 632	44 991
2010	112.31	31.65	80.66	1 685	34 468	33 052
2011	113.55	33.80	79.76	1 508	28 907	27 352
2012	114.66	36.06	78.60	1 292	25 882	24 354
2013	110.64	35.82	74.82	1 038	24 209	22 892
2014	108.93	36.39	72.54	882	20 395	19 087
2015	106.85	35.47	71.38	666	15 747	14 603
2016	96.73	27.53	69.20	500	13 409	12 368
2017	92.40	26.37	66.03	227	7 261	6 524
2018	87.92	23.85	64.07	139	5 947	5 090

表3-6

历年粮食、棉花、油料单产
YIELD OF GRAIN CROPS, COTTON AND OIL-BEARING CROPS PER HECTARE OVER THE YEARS

单位：公斤/公顷 (kg/hectare)

年份 Year	粮食 Grain Crops	夏粮 Summer Grain	秋粮 Autumn Grain	棉花 Cotton	油料 Oil-bearing Crops	# 油菜籽 Rapeseeds
1949	1 594	464	2 250	100	361	360
1952	2 370	762	3 406	240	540	528
1957	2 285	870	3 231	358	581	568
1962	3 013	1 556	3 967	351	503	497
1965	4 213	2 146	5 473	858	1 084	1 052
1970	3 739	2 068	4 487	772	1 368	1 354
1975	3 752	2 373	4 291	773	1 261	1 201
1978	4 022	3 714	4 979	761	1 907	1 897
1980	4 233	4 232	4 233	742	1 586	1 579
1985	4 765	2 994	5 916	957	1 565	1 562
1990	6 015	3 825	7 605	1 112	1 888	1 887
1995	6 663	4 157	8 332	1 583	2 168	2 166
2000	6 680	3 833	8 316	1 038	2 048	2 037
2001	6 814	3 137	8 592	1 089	1 753	1 735
2002	6 684	2 953	8 646	987	1 489	1 468
2003	6 497	2 974	8 408	1 036	1 583	1 553
2004	7 023	3 991	8 356	1 173	2 188	2 165
2005	6 521	4 193	7 615	1 033	2 095	2 086
2006	6 812	4 159	8 299	1 051	2 262	2 254
2007	6 134	4 131	7 411	1 029	2 288	2 280
2008	6 981	4 812	8 415	1 065	2 405	2 389
2009	7 064	4 705	8 685	1 057	2 393	2 380
2010	7 112	4 725	8 872	1 060	2 382	2 369
2011	7 230	4 975	8 947	1 085	2 481	2 478
2012	7 294	5 149	9 016	1 095	2 565	2 556
2013	7 321	5 237	9 044	1 081	2 614	2 610
2014	7 307	5 311	9 005	1 103	2 608	2 604
2015	7 340	5 333	9 028	1 110	2 611	2 608
2016	6 753	4 283	8 764	1 111	2 483	2 469
2017	6 837	4 437	8 720	1 083	2 561	2 558
2018	7 063	4 591	8 834	1 069	2 509	2 483

表3-7

历年蚕桑、茶叶、水果生产情况
STATISTICS ON SILKWORM COCOONS, TEA AND FRUITS OVER THE YEARS

年份 Year	蚕桑 Silkworm Cocoons and Mulberry		茶叶 Tea		水果 Fruits	
	桑园面积(公顷) Mulberry Field Area (hectare)	蚕茧产量(吨) Output of Silkworm Cocoons (ton)	茶园面积(公顷) Tea Field Area (hectare)	总产量(吨) Total Output (ton)	果园面积(公顷) Area of Orchards (hectare)	总产量(吨) Total Output (ton)
1949	7 051	1 797	117	66	1 096	6 785
1952	7 360	3 047	117	77	1 184	7 584
1957	7 191	2 510	121	47	1 321	8 257
1962	5 843	943	208	90	1 517	12 213
1965	5 745	1 917	212	137	1 599	16 236
1970	7 051	4 520	210	190	1 706	19 039
1975	7 046	4 340	314	261	2 098	23 357
1978	6 115	3 325	393	286	2 440	18 653
1980	6 065	4 784	401	286	2 778	17 407
1985	6 868	5 663	417	265	5 771	39 113
1990	7 973	9 785	360	369	4 853	42 280
1995	9 275	12 435	421	262	6 796	62 096
2000	6 188	7 291	469	258	6 080	59 203
2001	6 090	7 397	570	249	6 286	78 523
2002	5 333	5 785	679	235	6 523	67 918
2003	4 164	3 437	1 530	399	6 554	79 307
2004	3 918	3 512	1 815	315	6 191	73 084
2005	3 895	2 771	1 955	348	6 708	74 138
2006	3 881	3 008	2 106	381	7 029	76 023
2007	3 879	2 478	2 120	385	7 554	79 767
2008	3 853	1 654	2 207	397	8 712	91 102
2009	3 745	915	2 296	403	9 627	103 064
2010	3 618	638	2 344	338	10 214	96 953
2011	3 474	558	2 400	349	10 791	103 082
2012	3 601	495	2 416	375	10 866	105 993
2013	2 070	396	2 403	383	11 155	110 763
2014	2 067	357	2 400	374	11 343	114 928
2015	2 047	295	2 430	364	11 444	104 156
2016	2 030	237	2 430	357	11 132	95 595
2017	2 030	199	2 433	360	10 516	105 125
2018	2 030	193	2 619	401	9 541	98 532

表3-8

历年牧业、渔业生产情况
STATISTICS ON LIVESTOCK AND FISHERY OVER THE YEARS

年 份 Year	猪（万头）Hogs（10 000 heads）			年末存栏 Livestock Being Raised at Year-end			牛奶产量（吨）Output of Cow Milk（ton）	水产品产量（吨）Output of Aquatic Products(ton)
	年末存栏 Hog Being Raised at Year-end	肉猪出栏 Slaughtered Hogs	猪肉产量（吨）Output of Pork（ton）	牛（万头）Cattle and Buffaloes (10 000 heads)	羊（万只）Sheep and Goats (10 000 heads)	家禽（万只）Poultry (10 000 heads)		
1949	23.21	11.80		8.59	18.73	120.23		14 977
1952	37.98	22.16		10.18	26.86	178.32		21 470
1957	81.58	40.40		9.45	41.96	278.11		30 998
1962	71.52	25.67		6.69	58.40	162.37		26 672
1965	155.04	120.68		6.24	42.18	169.81		32 817
1970	214.19	117.68		6.20	49.28	203.55		44 765
1975	245.64	178.35		3.55	47.57	269.22	1 934	61 845
1978	264.31	185.66		2.74	45.58	418.93	2 375	82 249
1980	250.34	310.14	129 457	2.43	48.53	453.57	4 110	87 119
1985	186.01	210.41	110 498	0.79	24.00	1 012.16	10 155	158 774
1990	154.62	193.54	101 418	0.62	41.00	1 048.48	16 069	217 276
1995	111.73	177.46	104 321	0.34	49.38	1 008.51	12 316	284 097
2000	104.75	198.50	111 075	0.86	35.92	971.05	43 742	345 139
2001	98.71	204.74	115 631	1.89	36.16	1 109.73	80 453	354 308
2002	88.78	188.12	107 976	2.65	32.12	1 181.12	105 095	357 221
2003	75.89	178.49	93 809	2.47	27.05	1 067.30	100 266	338 707
2004	76.00	160.82	85 617	2.26	21.75	1 060.91	108 812	311 884
2005	73.85	139.91	86 274	2.40	13.08	1 202.80	94 651	316 523
2006	66.05	136.64	99 935	2.29	5.89	929.61	100 547	299 882
2007	70.87	122.24	92 499	2.30	4.67	1 050.83	98 129	292 785
2008	77.93	110.66	79 204	2.68	4.88	1 113.06	91 983	290 637
2009	82.37	117.34	88 876	2.32	6.49	1 120.89	91 019	273 498
2010	83.51	117.70	84 487	2.35	7.90	1 093.48	91 675	277 049
2011	85.34	118.49	86 164	2.34	7.77	991.09	92 577	284 083
2012	84.97	113.44	84 543	2.28	8.58	853.76	92 524	288 433
2013	85.98	106.15	79 751	2.20	9.87	787.92	95 060	276 955
2014	76.69	103.46	75 525	2.39	10.73	656.68	101 224	267 039
2015	66.44	94.89	70 423	2.36	12.96	657.45	113 774	262 057
2016	60.34	84.46	61 778	2.15	10.36	651.87	102 957	254 918
2017	29.54	69.45	51 027	1.54	5.65	315.75	78 898	234 122
2018	13.66	35.63	25 351	0.99	4.30	210.38	71 550	195 644

表3-9

农村基本情况 (2018年末)

项　目		Item		全　市 Whole Municipality
农村组织		**Village Units**		
镇政府	(个)	Town Governments	(unit)	52
村民委员会		Number of Villagers' Committees		1 025
乡村户数、人口		**Households and Rural Population**		
乡村总户数	(万户)	Number of Households	(10 000 households)	87.34
乡村总人口	(万人)	Rural Population	(10 000 persons)	283.26
年末乡村实有从业人员		**Rural Employees of year-end**		
合　计		Total		171.58
1.按性别分		Grouped by Sex		
男劳动力		Male		88.62
女劳动力		Female		82.96
2.按行业分		Grouped by Sector		
农林牧渔业		Farming, Forestry, Animal Husbandry and Fishery		21.02
工　业		Industry		104.35
建筑业		Construction		9.65
交通运输、仓储和邮政业		Transportation, Logistics and Postal		5.45
信息传输、计算机服务和软件业		Information Transmission, Software and Information Technology Services		1.33
批发和零售业		Wholesale and Retail Trade Services		10.43
住宿和餐饮业		Accommodation and Catering Services		4.62
金融、保险业		Banking and Insurance		1.04
房地产、社会服务业		Real Estate and Social Services		2.43
卫生、体育、社会福利业		Health Care, Sporting and Social Welfare		1.15
文、教、艺术和广播影视业		Culture, Education and Arts, Radio, Film and Television		1.06
科研和综合技术服务业		Scientific Research and Polytechnical Services		0.31
乡镇经济组织管理		Rural Economic Management		1.25
其　他		Others		7.49

BASIC CONDITIONS OF COUNTRYSIDE (END OF 2018)

市 区 Urban Area	# 吴江区 Wujiang District	常 熟 Changshu	张家港 Zhangjiagang	昆 山 Kunshan	太 仓 Taicang
20	7	8	8	10	6
436	249	214	153	149	73
32.57	15.41	17.72	20.06	10.42	6.57
107.79	50.03	57.02	59.27	36.01	23.17
65.32	29.81	38.38	31.77	20.92	15.19
34.18	15.13	19.42	16.64	10.64	7.74
31.14	14.68	18.96	15.13	10.28	7.45
10.19	3.59	3.42	3.12	1.60	2.69
36.50	18.19	24.05	21.00	12.94	9.86
4.39	2.05	2.07	1.54	1.08	0.57
2.02	0.87	1.16	1.30	0.60	0.37
0.54	0.28	0.27	0.22	0.24	0.06
4.71	1.97	2.36	1.71	1.34	0.31
1.88	0.66	0.84	0.75	0.98	0.17
0.39	0.14	0.24	0.16	0.16	0.09
0.48	0.26	0.72	0.36	0.78	0.09
0.36	0.15	0.32	0.16	0.24	0.07
0.32	0.09	0.40	0.12	0.15	0.07
0.11	0.05	0.07	0.07	0.04	0.02
0.51	0.25	0.34	0.23	0.11	0.06
2.92	1.26	2.12	1.03	0.66	0.76

表3-10

农林牧渔业总产值 (2018年)
GROSS OUTPUT VALUE OF FARMING, FORESTRY, ANIMAL HUSBANDRY AND FISHERY (2018)

单位：万元 (可比价格 at Comparable Price) (10 000 yuan)

地　区	Region	总产值 Gross Output Value	农　业 Farming	林　业 Forestry	牧　业 Animal Husbandry	渔　业 Fishery	农林牧渔服务业 Services
全　市	**Whole Municipality**	**4 074 471**	**1 741 298**	**240 637**	**256 977**	**1 345 285**	**490 274**
市　区	Urban Area	1 505 997	503 201	52 049	74 219	680 789	195 739
# 吴江区	Wujiang	771 245	303 812	26 520	64 936	322 922	53 055
常　熟	Changshu	745 863	437 907	27 288	38 321	146 986	95 361
张家港	Zhangjiagang	591 268	341 114	75 455	43 871	45 059	85 769
昆　山	Kunshan	564 659	170 154	48 281	7 080	304 652	34 492
太　仓	Taicang	666 684	288 922	37 564	93 486	167 799	78 913

表3-11

农林牧渔业总产值 (2018年)
GROSS OUTPUT VALUE OF FARMING, FORESTRY, ANIMAL HUSBANDRY AND FISHERY (2018)

单位：万元 (10 000 yuan)

地　区	Region	总产值 Gross Output Value	农　业 Farming	林　业 Forestry	牧　业 Animal Husbandry	渔　业 Fishery	农林牧渔服务业 Services
全　市	**Whole Municipality**	**4 100 858**	**1 776 435**	**245 678**	**240 964**	**1 344 111**	**493 670**
市　区	Urban Area	1 513 735	514 401	53 331	68 572	680 532	196 899
# 吴江区	Wujiang	774 068	311 246	27 307	60 046	322 643	52 826
常　熟	Changshu	750 944	444 084	27 804	35 972	146 762	96 322
张家港	Zhangjiagang	597 777	348 628	76 837	41 245	44 941	86 126
昆　山	Kunshan	568 708	173 847	49 155	6 603	304 343	34 760
太　仓	Taicang	669 694	295 475	38 551	88 572	167 533	79 563

表3-12

农林牧渔业增加值 (2018年)
VALUE ADDED OF FARMING, FORESTRY, ANIMAL HUSBANDRY AND FISHERY (2018)

单位：万元 (10 000 yuan)

项 目	Item	总产值 Gross Output Value	中间消耗 Depreciation	增加值 Value-added	增加值率 (%) Value-adding Rate (%)
总 计	**Total**	**4 100 858**	**1 700 720**	**2 400 138**	**58.5**
农 业	Farming	1 776 435	610 682	1 165 753	65.6
林 业	Forestry	245 678	112 126	133 552	54.4
牧 业	Animal Husbandry	240 964	137 578	103 386	42.9
渔 业	Fishery	1 344 111	606 828	737 283	54.9
农林牧渔服务业	Services	493 670	233 506	260 164	52.7

表3-13

分地区农林牧渔业增加值 (2018年)
VALUE ADDED OF FARMING, FORESTRY, ANIMAL HUSBANDRY AND FISHERY BY REGION (2018)

单位：万元 (10 000 yuan)

地 区	Region	增加值 Value-added	农 业 Farming	林 业 Forestry	牧 业 Animal Husbandry	渔 业 Fishery	农林牧渔服务业 Services
全 市	**Whole Municipality**	**2 400 138**	**1 165 753**	**133 552**	**103 386**	**737 283**	**260 164**
市 区	Urban Area	872 740	339 440	28 000	26 702	374 469	104 129
# 吴江区	Wujiang	454 978	219 434	15 221	23 540	172 825	23 958
常 熟	Changshu	452 193	288 563	15 460	14 328	80 688	53 154
张家港	Zhangjiagang	344 712	222 974	41 344	17 423	24 568	38 403
昆 山	Kunshan	336 421	117 694	27 035	2 773	168 758	20 161
太 仓	Taicang	394 072	197 082	21 713	42 160	88 800	44 317

表3-14

农作物播种面积（2018年）
SOWN AREAS OF FARM CROPS (2018)

单位：千公顷 (1 000 hectares)

项　目	Item	全　市 Whole Municipality	市　区 Urban Area	#吴江区 Wujiang District	常　熟 Changshu	张家港 Zhang-jiagang	昆　山 Kunshan	太　仓 Taicang
农作物总播种面积	**Total Sown Area**	**217.79**	**49.74**	**36.18**	**58.93**	**52.32**	**19.55**	**37.25**
一、粮食作物	**Grain Crops**	**124.47**	**26.29**	**20.53**	**33.06**	**33.56**	**12.62**	**18.94**
（一）夏收粮食	Summer Grain	51.94	8.19	6.78	14.66	15.85	5.05	8.19
1.夏收谷物	Summer Cereal	50.96	8.14	6.78	14.37	15.64	4.96	7.85
（1）小　麦	Wheat	50.95	8.14	6.78	14.37	15.63	4.96	7.85
（2）元　麦	Hull-less Barley	0.01	–	–	–	0.01	–	–
（3）大　麦	Barley	–	–	–	–	–	–	–
2.夏收豆类	Summer Beans	0.98	0.05	–	0.29	0.21	0.09	0.34
（二）秋收粮食	Autumn Grain	72.53	18.10	13.75	18.40	17.71	7.57	10.75
1.秋收谷物	Autumn Cereal	69.15	17.70	13.49	17.82	16.45	7.31	9.87
（1）稻　谷	Rice	68.05	17.70	13.49	17.48	16.21	7.25	9.41
#单季晚稻	Single Late Rice	68.05	17.70	13.49	17.48	16.21	7.25	9.41
（2）玉　米	Corn	1.10	–	–	0.34	0.24	0.06	0.46
（3）其他谷物	Others	–	–	–	–	–	–	–
2.秋收豆类	Autumn Beans	2.87	0.38	0.26	0.42	1.13	0.22	0.72
（1）大　豆	Soybeans	2.54	0.38	0.26	0.35	1.12	0.16	0.53
（2）杂　豆	Others	0.33	–	–	0.07	0.01	0.06	0.19
3.秋收薯类	Autumn Tubers	0.51	0.02	–	0.16	0.13	0.04	0.16
二、油　料	**Oil-bearing Crops**	**2.37**	**0.07**	**0.06**	**0.72**	**0.84**	**0.23**	**0.51**
#油菜籽	Rapeseeds	2.05	0.07	0.06	0.68	0.70	0.22	0.38
三、棉　花	**Cotton**	**0.13**	–	–	**0.05**	**0.03**	**0.01**	**0.04**
四、麻　类	**Fiber Crops**	–	–	–	–	–	–	–
五、糖　料	**Sugar Crops**	**0.03**	–	–	–	**0.02**	–	**0.01**
六、药　材	**Crude Drugs**	**0.05**	–	–	–	**0.03**	**0.02**	–
七、蔬菜、瓜类	**Vegetables and Melon Crops**	**77.42**	**20.91**	**13.62**	**24.16**	**11.30**	**4.64**	**16.41**
八、其他农作物	**Others**	**13.32**	**2.47**	**1.97**	**0.94**	**6.54**	**2.03**	**1.34**
#青饲料	Green Fodder	1.70	0.97	0.96	0.35	0.03	0.08	0.27
绿　肥	Green Manure	3.21	1.01	1.01	0.35	0.34	1.48	0.03
附：常年蔬菜地	**In Addition Vegetable Gardens**	**23.27**	**6.45**	**4.50**	**7.21**	**3.24**	**1.17**	**5.20**

表3-15

农产品总产量（2018年）
TOTAL YIELD OF FARM CROPS (2018)

单位：吨 (ton)

项 目	Item	全 市 Whole Municipality	市 区 Urban Area	# 吴江区 Wujiang District	常 熟 Changshu	张家港 Zhang-jiagang	昆 山 Kunshan	太 仓 Taicang
一、粮食作物	**Grain Crops**	**879 178**	**199 106**	**155 667**	**229 591**	**226 036**	**92 539**	**131 906**
（一）夏收粮食	Summer Grain	238 468	36 231	30 937	65 132	75 867	23 248	37 990
1.夏收谷物	Summer Cereal	235 238	36 117	30 937	64 018	75 335	22 900	36 868
（1）小 麦	Wheat	235 208	36 117	30 937	64 018	75 305	22 900	36 868
（2）元 麦	Hull-less Barley	30	–	–	–	30	–	–
（3）大 麦	Barley	–	–	–	–	–	–	–
2.夏收豆类	Summer Beans	3 230	114	–	1 114	532	348	1 122
（二）秋收粮食	Autumn Grain	640 710	162 875	124 730	164 459	150 169	69 291	93 916
1.秋收谷物	Autumn Cereal	627 987	161 389	123 838	161 407	146 454	68 133	90 604
（1）稻 谷	Rice	621 375	161 389	123 838	159 260	145 039	67 751	87 936
# 单季晚稻	Single Late Rice	621 375	161 389	123 838	159 260	145 039	67 751	87 936
（2）玉 米	Corn	6 612	–	–	2 147	1 415	382	2 668
（3）其他谷物	Others	–	–	–	–	–	–	–
2.秋收豆类	Autumn Beans	9 507	1 386	892	1 840	2 831	858	2 592
（1）大 豆	Soybeans	8 207	1 386	892	1 449	2 804	660	1 908
（2）杂 豆	Others	1 300	–	–	391	27	198	684
3.秋收薯类	Autumn Tubers	3 216	100	–	1 212	884	300	720
二、油 料	**Oil-bearing Crops**	**5 947**	**163**	**143**	**1 856**	**2 104**	**504**	**1 320**
# 油菜籽	Rapeseeds	5 090	163	143	1 718	1 815	489	905
三、棉 花	**Cotton**	**139**	–	–	**50**	**17**	**22**	**50**
四、麻 类	**Fiber Crops**	–	–	–	–	–	–	–
五、糖 料	**Sugar Crops**	**936**	–	–	–	**519**	–	**417**
六、蔬 菜	**Vegetable**	**2 143 562**	**492 741**	**318 837**	**748 240**	**266 253**	**124 508**	**511 820**

表3-16

农产品单产（2018年）
YIELD OF FARM CROPS PER HECTARE (2018)

单位：公斤/公顷 (kg/hectare)

项　目	Item	全市 Whole Municipality	市区 Urban Area	#吴江区 Wujiang District	常熟 Changshu	张家港 Zhang-jiagang	昆山 Kunshan	太仓 Taicang
一、粮食作物	**Grain Crops**	**7 063**	**7 573**	**7 582**	**6 945**	**6 735**	**7 333**	**6 964**
（一）夏收粮食	Summer Grain	4 591	4 424	4 563	4 443	4 787	4 604	4 639
1.夏收谷物	Summer Cereal	4 616	4 437	4 563	4 455	4 817	4 617	4 697
（1）小　麦	Wheat	4 616	4 437	4 563	4 455	4 818	4 617	4 697
（2）元　麦	Hull-less Barley	3 000	–	–	–	3 000	–	–
（3）大　麦	Barley	–	–	–	–	–	–	–
2.夏收豆类	Summer Beans	3 296	2 280	–	3 841	2 533	3 867	3 300
（二）秋收粮食	Autumn Grain	8 834	8 999	9 071	8 938	8 479	9 153	8 736
1.秋收谷物	Autumn Cereal	9 082	9 118	9 180	9 058	8 903	9 321	9 180
（1）稻　谷	Rice	9 131	9 118	9 180	9 111	8 948	9 345	9 345
# 单季晚稻	Single Late Rice	9 131	9 118	9 180	9 111	8 948	9 345	9 345
（2）玉　米	Corn	6 011	–	–	6 315	5 896	6 367	5 800
（3）其他谷物	Others	–	–	–	–	–	–	–
2.秋收豆类	Autumn Beans	3 313	3 647	3 431	4 381	2 505	3 900	3 600
（1）大　豆	Soybeans	3 231	3 647	3 431	4 140	2 504	4 125	3 600
（2）杂　豆	Others	3 939	–	–	5 586	2 700	3 300	3 600
3.秋收薯类	Autumn Tubers	6 306	5 000	–	7 575	6 800	7 500	4 500
二、油　料	**Oil-bearing Crops**	**2 509**	**2 329**	**2 383**	**2 578**	**2 505**	**2 191**	**2 588**
# 油菜籽	Rapeseeds	2 483	2 329	2 383	2 526	2 593	2 223	2 382
三、棉　花	**Cotton**	**1 069**	–	–	**1 000**	**567**	**2 200**	**1 250**
四、麻　类	**Fiber Crops**	–	–	–	–	–	–	–
五、糖　料	**Sugar Crops**	**31 200**	–	–	–	**25 950**	–	**41 700**
六、蔬　菜	**Vegetable**	**30 242**	**26 322**	**26 838**	**32 141**	**28 598**	**32 173**	**32 600**

表3-17

渔业生产情况 (2018年)
STATISTICS ON FISHERY (2018)

项 目	Item	全 市 Whole Municipality	市 区 Urban Area	#吴江区 Wujiang District	常 熟 Changshu	张家港 Zhang-jiagang	昆 山 Kunshan	太 仓 Taicang
基本情况	**Basic Conditions**							
渔业村数 (个)	Number of Fishing Villages (unit)	46	36	15	–	–	10	–
渔业户数 (户)	Number of Fishing Households (household)	24 602	14 852	4 622	3 690	216	4 125	1 719
# 海 洋	Seawater	45	–	–	–	45	–	–
渔业人口 (人)	Population in Fishery (person)	103 992	67 393	14 813	14 297	1 400	16 487	4 415
渔业劳动力	Fishery Labor Force	68 875	46 025	13 716	9 318	751	9 080	3 701
# 专业劳动力	Specialized Labor Force	51 198	31 970	7 124	7 643	626	8 290	2 669
# 捕捞专业	Fish Catching	6 212	3 726	830	475	134	1 440	437
养殖专业	Aquaculture	43 211	26 552	5 952	7 140	480	6 850	2 189
水产品产量 (吨)	**Output of Aquatic Products** (ton)	**195 644**	**115 961**	**68 726**	**25 055**	**13 272**	**29 417**	**11 939**
海洋产品	Seawater Aquatic Products	3 248	–	–	2 088	–	–	1 160
淡水产品	Freshwater Aquatic Products	192 396	115 961	68 726	22 967	13 272	29 417	10 779
捕 捞	Fish Catching	19 943	11 788	2 466	2 622	745	866	3 922
养 殖	Aquaculture	175 701	104 173	66 260	22 433	12 527	28 551	8 017
渔 船	**Fishing Boat**							
机动渔船 (艘)	Motorized Fishing Boats (unit)	6 539	6 268	2 070	73	31	160	7
(吨)	(ton)	20 824	15 595	3 326	2 696	691	243	1 599
(千瓦)	(kw)	80 595	70 193	20 251	4 385	1 370	2 544	2 103
非机动渔船 (艘)	Non-motorized Fishing Boats (unit)	10 972	8 506	818	310	44	745	1 367
(载吨)	(ton)	24 994	22 362	3 328	185	22	1 960	465
淡水养殖面积 (千公顷)	**Freshwater Raise Areas**(1 000 hectares)	**51.29**	**35.61**	**18.33**	**6.46**	**0.91**	**6.46**	**1.85**
# 池塘面积	Pond Area	29.34	15.80	8.88	6.46	0.91	4.32	1.85

表3-18

牧业生产情况 (2018年)
STATISTICS ON LIVESTOCK (2018)

项　　目	Item	全　市 Whole Municipality	市　区 Urban Area	#吴江区 Wujiang District	常　熟 Changshu	张家港 Zhang-jiagang	昆　山 Kunshan	太　仓 Taicang
当年出栏数	**Slaughtered Livestock of the Year**							
牛　(万头)	Cattle and Buffaloes (10 000 heads)	–	–	–	–	–	–	–
猪	Hogs	35.63	12.17	10.20	7.99	5.44	0.33	9.70
羊　(万只)	Sheep and Goats (10 000 heads)	5.17	1.87	1.58	1.35	0.48	0.07	1.40
#山　羊	Goats	1.41	0.39	0.30	0.18	0.35	0.07	0.42
家　禽	Poultry	927.49	98.92	79.53	39.32	70.48	5.97	712.80
兔	Rabbit	1.73	0.97	0.97	–	0.33	–	0.43
年末存栏数	**Livestock Being Raised at Year-end**							
牛　(万头)	Cattle and Buffaloes (10 000 heads)	0.99	–	–	0.38	0.32	–	0.29
猪	Hogs	13.66	1.18	0.54	4.21	2.59	0.18	5.50
羊　(万只)	Sheep and Goats (10 000 heads)	4.30	1.19	0.91	1.49	0.43	0.04	1.15
#山　羊	Goats	1.37	0.28	0.20	0.20	0.40	0.04	0.45
家　禽	Poultry	210.38	44.96	40.55	20.43	40.87	2.34	101.78
兔	Rabbit	0.97	0.67	0.67	–	0.16	–	0.14
产　量　(吨)	**Output of Meat** (ton)							
牛　肉	Beef	–	–	–	–	–	–	–
猪　肉	Pork	25 351	8 422	7 138	5 598	4 310	231	6 790
羊　肉	Mutton	880	322	274	288	64	10	196
#山羊肉	Goat Mutton	194	53	44	27	45	10	59
禽　肉	Poultry	12 223	1 792	1 466	599	1 158	120	8 554
兔　肉	Rabbit	37	17	17	–	11	–	9
奶　类	Milk	71 550	–	–	24 042	19 226	10 060	18 222
#牛　奶	Cow Milk	71 550	–	–	24 042	19 226	10 060	18 222
绵羊毛	Sheep Wool	17.24	4.24	4.24	13.00	–	–	–
蜂　蜜	Honey	738	577	6	42	48	13	58
禽　蛋	Poultry Eggs	9 233	3 264	2 736	1 809	3 169	54	937

表3-19

林业、蚕桑、茶叶、水果生产情况（2018年）
STATISTICS ON FORESTRY, SILKWORM COCOONS, TEA AND FRUITS PRODUCTION (2018)

项目	Item	全市 Whole Municipality	市区 Urban Area	#吴江区 Wujiang District	常熟 Changshu	张家港 Zhangjiagang	昆山 Kunshan	太仓 Taicang
林业	**Forestry**							
造林面积（公顷）	Build Forestry Areas (hectare)	501	112	61	58	70	208	53
育苗面积（公顷）	Raise Seedlings Areas (hectare)	7 151	5 267	2 990	646	708	322	208
林木采伐（立方米）	Timber Cut (cu.m)	6 646	5 646	5 358	150	839	–	11
年末实有林地面积(公顷)	Actual Forestry Areas (year-end) (hectare)	103 072	55 329	19 598	14 753	11 991	13 094	7 905
蚕桑	**Silkworm Cocoons and Mulberry**							
蚕茧产量（吨）	Output of Silkworm Cocoons (ton)	193	193	193	–	–	–	–
年末实有桑园面积（公顷）	Mulberry Field Area (year-end) (hectare)	2 030	2 030	2 030	–	–	–	–
茶叶	**Tea**							
茶叶产量（吨）	Output of Tea (ton)	401	353	–	39	9	–	–
#绿毛茶	Green Tea	310	263	–	39	9	–	–
年末实有茶园面积（公顷）	Tea Field Area (year-end) (hectare)	2 619	2 441	–	131	47	–	–
水果	**Fruits**							
水果产量（吨）	Output of Fruits (ton)	98 532	46 305	13 208	12 596	22 145	11 939	5 547
#柑桔	Citrus	18 794	11 711	7 830	194	6 302	457	130
梨	Pears	12 526	5 855	2 350	1 257	2 566	2 149	700
葡萄	Grapes	27 335	5 593	1 502	8 488	4 281	6 583	2 390
年末实有果园面积（公顷）	Area of Orchards (year-end) (hectare)	9 541	6 511	737	732	1 192	638	468
#柑桔	Citrus	1 404	1 223	400	15	149	10	7
梨	Pears	953	489	124	105	160	108	91
葡萄	Grapes	1 534	373	100	420	231	382	128

表3-20 农业机械化、化学化及农田水利化情况（2018年）

指　标		Item		全　市 Whole Municipality
一、农业机械化情况		**Statistics on Agricultural Machinery**		
（一）机耕面积	(千公顷)	Area Ploughed by Tractors	(1 000 hectares)	140.62
（二）机播面积		Seeded Area by Tractors		106.08
#机插水稻面积		Rice Planted Area by Transplanters		57.11
机播水稻面积		Seeded Rice Area by Tractors		3.48
（三）机收面积		Harvest Area by Tractors		118.29
#机收水稻面积		Rice Harvest Area by Tractors		67.40
（四）机械脱粒粮食数量	(万吨)	Amount of Grain Crops Shelling by Thresher	(10 000 tons)	83.06
二、农用化肥、农药施用量		**Use of Agricultural Fertilizers and Insecticides**		
化　肥（折纯量）	(吨)	Chemical Fertilizer (pure)	(ton)	64 428
农　药		Agricultural Chemical Insecticides		3 458
三、农村用电量	(万千瓦时)	**Electricity Consumed in Rural Area**	(10 000 kwh)	**5 995 437**
四、农田水利建设情况		**Irrigation and Water Conservancy**		
有效灌溉面积	(千公顷)	Effective Irrigation Area	(1 000 hectares)	166.57

STATISTICS ON AGRICULTURAL MACHINERY, CHEMICAL APPLICATION AND IRRIGATION OF FARMING LAND (2018)

市 区 Urban Area	# 吴江区 Wujiang District	常 熟 Changshu	张家港 Zhangjiagang	昆 山 Kunshan	太 仓 Taicang
27.32	20.33	40.08	32.06	12.13	29.03
21.06	16.82	27.96	31.21	11.19	14.66
26.02	11.33	14.89	14.87	0.56	0.77
0.79	0.43	0.85	0.35	1.40	0.10
25.64	20.14	31.92	31.21	12.21	17.32
17.46	13.36	17.48	15.79	7.25	9.41
18.86	14.30	19.62	22.33	9.11	13.15
16 891	9 132	21 756	10 610	6 850	8 321
891	420	1 496	486	292	293
2 265 630	**1 548 775**	**798 937**	**1 237 739**	**1 097 329**	**595 802**
48.26	23.17	41.10	30.63	15.30	31.28

表3-21

主要农业机械拥有量 (2018年末)

项　目		Item		全　市 Whole Municipality
一、农业机械总动力	(万千瓦)	**Total Power of Agricultural Machinery**	(10 000 kw)	**159.87**
# 柴油机		Diesel Engines		85.07
电动机		Motor		46.47
二、主要农业机械		**Main Agricultural Machinery**		
1.大中型拖拉机	(台)	Large and Medium Tractors	(unit)	4 878
	(万千瓦)		(10 000 kw)	25.51
2.小型拖拉机	(台)	Mini-tractors	(unit)	516
	(万千瓦)		(10 000 kw)	0.72
3.机动水稻插秧机	(台)	Rice Transplanters	(unit)	3 609
4.机动值保机械		Mobile Plant Protection Machinery		38 018
	(万千瓦)		(10 000 kw)	4.27
5.农用水泵	(万台)	Agricultural Water Pump	(10 000 units)	3.36
6.节水灌溉类机械	(套)	Equipment in Water-saving Irrigation	(set)	1 671
7.联合收割机	(台)	Combine Harvesters	(unit)	2 556
8.机动脱粒机		Motorized Huller		10 738
9.渔业机械		Machinery of Fishery		50 305
	(万千瓦)		(10 000 kw)	18.68

POSSESSION OF AGRICULTURAL MACHINERY (END OF 2018)

市 区 Urban Area	# 吴江区 Wujiang District	常 熟 Changshu	张家港 Zhangjiagang	昆 山 Kunshan	太 仓 Taicang
58.97	**26.64**	**31.70**	**30.15**	**17.93**	**21.12**
26.92	14.65	18.34	18.15	9.38	12.28
12.11	6.92	11.70	7.46	7.64	7.57
1 112	836	1 232	854	573	1 107
5.79	4.17	6.38	4.68	3.15	5.51
257	225	100	16	116	27
0.37	0.34	0.16	0.03	0.13	0.02
718	572	1 162	839	333	557
10 065	2 623	17 152	5 296	2 309	3 196
1.16	0.57	1.14	1.04	0.28	0.65
1.36	0.85	0.92	0.44	0.17	0.47
528	–	537	–	176	430
398	279	717	705	226	510
1 036	920	8 192	–	–	1 510
24 030	15 110	8 350	2 547	11 868	3 510
11.01	5.84	1.97	0.34	2.75	2.62

表3-22

分镇（涉农街道）基本情况 (2018年)

镇（街道） Towns （Sub-districts）		行政区域面积（公顷） The Administrative Area (hectare)	年末人口（人） Population Year-end (person)	年末耕地面积（公顷） Cultivated Area Year-end (hectare)	#高标准农田 High Standard Farmland Area	农机总动力（千瓦） Total Agricultural Machinery Power (kw)
吴中区	**Wuzhong District**					
越溪街道	Yuexi Sub-district	4 880	93 267	148	–	1350
横泾街道	Hengjing Sub-district	5 223	64 113	750	388	4931
香山街道	Xiangshan Sub-district	2 700	38 618	272	–	191
甪直镇	Luzhi Town	12 081	137 403	2 014	624	23 316
木渎镇	Mudu Town	7 459	322 472	80	–	800
胥口镇	Xukou Town	3 586	91 458	225	68	1 080
东山镇	Dongshan Town	9 600	56 091	474	140	34 544
光福镇	Guangfu Town	6 156	48 219	1 340	71	22 025
金庭镇	Jinting Town	8 342	45 266	779	40	6 753
临湖镇	Linhu Town	5 430	91 216	1 453	620	17 761
相城区	**XiangchengDistrict**					
太平街道	Taiping Sub-district	4 335	45 945	441	–	6 100
黄桥街道	Huangqiao Sub-district	2 308	58 054	198	–	198
北桥街道	Beiqiao Sub-district	4 752	57 438	976	216	6 782
漕湖街道	Caohu Sub-district	5 240	24 671	161	16	2 203
望亭镇	Wangting Town	4 406	62 197	1 345	516	5 769
黄埭镇	Huangdai Town	5 600	123 793	506	388	1 668
渭塘镇	Weitang Town	3 936	83 514	786	188	825
阳澄湖镇	Yangchenghu Town	6 284	62 361	1 209	75	22 245
阳澄湖生态休闲旅游度假区	Yangcheng Lake Ecological Leisure Tourism Resort	6 172	16 653	862	43	3 046
高新区、虎丘区	**New&Hi-techZone,HuqiuDistrict**					
镇湖街道	Zhenhu Sub-district	2 020	26 051	453	–	3 030
东渚街道	Dongzhu Sub-district	2 002	37 250	377	24	8 000
浒墅关镇	Xushuguan Town	3 000	64 861	380	97	1 500
通安镇	Tongan Town	3 698	96 714	1 326	584	1 806

BASIC SITUATION BY TOWNS (STREETS CONTAINING AGRICULTURE)（2018）

农作物播种面积(公顷) Sown Area of Farm Crops (hectare)	# 粮食作物 Grain Crops	# 蔬菜作物 Vegetables Crops	粮食总产量(吨) Total Output of Grain (ton)	蔬菜总产量(吨) Total Output of Vegetables (ton)	企业个数(个) Number of Enterprises (unit)	#规模以上工业 Number of Enterprises Above Designated
252	54	108	297	2 769	3 181	58
829	409	420	4080	16 340	1 035	55
18	–	18	–	520	645	4
1 750	794	913	5 800	23 238	5 101	140
175	–	12	–	350	10 321	90
201	106	95	792	3 040	3 312	142
322	5	317	35	5 098	923	34
176	80	96	547	2 395	881	19
680	80	380	760	10 562	517	6
1 233	710	404	6 596	7 883	2 622	72
334	123	211	827	5 420	4 075	44
53	20	33	135	522	2 107	62
893	415	400	2 884	7 473	2 491	91
576	479	98	1 400	3 334	735	52
976	429	470	4 128	6 830	3 103	64
750	660	70	3 907	2 399	3 877	156
496	64	315	489	6 686	2 265	100
1 152	208	310	1 099	3 734	1 139	66
391	318	60	2 095	1 529	589	6
420	35	145	282	4 110	116	2
164	67	97	397	2 290	209	4
720	558	105	3 296	3 031	2 118	100
297	228	68	1 842	1 848	1 674	56

表3-22 续表 1

镇（街道） Towns （Sub-districts）		行政区域面积 (公顷) The Administrative Area (hectare)	年末人口 (人) Population Year-end (person)	年末耕地面积 (公顷) Cultivated Area Year-end (hectare)	# 高标准农田 High Standard Farmland Area	农机总动力 (千瓦) Total Agricultural Machinery Power (kw)
吴江区	**WuJiang District**					
松陵镇	Songling Town	19 872	279 353	4 296	177	38 233
平望镇	Pingwang Town	13 565	124 958	4 650	2 900	13 000
盛泽镇	Shengze Town	14 774	198 070	3 023	1 685	52 000
七都镇	Qidu Town	8 620	83 270	2 886	245	33 200
震泽镇	Zhenze Town	9 561	89 300	3 524	1 667	41 250
桃源镇	Taoyuan Town	9 060	79 684	3 688	80	5 042
黎里镇	Lili Town	25 800	179 379	5 113	1 228	74 800
吴江经济技术开发区	Wujiang Economic and Technological Development Zone	17 300	316 174	2 934	840	22 000
常　熟	**ChangShu**					
虞山街道	Yushan Sub-district	6 270	207 486	239	–	128
常福街道	Changfu Sub-district	8 660	119 723	2 446	1 744	7 326
琴川街道	Qinchuan Sub-district	4 870	214 329	158	–	560
莫城街道	Mocheng Sub-district	4 080	138 766	961	533	5 170
碧溪街道	Bixi Sub-district	11 379	152 237	3 347	2 673	10 316
东南街道	Dongnan Sub-district	2 798	41 014	–	–	–
梅李镇	Meili Town	8 084	109 178	3 018	176	8 043
海虞镇	Haiyu Town	10 997	123 779	3 564	2 247	7 727
古里镇	Guli Town	9 646	107 380	2 203	2 203	28 936
沙家浜镇	Shajiabang Town	7 024	58 391	1 984	333	9 306
支塘镇	Zhitang Town	12 896	83 232	5 352	5 352	32 420
董浜镇	Dongbang Town	6 261	65 342	2 763	2 763	12 321
辛庄镇	Xinzhuang Town	10 426	103 156	3 336	540	10 756
尚湖镇	Shanghu Town	11 250	106 960	3 529	1 767	21 850
张家港	**ZhangJiaGang**					
杨舍镇	Yangshe Town	15 309	416 753	3 400	148	24 684

Continued 1

农作物播种面积(公顷) Sown Area of Farm Crops (hectare)	# 粮食作物 Grain Crops	# 蔬菜作物 Vegetables Crops	粮食总产量(吨) Total Output of Grain (ton)	蔬菜总产量(吨) Total Output of Vegetables (ton)	企业个数(个) Number of Enterprises (unit)	#规模以上工业 Number of Enterprises Above Designated
3 440	1 962	1 340	14 399	37 736	14 083	96
5 700	3 663	1 145	27 079	26 742	3 798	119
2 781	2 714	67	20 579	3 010	17 768	305
890	310	403	2 655	9 548	984	99
3 499	2 814	44	20 566	2 180	2 395	81
656	524	132	4 412	5 537	1 686	108
7 423	6 961	401	33 421	10 060	6 112	285
2 600	1 485	1 115	11 347	52 629	6 465	359
199	198	1	2 684	23	5 673	12
4 613	4 113	500	25 697	9 672	4 156	163
245	245	–	2 350	536	8 715	9
1 321	1 130	169	7 341	5 188	5 539	27
5 943	786	4 844	4 453	94 718	3 455	241
–	–	–	–	–	4 598	141
5 941	2 838	2 644	21 050	128 449	1 659	91
6 070	5 293	669	36 349	19 758	2 493	122
3 928	3 546	377	26 670	21 250	2 467	125
192	134	55	981	1 773	801	62
8 823	5 965	2 736	39 624	58 665	2 550	96
7 276	1 078	6 064	7 199	173 298	1 018	59
4 166	2 728	752	18 837	13 509	2 408	101
7 974	7 064	480	51 894	7 866	1 796	94
3 724	2 467	796	16 719	15 171	11 729	300

表3-22 续表 2

镇（街道） Towns （Sub-districts）		行政区域面积 (公顷) The Administrative Area (hectare)	年末人口 (人) Population Year-end (person)	年末耕地面积 (公顷) Cultivated Area Year-end (hectare)	#高标准农田 High Standard Farmland Area	农机总动力 (千瓦) Total Agricultural Machinery Power (kw)
塘桥镇	Tangqiao Town	9 427	150 560	3 892	1 020	38 965
金港镇	JinGang Town	13 161	324 827	2 930	1 000	31 368
锦丰镇	Jinfeng Town	11 432	187 016	4 542	357	35 618
乐余镇	Leyu Town	7 861	92 903	3 906	80	23 679
凤凰镇	Fenghuang Town	7 879	122 906	2 728	970	53 142
南丰镇	Nanfeng Town	6 246	81 533	2 694	1 729	31 234
大新镇	Daxin Town	4 048	73 923	1 682	42	16 075
昆 山	**KunShan**					
玉山镇	Yushan Town	11 800	472 223	890	806	7 094
巴城镇	Bacheng Town	15 700	104 405	1 095	272	28 260
周市镇	Zhoushi Town	7 943	146 255	875	400	15 993
陆家镇	Lujia Town	3 546	97 734	328	306	2 272
花桥镇	Huaqiao Town	5 009	129 767	446	246	5 169
淀山湖镇	Dianshanhu Town	6 584	65 046	1 243	655	16 667
张浦镇	Zhangpu Town	10 904	132 414	2 730	1 893	32 738
周庄镇	Zhouzhuang Town	3 605	33 301	498	340	18 260
千灯镇	Qiandeng Town	7 853	152 005	1 408	1 159	21 004
锦溪镇	Jinxi Town	9 069	51 966	1 538	910	33 654
昆山经济技术开发区	Kunshan Economic and Technological Development Zone	11 500	382 514	861	–	12 353
太 仓	**TaiCang**					
城厢镇	Chengxiang Town	5 295	164 343	1 930	1 333	25 000
沙溪镇	Shaxi Town	13 240	144 706	6 028	2 906	27 508
浏河镇	Liuhe Town	6 459	99 256	3 177	1 985	13 152
浮桥镇	Fuqiao Town	14 444	133 803	4 362	1 120	24 681
璜泾镇	Huangjing Town	8 355	79 462	4 184	2 646	23 120
双凤镇	Shuangfeng Town	6 250	59 670	2 274	1 946	14 687

Continued 2

农作物播种面积(公顷) Sown Area of Farm Crops (hectare)	# 粮食作物 Grain Crops	# 蔬菜作物 Vegetables Crops	粮食总产量(吨) Total Output of Grain (ton)	蔬菜总产量(吨) Total Output of Vegetables (ton)	企业个数(个) Number of Enterprises (unit)	#规模以上工业 Number of Enterprises Above Designated
5 200	4 600	480	32 501	21 025	2 296	135
4 277	2 924	884	19 758	21 774	14 426	350
6 735	4 761	1 536	31 685	57 985	4 578	93
8 505	5 216	1 856	35 526	57 707	2 556	70
4 194	2 849	377	19 926	8 016	2 310	131
5 212	3 194	954	21 421	20 426	1 243	24
2 342	1 651	409	10 604	10 127	812	50
1 867	1 448	378	10 738	11 449	9 125	310
2 060	943	480	7 081	11 072	5 478	189
1 620	759	739	5 866	18 514	4 634	208
848	597	167	4 286	5 020	2 568	91
530	296	29	2 500	749	8 397	65
1 799	1 443	216	10 812	6 684	1 990	116
3 494	2 146	1 150	16 088	42 959	8 175	262
1 043	498	182	3 926	5 685	1 057	16
2 528	1 827	285	13 444	7 035	5 069	237
1 800	1 534	266	11 351	9 060	1 514	92
1 180	1 071	109	7 916	3 116	23 786	436
2 442	1 744	616	12 255	9 532	5 153	97
7 855	3 909	3 725	29 050	133 200	3 435	150
8 376	2 311	2 709	13 999	28 961	1 562	84
7 625	4 528	2 003	29 808	59 985	4 058	157
5 475	3 750	1 725	26 007	52 802	1 805	144
2 927	1 460	1 467	10 313	27 625	1 934	93

表3-22 续表 3

镇（街道）	Towns （Sub-districts）	企业从业人员(人) Laborers of Enterprises (person)	工业总产值(万元) Gross Industrial Output Value (10 000 yuan)	# 规模以上工业 Gross Industrial Output Value Above Designated Size	固定资产投资完成额(万元) Value of Investment in Fixed Assets (10 000 yuan)
吴中区	**Wuzhong District**				
越溪街道	Yuexi Sub-district	37 000	1 032 253	639 997	146 298
横泾街道	Hengjing Sub-district	27 909	856 019	534 055	40 299
香山街道	Xiangshan Sub-district	5 956	38 880	14 779	163 527
甪直镇	Luzhi Town	67 322	2 308 141	1 486 879	128 598
木渎镇	Mudu Town	128 032	1 751 293	963 211	538 040
胥口镇	Xukou Town	55 966	2 520 353	2 044 074	161 494
东山镇	Dongshan Town	15 104	1 036 818	920 765	60 021
光福镇	Guangfu Town	16 816	485 683	378 909	38 300
金庭镇	Jinting Town	6 745	90 175	58 782	44 500
临湖镇	Linhu Town	47 190	1 299 100	827 500	112 000
相城区	**XiangchengDistrict**				
太平街道	Taiping Sub-district	25 620	872 240	622 063	57 086
黄桥街道	Huangqiao Sub-district	41 285	1 418 570	673 536	83 318
北桥街道	Beiqiao Sub-district	26 112	1 080 257	795 933	57 976
漕湖街道	Caohu Sub-district	18 211	1 280 375	1 252 462	567 838
望亭镇	Wangting Town	39 742	1 045 260	669 851	162 830
黄埭镇	Huangdai Town	69 869	4 758 098	3 554 445	329 526
渭塘镇	Weitang Town	40 971	1 972 505	1 762 120	243 777
阳澄湖镇	Yangchenghu Town	37 005	1 055 623	549 014	197 047
阳澄湖生态休闲旅游度假区	Yangcheng Lake Ecological Leisure Tourism Resort	6 755	93 250	61 386	20 052
高新区、虎丘区	**New&Hi-echZone,HuqiuDistrict**				
镇湖街道	Zhenhu Sub-district	2 130	17 900	8 400	17 700
东渚街道	Dongzhu Sub-district	5 950	135 800	47 742	15 400
浒墅关镇	Xushuguan Town	41 008	1 704 110	1 666 500	717 450
通安镇	Tongan Town	26 543	1 189 900	862 400	339 965

Continued 3

地区生产总值(万元) Gross Domestic Product (10 000 yuan)	第一产业 Primary Industry	第二产业 Secondary Industry	第三产业 Tertiary Industry	财政总收入(万元) Total Revenue (10 000 yuan)	# 一般公共预算收入 General Public Budget Revenue	农村常住居民人均可支配收入(元) Per Capita Net Income of Rural Resident (yuan)
327 996	2 595	205 418	119 983	11 415	11 071	40 942
386 047	20 843	207 230	157 974	82 490	39 596	36 064
201334	970	24 859	175 505	441 424	49 124	35 395
1 109 328	9 536	563 243	536 549	412 902	143 427	37 420
1 792 600	3 000	766 400	1 023 200	433 059	248 842	37 680
1 180 246	32 028	667 653	480 565	202 306	114 674	38 462
358 091	25 508	187 556	145 027	52 684	28 194	38 602
335 086	16 858	127 227	191 001	59 436	21 068	38 740
234 986	24 609	25 797	184 580	51 287	8 095	25 022
704 300	26 500	286 800	391 000	104 955	61 550	35 423
472 270	7 202	213 856	251 212	109 192	61 002	33 941
754 023	3 087	363 245	387 691	349 284	76 730	32 193
483 687	8 981	275 816	198 890	-	-	38 288
224 232	1 855	188 392	33 985	10 920	10 920	38 077
533 409	3 791	264 934	264 684	117 198	63 444	34 817
1 795 076	28 721	1 036 914	729 441	272 356	144 025	29 715
808 047	6 830	409 076	392 141	161 830	78 510	36 995
676 084	37 027	320 042	319 015	120 678	52 855	35 068
60 074	2 720	23 650	33 704	22 825	4 720	38 322
43 200	4 850	10 800	27 550	20 438	17 884	34 305
34 392	2 380	21 820	10 192	31 050	19 130	30 361
574 300	2 240	376 143	195 917	584 147	113 626	29 370
451 600	10 633	268 800	172 167	159 265	50 894	35 498

表3-22 续表 4

镇（街道）	Towns （Sub-districts）	企业从业人员(人) Laborers of Enterprises (person)	工业总产值(万元) Gross Industrial Output Value (10 000 yuan)	# 规模以上工业 Gross Industrial Output Value Above Designated Size	固定资产投资完成额(万元) Value of Investment in Fixed Assets (10 000 yuan)
吴江区	**WuJiang District**				
松陵镇	Songling Town	123 900	2 214 700	1 399 663	1 945 521
平望镇	Pingwang Town	92 154	3 942 172	2 798 942	336 873
盛泽镇	Shengze Town	143 859	8 940 100	6 526 300	786 715
七都镇	Qidu Town	32 150	4 459 647	3 478 525	239 096
震泽镇	Zhenze Town	49 700	1 882 700	1 414 400	226 259
桃源镇	Taoyuan Town	46 750	1 693 419	1 042 917	199 776
黎里镇	Lili Town	113 744	6 869 903	4 946 330	715 077
吴江经济技术开发区	Wujiang Economic and Technological Development Zone	194 571	16 409 300	14 008 418	1 317 896
常　熟	**ChangShu**				
虞山街道	Yushan Sub-district	48 879	165 560	135 760	267 294
常福街道	Changfu Sub-district	88 256	5 802 929	5 370 042	513 907
琴川街道	Qinchuan Sub-district	72 720	573 300	223 577	916 800
莫城街道	Mocheng Sub-district	45 605	738 000	247 773	88 665
碧溪街道	Bixi Subdistrict	102 772	11 173 590	10 521 453	1 056 921
东南街道	Dongnan Sub-district	90 723	6 785 729	6 377 068	573 848
梅李镇	Meili Town	48 531	3 520 000	3 233 500	120 400
海虞镇	Haiyu Town	43 642	2 635 300	2 232 190	322 251
古里镇	Guli Town	50 831	3 018 416	2 139 660	243 454
沙家浜镇	Shajiabang Town	39 284	2 653 724	2 255 665	126 635
支塘镇	Zhitang Town	32 516	1 637 202	1 129 033	188 564
董浜镇	Dongbang Town	27 793	948 000	639 616	125 434
辛庄镇	Xinzhuang Town	49 762	2 805 000	2 059 145	239 950
尚湖镇	Shanghu Town	42 685	1 653 656	1 028 475	116 540
张家港	**ZhangJiaGang**				
杨舍镇	Yangshe Town	237 030	8 566 031	7 203 959	2 001 293

Continued 4

地区生产总值 (万元) Gross Domestic Product (10 000 yuan)	第一产业 Primary Industry	第二产业 Secondary Industry	第三产业 Tertiary Industry	财政总收入 (万元) Total Revenue (10 000 yuan)	# 一般公共预算收入 General Public Budget Revenue	农村常住居民人均可支配收入(元) Per Capita Net Income of Rural Resident (yuan)
3 093 929	60 869	973 870	2 059 190	697 750	410 500	32 194
1 597 911	22 789	903 279	671 843	199 666	110 198	37 445
4 311 260	20 739	1 956 344	2 334 177	706 719	350 239	41 302
1 115 320	44 840	597 330	473 150	107 722	62 552	32 194
1 355 410	64 600	735 410	555 400	149 538	79 809	33 820
784 110	38 260	401 626	344 224	109 200	91 200	31 280
2 852 360	65 550	1 608 920	1 177 890	624 489	263 404	32 194
4 632 305	44 247	3 494 834	1 093 224	1 268 691	520 273	31 962
802 823	941	231 042	570 840	186 448	114 469	39 096
1 314 748	8 575	1 024 784	281 389	437 072	177 328	33 805
2 242 046	1 154	454 440	1 786 452	458 590	269 819	33 750
1 290 902	4 375	188 747	1 097 780	64 896	37 946	37 044
4 623 375	19 740	3 448 688	1 154 947	1 111 521	440 617	36 465
1 906 947	–	1 586 187	320 760	559 343	281 752	36 000
847 255	34 500	600 500	212 255	205 131	110 420	37 742
1 043 796	26 449	663 455	353 892	258 136	115 243	32 820
1 105 320	28 268	717 531	359 521	298 652	88 084	36 870
903 926	38 970	628 700	236 256	173 945	76 901	34 180
760 328	36 260	374 188	349 880	85 983	56 353	37 411
378 275	33 786	198 421	146 068	48 816	27 184	37 680
754 558	22 841	560 741	170 976	207 041	67 408	34 904
787 985	23 970	458 818	305 197	118 231	48 329	32 820
8 081 406	49 800	2 751 600	5 280 006	1 160 358	631 578	37 584

表3-22 续表 5

镇（街道） Towns （Sub-districts）		企业从业人员(人) Laborers of Enterprises (person)	工业总产值(万元) Gross Industrial Output Value (10 000 yuan)	# 规模以上工业 Gross Industrial Output Value Above Designated Size	固定资产投资完成额(万元) Value of Investment in Fixed Assets (10 000 yuan)
塘桥镇	Tangqiao Town	83 125	3 160 000	2 030 000	284 500
金港镇	JinGang Town	185 786	14 410 235	12 248 708	792 965
锦丰镇	Jinfeng Town	97 991	18 893 926	17 612 400	689 959
乐余镇	Leyu Town	30 307	1 102 570	771 100	53 600
凤凰镇	Fenghuang Town	50 102	3 325 800	2 496 600	212 510
南丰镇	Nanfeng Town	36 958	5 133 000	4 902 500	78 800
大新镇	Daxin Town	22 969	855 500	482 900	142 600
昆 山	**KunShan**				
玉山镇	Yushan Town	246 058	12 807 619	11 577 619	1 494 752
巴城镇	Bacheng Town	59 696	3 400 156	2 694 329	488 295
周市镇	Zhoushi Town	97 102	4 779 876	3 467 696	499 926
陆家镇	Lujia Town	63 462	2 853 327	2 734 050	123 449
花桥镇	Huaqiao Town	107 135	1 808 620	1 534 552	986 512
淀山湖镇	Dianshanhu Town	39 651	2 240 057	1 976 598	161 248
张浦镇	Zhangpu Town	110 403	5 752 199	4 312 199	309 646
周庄镇	Zhouzhuang Town	13 410	308 710	166 421	119 315
千灯镇	Qiandeng Town	85 520	5 278 031	4 143 031	374 091
锦溪镇	Jinxi Town	73 418	3 315 211	3 123 234	260 135
昆山经济技术开发区	Kunshan Economic and Technological Development Zone	476 343	48 237 623	46 785 655	2 194 578
太 仓	**TaiCang**				
城厢镇	Chengxiang Town	58 012	1 381 090	1 056 537	410 594
沙溪镇	Shaxi Town	78 855	2 814 500	2 110 848	339 843
浏河镇	Liuhe Town	42 176	1 242 000	953 255	405 157
浮桥镇	Fuqiao Town	84 128	8 525 789	7 725 349	1 023 176
璜泾镇	Huangjing Town	35 482	2 147 200	1 610 366	141 528
双凤镇	Shuangfeng Town	36 876	1 227 419	957 387	130 576

Continued 5

地区生产总值 (万元) Gross Domestic Product (10 000 yuan)	第一产业 Primary Industry	第二产业 Secondary Industry	第三产业 Tertiary Industry	财政总收入 (万元) Total Revenue (10 000 yuan)	# 一般公共预算收入 General Public Budget Revenue	农村常住居民人均可支配收入(元) Per Capita Net Income of Rural Resident (yuan)
1 896 000	32 800	1 010 600	852 600	151 009	89 146	36 897
7 441 346	37 035	3 677 218	3 727 093	1 145 663	594 793	38 164
6 494 000	41 700	4 787 900	1 664 400	929 706	484 277	38 682
489 100	30 000	263 700	195 400	51 229	43 994	34 450
1 158 200	35 800	660 200	462 200	150 001	84 858	38 500
1 381 200	47 600	925 500	408 100	306 134	152 189	37 358
395 700	19 300	218 500	157 900	53 959	30 717	33 401
7 623 547	24 250	3 638 259	3 961 038	1 701 459	900 928	44 481
1 803 324	47 325	833 957	922 042	275 810	211 215	40 462
2 648 800	14 500	1 463 300	1 171 000	659 994	307 655	39 008
1 580 136	2 586	956 519	621 031	272 629	151 350	43 062
3 050 644	5 800	454 320	2 590 524	869 381	414 033	42 018
1 006 016	15 584	462 808	527 624	192 070	111 238	33 847
2 308 514	43 501	1 471 613	793 400	578 376	250 872	40 396
489 600	7 204	153 196	329 200	94 837	33 723	37 977
2 096 007	21 077	1 314 771	760 159	363 524	208 799	42 608
861 447	21 010	496 025	344 412	141 024	81 332	36 389
14 854 040	14 000	10 260 088	4 579 952	1 205 463	1 116 159	42 336
1 512 533	31 280	423 852	1 057 401	131 650	112 466	32 458
1 349 671	77 286	627 097	645 288	163 184	89 752	39 344
1 010 200	26 578	445 195	538 427	259 083	70 450	34 233
3 229 701	58 827	2 385 973	784 901	554 892	327 812	34 573
861 561	28 797	421 918	410 846	54 712	36 380	42 442
412 807	42 292	198 098	172 417	112 499	43 412	29 540

主 要 统 计 指 标 解 释

农林牧渔业总产值 指以货币表现的农、林、牧、渔业全部产品和对农林牧渔业生产活动进行的各种支持性服务活动的价值总量，它反映一定时期内农林牧渔业生产总规模和总成果。1957年以前的农林牧渔业总产值中包括了厩肥和农民自给性手工业(如农民自制衣服、鞋、袜，自己从事粮食初步加工等)。1958年及以后，林业中增加了村及村以下竹木采伐产值；牧业中取消了厩肥产值；副业中取消了农民自给性手工业产值，增加了村及村以下办的工业产值； 渔业中增加了海洋捕捞水产品产值。1980年及以后，在副业中增加了农民家庭兼营工业商品部分的产值。从1984年起村及村以下工业产值划归工业。从1993年起取消副业，将野生动物的捕猎划入牧业，野生植物采集和农民家庭兼营商品性工业划归农业。从2003年起，执行新的国民经济行业分类标准，农林牧渔业总产值中包括了农林牧渔服务业产值。林业中增加了森林采运业产值。农业中取消了家庭兼营商品性工业产值，将野生林产品的采集划归林业。

农林牧渔业总产值的计算方法通常是按农、林、牧、渔业产品及其副产品的产量分别乘以各自单位产品价格求得；少数生产周期较长，当年没有产品或产品产量不易统计的，则采用间接方法匡算其产值；然后将四业产品产值及农林牧渔服务业产值相加即为农林牧渔业总产值。

粮食产量 指全社会的产量。包括国有经济经营的、集体统一经营的和农民家庭经营的粮食产量，还包括工矿企业办的农场和其他生产单位的产量。粮食除包括稻谷、小麦、玉米、高粱、谷子及其他杂粮外，还包括薯类和豆类。其产量计算方法，豆类按去豆荚后的干豆计算；薯类(包括甘薯和马铃薯，不包括芋头和木薯)1963年以前按每4公斤鲜薯折1公斤粮食计算，从1964年开始改为按5公斤鲜薯折1公斤粮食计算。城市郊区作为蔬菜的薯类(如马铃薯等)按鲜品计算，并且不作粮食统计。其他粮食一律按脱粒后的原粮计算。1989年以前全国粮食产量数据主要靠全面报表取得，1989年开始使用抽样调查数据。

棉花产量 指全社会的产量。包括春播棉和夏播棉。产量按皮棉计算。不包括木棉。

油料产量 指全部油料作物的生产量。包括花生、油菜籽、芝麻、向日葵籽、胡麻籽（亚麻籽）和其他油料。不包括大豆、木本油料和野生油料。花生以带壳干花生计算。

水产品产量 指人工养殖的水产品和天然生长的水产品的捕捞量。包括海水的鱼类、虾蟹类、贝类和藻类以及内陆水域的鱼类、虾蟹类和贝类，不包括淡水生植物。水产品产量是通过各级农业和统计部门逐级上报取得数据。1995年及以前，贝类中牡蛎按鲜肉计算；蚶、蛤、蛙按5斤鲜品折1斤计算。1996年以后则统一按鲜品计算。

猪、牛、羊肉产量 指当年出栏并已屠宰、除去头蹄下水后带骨肉(即胴体重)的重量。包括全社会范围内的产量。

期初(末)畜禽存栏头(只)数 指报告期初(末)农村各种合作经济组织和国营农场、农民个人、机关、团体、学校、工矿企业、部队等单位以及城镇居民饲养的大牲畜、猪、羊、家禽等畜禽的存栏数。

农作物播种面积 指实际播种或移植有农作物的面积。凡是实际种植有农作物的面积，不论种植在耕地上还是种植在非耕地上，均包括在农作物播种面积中。在播种季节基本结束后，因遭灾而重新改种和补种的农作物面积，也包括在内。它是反映我国耕地面积利用情况的一个重要指标。目前，农作物播种面积主要包括粮食、棉花、油料、糖料、麻类、烟叶、蔬菜和瓜类、药材和其他农作物九大类。

有效灌溉面积 指具有一定的水源，地块比较平整，灌溉工程或设备已经配套，在一般年景下，当年能够进行正常灌溉的耕地面积。在一般情况下，有效灌溉面积应等于灌溉工程或设备已经配备，能够进行正常灌溉的水田和水浇地面积之和。它是反映我国耕地抗旱能力的一个重要指标。

农用化肥施用量 指本年内实际用于农业生产的化肥数量，包括氮肥、磷肥、钾肥和复合肥。化肥施用量要求按折纯量计算数量。折纯量是指把氮肥、磷肥、钾肥分别按含氮、含五氧化二磷、含氧化钾的百分之百成份进行折算后的数量。复合肥按其所含主要成分折算。公式为：

折纯量=实物量×某种化肥有效成份含量的百分比

农业机械总动力 指主要用于农、林、牧、渔业的各种动力机械的动力总和。包括耕作机械、排灌机械、收获机械、农用运输机械、植物保护机械、牧业机械、林业机械、渔业机械和其他农业机械〔内燃机按引擎马力折成瓦(特)计算、电动机按功率折成瓦(特)计算〕。不包括专门用于乡、镇、村、组办工业、基本建设、非农业运输、科学试验和教学等非农业生产方面用的动力机械与作业机械。这个指标的统计数据主要来源于农机部门。

乡村户数 指长期(一年以上)居住在乡镇(不包括城关镇)行政管理区域内的住户，还包括居住在城关镇所辖行政村范围内的农村住户。户口不在本地而在本地居住一年及以上的住户也包括在本地农村住户内；有本地户口，但举家外出谋生一年以上的住户，无论是否保留承包耕地都不包括在本地农村住户范围内。不包括乡村地区内的国有经济的机关、团体、学校、企业、事业单位的集体户。

乡村人口数 指乡村地区常住居民户数中的常住人口数，即经常在家或在家居住6个月以上，而且经济和生活与本户连成一体的人口。外出从业人员在外居住时间虽然在6个月以上，但收入主要带回家中，经济与本户连为一体，仍视为家庭常住人口；在家居住，生活和本户连成一体的国家职工、退休人员也为家庭常住人口。但是现役军人、中专及以上(走读生除外)的在校学生、以及常年在外(不包括探亲、看病等)且已有稳定的职业与居住场所的外出从业人员，不应当作家庭常住人口。

乡村从业人员 指乡村人口中实际参加生产经营活动并取得实物或货币收入的人员，包括劳动年龄内经常参加劳动的人员，也包括超过劳动年龄但经常参加劳动的人员，但不包括户口在家的在外学生、现役军人和丧失劳动能力的人，也不包括待业人员和家务劳动者。从业人员按从事主业时间最长（时间相同按收入）分为农林牧渔业从业人员、工业从业人员、建筑业从业人员、交通运输业、仓储及邮电通信业从业人员、批零贸易业、餐饮业从业人员、其他非农行业从业人员。

EXPLANATORY NOTES ON MAIN STATISTICAL INDICATORS

Gross Output Value of Agriculture, Forestry, Animal Husbandry and Fishery refers to the total value of products of agriculture, forestry, animal husbandry and fishery, and total value of services in support of agriculture, forestry, animal husbandry and fishery activities. It reflects the total scale and results of agricultural production during a given period. Prior to 1957, China's gross agricultural output value included barnyard manure and handicraft products for self-consumption (clothes, shoes, stockings, and initial grain processing undertaken by peasants). Since 1958, cutting and felling of bamboo and trees by villages and other cooperative organizations under villages have been included in forestry; value of barnyard manure has been excluded from animal husbandry; self consumed handicrafts have not been included from sideline occupations, while the output value of industries run by villages and cooperative organizations under village has been included in sideline occupations; and the output value of fish catches by motor fishing boats has been added to fishery. Since 1980, the value of handicraft products made for sale by individuals in households has been added to sideline occupations. Since 1984, industries run by villages and under villages have been included in the sector of industry. Since 1993, the subdivision of sideline occupations has been cancelled, and the hunting of wild animals has been classified into animal husbandry, and the gathering of wild plants and commodity industry run by rural household have been included in farming. A new industrial classification of economic activities was introduced in 2003. Under the new classification, value of services to agriculture, forestry, animal husbandry and fishery is included in the gross output value of agriculture, value of wood felling and transport is included in forestry, value of industrial output by rural households is not included in agriculture, and the collection of wild forest products is taken from agriculture and included in forestry.

Gross output value of agriculture is obtained by multiplying the output of each product or by-product by its price, resulting in the output value of each single item. For a small number of products, annual output of which is not available or difficult to get due to the long production (growing) process involved, the output value is estimated through an indirect approach. The sum of output values of all products of agriculture, forestry, animal husbandry and fishery and services in support to those industries is then equal to the gross output value of agriculture.

Grain Output refers to the total output in the whole country including grains produced by State farms, collective units, rural households, as well as by farms affiliated to industrial and mining enterprises and other production units. Grain includes rice, wheat, corn, sorghum, millet and other miscellaneous grains as well as tubers and beans. Output of beans refers to dry beans without pods. The output of tubers (sweet potatoes and potatoes, not including taros and cassava) are converted into that of grain at the ratio 4:1, i.e. 4 kilograms of fresh tubers were equivalent to 1 kilogram of grain up to 1963. Since 1964 the ratio for conversion has been 5:1. Tubers supplied as vegetables (such as potatoes) in cities and suburbs are calculated as fresh vegetables and their output is not included in the output of grain. Output of all other grains refers to husked grain. Data on grain production before 1989 were obtained through the Comprehensive Statistical Reporting System. Since 1989, data from sample surveys are used.

Cotton Output refers to cotton production in the whole country including cotton planted in spring and in autumn. Output is measured as the weight of ginned cotton. Kapok is not included.

Output of Oil-bearing Crops refers to the total production of oil-bearing crops of various kinds, including peanuts (dry, in shell), rapeseeds, sesame, sunflower seeds, flax seeds, and other oil-bearing crops. Soybeans, oil-bearing woody plants, and wild oil-bearing crops are not included.

Output of Aquatic Products refers to catches of both artificially cultured and naturally grown aquatic products, including fish, shrimps, crabs and shellfish in sea and inland water as well as seaweed. Freshwater plants are not included.

Output of Pork, Beef, and Mutton refers to the meat of slaughtered hogs, cattle, sheep and goats with head, feet, and offal taken away. Data refers to the production of the whole country.

Number of Livestock or Poultry in Stock at Beginning (or End) of Period refers to the total number of large animals, pigs, sheep, fowls, etc. raised by rural cooperative organizations, State farms, rural individuals, government agencies, schools, industrial and mining enterprises, army, and urban residents at the beginning (or end) of the reference period.

Sown Area of Crops refers to area of land sown or transplanted with crops regardless of being in cultivated area or non-cultivated area. Area of land re-sown due to natural disasters is also included. This is an important indicator that can reflect the utilization condition of the cultivated land in China. At present, the sown area of crops mainly include the following 9 categories of crops: grain, cotton, oil-bearing crops, sugar crops, flax crops, tobacco, vegetables and melons, medicinal materials and other farm crops.

Irrigated Area refers to area of land that are effectively irrigated, i.e. relatively level land, where there are water sources or complete sets of irrigation facilities to lift and move adequate water for irrigation purpose under normal conditions. Under normal situations, irrigated area is the sum of watered fields and irrigated fields where irrigation systems or equipment have been installed for regular irrigation purpose. This important indicator reflects drought resistance capacity of the cultivated land in China.

Consumption of Chemical Fertilizers in Agriculture refers to the quantity of chemical fertilizers applied in agriculture in the year, including nitrogenous fertilizer, phosphate fertilizer, potash fertilizer, and compound fertilizer. The consumption of chemical fertilizers is calculated in terms of volume of effective components by means of converting the gross weight of the respective fertilizers into weight containing effective component (e.g. nitrogen content in nitrogenous fertilizer, phosphorous pentoxide contents in phosphate fertilizer, and potassium oxide contents in potash fertilizer). Compound fertilizer is converted in regard to its major components. The formula is:

Volume of effective component= physical quantity× effective component of certain chemical fertilizer (%)

Total Power of Agricultural Machinery refers to total mechanical power of machinery used in agriculture, forestry, animal husbandry and fishery, including machinery for ploughing, irrigation and drainage, harvesting, transport, plant protection, animal husbandry, forestry and fishery and other agricultural machineries. (For the power of internal combustion engines, it is converted from its horsepower into watts while for electric motors the output power is converted into watts.) Machinery employed for non-agricultural purposes, such as the machines used in township-run and village-run industry, construction, non-agricultural transport, scientific experiments and teaching, are not included. Data are mainly from agricultural machinery agencies.

Number of Households in Villages refers to households resident on a long term basis (i.e. 1 year or more) in administrative districts in townships (not including urban townships), including rural households resident in areas under the jurisdiction of urban townships. Households whose household registration is not in the locality yet resident for one year or more are included among the rural households. Households having local household registration yet the whole household having left for somewhere else for work for one year or more, whether still retaining contracted farmland, are not included among the local rural households. Also not included are collective households associated with institutions of the State economy, organizations, schools and enterprises.

Number of Residents of Villages refers to the number of usual residents in usual resident households in rural areas. These are persons who are regularly at home or are at home for 6 months or more and economically and socially integrated with the household. For persons who are away from home for employment for more than 6 months yet the main income is brought back home and thus economically integrated with the household, the person is still considered as a usual resident of the household. National employee and retired personnel who reside at home and whose living is integrated with the household are also considered as usual residents. However, serving military personnel, students at secondary technical level or above (unless commuting between school and home), employed persons who are regularly elsewhere the year round (except visiting relatives or receiving medical attention) and having a stable job and residence should not be considered as usual resident of the household.

Rural Persons Engaged refer to persons in the rural labour force aged over 16 years who are engaged in actual production and management activities and receive payment in kind or wages, including those covered within the labour force age bracket and regularly participating in production activities, and those who are out of the labour force age bracket yet also participating in production activities regularly. Students studying in other places with their permanent residence registered in local areas, servicemen and persons incapable of working are not included. Also not included are those who are waiting for jobs and those engaged in housework. Persons employed are classified as persons engaged in agriculture, forestry, animal husbandry or fishery activities; persons engaged in industrial activities; persons engaged in construction activities; persons engaged in transport, storage and telecommunications activities; persons engaged in wholesale and retail trade and catering activities; and persons engaged in other non-agriculture activities. In case the person is engaged in more than one type of work, classification is according to the industry in which he works most of the time (where time is the same income would be the criterion).

四、工 业

CHAPTER 4
INDUSTRY

4 工 业 INDUSTRY

主要统计指标 MAJOR STATISTICAL INDICATORS

2018年末规模以上工业企业单位数	Number of Industrial Enterprises Above Designated Size	10 393	个	unit
2018年规模以上工业总产值	Gross Industrial Output Value Above Designated Size	33 354.01	亿元	100 million yuan
比上年增长	Increase Over Last Year	6.1	%	
按轻重工业分	Grouped by Light and Heavy Industry			
轻工业	Light Industry	7 601.63	亿元	100 million yuan
重工业	Heavy Industry	25 752.38	亿元	100 million yuan
按企业规模分	Grouped by Size of Enterprises			
大型企业	Large	15 400.97	亿元	100 million yuan
中型企业	Medium-sized	7 831.86	亿元	100 million yuan
小型企业	Small	9 903.20	亿元	100 million yuan
微型企业	Micro	217.98	亿元	100 million yuan

表4-1

历年规模以上工业企业主要经济指标

单位：万元

年　份 Year	企业单位数(个) Number of Enterprises (unit)	工业总产值 Gross Industrial Output Value	按轻重工业分 Grouped by Light and Heavy Industry		按企业规模分	
			轻工业 Light Industry	重工业 Heavy Industry	大型企业 Large	中型企业 Medium-sized
1998	2 994	16 256 934	8 893 282	7 363 652	2 995 207	2 609 044
1999	3 002	19 263 441	10 156 195	9 107 246	3 414 152	2 716 347
2000	3 112	23 965 052	11 436 139	12 528 913	3 904 674	3 109 090
2001	3 735	27 847 905	12 809 043	15 038 862	7 135 751	8 218 624
2002	4 112	34 658 727	15 444 514	19 214 212	8 539 021	9 757 505
2003	4 553	49 765 080	17 678 551	32 086 529	16 870 145	19 628 859
2004	5 044	73 075 445	23 975 758	49 099 687	21 811 989	29 610 744
2005	6 743	99 085 843	33 334 762	65 751 081	35 539 278	38 002 461
2006	7 485	125 385 124	41 050 258	84 334 866	47 091 734	45 881 307
2007	8 632	159 089 177	49 727 549	109 361 628	60 631 093	56 618 033
2008	9 959	186 301 295	53 942 361	132 358 934	71 641 117	59 368 646
2009	13 720	202 844 954	57 460 526	145 384 428	85 074 954	61 423 155
2010	13 538	246 516 665	67 657 641	178 859 024	105 149 095	74 590 048
2011	9 904	277 787 533	73 490 164	204 297 369	124 795 596	83 096 116
2012	10 444	287 455 409	73 916 098	213 539 311	157 579 505	55 970 829
2013	10 776	302 762 935	78 901 611	223 861 324	164 846 417	59 803 476
2014	10 432	303 221 722	78 318 071	224 903 651	159 625 055	63 898 002
2015	10 062	302 492 460	76 331 670	226 160 789	164 584 505	62 412 235
2016	9 616	307 139 889	76 958 330	230 181 558	164 641 653	64 968 586
2017	9 840	314 687 731	75 302 913	239 384 818	151 710 613	73 315 389
2018	10 393	333 540 080	76 016 264	257 523 816	154 009 712	78 318 578

注:1.2011年起规模以上工业企业调整为主营业务收入2000万元及以上企业。
2.2012年起企业规模按新标准划分为大型、中型、小型和微型。

MAIN ECONOMIC INDICATORS OF INDUSTRIAL ENTERPRISES ABOVE DESIGNATED SIZE OVER THE YEARS

(10 000 yuan)

Grouped by Size of Enterprises		资产总计 Total Assets	负债合计 Total Liabilities	主营业务收入 Major Business Revenue	利润总额 Total Profits	利税总额 Total Taxes and Profits
小型企业 Small	微型企业 Micro					
10 652 683		18 824 205	11 446 462	14 720 068	305 919	832 170
13 132 942		21 088 922	12 862 606	17 582 236	538 669	1 163 234
16 951 288		23 469 761	14 223 651	22 457 228	971 628	1 840 854
12 493 530		27 834 921	16 089 038	26 436 769	1 254 486	2 285 154
16 362 201		32 787 791	19 271 033	33 296 973	1 589 106	2 622 662
13 266 076		44 603 074	27 858 508	49 248 746	2 194 415	3 433 163
21 652 712		57 899 546	36 388 012	71 467 733	3 095 635	4 458 494
25 544 104		81 219 897	50 593 501	98 744 108	4 229 922	5 973 209
32 412 083		99 966 153	60 878 731	125 330 162	5 914 347	8 081 296
41 840 051		123 284 593	74 852 459	158 259 327	7 958 634	10 817 112
55 291 532		136 202 182	78 879 841	183 794 211	8 956 435	13 301 381
56 346 845		162 583 329	93 080 572	200 107 317	10 388 855	15 248 361
66 777 522		193 511 382	111 436 678	245 775 123	15 070 575	19 882 807
69 895 821		218 219 248	128 799 568	278 989 060	14 847 255	20 293 774
69 743 737	4 161 338	233 314 843	134 747 950	289 987 963	12 515 742	18 163 524
75 574 904	2 538 139	251 288 272	143 233 671	302 249 211	13 501 159	19 375 338
77 209 688	2 488 977	261 089 659	144 008 220	303 972 668	14 601 276	20 740 808
73 658 725	1 836 995	268 957 448	142 682 003	297 686 520	15 290 361	20 751 530
75 889 501	1 640 149	283 565 028	148 380 223	303 801 818	17 727 401	23 882 390
88 139 086	1 522 643	302 036 993	158 759 894	320 058 558	20 021 491	25 892 798
99 031 993	2 179 798	322 234 396	169 230 901	341 084 012	20 940 474	28 215 138

Note: 1.In 2011, industrial enterprises above Designated Size refers to enterprise with main business income above 20 million yuan.
2.From 2012, the enterprise size divide into large, medium-sized, small and micro by new standard.

表4-2 规模以上工业企业主要经济指标 (2018年)

单位：万元

项　　目	Item	企业单位数(个) Number of Enterprises (unit)
总　　计	**Total**	**10 393**
一、按登记注册类型分	**Grouped by Registration Status**	
国有企业	State-owned Enterprises	2
集体企业	Collective-owned Enterprises	9
股份合作企业	Share-holding Cooperative Enterprises	15
联营企业	Joint Ownership Enterprises	2
有限责任公司	Limited Liability Corporations	640
股份有限公司	Share-holding Corporations Ltd.	269
私营企业	Private Enterprises	5 399
其他企业	Other Enterprises	–
港澳台投资企业	Enterprises with Investment from HongKong, Macao and Taiwan	1 157
外商投资企业	Enterprises with Foreign Investment	2 900
二、按轻重工业分	**Grouped by Light and Heavy Industry**	
轻工业	Light Industry	4 080
重工业	Heavy Industry	6 313
三、按企业规模分	**Grouped by Size of Enterprises**	
大型企业	Large	372
中型企业	Medium-sized	1 512
小型企业	Small	8 105
微型企业	Micro	404
四、按行业类别分	**Grouped by Sector**	
非金属矿采选业	Nonmetal Minerals Mining and Dressing	1
农副食品加工业	Agricultural and Sideline Food Processing	53
食品制造业	Food Production	58
酒、饮料和精制茶制造业	Wine, Beverage and Refined Tea Manufacturing	20
烟草制品业	Manufacture of Tobacco	1
纺织业	Textile Industry	1 260

MAIN ECONOMIC INDICATORS OF INDUSTRIAL ENTERPRISES ABOVE DESIGNATED SIZE (2018)

(10 000 yuan)

# 亏损企业 Loss Making Enterprises	工业总产值 Gross Industrial Output Value	工业销售产值 Value of Industrial Products Sales	# 出口交货值 Delivery Value for Export	资产总计 Total Assets	# 流动资产合计 Circulating Funds	# 应收帐款 Net Account Income
1 783	**333 540 080**	**331 811 246**	**125 111 848**	**322 234 396**	**202 292 887**	**74 185 931**
1	36 180	36 180	–	272 541	53 681	787
2	60 361	61 499	3 333	44 330	36 538	18 537
1	214 067	208 757	–	323 144	209 110	91 269
–	32 786	30 649	1 711	38 092	29 971	1 157
104	33 630 852	33 734 841	5 252 695	36 875 729	19 987 494	6 366 568
22	14 376 024	14 324 018	2 690 713	24 963 801	13 316 430	3 967 116
772	79 963 300	79 238 839	11 682 754	84 206 542	53 786 446	17 190 442
–	–	–	–	–	–	–
242	62 147 950	61 646 339	35 270 329	52 013 361	35 086 212	14 778 901
639	143 078 560	142 530 125	70 210 313	123 496 856	79 787 006	31 771 154
729	76 016 264	75 609 864	17 914 660	73 706 118	45 768 638	13 749 327
1 054	257 523 816	256 201 382	107 197 188	248 528 278	156 524 250	60 436 604
45	154 009 712	153 624 695	85 026 016	137 258 060	84 581 234	31 977 423
192	78 318 578	77 610 814	22 942 321	84 633 315	51 412 368	18 456 185
1 443	99 031 993	98 376 173	16 862 914	98 100 819	64 695 039	23 187 507
103	2 179 798	2 199 564	280 597	2 242 201	1 604 247	564 816
–	18 300	19 326	–	47 627	16 575	2 003
12	3 018 503	3 077 437	16 924	1 967 349	1 330 280	245 005
8	2 526 723	2 404 690	135 762	1 646 564	866 113	252 526
6	629 645	633 376	846	686 338	315 155	93 189
–	12 921	12 802	–	34 975	6 421	–
180	13 125 489	13 101 382	2 289 359	12 743 876	7 940 797	2 039 204

表4-2 续表 1

单位：万元

项 目	Item	# 产成品 Manufactured Products
总 计	**Total**	**17 171 940**
一、按登记注册类型分	**Grouped by Registration Status**	
国有企业	State-owned Enterprises	–
集体企业	Collective-owned Enterprises	2 140
股份合作企业	Share-holding Cooperative Enterprises	12 605
联营企业	Joint Ownership Enterprises	6 083
有限责任公司	Limited Liability Corporations	1 539 388
股份有限公司	Share-holding Corporations Ltd.	1 075 049
私营企业	Private Enterprises	5 180 989
其他企业	Other Enterprises	–
港澳台投资企业	Enterprises with Investment from HongKong, Macao and Taiwan	2 447 769
外商投资企业	Enterprises with Foreign Investment	6 907 916
二、按轻重工业分	**Grouped by Light and Heavy Industry**	
轻工业	Light Industry	5 223 007
重工业	Heavy Industry	11 948 933
三、按企业规模分	**Grouped by Size of Enterprises**	
大型企业	Large	6 335 762
中型企业	Medium-sized	4 861 615
小型企业	Small	5 839 414
微型企业	Micro	135 149
四、按行业类别分	**Grouped by Sector**	
非金属矿采选业	Nonmetal Minerals Mining and Dressing	1 525
农副食品加工业	Agricultural and Sideline Food Processing	124 211
食品制造业	Food Production	103 711
酒、饮料和精制茶制造业	Wine, Beverage and Refined Tea Manufacturing	21 921
烟草制品业	Manufacture of Tobacco	–
纺织业	Textile Industry	1 271 601

Continued 1

(10 000 yuan)

固定资产原价 Original Value of Fixed Assets	累计折旧 Accumulative Total Depreciation	负债合计 Total Liabilities	所有者权益合计 Total Creditors Equity	# 实收资本 Total Capital Hold	主营业务收入 Major Business Revenue
152 658 519	**78 172 655**	**169 230 901**	**153 003 419**	**81 041 869**	**341 084 012**
354 473	177 655	117 893	154 648	17 915	36 151
23 832	16 450	34 162	10 169	3 863	62 699
151 084	89 921	114 828	208 315	49 243	206 318
16 225	8 818	6 031	32 061	1 788	30 645
18 705 978	7 706 801	21 764 055	15 111 672	9 242 326	35 066 617
6 691 795	3 247 146	11 591 586	13 372 213	4 404 475	14 972 841
31 397 690	15 349 557	48 787 097	35 419 403	14 922 340	84 275 644
–	–	–	–	–	–
25 799 428	13 710 994	26 151 884	25 861 470	13 265 409	62 056 559
69 518 014	37 865 314	60 663 366	62 833 467	39 134 511	144 376 539
37 220 866	18 840 683	39 652 449	34 053 639	20 046 706	77 976 905
115 437 653	59 331 972	129 578 453	118 949 779	60 995 162	263 107 107
67 863 056	37 050 165	73 562 540	63 695 519	29 345 712	157 299 445
40 929 489	19 955 589	41 689 123	42 944 184	21 514 705	79 734 206
43 283 507	20 905 119	52 698 928	45 401 828	29 647 140	101 817 282
582 467	261 783	1 280 310	961 888	534 312	2 233 079
36 006	20 003	20 394	27 233	10 000	19 326
774 516	395 418	917 619	1 049 731	450 577	3 793 237
1 009 545	424 544	906 823	739 740	630 220	2 424 977
647 238	359 844	266 946	419 392	309 980	650 295
43 285	25 935	1 810	33 165	36 286	12 802
7 047 814	3 643 311	8 016 212	4 727 655	2 901 567	13 110 411

表4-2 续表 2

单位：万元

项　　目	Item	主营业务成本 Major Business Cost
总　　计	**Total**	**292 952 799**
一、按登记注册类型分	**Grouped by Registration Status**	
国有企业	State-owned Enterprises	17 494
集体企业	Collective-owned Enterprises	58 930
股份合作企业	Share-holding Cooperative Enterprises	175 368
联营企业	Joint Ownership Enterprises	23 601
有限责任公司	Limited Liability Corporations	30 049 052
股份有限公司	Share-holding Corporations Ltd.	12 186 347
私营企业	Private Enterprises	71 767 503
其他企业	Other Enterprises	–
港澳台投资企业	Enterprises with Investment from HongKong, Macao and Taiwan	54 527 163
外商投资企业	Enterprises with Foreign Investment	124 147 341
二、按轻重工业分	**Grouped by Light and Heavy Industry**	
轻工业	Light Industry	64 977 494
重工业	Heavy Industry	227 975 305
三、按企业规模分	**Grouped by Size of Enterprises**	
大型企业	Large	139 418 276
中型企业	Medium-sized	64 811 306
小型企业	Small	86 691 078
微型企业	Micro	2 032 139
四、按行业类别分	**Grouped by Sector**	
非金属矿采选业	Nonmetal Minerals Mining and Dressing	12 504
农副食品加工业	Agricultural and Sideline Food Processing	3 481 482
食品制造业	Food Production	1 338 621
酒、饮料和精制茶制造业	Wine, Beverage and Refined Tea Manufacturing	519 169
烟草制品业	Manufacture of Tobacco	6 882
纺织业	Textile Industry	11 862 372

Continued 2

(10 000 yuan)

主营业务税金及附加 Pre-tax and Related Payment of Major Business	营业利润 Business Profits	利润总额 Total Profits	亏损企业亏损总额 Total Deficit of Loss-Making Enterprises	利税总额 Total Taxes and Profits	应交增值税 Value Added Tax Payable
1 537 245	**20 546 202**	**20 940 474**	**2 192 571**	**28 215 138**	**5 709 102**
499	2 263	2 412	794	4 167	1 256
216	75	245	154	1 705	1 244
787	12 599	18 521	696	25 773	6 464
176	2 176	2 383	–	3 018	460
146 707	2 536 029	2 514 313	191 994	3 420 956	754 053
76 258	1 369 488	1 427 778	33 171	1 760 919	255 543
381 581	5 090 331	5 211 256	370 380	7 515 351	1 917 650
–	–	–	–	–	–
218 911	3 592 950	3 654 047	342 678	4 727 159	851 124
712 111	7 940 291	8 109 519	1 252 705	10 756 090	1 921 308
367 433	4 483 683	4 589 507	650 573	6 560 514	1 598 466
1 169 813	16 062 519	16 350 967	1 541 999	21 654 624	4 110 635
647 003	9 190 194	9 243 587	639 541	11 635 565	1 737 817
397 687	6 312 643	6 452 864	382 928	8 442 404	1 582 742
484 353	5 029 806	5 221 925	1 096 990	8 068 330	2 350 133
8 202	13 559	22 098	73 113	68 839	38 410
609	927	2 527	–	4 911	1 775
5 801	154 165	155 925	10 919	190 176	28 344
15 562	97 126	98 067	133 439	191 328	77 647
16 058	52 279	55 812	4 395	102 874	30 646
402	952	960	–	2 542	1 179
53 582	363 284	406 852	55 670	717 418	256 286

表4-2 续表 3

单位：万元

项　　目	Item	企业单位数 (个) Number of Enterprises (unit)
纺织服装、服饰业	Garments and Apparel Industry	352
皮革、毛皮、羽毛及其制品和制鞋业	Leather, Fur, Wool and Shoes Products	51
木材加工和木、竹、藤、棕、草制品业	Wood Processing, Wood, Bamboo, Rattan and Coir Products Straw Products	50
家具制造业	Furniture Manufacturing	76
造纸和纸制品业	Papermaking and Paper Products	174
印刷和记录媒介复制业	Printing and Record Duplicating	158
文教、工美、体育和娱乐用品制造业	Stationary,Educational, Industrial arts, Sports and Entertainment products	123
石油、煤炭及其他燃料加工业	Oil, Coal and Other Fuel Processing Industries	23
化学原料和化学制品制造业	Raw Chemical Materials and Chemical Products	565
医药制造业	Medical and Pharmaceutical Products	105
化学纤维制造业	Chemical Fiber Manufacturing	339
橡胶和塑料制品业	Rubber and Plastic Products	794
非金属矿物制品业	Nonmetal Mineral Products	337
黑色金属冶炼和压延加工业	Smelting and Pressing of Ferrous Metals	139
有色金属冶炼和压延加工业	Smelting and Pressing of Nonferrous Metals	242
金属制品业	Metal Products	823
通用设备制造业	General Equipment Manufacture	1 049
专用设备制造业	Special Purposes Equipment Manufacturing	759
汽车制造业	Automobile Manufacturing	519
铁路、船舶、航空航天和其他运输设备制造业	Railway, Ship, Aerospace and Other Transportation Equipment Manufacturing	116
电气机械和器材制造业	Electric Equipment and Machinery Manufacturing	749
计算机、通信和其他电子设备制造业	Computer Telecommunications and Other Electronic Equipment Manufacture	1 105
仪器仪表制造业	Instruments, Meters Machinery	199
其他制造业	Other Products Manufacture	20
废弃资源综合利用业	Comprehensive Utilization of Waste Resources	30
金属制品、机械和设备修理业	Metal Products, Machinery and Equipment Repair	4
电力、热力生产和供应业	Production and Supply of Electricity and Thermal Power	43
燃气生产和供应业	Production and Supply of Gas	27
水的生产和供应业	Production and Supply of Water	29

Continued 3

(10 000 yuan)

# 亏损企业 Loss Making Enterprises	工业总产值 Gross Industrial Output Value	工业销售产值 Value of Industrial Products Sales	# 出口交货值 Delivery Value for Export	资产总计 Total Assets	# 流动资产合计 Circulating Funds	# 应收帐款 Net Account Income
83	4 125 062	3 977 296	1 332 766	3 447 935	2 559 779	905 717
15	428 009	426 963	294 330	337 010	252 302	91 288
9	488 979	492 092	58 224	997 929	653 387	162 881
22	909 803	917 392	459 479	830 320	551 020	193 310
28	7 133 142	7 211 974	571 306	8 500 923	4 974 385	1 238 894
31	2 306 002	2 292 515	624 424	2 425 170	1 405 559	662 205
24	1 850 635	1 825 722	845 018	1 920 455	1 270 016	307 448
5	916 254	901 844	–	681 983	445 628	128 023
93	20 185 887	20 233 383	3 335 925	21 796 379	12 308 577	4 323 103
14	2 930 979	3 004 361	426 382	3 814 628	2 409 876	581 848
63	11 284 463	11 153 989	561 292	10 883 329	5 928 762	921 623
133	12 152 419	12 048 631	3 517 935	11 906 878	7 514 291	3 123 054
48	5 926 316	5 923 013	557 072	6 531 675	4 473 799	2 316 537
23	21 975 073	22 314 961	2 638 781	22 566 366	12 039 995	645 149
49	7 119 940	7 197 618	630 517	4 480 115	2 902 703	991 968
128	11 315 491	11 258 576	2 654 266	12 275 800	7 874 381	2 999 574
131	26 962 237	26 662 108	9 063 642	26 026 616	18 424 397	6 843 955
124	14 034 082	13 788 170	4 095 598	17 445 837	12 346 052	4 392 752
127	19 105 235	19 026 034	3 244 869	20 154 011	11 383 426	4 658 136
33	3 089 873	3 011 652	1 260 767	2 977 387	2 001 767	696 938
139	25 057 837	25 063 148	8 478 547	30 053 133	19 813 178	7 862 639
216	102 316 137	101 402 308	77 107 093	75 443 379	52 108 627	25 673 316
21	4 689 270	4 558 108	869 305	4 933 180	3 678 787	1 209 907
5	141 352	139 406	33 172	136 806	100 319	28 034
5	329 199	300 871	4 096	362 247	210 939	37 553
–	23 715	23 529	4 148	30 369	27 181	4 090
2	4 207 114	4 201 165	–	8 040 816	1 852 401	420 119
2	2 704 094	2 713 419	–	3 138 055	1 526 810	97 696
4	499 902	491 986	–	2 968 938	779 201	36 248

表4-2 续表 4

单位：万元

项　　目	Item	# 产成品 Manufactured Products
纺织服装、服饰业	Garments and Apparel Industry	374 388
皮革、毛皮、羽毛及其制品和制鞋业	Leather, Fur, Wool and Shoes Products	24 216
木材加工和木、竹、藤、棕、草制品业	Wood Processing, Wood, Bamboo, Rattan and Coir Products Straw Products	70 024
家具制造业	Furniture Manufacturing	63 353
造纸和纸制品业	Papermaking and Paper Products	287 966
印刷和记录媒介复制业	Printing and Record Duplicating	110 929
文教、工美、体育和娱乐用品制造业	Stationary,Educational, Industrial arts, Sports and Entertainment products	203 332
石油、煤炭及其他燃料加工业	Oil, Coal and Other Fuel Processing Industries	37 188
化学原料和化学制品制造业	Raw Chemical Materials and Chemical Products	1 068 428
医药制造业	Medical and Pharmaceutical Products	355 511
化学纤维制造业	Chemical Fiber Manufacturing	789 454
橡胶和塑料制品业	Rubber and Plastic Products	732 134
非金属矿物制品业	Nonmetal Mineral Products	371 664
黑色金属冶炼和压延加工业	Smelting and Pressing of Ferrous Metals	1 361 252
有色金属冶炼和压延加工业	Smelting and Pressing of Nonferrous Metals	293 139
金属制品业	Metal Products	592 323
通用设备制造业	General Equipment Manufacture	1 509 316
专用设备制造业	Special Purposes Equipment Manufacturing	952 369
汽车制造业	Automobile Manufacturing	1 133 056
铁路、船舶、航空航天和其他运输设备制造业	Railway, Ship, Aerospace and Other Transportation Equipment Manufacturing	166 231
电气机械和器材制造业	Electric Equipment and Machinery Manufacturing	1 312 142
计算机、通信和其他电子设备制造业	Computer Telecommunications and Other Electronic Equipment Manufacture	3 469 807
仪器仪表制造业	Instruments, Meters Machinery	300 085
其他制造业	Other Products Manufacture	23 446
废弃资源综合利用业	Comprehensive Utilization of Waste Resources	33 289
金属制品、机械和设备修理业	Metal Products, Machinery and Equipment Repair	3 775
电力、热力生产和供应业	Production and Supply of Electricity and Thermal Power	19
燃气生产和供应业	Production and Supply of Gas	8 445
水的生产和供应业	Production and Supply of Water	1 695

Continued 4

(10 000 yuan)

固定资产原价 Original Value of Fixed Assets	累计折旧 Accumulative Total Depreciation	负债合计 Total Liabilities	所有者权益合计 Total Creditors Equity	# 实收资本 Total Capital Hold	主营业务收入 Major Business Revenue
1 081 153	582 162	2 144 907	1 303 028	683 627	4 033 525
124 432	72 666	157 521	179 489	113 390	426 889
145 195	63 961	544 739	453 189	289 651	529 582
330 784	141 487	422 981	407 338	273 248	981 612
5 226 572	2 983 485	4 184 922	4 316 000	3 130 811	7 153 873
1 491 072	794 837	1 199 492	1 225 677	601 188	2 320 856
745 955	399 298	1 030 638	889 815	435 326	2 361 983
306 856	149 797	253 801	428 182	383 937	902 540
11 925 037	5 452 198	9 868 593	11 927 781	6 802 675	21 227 574
1 803 217	793 150	1 696 164	2 118 463	1 319 767	3 021 013
6 178 273	3 216 353	7 089 743	3 793 584	2 644 089	11 755 274
6 903 518	3 512 033	5 146 180	6 760 690	3 977 216	12 099 267
3 412 052	1 889 447	3 471 656	3 060 017	2 065 358	5 960 205
12 339 194	7 553 255	12 386 283	10 180 081	2 402 049	25 633 201
1 852 959	943 417	2 360 304	2 119 809	1 459 367	7 366 465
4 675 563	2 250 143	5 946 512	6 329 283	3 479 646	11 270 491
9 341 709	4 668 960	12 591 179	13 435 431	6 065 710	26 954 852
5 984 335	2 730 340	8 522 382	8 923 447	3 705 517	13 941 842
9 527 072	4 205 005	10 496 824	9 657 183	5 959 411	19 109 888
1 122 372	503 198	1 484 028	1 493 358	638 065	3 049 510
8 408 325	3 986 194	15 661 943	14 391 181	7 039 595	26 806 334
36 507 353	20 158 498	41 725 292	33 718 082	18 793 152	101 590 064
1 324 012	603 059	2 234 900	2 698 278	1 032 050	4 586 094
70 045	38 839	104 381	32 425	42 475	175 885
181 858	90 028	236 921	125 326	122 259	344 512
3 225	1 314	21 827	8 542	8 869	24 359
8 373 307	4 032 353	4 684 811	3 356 004	2 068 281	4 187 193
827 859	288 820	1 584 615	1 553 441	505 614	2 755 897
2 886 813	1 199 305	1 847 559	1 121 379	660 897	502 188

表4-2 续表 5

单位：万元

项　　目	Item	主营业务成本 Major Business Cost
纺织服装、服饰业	Garments and Apparel Industry	3 392 927
皮革、毛皮、羽毛及其制品和制鞋业	Leather, Fur, Wool and Shoes Products	388 302
木材加工和木、竹、藤、棕、草制品业	Wood Processing, Wood, Bamboo, Rattan and Coir Products Straw Products	443 982
家具制造业	Furniture Manufacturing	823 280
造纸和纸制品业	Papermaking and Paper Products	5 804 950
印刷和记录媒介复制业	Printing and Record Duplicating	1 864 225
文教、工美、体育和娱乐用品制造业	Stationary,Educational, Industrial arts, Sports and Entertainment products	2 058 430
石油、煤炭及其他燃料加工业	Oil, Coal and Other Fuel Processing Industries	760 089
化学原料和化学制品制造业	Raw Chemical Materials and Chemical Products	16 824 394
医药制造业	Medical and Pharmaceutical Products	1 627 326
化学纤维制造业	Chemical Fiber Manufacturing	10 770 145
橡胶和塑料制品业	Rubber and Plastic Products	9 950 203
非金属矿物制品业	Nonmetal Mineral Products	4 997 182
黑色金属冶炼和压延加工业	Smelting and Pressing of Ferrous Metals	22 239 986
有色金属冶炼和压延加工业	Smelting and Pressing of Nonferrous Metals	6 890 220
金属制品业	Metal Products	9 496 323
通用设备制造业	General Equipment Manufacture	21 867 158
专用设备制造业	Special Purposes Equipment Manufacturing	10 824 665
汽车制造业	Automobile Manufacturing	15 776 066
铁路、船舶、航空航天和其他运输设备制造业	Railway, Ship, Aerospace and Other Transportation Equipment Manufacturing	2 497 821
电气机械和器材制造业	Electric Equipment and Machinery Manufacturing	22 751 993
计算机、通信和其他电子设备制造业	Computer Telecommunications and Other Electronic Equipment Manufacture	93 458 865
仪器仪表制造业	Instruments, Meters Machinery	3 352 956
其他制造业	Other Products Manufacture	147 389
废弃资源综合利用业	Comprehensive Utilization of Waste Resources	297 598
金属制品、机械和设备修理业	Metal Products, Machinery and Equipment Repair	17 223
电力、热力生产和供应业	Production and Supply of Electricity and Thermal Power	3 612 399
燃气生产和供应业	Production and Supply of Gas	2 460 517
水的生产和供应业	Production and Supply of Water	335 155

Continued 5

(10 000 yuan)

主营业务税金及附加 Pre-tax and Related Payment of Major Business	营业利润 Business Profits	利润总额 Total Profits	亏损企业亏损总额 Total Deficit of Loss-Making Enterprises	利税总额 Total Taxes and Profits	应交增值税 Value Added Tax Payable
20 194	121 160	124 010	32 718	226 689	82 317
2 341	-3 981	4 005	6 061	10 221	3 874
5 567	7 254	7 365	20 292	29 927	16 951
6 037	30 268	28 444	12 776	55 014	20 461
33 775	635 692	635 205	31 345	863 487	194 225
13 783	163 805	168 104	18 281	242 441	60 364
10 676	54 812	59 983	16 439	91 279	20 470
29 141	72 150	72 179	5 655	127 992	26 673
101 578	2 075 636	2 089 133	125 377	2 768 651	575 601
30 108	253 265	268 587	80 153	490 416	191 174
30 841	551 167	526 819	62 519	710 504	152 707
64 275	837 328	860 762	88 711	1 185 644	259 598
34 563	366 487	373 079	38 315	620 082	212 065
126 546	2 301 891	2 250 623	39 311	2 904 309	526 486
16 502	129 273	135 320	16 571	210 611	57 831
57 277	640 750	652 498	84 411	977 252	266 959
140 360	2 269 597	2 318 585	113 033	2 977 553	516 222
81 054	1 247 792	1 289 892	85 746	1 678 511	306 513
200 291	1 337 782	1 353 286	297 505	1 934 068	377 958
11 443	279 623	296 352	37 777	360 023	52 152
105 722	1 714 705	1 733 463	193 860	2 173 291	332 099
245 598	3 483 693	3 625 697	558 061	4 547 099	668 294
27 509	565 614	575 263	8 623	727 693	123 827
891	-2 080	-1 424	6 320	4 856	5 374
1 556	22 754	28 826	833	41 263	10 877
103	1 485	1 473	–	2 407	832
34 226	409 416	419 114	1 280	650 278	194 543
5 414	210 266	218 755	4 685	254 718	30 291
7 861	99 866	104 933	1 489	139 610	26 488

表4-3 规模以上国有及国有控股工业企业主要经济指标 (2018年)

单位：万元

项　　目	Item	企业单位数(个) Number of Enterprises (unit)	# 亏损企业 Loss Making Enterprises
总　　计	**Total**	**144**	**22**
非金属矿采选业	Nonmetal Minerals Mining and Dressing	1	–
农副食品加工业	Agricultural and Sideline Food Processing	1	1
酒、饮料和精制茶制造业	Wine, Beverage and Refined tea manufacturing	1	–
烟草制品业	Manufacture of Tobacco	1	–
纺织业	Textile Industry	1	–
纺织服装、服饰业	Garments and Apparel Industry	3	2
造纸和纸制品业	Papermaking and Paper Products	1	–
印刷和记录媒介复制业	Printing and Record Duplicating	–	–
文教、工美、体育和娱乐用品制造业	Printing and Record Duplicating	1	1
石油、煤炭及其他燃料加工业	Oil, Coal and Other Fuel Processing Industries	1	–
化学原料和化学制品制造业	Raw Chemical Materials and Chemical Products	17	2
医药制造业	Medical and Pharmaceutical Products	2	–
橡胶和塑料制品业	Rubber and Plastic Products	3	1
非金属矿物制品业	Nonmetal Mineral Products	14	–
黑色金属冶炼和压延加工业	Smelting and Pressing of Ferrous Metals	4	1
有色金属冶炼和压延加工业	Smelting and Pressing of Nonferrous Metals	5	1
金属制品业	Manufacture of Metal Products	3	–
通用设备制造业	General Equipment Manufacture	15	6
专用设备制造业	For Special Purposes Equipment Manufacturing	7	1
汽车制造业	Automobile Manufacturing	2	–
铁路、船舶、航空航天和其他运输设备制造业	Transport Equipment Manufacturing	2	–
电气机械和器材制造业	Electric Equipment and Machinery Manufacturing	7	1
计算机、通信和其他电子设备制造业	Computer Telecommunications and Other Electronic Equipment Manufacture	9	1
仪器仪表制造业	Instruments, Meters Machinery	5	2
金属制品、机械和设备修理业	Metal Products, Machinery and Equipment Repair	1	–
电力、热力生产和供应业	Production and Supply of Electricity and Thermal Power	14	–
燃气生产和供应业	Production and Supply of Gas	9	–
水的生产和供应业	Production and Supply of Water	14	2

MAIN ECONOMIC INDICATORS OF STATE-OWNED ENTERPRISES AND SHARE HOLDING INDUSTRIAL ENTERPRISES ABOVE DESIGNATED SIZE (2018)

(10 000 yuan)

工业总产值 Gross Industrial Output Value	工业销售产值 Value of Industrial Products Sales	# 出口交货值 Delivery Value for Export	资产总计 Total Assets	# 流动资产合计 Circulating Funds	累计折旧 Accumulative Depreciation	负债合计 Total Liabilities
10 069 047	**9 911 276**	**1 664 750**	**12 903 702**	**5 906 482**	**4 851 692**	**7 166 234**
18 300	19 326	–	47 627	16 575	20 003	20 394
7 207	7 236	–	16 322	13 530	4 850	11 934
41 550	42 675	–	96 990	63 011	64 579	9 864
12 921	12 802	–	34 975	6 421	25 935	1 810
26 960	26 306	–	8 269	5 727	1 982	5 734
26 714	26 507	11 911	31 244	22 573	13 666	11 561
115 233	116 903	–	157 326	64 797	142 961	10 417
–	–	–	–	–	–	–
30 104	28 530	–	36 283	16 849	14 420	18 226
218 427	214 229	–	74 053	50 392	29 362	10 703
1 135 399	1 103 229	335 787	1 173 955	522 514	315 531	563 987
50 443	48 028	–	60 147	39 571	7 412	47 578
78 188	71 774	13 314	63 937	34 911	15 345	40 449
539 299	562 665	25 385	547 193	371 254	93 436	272 883
616 399	582 767	9 267	621 889	375 367	238 653	449 070
1 287 946	1 229 031	51 209	357 753	235 707	58 679	245 934
103 964	104 943	3 110	107 925	65 190	20 895	45 338
787 112	774 463	243 950	1 007 593	704 366	91 257	676 494
252 911	260 019	10 294	672 335	374 994	50 057	497 390
166 967	163 437	44 710	168 810	101 944	9 827	116 908
37 561	38 397	–	54 864	39 664	1 482	28 369
337 822	342 443	23 197	450 761	264 944	31 534	282 292
1 362 695	1 344 282	882 321	1 957 760	1 236 673	968 900	1 163 354
77 175	73 512	10 294	105 456	78 121	10 692	74 390
7 683	7 683	–	10 590	9 837	430	9 305
1 725 323	1 722 656	–	2 363 775	378 823	1 695 538	1 122 727
730 188	720 544	–	1 010 030	523 159	158 731	430 418
274 559	266 892	–	1 665 841	289 572	765 538	998 708

表4-3 续表

单位：万元

项　　目	Item	所有者权益合　计 Creditors Equity	# 实收资本 Total Capital Hold
总　计	**Total**	**5 737 468**	**3 827 951**
非金属矿采选业	Nonmetal Minerals Mining and Dressing	27 233	10 000
农副食品加工业	Agricultural and Sideline Food Processing	4 389	12 697
酒、饮料和精制茶制造业	Wine, Beverage and Refined tea manufacturing	87 126	73 154
烟草制品业	Manufacture of Tobacco	33 165	36 286
纺织业	Textile Industry	2 535	1 337
纺织服装、服饰业	Garments and Apparel Industry	19 683	6 961
造纸和纸制品业	Papermaking and Paper Products	146 909	84 000
印刷和记录媒介复制业	Printing and Record Duplicating	–	–
文教、工美、体育和娱乐用品制造业	Printing and Record Duplicating	18 057	7 939
石油、煤炭及其他燃料加工业	Oil, Coal and Other Fuel Processing Industries	63 350	63 350
化学原料和化学制品制造业	Raw Chemical Materials and Chemical Products	609 968	247 768
医药制造业	Medical and Pharmaceutical Products	12 568	10 920
橡胶和塑料制品业	Rubber and Plastic Products	23 488	21 131
非金属矿物制品业	Nonmetal Mineral Products	274 310	132 342
黑色金属冶炼和压延加工业	Smelting and Pressing of Ferrous Metals	172 819	515 800
有色金属冶炼和压延加工业	Smelting and Pressing of Nonferrous Metals	111 819	118 487
金属制品业	Manufacture of Metal Products	62 588	62 032
通用设备制造业	General Equipment Manufacture	331 099	194 464
专用设备制造业	For Special Purposes Equipment Manufacturing	174 944	112 377
汽车制造业	Automobile Manufacturing	51 903	26 322
铁路、船舶、航空航天和其他运输设备制造业	Transport Equipment Manufacturing	26 495	21 000
电气机械和器材制造业	Electric Equipment and Machinery Manufacturing	168 469	57 680
计算机、通信和其他电子设备制造业	Computer Telecommunications and Other Electronic Equipment Manufacture	794 406	798 117
仪器仪表制造业	Instruments, Meters Machinery	31 066	18 615
金属制品、机械和设备修理业	Metal Products, Machinery and Equipment Repair	1 285	1 000
电力、热力生产和供应业	Production and Supply of Electricity and Thermal Power	1 241 047	765 450
燃气生产和供应业	Production and Supply of Gas	579 612	76 885
水的生产和供应业	Production and Supply of Water	667 134	351 836

Continued

(10 000 yuan)

主营业务收入 Major Business Revenue	主营业务成本 Major Business Cost	主营业务税金及附加 Pre-tax and Related Payment of Major Business	营业利润 Business Profits	利润总额 Total Profits	亏损企业亏损总额 Total Deficit of Loss-Making Enterprises	利税总额 Total Taxes and Profits	应交增值税 Value Added Tax Payable
10 031 920	**8 678 573**	**49 093**	**632 960**	**643 610**	**46 820**	**912 458**	**216 108**
19 326	12 504	609	927	2 527	–	4 911	1 775
7 236	6 449	71	-954	-1 000	1 000	-545	384
42 675	33 285	5 430	2 915	2 916	–	11 670	3 324
12 802	6 882	402	952	960	–	2 542	1 179
26 961	24 883	72	329	331	–	694	291
26 512	18 799	308	-136	-79	591	1 704	1 475
120 760	67 385	1 157	30 528	30 720	–	38 982	7 104
–	–	–	–	–	–	–	–
28 333	28 406	78	-3 452	-3 439	3 439	-3 840	-479
179 430	164 143	1 048	8 572	8 573	–	10 965	1 344
1 145 020	917 456	4 725	133 792	132 975	2 749	161 429	23 665
48 030	18 176	554	1 064	972	–	5 862	4 337
73 633	65 238	353	458	578	398	1 247	316
560 593	449 587	3 320	58 611	59 138	–	82 374	19 916
591 403	558 275	1 273	4 396	622	1 617	11 360	8 946
1 339 102	1 314 500	946	922	715	838	1 783	122
101 771	89 509	723	4 917	5 968	–	8 819	2 127
772 740	669 796	3 432	-179	5 068	28 605	19 411	10 911
253 709	207 801	1 534	12 015	13 475	139	19 976	4 614
163 437	133 213	446	20 955	20 963	–	22 567	1 159
41 199	34 136	282	2 690	2 700	–	4 906	1 904
323 170	288 298	1 144	7 866	7 949	2 190	16 310	7 217
1 335 083	1 173 032	2 789	63 197	66 576	2 854	82 408	13 030
72 337	54 039	544	4 203	1 194	1 231	4 579	2 841
7 658	7 440	49	61	61	–	366	256
1 718 377	1 564 235	11 383	115 002	117 242	–	202 286	71 273
746 368	597 715	2 429	117 104	119 282	–	134 983	13 014
274 255	173 392	3 990	46 202	46 625	1 169	64 709	14 064

表4-4 规模以上民营工业企业主要经济指标（2018年）

单位：万元

项　　目	Item	企业单位数（个）Number of Enterprises (unit)	# 亏损企业 Loss Making Enterprises
总　　计	**Total**	**6 214**	**887**
农副食品加工业	Agricultural and Sideline Food Processing	32	5
食品制造业	Food Production	24	–
酒、饮料和精制茶制造业	Wine, Beverage and Refined tea manufacturing	4	1
纺织业	Textile Industry	1 078	146
纺织服装、服饰业	Garments and Apparel Industry	260	54
皮革、毛皮、羽毛及其制品和制鞋业	Leather, Fur, Wool and Shoes Products	25	4
木材加工和木、竹、藤、棕、草制品业	Wood Processing, Wood, Bamboo, Rattan and Coir Products Straw Products	38	7
家具制造业	Furniture Manufacturing	46	13
造纸和纸制品业	Papermaking and Paper Products	111	13
印刷和记录媒介复制业	Printing and Record Medium Reproduction	107	21
文教、工美、体育和娱乐用品制造业	Stationary,Educational, Industrial arts, Sports and Entertainment products	70	10
石油、煤炭及其他燃料加工业	Oil, Coal and Other Fuel Processing Industries	16	3
化学原料和化学制品制造业	Raw Chemical Materials and Chemical Products	255	33
医药制造业	Medical and Pharmaceutical Products	68	6
化学纤维制造业	Chemical Fiber	313	54
橡胶和塑料制品业	Rubber and Plastic Products	458	54
非金属矿物制品业	Nonmetal Mineral Products	221	28
黑色金属冶炼和压延加工业	Smelting and Pressing of Ferrous Metals	98	13
有色金属冶炼和压延加工业	Smelting and Pressing of Nonferrous Metals	174	35
金属制品业	Metal Products	564	69
通用设备制造业	General Equipment Manufacture	570	66
专用设备制造业	Special Purposes Equipment Manufacturing	428	61
汽车制造业	Automobile Manufacturing	200	34
铁路、船舶、航空航天和其他运输设备制造业	Railway, Ship, Aerospace and Other Transportation Equipment Manufacturing	48	15
电气机械和器材制造业	Electric Equipment and Machinery Manufacturing	450	68
计算机、通信和其他电子设备制造业	Computer Telecommunications and Other Electronic Equipment Manufacture	382	57
仪器仪表造业	Instruments, Meters, Machinery	99	6
其他制造业	Other Industry	8	1
废弃资源综合利用业	Comprehensive Utilization of Waste Resources	18	3
金属制品、机械和设备修理业	Metal Products, Machinery and Equipment Repair	2	–
电力、热力生产和供应业	Production and Supply of Electric Power and Heat Energy	23	2
燃气生产和供应业	Production and Supply of Gas	12	2
水的生产和供应业	Production and Supply of Water	12	3

MAIN ECONOMIC INDICATORS OF PRIVATE AND INDIVIDUAL INDUSTRIAL ENTERPRISES ABOVE DESIGNATED SIZE (2018)

(10 000 yuan)

工业总产值 Gross Industrial Output Value	工业销售产值 Value of Industrial Products Sales	# 出口交货值 Delivery Value for Export	资产总计 Total Assets	# 流动资产合计 Circulating Funds	累计折旧 Accumulative Depreciation	负债合计 Total Liabilities
120 110 673	**119 513 081**	**19 007 506**	**136 671 953**	**83 167 916**	**22 932 409**	**77 104 533**
681 813	684 203	14 181	329 282	246 811	56 097	176 382
358 998	358 967	12 848	329 389	167 116	75 796	137 048
124 048	120 145	–	157 612	86 049	33 933	32 343
10 196 921	10 156 674	1 366 312	9 489 196	5 803 169	2 469 405	6 298 671
2 608 556	2 618 111	744 563	1 903 503	1 250 943	316 424	1 289 816
151 074	144 048	69 121	90 227	76 041	26 588	46 553
271 438	272 063	11 864	647 498	365 257	27 268	340 205
410 924	406 335	170 624	398 678	264 359	51 474	245 510
1 464 686	1 467 428	65 386	906 675	618 971	146 505	518 040
1 220 400	1 216 658	251 704	1 258 640	750 733	370 113	682 093
758 930	745 243	190 656	825 987	560 314	103 136	538 523
179 900	166 145	–	162 087	73 638	18 682	79 742
7 197 908	7 153 158	688 534	9 025 711	5 131 892	1 150 807	4 597 930
1 058 194	1 002 784	154 118	1 143 921	720 783	221 403	573 956
10 396 169	10 288 231	387 390	9 586 429	5 320 109	2 689 103	6 244 932
5 142 078	5 056 678	977 755	4 510 613	3 080 073	647 121	2 376 380
2 981 790	2 951 945	98 261	2 958 507	2 346 897	394 512	1 922 828
17 895 719	18 322 345	2 120 578	19 926 159	10 571 440	6 216 006	10 822 880
3 593 176	3 551 219	217 095	2 115 429	1 325 270	268 402	1 230 337
6 475 679	6 445 131	835 069	7 436 056	4 562 317	980 328	4 000 157
7 416 734	7 330 469	1 359 928	8 932 656	5 931 802	1 030 164	4 451 093
4 655 531	4 574 966	860 159	6 307 091	4 417 438	697 445	3 492 218
3 597 226	3 634 266	402 454	4 636 796	2 989 052	548 710	2 808 165
670 144	640 815	91 322	773 442	537 402	54 609	420 522
12 586 429	12 523 617	2 475 281	18 644 250	11 743 364	1 432 988	10 265 081
13 007 701	12 791 299	5 077 543	17 290 739	10 405 551	1 659 146	9 263 871
2 148 972	2 041 135	346 787	2 648 570	2 017 385	111 098	1 295 722
52 627	51 725	13 828	34 328	19 634	7 783	20 689
232 612	202 379	–	265 336	149 277	47 258	209 606
13 247	13 247	4 148	15 536	14 557	574	11 719
1 303 204	1 305 090	–	2 942 218	963 170	927 989	2 073 626
1 132 588	1 151 558	–	446 944	268 274	22 838	258 963
125 257	125 008	–	532 449	388 829	128 707	378 935

表4-4 续表

单位：万元

项　　目	Item	所有者权益合　计 Creditors Equity	# 实收资本 Total Capital Hold
总　　计	**Total**	**59 567 375**	**25 837 696**
农副食品加工业	Agricultural and Sideline Food Processing	152 901	66 232
食品制造业	Food Production	192 340	134 936
酒、饮料和精制茶制造业	Wine, Beverage and Refined tea manufacturing	125 268	9 543
纺织业	Textile Industry	3 190 517	1 727 388
纺织服装、服饰业	Garments and Apparel Industry	613 687	346 362
皮革、毛皮、羽毛及其制品和制鞋业	Leather, Fur, Wool and Shoes Products	43 674	29 076
木材加工和木、竹、藤、棕、草制品业	Wood Processing, Wood, Bamboo, Rattan and Coir Products Straw Products	307 293	194 405
家具制造业	Furniture Manufacturing	153 168	95 702
造纸和纸制品业	Papermaking and Paper Products	388 635	215 632
印刷和记录媒介复制业	Printing and Record Medium Reproduction	576 547	272 546
文教、工美、体育和娱乐用品制造业	Stationary,Educational, Industrial arts, Sports and Entertainment products	287 464	124 219
石油、煤炭及其他燃料加工业	Oil, Coal and Other Fuel Processing Industries	82 345	46 960
化学原料和化学制品制造业	Raw Chemical Materials and Chemical Products	4 427 780	2 042 478
医药制造业	Medical and Pharmaceutical Products	569 964	278 125
化学纤维制造业	Chemical Fiber	3 341 496	2 089 266
橡胶和塑料制品业	Rubber and Plastic Products	2 134 230	1 029 839
非金属矿物制品业	Nonmetal Mineral Products	1 035 677	544 433
黑色金属冶炼和压延加工业	Smelting and Pressing of Ferrous Metals	9 103 279	955 863
有色金属冶炼和压延加工业	Smelting and Pressing of Nonferrous Metals	885 090	464 289
金属制品业	Metal Products	3 435 895	1 717 596
通用设备制造业	General Equipment Manufacture	4 481 560	2 074 917
专用设备制造业	Special Purposes Equipment Manufacturing	2 814 868	1 232 220
汽车制造业	Automobile Manufacturing	1 828 630	878 009
铁路、船舶、航空航天和其他运输设备制造业	Railway, Ship, Aerospace and Other Transportation Equipment Manufacturing	352 920	158 544
电气机械和器材制造业	Electric Equipment and Machinery Manufacturing	8 379 164	3 835 238
计算机、通信和其他电子设备制造业	Computer Telecommunications and Other Electronic Equipment Manufacture	8 026 867	3 858 455
仪器仪表造业	Instruments, Meters, Machinery	1 352 847	454 086
其他制造业	Other Industry	13 640	10 285
废弃资源综合利用业	Comprehensive Utilization of Waste Resources	55 730	61 098
金属制品、机械和设备修理业	Metal Products, Machinery and Equipment Repair	3 817	3 800
电力、热力生产和供应业	Production and Supply of Electric Power and Heat Energy	868 591	628 673
燃气生产和供应业	Production and Supply of Gas	187 982	178 536
水的生产和供应业	Production and Supply of Water	153 514	78 948

Continued

(10 000 yuan)

主营业务收入 Major Business Revenue	主营业务成本 Major Business Cost	主营业务税金及附加 Pre-tax and Related Payment of Major Business	营业利润 Business Profits	利润总额 Total Profits	亏损企业亏损总额 Total Deficit of Loss-Making Enterprises	利税总额 Total Taxes and Profits	应交增值税 Value Added Tax Payable
126 418 028	**107 138 874**	**562 583**	**8 486 111**	**8 644 497**	**560 428**	**11 947 934**	**2 732 392**
705 070	627 469	1 572	34 418	35 794	2 045	45 155	7 764
410 074	325 624	2 079	29 874	29 698	–	44 059	12 283
134 646	88 380	2 748	26 336	26 092	331	36 629	7 790
10 159 595	9 258 306	39 021	262 203	304 525	32 610	545 835	201 813
2 681 571	2 325 021	12 081	41 262	41 282	22 217	116 190	62 667
146 191	140 387	661	-5 416	1 928	1 693	5 669	3 077
266 454	223 779	2 483	-1 963	-1 609	16 646	9 614	8 697
421 158	343 357	2 620	17 563	17 531	5 017	32 961	12 793
1 461 424	1 305 214	4 250	43 810	45 708	5 442	78 926	28 842
1 251 284	1 065 740	6 016	58 215	67 495	5 738	104 109	30 524
1 273 708	1 163 391	3 759	22 397	25 439	2 351	44 871	15 586
181 066	155 337	871	6 243	6 350	1 010	11 345	4 124
7 770 294	5 988 103	38 229	889 086	903 768	19 927	1 186 662	243 781
992 198	614 034	7 798	81 606	86 896	8 716	140 882	46 034
10 793 081	9 875 330	27 118	558 648	533 445	33 118	705 161	144 481
5 067 117	4 241 688	22 228	332 891	341 469	17 767	468 778	104 484
2 956 693	2 570 391	14 287	125 636	127 991	16 498	246 912	104 407
21 625 718	18 460 853	117 423	2 274 670	2 227 412	14 003	2 838 060	493 090
3 602 218	3 417 698	7 435	28 678	33 566	9 186	71 778	30 601
6 455 089	5 557 529	29 047	268 093	275 464	45 856	477 172	172 311
7 373 339	5 968 667	39 502	465 798	489 151	39 574	719 191	189 016
4 554 339	3 412 668	32 112	382 055	408 523	25 619	591 505	150 560
3 711 925	3 052 765	19 031	249 325	258 489	33 153	375 934	98 228
654 722	541 503	2 457	13 839	14 024	28 170	27 078	10 542
14 010 611	11 859 849	50 919	883 006	897 304	103 364	1 152 974	204 252
12 781 391	10 618 775	51 232	879 081	909 448	61 569	1 159 830	198 098
2 074 339	1 385 186	13 516	299 413	309 833	1 306	395 452	71 240
52 802	46 388	258	1 228	1 277	79	2 206	657
245 103	213 310	971	15 874	21 674	343	29 671	7 022
13 247	8 143	52	1 387	1 355	–	1 617	210
1 312 116	1 067 740	8 659	172 244	174 226	1 280	240 875	57 983
1 151 629	1 124 384	450	4 434	4 510	4 685	9 266	4 306
127 818	91 866	1 698	24 179	24 440	1 114	31 566	5 131

表4-5 规模以上外商和港澳台商投资工业企业主要经济指标 (2018年)

单位：万元

指　标	Item	企业单位数(个) Number of Enterprises (unit)	#亏损企业 Loss Making Enterprises
总　计	**Total**	**4 057**	**881**
农副食品加工业	Agricultural and Sideline Food Processing	20	6
食品制造业	Food Production	34	8
酒、饮料和精制茶制造业	Wine, Beverage and Refined tea manufacturing	15	5
纺织业	Textile Industry	181	34
纺织服装、服饰业	Garments and Apparel Industry	90	28
皮革、毛皮、羽毛及其制品和制鞋业	Leather, Fur, Wool and Shoes Products	26	11
木材加工和木、竹、藤、棕、草制品业	Timber Processing, Bamboo, Cane, Palm Fiber and Straw Products	12	2
家具制造业	Furniture Manufacturing	30	9
造纸和纸制品业	Papermaking and Paper Products	62	15
印刷和记录媒介复制业	Printing and Record Medium Reproduction	51	10
文教、工美、体育和娱乐用品制造业	Stationary,Educational, Industrial arts, Sports and Entertainment products	53	14
石油、煤炭及其他燃料加工业	Oil, Coal and Other Fuel Processing Industries	6	2
化学原料和化学制品制造业	Raw Chemical Materials and Chemical Products	294	58
医药制造业	Medical and Pharmaceutical Products	35	8
化学纤维制造业	Chemical Fiber	26	9
橡胶和塑料制品业	Rubber and Plastic Products	335	78
非金属矿物制品业	Nonmetal Mineral Products	102	20
黑色金属冶炼和压延加工业	Smelting and Pressing of Ferrous Metals	37	9
有色金属冶炼和压延加工业	Smelting and Pressing of Nonferrous Metals	65	13
金属制品业	Metal Products	256	59
通用设备制造业	Ordinary Equipment Manufactory Trade	466	60
专用设备制造业	Special Purposes Equipment Manufacturing	325	62
汽车制造业	Automobile Manufacturing	317	93
铁路、船舶、航空航天和其他运输设备制造业	Railway, Ship, Aerospace and Other Transportation Equipment Manufacturing	67	18
电气机械和器材制造业	Electric Equipment and Machinery	294	71
计算机、通信和其他电子设备制造业	Computer Telecommunications and Other Electronic Equipment Manufacture	716	159
仪器仪表制造业	Instruments, Meters Machinery	97	14
其他制造业	Others Industry	12	4
废弃资源综合利用业	Comprehensive Utilization of Waste Resources	12	2
金属制品、机械和设备修理业	Metal Products, Machinery and Equipment Repair	1	–
电力、热力生产和供应业	Production and Supply of Electric Power and Heat Energy	6	–
燃气生产和供应业	Production and Supply of Gas	7	–
水的生产和供应业	Production and Supply of Water	7	–

MAIN ECONOMIC INDICATORS OF INDUSTRIAL ENTERPRISES ABOVE DESIGNATED SIZE WITH FOREIGN INVESTMENT AND INVESTMENT FROM HONG KONG, MACAO AND TAIWAN (2018)

(10 000 yuan)

工业总产值 Gross Industrial Output Value	工业销售产值 Value of Industrial Products Sales	# 出口交货值 Delivery Value for Export	资产总计 Total Assets	# 流动资产合计 Circulating Funds	累计折旧 Accumulative Depreciation	负债合计 Total Liabilities
205 226 511	**204 176 464**	**105 480 642**	**175 510 217**	**114 873 218**	**51 576 308**	**86 815 250**
2 329 483	2 385 998	2 744	1 621 745	1 069 939	334 472	729 304
2 167 725	2 045 723	122 914	1 317 175	698 997	348 748	769 775
464 048	470 556	846	431 737	166 095	261 333	224 738
2 901 608	2 918 402	923 048	3 246 411	2 131 902	1 171 924	1 711 807
1 503 190	1 345 939	588 203	1 521 451	1 291 331	257 913	846 807
276 935	282 915	225 209	246 783	176 261	46 078	110 968
217 541	220 029	46 360	350 431	288 131	36 694	204 535
498 879	511 057	288 855	431 643	286 661	90 013	177 471
5 553 223	5 627 643	505 921	7 436 922	4 290 618	2 694 020	3 656 465
1 085 601	1 075 858	372 720	1 166 530	654 826	424 724	517 399
1 091 705	1 080 479	654 362	1 094 468	709 702	296 163	492 115
517 927	521 471	–	445 842	321 598	101 754	163 356
12 087 064	12 173 723	2 433 696	11 765 916	6 763 199	4 067 377	4 758 402
1 822 342	1 953 549	272 264	2 610 560	1 649 523	564 336	1 074 630
888 294	865 758	173 902	1 296 900	608 653	527 250	844 812
6 999 641	6 982 029	2 538 586	7 377 021	4 428 479	2 861 359	2 758 946
2 405 227	2 408 402	433 426	3 025 974	1 755 649	1 401 498	1 275 945
3 462 955	3 409 850	508 936	2 018 317	1 093 188	1 098 595	1 114 334
2 350 280	2 512 907	413 423	2 130 068	1 406 593	643 308	969 746
4 735 848	4 708 502	1 816 087	4 731 818	3 246 875	1 248 920	1 901 017
18 862 937	18 660 951	7 517 410	16 192 007	11 872 790	3 549 797	7 527 160
9 245 652	9 073 196	3 225 145	10 964 071	7 828 524	2 004 075	4 935 196
15 341 042	15 228 331	2 797 705	15 348 405	8 292 430	3 646 468	7 571 751
2 396 056	2 347 163	1 169 446	2 175 441	1 447 371	447 593	1 045 773
12 243 439	12 314 780	6 003 190	11 040 988	7 863 827	2 538 175	5 180 540
88 897 415	88 202 757	71 910 108	57 539 750	41 383 301	18 381 765	32 235 873
2 478 668	2 458 738	512 699	2 193 433	1 594 693	482 976	871 578
88 725	87 682	19 343	102 478	80 685	31 056	83 692
96 587	98 492	4 096	96 911	61 661	42 770	27 314
2 785	2 599	–	4 242	2 787	310	803
1 178 588	1 173 419	–	2 734 824	510 408	1 408 825	1 488 458
863 678	863 678	–	1 715 942	746 400	116 440	906 880
171 425	163 888	–	1 134 014	150 121	449 579	637 661

表4-5 续表

单位：万元

项目	Item	所有者权益合计 Creditors Equity	# 实收资本 Total Capital Hold
总计	**Total**	**88 694 937**	**52 399 920**
农副食品加工业	Agricultural and Sideline Food Processing	892 441	371 647
食品制造业	Food Production	547 400	495 284
酒、饮料和精制茶制造业	Wine, Beverage and Refined tea manufacturing	206 999	227 284
纺织业	Textile Industry	1 534 603	1 172 842
纺织服装、服饰业	Garments and Apparel Industry	674 643	334 960
皮革、毛皮、羽毛及其制品和制鞋业	Leather, Fur, Wool and Shoes Products	135 815	84 314
木材加工和木、竹、藤、棕、草制品业	Timber Processing, Bamboo, Cane, Palm Fiber and Straw Products	145 896	95 247
家具制造业	Furniture Manufacturing	254 171	177 546
造纸和纸制品业	Papermaking and Paper Products	3 780 456	2 831 180
印刷和记录媒介复制业	Printing and Record Medium Reproduction	649 131	328 642
文教、工美、体育和娱乐用品制造业	Stationary,Educational, Industrial arts, Sports and Entertainment products	602 351	311 108
石油、煤炭及其他燃料加工业	Oil, Coal and Other Fuel Processing Industries	282 487	273 627
化学原料和化学制品制造业	Raw Chemical Materials and Chemical Products	7 007 512	4 553 729
医药制造业	Medical and Pharmaceutical Products	1 535 931	1 030 722
化学纤维制造业	Chemical Fiber	452 088	554 824
橡胶和塑料制品业	Rubber and Plastic Products	4 618 072	2 937 376
非金属矿物制品业	Nonmetal Mineral Products	1 750 030	1 388 583
黑色金属冶炼和压延加工业	Smelting and Pressing of Ferrous Metals	903 983	930 385
有色金属冶炼和压延加工业	Smelting and Pressing of Nonferrous Metals	1 160 320	922 777
金属制品业	Metal Products	2 830 801	1 700 018
通用设备制造业	Ordinary Equipment Manufactory Trade	8 664 845	3 818 328
专用设备制造业	Special Purposes Equipment Manufacturing	6 028 871	2 429 083
汽车制造业	Automobile Manufacturing	7 776 651	5 055 081
铁路、船舶、航空航天和其他运输设备制造业	Railway, Ship, Aerospace and Other Transportation Equipment Manufacturing	1 129 667	469 521
电气机械和器材制造业	Electric Equipment and Machinery	5 860 444	3 160 416
计算机、通信和其他电子设备制造业	Computer Telecommunications and Other Electronic Equipment Manufacture	25 303 874	14 787 167
仪器仪表制造业	Instruments, Meters Machinery	1 321 855	567 432
其他制造业	Others Industry	18 785	32 190
废弃资源综合利用业	Comprehensive Utilization of Waste Resources	69 596	61 161
金属制品、机械和设备修理业	Metal Products, Machinery and Equipment Repair	3 439	4 069
电力、热力生产和供应业	Production and Supply of Electric Power and Heat Energy	1 246 365	674 158
燃气生产和供应业	Production and Supply of Gas	809 062	264 993
水的生产和供应业	Production and Supply of Water	496 354	354 228

Continued

(10 000 yuan)

主营业务收入 Major Business Revenue	主营业务成本 Major Business Cost	主营业务税金及附加 Pre-tax and Related Payment of Major Business	营业利润 Business Profits	利润总额 Total Profits	亏损企业亏损总额 Total Deficit of Loss-Making Enterprises	利税总额 Total Taxes and Profits	应交增值税 Value Added Tax Payable
206 433 098	**178 674 504**	**931 022**	**11 533 242**	**11 763 567**	**1 595 383**	**15 483 249**	**2 772 432**
3 080 931	2 847 564	4 159	120 701	121 131	7 874	145 567	20 196
2 014 903	1 012 997	13 483	67 252	68 369	133 439	147 269	65 364
472 973	397 505	7 881	23 028	26 804	4 064	54 575	19 533
2 923 855	2 579 183	14 488	100 753	101 997	23 060	170 889	54 182
1 338 704	1 060 664	7 955	79 813	82 591	10 126	108 742	18 188
280 698	247 915	1 680	1 434	2 077	4 369	4 553	796
263 128	220 203	3 084	9 216	8 974	3 646	20 313	8 255
560 454	479 923	3 416	12 705	10 913	7 759	22 053	7 668
5 571 690	4 432 350	28 368	561 353	558 777	25 903	745 579	158 279
1 069 572	798 485	7 767	105 590	100 609	12 543	138 332	29 840
1 088 275	895 039	6 917	32 415	34 543	14 088	46 408	4 884
542 045	440 609	27 221	57 335	57 256	4 645	105 682	21 205
12 510 116	10 052 802	59 876	1 085 216	1 084 660	102 702	1 453 831	307 906
1 980 785	995 115	21 756	170 596	180 720	71 437	343 672	140 804
962 193	894 815	3 723	-7 481	-6 626	29 401	5 344	8 227
7 022 227	5 698 896	41 993	504 834	519 691	70 547	717 400	155 304
2 442 919	1 977 205	16 957	182 241	185 950	21 817	290 796	87 742
3 416 080	3 220 858	7 850	22 825	22 590	23 691	54 890	24 449
2 518 296	2 242 148	8 482	100 556	101 848	6 547	138 246	27 133
4 713 630	3 849 285	27 506	367 740	371 066	38 555	491 262	92 520
18 912 889	15 318 206	97 641	1 803 293	1 827 869	45 308	2 243 258	316 884
9 249 298	7 294 954	48 278	860 054	874 773	59 988	1 074 977	151 540
15 234 526	12 590 088	180 814	1 067 502	1 073 835	264 352	1 535 566	278 571
2 368 312	1 932 780	8 765	264 817	281 357	9 607	330 457	40 314
12 590 602	10 717 404	53 957	822 088	826 445	90 496	1 004 186	122 277
88 405 217	82 503 485	191 930	2 580 881	2 690 045	496 492	3 350 987	462 567
2 454 570	1 925 787	13 499	262 040	264 278	6 197	328 162	50 154
123 083	101 001	633	-3 308	-2 701	6 241	2 650	4 717
99 410	84 288	585	6 880	7 152	490	11 591	3 855
3 454	1 641	2	37	57	–	424	365
1 156 700	980 425	14 184	122 170	127 646	–	207 117	65 287
888 862	760 117	2 735	94 188	100 421	–	116 471	13 316
172 704	120 768	3 439	54 477	58 452	–	72 002	10 111

表4-6

规模以上工业高新技术产业主要经济指标 (2018年)
MAIN ECONOMIC INDICATORS OF HI-TECH MANUFACTURING INDUSTRY ABOVE THE DESIGNATED SIZE(2018)

项　　目	Item	全　市 Whole Municipality
企业单位数　(个)	**Number of Enterprises　(unit)**	**3 624**
工业总产值　(万元)	**Gross Industrial Output Value Total (10 000 yuan)**	**157 765 253**
按行业分	**Grouped by Sector**	
航空航天制造业	Aviation and Aerospace	800 640
电子计算机及办公设备制造业	Computer and Manufacturing of Office Appliance	16 202 508
电子及通讯设备制造业	Electronics and Communications Equipment	58 954 648
医药制造业	Biomedical Manufacturing	5 136 346
仪器仪表制造业	Instrument Manufacturing	5 367 541
智能装备制造业	Intelligent Equipment Manufacturing Industry	35 655 830
新材料制造业	New Material Production Industry	26 227 403
新能源制造业	New Energy Manufacturing	9 420 338
按地区分	**Grouped by Region**	
市　区	Urban Area	81 159 820
# 吴江区	Wujiang District	15 746 239
常　熟	Changshu	13 089 635
张家港	Zhangjiagang	12 392 590
昆　山	Kunshan	40 238 428
太　仓	Taicang	10 884 779
产销率　(%)	**Proportion of Products Sold　(%)**	**99.10**

表4-7

规模以上工业新兴产业主要经济指标（2018年）
MAIN ECONOMIC INDICATORS OF EMERGING INDUSTRIES ABOVE DESIGNATED SIZE(2018)

项 目	Item	全 市 Whole Municipality
企业单位数 （个）	**Number of Enterprises (unit)**	**2 842**
工业总产值 （万元）	**Gross Industrial Output Value Total (10 000 yuan)**	**173 277 901**
按行业分	**Grouped by Sector**	
新型平板显示	New Flat Panel Displays	28 876 413
新材料	New Materials	49 190 428
智能电网和物联网	Smart Grid and Internet Of Things	15 903 281
高端装备制造	High-End Equipment Manufacturing	39 002 978
节能环保	Energy Saving and Environmental Protection	12 620 383
新能源	New Energy	10 845 913
生物技术和新医药	Biotechnology and New Medicines	8 343 366
集成电路	Integrated Circuit	8 495 140
按地区分	**Grouped by Region**	
市 区	Urban Area	79 493 588
# 吴江区	Wujiang District	18 936 938
常 熟	Changshu	18 801 394
张家港	Zhangjiagang	22 739 434
昆 山	Kunshan	39 501 597
太 仓	Taicang	12 741 888
产销率 (%)	**Proportion of Products Sold (%)**	**101.77**

表4-8

规模以上工业企业主要经济效益指标 (2018年)

单位：%

项　目	Item	总资产贡献率 Total Assets Contribution Ratio
总　计	**Total**	**9.38**
一、按轻重工业分	**Grouped by Light and Heavy Industry**	
轻工业	Light Industry	9.68
重工业	Heavy Industry	9.29
二、按行业类别分	**Grouped by Sector**	
非金属矿采选业	Nonmetal Minerals Mining and Dressing	10.34
农副食品加工业	Agricultural and Sideline Food Processing	10.00
食品制造业	Food Production	12.56
酒、饮料和精制茶制造业	Wine, Beverage and Refined tea manufacturing	15.53
烟草制品业	Manufacture of Tobacco	7.27
纺织业	Textile Industry	6.84
纺织服装、服饰业	Garments and Apparel Industry	7.36
皮革、毛皮、羽毛及其制品和制鞋业	Leather, Fur, Wool Products	3.92
木材加工和木、竹、藤、棕、草制品业	Wood Processing, Wood, Bamboo, Rattan and Coir Products Straw Products	4.96
家具制造业	Furniture Manufacturing	7.06
造纸和纸制品业	Papermaking and Paper Products	10.99
印刷和记录媒介的复制业	Printing and Record Duplicating	10.47
文教、工美、体育和娱乐用品制造业	Stationary,Educational, Industrial Arts, Sports and Entertainment Products	5.28
石油、煤炭及其他燃料加工业	Oil, Coal and Other Fuel Processing Industries	19.14

MAIN INDICATORS OF ECONOMIC BENEFIT OF INDUSTRIAL ENTERPRISES ABOVE DESIGNATED SIZE (2018)

(%)

规模以上工业 Enterprises Above Designated Size				# 民营工业 Private and Individual	
成本费用利润率 Rate Between Profit and Cost	资产负债率 Assets Liability Ratio	固定资产净值率 New Value Added in Fixed Asset	产销率 Proportion of Products Sold	总资产贡献率 Total Assets Contribution Ratio	成本费用利润率 Rate Between Profit and Cost
6.34	**52.52**	**48.79**	**99.48**	**9.69**	**6.96**
6.04	53.80	49.38	99.47	9.49	5.13
6.43	52.14	48.60	99.49	9.76	7.84
13.62	42.82	44.44	105.61	–	–
4.25	46.64	48.95	101.95	14.37	5.29
4.40	55.07	57.95	95.17	13.79	7.73
9.26	38.89	44.40	100.59	23.34	24.13
6.32	5.17	40.08	99.08	–	–
3.04	62.90	48.31	99.82	7.08	2.90
3.05	62.21	46.15	96.42	7.25	1.53
0.93	46.74	41.60	99.76	7.29	1.27
1.36	54.59	55.95	100.64	3.87	-0.59
2.97	50.94	57.23	100.83	9.10	4.32
9.38	49.23	42.92	101.11	9.38	3.19
7.75	49.46	46.69	99.42	9.05	5.60
2.55	53.67	46.47	98.65	6.03	2.02
8.48	37.22	51.18	98.43	7.93	3.61

表4-8 续表 1

单位：%

项　　目	Item	# 民营工业 资产负债率 Assets Liability Ratio
总　　计	**Total**	**56.42**
一、按轻重工业分	**Grouped by Light and Heavy Industry**	
轻工业	Light Industry	60.64
重工业	Heavy Industry	54.88
二、按行业类别分	**Grouped by Sector**	
非金属矿采选业	Nonmetal Minerals Mining and Dressing	–
农副食品加工业	Agricultural and Sideline Food Processing	53.57
食品制造业	Food Production	41.61
酒、饮料和精制茶制造业	Wine, Beverage and Refined tea manufacturing	20.52
烟草制品业	Manufacture of Tobacco	–
纺织业	Textile Industry	66.38
纺织服装、服饰业	Garments and Apparel Industry	67.76
皮革、毛皮、羽毛及其制品业	Leather, Fur, Wool Products	51.60
木材加工和木、竹、藤、棕、草制品业	Wood Processing, Wood, Bamboo, Rattan and Coir Products Straw Products	52.54
家具制造业	Furniture Manufacturing	61.58
造纸和纸制品业	Papermaking and Paper Products	57.14
印刷和记录媒介的复制业	Printing and Record Duplicating	54.19
文教、工美、体育和娱乐用品制造业	Stationary,Educational,Industrial arts, Sports and Entertainment products	65.20
石油、煤炭及其他燃料加工业	Oil, Coal and Other Fuel Processing Industries	49.20

Continued 1

(%)

Private and Individual		# 外商和港澳台商 Enterprises with Investment from Foreign ,Hong Kong,Macao and Taiwan				
固定资产净值率 New Value Added in Fixed Asset	产销率 Proportion of Products Sold	总资产贡献率 Total Assets Contribution Ratio	成本费用利润率 Rate Between Profit and Cost	资产负债率 Assets Liability Ratio	固定资产净值率 New Value Added in Fixed Asset	产销率 Proportion of Products Sold
53.71	**99.50**	**9.20**	**5.94**	**49.46**	**45.89**	**99.49**
52.42	99.10	9.86	7.06	47.22	47.17	99.86
54.35	99.70	9.02	5.71	50.06	45.54	99.41
–	–	–	–	–	–	–
53.53	100.35	9.25	4.05	44.97	48.27	102.43
60.78	99.99	12.25	3.71	58.44	57.28	94.37
54.66	96.85	13.47	5.91	52.05	45.80	101.40
–	–	–	–	–	–	–
50.27	99.61	6.12	3.56	52.73	43.61	100.58
50.82	100.37	7.51	6.10	55.66	39.37	89.54
30.99	95.35	2.69	0.74	44.97	46.36	102.16
54.58	100.23	6.98	3.36	58.37	56.92	101.14
58.81	98.88	5.17	1.97	41.12	56.27	102.44
57.11	100.19	10.90	10.64	49.17	42.82	101.34
50.48	99.69	12.00	10.43	44.35	42.88	99.10
55.25	98.20	4.71	3.15	44.96	42.55	98.97
65.06	92.35	24.01	12.16	36.64	50.18	100.68

表4-8 续表 2

单位：%

项　　目	Item	总资产贡献率 Total Assets Contribution Ratio
化学原料和化学制品制造业	Raw Chemical Materials and Chemical Products	13.44
医药制造业	Medical and Pharmaceutical Products	13.36
化学纤维制造业	Chemical Fiber Manufacturing	8.04
橡胶和塑料制品业	Rubber and Plastic Products	10.48
非金属矿物制品业	Nonmetal Mineral Products	10.02
黑色金属冶炼和压延加工业	Smelting and Pressing of Ferrous Metals	13.80
有色金属冶炼和压延加工业	Smelting and Pressing of Nonferrous Metals	5.90
金属制品业	Metal Products	9.05
通用设备制造业	General Equipment Manufacture	11.69
专用设备制造业	Special Purposes Equipment Manufacturing	9.93
汽车制造业	Automobile Manufacturing	10.07
铁路、船舶、航空航天和其他运输设备制造业	Railway, Ship, Aerospace and Other Transportation Equipment Manufacturing	12.22
电气机械和器材制造业	Electric Equipment and Machinery Manufacturing	7.89
计算机、通信和其他电子设备制造业	Computer Telecommunications and Other Electronic Equipment Manufacture	6.32
仪器仪表制造业	Instruments, Meters Machinery	14.95
其他制造业	Other Products Manufacture	4.86
废弃资源综合利用业	Comprehensive Utilization of Waste Resources	12.19
金属制品、机械和设备修理业	Metal Products, Machinery and Equipment Repair	12.46
电力、热力生产和供应业	Manufacture and Supply of Electricity and Thermal Power	9.88
燃气生产和供应业	Manufacture and Supply of Gas	8.81
水的生产和供应业	Manufacture and Supply of Water	5.26

Continued 2

(%)

规模以上工业 Enterprises Above Designated Size				# 民营工业 Private and Individual	
成本费用利润率 Rate Between Profit and Cost	资产负债率 Assets Liability Ratio	固定资产净值率 New Value Added in Fixed Asset	产销率 Proportion of Products Sold	总资产贡献率 Total Assets Contribution Ratio	成本费用利润率 Rate Between Profit and Cost
10.72	45.28	54.28	100.24	14.11	12.71
9.50	44.46	56.01	102.50	13.10	9.51
4.37	65.14	47.94	98.84	8.95	4.82
7.53	43.22	49.13	99.15	11.19	7.12
6.59	53.15	44.62	99.94	9.01	4.50
8.72	54.89	38.79	101.55	15.18	10.24
1.71	52.68	49.09	101.09	4.84	0.81
6.01	48.44	51.87	99.50	7.26	4.38
9.30	48.38	50.02	98.89	8.55	6.96
9.95	48.85	54.38	98.25	9.98	9.69
7.36	52.08	55.86	99.59	9.02	7.09
10.59	49.84	55.17	97.47	4.00	2.15
6.70	52.11	52.59	100.02	7.09	6.58
3.65	55.31	44.78	99.11	7.55	7.41
14.02	45.30	54.45	97.20	15.20	16.96
-0.80	76.30	44.55	98.62	7.17	2.48
8.81	65.40	50.50	91.39	12.07	9.24
6.46	71.87	59.25	99.22	19.43	11.48
10.36	58.26	51.84	99.86	10.07	14.71
8.26	50.50	65.11	100.34	2.51	0.39
19.64	62.23	58.46	98.42	6.58	18.48

表4-8 续表 3

单位：%

项　目	Item	# 民营工业 资产负债率 Assets Liability Ratio
化学原料和化学制品制造业	Raw Chemical Materials and Chemical Products	50.94
医药制造业	Medical and Pharmaceutical Products	50.17
化学纤维制造业	Chemical Fiber Manufacturing	65.14
橡胶和塑料制品业	Rubber and Plastic Products	52.68
非金属矿物制品业	Nonmetal Mineral Products	64.99
黑色金属冶炼和压延加工业	Smelting and Pressing of Ferrous Metals	54.31
有色金属冶炼和压延加工业	Smelting and Pressing of Nonferrous Metals	58.16
金属制品业	Metal Products	53.79
通用设备制造业	General Equipment Manufacture	49.83
专用设备制造业	Special Purposes Equipment Manufacturing	55.37
汽车制造业	Automobile Manufacturing	60.56
铁路、船舶、航空航天和其他运输设备制造业	Railway, Ship, Aerospace and Other Transportation Equipment Manufacturing	54.37
电气机械和器材制造业	Electric Equipment and Machinery Manufacturing	55.06
计算机、通信和其他电子设备制造业	Computer Telecommunications and Other Electronic Equipment Manufacture	53.58
仪器仪表制造业	Instruments, Meters Machinery	48.92
其他制造业	Other Products Manufacture	60.27
废弃资源综合利用业	Comprehensive Utilization of Waste Resources	79.00
金属制品、机械和设备修理业	Metal Products, Machinery and Equipment Repair	75.43
电力、热力生产和供应业	Manufacture and Supply of Electricity and Thermal Power	70.48
燃气生产和供应业	Manufacture and Supply of Gas	57.94
水的生产和供应业	Manufacture and Supply of Water	71.17

Continued 3

(%)

Private and Individual		# 外商和港澳台商 Enterprises with Investment from Foreign ,Hong Kong,Macao and Taiwan				
固定资产净值率 New Value Added in Fixed Asset	产销率 Proportion of Products Sold	总资产贡献率 Total Assets Contribution Ratio	成本费用利润率 Rate Between Profit and Cost	资产负债率 Assets Liability Ratio	固定资产净值率 New Value Added in Fixed Asset	产销率 Proportion of Products Sold
63.62	99.38	12.94	9.42	40.44	49.25	100.72
54.17	94.76	13.52	9.69	41.16	56.85	107.20
47.43	98.96	1.28	-0.68	65.14	50.41	97.46
61.79	98.34	10.07	7.84	37.40	44.92	99.75
48.67	99.00	10.02	8.06	42.17	42.24	100.13
38.52	102.38	3.88	0.65	55.21	39.83	98.47
56.81	98.83	7.38	4.12	45.53	44.08	106.92
56.83	99.53	11.85	8.30	40.18	47.21	99.42
58.84	98.84	13.95	10.61	46.49	45.89	98.93
61.07	98.27	9.95	10.16	45.01	51.45	98.13
63.23	101.03	10.34	7.36	49.33	54.46	99.27
68.76	95.62	15.19	13.26	48.07	52.24	97.96
61.20	99.50	9.31	6.87	46.92	44.88	100.58
66.22	98.34	5.95	3.10	56.02	41.32	99.22
70.63	94.98	15.04	11.89	39.74	47.84	99.20
62.03	98.29	4.08	-2.13	81.67	37.32	98.82
57.48	87.00	12.52	7.71	28.19	39.51	101.97
62.34	100.00	10.00	1.66	18.94	66.01	93.32
60.51	100.14	10.02	11.77	54.43	48.29	99.56
50.78	101.67	7.98	11.81	52.85	72.36	100.00
47.82	99.80	7.09	32.35	56.23	62.96	95.60

表4-9 分地区规模以上工业企业主要经济指标 (2018年)

单位：万元

项　目	Item	企业单位数(个) Number of Enterprises (unit)	# 亏损企业 Loss Making Enterprises	主营业务收入 Major Business Revenue	资产总计 Total Assets
全　市	**Whole Municipality**	**10 393**	**1 783**	**341 084 012**	**322 234 396**
按地区分	**Grouped by Region**				
市　区	Urban Area	4 721	702	144 881 512	139 740 400
常　熟	Changshu	1 373	222	38 261 224	42 451 245
张家港	Zhangjiagang	1 197	276	49 875 500	51 267 451
昆　山	Kunshan	2 100	385	84 939 122	66 660 476
太　仓	Taicang	1 002	198	23 126 653	22 114 824
在市区中	**In Urban Area**				
姑苏区	Gusu District	13	1	420 078	782 173
吴中区	Wuzhong District	903	134	15 138 940	16 894 050
相城区	Xiangcheng District	742	99	12 780 266	12 499 740
高新区、虎丘区	New Hi-tech Zone & Huqiu District	743	116	32 265 077	26 572 160
工业园区	Industrial Park	794	127	47 275 014	45 556 869
吴江区	Wujiang District	1 526	225	37 002 138	37 435 407

MAIN ECONOMIC INDICATORS OF INDUSTRIAL ENTERPRISES ABOVE DESIGNATED SIZE BY REGION (2018)

(10 000 yuan)

负债合计 Total Liabilities	所有者权益合计 Creditors Equity	# 实收资本 Total Capital Hold	利税总额 Total taxes and Profits	利润总额 Total Profits	亏损企业亏损总额 Total Deficit of Loss-Making Enterprises
169 230 901	**153 003 419**	**81 041 869**	**28 215 138**	**20 940 474**	**2 192 571**
71 095 790	68 644 577	35 910 412	12 504 298	9 483 164	846 988
23 401 753	19 049 480	13 083 947	3 207 868	2 203 582	438 045
28 261 040	23 006 404	9 001 646	5 058 535	3 786 307	189 348
34 808 025	31 852 433	17 024 213	5 219 303	3 894 394	546 070
11 664 293	10 450 524	6 021 651	2 225 134	1 573 028	172 121
266 252	515 921	133 693	58 356	47 436	755
8 670 405	8 223 639	3 987 110	1 364 267	950 598	101 746
6 817 823	5 681 911	3 109 329	973 759	634 401	63 570
13 322 250	13 249 904	7 222 890	2 242 593	1 775 706	154 281
20 973 739	24 583 124	12 364 675	4 874 166	3 865 416	364 341
21 045 321	16 390 077	9 092 715	2 991 158	2 209 607	162 295

表4-10

分地区、分经济类型规模以上工业企业主要经济效益指标（2018年）

单位：%

项　　目	Item	经济效益综合指数 Comprehensive Index on Economic Return	总资产贡献率 Ratio of Total Assets to Industrial Output Value
总　　计	**Total**	**262.64**	**9.38**
按地区分	**Grouped by Region**		
市　区	Urban Area	256.77	9.49
常　熟	Changshu	271.35	8.29
张家港	Zhangjiagang	359.19	10.90
昆　山	Kunshan	228.67	8.17
太　仓	Taicang	284.69	10.87
在市区中	**In Urban Area**		
姑苏区	Gusu District	331.36	7.72
吴中区	Wuzhong District	217.76	8.54
相城区	Xiangcheng District	212.10	8.53
高新区、虎丘区	New Hi-tech Zone & Huqiu District	291.13	8.63
工业园区	Industrial Park	320.24	11.22
吴江区	Wujiang District	213.97	8.78
按经济类型分	**Grouped by Ownership**		
国有经济	State-owned	395.93	7.59
民营经济	Private and Individual	248.02	9.69
外商及港澳台经济	Enterprises with Investment from Foreign ,Hong Kong,Macao and Taiwan	268.96	9.20

MAIN INDICATORS OF ECONOMIC BENEFIT OF INDUSTRIAL ENTERPRISES ABOVE DESIGNATED SIZE BY REGION AND OWNERSHIP (2018)

(%)

成本费用利润率 Rate Between Profit and Cost	资产负债率 Assets Liability Ratio	固定资产净值率 New Value Added in Fixed Asset	产销率 Proportion of Products Sold	资本保值增值率 Rate of the Preserved Value and Increased Value of Capital	流动资产周转次数(次) Number of Times of Turnover of Circulating Fund (time)
6.34	**52.52**	**48.79**	**99.48**	**106.50**	**1.73**
6.86	50.88	47.64	99.22	105.63	1.63
5.88	55.13	52.48	98.54	106.87	1.60
7.62	55.12	46.79	101.04	108.89	1.89
4.73	52.22	49.59	99.61	107.88	1.88
7.02	52.74	50.90	99.16	102.52	1.87
11.40	34.04	60.94	100.01	104.97	1.86
6.58	51.32	50.57	98.75	109.65	1.35
5.06	54.54	50.99	99.53	105.50	1.62
5.78	50.14	45.03	99.17	107.60	1.78
8.72	46.04	43.54	99.47	102.69	1.64
6.17	56.22	52.76	99.01	106.72	1.65
6.56	55.51	50.80	98.43	115.20	1.77
6.96	56.42	53.71	99.50	110.19	1.59
5.94	49.46	45.89	99.49	103.85	1.83

表4-11

规模以上工业主要产品产量 (2018年)

产品名称		Name of Products		全 市 Whole Municipality
饲 料	(吨)	Fodder	(ton)	2 880 843
精制食用植物油		Refined Edible Vegetable Oil		1 707 899
乳制品		Dairy Products		177 988
大 米		Rice		49 607
饮料酒	(千升)	Drinks	(1 000 liters)	455 754
纱	(吨)	Yarn	(ton)	554 992
布	(万米)	Cloth	(10 000 meters)	69 221
绒线（毛线）	(吨)	Knitting Wool	(ton)	52 519
毛机织物（呢绒）	(万米)	Wool Fabrics	(10 000 meters)	6 671
印染布		Printing and Dyeing Cloth		137 939
蚕丝及交织机织物(含蚕丝≥50%)		Silk and Woven Fabrics (Including Silk ≥ 50%)		478
服 装	(万件)	Garment	(10 000 pieces)	44 447
皮革鞋靴	(万双)	Leather Footwear	(10 000 pairs)	762
人造板	(立方米)	Artificial Board	(cu.m)	208 919
家 具	(件)	Furniture	(piece)	5 607 132
机制纸及纸板（外购原纸加工除外）	(吨)	Machine Made Paper	(ton)	5 848 604
焦 炭	(万吨)	Coke	(10 000 tons)	494
硫酸（折100%）	(吨)	Sulfuric Acid (100%)	(ton)	1 896 459
纯碱（碳酸钠）		Soda Ash		1 334 893
合成氨(无水氨)		Synthetic Ammonia		832 117
农用氮、磷、钾化学肥料总计(折纯)		Agricultural Chemical Fertilizers (Pure)		517 290
化学农药原药(折有效成分100%)		Chemicals and Pesticides (Active Ingredient 100% Discount)		9 386
涂 料		Paint		741 587
初级形态的塑料		Primary form of Plastic		899 009

MAJOR PRODUCTS OUTPUT OF INDUSTRIAL ENTERPRISES ABOVE DESIGNATED SIZE (2018)

市 区 Urban Area	# 吴江区 Wujiang District	常 熟 Changshu	张家港 Zhangjiagang	昆 山 Kunshan	太 仓 Taicang
45 982	–	13 154	2 821 708	–	–
43 803	43 803	57 650	1 597 927	8 519	–
150 467	–	–	27 521	–	–
–	–	–	49 607	–	–
214 041	–	–	55 748	185 964	–
93 577	88 194	34 898	381 730	1 461	43 327
37 733	35 423	1 171	19 200	4 493	6 624
–	–	1 760	50 759	–	–
–	–	225	6 447	–	–
39 496	18 581	71 780	26 337	326	–
478	478	–	–	–	–
21 164	5 423	3 743	14 211	4 055	1 274
762	762	–	–	–	–
108 793	–	80 458	9 743	9 925	–
1 685 301	1 169 297	129 725	–	3 569 037	223 069
1 695 932	–	1 256 052	78 060	26 064	2 792 496
–	–	–	494	–	–
–	–	258 291	1 619 643	18 525	–
–	–	–	627 980	706 913	–
–	–	–	529 807	302 310	–
–	–	–	321 937	195 353	–
	–	–	9 386	–	–
311 920	32 150	–	205 582	216 580	7 506
339 712	85 278	75 900	272 259	70 140	140 998

表4-11 续表 1

产品名称		Name of Products		全 市 Whole Municipality
化学药品原药	(吨)	Original Drug Chemicals (Chemical Medicine)	(ton)	9 461
化学纤维		Chemical Fiber		6 778 485
橡胶轮胎外胎	(条)	Tires	(piece)	64 515 527
塑料制品	(吨)	Plastic Products	(ton)	1 460 528
水　泥		Cement		10 040 539
平板玻璃	(重量箱)	Plate Glass	(wt.cases)	15 020 572
生　铁	(吨)	Pig Iron	(ton)	26 601 621
粗　钢		Raw Steel		37 432 349
钢　材		Rolled Steel		45 926 591
金属切削机床	(台)	Metal-cutting Machines	(unit)	10 096
# 数控金属切削机床		CNC Metal Cutting Machine		3 739
阀　门	(吨)	Valves	(ton)	186 201
滚动轴承	(万套)	Rolling Bearing	(10 000 sets)	126 549
模　具	(套)	Mould	(set)	877 045
汽　车	(辆)	Trucks	(coach)	148 028
改装汽车		Refit Trucks		3 066
两轮脚踏自行车		Two-wheel Pedal Bicycles		3 851 394
交流电动机	(千瓦)	Alternating Current Motor	(kw)	8 819 487
变压器	(千伏安)	Transformer	(kva)	19 078 050
通信及电子网络用电缆	(对千米)	Communication Cables	(pair km)	3 999 506
电力电缆	(千米)	Electric Power Cables	(km)	1 007 050
光　缆	(芯千米)	Optic Fiber	(core kilometer)	44 662 609
锂离子电池	(只)	Lithium-Ion Batteries	(piece)	390 673 926
家用电冰箱(家用冷冻冷藏箱)	(台)	Household Refrigerator (Household Refrigerated Freezers)	(unit)	832 689
家用冷柜(家用冷冻箱)		Household Refrigerators (Household Freezers)		461 054

Continued 1

市　区 Urban Area	# 吴江区 Wujiang District	常　熟 Changshu	张家港 Zhangjiagang	昆　山 Kunshan	太　仓 Taicang
4 320	102	662	512	1 636	2 331
4 640 237	4 264 665	282 997	601 148	–	1 254 103
2 687 148	–	12 772 945	4 366 266	44 689 168	–
639 489	85 811	2 150	587 909	174 092	56 888
3 517 364	3 125 237	–	2 808 769	1 649 319	2 065 087
4 513 854	–	–	–	10 506 718	–
394 301	–	–	26 207 320	–	–
704 967	–	3 001 700	33 725 682	–	–
956 913	203 405	5 925 226	38 950 681	93 771	–
7 811	1 641	706	324	1 255	–
2 207	–	706	–	826	–
176 612	1 347	–	–	9 589	–
32 682	–	6 900	8 711	15 449	62 807
25 813	259	800 901	2 193	47 943	195
11 360	–	136 668	–	–	–
518	–	1 445	109	994	–
–	–	–	99 315	2 921 684	830 395
3 893 516	2 399 443	–	–	–	4 925 971
19 078 050	15 021 002	–	–	–	–
2 524 342	2 524 342	6 553	1 461 839	6 772	–
741 628	151 859	182 666	20 018	62 738	–
35 966 148	35 966 148	7 976 994	–	719 467	–
132 407 050	38 904 502	35 651 115	152 451 147	70 164 614	–
789 392	–	43 297	–	–	–
–	–	461 054	–	–	–

表4-11 续表 2

产品名称		Name of Products		全 市 Whole Municipality
房间空气调节器	(台)	Room Air Conditioner	(unit)	4 224 206
家用电风扇		Household Electric Fan		342 310
家用吸排油烟机		Household Smoke Absorbers		142 681
家用洗衣机		Household Washing Machines		2 177 873
家用吸尘器		Household Dust Catcher		54 191 400
家用燃气灶具		Household Gas Utensile		143 063
家用燃气热水器		Household Water Heater		168 516
移动通信手持机(手机)		Mobile Phone		42 840 254
微型计算机设备		Micro-Computer Equipment		61 057 736
# 笔记本计算机		Laptop Computer		40 469 053
显示器		Monitors		47 962 617
# 平板显示器		Flat Panel Displays		28 391 815
集成电路	(万块)	Integrated Circuit	(10 000 pieces)	222 564
光电子器件	(万只、片、套)	Optoelectronic Devices	(10 000 pieces,sets)	2 164 495
# 发光二极管(LED管)	(万只)	Light Emitting Diode (LED)	(10 000 units)	1 780 774
电子元件		Electronic Components		139 869 886
印制电路板	(平方米)	Printed Circuit Board	(sq.m)	115 724 114
彩色电视机	(台)	Color TV Sets	(unit)	11 937 481
# 液晶(LCD)电视机		Liquid Crystal (LCD) TV Sets		11 937 481
工业自动调节仪表与控制系统	(台、套)	Industrial Automatically-Adjusting Instrumentation and Control System	(unit,set)	5 240 442
照相机	(台)	Cameras	(unit)	9 250 775
# 数码照相机		Digital Camera		3 593 079
发电量	(亿千瓦时)	Power Generation	(100 million kwh)	1 089. 88

Continued 2

市 区 Urban Area	# 吴江区 Wujiang District	常 熟 Changshu	张家港 Zhangjiagang	昆 山 Kunshan	太 仓 Taicang
4 224 206	–	–	–	–	–
31 190	–	–	–	311 120	–
–	–	–	–	142 681	–
2 177 873	–	–	–	–	–
54 191 400	1 180 405	–	–	–	–
–	–	–	–	143 063	–
–	–	–	–	168 516	–
3 252 525	1 798 003	–	–	39 587 729	–
16 087 887	–	–	–	44 969 849	–
2 614 140	–	–	–	37 854 913	–
47 962 617	6 747 864	–	–	–	–
28 391 815	6 592 990	–	–	–	–
221 181	85 961	–	–	1 383	–
2 133 185	1 839 054	4 976	1 683	24 651	–
1 780 774	1 780 774	–	–	–	–
138 326 423	903 841	1 292 901	60	239 352	11 150
97 412 242	–	826 300	–	17 485 572	–
8 735 780	4 626 706	–	–	3 201 701	–
8 735 780	4 626 706	–	–	3 201 701	–
5 236 347	274 951	–	3 733	362	–
7 104 141	–	–	–	2 146 634	–
1 446 445	–	–	–	2 146 634	–
261. 07	55. 39	307. 68	247. 42	15. 73	257. 97

表4-12

全市工业主营业务收入百强企业（2018年）
TOP 100 ENTERPRISES OF THE MAJOR BUSINESS REVENUE (2018)

序　号 No.	企业名称 Name of Enterprises	所在地区 Location	序　号 No.	企业名称 Name of Enterprises	所在地区 Location
1	江苏沙钢集团有限公司	张家港	26	南亚电子材料（昆山）有限公司	昆　山
2	世硕电子（昆山）有限公司	昆　山	27	昆山联滔电子有限公司	昆　山
3	仁宝信息技术（昆山）有限公司	昆　山	28	金红叶纸业集团有限公司	工业园区
4	名硕电脑（苏州）有限公司	高新区、虎丘区	29	苏州三星电子液晶显示科技有限公司	工业园区
5	江苏永钢集团有限公司	张家港	30	中达电子（江苏）有限公司	吴江区
6	仁宝资讯工业（昆山）有限公司	昆　山	31	牧田（昆山）有限公司	昆　山
7	纬新资通（昆山）有限公司	昆　山	32	伟创力电子技术（苏州）有限公司	工业园区
8	达富电脑（常熟）有限公司	常　熟	33	瑞仪光电（苏州）有限公司	吴江区
9	博世汽车部件（苏州）有限公司	工业园区	34	立讯电子科技（昆山）有限公司	昆　山
10	通力电梯有限公司	昆　山	35	昆山丘钛微电子科技有限公司	昆　山
11	常熟市龙腾特种钢有限公司	常　熟	36	高创（苏州）电子有限公司	吴江区
12	苏州佳世达电通有限公司	高新区、虎丘区	37	太仓东华能源燃气有限公司	太　仓
13	张家港浦项不锈钢有限公司	张家港	38	张家港万达薄板有限公司	张家港
14	纬创资通（昆山）有限公司	昆　山	39	常熟阿特斯阳光电力科技有限公司	常　熟
15	奇瑞捷豹路虎汽车有限公司	常　熟	40	江苏骏马集团有限责任公司	张家港
16	中粮东海粮油工业（张家港）有限公司	张家港	41	江苏亨通精工金属材料有限公司	吴江区
17	舍弗勒（中国）有限公司	太　仓	42	苏州三星电子有限公司	工业园区
18	江苏恒力化纤股份有限公司	吴江区	43	苏州三星电子电脑有限公司	工业园区
19	三一重机有限公司	昆　山	44	昆山德力铜业有限公司	昆　山
20	苏州三星显示有限公司	工业园区	45	东华能源（张家港）新材料有限公司	张家港
21	江苏国望高科纤维有限公司	吴江区	46	苏州盛虹纤维有限公司	吴江区
22	长春化工（江苏）有限公司	常　熟	47	康宝莱（中国）保健品有限公司	工业园区
23	纬视晶光电（昆山）有限公司	昆　山	48	烨辉（中国）科技材料有限公司	常　熟
24	张家港联合铜业有限公司	张家港	49	江苏亨通光电股份有限公司	吴江区
25	玖龙纸业（太仓）有限公司	太　仓	50	微盟电子（昆山）有限公司	昆　山

表4-12 续表 Continued

序 号 No.	企业名称 Name of Enterprises	所在地区 Location	序 号 No.	企业名称 Name of Enterprises	所在地区 Location
51	张家港康得新光电材料有限公司	张家港	76	安波福电子（苏州）有限公司	工业园区
52	苏州腾晖光伏技术有限公司	常 熟	77	金龙联合汽车工业（苏州）有限公司	工业园区
53	佳能（苏州）有限公司	高新区、虎丘区	78	中磊电子（苏州）有限公司	工业园区
54	富士康（昆山）电脑接插件有限公司	昆 山	79	三菱电机汽车部件（中国）有限公司	常 熟
55	益江（张家港）粮油工业有限公司	张家港	80	芬欧汇川(中国)有限公司	常 熟
56	三星电子（苏州）半导体有限公司	工业园区	81	牧田（中国）有限公司	昆 山
57	苏州维信电子有限公司	吴中区	82	伟创力电脑(苏州)有限公司	吴中区
58	江苏亨通线缆科技有限公司	吴江区	83	淳华科技（昆山）有限公司	昆 山
59	苏州长城开发科技有限公司	工业园区	84	苏州旭创科技有限公司	工业园区
60	苏州东山精密制造股份有限公司	吴中区	85	天弘（苏州）科技有限公司	工业园区
61	中达电子零组件（吴江）有限公司	吴江区	86	苏州佳世达电子有限公司	高新区、虎丘区
62	优美科汽车催化剂（苏州）有限公司	工业园区	87	威刚科技（苏州）有限公司	工业园区
63	东吴黄金集团有限公司	工业园区	88	苏州三星电子家电有限公司	工业园区
64	观致汽车有限公司	常 熟	89	乐金电子（昆山）有限公司	昆 山
65	江苏理文造纸有限公司	常 熟	90	苏州璨宇光学有限公司	工业园区
66	亚旭电子科技（江苏）有限公司	吴江区	91	江苏亨通电力电缆有限公司	吴江区
67	利乐包装（昆山）有限公司	昆 山	92	澳洋集团有限公司	张家港
68	张家港沙洲电力有限公司	张家港	93	苏州松下半导体有限公司	高新区、虎丘区
69	江苏宝洁有限公司	太 仓	94	苏州佳世达光电有限公司	高新区、虎丘区
70	江苏常熟发电有限公司	常 熟	95	浦项（苏州）汽车配件制造有限公司	昆 山
71	苏州汇川技术有限公司	吴中区	96	仁宝网路资讯（昆山）有限公司	昆 山
72	罗技科技（苏州）有限公司	高新区、虎丘区	97	科沃斯机器人股份有限公司	吴中区
73	康硕电子（苏州）有限公司	高新区、虎丘区	98	上海华电电力发展有限公司望亭发电分公司	相城区
74	苏州欧菲光科技有限公司	相城区	99	启新通讯（昆山）有限公司	昆 山
75	正新橡胶（中国）有限公司	昆 山	100	仁宝视讯电子（昆山）有限公司	昆 山

表4-13

全市工业利税总额百强企业 (2018年)
TOP 100 ENTERPRISES OF THE TOTAL TAXES AND PROFITS (2018)

序号 No.	企业名称 Name of Enterprises	所在地区 Location	序号 No.	企业名称 Name of Enterprises	所在地区 Location
1	江苏沙钢集团有限公司	张家港	26	卫材（中国）药业有限公司	工业园区
2	江苏永钢集团有限公司	张家港	27	张家港沙洲电力有限公司	张家港
3	博世汽车部件（苏州）有限公司	工业园区	28	天齐锂业（江苏）有限公司	张家港
4	通力电梯有限公司	昆　山	29	惠氏制药有限公司	吴中区
5	奇瑞捷豹路虎汽车有限公司	常　熟	30	东华能源（张家港）新材料有限公司	张家港
6	江苏宝洁有限公司	太　仓	31	艾默生环境优化技术（苏州）有限公司	工业园区
7	张家港康得新光电材料有限公司	张家港	32	大金空调（苏州）有限公司	工业园区
8	玖龙纸业（太仓）有限公司	太　仓	33	苏州盛虹纤维有限公司	吴江区
9	江苏恒力化纤股份有限公司	吴江区	34	苏州旭创科技有限公司	工业园区
10	江苏理文造纸有限公司	常　熟	35	苏州汇川技术有限公司	吴中区
11	常熟市龙腾特种钢有限公司	常　熟	36	江苏常熟发电有限公司	常　熟
12	舍弗勒（中国）有限公司	太　仓	37	常熟三爱富中昊化工新材料有限公司	常　熟
13	南亚电子材料（昆山）有限公司	昆　山	38	索特传动设备有限公司	常　熟
14	长春化工（江苏）有限公司	常　熟	39	中粮东海粮油工业（张家港）有限公司	张家港
15	江苏亨通光导新材料有限公司	吴江区	40	苏州三星显示有限公司	工业园区
16	克诺尔车辆设备（苏州）有限公司	高新区、虎丘区	41	正新橡胶（中国）有限公司	昆　山
17	三一重机有限公司	昆　山	42	华润电力（常熟）有限公司	常　熟
18	国巨电子（中国）有限公司	高新区、虎丘区	43	盛虹集团有限公司	吴江区
19	昆山联滔电子有限公司	昆　山	44	沪士电子股份有限公司	昆　山
20	江苏国望高科纤维有限公司	吴江区	45	安波福电子（苏州）有限公司	工业园区
21	三星电子（苏州）半导体有限公司	工业园区	46	和舰芯片制造（苏州）股份有限公司	工业园区
22	利乐包装（昆山）有限公司	昆　山	47	立讯电子科技（昆山）有限公司	昆　山
23	牧田（昆山）有限公司	昆　山	48	名硕电脑（苏州）有限公司	高新区、虎丘区
24	康宝莱（中国）保健品有限公司	工业园区	49	霍尼韦尔特性材料和技术(中国)有限公司	张家港
25	常熟开关制造有限公司(原常熟开关厂)	常　熟	50	通鼎互联信息股份有限公司	吴江区

表4-13 续表 Continued

序 号 No.	企业名称 Name of Enterprises	所在地区 Location	序 号 No.	企业名称 Name of Enterprises	所在地区 Location
51	3M材料技术（苏州）有限公司	工业园区	76	昆山龙腾光电有限公司	昆 山
52	莱克电气股份有限公司	高新区、虎丘区	77	碧辟（中国）工业油品有限公司	太 仓
53	苏州西门子电器有限公司	高新区、虎丘区	78	日立汽车系统（苏州）有限公司	工业园区
54	苏州富强科技有限公司	高新区、虎丘区	79	科沃斯机器人股份有限公司	吴中区
55	迈锐精密科技（苏州）有限公司	工业园区	80	三菱电机汽车部件（中国）有限公司	常 熟
56	苏州东瑞制药有限公司	吴中区	81	三菱电机自动化机器制造(常熟)有限公司	常 熟
57	埃克森美孚（太仓）石油有限公司	太 仓	82	康力电梯股份有限公司	吴江区
58	富翔精密工业（昆山）有限公司	昆 山	83	苏州华科电子有限公司	工业园区
59	金华盛纸业（苏州工业园区）有限公司	工业园区	84	中达电子零组件（吴江）有限公司	吴江区
60	飞旭电子（苏州）有限公司	吴江区	85	双狮（张家港）精细化工有限公司	张家港
61	耐世特汽车系统（苏州）有限公司	工业园区	86	贝克曼库尔实验系统（苏州）有限公司	工业园区
62	SEW-传动设备（苏州）有限公司	工业园区	87	华能太仓发电有限责任公司	太 仓
63	苏州明纬科技有限公司	相城区	88	太仓港协鑫发电有限公司	太 仓
64	江苏理文化工有限公司	常 熟	89	卡特彼勒（苏州）有限公司	工业园区
65	金红叶纸业集团有限公司	工业园区	90	牧田（中国）有限公司	昆 山
66	江苏亨通光电股份有限公司	吴江区	91	康美包（苏州）有限公司	工业园区
67	苏州碧迪医疗器械有限公司	工业园区	92	康普通讯技术（中国）有限公司	工业园区
68	丰田汽车（常熟）零部件有限公司	常 熟	93	台光电子材料（昆山）有限公司	昆 山
69	江苏骏马集团有限责任公司	张家港	94	苏州三星电子液晶显示科技有限公司	工业园区
70	常熟市汽车饰件股份有限公司	常 熟	95	加通汽车内饰（常熟）有限公司	常 熟
71	膳魔师（中国）家庭制品有限公司	昆 山	96	昆山康龙电子科技有限公司	昆 山
72	苏州绿叶日用品有限公司	高新区、虎丘区	97	博格华纳汽车零部件（江苏）有限公司	太 仓
73	莱顿汽车部件（苏州）有限公司	工业园区	98	中达电子（江苏）有限公司	吴江区
74	必成玻璃纤维（昆山）有限公司	昆 山	99	苏州三星电子电脑有限公司	工业园区
75	富士和机械工业（昆山）有限公司	昆 山	100	马斯特模具（昆山）有限公司	昆 山

表4-14

全市工业利润总额百强企业（2018年）
TOP 100 ENTERPRISES OF THE TOTAL PROFITS (2018)

序 号 No.	企业名称 Name of Enterprises	所在地区 Location	序 号 No.	企业名称 Name of Enterprises	所在地区 Location
1	江苏沙钢集团有限公司	张家港	26	常熟开关制造有限公司（原常熟开关厂）	常 熟
2	江苏永钢集团有限公司	张家港	27	苏州旭创科技有限公司	工业园区
3	博世汽车部件（苏州）有限公司	工业园区	28	常熟三爱富中昊化工新材料有限公司	常 熟
4	通力电梯有限公司	昆 山	29	艾默生环境优化技术（苏州）有限公司	工业园区
5	江苏宝洁有限公司	太 仓	30	苏州盛虹纤维有限公司	吴江区
6	张家港康得新光电材料有限公司	张家港	31	三星电子（苏州）半导体有限公司	工业园区
7	奇瑞捷豹路虎汽车有限公司	常 熟	32	苏州三星显示有限公司	工业园区
8	江苏恒力化纤股份有限公司	吴江区	33	中粮东海粮油工业（张家港）有限公司	张家港
9	玖龙纸业（太仓）有限公司	太 仓	34	张家港沙洲电力有限公司	张家港
10	舍弗勒（中国）有限公司	太 仓	35	和舰芯片制造（苏州）股份有限公司	工业园区
11	江苏理文造纸有限公司	常 熟	36	立讯电子科技（昆山）有限公司	昆 山
12	江苏亨通光导新材料有限公司	吴江区	37	霍尼韦尔特性材料和技术（中国）有限公司	张家港
13	南亚电子材料（昆山）有限公司	昆 山	38	江苏亨通光电股份有限公司	吴江区
14	长春化工（江苏）有限公司	常 熟	39	沪士电子股份有限公司	昆 山
15	三一重机有限公司	昆 山	40	东华能源（张家港）新材料有限公司	张家港
16	国巨电子（中国）有限公司	高新区、虎丘区	41	名硕电脑（苏州）有限公司	高新区、虎丘区
17	昆山联滔电子有限公司	昆 山	42	惠氏制药有限公司	吴中区
18	常熟市龙腾特种钢有限公司	常 熟	43	苏州汇川技术有限公司	吴中区
19	克诺尔车辆设备（苏州）有限公司	高新区、虎丘区	44	莱克电气股份有限公司	高新区、虎丘区
20	江苏国望高科纤维有限公司	吴江区	45	索特传动设备有限公司	常 熟
21	牧田（昆山）有限公司	昆 山	46	苏州明纬科技有限公司	相城区
22	康宝莱（中国）保健品有限公司	工业园区	47	安波福电子（苏州）有限公司	工业园区
23	利乐包装（昆山）有限公司	昆 山	48	卫材（中国）药业有限公司	工业园区
24	大金空调（苏州）有限公司	工业园区	49	耐世特汽车系统（苏州）有限公司	工业园区
25	天齐锂业（江苏）有限公司	张家港	50	迈锐精密科技（苏州）有限公司	工业园区

表4-14 续表 Continued

序 号 No.	企业名称 Name of Enterprises	所在地区 Location	序 号 No.	企业名称 Name of Enterprises	所在地区 Location
51	3M材料技术（苏州）有限公司	工业园区	76	中达电子零组件（吴江）有限公司	吴江区
52	飞旭电子（苏州）有限公司	吴江区	77	牧田（中国）有限公司	昆 山
53	苏州西门子电器有限公司	高新区、虎丘区	78	三菱电机自动化机器制造（常熟）有限公司	常 熟
54	苏州富强科技有限公司	高新区、虎丘区	79	日立汽车系统（苏州）有限公司	工业园区
55	正新橡胶（中国）有限公司	昆 山	80	康力电梯股份有限公司	吴江区
56	华润电力（常熟）有限公司	常 熟	81	江苏常熟发电有限公司	常 熟
57	通鼎互联信息股份有限公司	吴江区	82	台光电子材料（昆山）有限公司	昆 山
58	富翔精密工业（昆山）有限公司	昆 山	83	友达光电（苏州）有限公司	工业园区
59	金华盛纸业（苏州工业园区）有限公司	工业园区	84	贝克曼库尔实验系统（苏州）有限公司	工业园区
60	膳魔师（中国）家庭制品有限公司	昆 山	85	常熟阿特斯阳光电力科技有限公司	常 熟
61	江苏理文化工有限公司	常 熟	86	必成玻璃纤维（昆山）有限公司	昆 山
62	SEW-传动设备（苏州）有限公司	工业园区	87	加通汽车内饰（常熟）有限公司	常 熟
63	昆山龙腾光电有限公司	昆 山	88	马斯特模具（昆山）有限公司	昆 山
64	富士和机械工业（昆山）有限公司	昆 山	89	埃克森美孚（太仓）石油有限公司	太 仓
65	苏州华科电子有限公司	工业园区	90	佳能（苏州）有限公司	高新区、虎丘区
66	丰田汽车（常熟）零部件有限公司	常 熟	91	苏州绿叶日用品有限公司	高新区、虎丘区
67	苏州碧迪医疗器械有限公司	工业园区	92	苏州纽威阀门股份有限公司	高新区、虎丘区
68	科沃斯机器人股份有限公司	吴中区	93	苏州三星电子电脑有限公司	工业园区
69	常熟市汽车饰件股份有限公司	常 熟	94	禧玛诺（昆山）自行车零件有限公司	昆 山
70	苏州东瑞制药有限公司	吴中区	95	苏州安洁科技股份有限公司	吴中区
71	莱顿汽车部件（苏州）有限公司	工业园区	96	金红叶纸业集团有限公司	工业园区
72	卡特彼勒（苏州）有限公司	工业园区	97	旺诠科技（昆山）有限公司	昆 山
73	康普通讯技术（中国）有限公司	工业园区	98	双狮（张家港）精细化工有限公司	张家港
74	盛虹集团有限公司	吴江区	99	阿科玛（常熟）氟化工有限公司	常 熟
75	三菱电机汽车部件（中国）有限公司	常 熟	100	苏州市佳禾食品工业有限公司	吴江区

表4-15

全市工业资产总计百强企业（2018年）
TOP 100 ENTERPRISES OF THE TOTAL ASSETS (2018)

序 号 No.	企业名称 Name of Enterprises	所在地区 Location	序 号 No.	企业名称 Name of Enterprises	所在地区 Location
1	江苏沙钢集团有限公司	张家港	26	金华盛纸业（苏州工业园区）有限公司	工业园区
2	江苏永钢集团有限公司	张家港	27	苏州三星电子液晶显示科技有限公司	工业园区
3	世硕电子（昆山）有限公司	昆　山	28	长春化工（江苏）有限公司	常　熟
4	达富电脑（常熟）有限公司	常　熟	29	东华能源股份有限公司	张家港
5	金红叶纸业集团有限公司	工业园区	30	玖龙纸业（太仓）有限公司	太　仓
6	名硕电脑（苏州）有限公司	高新区、虎丘区	31	仁宝信息技术（昆山）有限公司	昆　山
7	江苏亨通光电股份有限公司	吴江区	32	舍弗勒（中国）有限公司	太　仓
8	张家港康得新光电材料有限公司	张家港	33	昆山国显光电有限公司	昆　山
9	苏州东山精密制造股份有限公司	吴中区	34	纬新资通（昆山）有限公司	昆　山
10	三一重机有限公司	昆　山	35	江苏常熟发电有限公司	常　熟
11	奇瑞捷豹路虎汽车有限公司	常　熟	36	通鼎互联信息股份有限公司	吴江区
12	观致汽车有限公司	常　熟	37	江苏骏马集团有限责任公司	张家港
13	通力电梯有限公司	昆　山	38	昆山联滔电子有限公司	昆　山
14	江苏恒力化纤股份有限公司	吴江区	39	常熟阿特斯阳光电力科技有限公司	常　熟
15	张家港沙洲电力有限公司	张家港	40	东华能源（张家港）新材料有限公司	张家港
16	博世汽车部件（苏州）有限公司	工业园区	41	纬创资通（昆山）有限公司	昆　山
17	苏州腾晖光伏技术有限公司	常　熟	42	陶氏硅氧烷（张家港）有限公司	张家港
18	南亚电子材料（昆山）有限公司	昆　山	43	伟创力电子技术（苏州）有限公司	工业园区
19	江苏中利集团股份有限公司	常　熟	44	苏州安洁科技股份有限公司	吴中区
20	苏州胜利精密制造科技股份有限公司	高新区、虎丘区	45	天顺风能（苏州）股份有限公司	太　仓
21	太仓港协鑫发电有限公司	太　仓	46	苏州佳世达电通有限公司	高新区、虎丘区
22	友达光电(昆山)有限公司	昆　山	47	波司登羽绒服装有限公司	常　熟
23	江苏国望高科纤维有限公司	吴江区	48	纬视晶光电（昆山）有限公司	昆　山
24	常熟市龙腾特种钢有限公司	常　熟	49	昆山龙腾光电有限公司	昆　山
25	澳洋集团有限公司	张家港	50	立讯电子科技（昆山）有限公司	昆　山

表4-15 续表 Continued

序 号 No.	企业名称 Name of Enterprises	所在地区 Location	序 号 No.	企业名称 Name of Enterprises	所在地区 Location
51	张家港浦项不锈钢有限公司	张家港	76	苏州三星电子电脑有限公司	工业园区
52	芬欧汇川(中国)有限公司	常 熟	77	江苏常铝铝业股份有限公司	常 熟
53	金龙联合汽车工业（苏州）有限公司	工业园区	78	盛虹集团有限公司	吴江区
54	正新橡胶（中国）有限公司	昆 山	79	苏州协鑫光伏科技有限公司	高新区、虎丘区
55	苏州三星显示有限公司	工业园区	80	苏州旭创科技有限公司	工业园区
56	高创（苏州）电子有限公司	吴江区	81	康力电梯股份有限公司	吴江区
57	上海华电电力发展有限公司望亭发电分公司	相城区	82	苏州阿特斯阳光电力科技有限公司	高新区、虎丘区
58	苏州维信电子有限公司	吴中区	83	中交天和机械设备制造有限公司	常 熟
59	苏州长城开发科技有限公司	工业园区	84	江苏亨通电力电缆有限公司	吴江区
60	苏州春兴精工股份有限公司	工业园区	85	苏州纽威阀门股份有限公司	高新区、虎丘区
61	江苏鹿港文化股份有限公司	张家港	86	苏州欧菲光科技有限公司	相城区
62	国巨电子（中国）有限公司	高新区、虎丘区	87	张家港华兴电力有限公司	张家港
63	昆山丘钛微电子科技有限公司	昆 山	88	礼来苏州制药有限公司	工业园区
64	三星电子（苏州）半导体有限公司	工业园区	89	常熟市汽车饰件股份有限公司	常 熟
65	江苏理文造纸有限公司	常 熟	90	江苏亨通线缆科技有限公司	吴江区
66	苏州汇川技术有限公司	吴中区	91	常熟风范电力设备股份有限公司	常 熟
67	仁宝资讯工业（昆山）有限公司	昆 山	92	牧田（昆山）有限公司	昆 山
68	烨辉（中国）科技材料有限公司	常 熟	93	富士康（昆山）电脑接插件有限公司	昆 山
69	沪士电子股份有限公司	昆 山	94	华灿光电（苏州）有限公司	张家港
70	和舰芯片制造（苏州）股份有限公司	工业园区	95	江苏银河电子股份有限公司	张家港
71	苏州海陆重工股份有限公司	张家港	96	香塘集团有限公司	太 仓
72	江苏华昌化工股份有限公司	张家港	97	矽品科技（苏州）有限公司	工业园区
73	富翔精密工业（昆山）有限公司	昆 山	98	昆山科森科技股份有限公司	昆 山
74	中粮东海粮油工业（张家港）有限公司	张家港	99	江苏亨通光导新材料有限公司	吴江区
75	瑞仪光电（苏州）有限公司	吴江区	100	科沃斯机器人股份有限公司	吴中区

主 要 统 计 指 标 解 释

工业 指从事自然资源的开采，对采掘品和农产品进行加工和再加工的物质生产部门。具体包括：(1)对自然资源的开采，如采矿、晒盐等(但不包括禽兽捕猎和水产捕捞)；(2)对农副产品的加工、再加工，如粮油加工、食品加工、缫丝、纺织、制革等；(3)对采掘品的加工、再加工，如炼铁、炼钢、化工生产、石油加工、机器制造、木材加工等，以及电力、自来水、煤气的生产和供应等；(4)对工业品的修理、翻新，如机器设备的修理、交通运输工具(如汽车)的修理等。

工业统计调查单位为独立核算法人工业企业。

独立核算法人工业企业指从事工业生产经营活动的单位。独立核算法人工业企业应同时具备以下条件：①依法成立，有自己的名称、组织机构和场所，能够承担民事责任；②独立拥有和使用资产，承担负债，有权与其他单位签订合同；③独立核算盈亏，并能够编制资产负债表。

本年鉴中涉及的企业登记注册类型：

国有及国有控股企业 指国有企业加上国有控股企业。国有企业是指企业全部资产归国家所有，并按《中华人民共和国企业法人登记管理条例》规定登记注册的非公司制的经济组织。不包括有限责任公司中的国有独资公司。国有控股企业包括：（1）在企业的全部实收资本中，国有经济成分的出资人拥有的实收资本（股本）所占企业全部实收资本（股本）的比例大于50%的国有绝对控股。（2）在企业的全部实收资本中，国有经济成分的出资人拥有的实收资本（股本）所占比例虽未大于50%，但相对大于其他任何一方经济成分的出资人所占比例的国有相对控股；或者虽不大于其他经济成分，但根据协议规定拥有企业实际控制权的国有协议控股。（3）投资双方各占50%，且未明确由谁绝对控股的企业，若其中一方为国有经济成分的，一律按国有控股处理。

集体企业 指企业资产归集体所有，并按《中华人民共和国企业法人登记管理条例》规定登记注册的经济组织。

股份合作企业 指以合作制为基础，由企业职工共同出资入股，吸收一定比例的社会资产投资组建，实行自主经营，自负盈亏，共同劳动，民主管理，按劳分配与按股分红相结合的一种集体经济组织。

联营企业 指两个及两个以上相同或不同所有制性质的企业法人或事业单位法人，按自愿、平等、互利的原则，共同投资组成的经济组织。联营企业包括国有联营企业、集体联营企业、国有与集体联营企业和其他联营企业。

国有联营企业：指所有联营单位均为国有。

集体联营企业：指所有联营单位均为集体。

国有与集体联营企业：指联营单位既有国有也有集体。

其他联营企业：指上述三种联营企业之外的其他联营形式的企业。

有限责任公司 指根据《中华人民共和国公司登记管理条例》规定登记注册，由两个以上，五十个以下的股东共同出资，每个股东以其所认缴的出资额对公司承担有限责任，公司以其全部资产对其债务承担责任的经济组织。有限责任公司包括国有独资公司以及其他有限责任公司。

股份有限公司 指根据《中华人民共和国公司登记管理条例》规定登记注册，其全部注册资本由等额股份构成并通过发行股票筹集资本，股东以其认购的股份对公司承担有限责任，公司以其全部资产对其债务承担责任的经济组织。

私营企业 指由自然人投资设立或由自然人控股，以雇佣劳动为基础的营利性经济组织。包括按照《公司法》、《合伙企业法》、《私营企业暂行条例》以及《个人独资企业法》规定登记注册的私营独资企业、私营合伙企业、私营有限责任公司、私营股份有限公司和个人独资企业。

港、澳、台商投资企业 指企业注册登记类型中的港、澳、台资合资、合作、独资经营企业和股份有限公司之和。

外商投资企业 指企业注册登记类型中的中外合资、合作经营企业、外资企业和外商投资股份有限公司之和。

轻工业 指主要提供生活消费品和制作手工工具的工业。按其所使用的原料不同，可分为两大类：(1)以农产品为原料的轻工业，是指直接或间接以农产品为基本原料的轻工业。主要包括食品制造、饮料制造、烟草加工、纺织、缝纫、皮革和毛皮制作、造纸以及印刷等工业；(2)以非农产品为原料的轻工业，是指以工业品为原料的轻工业。主要包括文教体育用品、化学药品制造、合成纤维制造、日用化学制品、日用玻璃制品、日用金属制品、手工工具制造、医疗器械制造、文化和办公用机械制造等工业。

重工业 指为国民经济各部门提供物质技术基础的主要生产资料的工业。按其生产性质和产品用途，可以分为下列三类：(1)采掘(伐)工业，是指对自然资源的开采，包括石油开采、煤炭开采、金属矿开采、非金属矿开采等工业；(2)原材料工业，指向国民经济各部门提供基本材料、动力和燃料的工业。包括金属冶炼及加工、炼焦及焦炭、化学、化工原料、水泥、人造板以及电力、石油和煤炭加工等工业；(3)加工工业，是指对工业原材料进行再加工制造的工业。包括装备国民经济各部门的机械设备制造工业、金属结构、水泥制品等工业，以及为农业提供的生产资料如化肥、农药等工业。

根据上述划分原则，修理业中以重工业产品为修理作业对象的划为重工业，反之划为轻工业。

工业总产值

指工业企业在报告期内生产的以货币形式表现的工业最终产品和提供工业劳务活动的总价值量。

（1）工业总产值计算应遵循的原则

①工业生产的原则。即凡是企业在报告期内生产的最终产品和提供的劳务，均应包括在内。其中的最终产品，不管是否在报告期内销售，只要是报告期内生产的，就应包括在内。凡不是工业生产的产品，均不得计入工业总产值。

②最终产品的原则。即企业生产的成品价值必须是本企业生产的，经检验合格不需再进行任何加工的最终产品。企业对外销售的半成品也应视为最终产品计入工业总产值。而在本企业内各车间转移的半成品和在制品只能计算其期末期初差额价值。

③“工厂法”原则。即以法人工业企业作为一个整体计算工业总产值，是其报告期内生产的最终产品和提供劳务的总价值量。

（2）工业总产值的内容

包括三部分：生产的成品价值、对外加工费收入、自制半成品在制品期末期初差额价值。

①成品价值：指企业在报告期内生产，并在报告期内不再进行加工，经检验合格、包装入库的已经销售和准备销售的全部工业成品（包括半成品）价值合计。成品价值包括企业生产的自制设备及提供给本企业在建工程、其他非工业部门和生活福利部门等单位使用的成品价值，但不包括用订货者来料加工的成品（半成品）价值。

工业总产值是按现行价格计算的。成品价值按成品实物量乘以报告期不含应交增值税（销项税额）的产品实际销售平均单价计算。会计核算中按成本价格转账的自制设备和自产自用的成品，按成本价格计算成品价值。

②对外加工费收入：指企业在报告期内完成的对外承做的工业品加工（包括用订货者来料加工生产）的加工费收入和对外工业品修理作业所收取的加工费收入和对内非工业部门提供的加工修理、设备安装等收入。对外加工费收入按不含应交增值税（销项税额）的价格计算。

对于以对外加工生产为主，对外加工费收入所占比重较大的企业，如果对外加工费收入出现跨报告期支付的情况，为保证总产值生产口径计算的准确性，则应将对外加工费收入按实际情况调整，记录本报告期应实际收取的对外加工费收入。

③自制半成品在制品期末期初差额价值。为了使工业总产值与工业中间投入中的物耗价值一致，以便同口径地计算工业增加值，规定本指标的计算原则是：凡是企业会计产品成本核算中计算半成品、在制品成本，则工业总产值中必须包括自制半成品在制品期末期初差额价值。反之则不包括。

自制半成品在制品期末期初差额价值等于自制半成品在制品期末价值减去期初价值后的余额，如果期末价值小于期初价值，该指标为负值，企业在计算产值时，应按负值计算，不能作为零处理。

（3）工业总产值计算的几种具体规定

①凡自备原材料（包括自备零部件）生产，不论其加工繁简程度如何，一律按全价，即包括自备原材料的价值，计算工业总产值。

②凡来料加工，加工企业只收取加工费，则加工企业一律按财务上结算的加工费计算工业总产值，即不包括定货者来料的价值。一般分两种情况：a、工业企业之间的来料加工，加工企业（即承包单位）按财务上结算的加工费计算工业总产值；委托加工的企业（即发包单位）按全价计算工业总产值。b、工业企业与非工业企业之间的来料加工，当工业企业作为加工企业时一律按加工费计算工业总产值。

③自制半成品、在制品期末期初差额价值，原则上应计入工业总产值，但如果会计产品成本核算中不计算自制半成品、在制品成本，则不计入工业总产值；如果会计产品成本核算中计算自制半成品、在制品成本的，则计入工业总产值。

区分来料加工与自备原材料生产的依据是加工企业与委托加工企业间的财务结算关系。如果委托企业提供原材料而不与加工企业结算，加工企业收取加工费，产品返回委托企业销售，则这种模式是来料加工；如果委托加工企业提供的原材料与加工企业是结算的，制成品由加工企业返给委托企业也是结算的，则这种模式是自备原材料生产。

资产总计 指企业过去的交易或者事项形成的、由企业拥有或者控制的、预期会给企业带来经济利益的资源。资产一般按流动性（资产的变现或耗用时间长短）分为流动资产和非流动资产。其中流动资产可分为货币资金、交易性金融资产、应收票据、应收账款、预付款项、其他应收款、存货等；非流动资产可分为长期股权投资、固定资产、无形资产及其他非流动资产等。根据会计“资产负债表”中“资产总计”项目的期末余额数填报。

执行《企业会计准则》或《小企业会计准则》的企业：资产总计=流动资产合计+非流动资产合计；执行其他企业会计制度的企业资产包括流动资产、长期投资、固定资产、无形资产和其他资产等。

流动资产合计 资产满足以下条件之一应归为流动资产：（1）预计在一个正常营业周期中变现、出售或耗用，主要包括存货、应收账款等；（2）主要为交易目的而持有；（3）预计在资产负债表日起一年内（含一年）变现；（4）自资产负债日起一年内，交换其他资产或清偿负债的能力不受限制的现金或现金等价物。包括货币资金、应收票据、应收账款、存货等项目。根据会计“资产负债表”中“流动资产合计”项目的期末余额数填报。

固定资产原价 指固定资产的成本，包括企业在购置、自行建造、安装、改建、扩建、技术改造某项固定资产时所发生的全部支出总额。根据会计“固定资产”科目的期末借方余额填报。

负债合计 指企业过去的交易或者事项形成的，预期会导致经济利益流出企业的现时义务。负债一般按偿还期长短分为流动负债和非流动负债。根据会计“资产负债表”中“负债合计”项目的期末余额数填报。

执行《企业会计准则》或《小企业会计准则》的企业：负债合计=流动负债合计+非流动负债合计；执行其他企业会计制度的企业负债包括流动负债和长期负债。

所有者权益合计 指企业资产扣除负债后由所有者享有的剩余权益。公司的所有者权益又称股东权益。包括实收资本、资本公积、盈余公积、未分配利润等。根据会计“资产负债表”中“所有者权益合计”项目的期末余额数填报。

主营业务收入 指企业确认的销售商品、提供劳务等主营业务的收入。根据会计“主营业务收入”科目的本年各月贷方余额（结转前）之和填报。如未设置该科目，以“营业收入”代替填报。

主营业务成本 指企业经营主要业务所发生的成本总额。根据会计“主营业务成本”科目的本年各月借方余额（结转前）之和填报。如未设置该科目，以“营业成本”代替填报。

主营业务税金及附加 指企业经营主要业务应负担的消费税、城市维护建设税、资源税、教育费附加及房产税、土地使用税、车船使用税、印花税等相关税费。根据会计“主营业务税金及附加”科目的本年各月借方余额（结转前）之和填报。如未设置该科目，以“税金及附加”代替填报。

利润总额 指企业在一定会计期间的经营成果，是生产经营过程中各种收入扣除各种耗费后的盈余，反映企业在报告期内实现的盈亏总额。利润总额为营业利润加上营业外收入，减去营业外支出后的金额，根据会计“利润表”中“利润总额”项目的本年累计数填报。

应交增值税 指按照税法规定，以销售货物、服务、无形资产、不动产或提供加工、修理修配劳务的增值额和货物进口金额为计税依据而课征的一种流转税。填报本指标时，应按权责发生制核算企业本期应负担的增值税。

从业人员平均人数 指报告期内（年度、季度、月度）平均拥有的从业人员数。

总资产贡献率 反映企业全部资产的获利能力，是企业经营业绩和管理水平的集中体现，是评价和考核企业盈利能力的核心指标。计算公式为：

$$\text{总资产贡献率}(\%)=\frac{\text{利润总额}+\text{税金总额}+\text{利息支出}}{\text{平均资金总额}}\times 100\%$$

公式中：税金总额为产品销售税金及附加与应交增值税之和；平均资产总额为期初期末资产之和的算术平均值。

资产负债率 该指标既反映企业经营风险的大小，也反映企业利用债权人提供的资金从事经营活动的能力。计算公式为：

$$\text{资产负债率}(\%)=\frac{\text{负债总额}}{\text{资产总额}}\times 100\%$$

资产与负债均为报告期期末数。

流动资产周转次数 指一定时期内流动资产完成的周转次数，反映投入工业企业流动资金的周转速度。计算公式为：

$$\text{流动资产周转次数}=\frac{\text{产品销售收入}}{\text{全部流动资产平均余额}}$$

公式中：全部流动资产平均余额为期初和期末的流动资产之和的算术平均值。

成本费用利润率 反映企业投入的生产成本及费用的经济效益，同时也反映企业降低成本所取得的经济效益。计算公式为：

$$\text{成本费用利润率}(\%)=\frac{\text{利润总额}}{\text{成本费用总额}}\times 100\%$$

公式中：成本费用总额为产品销售成本、销售费用、管理费用、财务费用之和。

产品销售率 该指标反映工业产品已实现销售的程度，是分析工业产销衔接情况，研究工业产品满足社会需求的指标。计算公式为：

$$\text{产品销售率}(\%)=\frac{\text{工业销售产值}}{\text{工业总产值(现价)}}\times 100\%$$

资产保值增值率 该指标反映企业净资产的变动状况，是企业发展能力的集中体现。计算公式为：

$$\text{资本保值增值率}=\frac{\text{报告期期末所有者权益}}{\text{上年同期期末所有者权益}}\times 100\%$$

所有者权益等于资产总计减负债总计。

固定资产净值率 指企业固定资产净值与固定资产原值的比率，是反映固定资产新旧程度的一种指标。计算公式为：

$$\text{固定资产净值率}=\frac{\text{固定资产净值}}{\text{固定资产原值}}\times 100\%$$

EXPLANATORY NOTES ON MAIN STATISTICAL INDICATORS

Industry refers to the material production sector which is engaged in the extraction of natural resources and processing and reprocessing of minerals and agricultural products, including (1) extraction of natural resources, such as mining, salt production (but not including hunting and fishing); (2) processing and reprocessing of farm and sideline produces, such as rice husking, flour milling, wine making, oil pressing, silk reeling, spinning and weaving, and leather making; (3) manufacture of industrial products, such as steel making, iron smelting, chemicals manufacturing, petroleum processing, machine building, timber processing; water and gas production and electricity generation and supply; (4)repairing of industrial products such as the repairing of machinery and means of transport (including cars).

In industrial statistics surveys, the units of enquiry are corporate industrial enterprises with independent accounting systems.

Corporate industrial enterprises with independent accounting systems refer to enterprises engaging in industrial production activities, which meet the following requirements: (1) They are established legally, having their own names, organizations, location and able to take civil liability; (2) They possess and use their assets independently, assume liabilities and are entitled to sign contracts with other units; (3) They are financially independent and compile their own balance sheets.

Enterprises covered in the industrial statistics in the Yearbook include the following categories by their registration:

State-owned and State-holding Enterprises refer to state-owned enterprises plus State-holding enterprises. State-owned enterprises refer to non-corporate economic organizations whose entire assets of the enterprise are owned by the state and which are registered in accordance with "The Regulations of the People's Republic of China on the Registration and Management of Enterprise Legal Persons". They do not include state-owned sole proprietorship companies in limited liability companies. State-owned holding enterprises include: (1) state-owned absolute holding enterprises in which in the total paid-in capital of an enterprise, the state-owned economic entity's paid-in capital (share capital) is more than 50% of the enterprise's total paid-in capital (share capital). (2) state-owned relative holding enterprises in which in the total paid-in capital of an enterprise, the share of the paid-in capital (share capital) owned by the contributor of the state-owned economy is not more than 50% but is relatively larger than any other contributor of the economic composition; or state-owned agreement holding enterprises in which in the total paid-in capital of an enterprise, the share of paid-in capital (share capital) owned by the contributor of the state-owned economy is not more than other economic components, but has actual control of the enterprise in accordance with the agreement. (3) enterprises in which each investor holds 50% of the shares and it is not clear who is absolutely holding, if one of them is a state-owned economy shall be treated as state-owned holding enterprises.

Collective Enterprises refer to economic organizations whose assets are collectively owned and which are registered in accordance with "The Regulations of the People's Republic of China on the Registration and Management of Enterprise Legal Persons".

Share-holding Cooperative Enterprise refers to a collective economic organization which is based on the cooperative system and set up with its employees jointly investing in shares and absorbing a certain proportion of social assets to invest in, and carries out self-management, assuming sole responsibility for profits and losses, working together, managing democratically, and combining the distribution according to work with the distribution of dividends according to shares.

Joint-operation Enterprises refer to economic organizations which are formed by two or more enterprise legal persons or institutional legal persons of the same or different types of ownership, on the principle of voluntariness, equality and mutual benefit, and with joint investment. Associated enterprises include state-owned joint ventures, collective joint ventures, state-owned and collective joint ventures and other joint ventures.

State-owned joint ventures: refer to all affiliates being state-owned.

Collective joint ventures: refer to all associates being collectives.

State-owned and collective joint ventures: refer to joint ventures being both state-owned and collectives.

Other joint ventures: refer to enterprises in joint ventures other than the above-mentioned three joint ventures.

Limited Liability Company refers to an economic organization which is registered in accordance with "The Regulations of the People's Republic of China on the Administration of the Registration of Companies" and is jointly funded by more than two and fewer than 50 shareholders, with each shareholder assuming limited liability for the company on the basis of his subscribed contribution and the company assuming responsibility for its debt with all its assets. Limited liability companies also include state-owned sole proprietorship companies and other limited liability companies.

Company Limited by Shares refers to an economic organization which is registered in accordance with "The Regulations of the People's Republic of China on the Administration of the Registration of Companies" and in which all its registered capital consists of the same number of shares and its capital is raised through the issuance of shares, with each shareholder assuming limited liability for the company on the basis of the shares he buys and the company assuming responsibility for its debt with all its assets.

Private Enterprise refers to a profit-making economic organization that is established by natural persons or controlled by natural persons and is based on wage labor. Private enterprises include privately owned enterprises, private partnership enterprises, private limited liability companies, private limited companies, and individually owned enterprises registered in accordance with the provisions of "The Company Law", "The Partnership Enterprise Law", "The Provisional Regulations for Private Enterprises", and "The Individually Owned Enterprise Law".

Enterprises with Funds from Hong Kong, Macao and Taiwan refers to all industrial enterprises registered as the joint-venture, cooperative, sole (exclusive) investment industrial enterprises and limited liability corporations with funds from Hong Kong, Macao and Taiwan.

Foreign Funded Enterprises refer to all industrial enterprises registered as the joint-venture, cooperative, sole (exclusive) investment industrial enterprises and limited liability corporations with foreign funds.

Light Industry refers to the industry that produces consumer goods and hand tools. It consists of two categories, depending on the materials used:

(1) Industries using farm products as raw materials. These are the branches of light industry which directly or indirectly use farm products as basic raw materials, including the manufacture of food and beverages, tobacco processing, textile, clothing, fur and leather manufacturing, paper making, printing, etc.

(2) Industries using non-farm products as raw materials. These are the branches of light industry which use manufactured goods as raw materials, including the manufacture of cultural, educational articles and sports goods, chemicals, synthetic fibre, chemical products for daily use, glass products for daily use, metal products for daily use, hand tools, medical apparatus and instruments, and the manufacture of cultural and office machinery.

Heavy Industry refers to the industry which produces capital goods, and provides various sectors of the national economy with necessary material and technical basis for production. It consists of the following three branches according to the purpose of production or the use of products:

(1) Mining, quarrying and logging industry, which refers to the industry that extracts natural resources, including extraction of petroleum, coal, metal and non-metal ores.

(2) Raw materials industry refers to the industry that provides various sectors of the national economy with raw materials, fuels and power. It includes smelting and processing of metals, coking and coke chemistry, chemical materials and building materials such as cement, plywood, and power, petroleum refining and coal dressing.

(3) Manufacturing industry which refers to the industry that processes raw materials. It includes machine-building industries which equip sectors of the national economy; industries producing metal structure and cement products; and industries producing means of agricultural production, such as chemical fertilizers and pesticides.

In accordance with the above principles of classification, the repairing trades, which are engaged primarily in repairing products of heavy industry, are classified as heavy industry while those which are engaged in repairing products of light industry are classified as light industry.

Gross Industrial Output Value

It refers to the total value of the industrial end products produced in the form of currency and the industrial labor services provided by an industrial enterprise during the reporting period.

(1) Principles to be followed in the calculation of total industrial output value

① The principle of industrial production is that all the final products produced and services provided by the enterprise during the reporting period should be included. The final product, whether or not it is sold during the reporting period, should be included as long as it is produced during the reporting period. Any product that is not industrially produced cannot be included in the total industrial output value.

② The principle of the final product is that the value of the finished product produced by the enterprise must be the final product produced by the enterprise and no further processing is required after passing inspection. The semi-finished product sold externally by the enterprise should also be regarded as the final product in the total industrial output value. However, the value of their initial balance at the end of the period can only be calculated for the semi-finished products and the products being manufactured transferred in all the workshops within the enterprise.

③ The "factory law" principle is that the total industrial output value of a legal person industrial enterprise as a whole is the total value of the final products and the services provided by the enterprise during the reporting period.

(2) The content of total industrial output value includes three parts:

the value of finished products, the income of external processing fees, and the value of their initial balance at the end of the period for the self-made semi-finished products and the products being manufactured.

① The value of finished products: refers to the total value of all the industrial finished products (including semi-finished products) produced by an enterprise during the reporting period and requiring no further processing during the reporting period sold or ready for sale after being inspected and packed into the warehouse. The value of finished products includes the value of the self-made equipment produced by the enterprise and the value of finished products used by the enterprise's construction in progress, other non-industrial sectors and life welfare departments, but does not include the value of the finished products (semi-finished products) processed with the material from the orderer.

The total industrial output value is based on the current price. The value of the finished product is calculated by multiplying the physical quantity of the finished product by the average unit price of the product that does not include the value-added tax (output tax amount) payable during the reporting period. In the accounting calculation the value of the finished product is calculated according to the cost price for the self-made equipment or the self-produced and used finished product that is transferred at a cost price.

②The income of external processing fees: refers to the income of fees from the processing of industrial products externally undertaken (including the processing of the materials from the orderer) by an enterprise during the reporting period and the income of processing fees received from external industrial product repair operations and the income from the processing, repair, equipment installation and so on provided for internal non-industrial departments. The income of external processing fees is calculated at the price that does not include value-added tax (output tax amount) payable.

For enterprises with external processing production as the main factor, and the proportion of external processing fee income is relatively large, if the external processing fee income occurs across the reporting period, in order to ensure the accuracy of the calculation of the production value of the total output value, the external processing fee income should be adjusted according to actual conditions and the external processing fee income that should actually be collected during the reporting period is recorded.

③ The balance of the value of self-made semi-finished products or products being manufactured at the end and beginning of the period. In order to make the industrial output value consistent with the material consumption value of the intermediate input of industry, in order to calculate the industrial added value in the same way, the principle for calculating this indicator is: when calculating the cost of semi-finished products and products being manufactured in the accounting of enterprise accounting products, the total industrial output value must include the value of the initial balance at the end of the period of self-made semi-finished products or products being manufactured. The contrary does not include.

The balance of the value of self-made semi-finished products or products being manufactured at the beginning and end of the period is equal to the balance of the value of the self-made semi-finished products or products being manufactured at the end of the period minus their value at the beginning of the period. If the value at the end of the period is less than the value at the beginning of the period, this indicator is negative. When the enterprise calculates the production value, it shall calculate it as a negative value and cannot treat it as zero.

(3) Several specific regulations for the calculation of total industrial output value

① Where the production of self-provided raw materials (including self-provided parts and components) is irrespective of the degree of complication of its processing, the full value shall be calculated, that is, the value of the self-prepared raw materials shall be used to calculate the total industrial output value.

② Where the processing of incoming materials, the processing enterprise only charges processing fees, the processing enterprise shall calculate the total industrial output value in accordance with financial settlement processing fees, that is, the value of the orderer's incoming materials shall not be included. There are two general situations: a. for the processing of incoming materials between industrial enterprises, the processing enterprise (that is, the contracting unit) calculates the total industrial output value according to the financially settled processing fees; the enterprise that commissions processing (that is, the outsourcing unit) calculates the total industrial output value according to the full price. b. for the processing of incoming materials between an industrial enterprise and a non-industrial enterprise, when the industrial enterprise is used as a processing enterprise, its total industrial output value shall be calculated according to the processing fees.

③ The balance of the value of self-made semi-finished products or products being manufactured at the beginning and end of the period shall, in principle, be included in the total industrial output value. However, if the costs of self-made semi-finished products or products being manufactured are not calculated in the accounting product costing, it shall not be included in the total industrial output value; if the costs of self-made semi-finished products or products being manufactured are calculated in the accounting product costing, it shall be included in the total industrial output value.

The basis for distinguishing between processing of raw materials and production of self-provided raw materials is the financial settlement relationship between the processing enterprise and the enterprise that commissions processing. If the enterprise that commissions processing provides raw materials without settlement with the processing enterprise, the processing enterprise charges the processing fee, and the product is returned to the enterprise that commissions processing for sales, this mode is called processing; if the raw materials provided by the enterprise that commissions processing is settled with the processing enterprise, and the finished product is returned to the enterprise that commissions processing by the processing enterprise and also settled, this mode is called production of raw materials.

Total Assets refers to the resources formed by the enterprise's past transactions or events, owned or controlled by the enterprise and expected to bring economic benefits to the enterprise. Assets are generally classified into current assets and non-current assets based on liquidity (realization of assets or asset consumption time). Of them, current assets can be divided into monetary funds, transactional financial assets, bills receivable, accounts receivable, prepayments, other receivables, inventory, etc; non-current assets can be divided into long-term equity investments, fixed assets, intangible assets and other non-current assets. The report is based on the closing balance of the item "Asset Total" in the "Balance Sheet" of the accounting.

Enterprises that implement the "Accounting Standards for Business" or the "Accounting Standards for Small Business" : total assets = total current assets + total non-current assets; corporate assets that implement other enterprise accounting systems include current assets, long-term investments, fixed assets, intangible assets, and others assets.

Total Current Assets refers to an asset that meets one of the following conditions is classified as a current asset: (1) it is expected to be realized, sold or consumed in a normal operating cycle, mainly including inventory, accounts receivable; (2) it is mainly held for trading purposes; (3) it is expected to be realized within one year (including one year) from the balance sheet date; (4) within one year from the date of the assets and liabilities, cash or cash equivalents that are not limited in their ability to exchange other assets or settle their liabilities. It includes currency funds, bills receivable, accounts receivable, inventory and other items. The report is based on the closing balance of the item "Current Asset Total" in the "Balance Sheet" of the accounting.

Original Value of Fixed Assets refers to the cost of the fixed assets, including the total expenditure incurred by the enterprise when it purchases, self-builds, installs, reconstructs, expands, and technically transforms a certain fixed asset. The report is based on the closing debit balance of the accounting "fixed assets" account.

Total Liabilities refer to the current obligations of the enterprise formed from past transactions or events that are expected to result in the outflow of economic benefits from the enterprise. Liabilities are generally divided into current liabilities and non-current liabilities according to the length of the repayment period. The report is based on the closing balance of the item "Total Liabilities" in the "Balance Sheet" of the accounting.

Enterprises that implement the "Accounting Standards for Business" or the "Accounting Standards for Small Business": Total debt = total current liabilities + total non-current liabilities; corporate liabilities that implement other corporate accounting systems include current liabilities and long-term liabilities.

Total Ownership Equity refers to the residual equity that the owners of the enterprise's assets enjoy after deducting liabilities. The company's owners' equity is also called shareholders' equity. It includes paid-in capital, capital reserves, surplus reserves, undistributed profits, etc. The report is based on the closing balance of the item "Total Ownership Equity" in the "Balance Sheet" of the accounting.

Main Business Income refers to income from principal businesses such as sales of goods and provision of labor services confirmed by the enterprise. The report shall be based on the sum of the credit balance (before the carry-over) for each month of the current year in the item "Main Business Income" of the accounting. If this account is not set up, "Business Income" is used instead in reporting.

Main Operating Cost refers to the total cost incurred by the enterprise's main business operations. The report shall be based on the sum of the debit balance (before the carry-over) for each month of the current year in the item "Main Operating Cost" of the accounting. If this account is not set up, "Business Cost" is used instead in reporting.

Main Business Taxes and Surcharges refer to the related taxes such as consumption tax, city maintenance and construction tax, resource tax, education surtax, and real estate tax, land use tax, vehicle and vessel use tax, and stamp tax that should be borne by the enterprise's main business operations. The report shall be based on the sum of the debit balance (before the carry-over) for each month of the current year in the item "Main Business Taxes and Surcharges" of the accounting. If this account is not set up, "Taxes and Surcharges" is used instead in reporting.

Total Profit refers to the operating results of an enterprise during a certain accounting period. It is the surplus of various incomes after deduction of various expenses in the production and operation process, and reflects the total amount of profits and losses realized by the enterprise during the reporting period. The total profit is calculated as operating profit plus non-operating income, minus the non-operating expenses. It is reported in accordance with the accumulated amount of the item "Total Profit" in the accounting "Income Statement".

Value-added Tax (VAT) Payable refers to a turnover tax that is levied on the basis of taxation in accordance with the provisions of the tax law, with the value-added amount for the sale of goods, services, intangible assets, real estate or the provision of processing, repair and repair services, and the amount of goods imported. When reporting this indicator, the enterprise should calculate the value-added tax that should be borne by the enterprise according to the accrual basis.

Average Number of Employees refers to the average number of employees during the reporting period (annual, quarterly, monthly).

Ratio of Profits, Taxes and Interests to Average Assets reflects the profit-making capability of all assets of the enterprise and is a key indicator manifesting the performance and management and evaluating the profit-making potential of the enterprise. It is calculated as follows:

$$\text{Ratio of Profits, Taxes and Interests to Average Assets (\%)} = \frac{\text{total profits + total taxes + interest payment}}{\text{average assets}} \times 100\%$$

In the above formula, total taxes is the sum of tax and extra charges on the sales of products and value-added tax payable; and average assets is the arithmetic mean of the sum of beginning assets and ending assets.

Ratio of Debts to Assets reflects both the operation risk and the capability of the enterprise in making use of the capital from the creditors. It is calculated as follows:

$$\text{Ratio of Debts to Assets (\%)} = \frac{\text{total debts}}{\text{total assets}} \times 100\%$$

Both assets and debts are figures at the end of the reference period.

Turnover of Working Capital refers to the number of times of turnover of working capital in a given period of time, which reflects the speed of the turnover of working capital of industrial enterprises, and is calculated as follows:

$$\text{Turnover of Working Capital} = \frac{\text{sales revenue of products}}{\text{average balance of total working capital}}$$

In the above formula, average balance of total working capital refers to the arithmetic mean of the sum of working capital at the beginning and at the end of the reference period.

Ratio of Profits to Total Industrial Costs refers to the ratio of profits realized in a given period to the total costs in the same period, which reflects the economic efficiency of input cost and is calculated as follows:

$$\text{Ratio of Profits to Total Industrial Cost (\%)} = \frac{\text{total profits}}{\text{total costs}} \times 100\%$$

Total costs in the above formula are the sum of cost of products sold, marketing cost, management cost and financial cost.

Sales Ratio of Products is an indicator reflecting the actual sale of industrial products, analyzing the production-selling and supply-demand relations. It is calculated as:

$$\text{Sales Ratio of Products (\%)} = \frac{\text{value of industrial sales}}{\text{gross industrial output value (current prices)}} \times 100\%$$

Asset Value Increment Rate The index reflects the status of changes of the net assets of an enterprise, and is the concentrated reflection of the enterprise's development ability. The calculation formula is:

$$\text{Asset Value Increment Rate} = \frac{\text{The owner's equity at the end of the reporting period}}{\text{The owner's equity at the end of the same period last year}} \times 100\%$$

An owner's equity is equal to the total assets minus total liabilities.

Rate of Net Value of Fixed Assets refers to the ratio of the net value of the fixed assets of an enterprise and the value of its fixed assets, and is a measure reflecting the old and new conditions of the fixed assets. The calculation formula is:

$$\text{Rate of Net Value of Fixed Assets} = \frac{\text{The net value of the fixed assets}}{\text{The value of the fixed assets}} \times 100\%$$

五、建 筑 业

CHAPTER 5
CONSTRUCTION

5 建 筑 业
CONSTRUCTION

主 要 统 计 指 标
MAJOR STATISTICAL INDICATORS

2018年末建筑企业数	Number of Construction Enterprise	1 345	个	unit
2018年建筑业总产值	Gross Output Value of Construction	2 411.75	亿元	100 million yuan
比上年增长	Increase Over Last Year	23.4	%	
2018年竣工产值	Output Value of Buildings Completed	1 706.51	亿元	100 million yuan
比上年增长	Increase Over Last Year	10.6	%	
2018年房屋建筑施工面积	Floor Space of Buildings Under Construction	10 418.56	万平方米	10 000 sq.m.
比上年增长	Increase Over Last Year	11.5	%	
2018年房屋建筑竣工面积	Floor Space of Buildings Completed	2 768.89	万平方米	10 000 sq.m.
比上年增长	Increase Over Last Year	-5.1	%	
2018年建筑业全员劳动生产率	Overall Labor Productivity of Construction	39.21	万元/人	10 000 yuan/person
比上年增长	Increase Over Last Year	18.8	%	

表5-1 分地区、分行业建筑业生产情况 (2018年)

指 标		Item		全 市 Whole Municipality	市 区 Urban Area
企业数	(个)	Number of Enterprises	(unit)	1 345	801
签订的合同额	(万元)	Contractual Value	(10 000 yuan)	45 976 200	34 117 573
建筑业总产值		Gross Output Value of Construction		24 117 455	17 662 241
# 装饰装修产值		Decorate and Materials Construction		5 193 245	4 836 852
# 在外省完成的产值		Output Value of Buildings Completed outside of Jiangsu province		7 401 445	6 543 925
# 建筑工程		Construction		21 982 475	16 116 880
安装工程		Installation		1 951 573	1 395 853
其他产值		Others		183 407	149 508
竣工产值		Output Value of Buildings Completed		17 065 149	12 536 036
房屋建筑施工面积	(万平方米)	Floor Space of Buildings Under Construction	(10 000 sq.m)	10 418.56	5 712.71
# 本年新开工		Beginning Projects in this Year		4 072.61	2 357.24
房屋建筑竣工面积		Floor Space of Buildings Completed		2 768.89	1 491.80
从业人员平均人数	(人)	Average Employed Persons	(person)	615 026	416 958
全员劳动生产率	(万元/人)	Overall Labor Productivity	(10 000 yuan/person)	39.21	42.36

STATISTICS ON CONSTRUCTION BY REGION AND SECTOR (2018)

按地区分 Grouped by Region					按行业分 Grouped by Sector			
# 吴江区 Wujiang District	常熟 Changshu	张家港 Zhangjiagang	昆山 Kunshan	太仓 Taicang	房屋建筑业 Housing Construction	土木工程建筑业 Civil Engineering Construction	建筑安装业 Installation of Lines, Pipelines and Equipment	建筑装饰和其他建筑业 Decoration and Other Construction
145	130	142	191	81	359	354	289	343
2 206 728	2 898 363	3 035 217	5 189 210	735 837	18 545 668	17 260 409	2 584 823	7 585 300
1 256 124	1 600 721	1 477 468	2 861 715	515 312	9 013 510	7 538 874	1 935 144	5 629 927
65 821	135 378	52 414	111 387	57 215	167 099	11 162	40 174	4 974 809
103 404	201 613	176 585	451 946	27 377	1 088 108	2 835 360	632 748	2 845 230
1 148 507	1 501 159	1 353 498	2 519 207	491 731	8 886 071	7 017 486	572 066	5 506 852
86 787	97 610	119 090	321 899	17 121	76 916	414 178	1 355 967	104 512
20 830	1 951	4 880	20 609	6 459	50 524	107 210	7 111	18 563
1 140 188	1 055 229	1 128 862	1 957 919	387 102	6 111 732	4 307 476	1 509 550	5 136 391
785.20	1 329.40	1 259.50	1 816.26	300.70	10 027.34	233.98	113.76	43.49
314.94	623.97	427.12	576.51	87.77	3 901.63	100.40	37.75	32.84
305.30	325.83	307.60	541.01	102.65	2 638.11	80.49	38.45	11.84
44 439	46 515	46 641	85 750	19 162	285 415	124 984	52 436	152 191
28.27	34.41	31.68	33.37	26.89	31.58	60.32	36.90	36.99

表5-2 分登记注册类型建筑业生产情况 (2018年)

指　　标		Item		总　计 Total	国有企业 State-owned Enterprises
企业数	(个)	Number of Enterprises	(unit)	1 345	3
签订的合同额	(万元)	Contractual Value	(10 000 yuan)	45 976 200	27 130
建筑业总产值		Gross Output Value of Construction		24 117 455	13 529
# 装饰装修产值		Decorate and Materials Construction		5 193 245	–
# 在外省完成的产值		Output Value of Buildings Completed outside of Jiangsu province		7 401 445	–
# 建筑工程		Construction		21 982 475	5 099
安装工程		Installation		1 951 573	8 430
其他产值		Others		183 407	–
竣工产值		Output Value of Buildings Completed		17 065 149	5 099
房屋建筑施工面积	(万平方米)	Floor Space of Buildings Under Construction	(10 000 sq.m)	10 418.56	–
# 本年新开工		Beginning Projects in this Year		4 072.61	–
房屋建筑竣工面积		Floor Space of Buildings Completed		2 768.89	–
从业人员平均人数	(人)	Average Employed Persons	(person)	615 026	678
全员劳动生产率	(万元/人)	Overall Labor Productivity	(10 000 yuan/person)	39.21	19.95

STATISTICS ON CONSTRUCTION BY TYPE OF REGISTRATION (2018)

集体企业 Collective-owned Enterprises	股份合作企业 Share-holding Cooperative Enterprises	有限责任公司 Limited Liability Corporations	股份有限公司 Share-holding Corporations Ltd.	私营企业 Private Enterprises	港澳台商投资企业 Enterprises With Investment From HongKong, Macao and Taiwan	外商投资企业 Enterprises with Foreign Investment	其他企业 Other Enterprises
4	3	109	29	1 171	9	16	1
59 172	7 614	15 958 360	9 303 971	19 591 879	246 009	765 677	16 390
55 961	5 541	6 532 074	5 364 209	11 528 089	149 299	463 227	5 527
44 599	–	440 829	3 185 430	1 522 386	–	–	–
13 956	–	2 591 430	2 494 610	1 968 097	7 770	323 052	2 530
54 514	5 541	6 211 395	5 302 813	10 254 265	117 807	31 042	
–	–	309 207	60 329	1 107 601	28 294	432 185	5 527
1 448	–	11 472	1 067	166 224	3 197	–	–
57 395	13	3 056 511	4 107 936	9 387 879	122 416	319 843	8 057
7.89	7.00	1 728.32	1 581.76	7 069.83	7.93	15.83	–
3.10	–	711.12	659.83	2 686.84	6.64	5.08	–
4.78	–	493.22	268.22	1 984.47	5.22	12.98	–
3 838	141	111 906	104 421	380 625	1 654	11 674	89
14.58	39.30	58.37	51.37	30.29	90.27	39.68	62.10

表5-3

分地区、分行业建筑业财务状况 (2018年)

单位：万元

指 标	Item	全 市 Whole Municipality	按 市 区 Urban Area	 #吴江区 WujiangDistrict
年末资产负债	**Asset and Liabilities at Year-end**			
流动资产	Circulating Assets	22 902 442	15 015 368	1 337 979
# 存 货	Stocks	5 366 865	2 822 695	313 008
固定资产原价	Original Value of Fixed Assets	2 291 715	1 476 486	147 429
累计折旧	Accumulative Total Depreciation	1 185 727	772 093	77 284
# 本年折旧	Depreciation Within the Year	133 535	84 675	10 649
在建工程	Project Under Construction	101 073	66 600	5 964
资产总计	Total Assets	25 991 673	17 239 134	1 468 023
流动负债	Liquid Liabilities	16 156 506	10 810 538	795 560
非流动负债合计	Total Non Liquid Liabilities	454 373	371 397	42 683
负债合计	Total Liabilities	16 673 999	11 224 723	841 116
所有者权益	Creditors' Equity	9 317 674	6 014 411	626 907
# 实收资本	Actual Capital Hold	4 637 615	2 847 776	362 648
国家资本	State Capital	283 610	229 744	–
集体资本	Collective Capital	75 614	40 526	5 580
法人资本	Corporation Capital	1 422 873	971 272	111 824
个人资本	Individual Capital	2 715 217	1 481 849	237 524
港澳台资本	Capital from HongKong, Macao and Taiwan	36 623	32 120	7 720
外商资本	Foreign Capital	103 678	92 265	–
损益及分配	**Expenditure, Income and Distribution**			
主营业务收入	Main Business Income	22 756 569	16 285 159	1 213 798
主营业务成本	Main Business Cost	20 354 930	14 502 692	1 081 452
主营业务税金及附加	Main Business Taxes and Surcharges	89 173	60 318	7 877
其他业务利润	Profits of Other Business	41 176	26 061	2 123
管理费用	Management Fee	1 076 264	787 331	55 043
财务费用	Financial Expenses	128 318	86 660	8 683
营业利润	Operating Profit	1 027 341	742 770	55 949
利润总额	Total Profit	1 029 627	746 031	54 532
应交所得税	Income Tax Payable	205 660	138 977	11 874
人工成本及增值税	**Labor Cost and Value Added Tax**			
应付职工薪酬(本年贷方累计发生额)	Employee Compensation Payable (the Cumulative Amount of Credits)	3 545 760	2 385 727	253 778
应交增值税	Value Added Tax Payable	500 777	349 550	36 453

FINANCIAL CONDITIONS OF CONSTRUCTION BY REGION AND SECTOR (2018)

(10 000 yuan)

地区分 Grouped by Region				按行业分 Grouped by Sector			
常熟 Changshu	张家港 Zhangjiagang	昆山 Kunshan	太仓 Taicang	房屋建筑业 Housing Construction	土木工程建筑业 Civil Engineering Construction	建筑安装业 Installation of Lines, Pipelines and Equipment	建筑装饰和其他建筑业 Decoration and Other Construction
1 971 346	1 948 057	3 427 681	539 990	7 871 350	7 257 102	2 421 137	5 352 853
612 948	581 706	1 195 785	153 731	2 385 691	1 811 130	812 804	357 241
169 224	210 726	342 450	92 829	640 924	1 004 100	236 304	410 386
96 769	107 951	160 133	48 781	295 319	625 099	107 629	157 679
10 491	13 201	19 792	5 377	36 069	57 012	17 969	22 485
965	16 395	6 376	10 737	47 425	25 769	18 146	9 733
2 103 627	2 159 011	3 864 680	625 221	8 678 139	8 422 235	2 706 335	6 184 965
1 300 672	1 375 285	2 408 060	261 952	5 558 157	5 251 725	1 693 355	3 653 269
27 333	40 131	10 885	4 627	92 004	271 790	7 104	83 475
1 329 670	1 420 665	2 422 501	276 440	5 676 231	5 544 937	1 707 271	3 745 560
773 957	738 347	1 442 179	348 781	3 001 908	2 877 297	999 064	2 439 404
363 252	411 338	826 347	188 903	1 662 841	1 610 201	495 593	868 979
8 100	5 250	39 716	800	5 000	262 907	12 938	2 765
8 408	20 664	2 000	4 017	17 522	47 694	4 417	5 981
108 263	106 030	193 638	43 670	424 363	507 602	181 520	309 387
238 482	279 394	577 305	138 188	1 195 826	783 059	248 991	487 342
–	–	2 276	2 228	2 228	7 720	26 676	–
–	–	11 412	–	17 903	1 219	21 052	63 504
1 552 530	1 534 024	2 830 135	554 721	8 097 705	7 182 460	2 067 121	5 409 283
1 409 409	1 380 212	2 567 165	495 452	7 535 779	6 507 003	1 769 217	4 542 932
6 714	5 900	12 573	3 668	32 689	28 592	10 713	17 179
2 596	3 173	7 720	1 627	14 428	5 603	10 827	10 319
57 715	77 189	122 526	31 502	260 695	315 012	154 508	346 049
12 192	13 371	12 430	3 666	58 429	44 048	3 971	21 870
65 925	62 960	133 689	21 996	227 924	281 309	127 984	390 124
69 212	59 044	133 849	21 491	231 221	280 167	125 741	392 499
16 861	14 456	31 572	3 793	56 207	60 346	26 182	62 924
300 818	265 448	488 237	105 531	1 746 805	685 218	243 367	870 371
31 239	32 565	73 126	14 298	161 859	152 806	42 229	143 884

表5-4

分登记注册类型建筑业财务状况 (2018年)

单位：万元

指　　标	Item	总　计 Total	国有企业 State-owned Enterprises
年末资产负债	**Asset and Liabilities at Year-end**		
流动资产	Circulating Assets	22 902 442	30 967
# 存　货	Stocks	5 366 865	8 175
固定资产原价	Original Value of Fixed Assets	2 291 715	19 584
累计折旧	Accumulative Total Depreciation	1 185 727	2 732
# 本年折旧	Depreciation Within the Year	133 535	549
在建工程	Project Under Construction	101 073	–
资产总计	Total Assets	25 991 673	50 720
流动负债	Liquid Liabilities	16 156 506	29 992
非流动负债合计	Total Non Liquid Liabilities	454 373	–
负债合计	Total Liabilities	16 673 999	29 992
所有者权益	Creditors' Equity	9 317 674	20 728
# 实收资本	Actual Capital Hold	4 637 615	10 400
国家资本	State Capital	283 610	8 400
集体资本	Collective Capital	75 614	–
法人资本	Corporation Capital	1 422 873	2 000
个人资本	Individual Capital	2 715 217	–
港澳台资本	Capital from HongKong, Macao and Taiwan	36 623	–
外商资本	Foreign Capital	103 678	–
损益及分配	**Expenditure, Income and Distribution**		
主营业务收入	Main Business Income	22 756 569	12 999
主营业务成本	Main Business Cost	20 354 930	10 178
主营业务税金及附加	Main Business Taxes and Surcharges	89 173	43
其他业务利润	Profits of Other Business	41 176	951
管理费用	Management Fee	1 076 264	2 651
财务费用	Financial Expenses	128 318	-38
营业利润	Operating Profit	1 027 341	1 020
利润总额	Total Profit	1 029 627	1 029
应交所得税	Income Tax Payable	205 660	170
人工成本及增值税	**Labor Cost and Value Added Tax**		
应付职工薪酬(本年贷方累计发生额)	Employee Compensation Payable (the Cumulative Amount of Credits)	3 545 760	4 875
应交增值税	Value Added Tax Payable	500 777	287

FINANCIAL CONDITIONS OF CONSTRUCTION BY TYPE OF REGISTRATION (2018)

(10 000 yuan)

集体企业 Collective-owned Enterprises	股份合作制企业 Share-holding Cooperative Enterprises	有限责任公司 Limited Liability Corporations	股份有限公司 Share-holding Corporations Ltd.	私营企业 Private Enterprises	港澳台商投资企业 Enterprises With Investment From HongKong, Macao and Taiwan	外商投资企业 Enterprises with Foreign Investment	其他企业 others Enterprises
97 126	7 538	5 741 792	4 313 450	11 976 832	268 399	454 612	11 725
7 034	920	1 548 826	406 825	3 202 422	45 100	147 268	296
2 554	709	525 669	265 116	1 415 978	38 809	23 297	–
1 610	403	277 442	95 544	778 131	18 643	11 220	–
180	15	36 234	12 083	80 674	2 663	1 138	–
35	–	8 679	19 216	67 646	4 813	684	–
98 804	8 059	6 382 112	5 141 098	13 495 675	305 976	496 554	12 676
76 638	4 180	4 641 067	3 146 865	7 786 735	179 102	280 738	11 190
5	–	101 115	217 214	94 943	41 000	97	–
76 643	4 181	4 743 823	3 364 579	7 941 989	220 768	280 835	11 190
22 161	3 878	1 638 289	1 776 519	5 553 686	85 208	215 719	1 487
8 334	1 468	835 780	463 602	3 208 816	48 363	59 652	1 200
–	–	265 721	9 489	–	–	–	–
8 334	600	60 233	4 417	2 030	–	–	–
–	–	313 489	144 122	937 808	23 260	993	1 200
–	868	196 337	242 070	2 267 866	–	8 076	–
–	–	–	–	–	25 103	11 520	–
–	–	–	63 504	1 111	–	39 062	–
52 331	5 842	6 026 132	4 795 101	11 150 483	150 142	546 166	17 374
46 900	4 995	5 538 564	4 142 289	10 003 886	129 161	464 649	14 309
152	100	16 656	11 816	57 992	574	1 795	45
301	19	8 843	8 604	22 166	204	90	–
2 599	454	226 608	258 699	546 767	9 740	28 319	429
1 560	–	24 828	17 179	82 829	2 766	-802	-4
1 372	312	240 236	310 550	419 547	8 226	43 812	2 267
1 287	311	238 861	313 419	422 824	8 072	41 558	2 267
290	35	50 621	51 036	93 124	1 369	8 668	347
20 399	467	708 894	803 628	1 955 737	9 815	41 168	778
1 333	27	104 017	106 492	278 490	4 581	5 253	298

表5-5

劳务分包建筑企业生产经营情况 (2018年) BUSINESS STATUS OF SUBCONTRACTING CONSTRUCTION ENTERPRISES (2018)

单位：万元 (10 000 yuan)

类别	Type	企业数(个) Number of Enterprises (unit)	建筑业总产值 Gross Output Value of Construction	营业收入合计 Total Business Revenue	#主营业务收入 Major Business Revenue	资产合计 Total Assets	负债合计 Total Liabilities
全　市	**Whole Municipality**	**52**	**143 307**	**144 022**	**143 974**	**138 429**	**119 083**
按地区分	**Grouped by Region**						
市　区	Urban Area	10	73 695	74 129	74 129	81 202	75 453
# 吴江区	Wujiang District	1	763	820	820	498	31
常　熟	Changshu	8	7 651	7 377	7 328	6 130	3 262
张家港	Zhangjiagang	28	56 444	60 868	60 868	47 714	37 818
昆　山	Kunshan	4	5 175	1 306	1 306	2 557	1 774
太　仓	Taicang	2	342	342	342	827	777
按行业分	**Grouped by Sector**						
房屋建筑业	Housing Construction	15	19 954	25 474	25 426	30 223	25 424
土木工程建筑业	Civil Engineering Construction	3	42 373	39 520	39 520	3 349	1 400
建筑安装业	Construction Installation	3	2 908	2 322	2 321	1 747	862
建筑装饰和其他建筑业	Decoration and Other Construction	31	78 072	76 707	76 707	103 110	91 398

表5-5 续表 Continued

单位：万元 (10 000 yuan)

类别	Type	实收资本 Actual Capital Hold	利润总额 Total Profits	税金及附加 Taxes and Extra Charges Project Settlement Accounts	从业人员(人) Number of Employed Persons (person)	计算劳动生产率人数(人) Number of Persons Overall Labor Productivity (person)	应付职工薪酬 Deal with the employee payment
全　市	**Whole Municipality**	**10 754**	**2 029**	**732**	**15 936**	**21 102**	**93 521**
按地区分	**Grouped by Region**						
市　区	Urban Area	2 239	473	271	7 410	13 629	54 844
# 吴江区	Wujiang District	50	111	10	23	21	185
常　熟	Changshu	1 768	161	42	591	612	1 974
张家港	Zhangjiagang	6 247	1 363	335	6 422	5 191	29 262
昆　山	Kunshan	450	32	84	1 455	1 588	7 098
太　仓	Taicang	50	1	1	58	82	343
按行业分	**Grouped by Sector**						
房屋建筑业	Housing Construction	3 704	140	171	4 117	2 576	18 492
土木工程建筑业	Civil Engineering Construction	1 151	22	144	4 087	9 798	40 674
建筑安装业	Construction Installation	500	29	11	498	433	1 466
建筑装饰和其他建筑业	Decoration and Other Construction	5 399	1 839	407	7 234	8 295	32 889

表5-6

全市建筑业总产值三十强企业（2018年）
TOP 30 ENTERPRISES OF THE GROSS OUTPUT VALUE OF CONSTRUCTION (2018)

序号 No.	企业名称 Name of Enterprises	所在地区 Location	资质等级 Qualification Grade
1	苏州金螳螂建筑装饰股份有限公司	工业园区	专业承包一级
2	中亿丰建设集团股份有限公司	相城区	总承包特级
3	中铁四局集团第二工程有限公司	相城区	总承包一级
4	中交一公局第二工程有限公司	高新区、虎丘区	总承包一级
5	中铁二十局集团第一工程有限公司	高新区、虎丘区	总承包一级
6	苏州第一建筑集团有限公司	姑苏区	总承包特级
7	江苏金土木建设集团有限公司	常熟市	总承包特级
8	中铁十局集团第五工程有限公司	高新区、虎丘区	总承包一级
9	苏州柯利达装饰股份有限公司	高新区、虎丘区	专业承包一级
10	苏州嘉盛建设工程有限公司	吴中区	总承包特级
11	苏州美瑞德建筑装饰有限公司	姑苏区	专业承包一级
12	江苏金都建工集团有限公司	昆山市	总承包一级
13	振华集团（昆山）建设工程股份有限公司	昆山市	总承包一级
14	亚翔系统集成科技（苏州）股份有限公司	工业园区	专业承包一级
15	苏州园林发展股份有限公司	工业园区	专业承包一级
16	苏州中车建设工程有限公司	工业园区	总承包一级
17	南方雄狮创建集团股份有限公司	吴中区	专业承包二级
18	苏州工业设备安装集团有限公司	姑苏区	总承包一级
19	苏州第五建筑集团有限公司	姑苏区	总承包一级
20	苏州建设（集团）有限责任公司	姑苏区	总承包一级
21	天合建设集团有限公司	昆山市	总承包一级
22	苏州苏明装饰股份有限公司	相城区	专业承包一级
23	苏州交通工程集团有限公司	相城区	总承包一级
24	江苏德丰建设集团有限公司	张家港市	总承包特级
25	江苏兴港建设集团有限公司	张家港市	总承包一级
26	苏州建鑫建设集团有限公司	高新区、虎丘区	总承包一级
27	江苏城南建设集团有限公司	昆山市	总承包一级
28	吴江市建设工程（集团）有限公司	吴江区	总承包一级
29	苏州狮山建筑安装工程有限公司	相城区	总承包一级
30	苏州建筑工程集团有限公司	工业园区	总承包一级

主 要 统 计 指 标 解 释

建筑业统计单位 指从事房屋、构筑物建造和设备安装活动的法人企业。建筑业法人企业应具有建筑业资质并能够独立核算，同时其应具备以下条件：①依法成立，有自己的名称、组织机构和场所，能够承担民事责任；②独立拥有和使用资产，承担负债，有权与其他单位签订合同；③独立核算盈亏，能够编制资产负债表。

建筑业总产值 是以货币形式表现的建筑业企业在一定时期内生产的建筑业产品和提供的服务的总和。建筑业总产值包括：

(1) 建筑工程产值：指列入建筑工程预算内的各种工程价值。

(2) 安装工程产值：指设备安装工程价值，不包括被安装设备本身的价值。

(3) 其他产值：建筑业总产值中除建筑工程、安装工程以外的产值。包括房屋构筑物修理产值、非标准设备制造产值、总包企业向分包企业收取的管理费以及不能明确划分的施工活动所完成的产值。

a.房屋构筑物修理产值：指房屋和构筑物修理所完成的产值，但不包括被修理房屋、构筑物本身价值和生产设备的修理产值。

b.非标准设备制造产值：指加工制造没有定型的非标准生产设备的加工费和原材料价值(如化工厂、炼油厂用的各种罐、槽，矿井生产统一使用的各种漏斗、三角槽、阀门等)以及附属加工厂为本企业承建工程制作的非标准设备的价值。

房屋建筑施工面积 指在报告期内施过工的全部房屋建筑面积，包括本期新开工的房屋面积、上期施工跨入本期继续施工的房屋面积、上期停缓建在本期恢复施工的房屋面积、本期竣工的房屋面积及本期施工后又停缓建的房屋面积。

房屋建筑竣工面积 指在报告期内房屋建筑按照设计要求全部完工，达到了使用条件，经验收鉴定合格，正式移交使用单位的房屋建筑面积。

主营业务收入 指企业(或单位)按承包工程实现的工程价款结算收入，以及向发包单位收取的除工程价款以外的按规定列作营业收入的各种款项，如临时设施费、劳动保险费、施工机械调迁费等以及向发包单位收取的各种索赔款。

EXPLANATORY NOTES ON MAIN STATISTICAL INDICATORS

Statistical Unit in the Construction Industry refers to a corporate enterprise engaged in the construction of buildings and structures and in the installation of equipment. A corporate construction enterprise should have qualification certificates with independent accounting system, and should meet the following 3 requirements: a) being set up in line with relevant legal basis, having its full name, organization and location, and capable of taking civil liabilities; b) independently possessing and using its assets and assuming its liabilities, and entitled to sign contracts with other institutions; and c) making independent accounts of its profits and losses, and capable of compiling its own balance sheet.

Gross Output Value of Construction refers to total of construction products and services, expressed in money terms, produced or rendered by construction and installation enterprises during a given period of time. It includes:

(1) Output value of construction projects: the value of projects covered by the project budgets;

(2) Output value of installation projects: the value of the installation of equipment, (excluding the value of the equipment to be installed);

(3) Other output values: the output value of construction industry apart from that of construction projects and installation projects. It includes: output value of repair of buildings and structures; output value of non-standard equipment manufacturing; overhead expenses received by contracted enterprises from the sub-contracted enterprises and the completed output value of construction activities for which there is no clear definition.

a. Output value of repair of buildings and structures: the value created through the repairs of buildings or structures. It does not include the value of buildings or structures being repaired and the value of the repair of production equipment;

b. Output value of manufactured non-standard equipment: the value of non-standard production equipment, including raw materials and manufacturing cost, made for the construction project (i.e., chemical plant; kettles or tanks used by refineries; various fillers, triangle tanks, valves used by mines). It also includes the output value of equipment manufactured by subsidiary workshops.

Floor Space of Buildings Under Construction refers to floor space of buildings under construction during the reference period, including the floor space of buildings for which construction has newly started; buildings for which construction has started earlier and is continuing during the reference period; and buildings for which construction has been suspended earlier but has restarted during the reference period; buildings completed during the reference period; and buildings under construction but construction has subsequently been during the reference period.

Floor Space of Buildings Completed refers to the floor space of buildings that are completed in the reference period in accordance with the requirements of the design, up to the standard for being put into use, and having been checked and accepted by departments concerned as qualified ones.

Main Business Income refers to the income received by the construction enterprise from the contracted project through settlement procedures, and other charges to the contractor as operational costs in addition to the value of the project, such as temporary facility fee, labour insurance premium , moving cost of construction equipment, as well as various types of claims to the contractor.

六、运输 邮电业

CHAPTER 6
TRANSPORTATION，POST AND TELECOMMUNICATION

6 运输　邮电业 TRANSPORTATION, POST AND TELECOMMUNICATION

主要统计指标 MAJOR STATISTICAL INDICATORS

2018年全社会公路水运客运量	Total Passenger Traffic of Highways and Waterways	29 762	万人次	10 000 person-times
比上年增长	Increase Over Last Year	-6.7	%	
2018年全社会公路水运货运量	Total Freight Traffic of Highways and Waterways	16 159	万吨	10 000 tons
比上年增长	Increase Over Last Year	8.2	%	
2018年苏州港货物吞吐量	Cargo Handled at Suzhou Ports	53 227	万吨	10 000 tons
比上年增长	Increase Over Last Year	-12.0	%	
2018年苏州港集装箱吞吐量	Volume of Container Handled at Suzhou Ports	635.51	万标箱	10 000 teu
比上年增长	Increase Over Last Year	8.2	%	
2018年末私家车拥有量	Number of Private Motor Vehicles	330.11	万辆	10 000 coach
比上年增长	Increase Over Last Year	9.1	%	
2018年邮电业务总收入	Total Revenue of Postal and Telecommunication Services	397.94	亿元	100 million yuan
比上年增长	Increase Over Last Year	12.4	%	

表6-1

部分年份全社会交通运输量
TOTAL TRAFFIC OF PARTIAL YEARS

项　目	Item	2014年	2015年	2016年	2017年	2018年
铁　路	**Railway**					
客运量　(万人次)	Passenger Traffic (10 000 person-times)	7 026.19	7 536.38	8 138.93	8 983.36	9 430.53
发送量	Number of Passengers Dispatched	3 496.38	3 742.43	4 059.05	4 485.10	4 704.44
到达量	Amount at the Time of Arrival	3 529.81	3 793.95	4 079.88	4 498.26	4 726.09
货运量　(万吨)	Freight Traffic (10 000 tons)	221.84	178.40	185.97	188.44	175.91
发送量	Volume of Freight Dispatched	67.17	66.78	82.32	77.66	62.43
到达量	Amount at the Time of Arrival	154.67	111.62	103.65	110.78	113.48
旅客周转量(万人公里)	Passenger-kilometers (10 000 person-km)	1 496 579	1 612 785	1 749 870	1 862 374	1 972 917
发送量	Number of Passengers Dispatched	744 729	800 880	872 696	948 091	993 550
到达量	Amount at the Time of Arrival	751 850	811 905	877 174	914 283	979 367
货物周转量(万吨公里)	Freight Ton-kilometers (10 000 ton-km)	141 515	113 600	118 307	119 318	111 819
发送量	Number of Passengers Dispatched	41 444	41 270	51 038	47 767	38 402
到达量	Amount at the Time of Arrival	100 071	72 330	67 269	71 551	73 418
公　路	**Highways**					
客运量　(万人次)	Passenger Traffic (10 000 person-times)	39 432	34 110	31 589	31 272	29 123
货运量　(万吨)	Freight Traffic (10 000 tons)	11 855	11 814	12 287	13 614	14 787
旅客周转量　(万人公里)	Passenger-kilometers (10 000 person-km)	1 374 907	1 318 903	1 217 335	1 256 441	1 206 134
货物周转量　(万吨公里)	Freight Ton-kilometers (10 000 ton-km)	1 579 367	1 665 643	1 732 654	1 937 652	2 088 144
水　运	**Waterways**					
客运量　(万人次)	Passenger Traffic (10 000 person-times)	526	535	541	631	639
货运量　(万吨)	Freight Traffic (10 000 tons)	1 098	1 191	1 221	1 323	1 372
旅客周转量　(万人公里)	Passenger-kilometers (10 000 person-km)	4 847	4 925	4 974	5 673	5 752
货物周转量　(万吨公里)	Freight Ton-kilometers (10 000 ton-km)	425 701	469 519	512 808	558 434	590 068
地方港口吞吐量　(万吨)	Cargo Handled at Local Ports (10 000 tons)	55 033	61 092	65 032	68 125	61 295
# 苏州港港口吞吐量	Cargo Handled at Suzhou Port	47 792	53 990	57 937	60 456	53 227

表6-2

部分年份公路和航道通航里程
LENGTH OF HIGHWAYS AND NAVIGABLE INLAND WATERWAYS OF PARTIAL YEARS

项　目	Item	2014年	2015年	2016年	2017年	2018年
一、公路总里程 (公里)	**Total Length of Highways** (km)	**13 212.1**	**13 238.8**	**13 207.5**	**12 658.3**	**12 173.2**
1. 按技术等级分	Rated by Technical Standards					
高　速	Express-way	550.2	550.2	598.3	598.3	598.3
一　级	A Qualification	1 706.7	1 704.3	1 748.8	1 707.4	1 790.7
二　级	B Qualification	4 114.4	4 149.3	4 099.7	4 063.4	4 148.5
三　级	C Qualification	2 407.4	2 405.4	2 366.9	2 358.2	2 371.9
四　级	D Qualification	4 433.4	4 429.6	4 393.8	3 931.0	3 263.8
2.按行政等级分	Grouped by Grade of Administration					
国　道	State Highway	496.0	496.0	824.6	824.6	824.6
省　道	Provincial Highway	928.6	928.6	639.8	982.5	986.6
县　道	County Highway	1 634.5	1 629.6	1 650.7	1 342.1	1 871.7
乡　道	Rural Highway	4 083.8	4 091.6	4 055.4	3 940.7	3 735.5
村　道	Village Highway	6 029.5	6 053.3	5 997.4	5 534.1	4 720.6
专用公路	Specialized Highway	39.7	39.7	39.7	34.2	34.2
3. 按路面标准分	Grouped by Standard of Road Surface					
高　级	High	13 085.3	13 115.4	13 181.5	12 632.4	12 160.6
中级、低级	Medium and Low	126.8	123.4	25.9	25.9	12.6
二、公路桥梁 (座)	**Highway Bridges** (unit)	**9 704**	**9 721**	**9 754**	**9 743**	**9 600**
(米)	(m)	**500 193**	**493 695**	**550 356**	**583 059**	**593 043**
三、内河航道通航里程 (公里)	**Length of Navigable Inland Waterways** (km)	**2 787.0**	**2 786.0**	**2 786.0**	**2786.4**	**2 786.4**
# 水深 1 米以上里程	Depths of One Meter and Over	2 638.9	2 638.4	2 638.4	2638.4	2 638.4
四、通航河流上建筑物 (座)	**Construction in Navigable Waterways** (unit)	**110**	**110**	**111**	**111**	**118**
1.永久性闸坝	Permanent Gate and Dam	49	49	49	49	54
2.船　闸	Lock Gate	7	7	8	8	8
3.套　闸	Gate Set	54	54	54	54	56
五、内河航道上设立的航标	**Navigation Mark in Inland Waterways**	**171**	**159**	**159**	**166**	**166**
# 发光的	Luminary	158	159	159	166	166

表6-3

部分年份全社会船舶数
TOTAL NUMBER OF TRANSPORT VESSELS OF PARTIAL YEARS

指　标		Item		2014年	2015年	2016年	2017年	2018年
客　船	(艘)	**Passenger Ship**	(unit)	**122**	**147**	**147**	**176**	**174**
	(客位)		(seat)	5 292	10 939	11 458	15 340	15 554
	(千瓦)		(kw)	12 451	21 919	22 894	31 148	31 320
货　船	(艘)	**Cargo Ship**	(unit)	**208**	**187**	**167**	**155**	**151**
	(吨位)		(ton)	116 486	130 030	135 664	107 038	106 446
	(千瓦)		(kw)	65 847	63 885	63 341	52 071	50 644
拖　船	(艘)	**Tug Boat**	(unit)	**5**	**2**	**6**	**3**	**2**
	(千瓦)		(kw)	1 064	440	11 474	4 636	4 416
驳　船	(艘)	**Barges**	(unit)	**41**	**27**	**36**	**10**	**1**
	(吨位)		(ton)	6 560	4 960	13 040	7 240	54

注：原既可装货也可以载客的渡船作为货船统计，从2015年起纳入客船统计。
Note：The ferry which can carry both goods and passengers was as the cargo ship statistics, from 2015 onwards, the ferry is as the passenger ship statistics.

表6-4

分地区机动车拥有量(2018年末)
CIVIL MOTOR VEHICLES BY REGION (END OF 2018)

单位：辆　　(coach)

地　区　Region	机动车总计 Total Motor Vehicles	# 汽　车 Vehicles	# 私家客车 Personal Passenger Vehicles	# 私家货车 Personal Freight Trucks	年末汽车驾驶员(人) The Number of Car Drivers (person)	年内汽车上牌数 The number of Auto Registration in 2018	年内汽车驾驶员领证(人) Driver's license number in 2018 (persons)
全　市 Whole Municipality	**4 034 238**	**3 910 639**	**3 277 477**	**23 643**	**4 113 468**	**453 862**	**272 053**
市　区　Urban Area	2 195 925	2 153 323	1 797 692	9 813	2 166 771	254 882	145 073
#吴江区 Wujiang District	414 332	389 978	341 464	4 898	436 186	47 010	30 471
常　熟　Changshu	495 650	472 716	412 858	4 077	569 794	46 130	38 053
张家港　Zhangjiagang	423 364	401 636	339 539	6 207	454 256	39 633	24 518
昆　山　Kunshan	658 175	643 227	527 897	1 571	638 750	86 244	45 954
太　仓　Taicang	261 124	239 737	199 491	1 975	283 897	26 973	18 455

表6-5

历年全社会客运情况
TOTAL PASSENGER TRAFFIC OVER THE YEARS

年　份 Year	客运量 (万人次) Passenger Traffic (10 000 person-times)	公　路 Highways	水　运 Waterways	旅客周转量 (万人公里) Passenger-kilometers (10 000 person-km)	公　路 Highways	水　运 Waterways	铁路旅客发送量 (万人次) Number of Passengers Dispatched on Railway (10 000 person-times)
1949	56	45	11	1 486	1 299	187	
1952	383	167	216	8 651	3 232	5 419	
1957	2 270	1 887	383	26 754	18 024	8 730	
1962	1 486	845	641	39 595	23 076	16 519	366.45
1965	1 101	676	425	24 381	15 425	8 956	208.86
1970	1 724	1 054	670	33 280	21 241	12 039	226.06
1975	2 919	2 091	828	55 339	39 726	15 613	316.63
1978	3 296	2 477	819	64 766	48 775	15 991	356.44
1980	4 813	4 034	779	96 041	74 404	21 637	520.21
1985	6 757	6 340	417	188 795	165 851	22 944	745.40
1990	6 764	6 516	247	232 799	218 521	14 278	755.78
1995	18 945	18 840	104	628 147	620 152	7 995	917.64
2000	18 559	18 447	112	1 013 554	1 009 983	3 571	940.23
2001	19 508	19 394	114	1 064 044	1 060 708	3 336	1 043.47
2002	21 031	20 935	96	1 199 190	1 196 358	2 832	1 161.83
2003	22 921	22 835	86	1 518 126	1 515 701	2 425	1 211.27
2004	25 292	25 265	27	1 792 342	1 791 228	1 114	1 481.92
2005	30 707	30 703	4	1 919 138	1 918 713	425	1 663.78
2006	35 186	35 182	4	2 149 435	2 149 035	400	1 707.07
2007	40 163	40 163	-	2 498 592	2 498 592	-	1 625.41
2008	45 386	45 386	-	2 855 005	2 855 005	-	1 893.33
2009	39 338	39 263	75	1 679 103	1 678 269	834	1 939.87
2010	56 475	56 392	83	2 412 841	2 411 917	924	2 044.68
2011	63 793	63 699	94	2 746 339	2 745 297	1 042	2 274.68
2012	68 998	68 895	103	3 077 391	3 076 263	1 128	2 627.98
2013老口径	71 798	71 696	102	3 212 308	3 211 241	1 067	3 035.07
2013新口径	39 584	39 050	534	1 373 225	1 368 347	4 878	
2014	39 958	39 432	526	1 379 754	1 374 907	4 847	3 496.38
2015	34 645	34 110	535	1 323 828	1 318 903	4 925	3 742.43
2016	32 130	31 589	541	1 222 309	1 217 335	4 974	4 059.05
2017	31 903	31 272	631	1 262 114	1 256 441	5 673	4 485.10
2018	29 762	29 123	639	1 211 886	1 206 134	5 752	4 704.44

注：新口径公路客运量不包括公交车和出租车的运输量。

Note:The new caliber of passenger traffic of highways didn't include that of buses and taxis.

表6-6

历年全社会货运情况
TOTAL FREIGHT TRAFFIC OVER THE YEARS

单位：万吨 (10 000 tons)

年份 Year	货运量 Freight Traffic	公路 Highways	水运 Waterways	货物周转量（万吨公里）Freight Ton-kilometers (10 000 ton-km)	公路 Highways	水运 Waterways	铁路货物发送量 Volume of Freight Dispatched on Railway	铁路货物到达量 Volume of Freight Arrived on Railway
1949	55	1	54	2 419	26	2 393		
1952	209	34	175	8 995	257	8 738		
1957	365	21	344	19 991	287	19 704		
1962	501	78	422	19 753	883	18 870	35.03	141.85
1965	777	108	668	35 314	1 128	34 186	41.61	222.96
1970	926	122	805	56 138	1 432	54 706	52.33	250.44
1975	1 645	226	1 419	92 848	3 392	89 456	79.54	317.52
1978	2 195	329	1 866	115 434	6 086	109 348	87.28	465.79
1980	2 712	399	2 313	138 610	8 663	129 947	92.93	541.90
1985	6 041	871	5 170	258 795	24 060	234 735	124.05	630.52
1990	3 211	746	2 465	208 573	26 187	182 386	116.43	557.97
1995	8 561	4 746	3 815	496 290	190 242	306 048	164.13	740.91
2000	7 816	4 567	3 248	458 916	245 987	212 929	159.37	391.51
2001	7 988	4 738	3 250	464 030	254 699	209 331	174.53	564.09
2002	8 350	5 010	3 340	478 850	275 550	203 300	164.44	703.81
2003	7 354	5 389	1 965	454 889	334 060	120 829	165.94	838.26
2004	8 833	6 941	1 892	522 670	397 170	125 500	167.72	800.78
2005	10 393	7 762	2 631	684 229	515 208	169 021	145.92	741.27
2006	11 099	8 891	2 208	746 045	590 016	156 029	147.15	644.36
2007	11 834	9 958	1 876	820 219	656 395	163 824	131.30	632.35
2008	12 631	10 863	1 768	902 918	733 993	168 925	127.61	494.50
2009	11 370	10 820	550	1 032 213	887 006	145 207	118.40	452.66
2010	13 417	12 768	649	1 237 387	1 037 797	199 590	90.94	400.06
2011	15 602	14 798	804	1 498 375	1 200 220	298 155	93.00	406.34
2012	17 325	16 441	884	1 705 084	1 357 255	347 829	93.78	311.43
2013老口径	18 504	17 568	936	1 818 741	1 445 420	373 321	83.53	195.79
2013新口径	11 786	10 799	987	1 817 314	1 435 496	381 818		
2014	12 953	11 855	1 098	2 005 068	1 579 367	425 701	67.17	154.67
2015	13 005	11 814	1 191	2 135 162	1 665 643	469 519	66.78	111.62
2016	13 508	12 287	1 221	2 245 462	1 732 654	512 808	82.32	107.04
2017	14 937	13 614	1 323	2 496 086	1 937 652	558 434	77.66	110.78
2018	16 159	14 787	1 372	2 678 212	2 088 144	590 068	62.43	113.48

注：新口径公路货运量不包含农用车和拖拉机的运输量。
Note: The new caliber of Freight traffic of highways didn't include that of agricultural vehicles and tractors.

表6-7

分 地 区 客 运 量 (2018年)
PASSENGER TRAFFIC BY REGION (2018)

地　区	Region	客运量 (万人次) Passenger Traffic (10 000 person-times)	公　路 Highways	水　运 Waterways	旅客周转量 (万人公里) Passenger-kilometers (10 000 person-km)	公　路 Highways	水　运 Waterways
全　市	**Whole Municipality**	**29 762**	**29 123**	**639**	**1 211 886**	**1 206 134**	**5 752**
市　区	Urban Area	16 989	16 673	316	693 369	690 529	2 840
# 吴江区	Wujiang District	2 979	2 927	52	121 676	121 203	473
常　熟	Changshu	3 318	3 253	65	135 305	134 720	585
张家港	Zhangjiagang	3 002	2 886	116	120 573	119 527	1 046
昆　山	Kunshan	3 795	3 733	62	155 145	154 583	562
太　仓	Taicang	2 658	2 578	80	107 494	106 775	719

表6-8

分 地 区 货 运 量 (2018年)
FREIGHT TRAFFIC BY REGION (2018)

地　区	Region	货运量 (万吨) Freight Traffic (10 000 tons)	公　路 Highways	水　运 Waterways	货物周转量 (万吨公里) Freight-kilometers (10 000 ton-km)	公　路 Highways	水　运 Waterways
全　市	**Whole Municipality**	**16 159**	**14 787**	**1 372**	**2 678 212**	**2 088 144**	**590 068**
市　区	Urban Area	8 718	8 157	561	1 393 238	1 151 890	241 349
# 吴江区	Wujiang District	1 369	1 255	114	226 380	177 231	49 149
常　熟	Changshu	1 740	1 536	205	304 907	216 893	88 014
张家港	Zhangjiagang	2 176	1 917	259	381 910	270 722	111 189
昆　山	Kunshan	1 729	1 615	114	277 068	227 995	49 073
太　仓	Taicang	1 796	1 562	233	321 088	220 645	100 443

表6-9

苏州港码头泊位和吞吐量 (2018年)
NUMBER OF BERTHS AND THROUGHPUT OF SUZHOU PORT (2018)

项　目	Item	合 计 Total	常熟港区 Changshu Port	张家港港区 Zhangjiagang Port	太仓港区 Taicang Port
码头泊位个数 (个)	**Number of Berths** (unit)	**298**	**52**	**162**	**84**
# 万吨级以上	10 000 Ton Class	130	21	73	36
# 公用码头	Public Berths	168	32	67	69
# 集装箱码头	Containen Berths	16	2	4	10
货物吞吐量 (万吨)	Cargo at Ports Throughput (10 000 tons)	**53 227**	**6 970**	**23 373**	**22 884**
# 外　贸	Freight Trade	13 893	1 246	5 463	7 184
集装箱吞吐量(万标箱)	International Containes (10 000TEU)	**635.51**	**25.47**	**102.92**	**507.11**
重　量 (万吨)	Weight (10 000 tons)	8 885.79	251.96	1 348.33	7 285.50
# 货　物	Freight	7 614.86	201.02	1 142.49	6 271.36

注:标箱指折合20英尺标准箱，英文缩写TEU。　Note:TEU is the abbreviation, Which refers to 20-foot equivalent unit.

表6-10

苏州港集装箱吞吐量 (2018年)
VOLUME OF CONTAINER HANDLED OF SUZHOU PORT (2018)

项　目	Item	合 计 Total	其中 of which		按航线分 Grouped by Routes		
			进 港 In-Port	出 港 Out-Port	国际航线 International Routes	内支线 Ports of Inland Rivers	国内航线 Domestic Routes
箱量合计 (标箱)	**Total Containers** (TEU)	**6 355 073**	**3 076 721**	**3 278 352**	**788 685**	**2 122 420**	**3 443 968**
空箱小计	Light Case Subtotal	1 376 751	639 744	737 007	223 567	415 000	738 184
# 45英尺箱 (箱)	45-foot equivalent unit (unit)	5 120	121	4 999	1 271	716	3 133
40英尺箱	40-foot equivalent unit	369 121	163 258	205 863	78 533	149 217	141 371
20英尺箱	20-foot equivalent unit	626 981	312 951	314 030	63 633	114 955	448 393
重箱小计 (标箱)	Heavy Case Subtotal (TEU)	4 978 322	2 436 977	2 541 345	565 119	1 707 420	2 705 783
# 45英尺箱 (箱)	45-foot equivalent unit (unit)	819	664	155	10	712	97
40英尺箱	40-foot equivalent unit	1 283 921	630 918	653 003	214 801	612 500	456 620
20英尺箱	20-foot equivalent unit	2 408 568	1 173 615	1 234 953	135 425	480 818	1 792 325
重量合计 (吨)	**Total Weight** (ton)	**88 857 912**	**45 254 985**	**43 602 927**	**6 153 471**	**24 233 914**	**58 470 527**
# 货　重	Freight Weight	76 148 649	39 100 694	37 047 955	4 629 577	20 113 148	51 405 924

表6-11

苏州港进出港口货物分类流向一览 (2018年)
FREIGHT HANDLED AT SUZHOU PORT BY DIRECTION (2018)

单位：万吨 (10 000 tons)

类 别	Type	总 计 Total	总计中 In Total 进 港 Arrival	出 港 Departure
总 计	**Total**	**53 226.85**	**32 467.56**	**20 759.29**
1.煤炭及其制品	Coal and Its Products	13 846.13	9 439.81	4 406.32
2.石油、天然气及制品	Petroleum, Natural Gas and Related Products	911.01	543.28	367.73
3.金属矿石	Metal Ores	13 175.45	9 026.67	4 148.78
# 铁矿石	Iron Ore	10 738.79	7 292.36	3 446.43
4.钢 铁	Iron and Steel	3 200.88	1 068.07	2 132.81
# 钢 材	Rolled Steel	2 418.93	428.33	1 990.60
5.矿物性建筑材料	Mineral Building Materials	5 241.84	2 574.75	2 667.09
6.水 泥	Cement	129.70	9.85	119.85
7.木 材	Timber	1 714.55	1 443.69	270.86
# 原 木	Log	1 315.96	1 105.62	210.35
8.非金属矿石	Nonmetal Ores	133.55	115.36	18.19
9.化学肥料及农药	Chemical Fertilizers and Pesticides	234.19	119.74	114.45
10.盐	Salt	15.00	14.50	0.50
11.粮 食	Grain	1 038.77	707.83	330.94
# 黄 豆	Bean	557.80	443.33	114.47
12.机械、设备、电器	Machine, Equipment and Wiring	357.09	47.87	309.22
13.化工原料及制品	Chemical Industry Materials and Products	2 510.66	1 819.82	690.84
14.有色金属	Nonferrous Metals	17.62	10.46	7.16
15.轻工、医药产品	Products of Light Industry and Medicine & Pharmacy	712.03	460.02	252.01
16.农林牧渔业产品	The Output of Agricultural Products	435.10	166.11	268.99
17.其 他	Others	9 553.28	4 899.71	4 653.57
# 集装箱重量	Container Weight	8 885.79	4 525.50	4 360.29
# 滚装船汽车吞吐量(标辆)	Car Throughput (Standard Vehicle) on Roll-on Ships	119 637	90 772	28 865

表6-12

邮政电信基本情况（2018年）

项　目		Item		全　市 Whole Municipality
一、邮电业务总收入	(亿元)	**Business Income of Post & Telecommunications**	(100 million yuan)	**397.94**
电信业务总收入		Business Income of Telecommunications		216.37
邮政业务总收入		Business Income of Post		181.57
# 快递业务收入		Business Income of Express		156.21
二、邮政行业分类业务量		**Business Volume of Postal Service**		
函　件(邮政系统)	(万件)	Number of Letters (Postal System)	(10 000 pcs)	9 441
包　裹		Number of Package		36.57
快递业务量		Business Volume of Express		124 939
报刊杂志累计数	(万份)	Number of Newspapers and Magazines Circulation	(10 000 copies)	26 792
三、电信业务主要指标		**Main Indicators on Telecommunications**		
固定电话用户	(户)	Fixed Telephone Subscribers	(household)	2 488 704
移动电话用户		Number of Mobile Telephone Subscribers		18 556 413
# 3G用户		3G users		468 407
# 4G用户		4G users		14 855 747
移动互联网用户		Mobile Internet Users		15 509 661
固定互联网宽带接入用户		Fixed Internet Broadband Access Users		6 229 436

注:邮政业务总收入中包含规模以上快递公司快递业务收入，但未包括邮政储蓄银行直接营业收入。

POSTS AND TELECOMMUNICATIONS (2018)

市　区 Urban Area	# 吴江区 Wujiang District	常　熟 Changshu	张家港 Zhangjiagang	昆　山 Kunshan	太　仓 Taicang
235.70	**35.64**	**49.79**	**27.79**	**65.87**	**18.78**
121.80	23.63	23.56	19.65	39.03	12.32
113.90	12.01	26.23	8.14	26.84	6.46
97.39	9.48	22.75	6.33	24.11	5.63
8 569	74	222	112	475	63
26.38	1.25	0.95	3.70	1.99	3.55
60 125	8 828	31 173	5 136	23 582	4 923
14 222	2 180	4 208	2 826	3 492	2 044
1 373 374	245 449	318 392	235 493	406 624	154 821
10 579 406	1 952 123	2 063 104	1 757 244	3 091 372	1 065 287
270 475	43 551	53 516	41 805	73 557	29 054
8 433 074	1 580 036	1 628 097	1 396 099	2 544 199	854 278
8 803 371	1 650 629	1 720 650	1 456 991	2 638 169	890 480
3 204 321	651 736	756 964	709 311	1 164 936	393 904

Note: Business volume of post contain business volume of express company above designated size, but not contain the postal savings bank direct operating income.

主 要 统 计 指 标 解 释

公路里程 指在一定时期内实际达到《公路工程[WTBZ]技术标准JTJ01-88》规定的等级公路，并经公路主管部门正式验收交付使用的公路里程数。包括大中城市的郊区公路以及通过小城镇街道部分的公路里程和桥梁、渡口的长度，不包括大中城市的街道、厂矿、林区生产用道和农业生产用道的里程。两条或多条公路共同经由同一路段，只计算一次，不得重复计算里程长度。该指标可以反映公路建设的发展规模，也是计算运输网密度等指标的基础资料。

内河航道里程 也称内河通航里程，指在一定时期内，能通航运输船舶及排筏的天然河流、湖泊水库、运河及通航渠道的长度。包括全年季节性通航累计三个月以上的航道，不包括仅供零散流放竹、木排的河道。该指标可以反映内河水运网的规模、水平和发展情况。

货(客)运量 指在一定时期内，各种运输工具实际运送的货物(旅客)数量。货运按吨计算，客运按人计算。货物不论运输距离长短、货物类别，均按实际重量统计。旅客不论行程远近或票价多少，均按一人一次客运量统计；半价票、儿童票也按一人统计。

货物(旅客)周转量 指在一定时期内，由各种运输工具运送的货物(旅客)数量与其相应运输距离的乘积之总和。该指标可以反映运输业生产的总成果，也是编制和检查运输生产计划，计算运输效率、劳动生产率以及核算运输单位成本的主要基础资料。计算货物周转量通常按发出站与到达站之间的最短距离，也就是计费距离计算。计算公式为：

货物（旅客）周转量=∑（货物（旅客）运输量×运输距离）

民用汽车拥有量 指报告期末，在公安交通管理部门按照《机动车注册登记工作规范》，已注册登记领有民用车辆牌照的全部汽车数量。汽车拥有量统计的主要分类：根据汽车结构分为载客汽车、载货汽车及其他汽车；根据汽车所有者不同分为个人(私人)汽车、单位汽车；根据汽车的使用性质分为营运汽车、非营运汽车；根据汽车大小规格不同载客汽车分为大型、中型、小型和微型，载货汽车分为重型、中型、轻型和微型。

移动电话用户 指在电信运营企业营业网点办理开户登记手续，通过移动电话交换机进入移动电话网，占用移动电话号码的各类电话用户。包括GSM数字移动电话用户、CDMA数字移动电话用户和电信运营企业发行的报告期末已激活充值的能异地漫游的各种智能卡用户。

快递业务量 企业收寄的各类快递业务总数量，由受理用户委托的企业负责统计。

快递业务量=国内同城快递业务量+国内异地快递业务量+港澳台快递业务量+国际快递业务量。

EXPLANATORY NOTES ON MAIN STATISTICAL INDICATORS

Length of Highways refers to the length of highways which are built in conformity with the grades specified by the highway engineering standard [Highways WTBZ-Technical Standard JTJ01-88]formulated by the Ministry of Communications, and have been formally checked and accepted by the departments of highways and put into use. The length of highways includes that of the suburb highways at large and medium-sized cities, highways passing through streets at small cities and towns, and also the length of bridges and ferry piers. It does not include the length of streets in big and medium-sized cities and highways built for the production purpose at factories, mines, forest areas and agricultural areas. If two or more highways go the same section of the way, the length of the section is only calculated for once and no duplication is allowed. The length of highways is an indicator to show the development of the scale of highway construction and to provide essential information to calculate the transport network density.

Length of Navigable Inland Waterways is an indicator reflecting the size and development of inland water network. It refers to the length of the natural rivers, lakes, reservoirs, canals, and ditches open to navigation during a given period, which enables transportation by ships and rafts. It includes the channels open to navigation for over an accumulated period of 3 months in a year, yet this does not include the river courses which are only used to float odd logs and bamboo rafts. This indicator can reflect the scale, level and development situation of the inland waterway network.

Freight (Passenger) Traffic refers to the volume of freight (passenger) transported with various means within a specific period of time. Freight transport is calculated in tons and passenger traffic is calculated in terms of number of persons. Freight transport is calculated in terms of the actual weight of the goods and takes no account of the type of freight and distance of travel. Passenger traffic is calculated by the principle that one person can be counted only once in one trip and takes no account of the travelling distance and ticket price. The passengers who travel with a half price ticket or a child's ticket is also calculated as one person.

Freight Ton-kilometres (Passenger-kilometres) refers to the sum of the product of the volume of transported cargo (passengers) multiplied by the transport distance. It is an important indicator to reflect the achievement of the transportation industry. This is an important indicator to show the total results of the transport industry; to prepare and examine the transport plan; and to serve as the main basic data for calculating the efficiency, labour productivity and unit cost of transport. Normally, the shortest distance between the departure station and the destination station (i.e., the payable distance) is the basis in calculating the freight ton-kilometres. The formula is as follows:

$$\begin{matrix}\text{Freight ton-kilometres} \\ \text{(passenger-kilometres)}\end{matrix} = \sum \begin{matrix}\text{freight} \\ \text{(passenger)traffic}\end{matrix} \times \begin{matrix}\text{distance of} \\ \text{transportation}\end{matrix}$$

Possession of Civil Motor Vehicles refer to the total numbers of vehicles that are registered and received vehicles license tags according to the *Work Standard for Motor Vehicles Registration* formulated by the Transport Management Office under the department of public security at the end of the reference period. They are divided into categories. According to the structure of motor vehicles, they are divided into passenger vehicles, trucks and others; according to ownership into private vehicles and vehicles for the unit's use; according to kind of usage into working vehicles and non-working vehicles; and according to size of vehicles into large passenger vehicles, medium-sized passenger vehicles, small passenger vehicles and mini passenger vehicles, heavy trucks, light-heavy trucks, light trucks and mini-trucks.

Mobile Telephone Subscribers refer to persons who have gone through registration procedures in the operation points of enterprises engaged in telecommunications and are hence connected with the mobile telephone communication network through the mobile telephone switchboards and occupy mobile phone numbers. Included are GSM digital mobile phone subscribers, CDMA digital mobile phone subscribers and subscribers to intelligent phone cards with roaming facility issued by telecommunications enterprises and which have been subscribed to and activated at the end of the reference period.

Business volume of express the total number of express services received by enterprises, count by enterprises who was entrusted by the user. Business volume of express= domestic express delivery business volume of same city + domestic express delivery business volume of different city + Hong Kong, Macao and Taiwan express business volume + International express delivery business volume.

七、贸易餐饮业

CHAPTER 7
TRADE AND CATERING BUSINESS

7 贸易餐饮业
TRADE AND CATERING BUSINESS

主要统计指标
MAJOR STATISTICAL INDICATORS

2018年社会消费品零售总额	Total Retail Sales of Consumer Goods	5 746.90	亿元	100 million yuan
比上年增长	Increase Over Last Year	7.4	%	
2018年批发和零售业零售额	Wholesale and Retail Sale Trades	5 034.59	亿元	100 million yuan
比上年增长	Increase Over Last Year	7.1	%	
2018年住宿和餐饮业零售额	Accommodation and Catering Trade	712.30	亿元	100 million yuan
比上年增长	Increase Over Last Year	9.0	%	
2018年限额以上批发和零售业	Enterprises Above Designated Size in Wholesale and Retail Trades			
商品购进总额	Total Purchases	16 829.67	亿元	100 million yuan
商品销售总额	Total Sales	18 623.41	亿元	100 million yuan
商品年末库存总额	Inventory (year-end)	782.86	亿元	100 million yuan
2018年限额以上住宿业营业总额	Total Business Turnover of Hotel Accommodation Above Designated Size	78.60	亿元	100 million yuan
2018年限额以上餐饮业营业总额	Total Business Turnover of Catering Trade Above Designated Size	93.95	亿元	100 million yuan
2018年亿元以上商品交易市场商品成交总额	Total Business Turnover of Transaction Markets Over 100 Million Yuan	7 986.33	亿元	100 million yuan
比上年增长	Increase Over Last Year	1.7	%	

表7-1

历年分地区社会消费品零售总额
TOTAL RETAIL SALES OF CONSUMER GOODS OVER THE YEARS BY REGION

单位：万元 (10 000 yuan)

年 份 Year	全 市 Whole Municipality	市 区 Urban Area	# 吴江区 Wujiang District	常 熟 Changshu	张家港 Zhangjiagang	昆 山 Kunshan	太 仓 Taicang
1949	23 818	15 576	3 604	2 867	1 562	2 067	1 746
1952	31 193	18 652	4 125	5 004	2 319	2 663	2 555
1957	35 788	22 027	3 615	5 863	2 533	2 627	2 738
1962	42 967	26 191	5 011	7 294	3 187	3 383	2 912
1965	48 564	27 345	5 103	8 510	4 977	3 912	3 820
1970	51 397	28 185	5 397	8 636	5 299	4 922	4 355
1975	77 612	44 546	8 102	12 415	8 418	6 140	6 093
1978	94 747	51 986	10 208	15 313	13 233	6 924	7 291
1980	156 707	84 305	17 124	26 894	20 571	11 114	13 823
1985	370 485	194 924	42 027	69 891	44 214	30 366	31 090
1990	721 514	375 196	72 891	147 881	75 660	65 017	57 760
1995	2 423 094	1 217 029	207 724	507 723	285 642	247 284	165 416
2000	4 281 714	2 293 890	345 989	756 715	458 523	516 558	256 028
2001	4 914 382	2 652 807	393 390	847 521	522 342	609 046	282 666
2002	5 713 157	3 113 126	456 687	975 385	600 748	703 170	320 728
2003	6 640 502	3 633 803	526 263	1 108 282	705 690	831 572	361 155
2004	7 768 800	4 255 432	613 551	1 296 788	820 809	980 079	415 692
2005	9 343 000	5 103 568	762 873	1 509 313	996 237	1 226 497	507 385
2006	11 236 000	6 099 528	952 656	1 764 594	1 211 273	1 536 685	623 920
2007	13 706 000	7 378 277	1 207 675	2 099 770	1 494 469	1 955 155	778 329
2008	17 488 000	9 318 800	1 620 000	2 629 000	1 949 000	2 557 000	1 034 200
2009	20 268 405	10 774 312	1 874 029	3 045 857	2 261 813	2 980 480	1 205 943
2010	24 020 199	12 759 030	2 229 679	3 601 883	2 678 564	3 566 414	1 414 308
2011	28 295 794	14 987 098	2 636 452	4 262 612	3 164 556	4 209 816	1 671 712
2012	32 409 679	16 820 177	3 080 430	4 995 373	3 707 280	4 936 190	1 950 659
2013	36 622 357	18 953 775	3 567 589	5 644 322	4 138 019	5 699 233	2 187 008
2014	40 998 329	21 337 066	3 924 952	6 186 745	4 583 222	6 500 862	2 390 434
2015	44 616 214	23 117 215	4 222 992	6 756 392	4 948 748	7 146 845	2 647 014
2016	49 367 885	25 585 002	4 676 567	7 407 789	5 351 641	8 150 370	2 873 083
2017	54 428 192	28 049 519	5 071 738	8 004 117	5 814 558	9 458 504	3 101 494
2018	57 468 970	29 558 995	5 358 580	8 249 156	6 058 728	10 217 657	3 384 434

表7-2

部分年份分行业社会消费品零售总额
TOTAL RETAIL SALES OF CONSUMER GOODS OF PARTIAL YEARS BY SECTOR

单位：万元 (10 000 yuan)

年份 Year	社会消费品零售总额 Total Retail Sales of Consumer Goods	# 批发和零售业 Wholesale and Retail Sale Trades	# 住宿和餐饮业 Accommodation and Catering Trade
1990	721 514	654 249	39 794
1995	2 423 094	2 177 435	207 724
2000	4 281 714	3 760 650	488 204
2005	9 343 000	8 119 628	1 179 960
2010	24 020 199	21 075 139	2 725 445
2011	28 295 794	24 764 557	3 213 714
2012	32 409 679	28 303 744	3 827 257
2013	36 622 357	31 972 397	4 303 595
2014	40 998 329	35 803 949	4 807 120
2015	44 616 214	39 196 633	5 419 581
2016	49 367 885	43 430 180	5 937 705
2017	54 428 192	47 894 429	6 533 763
2018	57 468 970	50 345 936	7 123 034

表7-3

分地区社会消费品零售总额 (2018年)
TOTAL RETAIL SALES OF CONSUMER GOODS BY REGION (2018)

单位：万元 (10 000 yuan)

地区 Region	社会消费品零售总额 Total Retail Sales of Consumer Goods	# 个体 Individual	按行业分 Grouped by Sector	
			批发和零售业 Wholesale and Retail Sale Trades	住宿和餐饮业 Accommodation and Catering Trade
全市 Whole Municipality	**57 468 970**	**22 830 151**	**50 345 936**	**7 123 034**
市区 Urban Area	29 558 995	10 123 658	26 533 408	3 025 587
姑苏区 Gusu District	9 688 419	3 877 772	8 800 646	887 773
吴中区 Wuzhong District	4 412 355	889 947	4 047 019	365 336
相城区 Xiangcheng District	2 258 884	657 894	1 989 253	269 631
高新区、虎丘区 New & Hi-tech Zone, Huqiu District	2 903 448	300 564	2 575 829	327 619
工业园区 Industrial Park	4 937 310	1 202 995	4 485 868	451 442
吴江区 Wujiang District	5 358 580	3 194 486	4 634 794	723 786
县级市 Cities at County Level	27 909 975	12 706 493	23 812 528	4 097 447
常熟 Changshu	8 249 156	5 054 658	7 500 682	748 474
张家港 Zhangjiagang	6 058 728	3 153 044	5 085 988	972 740
昆山 Kunshan	10 217 657	2 060 781	8 320 743	1 896 914
太仓 Taicang	3 384 434	2 438 009	2 905 115	479 319

表7-4

分月社会消费品零售总额（2018年）
RETAIL SALES OF CONSUMER GOODS BY MONTH (2018)

单位：万元 （10 000 yuan）

月　份	Month	全　市 Whole Municipality	市　区 Urban Area	# 吴江区 Wujiang District	常　熟 Changshu	张家港 Zhangjiagang	昆　山 Kunshan	太　仓 Taicang
总　计	**Total**	**57 468 970**	**29 558 995**	**5 358 580**	**8 249 156**	**6 058 728**	**10 217 657**	**3 384 434**
一季度	**1st Quarter**	**14 459 418**	**7 523 956**	**1 381 498**	**2 026 369**	**1 503 656**	**2 551 759**	**853 677**
1月	Jan.	5 350 236	2 794 964	506 293	751 306	522 522	966 343	315 101
2月	Feb.	4 202 042	2 223 445	395 490	594 611	449 968	678 526	255 492
3月	Mar.	4 907 141	2 505 547	479 715	680 452	531 166	906 890	283 085
二季度	**2nd Quarter**	**13 717 920**	**6 971 706**	**1 295 737**	**2 055 359**	**1 402 286**	**2 451 730**	**836 839**
4月	Apr.	4 347 712	2 197 081	431 985	668 077	431 576	780 026	270 952
5月	May.	4 723 664	2 415 394	414 531	700 215	501 365	812 279	294 411
6月	June	4 646 544	2 359 232	449 221	687 067	469 345	859 425	271 476
三季度	**3rd Quarter**	**13 955 194**	**7 145 110**	**1 306 291**	**2 046 538**	**1 457 010**	**2 465 925**	**840 611**
7月	July	4 567 393	2 306 313	430 313	679 007	488 516	805 132	288 425
8月	Aug.	4 712 600	2 419 151	423 596	692 080	473 193	848 604	279 572
9月	Sept.	4 675 201	2 419 646	452 382	675 451	495 301	812 190	272 613
四季度	**4th Quarter**	**15 336 438**	**7 918 223**	**1 375 053**	**2 120 889**	**1 695 777**	**2 748 243**	**853 306**
10月	Oct.	5 038 966	2 623 618	442 228	736 966	561 021	836 905	280 455
11月	Nov.	5 173 425	2 653 538	444 532	698 340	556 242	973 140	292 164
12月	Dec.	5 124 048	2 641 066	488 293	685 583	578 514	938 198	280 687

表7-5 限额以上批发和零售、住宿和餐饮法人企业基本情况 (2018年)

BASIC CONDITION OF WHOLESALE AND RETAIL, ACCOMMODATION AND CATERING CORPORATE ENTERPRISES ABOVE THE DESIGNATED SIZE (2018)

项　目	Item	法人企业数(个) Number of Corporation (unit)	零售或餐饮营业面积(平方米) Floor Space of Retail or Catering Business (sq.m)	年末从业人员(人) Year-end Employees (person)
总　计	**Total**	**4 002**	**6 759 481**	**274 960**
市　区	Urban Area	1 879	4 087 187	152 994
# 吴江区	Wujiang District	570	483 055	19 757
常　熟	Changshu	479	520 844	18 945
张家港	Zhangjiagang	779	625 469	30 694
昆　山	Kunshan	676	1 279 235	62 208
太　仓	Taicang	189	246 746	10 119
一、批发和零售业小计	**Wholesale Trades and Retail Sales**	**3 622**	**5 623 699**	**202 817**
按行业分	**Grouped by Sector**			
批发业	Wholesale Trades	2 746	1 097 793	104 737
零售业	Retail Sales	876	4 525 906	98 080
按地区分	**Grouped by Region**			
市　区	Urban Area	1 646	3 337 420	98 452
# 吴江区	Wujiang District	536	372 478	15 526
常　熟	Changshu	444	423 418	15 630
张家港	Zhangjiagang	748	538 761	25 740
昆　山	Kunshan	617	1 121 570	55 131
太　仓	Taicang	167	202 530	7 864
二、住宿和餐饮业小计	**Accommodation and Catering Trade**	**380**	**1 135 782**	**72 143**
按行业分	**Grouped by Sector**			
住宿业	Accommodation	178	518 315	28 948
餐饮业	Catering Trade	202	617 467	43 195
按地区分	**Grouped by Region**			
市　区	Urban Area	233	749 767	54 542
# 吴江区	Wujiang District	34	110 577	4 231
常　熟	Changshu	35	97 426	3 315
张家港	Zhangjiagang	31	86 708	4 954
昆　山	Kunshan	59	157 665	7 077
太　仓	Taicang	22	44 216	2 255

表7-6 限额以上批发和零售业商品购进、销售、库存总额（2018年）

单位：万元

项　目	Item	购进总额 Total Purchases
总　计	**Total**	**168 296 715**
一、批发业	**Wholesale Trades**	**147 287 480**
# 国有及国有控股	State-owned and State Holding Majority Shares	18 230 395
1. 按地区分	**Grouped by Region**	
市　区	Urban Area	41 707 028
# 吴江区	Wujiang District	17 159 680
常　熟	Changshu	9 858 028
张家港	Zhangjiagang	70 675 748
昆　山	Kunshan	15 920 210
太　仓	Taicang	9 126 465
2. 按登记注册类型分	**Grouped by Registration Status**	
国有企业	State-owned Enterprises	1 122 315
集体企业	Collective-owned Enterprises	62 672
股份合作企业	Share-holding Cooperative Enterprises	-
联营企业	Joint Ownership Enterprises	-
有限责任公司	Limited Liability Corporations	52 132 152
股份有限公司	Share-holding Cooperative Ltd.	1 785 574
私营企业	Private Enterprises	59 808 869
其他企业	Other Enterprises	-
港澳台商投资企业	Enterprises with Investment from HongKong, Macao and Taiwan	7 520 104
外商投资企业	Enterprises with Foreign Investment	24 855 795
3. 按主要行业分	**Grouped by Sector**	
农、林、牧、渔产品批发	Wholesale of Products of Agriculture, Forestry, Animal Husbandry, and Fishery	4 425 099
食品、饮料及烟草制品批发	Wholesale of Food, Beverages and Tobaccos	3 743 648
纺织、服装及日用品批发	Wholesale of Textiles, Garments and Daily Articles	35 304 199
# 服装批发	Wholesale of Garments	7 404 660
文化、体育用品及器材批发	Wholesale of Cultural, Sports and Appliances Goods	1 400 185

TOTAL PURCHASES, SALES AND INVENTORY OF WHOLESALE AND RETAIL TRADE ABOVE DESIGNATED SIZE (2018)

(10 000 yuan)

#进 口 Imports	销售总额 Total Sales	批 发 Wholesale	#出 口 Exports	零 售 Retail Sale	年末库存总额 Inventory (year-end)
17 189 304	**186 234 072**	**161 630 356**	**15 888 618**	**24 603 716**	**7 828 634**
16 387 608	**161 032 163**	**158 620 468**	**15 888 618**	**2 411 695**	**6 109 079**
558 876	19 183 624	18 700 416	2 165 443	483 207	785 263
2 420 317	47 708 922	45 795 476	3 036 154	1 913 445	1 809 633
72 272	17 833 954	17 823 516	833 782	10 438	176 973
56 204	10 761 070	10 657 193	790 572	103 876	857 246
6 729 153	72 875 106	72 831 163	4 840 215	43 943	1 998 097
6 801 970	17 656 655	17 471 787	6 966 686	184 868	840 643
379 965	12 030 411	11 864 849	254 990	165 562	603 460
–	1 614 108	1 599 171	–	14 937	88 098
–	58 591	56 769	29 429	1 822	12 391
–	–	–	–	–	–
–	–	–	–	–	–
7 146 707	54 061 349	53 386 624	4 652 560	674 725	2 107 324
115 273	1 839 195	1 831 834	295 171	7 361	204 138
624 503	63 893 263	63 469 709	3 902 822	423 554	2 101 058
–	–	–	–	–	–
449 419	10 677 367	10 346 035	130 201	331 331	733 355
8 051 707	28 888 290	27 930 326	6 878 435	957 965	862 714
3 423 832	4 434 131	4 433 863	5 996	268	412 902
130 844	4 698 874	4 637 726	28 926	61 148	234 655
1 075 439	41 954 290	40 294 450	5 542 662	1 659 840	1 868 163
890 338	9 869 290	8 847 454	3 312 975	1 021 836	546 866
6 874	1 600 005	1 543 700	107 642	56 305	101 853

表7-6 续表 1

单位：万元

项　　目	Item	购进总额 Total Purchases
医药及医疗器材批发	Wholesale of Medicines and Medical Appliances	2 577 469
矿产品、建材及化工产品批发	Wholesale of Mineral Products, Building Materials and Chemical Products	78 264 638
机械设备、五金交电及电子产品批发	Wholesale of Machinery, Hardware, Transport, Electric and Electronic Equipment	19 500 808
# 汽车及零配件批发	Wholesale of Automobiles and Spare parts	5 520 053
五金产品批发	Wholesale of Hardware Products	949 151
电气设备批发	Wholesale of Electrical Equipment	412 970
计算机、软件及辅助设备批发	Wholesale of Computers, Software and Auxiliary Equipment	6 431 027
通讯设备批发	Wholesale of Communication Equipment	602 024
贸易经纪与代理	Trade Management and Agency	612 241
其他批发	Other Wholesale	1 459 194
二、零售业	**Retail Trades**	**21 009 235**
# 国有及国有控股	State-owned and State Holding Majority Shares	2 251 456
1. 按地区分	**Grouped by Region**	
市　区	Urban Area	10 260 868
# 吴江区	Wujiang District	1 303 642
常　熟	Changshu	1 362 079
张家港	Zhangjiagang	1 246 666
昆　山	Kunshan	7 666 203
太　仓	Taicang	473 420
2. 按登记注册类型分	**Grouped by Registration Status**	
国有企业	State-owned Enterprises	26 548
集体企业	Collective-owned Enterprises	34 088
股份合作企业	Share-holding Cooperative Enterprises	2 609
联营企业	Joint Ownership Enterprises	8 084
有限责任公司	Limited Liability Corporations	5 945 995
股份有限公司	Share-holding Cooperative Ltd.	2 564 093
私营企业	Private Enterprises	7 190 795

Continued 1

(10 000 yuan)

# 进 口 Imports	销售总额 Total Sales	批 发 Wholesale	# 出 口 Exports	零 售 Retail Sale	年末库存总额 Inventory (year-end)
269 230	2 901 478	2 899 602	13 662	1 876	210 881
3 930 910	80 919 925	80 381 184	2 303 534	538 741	2 311 775
7 437 807	22 115 073	22 058 304	7 502 165	56 769	864 328
403 528	6 421 785	6 401 298	117 917	20 487	260 038
30 336	1 072 118	1 066 213	323 942	5 905	54 977
14 631	501 360	500 810	48 046	550	42 425
6 234 629	6 576 346	6 563 520	6 353 822	12 826	29 476
1 688	708 736	702 418	15 834	6 318	18 734
68 984	644 767	644 612	349 943	155	9 716
43 687	1 763 621	1 727 028	34 087	36 593	94 806
801 696	**25 201 909**	**3 009 889**	**–**	**22 192 020**	**1 719 555**
1	3 754 665	840 709	–	2 913 956	111 299
485 409	13 111 288	1 052 007	–	12 059 281	1 003 843
45 433	1 335 468	13 575	–	1 321 893	134 755
89 055	1 502 692	39 437	–	1 463 255	144 066
142 034	1 476 218	121 984	–	1 354 234	162 212
69 531	8 622 781	1 795 106	–	6 827 674	249 986
15 667	488 930	1 354	–	487 576	159 447
–	32 483	–	–	32 483	2 599
–	40 734	–	–	40 734	2 676
–	3 189	177	–	3 012	129
–	8 509	–	–	8 509	43
299 543	7 285 380	103 250	–	7 182 130	332 293
39 473	2 773 281	605 029	–	2 168 252	89 644
391 564	7 871 763	276 295	–	7 595 468	984 161

表7-6 续表 2

单位：万元

项　　目	Item	购进总额 Total Purchases
其他企业	Other Enterprises	5 595
港澳台商投资企业	Enterprises with Investment from HongKong, Macao and Taiwan	4 017 567
外商投资企业	Enterprises with Foreign Investment	1 213 861
3.按主要行业分	**Grouped by Sector**	
综合零售	Retail of Integrated	4 693 910
百货零售	Retail of Consumer Goods	974 133
超级市场零售	Retail of Supermarket	3 607 376
便利店零售	Retail by Convenience Stores	96 118
其他综合零售	Others Retail of Integrated	16 283
食品、饮料及烟草制品专门零售	Retail of Food, Beverages and Tobaccos	199 757
纺织、服装及日用品专门零售	Retail of Textiles, Garments and Daily Articles	541 071
文化、体育用品及器材专门零售	Retail of Culture, Sports Articles and Equipment	167 685
医药及医疗器材专门零售	Retail of Medicines and Medical Appliances	408 571
汽车、摩托车、燃料及零配件专门零售	Retail of Motor Vehicles, Motorcycles, Fuels and Parts	10 573 878
# 汽车新车零售	Retail of New Cars	8 008 988
家用电器及电子产品专门零售	Retail of Household Appliances and Electronic Products	686 250
# 日用家电零售	Retail of Household Appliances	235 718
计算机、软件及辅助设备零售	Retail of Computers, Software and Appliances	56 077
五金、家具及室内装修材料专门零售	Retail of Hardware Furniture and Materials for Ornament	51 346
无店铺及其他零售	Retail of Non-shop and Others	3 686 766
4.按经营方式分	**Grouped by Means of Operation**	
独立商店	Independent Shop	11 055 868
连锁商店总店	Central Shop of Chain Shops	5 653 695
连锁门店	Outlets of Chain Shops	442 691
其　他	Others	3 856 982
5.按零售业态分	**Grouped by Retail Size**	
百货商店	Department Store	1 076 909
超级市场	Supermarket	4 195 435
专业店	Special Store	6 330 723
专卖店	Monopoly Store	5 302 642
其　他	Others	4 103 526

Continued 2

(10 000 yuan)

# 进 口 Imports	销售总额 Total Sales	批 发 Wholesale	# 出 口 Exports	零 售 Retail Sale	年末库存总额 Inventory (year-end)
–	6 620	–	–	6 620	46
29 411	4 622 635	1 785 104	–	2 837 531	178 054
41 705	2 557 316	240 034	–	2 317 282	129 910
162	5 950 008	1 708 940	–	4 241 068	180 213
140	1 529 485	17	–	1 529 468	31 953
22	4 283 253	1 708 923	–	2 574 330	138 381
–	114 978	–	–	114 978	9 262
–	22 292	–	–	22 292	617
3 747	252 548	3 909	–	248 639	15 578
6 152	846 876	98 189	–	748 687	185 617
–	232 269	14 739	–	217 530	59 145
52	530 675	21 677	–	508 998	63 991
790 743	12 235 893	1 063 975	–	11 171 918	1 073 299
766 834	8 494 256	182 770	–	8 311 486	965 084
–	754 513	51 635	–	702 879	34 610
–	240 525	607	–	239 918	7 066
–	68 853	6 932	–	61 921	4 137
–	64 128	2 099	–	62 029	9 051
841	4 334 997	44 726	–	4 290 272	98 050
706 274	12 804 522	263 324	–	12 541 199	1 320 539
1	7 427 563	2 601 912	–	4 825 651	219 585
21	478 822	3 932	–	474 891	59 116
95 400	4 491 002	140 722	–	4 350 281	120 315
220	1 697 978	–	–	1 697 978	48 557
7 266	4 657 612	1 697 318	–	2 960 294	405 455
359 180	7 122 760	426 327	–	6 696 433	569 456
333 628	7 050 585	742 728	–	6 307 858	601 369
101 402	4 672 973	143 516	–	4 529 458	94 718

表7-7

限额以上住宿和餐饮业经营情况 (2018年)

项　目	Item	营业总额 (万元) Total Business Turnover (10 000 yuan)
总　计	**Total**	**1 725 518**
一、住宿业	**Accommodation**	**786 013**
# 国有及国有控股	State-owned and State Holding Majority Shares	222 436
1. 按地区分	**Grouped by Region**	
市　区	Urban Area	613 718
# 吴江区	Wujiang District	76 248
常　熟	Changshu	52 383
张家港	Zhangjiagang	55 175
昆　山	Kunshan	34 471
太　仓	Taicang	30 266
2. 按登记注册类型分	**Grouped by Registration Status**	
国有企业	State-owned Enterprises	85 658
集体企业	Collective-owned Enterprises	11 902
股份合作企业	Share-holding Cooperative Enterprises	650
联营企业	Joint Ownership Enterprises	–
有限责任公司	Limited Liability Corporations	374 656
股份有限公司	Share-holding Cooperative Ltd.	27 283
私营企业	Private Enterprises	152 898
其他企业	Other Enterprises	–
港澳台商投资企业	Enterprises with Investment from HongKong, Macao and Taiwan	53 738
外商投资企业	Enterprises with Foreign Investment	79 227
3. 按主要行业分	**Grouped by Sector**	
旅游饭店	Tourist Hotel	725 088
一般旅馆	Regular Hotel	58 036
其他住宿服务	Other Accommodation Service	2 888
4. 按星级分	**Grouped by Star Rated**	
五　星	Five Star	254 686
四　星	Four Star	125 685
三　星	Three Star	23 265
二　星	Two Star	2 748
一　星	One Star	–
其　他	Other	379 628

BUSINESS CONDITION OF ACCOMMODATION AND CATERING ENTERPRISES ABOVE DESIGNATED SIZE(2018)

				年末拥有床位数 (个)	年末拥有餐位数 (个)
客房收入 Room Rate Revenues	餐费收入 Catering Revenues	商品销售收入 Commodity Sales Revenues	其他收入 Others Revenues	Year-end Guest Beds (unit)	Dining Seats by the Year end (unit)
453 389	**1 165 882**	**44 854**	**61 392**	**87 532**	**323 121**
379 389	**349 247**	**9 966**	**47 410**	**74 247**	**120 607**
89 159	106 913	3 007	23 357	15 789	41 931
301 259	266 130	8 523	37 805	57 533	83 117
29 079	42 950	669	3 550	6 153	17 168
25 207	24 048	863	2 265	5 438	12 422
17 538	34 177	394	3 067	4 124	14 368
19 441	13 237	121	1 672	4 180	6 739
15 945	11 654	66	2 601	2 972	3 961
40 834	37 105	629	7 091	6 053	11 845
3 096	8 666	49	90	978	2 580
367	284	–	–	180	150
–	–	–	–	–	–
165 802	177 036	6 385	25 433	25 022	61 000
15 754	10 576	45	908	2 092	2 346
85 368	59 103	1 425	7 002	18 851	30 390
–	–	–	–	–	–
22 371	25 644	688	5 035	16 884	8 468
45 798	30 832	746	1 851	4 187	3 828
336 058	338 910	9 442	40 679	63 291	114 769
42 403	9 652	509	5 473	10 597	5 538
928	685	16	1 259	359	300
112 560	129 649	1 604	10 874	13 385	37 614
51 884	61 731	2 340	9 730	10 909	28 980
12 282	6 923	463	3 597	4 775	6 850
748	1 790	1	210	317	810
–	–	–	–	–	–
201 914	149 155	5 559	23 000	44 861	46 353

表7-7 续表

项　目	Item	营业总额(万元) Total Business Turnover (10 000 yuan)
二、餐饮业	**Catering Services**	**939 505**
# 国有及国有控股	State-owned and State Holding Majority Shares	32 876
1. 按地区分	**Grouped by Region**	
市　区	Urban Area	692 533
# 吴江区	Wujiang District	21 662
常　熟	Changshu	27 366
张家港	Zhangjiagang	57 317
昆　山	Kunshan	143 980
太　仓	Taicang	18 308
2. 按登记注册类型分	**Grouped by Registration Status**	
国有企业	State-owned Enterprises	6 410
集体企业	Collective-owned Enterprises	–
股份合作企业	Share-holding Cooperative Enterprises	–
联营企业	Joint Ownership Enterprises	398
有限责任公司	Limited Liability Corporations	132 983
股份有限公司	Share-holding Cooperative Ltd.	29 095
私营企业	Private Enterprises	387 521
其他企业	Other Enterprises	5 645
港澳台商投资企业	Enterprises with Investment from HongKong, Macao and Taiwan	30 547
外商投资企业	Enterprises with Foreign Investment	346 906
3. 按主要行业分	**Grouped by Sector**	
正餐服务	Dinner	501 497
快餐服务	Fast Food	311 975
饮料及冷饮服务	Beverage and Cold Drink Services	51 330
其他餐饮服务	Other	74 703
4. 按经营方式分	**Grouped by Management Forms**	
独立经营	Independent-stores	433 336
连锁经营总店	Chain-stores-General	332 073
连锁经营分店	Chain-stores-Branch	94 721
其　他	Other	79 375

Continued

客房收入 Room Rate Revenues	餐费收入 Catering Revenues	商品销售收入 Commodity Sales Revenues	其他收入 Others Revenues	年末拥有床位数(个) Year-end Guest Beds (unit)	年末拥有餐位数(个) Dining Seats by the Year end (unit)
74 000	**816 635**	**34 888**	**13 982**	**13 285**	**202 514**
10 118	21 178	471	1 109	1 613	7 255
21 870	627 407	32 658	10 598	3 196	143 246
1 491	19 007	115	1 048	391	9 600
1 539	25 608	212	8	526	6 325
12 530	43 189	324	1 274	2 336	15 754
34 067	107 080	1 482	1 351	6 186	31 727
3 995	13 351	212	751	1 041	5 462
904	5 269	101	136	580	2 200
–	–	–	–	–	–
–	–	–	–	–	–
–	362	36	–	–	120
31 489	90 623	1 233	9 638	4 452	25 747
–	26 235	2 328	532	–	10 480
30 325	326 133	28 863	2 202	6 348	109 235
2 372	3 273	–	–	338	1 600
5 477	23 805	89	1 175	806	4 965
3 433	340 936	2 238	299	761	48 167
74 000	384 358	30 590	12 549	13 285	121 878
–	311 755	177	43	–	49 316
–	48 177	2 179	974	–	6 893
–	72 345	1 942	416	–	24 427
64 925	352 307	4 504	11 601	11 119	105 716
–	305 342	25 713	1 017	–	45 752
–	89 682	4 507	532	–	14 138
9 076	69 304	164	831	2 166	36 908

表7-8 限额以上批发和零售法人企业主要财务指标 (2018年)

单位：万元

项　　目	Item	流动资产合计 Total Circulating Funds	固定资产原价 Original Value of Fixed Assets
总　　计	**Total**	**45 989 541**	**4 711 123**
一、批发业	**Wholesale Trades**	**39 357 818**	**2 394 695**
# 国有及国有控股	State-owned and State Holding Majority Shares	4 864 442	459 401
1. 按地区分	**Grouped by Region**		
市　区	Urban Area	13 221 678	1 079 575
# 吴江区	Wujiang District	3 753 114	151 680
常　熟	Changshu	3 575 137	266 340
张家港	Zhangjiagang	12 714 785	432 707
昆　山	Kunshan	5 987 849	376 610
太　仓	Taicang	3 858 369	239 463
2. 按登记注册类型分	**Grouped by Registration Status**		
国有企业	State-owned Enterprises	1 005 867	129 954
集体企业	Collective-owned Enterprises	25 087	6 993
股份合作企业	Share-holding Cooperative Enterprises	–	–
联营企业	Joint Ownership Enterprises	–	–
有限责任公司	Limited Liability Corporations	13 231 751	548 348
股份有限公司	Share-holding Cooperative Ltd.	1 057 495	85 597
私营企业	Private Enterprises	13 480 297	830 310
其他企业	Other Enterprises	–	–
港澳台商投资企业	Enterprises with Investment from HongKong, Macao and Taiwan	3 507 141	370 432
外商投资企业	Enterprises with Foreign Investment	7 050 179	423 061
3. 按主要行业分	**Grouped by Sector**		
农、林、牧、渔产品批发	Wholesale of Products of Agriculture, Forestry, Animal Husbandry, and Fishery	1 355 585	17 853
食品、饮料及烟草制品批发	Wholesale of Food, Beverages and Tobaccos	1 812 064	195 322
纺织、服装及日用品批发	Wholesale of Textiles, Garments and Daily Articles	11 095 145	959 235
# 服装批发	Wholesale of Garments	2 998 879	464 067
文化、体育用品及器材批发	Wholesale of Cultural, Sports Equipment and Appliances	673 105	39 001

MAIN FINANCIAL INDICATORS OF WHOLESALE AND RETAIL CORPORATION ABOVE DESIGNATED SIZE (2018)

(10 000 yuan)

累计折旧 Accumulative Total Depreciation	固定资产净值 Net Fixed Assets	资产总计 Total Assets	负债总计 Total Liabilities	所有者权益合计 Total Creditors Equity	营业收入 Business Revenue	# 主营业务收入 Major Business Revenue	营业成本 Business Cost
2 061 852	**2 647 313**	**58 289 780**	**43 165 467**	**15 125 529**	**161 953 230**	**161 159 581**	**149 987 742**
1 054 932	**1 338 479**	**48 522 038**	**35 451 719**	**13 070 413**	**139 725 990**	**139 417 604**	**130 401 190**
168 541	289 687	6 213 420	3 919 672	2 293 747	16 799 172	16 738 151	15 867 670
517 556	561 944	17 333 358	11 889 799	5 443 652	40 543 104	40 375 651	36 669 130
54 856	96 748	5 167 242	4 298 922	868 413	15 508 719	15 499 610	15 199 691
115 805	150 536	4 674 832	3 298 159	1 376 673	9 404 242	9 370 698	8 673 008
162 047	269 451	14 909 743	12 174 495	2 735 248	63 601 147	63 561 384	62 006 674
157 730	218 882	7 203 333	4 978 378	2 224 955	15 701 479	15 648 304	14 516 297
101 795	137 668	4 400 773	3 110 888	1 289 884	10 476 019	10 461 568	8 536 082
59 839	70 114	1 087 388	213 888	873 500	1 388 586	1 387 372	976 272
5 566	1 427	28 930	24 203	4 727	50 592	50 419	49 391
–	–	–	–	–	–	–	–
–	–	–	–	–	–	–	–
208 724	338 451	16 147 077	13 099 605	3 047 472	47 315 492	47 220 493	45 568 147
38 417	47 180	1 861 717	1 171 536	690 181	1 554 434	1 549 218	1 461 525
366 299	463 899	15 413 573	12 627 245	2 786 421	55 901 388	55 790 318	54 104 636
–	–	–	–	–	–	–	–
161 017	209 416	4 007 882	2 341 810	1 666 073	9 179 423	9 162 258	6 621 883
215 069	207 993	9 975 471	5 973 433	4 002 038	24 336 076	24 257 527	21 619 336
4 412	13 441	1 391 302	1 423 506	-32 205	4 011 434	4 010 641	3 961 217
93 638	101 686	2 168 148	1 065 895	1 102 254	4 103 814	4 090 452	3 466 025
414 618	544 541	14 261 079	9 985 113	4 275 851	36 100 181	36 041 156	31 096 830
211 338	252 729	4 339 717	2 637 750	1 701 967	9 023 038	9 002 904	6 600 744
24 955	14 047	1 086 044	570 970	515 075	1 429 926	1 399 154	1 289 130

表7-8 续表 1

单位：万元

项　　目	Item	流动资产合计 Total Circulating Funds	固定资产原价 Original Value of Fixed Assets
医药及医疗器材批发	Wholesale of Medicines and Medical Appliances	1 174 752	91 353
矿产品、建材及化工产品批发	Wholesale of Mineral Products, Building Materials and Chemical Products	14 514 432	678 506
机械设备、五金交电及电子产品批发	Wholesale of Machinery, Hardware, Transport, Electric and Electronic Equipment	7 865 915	374 223
# 汽车及零配件批发	Wholesale of Automobiles and Spare parts	1 946 619	46 336
五金产品批发	Wholesale of Hardware Products	309 458	28 415
电气设备批发	Wholesale of Electrical Equipment	675 055	65 711
计算机、软件及辅助设备批发	Wholesale of Computers, Software and Auxiliary Equipment	2 026 215	6 724
通讯设备批发	Wholesale of Communication Equipment	112 563	3 656
贸易经纪与代理	Trade Management and Agency	294 428	3 299
其他批发	Other Wholesale	572 392	35 902
二、零售业	**Retail Trades**	**6 631 724**	**2 316 428**
# 国有及国有控股	State-owned and State Holding Majority Shares	825 279	225 290
1. 按地区分	**Grouped by Region**		
市　区	Urban Area	3 790 287	1 431 712
# 吴江区	Wujiang District	385 985	84 756
常　熟	Changshu	465 980	145 665
张家港	Zhangjiagang	503 255	206 766
昆　山	Kunshan	1 670 557	469 695
太　仓	Taicang	201 644	62 591
2. 按登记注册类型分	**Grouped by Registration Status**		
国有企业	State-owned Enterprises	13 814	1 280
集体企业	Collective-owned Enterprises	8 954	4 432
股份合作企业	Share-holding Cooperative Enterprises	7 198	419
联营企业	Joint Ownership Enterprises	320	576
有限责任公司	Limited Liability Corporations	1 652 119	428 939
股份有限公司	Share-holding Cooperative Ltd.	743 097	235 421
私营企业	Private Enterprises	2 747 387	770 469

Continued 1

(10 000 yuan)

累计折旧 Accumulative Total Depreciation	固定资产净值 Net Fixed Assets	资产总计 Total Assets	负债总计 Total Liabilities	所有者权益合计 Total Creditors Equity	营业收入 Business Revenue	# 主营业务收入 Major Business Revenue	营业成本 Business Cost
36 140	55 213	1 338 681	921 906	416 775	2 528 457	2 514 296	2 280 700
303 389	373 908	17 482 117	13 967 564	3 514 761	69 900 902	69 757 331	68 253 893
156 925	217 298	9 743 194	6 815 987	2 927 207	19 506 421	19 462 741	18 087 013
22 928	23 408	2 865 361	1 531 012	1 334 349	4 976 394	4 971 205	4 343 097
15 703	12 712	331 170	212 046	119 124	968 233	967 694	897 236
23 475	42 237	808 454	554 272	254 183	496 634	496 232	442 066
2 609	4 114	2 033 007	1 938 068	94 939	6 509 790	6 504 329	6 443 447
1 899	1 756	116 101	80 995	35 106	611 170	608 314	547 488
2 269	1 030	304 751	249 760	54 991	589 461	589 235	567 121
18 585	17 317	746 722	451 018	295 703	1 555 395	1 552 599	1 399 261
1 006 920	**1 308 834**	**9 767 742**	**7 713 749**	**2 055 116**	**22 227 240**	**21 741 977**	**19 586 552**
108 020	117 270	1 278 983	1 221 673	57 310	3 296 971	3 224 880	3 044 999
600 916	829 734	5 885 506	4 633 544	1 251 962	11 485 005	11 244 374	10 217 819
37 604	46 033	467 000	363 203	103 797	1 078 251	1 055 292	970 063
62 877	82 788	634 687	429 116	205 571	1 338 792	1 304 191	1 159 647
88 502	118 652	762 547	570 693	192 976	1 276 462	1 244 404	1 135 562
234 714	234 981	2 225 228	1 865 442	359 785	7 674 005	7 519 441	6 680 832
19 912	42 679	259 776	214 954	44 822	452 977	429 567	392 693
1 082	198	15 184	2 526	12 658	21 061	20 888	16 905
2 763	1 669	11 920	3 042	8 877	35 715	35 186	30 816
305	114	7 313	1 374	5 939	2 741	2 741	2 271
348	228	548	19	529	7 310	7 310	6 964
195 319	234 008	2 359 691	1 914 919	445 894	6 497 524	6 390 539	5 581 260
98 449	136 972	1 043 599	987 737	55 862	2 473 852	2 448 174	2 304 144
311 700	457 707	3 649 674	2 812 072	837 602	7 077 022	6 904 296	6 288 519

表7-8 续表 2

单位：万元

项　　目	Item	流动资产合计 Total Circulating Funds	固定资产原价 Original Value of Fixed Assets
其他企业	Other Enterprises	–	–
港澳台商投资企业	Enterprises with Investment from HongKong, Macao and Taiwan	1 180 344	685 125
外商投资企业	Enterprises with Foreign Investment	278 491	189 770
3. 按主要行业分	**Grouped by Sector**		
综合零售	Retail of Integrated	1 337 344	1 176 810
百货零售	Retail of Consumer Goods	566 773	688 571
超级市场零售	Retail of Supermarket	697 132	475 584
便利店零售	Retail by Convenience Stores	43 205	12 448
其他综合零售	Others Retail of Integrated	30 234	208
食品、饮料及烟草制品专门零售	Wholesale of Foodstuff, Drink and Tobacco	110 373	43 498
纺织、服装及日用品专门零售	Wholesale of Textiles, Garments, Shoes and Hats	392 822	66 043
文化、体育用品及器材专门零售	Wholesale of Cultural, Sports Equipments and Appliances	137 746	55 096
医药及医疗器材专门零售	Wholesale of Medicines and Medical Appliances	210 664	23 948
汽车、摩托车、燃料及零配件专门零售	Wholesale of Timber	3 333 338	848 314
# 汽车新车零售	Retail of New Cars	2 532 469	608 464
家用电器及电子产品专门零售	Retail of Textiles, Garments, Shoes and Hats	271 585	38 574
# 日用家电零售	Retail of Household Appliances	73 998	22 936
计算机、软件及辅助设备零售	Retail of Computer, Software and Assistant Equipments	30 316	2 216
五金、家具及室内装修材料专门零售	Retail of Hardware Furniture and Materials for Ornament	22 195	4 031
无店铺及其他零售	Retail of Non-shop and Others	815 657	60 115
4. 按经营方式分	**Grouped by Means of Operation**		
独立商店	Independent shop	4 022 577	1 406 110
连锁商店总店	Central shop of chain shops	1 564 637	586 830
连锁门店	Chain Shop Outlets	16 429	8 434
其　他	Others	1 028 080	315 055
5. 按零售业态分	**Grouped by Retail Size**		
百货商店	Department Store	508 947	441 012
超级市场	Supermarket	760 919	539 212
专业店	Special Store	1 754 152	439 193
专卖店	Monopoly Store	2 517 642	562 988
其　他	Others	1 090 064	334 023

Continued 2

(10 000 yuan)

累计折旧 Accumulative Total Depreciation	固定资产净值 Net Fixed Assets	资产总计 Total Assets	负债总计 Total Liabilities	所有者权益合计 Total Creditors Equity	营业收入 Business Revenue	# 主营业务收入 Major Business Revenue	营业成本 Business Cost
–	–	–	–	–	–	–	–
323 534	361 590	2 105 752	1 654 073	451 680	4 020 270	3 906 403	3 481 692
73 421	116 349	574 062	337 987	236 076	2 091 745	2 026 438	1 873 981
529 675	647 519	2 689 542	2 216 851	473 814	5 346 154	5 145 510	4 570 221
219 376	469 195	1 317 722	947 562	370 161	1 435 354	1 351 829	1 173 470
305 218	170 754	1 282 913	1 195 555	88 480	3 788 584	3 677 000	3 319 077
4 917	7 526	58 629	53 227	5 402	102 568	97 209	64 558
164	44	30 278	20 506	9 772	19 649	19 473	13 116
20 281	23 217	145 215	85 290	59 925	225 481	220 430	184 004
31 476	34 567	552 420	496 132	56 287	640 149	632 173	458 530
27 996	27 100	234 122	135 630	98 493	206 778	199 174	161 504
11 729	12 218	239 200	154 741	84 460	470 695	464 584	362 395
346 223	500 976	4 647 711	3 583 069	1 064 642	10 994 151	10 772 412	10 156 719
236 676	370 674	3 517 121	2 536 377	980 744	7 768 761	7 586 233	7 133 696
12 557	26 075	329 625	215 870	113 754	655 694	633 296	577 806
3 544	19 393	114 948	85 002	29 946	231 953	225 605	206 011
1 344	930	33 617	16 884	16 734	64 804	62 168	55 989
2 241	1 789	25 734	24 201	1 533	47 184	47 026	37 432
24 742	35 373	904 173	801 966	102 207	3 640 955	3 627 372	3 077 940
598 697	806 743	5 920 674	4 313 658	1 608 138	11 577 244	11 284 085	10 187 308
340 829	245 996	2 382 232	2 158 510	223 722	6 630 384	6 479 976	5 959 193
3 874	4 561	23 510	30 634	- 7 124	70 010	69 216	55 379
63 520	251 535	1 441 327	1 210 947	230 380	3 949 603	3 908 700	3 384 672
191 185	249 827	992 740	637 550	355 190	1 363 260	1 295 333	1 128 763
324 149	215 451	1 435 298	1 318 493	117 927	3 985 047	3 868 185	3 481 201
188 866	249 487	2 325 972	1 808 640	517 332	5 844 516	5 756 121	5 321 702
228 586	334 128	3 460 258	2 589 156	871 102	6 927 877	6 759 270	6 217 632
74 134	259 942	1 553 474	1 359 910	193 565	4 106 541	4 063 068	3 437 254

表7-8 续表 3

单位：万元

项目	Item	#主营业务成本 Major Business Cost	税金及附加 Taxes and Extra Charges from Business	#主营业务税金及附加 Taxes and Extra Charges from Major Business
总计	**Total**	**149 500 442**	**395 270**	**391 104**
一、批发业	**Wholesale Trades**	**130 025 585**	**333 591**	**331 362**
# 国有及国有控股	State-owned and State Holding Majority Shares	15 837 998	190 563	189 971
1. 按地区分	**Grouped by Region**			
市区	Urban Area	36 508 093	238 639	237 752
# 吴江区	Wujiang District	15 182 374	5 906	5 852
常熟	Changshu	8 663 947	10 297	9 555
张家港	Zhangjiagang	61 929 510	36 369	35 887
昆山	Kunshan	14 399 815	18 318	18 203
太仓	Taicang	8 524 220	29 969	29 964
2. 按登记注册类型分	**Grouped by Registration Status**			
国有企业	State-owned Enterprises	976 178	183 035	183 002
集体企业	Collective-owned Enterprises	49 391	52	52
股份合作企业	Share-holding Cooperative Enterprises	–	–	–
联营企业	Joint Ownership Enterprises	–	–	–
有限责任公司	Limited Liability Corporations	45 515 550	27 114	25 652
股份有限公司	Share-holding Cooperative Ltd.	1 458 158	2 160	2 080
私营企业	Private Enterprises	53 905 258	38 626	38 137
其他企业	Other Enterprises	–	–	–
港澳台商投资企业	Enterprises with Investment from HongKong, Macao and Taiwan	6 534 041	42 920	42 807
外商投资企业	Enterprises with Foreign Investment	21 587 009	39 686	39 631
3. 按主要行业分	**Grouped by Sector**			
农、林、牧、渔产品批发	Wholesale of Products of Agriculture, Forestry, Animal Husbandry, and Fishery	3 961 065	643	629
食品、饮料及烟草制品批发	Wholesale of Food, Beverages and Tobaccos	3 382 487	186 769	186 712
纺织、服装及日用品批发	Wholesale of Textiles, Garments and Daily Articles	31 057 463	71 551	70 497
# 服装批发	Wholesale of Garments	6 595 137	31 964	31 962
文化、体育用品及器材批发	Wholesale of Cultural, Sports Equipment and Appliances	1 267 976	4 538	4 530

Continued 3

(10 000 yuan)

其他业务利润 Other Business Profits	销售费用 Cost Related With Sale	管理费用 Managerial Cost	财务费用 Financing Activities Cost	营业利润 Business Profits	利润总额 Total Profits	应交增值税 Value Added Tax Payable
327 715	**4 754 504**	**3 148 546**	**629 274**	**3 559 913**	**3 599 616**	**1 643 306**
124 588	**3 164 898**	**2 475 410**	**531 922**	**3 279 575**	**3 312 716**	**1 295 710**
13 689	245 800	90 720	62 969	367 273	380 016	94 076
67 830	1 168 313	1 055 500	194 632	1 453 744	1 473 523	572 800
7 481	86 816	62 193	104 577	85 242	88 184	38 759
19 995	448 415	90 866	42 274	232 615	233 170	84 047
13 766	540 632	220 962	209 662	571 438	564 978	278 663
15 723	546 419	270 861	43 479	390 048	407 216	159 277
7 274	461 119	837 221	41 875	631 730	633 830	200 923
631	18 566	28 611	-25 027	209 461	212 399	63 200
186	667	554	749	-623	1 037	125
–	–	–	–	–	–	–
–	–	–	–	–	–	–
25 986	798 126	192 149	216 452	545 943	553 174	209 863
2 059	56 842	28 545	33 204	-21 740	-21 683	19 264
45 646	747 046	483 017	230 029	371 372	362 156	388 274
–	–	–	–	–	–	–
8 613	756 515	914 509	25 160	887 469	890 088	280 850
41 467	787 136	828 024	51 354	1 287 692	1 315 545	334 134
–	7 066	4 735	14 975	-109 642	-109 036	3 572
5 240	179 930	57 183	-12 683	237 793	244 444	106 478
21 543	1 529 330	1 746 433	192 689	1 588 002	1 596 009	538 916
2 186	759 163	788 673	62 432	833 907	843 630	259 642
7 231	71 540	22 994	9 187	35 184	34 347	20 778

表7-8 续表 4

单位：万元

项　目	Item	#主营业务成本 Major Business Cost	税金及附加 Taxes and Extra Charges from Business	#主营业务税金及附加 Taxes and Extra Charges from Major Business
医药及医疗器材批发	Wholesale of Medicines and Medical Appliances	2 275 479	4 090	4 089
矿产品、建材及化工产品批发	Wholesale of Mineral Products, Building Materials and Chemical Products	68 050 313	42 635	41 606
机械设备、五金交电及电子产品批发	Wholesale of Machinery, Hardware, Transport, Electric and Electronic Equipment	18 064 675	20 650	20 584
# 汽车及零配件批发	Wholesale of Automobiles and Spare parts	4 340 906	7 852	7 846
五金产品批发	Wholesale of Hardware Products	896 672	867	865
电气设备批发	Wholesale of Electrical Equipment	442 039	663	663
计算机、软件及辅助设备批发	Wholesale of Computers, Software and Auxiliary Equipment	6 441 805	1 161	1 159
通讯设备批发	Wholesale of Communication Equipment	547 487	1 377	1 377
贸易经纪与代理	Trade Management and Agency	567 092	229	228
其他批发	Other Wholesale	1 399 036	2 487	2 487
二、零售业	**Retail Trades**	**19 474 857**	**61 678**	**59 743**
# 国有及国有控股	State-owned and State Holding Majority Shares	3 009 437	4 832	4 615
1. 按地区分	**Grouped by Region**			
市　区	Urban Area	10 151 357	39 388	37 952
# 吴江区	Wujiang District	966 843	1 632	1 582
常　熟	Changshu	1 154 702	3 926	3 639
张家港	Zhangjiagang	1 130 537	3 444	3 357
昆　山	Kunshan	6 655 320	13 762	13 636
太　仓	Taicang	382 941	1 159	1 159
2. 按登记注册类型分	**Grouped by Registration Status**			
国有企业	State-owned Enterprises	16 905	88	88
集体企业	Collective-owned Enterprises	30 812	78	78
股份合作企业	Share-holding Cooperative Enterprises	2 271	12	12
联营企业	Joint Ownership Enterprises	6 964	9	9
有限责任公司	Limited Liability Corporations	5 558 656	19 735	19 521
股份有限公司	Share-holding Cooperative Ltd.	2 300 604	4 785	4 582
私营企业	Private Enterprises	6 239 404	19 083	17 645

Continued 4

(10 000 yuan)

其他业务利润 Other Business Profits	销售费用 Cost Related With Sale	管理费用 Managerial Cost	财务费用 Financing Activities Cost	营业利润 Business Profits	利润总额 Total Profits	应交增值税 Value Added Tax Payable
5 717	109 624	47 250	15 726	78 312	78 278	38 677
65 251	533 801	306 070	253 904	777 919	781 547	348 623
17 788	604 920	257 312	51 587	658 227	669 555	205 531
4 523	381 263	49 242	-1 987	321 531	332 220	69 028
822	29 310	24 092	2 234	16 622	16 895	8 917
1 728	8 228	26 653	846	62 012	63 817	6 091
2 665	4 883	7 299	-40	63 330	63 384	2 259
1 335	31 408	16 059	1 700	13 622	13 712	13 148
135	7 734	7 026	2 121	5 999	6 088	5 597
1 683	120 954	26 406	4 416	7 781	11 485	27 538
203 128	**1 589 606**	**673 136**	**97 352**	**280 339**	**286 900**	**347 596**
20 391	177 483	23 723	6 033	40 149	42 751	19 576
116 945	732 106	332 927	63 326	141 759	145 917	179 783
11 393	60 076	27 183	5 706	14 227	15 197	24 701
25 252	76 679	44 508	11 206	44 563	45 373	26 671
16 716	76 020	44 767	11 200	10 592	8 856	38 024
37 507	678 036	231 374	8 019	73 797	76 618	95 673
6 708	26 765	19 560	3 602	9 628	10 137	7 446
-2	463	1 655	-43	1 975	2 032	423
542	1 498	1 321	70	1 561	1 535	610
–	215	57	1	185	252	97
–	198	3	–	137	137	53
52 320	628 813	185 383	28 956	63 553	66 306	115 747
18 724	91 516	35 793	1 604	36 327	37 374	16 332
87 686	409 095	246 271	48 930	78 066	77 214	149 330

表7-8 续表 5

单位：万元

项　　目	Item	#主营业务成本 Major Business Cost	税金及附加 Taxes and Extra Charges from Business	#主营业务税金及附加 Taxes and Extra Charges from Major Business
其他企业	Other Enterprises	–	–	–
港澳台商投资企业	Enterprises with Investment from HongKong, Macao and Taiwan	3 472 300	10 792	10 736
外商投资企业	Enterprises with Foreign Investment	1 846 942	7 096	7 072
3. 按主要行业分	**Grouped by Sector**			
综合零售	Retail of Integrated	4 557 050	21 253	20 078
百货零售	Retail of Consumer Goods	1 161 385	14 399	13 225
超级市场零售	Retail of Supermarket	3 318 411	6 460	6 458
便利店零售	Retail by Convenience Stores	64 138	356	356
其他综合零售	Others Retail of Integrated	13 116	39	39
食品、饮料及烟草制品专门零售	Wholesale of Foodstuff, Drink and Tobacco	183 130	924	764
纺织、服装及日用品专门零售	Wholesale of Textiles, Garments, Shoes and Hats	456 797	3 383	3 359
文化、体育用品及器材专门零售	Wholesale of Cultural, Sports Equipment and Appliances	161 307	4 248	4 229
医药及医疗器材专门零售	Wholesale of Medicines and Medical Appliances	362 137	1 909	1 882
汽车、摩托车、燃料及零配件专门零售	Wholesale of Timber	10 078 200	21 751	21 319
# 汽车新车零售	Retail of New Cars	7 081 211	17 564	17 233
家用电器及电子产品专门零售	Retail of Textiles, Garments, Shoes and Hats	569 277	1 374	1 356
# 日用家电零售	Retail of Household Appliances	203 532	681	678
计算机、软件及辅助设备零售	Retail of Computer, Software and Assistant Equipment	54 115	129	126
五金、家具及室内装修材料专门零售	Retail of Hardware Furniture and Materials for Ornament	37 420	119	119
无店铺及其他零售	Retail of Non-shop and Others	3 069 541	6 717	6 636
4. 按经营方式分	**Grouped by Means of Operation**			
独立商店	Independent shop	10 116 690	39 592	38 716
连锁商店总店	Central shop of chain shops	5 932 327	11 429	11 369
连锁门店	Chain Shop Outlets	55 379	263	263
其　他	Others	3 370 462	10 394	9 395
5. 按零售业态分	**Grouped by Retail Size**			
百货商店	Department Store	1 117 942	11 052	10 837
超级市场	Supermarket	3 480 544	7 544	7 543
专业店	Special Store	5 280 840	13 140	12 965
专卖店	Monopoly Storo	6 168 749	18 476	18 130
其　他	Others	3 426 782	11 466	10 268

Continued 5

(10 000 yuan)

其他业务利润 Other Business Profits	销售费用 Cost Related With Sale	管理费用 Managerial Cost	财务费用 Financing Activities Cost	营业利润 Business Profits	利润总额 Total Profits	应交增值税 Value Added Tax Payable
–	–	–	–	–	–	–
29 252	315 915	153 275	13 499	77 016	78 593	42 005
14 606	141 893	49 377	4 336	21 521	23 457	23 000
93 995	470 337	245 809	19 769	37 153	37 634	56 698
75 000	118 791	106 056	17 280	13 365	15 391	20 932
18 468	319 333	129 961	2 109	21 497	20 434	32 100
345	30 197	8 710	373	-1 138	-1 619	2 978
182	2 016	1 083	8	3 429	3 429	688
692	21 507	13 056	717	6 001	6 618	5 856
2 002	140 384	45 515	4 138	-11 850	-9 233	27 992
2 147	19 342	17 952	2 255	2 225	3 715	5 400
4 383	76 624	21 470	1 352	6 978	6 901	14 094
85 152	383 878	200 205	64 988	212 544	214 338	178 246
72 250	272 633	173 420	59 970	156 455	158 401	158 541
7 936	52 711	18 759	1 907	383	1 548	10 734
105	19 922	4 804	369	103	245	4 330
344	2 528	4 424	276	1 606	1 979	1 267
-2	5 731	4 293	227	-643	-564	1 030
6 821	419 092	106 077	1 999	27 548	25 943	47 546
149 446	693 558	374 846	86 312	234 445	243 364	222 983
23 643	457 874	162 671	3 085	47 818	46 757	61 911
758	15 494	676	135	-1 942	-1 969	1 915
29 282	422 680	134 943	7 820	17	-1 253	60 788
62 104	105 354	78 385	11 545	36 617	38 902	19 791
19 895	337 891	145 980	4 259	18 136	17 243	35 448
33 046	285 744	120 142	17 245	96 388	97 800	96 952
65 909	378 091	172 323	54 254	120 075	125 191	137 777
22 173	482 526	156 306	10 049	9 122	7 765	57 628

表7-9 限额以上住宿和餐饮法人企业主要财务指标 (2018年)

单位：万元

项　目	Item	流动资产合计 Total Circulating Funds	固定资产原价 Original Value of Fixed Assets
总　计	**Total**	**1 114 594**	**2 427 562**
一、住宿业	**Accommodation**	**783 107**	**2 021 492**
1. 按地区分	**Grouped by Region**		
市　区	Urban Area	561 044	1 532 816
# 吴江区	Wujiang District	85 310	350 933
常　熟	Changshu	66 531	191 078
张家港	Zhangjiagang	57 707	132 174
昆　山	Kunshan	33 505	100 963
太　仓	Taicang	64 319	64 461
2. 按登记注册类型分	**Grouped by Registration Status**		
国有企业	State-owned Enterprises	11 149	98 277
集体企业	Collective-owned Enterprises	16 590	27 737
股份合作企业	Share-holding Cooperative Enterprises	–	–
联营企业	Joint Ownership Enterprises	–	–
有限责任公司	Limited Liability Corporations	577 351	1 321 468
股份有限公司	Share-holding Cooperative Ltd.	4 488	48 156
私营企业	Private Enterprises	142 162	271 423
其他企业	Other Enterprises	–	–
港澳台商投资企业	Enterprises with Investment from HongKong, Macao and Taiwan	21 041	122 802
外商投资企业	Enterprises with Foreign Investment	10 325	131 630
3. 按星级分	**Grouped by Sear Rated**		
# 五　星	Five Star	207 627	846 846
四　星	Four Star	130 851	340 862
三　星	Three Star	39 136	73 231
二　星	Two Star	2 829	2 854

MAIN FINANCIAL INDICATORS OF ACCOMMODATION AND CATERING CORPORATION ABOVE DESIGNATED SIZE (2018)

(10 000 yuan)

累计折旧 Accumulative Total Depreciation	固定资产净值 Net Fixed Assets	资产总计 Total Assets	负债总计 Total Liabilities	所有者权益合计 Total Creditors Equity	营业收入 Business Revenue	#主营业务收入 Major Business Revenue	营业成本 Business Cost
907 873	**1 509 845**	**3 687 589**	**2 471 105**	**1 224 268**	**1 350 858**	**1 335 479**	**580 110**
728 226	**1 283 386**	**2 945 908**	**1 945 140**	**1 008 552**	**551 454**	**542 263**	**173 436**
536 491	977 186	2 251 518	1 379 698	879 604	403 380	398 675	116 161
112 815	238 118	394 923	314 482	80 441	64 763	64 643	18 906
62 364	128 714	241 831	239 602	2 229	49 096	48 071	15 743
77 441	63 992	186 688	146 551	40 137	39 206	38 478	17 158
28 095	72 868	144 436	81 753	62 682	29 626	28 060	15 289
23 836	40 626	121 436	97 535	23 901	30 147	28 980	9 085
41 835	56 442	110 001	30 416	79 584	24 734	23 635	12 763
17 730	10 007	39 294	23 573	15 721	10 022	10 021	3 046
–	–	–	–	–	–	–	–
–	–	–	–	–	–	–	–
430 718	900 008	2 161 123	1 321 737	847 170	321 287	316 344	92 924
23 379	24 777	33 328	19 166	14 162	14 416	14 229	4 466
99 657	171 781	420 006	405 208	14 798	122 827	120 549	43 564
–	–	–	–	–	–	–	–
59 670	63 132	97 861	62 198	35 663	36 948	36 265	9 693
55 237	57 240	84 295	82 842	1 454	21 221	21 220	6 981
336 381	491 313	907 768	693 107	214 661	177 828	175 854	44 316
121 009	229 111	790 749	240 739	557 794	108 889	104 954	44 356
28 394	44 837	114 618	76 038	38 580	23 362	23 095	11 492
2 277	577	3 454	3 304	150	2 706	2 706	983

表7-9 续表 1

单位：万元

项　目	Item	流动资产合计 Total Circulating Funds	固定资产原价 Original Value of Fixed Assets
二、餐饮业	**Catering Services**	**331 488**	**406 071**
1. 按地区分	**Grouped by Region**		
市　区	Urban Area	197 189	114 529
# 吴江区	Wujiang District	9 709	21 938
常　熟	Changshu	11 722	8 167
张家港	Zhangjiagang	57 707	132 174
昆　山	Kunshan	58 487	134 581
太　仓	Taicang	6 384	16 619
2. 按登记注册类型分	**Grouped by Registration Status**		
国有企业	State-owned Enterprises	2 004	3 566
集体企业	Collective-owned Enterprises	–	–
股份合作企业	Share-holding Cooperative Enterprises	–	–
联营企业	Joint Ownership Enterprises	322	207
有限责任公司	Limited Liability Corporations	113 213	103 511
股份有限公司	Share-holding Cooperative Ltd.	14 154	1 854
私营企业	Private Enterprises	152 072	180 943
其他企业	Other Enterprises	–	–
港澳台商投资企业	Enterprises with Investment from HongKong, Macao and Taiwan	19 480	56 871
外商投资企业	Enterprises with Foreign Investment	30 244	59 118
3. 按主要行业分	**Grouped by Sector**		
正　餐	Dinner	267 235	352 254
快　餐	Fast Food	24 322	38 956
饮料及冷饮服务	Beverage and Cold Drink Services	16 998	9 438
其他餐饮业	Other	22 933	5 422

Continued 1

(10 000 yuan)

累计折旧 Accumulative Total Depreciation	固定资产净值 Net Fixed Assets	资产总计 Total Assets	负债总计 Total Liabilities	所有者权益合计 Total Creditors Equity	营业收入 Business Revenue	#主营业务收入 Major Business Revenue	营业成本 Business Cost
179 647	**226 459**	**741 681**	**525 965**	**215 716**	**799 404**	**793 216**	**406 674**
47 973	57 333	351 373	195 008	156 365	618 290	614 985	312 500
7 158	14 815	29 435	18 626	10 808	17 990	17 092	10 805
4 313	3 854	18 660	14 268	4 391	25 922	25 904	17 620
77 441	63 992	186 688	146 551	40 137	39 206	38 478	17 158
45 283	89 298	164 468	147 391	17 077	98 056	96 052	50 218
4 637	11 982	20 492	22 746	-2 254	17 930	17 798	9 178
1 187	2 379	4 383	1 142	3 241	3 567	2 720	1 038
–	–	–	–	–	–	–	–
–	–	–	–	–	–	–	–
132	76	398	22	376	398	398	239
60 008	43 502	195 236	173 893	21 343	117 955	117 494	43 775
1 229	625	22 017	24 798	-2 781	28 415	27 926	14 451
78 112	102 867	312 208	229 520	82 688	363 248	360 830	209 506
–	–	–	–	–	–	–	–
10 043	46 829	80 325	54 752	25 572	21 202	20 683	6 737
28 937	30 182	127 115	41 839	85 276	264 619	263 166	130 927
150 701	201 587	602 559	464 746	137 813	423 664	419 594	195 304
22 089	16 867	73 719	28 280	45 439	288 796	287 348	151 510
4 258	5 181	35 806	17 710	18 095	15 084	14 606	5 058
2 598	2 824	29 597	15 228	14 369	71 860	71 668	54 802

表7-9 续表 2

单位：万元

项　　目	Item	#主营业务成本 Major Business Cost	税金及附加 Taxes and Extra Charges from Business	#主营业务税金及附加 Taxes and Extra Charges from Major Business
总　计	**Total**	**572 057**	**16 681**	**14 736**
一、住宿业	**Accommodation**	**171 202**	**12 864**	**11 520**
1. 按地区分	**Grouped by Region**			
市　区	Urban Area	115 460	10 780	9 541
# 吴江区	Wujiang District	18 903	1 913	1 910
常　熟	Changshu	15 519	913	913
张家港	Zhangjiagang	16 911	502	411
昆　山	Kunshan	14 453	279	278
太　仓	Taicang	8 860	391	377
2. 按登记注册类型分	**Grouped by Registration Status**			
国有企业	State-owned Enterprises	12 494	518	278
集体企业	Collective-owned Enterprises	3 046	14	14
股份合作企业	Share-holding Cooperative Enterprises	–	–	–
联营企业	Joint Ownership Enterprises	–	–	–
有限责任公司	Limited Liability Corporations	91 436	9 003	8 078
股份有限公司	Share-holding Cooperative Ltd.	4 466	293	293
私营企业	Private Enterprises	43 091	2 108	2 038
其他企业	Other Enterprises	–	–	–
港澳台商投资企业	Enterprises with Investment from HongKong Macao and Taiwan	9 690	544	544
外商投资企业	Enterprises with Foreign Investment	6 981	384	275
3. 按星级分	**Grouped by Sear Rated**			
# 五　星	Five Star	43 783	5 899	5 339
四　星	Four Star	42 969	1 404	1 108
三　星	Three Star	11 451	414	411
二　星	Two Star	983	42	41

Continued 2

(10 000 yuan)

其他业务利润 Other Business Profits	销售费用 Cost Related With Sale	管理费用 Managerial Cost	财务费用 Financing Activities Cost	营业利润 Business Profits	利润总额 Total Profits
6 136	**420 388**	**324 515**	**54 783**	**-28 441**	**-26 291**
3 651	**200 670**	**213 290**	**45 420**	**-76 985**	**-76 321**
1 971	160 333	159 597	35 850	-66 470	-65 893
118	29 879	25 035	2 871	-13 913	-13 584
625	15 021	18 386	3 843	-4 811	-4 746
455	13 745	10 735	3 148	-5 679	-5 558
107	6 262	11 581	616	-479	-508
494	5 309	12 990	1 962	454	383
439	5 956	8 320	134	-2 509	-2 448
15	5 529	1 101	281	170	180
–	–	–	–	–	–
–	–	–	–	–	–
1 037	119 663	138 297	31 106	-54 179	-53 910
177	4 517	4 835	211	92	129
993	43 334	40 357	8 545	-14 930	-14 446
–	–	–	–	–	–
30	16 188	10 202	2 426	-2 096	-2 191
960	5 483	10 178	2 717	-3 533	-3 637
816	64 168	72 915	15 928	-22 567	-22 596
1 228	37 207	42 297	789	-4 816	-4 834
132	5 455	9 029	1 105	-4 065	-4 017
–	1 343	395	6	-63	-66

表7-9 续表 3

单位：万元

项 目	Item	#主营业务成本 Major Business Cost	税金及附加 Taxes and Extra Charges from Business	#主营业务税金及附加 Taxes and Extra Charges from Major Business
二、餐饮业	**Catering Services**	**400 855**	**3 816**	**3 216**
1. 按地区分	**Grouped by Region**			
市 区	Urban Area	308 713	2 262	1 753
# 吴江区	Wujiang District	10 776	200	200
常 熟	Changshu	17 620	107	107
张家港	Zhangjiagang	16 911	502	411
昆 山	Kunshan	48 436	830	830
太 仓	Taicang	9 175	116	116
2. 按登记注册类型分	**Grouped by Registration Status**			
国有企业	State-owned Enterprises	1 038	18	18
集体企业	Collective-owned Enterprises	–	–	–
股份合作企业	Share-holding Cooperative Enterprises	–	–	–
联营企业	Joint Ownership Enterprises	239	2	2
有限责任公司	Limited Liability Corporations	42 295	1 358	858
股份有限公司	Share-holding Cooperative Ltd.	14 284	32	32
私营企业	Private Enterprises	206 579	1 950	1 950
其他企业	Other Enterprises	–	–	–
港澳台商投资企业	Enterprises with Investment from HongKong Macao and Taiwan	6 737	121	121
外商投资企业	Enterprises with Foreign Investment	129 682	336	235
3. 按主要行业分	**Grouped by Sector**			
正 餐	Dinner	193 294	3 137	2 627
快 餐	Fast Food	150 265	170	80
饮料及冷饮服务	Beverage and Cold Drink Services	5 058	131	131
其他餐饮业	Other	52 238	378	378

Continued 3

(10 000 yuan)

其他业务利润 Other Business Profits	销售费用 Cost Related With Sale	管理费用 Managerial Cost	财务费用 Financing Activities Cost	营业利润 Business Profits	利润总额 Total Profits
2 485	**219 718**	**111 225**	**9 363**	**48 544**	**50 031**
1 461	181 756	66 484	3 217	49 865	51 043
865	2 548	4 752	139	-534	-533
–	3 885	3 625	74	616	634
455	13 745	10 735	3 148	-5 679	-5 558
451	15 625	25 875	2 614	4 233	4 450
118	4 707	4 506	311	-490	-538
–	1 880	519	-10	121	126
–	–	–	–	–	–
–	–	–	–	–	–
–	81	34	–	43	35
687	43 478	22 593	4 631	2 469	3 099
227	8 117	5 490	1 103	-89	346
1 457	85 476	49 750	3 245	12 159	12 537
–	–	–	–	–	–
104	9 291	7 507	248	-2 708	-2 826
11	71 395	25 332	146	36 550	36 715
2 524	133 091	74 306	8 747	10 661	12 165
-150	72 688	26 687	234	37 222	37 356
63	8 490	1 206	252	-52	-155
48	5 449	9 026	131	714	665

表7-10

连锁总店经营情况 (2018年)

项　　目	Item	连锁总店数(个) Number of Chain Shops (unit)
总　　计	**Total**	**52**
一、批发业	**Wholesale Trades**	**1**
二、零售业	**Retail Trades**	**45**
1.按登记注册类型分	**Grouped by Registration Status**	
内资企业	Domestic Funded Enterprises	40
# 有限责任公司	Limited Liability Corporations	21
私营企业	Private Enterprises	16
港澳台商投资企业	Enterprises with Investment from HongKong, Macao and Taiwan	3
外商投资企业	Enterprises with Foreign Investment	2
2.按连锁经营业务分	**Grouped by Scope of Business**	
# 综合零售	Retail of Integrated	16
食品、饮料及烟草制品专门零售	Retail of Food, Beverages and Tobaccos	4
医疗及医疗器材专门零售	Retail of Medicines and Medical Appliances	16
家用电器及电子产品专门零售	Retail of Household Appliances and Electronic Products	4
3.按零售业态分	**Grouped by Retail Size**	
# 便利店	Convenience Store	4
超　市	Supermarket	11
专业店	Special Store	22
专卖店	Monopoly Store	5
三、住宿业	**Accommodation**	**1**
四、餐饮业	**Catering Services**	**5**
正　餐	Dinner	2
快　餐	Fast Food	2
饮料及冷饮服务	Beverage and Cold Drink Services	1
其　他	Other	–
附：外省在苏连锁门店	**Number of Chain Shops in Suzhou of Other Provinces**	–

BASIC STATISTICS OF CENTRAL SHOPS OF CHAIN STORES (2018)

连锁门店数(个) Number of Chain Shop Outlets (unit)	直营店 Factory Outlet	加盟店 Join-in Outlet	从业人员(人) Total Employment (person)	销售总额(营业额)(万元) Total Sales Business Income (10 000 yuan)	# 商品零售额 Retail Sale Trade
3 649	**2 514**	**1 135**	**55 626**	**6 228 253**	**3 994 321**
8	**8**	**–**	**103**	**4 088**	**1 021**
3 260	**2 125**	**1 135**	**36 829**	**5 929 931**	**3 702 944**
2 848	1 713	1 135	20 739	1 564 145	1 272 979
2 118	1 249	869	14 462	1 015 720	952 220
648	382	266	4 847	307 704	274 205
51	51	–	14 103	3 002 042	1 301 371
361	361	–	1 987	1 363 744	1 128 594
1 393	530	863	25 096	3 872 520	2 093 710
269	269	–	1 132	50 571	50 571
1 026	1 020	6	5 156	312 157	296 175
63	63	–	1 684	329 347	135 180
205	205	–	435	87 100	87 100
1 183	320	863	24 313	3 764 847	1 986 038
1 141	1 135	6	7 424	697 178	484 151
531	265	266	2 534	76 128	76 128
5	**5**	**–**	**89**	**2 965**	**60**
376	**376**	**–**	**18 605**	**291 270**	**290 296**
38	38	–	1 044	32 124	32 124
328	328	–	17 341	255 515	255 515
10	10	–	220	3 631	2 657
–	–	–	–	–	–
52	**51**	**1**	**3 764**	**497 403**	**427 137**

表7-11

亿元以上商品交易市场基本情况（2018年）
GENERAL INFORMATION OF COMMODITY EXCHANGE MARKET WITH TOTAL SALE OVER 100 MILLION YUAN (2018)

项目	Item	市场数(个) Number of Markets (unit)	年末已出租摊位数(个) Year-end Number of Hired Booths (unit)	商品成交额(万元) Transaction Value (10 000 yuan)	# 商品零售额 Consumer Goods Retail Sale
总计	Total	71	73 138	79 863 332	7 894 064
一、按经营环境分	Grouped by Form of Operation Environment				
露天式	Open Air	3	641	114 816	30 280
封闭式	Seal Off	55	65 214	46 280 393	7 455 950
其他	Others	13	7 283	33 468 123	407 834
二、按经营方式分	Grouped by Form of Operation				
批发	Whole sale	41	63 718	77 791 785	6 184 990
零售	Retail Sale	30	9 420	2 071 547	1 709 074
三、按市场类别分	Grouped by Category of Market				
综合市场	Integrated Market	4	1 171	233 695	66 044
生产资料综合市场	General Market	–	–	–	–
工业品综合市场	Industrial Products	1	348	18 296	18 230
农产品综合市场	Farm and Side-line Products	–	–	–	–
其他综合市场	Others	3	823	215 399	47 814
专业市场	Special Market	67	71 967	79 629 637	7 828 020
# 建材市场	Building Materials	6	2 179	286 036	185 790
金属材料市场	Metal Material	4	2 473	20 970 892	–
粮油市场	Grain and Oil	2	432	4 268 391	–
肉食禽蛋市场	Meat, Poultry and Eggs	3	975	397 398	122 408
水产品市场	Aquatic Products	3	634	528 075	64 900
蔬菜市场	Vegetables	2	1 186	169 154	19 143
食品饮料烟酒市场	Food, Beverage and Tobacco	1	409	512 648	–
纺织品服装鞋帽市场	Textile Products, Garments, Shoes and Hats	3	35 806	31 623 042	4 510 650
小商品市场	Small Commodities	1	2 310	750 000	225 000
家具市场	Furniture	5	4 216	972 051	175 003
汽车市场	Vehicles	2	278	856 380	807 634

主要统计指标解释

社会消费品零售总额 指企业（单位、个体户）通过交易直接售给个人、社会集团非生产、非经营用的实物商品金额，以及提供餐饮服务所取得的收入金额。个人包括城乡居民和入境人员，社会集团包括机关、社会团体、部队、学校、企事业单位、居委会或村委会等。

批发和零售业商品购进、销售、库存额 指各种登记注册类型的批发和零售业企业(单位)以本企业(单位)为总体的，从国内、国外市场购进的商品总量，销售和出口的商品总量，库存的商品总量等情况。该指标可以反映商品流转过程中商品的购进、销售、库存之间的比例关系和存在的问题。

商品购进额 指从本企业以外的单位和个人购进（包括从国外直接进口）作为转卖或加工后转卖的商品金额（含增值税）。商品购进包括：（1）从工农业生产者、批发和零售业企业、住宿和餐饮业企业、出版社或报社的出版发行部门和其他服务业企业购进的商品；（2）从机关团体、事业单位购进的商品；（3）从海关、市场管理部门购进的缉私和没收的商品；（4）从居民收购的废旧商品等。不包括：（1）企业为本单位自身经营用，不是作为转卖而购进的商品，如材料物资、包装物、低值易耗品、办公用品等；（2）未通过买卖行为而收入的商品，如接受其他部门移交的商品、借入的商品、收入代其他单位保管的商品、其他单位赠送的样品、加工回收的成品等；（3）经本单位介绍，由买卖双方直接结算，本单位只收取手续费的业务；（4）销售退回和买方拒付货款的商品；（5）商品溢余。

商品销售额 指对本单位以外的单位和个人出售的商品金额（包括售给本单位消费用的商品，含增值税）。商品销售包括（1）售给城乡居民和社会集团消费用的商品；（2）售给农业、工业、建筑业、服务业等国民经济各行业用于生产、经营用的商品，包括售予批发和零售业作为转卖或加工后转卖的商品；（3）对国（境）外直接出口的商品。不包括：（1）未通过买卖行为付出的商品，如随机构变动移交给其他企业单位的商品、借出的商品、归还受其他单位委托代保管的商品、付出的加工原料和赠送给其他单位的样品等；（2）经本单位介绍，由买卖双方直接结算，本单位只收取手续费的业务；（3）购货退回的商品；（4）商品损耗和损失；（5）出售本单位自用的废旧物资。

商品库存额 对于批发和零售业法人单位和个体经营户，是指报告期末取得所有权的全部商品金额（含增值税）；对于批发和零售业产业活动单位，是指报告期末实际在库且归属法人具有所有权的全部商品金额（含增值税）。库存商品包括：(1)存放在本单位(如门市部、批发站、采购站、经营处)的仓库、货场、货柜和货架中的商品；(2)挑选、整理、包装中的商品；(3)已记入购进而尚未运到本单位的商品，即发货单或银行承兑凭证已到而货未到的商品；(4)寄放他处的商品，如因购货方拒绝付款而暂时存在购货方的商品；(5)委托其他单位代销(未作销售或调出)尚未售出的商品；(6)代其他单位购进尚未交付的商品。不包括：所有权不属于本单位的商品；委托外单位加工的商品；外贸企业代理其他单位从国外进口，尚未付给订货单位的商品；代国家储备部门保管的商品。

住宿业 指为旅行者提供短期留宿场所的活动，有些单位只提供住宿，也有些单位提供住宿、饮食、商务、娱乐一体的服务，不包括主要按月或按年长期出租房屋住所的活动。

餐饮业 指通过即时制作加工、商业销售和服务性劳动等，向消费者提供食品和消费场所及设施的服务。

住宿和餐饮业营业额 指住宿和餐饮业单位在经营活动中因提供服务或销售商品等取得的收入。包括：客房收入、餐费收入、商品销售额（含增值税）和其他收入。其中，客房收入指住宿和餐饮业单位在经营活动中因提供住宿服务取得的收入。餐费收入指本单位为顾客提供就餐服务取得的收入，包括：经烹饪、调制加工后出售的各种食品，如主食、炒菜、凉拌菜等的收入。

亿元以上商品交易市场 指年成交额在亿元及以上的商品交易市场。商品交易市场是指经有关部门和组织批准设立，有固定场所、设施，有经营管理部门和监管人员，若干市场经营者入内，常年或实际开业三个月以上，集中、公开、独立地进行生活消费品、生产资料等现货商品交易以及提供相关服务的交易场所，包括各类消费品市场、生产资料市场等。

连锁总店（总部） 指负责连锁企业资源（商号、商誉、经营模式、服务标准、管理模式等等）的开发、配置、控制或使用等功能的企业核心管理机构。连锁经营是指经营同类商品或服务，使用统一商号的若干店铺，在同一总店（总部）的管理下，采取统一采购或特许经营等方式，实现规模效益的组织形式，包括直营连锁、特许连锁和自愿连锁三种形式。其中，直营连锁是指连锁店铺由连锁公司全资或控股开设，在总部的直接控制下，开展统一经营的连锁经营形式；特许连锁是指拥有注册商标、企业标志、专利、专有技术等经营资源的企业（特许人），以合同形式将其拥有的经营资源许可其他经营者（被特许人）使用，被特许人按合同约定在统一的经营模式下开展经营，并向特许人支付特许经营费用的连锁经营形式；自愿连锁是指若干个店铺或企业自愿组合起来，在不改变各自资产所有权关系的情况下，以同一个品牌形象面对消费者，以共同进货为纽带开展的连锁经营形式。

EXPLANATORY NOTES ON MAIN STATISTICAL INDICATORS

Total Retail Sales of Consumer Goods refer to the amount obtained by enterprises (units, self-employed individuals) through direct sales of non-production and non-business physical commodity to individuals, social institutions, and revenue from providing catering services. Individuals include rural and urban households, population from abroad, social institutions include government agencies, social organizations, military units, schools, institutions, neighbourhood (village) committees.

Purchase, Sales and Stock of Commodities by Wholesale and Retail Trades refer to the total volume of commodities purchased, total volume of sales and exports, and the stock of commodities by wholesale and retail enterprises (establishments) of different status of registration from domestic and overseas markets. This indicator reflects the relationship among purchase, sales and stock of commodities in the circulation of goods and reveals the existing problems.

Total Purchases of Commodities refer to the total value of purchases of commodities by enterprises (establishments) from other establishments or individuals (including direct import from abroad) for the purpose of re-selling, either with or without further processing of the commodities purchased. The commodities include: (1) commodities purchased from agricultural and industrial producer, wholesaler, retailer, publishing house and other service business; (2) commodities purchased from institutions and government departments; (3) confiscated goods purchased from the customs authorities or market management agencies; (4) second-hand goods and wastes purchased from residents; The commodities exclude (1) commodities purchased by enterprises (establishments) for use in their own business operation, commodities obtained without buying or selling procedures such as materials, consumable goods of low value, office appliance, etc. (2) received goods without trading, such as goods handed over from others, borrowed goods, preserved goods for others, donated goods from others, processed and retrieved goods, etc. (3) goods of direct settlement between buyer and seller with handling fees introduced by others, (4) goods returned or refused to pay by the buyer, (5) excessive goods.

Total Sales of Commodities refer to value of commodities sold by the establishments to other establishments and individuals (including goods sold for self consumption, including the value-added tax). The commodities include: (1) commodities sold to urban and rural residents and social groups for their consumption; (2) commodities sold to establishments in all industries for their production and operation, including agriculture, industry, construction, and catering services including commodities sold to wholesale and retail establishments for re-selling, with or without further processing; and (3) commodities for direct export to abroad. Excluded are (1) extended commodities without trading, such as goods handed over to other enterprises and institutions because of the change of organizations, lent goods, returned goods preserved for others, extended processing materials and samples donated to others, (2) goods of direct settlement between buyer and seller with handling fees introduced by others, (3) goods returned after purchase, (4) damaged and spoiled goods, (5) waste and used goods of self use,

Total Stock of Commodities For the legal entities and self-employed individuals engaged in wholesale and retail trade, it refers to total value (including VAT) of commodities possessed at the end of the reference period; and for wholesale and retail establishments, it refers to the value (including VAT) of all commodities actually in stock and owned by their legal persons at the end of reference period. The commodities in stock includes: (1) commodities located in storage, garages, counters, and shelves of operating places of wholesale and retail trades (such as sale stores, wholesale centres, procurement stations and operating offices); (2) commodities in the process of being selected, sorted, and packed; (3) commodities not arrived but recorded as purchase in the account, i.e. commodities not arrived but payment receipts for the commodities from the sellers or the banks arrived; (4) commodities deposited in other places rather than places mentioned above, for instance: commodities in the hold of purchasers temporarily due to the refusal of payment; (5) commodities entrusted to other units to sell but not sold yet; (6) commodities purchased for other units but not delivered yet. Commodities not included as stock are those not owned by the enterprises (units), commodities on commission for processing, imported commodities of agency of foreign trade enterprise but not yet delivered to ordering units and finally those put in stock on behalf of the state reserves units.

Hotel Services refer to the accommodation services provided to visitors. Some units may provide only accommodation while others provide a combination of accommodation, meals, business services and/or recreational facilities. It excludes activities related to the provision of long-term primary residences in facilities such as apartments typically leased on a monthly or annual basis.

Catering Services refer to the activities of providing foods, serving locations and facilities to customers through instant processing, commercial sales and service-type labor.

Business Revenue refers to revenue of hotels and catering services received from providing services or selling commodities through business activities, including income from hotels, from catering services, from selling of commodities (including VAT) and from other services. Income from hotels refers to income of hotels and catering services by providing lodging services through business activities. Income from catering services refers to income from providing catering services, including selling of cooked or prepared foods, such as staple food, cooked dishes, or cold dishes.

Large Commodity Markets with Transaction Value over 100 Million Yuan refers to the commodity markets with an annual transaction at and above 100 million. The commodity market refers to the markets approved and managed by related departments, where there are fixed sites, facilities, managers and administration offices, where there are a certain number of traders to operate for three month and above or all the year, where the commodities including the articles for daily consumption and capital goods and services are traded in a centralized, independent and open way. Such market includes markets of daily goods and market of capital goods, etc.

Chain Head Stores (headquarter) refer to the core leading stores responsible for development, allocation, administration and utilization of resources (name of stores, brand of stores, operation model, service standard, management way, etc.) of chain stores. Chain stores refers to the stores engaged in providing homogeneous commodities or services, with the central leadership of head store (headquarters) and guided by common policies, conduct centralized purchase and distributed selling of commodities, in order to gain better efficiency through standardized operation. The chain stores include regular chain stores, franchise chain stores and voluntary chain stores.

Regular Chain store refers to chain stores that are invested or controlled by the headquarters. They operate under direct and unified management from the headquarters.

Franchise chain store refers to the chain stores (franchisees) which are franchised with operation resources such as trade marks, names, patent and operation know-how by the franchisors in form of contract and pay the operation fees to the franchisors.

Voluntary chain store refers to the stores operate jointly on the voluntary bases while maintaining their status of independent legal entities with full ownership of their assets. They sell goods of same brand from same channel of resource to the consumers.

八、对外经济 国际旅游

CHAPTER 8
FOREIGN TRADE ECONOMY AND INTERNATIONAL TOURISM

8 对外经济　国际旅游
FOREIGN TRADE ECONOMY AND INTERNATIONAL TOURISM

主 要 统 计 指 标
MAJOR STATISTICAL INDICATORS

2018年进出口总额	Total Imports and Exports	3 541.14	亿美元	USD 100 million
比上年增长	Increase Over Last Year	12.0	%	
2018年出口总额	Total Exports	2 068.31	亿美元	USD 100 million
比上年增长	Increase Over Last Year	10.5	%	
2018年进口总额	Total Imports	1 472.83	亿美元	USD 100 million
比上年增长	Increase Over Last Year	14.2	%	
2018年新增注册外资金额	Value of Foreign Capital Signed Contracts	107.71	亿美元	USD 100 million
比上年增长	Increase Over Last Year	20.3	%	
2018年实际使用外资金额	Value of Foreign Capital Actually Used	45.25	亿美元	USD 100 million
比上年增长	Increase Over Last Year	0.5	%	
2018年接待境外游客	Number of Foreign Tourists	240.76	万人次	10 000 person-times
比上年增长	Increase Over Last Year	5.9	%	

表8-1

历年进出口总额及外贸依存度
TOTAL IMPORTS AND EXPORTS, FOREIGN TRADE DEPENDENCY OVER THE YEARS

单位：万美元 (USD 10 000)

年份 Year	进出口总额 Total Imports and Exports	出口 Exports	进口 Imports	外贸依存度(%) Foreign Trade Dependency(%)	出口依存度 Export Dependency	进口依存度 Import Dependency
1990	18 816	15 524	3 292	4.5	3.7	0.8
1991	38 002	31 002	7 000	8.6	7.0	1.6
1992	117 704	95 704	22 000	18.1	14.7	3.4
1993	195 860	84 077	111 783	21.5	9.2	12.3
1994	281 844	141 979	139 865	33.7	17.0	16.7
1995	459 223	233 491	225 732	42.5	21.6	20.9
1996	688 155	349 698	338 457	57.1	29.0	28.1
1997	863 611	464 677	398 934	63.2	34.0	29.2
1998	964 922	520 735	444 187	63.9	34.5	29.4
1999	1 255 482	692 776	562 706	76.5	42.2	34.3
2000	2 007 036	1 048 095	958 941	107.8	56.3	51.5
2001	2 366 160	1 230 679	1 135 481	111.3	57.9	53.4
2002	3 639 008	1 852 061	1 786 947	144.8	73.7	71.1
2003	6 566 313	3 263 377	3 302 936	194.0	96.4	97.6
2004	10 320 051	5 077 384	5 242 667	253.8	124.8	128.9
2005	14 058 895	7 277 472	6 781 423	275.9	142.8	133.1
2006	17 426 360	9 468 488	7 957 872	280.8	152.6	128.2
2007	21 179 567	11 888 422	9 291 145	272.3	152.8	119.5
2008	22 852 565	13 172 260	9 680 305	221.6	127.7	93.9
2009	20 144 633	11 408 529	8 736 104	175.3	99.3	76.0
2010	27 407 639	15 310 849	12 096 790	198.1	110.7	87.4
2011	30 086 256	16 723 345	13 362 911	178.5	99.2	79.3
2012	30 569 196	17 468 868	13 100 328	158.1	90.3	67.7
2013	30 934 780	17 570 638	13 364 142	145.2	82.5	62.7
2014	31 130 567	18 117 763	13 012 804	136.6	79.5	57.1
2015	30 534 957	18 145 930	12 389 027	128.8	76.6	52.3
2016	27 375 823	16 394 054	10 981 769	114.7	68.7	46.0
2017	31 607 895	18 716 062	12 891 833	123.5	73.2	50.3
2018	35 411 397	20 683 117	14 728 280	125.7	73.4	52.3

表8-2

分地区进出口总额(2018年)
TOTAL IMPORTS AND EXPORTS VALUE BY REGION (2018)

类别和地区	Type and Region	进出口总额 Total Imports and Exports	出口 Exports	进口 Imports
全市 （万元）	**Whole Municipality (10 000 yuan)**	**233 755 961**	**136 569 141**	**97 186 820**
市区	Urban Area	124 480 685	70 762 339	53 718 345
姑苏区	Gusu District	1 547 884	1 361 487	186 397
吴中区	Wuzhong District	5 830 492	4 056 199	1 774 294
相城区	Xiangcheng District	3 614 699	2 744 100	870 598
高新区、虎丘区	New & Hi-tech Zone, Huqiu District	30 080 436	19 046 214	11 034 222
工业园区	Industrial Park	68 319 301	32 950 763	35 368 537
吴江区	Wujiang District	15 087 873	10 603 576	4 484 297
常熟	Changshu	16 672 010	11 423 748	5 248 261
张家港	Zhangjiagang	24 012 646	11 531 615	12 481 031
昆山	Kunshan	58 980 443	38 414 185	20 566 258
太仓	Taicang	9 609 951	4 437 254	5 172 697
全市 （万美元）	**Whole Municipality (USD 10 000)**	**35 411 397**	**20 683 117**	**14 728 280**
市区	Urban Area	18 867 819	10 723 181	8 144 637
姑苏区	Gusu District	234 652	206 375	28 277
吴中区	Wuzhong District	883 370	614 431	268 938
相城区	Xiangcheng District	547 592	415 446	132 146
高新区、虎丘区	New & Hi-tech Zone, Huqiu District	4 555 796	2 882 659	1 673 137
工业园区	Industrial Park	10 357 148	4 995 446	5 361 701
吴江区	Wujiang District	2 289 262	1 608 824	680 438
常熟	Changshu	2 525 895	1 729 813	796 083
张家港	Zhangjiagang	3 646 692	1 751 777	1 894 915
昆山	Kunshan	8 913 973	5 805 248	3 108 725
太仓	Taicang	1 456 974	673 087	783 887
总计中：国有企业	**In Total: State-owned Enterprises**	**2 500 708**	**2 346 448**	**154 259**
民营企业	**Private Enterprises**	**7 321 620**	**4 495 782**	**2 825 838**
外商及港澳台商投资企业	**Enterprises with Investment from Foreign ,Hong Kong, Macao and Taiwan**	**25 588 935**	**13 840 883**	**11 748 052**
总计中：一般贸易	**In Total: Ordinary Trade**	**12 077 029**	**6 887 428**	**5 189 601**
加工贸易	**Processing Trade**	**17 555 561**	**10 123 591**	**7 431 970**

表8-3

分国别(地区)进出口总额 (2018年)
TOTAL IMPORTS AND EXPORTS VALUE BY COUNTRY AND REGION (2018)

单位：万美元 (USD 10 000)

国别和地区	Country and Region	进出口总额 Total Imports and Exports	出口 Exports	进口 Imports
总计	**Total**	**35 411 397**	**20 683 117**	**14 728 280**
亚洲	**Asia**	**19 642 703**	**8 534 391**	**11 108 313**
# 中国香港	HongKong, China	2 021 288	2 009 105	12 183
印度	India	610 435	551 094	59 341
日本	Japan	2 987 049	1 525 858	1 461 191
马来西亚	Malaysia	848 903	270 885	578 018
新加坡	Singapore	623 525	332 052	291 474
韩国	Republic of Korea	4 573 808	962 953	3 610 855
泰国	Thailand	629 386	347 766	281 621
阿拉伯联合酋长国	United Arab Emirates	275 091	181 879	93 212
中国台湾	Taiwan, China	3 073 317	712 546	2 360 771
非洲	**Africa**	**398 956**	**311 556**	**87 399**
欧洲	**Europe**	**5 885 769**	**4 403 680**	**1 482 089**
# 比利时	Belgium	164 338	129 650	34 687
英国	United Kingdom	620 991	537 262	83 729
德国	Germany	1 314 843	675 565	639 278
法国	France	374 714	259 896	114 818
意大利	Italy	327 125	215 379	111 746
荷兰	Netherlands	1 271 995	1 232 376	39 618
西班牙	Spain	192 567	152 873	39 694
芬兰	Finland	77 392	39 881	37 511
瑞士	Switzerland	101 452	32 859	68 593
南美洲	**South America**	**1 610 709**	**896 446**	**714 263**
# 巴西	Brazil	783 179	228 595	554 584
北美洲	**North America**	**6 931 568**	**6 087 952**	**843 615**
# 加拿大	Canada	411 884	304 623	107 261
美国	United States	6 519 669	5 783 315	736 354
大洋洲	**Oceania**	**940 307**	**449 073**	**491 234**
# 澳大利亚	Australia	855 783	404 558	451 225
总计中：东盟组织	**In Total: Association of Southeast Asian Nations**	**3 950 137**	**1 967 737**	**1 982 400**
欧盟组织	**European Union**	**5 468 899**	**4 113 022**	**1 355 877**

表8-4

分商品类章进出口总额 (2018年)
TOTAL IMPORTS AND EXPORTS OF GOODS OF SUB-CATEGORY CHAPTERS (2018)

单位：万美元 (USD 10 000)

商品名称	Item	进出口总额 Total Imports and Exports	出口 Exports	进口 Imports
总计	**Total**	**35 411 397**	**20 683 117**	**14 728 280**
活动物，动物产品	Live Animals, Animal Products	45 364	4 451	40 913
植物产品	Vegetable Products	529 487	5 883	523 604
动，植物油，脂，蜡及其分解产品	Animal or Vegetable Fats and Oils and their Cleavage Products	83 003	3 479	79 524
食品，饮料，酒及醋，烟草及制品	Prepared Foodstuffs; Beverages, Spirits And Vinegar; Tobacco and Manufactured Tobacco Substitutes	53 309	25 477	27 832
矿产品	Mineral Products	677 182	2 463	674 719
化学工业及其相关工业的产品	Products of The Chemical or Industries Allied	1 580 907	606 837	974 070
塑料及其制品，橡胶及其制品	Plastics and Articles Thereof Rubber and Articles Thereof	1 326 984	611 921	715 063
生皮，皮革，毛皮及其制品	Raw Hides and Skins, Leather, Fur Skins and Articles Thereof	88 351	76 707	11 644
木及木制品，其他编结材料制品	Wood and Articles of Wood; Other Plaiting Materials	78 209	20 688	57 521
纸浆，纸，纸板及其制品	Pulp of Paper，Paper and Paperboard and Articles Thereof	429 416	145 931	283 484
纺织原料及纺织制品	Textiles and Textile Articles	2 241 795	1 950 677	291 118
鞋帽伞杖鞭，羽毛制品，人造花	Footwear, Headgear, Umbrellas, Sun Umbrellas, Walking-Sticks, Seat-Sticks, Feathers and Articles Made ; Artificial Flowers	241 771	79 812	161 959
石料及其制品，陶瓷玻璃及制品	Articles of Stone, Ceramic Products; Glass and Glassware	223 473	99 496	123 977
珍珠，宝石，贵金属，仿首饰，硬币	Pearls, Precious , Precious Metals, Imitation Jewelry ; Coin	37 052	5 767	31 285
贱金属及其制品	Base Metals and Articles of Base Metal	1 699 990	1 046 778	653 212
机器，电子产品，电气设备及零件	Machinery, Electronic Products, Electrical Equipment and Parts	22 451 634	13 548 456	8 903 178
车辆，航空器，船舶及运输设备	Vehicles, Aircraft, Vessels And Associated Transport Equipment	832 991	634 085	198 906
光学，检测，医疗设备，钟表，乐器	Optical, Detection, Medical Equipment, Clocks and Watches, and Musical Instruments	1 897 419	948 019	949 400
武器，弹药及其零件，附件	Arms and Ammunition; Parts and Accessories Thereof	304	302	2
杂项制品	Miscellaneous Manufactured Articles	882 576	857 782	24 793
艺术品，收藏品及古物	Works of Art, Collectors' Pieces and Antiques	187	134	53
特殊交易品及未分类商品	Special Transaction Goods and Unclassified Goods	4 200	3 180	1 020
其他	Others	5 794	4 793	1 001
总计中：机电产品	**In Total: Mechanical and electrical products**	**26 504 681**	**16 247 821**	**10 256 860**
高新技术产品	**High-tech products**	**18 481 132**	**10 629 727**	**7 851 405**

表8-5

部分年份海外企业及服务外包
OVERSEAS BUSINESS CONDITIONS AND SERVICE OUTSOURCING OF PARTIAL YEAR

单位：万美元 (USD 10 000)

年份 Year	境外企业数（个） Number of Newly Approved Foreign Enterprises (unit)		新批中方境外投资额 New Registered Oversea Investment from China	服务外包 Services Outsourcing	
	新增 Newly Added	累计实有 Total		接包合同额 Access Package Contract Amount	离岸执行额 Offshore Executive Amount
2000	2	74	320		
2001	5	79	285		
2002	8	85	187		
2003	7	91	453		
2004	32	110	4 793		
2005	42	134	8 211		
2006	51	185	10 566		
2007	50	235	13 023		
2008	63	298	20 526		
2009	111	377	32 224	144 887	89 096
2010	118	495	47 446	226 842	126 934
2011	138	589	70 048	356 994	201 346
2012	187	744	122 163	559 619	305 409
2013	159	871	161 851	863 852	462 365
2014	209	1 034	170 029	1 038 857	548 585
2015	252	1 235	204 754	1 191 593	626 608
2016	334	1 509	320 896	1 284 545	668 847
2017	157	1 641	231 755	1 170 629	525 812
2018	239	1 835	268 150	1 179 042	482 559

表8-6

分地区海外企业情况（2018年）
OVERSEAS BUSINESS CONDITIONS BY REGION(2018)

地　　区	Region	境外企业数（个）Number of Newly Approved Foreign Enterprises (unit)		新批中方境外投资额（万美元）New Registered Oversea Investment from China (USD 10 000)
		新　增 Newly Added	累计实有 Total	
全　市	**Whole Municipality**	**239**	**1 835**	**268 150**
市　区	Urban Area	171	1 057	191 617
# 吴江区	Wujiang District	20	169	20 334
常　熟	Changshu	12	187	17 676
张家港	Zhangjiagang	29	280	39 665
昆　山	Kunshan	22	201	7 247
太　仓	Taicang	5	110	11 945

表8-7

分地区服务外包情况（2018年）
SERVICE OUTSOURCING BY REGION(2018)

地　　区	Region	新增企业(个) The New Enterprise (unit)	接包合同额(万美元) Access Package Contract Amount (USD 10 000)	离岸执行额(万美元) Offshore Executive Amount (USD 10 000)
全　市	**Whole Municipality**	**135**	**1 179 042**	**482 559**
市　区	Urban Area	116	861 542	368 959
# 吴江区	Wujiang District	1	10 261	8 067
常　熟	Changshu	1	23 077	20 686
张家港	Zhangjiagang	5	24 035	2 662
昆　山	Kunshan	6	183 428	55 743
太　仓	Taicang	7	86 960	34 509

表8-8

人民币对主要外币年平均汇价（中间价）
AVERAGE EXCHANGE RATE OF RMB YUAN AGAINST MAIN CONVERTIBLE CURRENCIES (MIDDLE PRICE)

单位：人民币元 (RMB yuan)

年 份 Year	100美元 100 US Dollars	100日元 100 Japanese Yen	100港元 100 Hong Kong Dollars	100欧元 100 Euro
1985	293.66	1.25	37.57	
1986	345.28	2.07	44.22	
1987	372.21	2.58	47.74	
1988	372.21	2.91	47.70	
1989	376.51	2.74	48.28	
1990	478.32	3.32	61.39	
1991	532.33	3.96	68.45	
1992	551.46	4.36	71.24	
1993	576.20	5.20	74.41	
1994	861.87	8.44	111.53	
1995	835.10	8.92	107.96	
1996	831.42	7.64	107.51	
1997	828.98	6.86	107.09	
1998	827.91	6.35	106.88	
1999	827.83	7.29	106.66	
2000	827.84	7.69	106.18	
2001	827.70	6.81	106.08	
2002	827.70	6.62	106.07	800.58
2003	827.70	7.15	106.24	936.13
2004	827.68	7.66	106.23	1 029.00
2005	819.17	7.45	105.30	1 019.53
2006	797.18	6.86	102.62	1 001.90
2007	760.40	6.46	97.46	1 041.75
2008	694.51	6.74	89.19	1 022.27
2009	683.10	7.30	88.12	952.70
2010	676.95	7.73	87.13	897.25
2011	645.88	8.11	82.97	900.11
2012	631.25	7.90	81.38	810.67
2013	619.28	6.33	79.85	822.19
2014	614.28	5.82	79.22	816.51
2015	622.84	5.16	80.34	691.41
2016	664.23	6.12	85.58	734.26
2017	675.18	6.02	86.64	763.03
2018	661.74	5.99	84.43	780.16

表8-9

历年使用外资情况
FOREIGN CAPITAL ACTUALLY USED OVER THE YEARS

单位：万美元 (USD 10 000)

年 份 Year	批准外资项目数(个) Number of Foreign Invested Enterprises Contracts Approved (unit)	新增注册外资金额 Newly Added Value of Foreign Capital Signed	实际使用外资金额 Amount of Foreign Capital Actually Used	历年累计开业外资企业数(个) Accumulative Total of Enterprises with Foreign Investment that Have that Have Entered Production or Operation The Years (unit)
1979~1984	63	2 691	...	
1985	55	8 730	1 070	
1990	164	14 361	6 954	172
1991	442	39 104	11 862	325
1992	3 069	476 095	85 973	1 804
1993	2 655	509 644	150 899	3 322
1994	1 270	463 143	219 086	4 379
1995	905	565 119	237 779	
1996	747	459 904	230 467	
1997	648	441 203	249 531	5 151
1998	520	431 694	307 180	4 285
1999	571	356 819	288 691	4 479
2000	943	467 787	288 338	4 761
2001	1 362	723 014	302 183	4 955
2002	2 465	1 006 655	481 398	5 511
2003	2 399	1 249 606	680 511	6 230
2004	2 282	1 470 260	503 314	7 028
2005	2 181	1 533 971	511 607	8 004
2006	2 281	1 592 383	610 462	10 218
2007	2 022	1 836 349	716 471	12 506
2008	1 462	1 638 953	813 262	12 253
2009	1 426	1 583 786	822 653	13 262
2010	1 537	1 691 980	853 511	14 127
2011	1 516	1 702 391	891 222	14 675
2012	1 189	1 516 828	916 490	15 138
2013	936	1 001 077	869 805	16 609
2014	905	857 856	811 978	16 859
2015	860	893 925	600 023	17 054
2016	784	572 513	484 938	17 214
2017	985	895 381	450 392	17 360
2018	1 013	1 077 109	452 492	16 205

注：2004年及以往年份实际利用外资为苏州市商务局上报数。2004年统计口径调整，2005年及以后年份数据为国家商务部反馈数。2013年起, 合同外资更名为新增注册外资。2014年起, 实际利用外资更名为实际使用外资。2015年起，实际使用外资不含中方股东境外中长期贷款。（下同）

Note: In 2004 and the previous year ,the data of foreign capital actually used in the table were report number by Suzhou Municipal Bureau of Commerce , the statistical caliber has been adjust. In 2005 they were feedback number by The State Department of Commerce. Starting from 2013, the contracted foreign investment was renamed as the newly registered foreign investment. Starting from 2014, the foreign investment actually utilized is renamed to the foreign investment actually used. Starting from 2015, the foreign investment actually utilized excludes offshore medium and long Term loans by foreign shareholders. (Same below)

表8-10

外商及港澳台商直接投资（2018年）

指　标	Item	全　市 Whole Municipality
新设外资项目数 (个)	**Number of Projects of Signed Contracts** (unit)	
本年新设项目数	Number of Projects of Signed Contracts in 2016	1 013
独资经营	Solely Owned Enterprises	696
合资经营	Joint Venture Enterprises	313
合作经营	Cooperative Operation Enterprises	1
股份有限公司	Share-holding Corporations Ltd.	3
历年累计批准项目数(未终止撤销企业)	Accumulative Total of Approved Enterprises The Years（Retired enterprises not being terminated0	22 824
批准外商注册外资金额 (万美元)	**Amount of Foreign Investment Contracts** (USD 10 000)	
本年新增注册外资	Amount of Foreign Investment Contracts Approved in 2016	1 077 109
独资经营	Solely Owned Enterprises	905 121
合资经营	Joint Venture Enterprises	148 566
合作经营	Cooperative Operation Enterprises	16 328
股份有限公司	Share-holding Corporations Ltd.	7 094
历年累计注册外资(未终止撤销企业)	Accumulative Foreign Contracts Investment The Years （Retired enterprises not being terminated0	22 814 232
实际使用外资金额 (万美元)	**Foreign Capital Actually Used** (USD 10 000)	
本年实际使用外资	Foreign Capital Actually Used in 2016	452 492
独资经营	Solely Owned Enterprises	356 831
合资经营	Joint Venture Enterprises	89 649
合作经营	Cooperative Operation Enterprises	2 088
股份有限公司	Share-holding Corporations Ltd.	3 924
历年累计实际使用外资	Total Amount of Foreign Capital Actually Used The Years	12 784 654
历年累计已开业投产的外资企业数 (个)	**Accumulative Total of Enterprises with Foreign Investment that Have Entered Production or Operation The Years** (unit)	**16 205**

DIRECT INVESTMENT FROM FOREIGN, HONG KONG, MACAO AND TAIWAN (2018)

市区 Urban Area	# 吴江 Wujiang	常熟 Changshu	张家港 Zhangjiagang	昆山 Kunshan	太仓 Taicang
552	64	72	46	276	67
343	41	51	29	220	53
208	22	21	17	54	13
1	1	–	–	–	–
–	–	–	–	2	1
12 125	2 348	1 381	1 338	6 230	1 750
508 707	62 753	119 645	81 365	234 184	133 208
415 974	45 163	74 969	77 570	209 805	126 803
70 829	17 210	45 586	3 898	22 492	5 761
16 328	96	–	–	–	–
5 576	284	-910	-103	1 887	644
13 953 952	1 985 755	2 053 588	1 378 420	3 867 780	1 560 492
247 652	45 084	48 680	39 512	72 676	43 972
178 266	24 661	30 930	37 593	69 725	40 317
64 711	17 419	16 912	1 534	2 837	3 655
1703	45	–	385	–	–
2 972	2 959	838	–	114	–
6 615 006	1 195 315	1 418 432	1 276 088	2 503 413	971 715
8 143	**1 480**	**986**	**952**	**4 755**	**1 369**

表8-11 外商及港澳台商投资企业国别(地区)分组 (2018年)

ENTERPRISES WITH INVESTMENT FROM FOREIGN，HONG KONG，MACAO AND TAIWAN BY COUNTRY (REGION)(2018)

单位：万美元 (USD 10 000)

地 区	Region	新设外资项目数(个) Number of Projects of Signed Contracts (unit)	新增注册外资金额 Newly Added Value of Foreign Capital Signed	实际使用外资金额 Amount of Foreign Capital Actually Used
分国别合计	**Sum by Country**	**1 013**	**1 077 109**	**452 492**
# 中国香港	HongKong,China	211	559 491	193 345
中国澳门	Macao,China	1	50	193
中国台湾	Taiwan,China	283	51 569	19 608
新加坡	Singapore	45	53 343	17 765
马来西亚	Malaysia	16	-876	12
日 本	Japan	39	21 683	27 217
韩 国	Republic of Korea	62	21 634	8 095
泰 国	Thailand	3	279	450
澳大利亚	Australia	10	1 013	41
法 国	France	4	3 489	1 635
意大利	Italy	22	3 176	2 163
德 国	Germany	54	24 717	15 012
英 国	United Kingdom	18	8 131	2 753
丹 麦	Denmark	3	5 897	233
瑞 士	Switzerland	5	7927	3 383
荷 兰	Netherlands	11	7 300	25 046
西班牙	Spain	4	2 546	2 001
美 国	United States	91	67 001	15 187
加拿大	Canada	37	1 518	587
维尔京群岛	Virgin Islands	11	28 741	8 364
开曼群岛	Cayman Islands	5	22 107	18 543
萨摩亚	Samoan	22	31 914	9 245
毛里求斯	Mauritius	–	87	4 442
文 莱	Brunei	–	-2 329	–
总计中：东盟组织	**In Total: Association of Southeast Asian Nations**	**65**	**50 671**	**18 227**
欧盟组织	**European Union**	**138**	**68 359**	**56 304**

表8-12

外商及港澳台商投资企业行业分组（2018年） ENTERPRISES WITH INVESTMENT FROM FOREIGN， HONG KONG，MACAO AND TAIWAN BY SECTOR (2018)

单位：万美元 (USD 10 000)

行　业	Sector	新设外资项目数（个） Number of Projects of Signed Contracts (unit)	新增注册外资金额 Newly Added Value of Foreign Capital Signed	实际使用外资金额 Amount of Foreign Capital Actually Used
分行业合计	**Sum by Sector**	**1 013**	**1077 109**	**452 492**
第一产业	**Primary Industry**	**4**	**1 117**	**32**
第二产业	**Secondary Industry**	**323**	**476 472**	**254 618**
# 制造业	Manufacturing	305	453 879	254 396
# 通用设备制造业	General Equipment Manufacture	64	49 331	46 159
计算机、通信和其他电子设备制造业	Computer Telecommunications and Other Electronic Equipment Manufacture	38	60 334	42 781
汽车制造业	Automobile Manufacturing	16	61 469	27 438
专用设备制造业	Special Purposes Equipment Manufacturing	73	44 787	19 817
电气机械和器材制造业	Electric Equipment and Machinery Manufacturing	26	45 795	12 614
医药制造业	Medical and Pharmaceutical Products	10	38 701	11 639
金属制品业	Metal Products	10	9 998	8 302
仪器仪表制造业	Instruments, Meters Machinery	14	6 567	1 207
纺织业	Textile Industry	6	114	629
建筑业	Construction	17	12 409	161
第三产业	**Tertiary Industry**	**686**	**599 520**	**197 842**
# 房地产业	Real Estate	15	181 158	101 213
租赁和商务服务业	Renting and Labor Services	81	113 701	30 991
批发和零售业	Wholesale and Retail Trade Services	300	73 433	16 931
交通运输、仓储和邮政业	Transportation, Logistics and Postal	15	30 696	15 999
科学研究和技术服务业	Scientific Research and Technical Services	134	52 552	12 654
金融业	Financial Industries	4	50 550	9 594
信息传输、软件和信息技术服务业	Information transmission, software and information technology services	86	49 141	6 226
水利、环境和公共设施管理业	Water Conservancy, Environment and Public Facilities Management	1	703	620
卫生和社会工作	Health Care and Social Work	–	605	533
居民服务、修理和其他服务业	Resident Services, Repairs and Other Services	6	1 336	101
住宿和餐饮业	Accommodation and Catering Services	23	37 089	80
文化、体育和娱乐业	Culture, Sports and Entertainment	13	1 754	45
教　育	Education	5	224	34

表8-13 国家级、省级开发区建设发展情况（2018年）

开发区名称	Development Zones	新设外资项目数（个） Number of Foreign Invested Enterprises Contracts Approved (unit)	新增注册外资（万美元） Newly Added Foreign Investment (USD 10 000)
总　计	**Total**	**788**	**877 412**
一、国家级开发区	**State Development Zones**	**729**	**765 568**
苏州工业园区	Suzhou Industrial Park	285	146 125
苏州高新技术产业开发区	Suzhou New and Hi-tech Development Zone	69	103 896
昆山经济技术开发区	Kunshan Economic and Technological Development Zone	87	81 802
张家港保税区	Zhangjiagang Bonded Area	20	30 377
苏州太湖国家旅游度假区	Suzhou Taihu National Tourism and Vacation Zone	5	25 915
昆山国家高新技术产业开发区	Kunshan New and Hi-tech industrial Development Zone	65	56 681
常熟经济技术开发区	Changshu Economic and Technological Development Zone	24	70 874
吴江经济技术开发区	Wujiang Economic and Technological Development Zone	26	25 778
太仓港经济技术开发区	Taicang Economic and Technological Development Zone	44	69 375
张家港经济技术开发区	Zhangjiagang Economicand Technological Development Zone	22	32 530
吴中经济技术开发区	Wuzhong Economic and Technological Development Zone	27	21 237
苏州浒墅关经济开发区	Xushuguan Economic Development Zone	8	40 165
相城经济开发区	Xiangcheng Economic Development Zone	24	59 733
常熟高新技术产业开发区	Changshu New and Hi-tech Industrial Development Zone	31	41 246
二、省级开发区	**Provincial Development Zones**	**59**	**111 844**
昆山旅游度假区	Kunshan Tourism and Holiday Zone	8	10 831
汾湖高新技术产业开发区	Foho New and Hi-tech Industrial Development Zone	9	12 105
昆山花桥经济开发区	Kunshan Huaqiao Economic Development Zone	42	88 908

注：苏州高新技术开发区中包含浒墅关经济开发区数据，下同。

CONSTRUCTION OF STATE AND PROVINCIAL DEVELOPMENT ZONES (2018)

实际使用外资 (万美元) Foreign Capital Actually Used (USD 10 000)	业务总收入 (万元) Total Business Revenue (10 000 yuan)	财政收入 (万元) Financial Revenue (10 000 yuan)	# 一般公共预算收入 General Public Budget Revenue	出口额 (万美元) Exports (USD 10 000)	进口额 (万美元) Imports (USD 10 000)
375 771	**566 089 000**	**32 744 991**	**14 686 839**	**18 082 581**	**13 408 982**
348 916	**524 684 500**	**30 365 502**	**13 421 229**	**17 657 791**	**13 177 163**
88 144	108 329 300	7 295 872	3 500 188	4 640 503	4 969 697
44 000	50 024 100	5 546 441	1 590 000	2 883 000	1 673 000
23 152	77 528 900	2 770 345	1 423 814	4 558 587	2 319 518
19 542	65 449 400	1 145 663	593 900	359 380	1 363 614
146	1 630 900	124 351	78 287	17 597	9 810
22 279	29 678 500	2 118 078	1 112 143	545 816	320 880
28 026	36 104 500	2 060 675	870 792	945 205	519 895
21 188	25 605 700	1 268 691	520 273	1 057 842	517 189
33 006	32 359 000	2 473 174	977 613	464 502	584 566
12 309	34 183 500	1 812 500	966 000	1 074 702	362 628
26 313	24 483 700	1 756 971	797 050	422 061	210 441
25 137	17 668 500	1 255 065	323 634	1 524 024	867 266
14 613	22 596 400	960 801	544 432	331 057	116 522
16 198	16 710 600	1 031 940	446 737	357 539	209 403
26 855	**41 404 500**	**2 379 489**	**1 265 610**	**424 790**	**231 819**
6 674	16 270 100	612 990	436 824	178 724	97 189
9 396	8 840 400	624 489	263 403	150 158	33 561
10 785	16 294 000	1 142 010	565 383	95 908	101 069

Note: The data of Suzhou New and Hi-tech Development Zone includes the data of Xushuguan Economic Development Zone, same as the following.

表8-14 国家级、省级开发区建设发展情况（至2018年累计）

开发区名称	Development Zones	已开发面积（平方公里）Area of Development (sq.km)	全社会固定资产投资（亿元）Total Value of Investment in Fixed Assets (100 million yuan)
总　计	**Total**	**1 092.82**	**40 816.47**
一、国家级开发区	**State Development Zones**	**997.26**	**37 259.78**
苏州工业园区	Suzhou Industrial Park	182.93	8 127.33
苏州高新技术产业开发区	Suzhou New and Hi-tech Development Zone	93.52	5 218.63
昆山经济技术开发区	Kunshan Economic and Technological Development Zone	62.59	3 340.74
张家港保税区	Zhangjiagang Bonded Area	60.00	1 771.99
苏州太湖国家旅游度假区	Suzhou Taihu National Tourism and Vacation Zone	62.59	457.31
昆山国家高新技术产业开发区	Kunshan New and Hi-tech industrial Development Zone	72.28	1 875.94
常熟经济技术开发区	Changshu Economic and Technological Development Zone	50.31	3 361.91
吴江经济技术开发区	Wujiang Economic and Technological Development Zone	56.70	1 917.92
太仓港经济技术开发区	Taicang Economic and Technological Development Zone	124.00	3 052.97
张家港经济技术开发区	Zhangjiagang Economicand Technological Development Zone	43.61	2 162.12
吴中经济技术开发区	Wuzhong Economic and Technological Development Zone	100.63	2 846.03
苏州浒墅关经济开发区	Xushuguan Economic Development Zone	47.12	1 089.16
相城经济开发区	Xiangcheng Economic Development Zone	55.46	1 939.42
常熟高新技术产业开发区	Changshu New and Hi-tech Industrial Development Zone	32.64	1 187.47
二、省级开发区	**Provincial Development Zones**	**95.56**	**3 556.69**
昆山旅游度假区	Kunshan Tourism and Holiday Zone	13.00	709.61
汾湖高新技术产业开发区	Foho New and Hi-tech Industrial Development Zone	24.96	1 335.47
昆山花桥经济开发区	Kunshan Huaqiao Economic Development Zone	57.60	1 511.61

CONSTRUCTION OF STATE AND PROVINCIAL DEVELOPMENT ZONES (BY 2018)

基础设施投入 (亿元) Investment In Infrastructure (100 million yuan)	期末内资企业数 (个) Number of Domestic Enterprise by Year End (unit)	内资企业注册资本额 (亿元) Registered Capital of Domestic Enterprise (100 million yuan)	期末注册外资企业数(个) Number of Enterprises with Foreign Investment that Have Registered by Year End (unit)	实际到账外资额 (亿美元) Foreign Capital Actually Used (USD 100 million)	期末从业人数 (万人) Number of Employee Persons by Year End (10 000 persons)
5 569.17	**325 337**	**27 478.40**	**18 983**	**1 079.15**	**475.39**
5 104.07	**289 852**	**25 345.19**	**16 445**	**996.26**	**422.31**
812.16	74 766	8 462.21	5 070	272.87	84.43
828.21	31 375	3 592.06	1 973	132.29	59.81
336.44	33 078	2 304.14	1 791	101.81	51.32
307.14	14 402	1 002.99	659	48.25	13.85
108.18	2 931	612.41	50	1.71	9.32
180.09	36 185	1 346.65	1 045	59.41	52.21
400.96	12 499	1 371.39	683	91.19	29.68
350.85	11 860	841.36	987	64.24	21.56
384.18	14 617	930.46	1 466	75.00	25.21
677.84	14 666	1 128.82	512	33.19	18.37
394.26	28 337	2 419.86	850	42.92	24.93
347.71	3 876	441.68	314	22.54	13.09
215.56	10 705	954.85	758	32.04	18.58
108.20	4 431	377.99	601	41.34	13.04
465.10	**35 485**	**2 133.21**	**2 538**	**82.89**	**53.08**
86.88	11 845	583.14	1 336	30.36	26.36
142.66	4 066	813.56	524	29.50	11.37
235.56	19 574	736.51	678	23.03	15.35

表8-15

部分年份国际旅游情况

项　　目		Item		1990年
一、旅游外汇收入	（万美元）	**Foreign Exchange Earnings of Tourism**	(USD 10 000)	**1 581**
二、接待境外游客	（万人次）	**Number of Foreign Tourists**	(10 000 person-times)	**27.84**
三、接待过夜境外游客		**Number of Foreign Tourists Staying Overnight**		**26.16**
外国人		Foreigners		8.07
港澳台同胞		Compatriots from HongKong, Macao and Taiwan		17.34
四、境外游客过夜人天数	（万人天）	**Person-days of Foreign Tourists Staying Overnight**	(10 000 person-days)	**31.93**
外国人		Foreigners		11.38
港澳台同胞		Compatriots from HongKong, Macao and Taiwan		19.75
五、接待过夜外国人分国别	（人次）	**Foreign Tourists Staying Overnight by Country**	(person-time)	
# 日　本		Japan		31 321
新加坡		Singapore		2 494
泰　国		Thailand		
印度尼西亚		Indonesia		
马来西亚		Malaysia		
美　国		United States		5 864
加拿大		Canada		
英　国		United Kingdom		2 314
法　国		France		3 606
德　国		Germany		2 367
意大利		Italy		
瑞　士		Switzerland		
澳大利亚		Australia		
六、接待能力		**Reception Capacity**		
星级宾馆	（家）	Star-rated Hotels	(unit)	12
星级宾馆床位	（张）	Number of Beds Star-rated Hotels	(unit)	3 212
附：旅游总收入	（亿元）	**The Total Income of Tourism**	(100 million yuan)	
# 国内旅游收入		Earnings form Domestic Tourism		
接待国内旅游人数	（万人次）	**Number of Received Domestic Tourists**	(10 000 person-times)	

注：2013年起国家旅游局对入境旅游统计口径进行调整，以社会住宿设施床位数为基础，并以公安部门的接待境外人员数据进行校核。

INTERNATIONAL TOURISM OF PARTIAL YEARS

2000年	2010年	2014年	2015年	2016年	2017年	2018年
20 135	**125 059**	**170 463**	**200 183**	**216 708**	**230 448**	**252 200**
71.41	**265.15**	**190.24**	**197.20**	**209.98**	**227.25**	**240.76**
55.73	**207.53**	**145.32**	**151.20**	**161.28**	**175.63**	**182.78**
37.58	147.23	82.75	84.43	91.08	97.45	103.21
18.15	60.30	62.57	66.77	70.20	78.18	79.57
88.32	**668.01**	**593.83**	**627.03**	**676.13**	**737.07**	**791.85**
62.67	453.03	304.48	309.80	334.84	352.36	379.98
25.65	214.98	289.35	317.23	341.29	384.71	411.87
114 870	426 352	198 511	158 794	161 423	168 820	161 899
19 217	57 832	31 136	29 961	26 873	24 559	24 610
7 595	24 363	8 756	6 059	8 195	5 601	5 542
4 688	21 808	17 658	12 342	11 809	10 672	8 326
36 570	59 078	48 859	29 117	24 024	19 398	17 490
36 027	192 581	83 013	125 740	130 890	132 622	138 968
4 312	43 358	27 698	21 520	14 109	15 373	16 619
10 823	44 071	24 124	22 367	17 798	17 780	17 923
20 920	38 428	22 571	18 193	15 650	18 457	18 745
10 604	68 084	44 555	65 468	63 816	65 541	66 985
7 555	20 422	15 106	18 233	17 195	17 576	17 447
1 926	5 808	3 898	4 296	3 484	4 385	3 728
5 779	33 131	18 575	13 510	12 916	14 411	15 199
67	159	132	123	110	104	95
14 816	41 183	35 850	39 414	37 511	32 567	31 612
141.88	**1 018.19**	**1 697.78**	**1 863.60**	**2 082.01**	**2 327.58**	**2 601.19**
125.22	917.76	1 574.81	1 728.79	1 932.50	2 161.32	2 416.48
1 496.05	**7 004.88**	**10 028.84**	**10 605.45**	**11 300.37**	**12 046.42**	**12 847.67**

Note: In 2013 the National Tourism Administration began to adjust the caliber of inbound tourism statistics, and it is based on the number of beds of the society's accommodation facilities and checked with the data of foreign tourists received in the police department.

表8-16

四星级及以上饭店、宾馆一览 (2018年末)
LIST OF HOTELS ABOVE 4-STAR STANDARD (END OF 2018)

单　位 Hotels and Restaurants	地　址 Address	电　话 Telephone Number	星级标准 Standard	客房数(间) Number of Guest Rooms (room)
苏州吴宫泛太平洋酒店	苏州市姑苏区新市路259号	65103388	五星	481
苏州雅都大酒店	苏州市姑苏区三香路488号	68291888	五星	327
苏州国泰南园宾馆	苏州市姑苏区十全街655号	67786778	五星	233
苏州万豪酒店	苏州市姑苏区干将西路1296号	82258888	五星	293
苏州怡景太湖高尔夫酒店	苏州市吴中区太湖国家旅游度假区墅里路2号	66217777	五星	118
苏州新城花园酒店	苏州市高新区狮山路1号	68250228	五星	457
苏州香格里拉大酒店	苏州市高新区塔园路168号	68080168	五星	390
苏州中茵皇冠假日酒店	苏州市工业园区星港街168号	67616688	五星	344
苏州工业园区金鸡湖大酒店	苏州市工业园区国宾路168号	62887878	五星	159
苏州工业园区阳澄湖澜廷度假酒店	苏州市工业园区阳澄湖半岛	62988888	五星	200
苏州金鸡湖凯宾斯基酒店	苏州市工业园区国宾路1号	62897888	五星	458
苏州维景国际大酒店	苏州市工业园区金鸡湖大道1355号	62800666	五星	475
苏州同里湖大饭店	苏州市吴江区九里湖路8号	63337888	五星	491
吴江东恒盛国际大酒店	苏州市吴江区文苑路88号	63928888	五星	422
吴江海悦花园大酒店	苏州市吴江区经济开发区运东大道1168号	63438888	五星	510
常熟虞山饭店	常熟市北门大街8号	52118888	五星	291
常熟天铭国际大酒店	常熟市海虞北路12号	52877777	五星	316
常熟皇冠假日酒店	常熟市开元大道6号	52729999	五星	269
常熟裕坤国贸酒店	常熟市珠江路176号	52988888	五星	286
常熟金海华丽嘉酒店	常熟市西门大街73号	52188888	五星	192
张家港国贸酒店	张家港市人民中路42号	58687788	五星	515

表8-16 续表 1 Continued 1

单 位 Hotels and Restaurants	地 址 Address	电 话 Telephone Number	星级标准 Standard	客房数(间) Number of Guest Rooms (room)
张家港华芳金陵国际酒店	张家港市长安中路388号	58811999	五星	398
张家港馨苑度假村	张家港市长安南路279号	58818888	五星	227
昆山一醉皇冠酒店	昆山市前进中路216号	57338888	五星	239
阳澄湖费尔蒙酒店	昆山市马鞍山西路3668号	57800888	五星	200
昆山瑞士大酒店	昆山市前进中路387号	57885788	五星	387
太仓花园酒店	太仓市人民北路11号	53531888	五星	251
太仓锦江国际大酒店	太仓市上海东路89号	53580000	五星	316
苏州胥城大厦	苏州市姑苏区三香路333号	68286688	四星	395
苏州冠云大酒店	苏州市姑苏区桐泾北路538号	68018118	四星	169
苏州市会议中心酒店	苏州市姑苏区道前街100号	65226691	四星	381
苏州园外楼饭店	苏州市姑苏区留园路477号	85888588	四星	182
苏州三元宾馆	苏州市姑苏区人民路887号	65113608	四星	96
苏州独墅湖书香世家会所酒店	苏州市吴中区通达路2699号	62795888	四星	184
苏州中华园大饭店	苏州市吴中区金山南路168号	66256666	四星	127
苏州山水度假村	苏州市吴中区东山镇西泾山	66399888	四星	130
苏州苏苑饭店	苏州市吴中区东吴北路130号	66018888-6635	四星	271
苏州南亚宾馆	苏州市相城区阳澄湖东路1号	65761688	四星	276
苏州金澄大酒店	苏州市相城区兴太路260号	65431888	四星	175
苏州桃园度假村	苏州市高新区金山东路68号	68018888	四星	210
苏州工业园区建屋国际酒店	苏州市工业园区星湖街金鸡湖商业广场	62966666	四星	177
苏州商旅美居酒店	苏州市工业园区凤里街336号	62967888	四星	193

表8-16 续表 2 Continued 2

单 位 Hotels and Restaurants	地 址 Address	电 话 Telephone Number	星级标准 Standard	客房数(间) Number of Guest Rooms (room)
苏州饭店（停业）	苏州市十全街345号	65204646	四星	
苏州新世纪大酒店	苏州姑苏区广济路38号	80988888	四星	192
吴江宾馆	苏州市吴江区鲈乡南路2155号	63420888	四星	232
吴江新世纪国际酒店	苏州市吴江区平望镇平波台3号	65059888	四星	79
吴江盛世锦江国际大酒店	苏州市吴江区盛泽镇盛泽大道88号	63139999	四星	158
吴江汉唐国际酒店	苏州市吴江区鲈乡南路1433号	63115555	四星	90
吴江松陵饭店	苏州市吴江区中山北路51号	63472888	四星	175
苏州新胜鸿国际酒店有限公司	苏州市吴江区盛泽镇舜新南路2008号	63477777	四星	126
常熟虞城大酒店	常熟市海虞南路64号	52777777	四星	280
常熟森林大酒店	常熟市虞山北路79号	52102888	四星	200
常熟旌逸国际酒店	常熟市东南开发区金都路1号	52111805	四星	144
张家港沙洲宾馆	张家港市暨阳中路170号	58810888	四星	242
张家港江南花园酒店	张家港市金港镇长江中路132号	58812569	四星	146
张家港市长江大酒店	张家港市金港镇长江西路99号	58318518	四星	200
昆山宾馆	昆山市人民北路99号	57888000	四星	196
昆山嘉顿国际饭店	昆山市马鞍山东路18号	57558888	四星	214
昆山威尼斯假日酒店	昆山市民权路18号	57016888	四星	240
太仓陆渡宾馆	太仓市陆渡镇号郑和中路78号	53459890	四星	244
太仓娄东宾馆	太仓市县府街6号	53712222	四星	284
太仓世代大酒店	太仓市县府东街30号	53587778	四星	112

表8-17

国际友好城市一览（2018年末）
LIST OF INTERNATIONAL SISTER CITIES OF SUZHOU (END OF 2018)

友好城市	Sister Cities	缔结时间 Time of Establishment of Relationship
苏州市	**Suzhou**	
意大利威尼斯市	Venice, Italy	1980年03月24日
加拿大维多利亚市	Victoria, Canada	1980年10月20日
日本池田市	Ikeda, Japan	1981年06月06日
日本金泽市	Kanazawa, Japan	1981年06月13日
美国波特兰市	Portland, USA	1988年06月07日
罗马尼亚图尔恰县	Tulcea, Romania	1995年09月20日
韩国全州市	Chonju, Republic of Korea	1996年03月21日
拉脱维亚里加市	Riga, Latvia	1997年09月22日
埃及伊斯梅利亚市	Ismailia, Egypt	1998年03月03日
法国格勒诺布尔市	Grenoble, France	1998年09月20日
荷兰奈梅亨市	Nijmegen, The Netherlands	1999年09月23日
丹麦埃斯比约市	Esbjerg, Denmark	2002年08月20日
巴西阿雷格里港市	Porto Alegre, Brazil	2004年06月22日
马达加斯加塔那那利佛市	Antananarivo, Madagascar	2005年11月29日
德国康斯坦茨市	Konstanz, Germany	2007年10月18日
新西兰陶波市	Taupo, New Zealand	2008年02月07日
澳大利亚洛根市	Logan, Australia	2009年11月09日
瑞典克鲁努贝里地区	Region Kronoberg, Sweden	2012年08月22日
波兰新松奇市	Nowy Sacz, Poland	2016年06月14日
刚果（布）黑角市	Pointe-Noire, Republic of the Congo	2016年07月05日
马尔代夫马累市	Male, Maldives	2016年07月15日

表8-17 续表 1 Continued 1

友好城市	Sister Cities	缔结时间 Time of Establishment of Relationship
比利时西弗兰德省	West Flanders, Belgium	2018年03月14日
姑苏区	**Gusu District**	
马耳他桑塔露西亚市	Santa Lucija, Malta	2001年11月09日
吴中区	**Wuzhong District**	
德国里萨市	Riesa, Germany	1999年08月16日
新西兰罗托鲁瓦市	Rotorua, New Zealand	2000年02月18日
美国南湖市	Southlake,USA	2014年12月05日
相城区	**Xiangcheng District**	
韩国荣州市	Yongju, Republic of Korea	1998年04月23日
瑞典维克舍市	Vaxjo, Sweden	2014年10月16日
吴江区	**Wujiang District**	
法国布尔昆-雅里昂市	Bourgoin - Jallieu, France	1993年10月07日
澳大利亚达博市	Dubbo, Australia	1995年06月07日
日本千叶市	Chiba, Japan	1996年10月10日
韩国华城市	Hwa Sung County, Republic of Korea	2000年09月27日
日本内滩町市	Uchinada, Japan	2006年10月08日
南非莫哈林市	Mogale, South Africa	2006年11月14日
美国马伯洛市	Marlboro Township,USA	2011年12月09日
德国西南普法尔茨区	South-West Pfalz，Germany	2017年10月30日
常熟市	**Changshu**	
日本绫部市	Ayabe, Japan	1989年05月12日

表8-17 续表 2 Continued 2

友好城市	Sister Cities	缔结时间 Time of Establishment of Relationship
日本萨摩川内市	Satsuma Sendai, Japan	1991年07月26日
澳大利亚汤斯维尔市	Townsville, Australia	1995年04月30日
美国惠蒂尔市	Whittier, USA	1995年05月12日
法国布莱斯特市	Brest, France	1996年07月16日
加拿大本拿比市	Burnaby, Canada	2009年07月20日
摩洛哥索维拉市	Essaouira, Morocco	2013年05月20日
韩国务安郡	MUAN-GUN, Republic of Korea	2016年10月21日
张家港市	**Zhangjiagang**	
澳大利亚波特兰市	Portland, Australia	1995年08月08日
日本丸龟市	Marugame, Japan	1999年05月28日
俄罗斯维亚基马市	Vyazama, Russia	2004年10月11日
美国丽浪多	Redondo Beach, USA	2007年05月21日
昆山市	**Kunshan**	
美国南艾尔蒙地市	South Elmonte, USA	1993年06月07日
纳米比亚赫鲁特方丹市	Grootfontein, Namibia	2003年07月21日
日本馆林市	Tatebayashi, Japan	2006年05月16日
澳大利亚彭里斯市	Australia, Penrith	2013年10月31日
芬兰许温凯市	Hyvinkaa, Finland	2016年05月20日
太仓市	**Taicang**	
意大利罗索里纳市	Rosolina, Italy	2000年02月23日
英国威勒尔市	Wirral, UK	2013年12月18日

主 要 统 计 指 标 解 释

进出口总额 指实际进出我国国境的货物总金额。包括对外贸易实际进出口货物，来料加工装配进出口货物，国家间、联合国及国际组织无偿援助物资和赠送品，华侨、港澳台同胞和外籍华人捐赠品，租赁期满归承租人所有的租赁货物，进料加工进出口货物，边境地方贸易及边境地区小额贸易进出口货物，中外合资企业、中外合作经营企业、外商独资经营企业进出口货物和公用物品，到、离岸价格在规定限额以上的进出口货样和广告品(无商业价值、无使用价值和免费提供出口的除外)，从保税仓库提取在中国境内销售的进口货物，以及其他进出口货物。该指标可以观察一个国家在对外贸易方面的总规模。我国规定出口货物按离岸价格统计，进口货物按到岸价格统计。

使用外资 指我国各级政府、部门、企业和其他经济组织通过对外借款、吸收外商直接投资以及用其他方式筹措的境外现汇、设备、技术等。

外商直接投资 指外国企业和经济组织或个人(包括华侨、港澳台胞以及我国在境外注册的企业)按我国有关政策、法规，用现汇、实物、技术等在我国境内开办外商独资企业、与我国境内的企业或经济组织共同举办中外合资经营企业、合作经营企业或合作开发资源的投资(包括外商投资收益的再投资)，以及经政府有关部门批准的项目投资总额内企业从境外借入的资金。

外商其他投资 指除对外借款和外商直接投资以外的各种利用外资的形式。包括企业在境内外股票市场公开发行的以外币计价的股票（目前主要是在香港证券市场发行的H股和在境内证券市场发行的B股）发行价总额，国际租赁进口设备的应付款，补偿贸易中外商提供的进口设备、技术、物料的价款，加工装配贸易中外商提供的进口设备、物料的价款。

对外直接投资 指我国国内投资者以现金、实物、无形资产等方式在国外及港澳台地区设立、购买国（境）外企业，并以控制该企业的经营管理权为核心的经济活动。

对外承包工程 指各对外承包公司以招标议标承包方式承揽的下列业务：(1)承包国外工程建设项目；(2)承包我国对外经援项目；(3)承包我国驻外机构的工程建设项目；(4)承包我国境内利用外资进行建设的工程项目；(5)与外国承包公司合营或联合承包工程项目时我国公司分包部分；(6)对外承包兼营的房屋开发业务。对外承包工程的营业额是以货币表现的本期内完成的对外承包工程的工作量，包括以前年度签订的合同和本年度新签订的合同在报告期内完成的工作量。

对外劳务合作 指以收取工资的形式向业主或承包商提供技术和劳动服务的活动。我国对外承包公司在境外开办的合营企业，中国公司同时又提供劳务的，其劳务部分也纳入劳务合作统计。劳务合作营业额按报告期内向雇主提交的结算数(包括工资、加班费和奖金等)统计。

旅游人数

(1)入境旅游人数：指报告期内来我国观光、度假、探亲访友、就医疗养、购物、参加会议或从事经济、文化、体育、宗教活动的外国人、港澳台同胞等入境游客。统计时，外国人、港澳台同胞每入境一次统计1人次。入境旅游人数包括入境过夜游客和入境一日游游客。

(2)出境人数：指中国（大陆）居民因公或因私出境前往其他国家、中国香港特别行政区、澳门特别行政区和台湾省观光、度假、探亲访友、就医疗养、购物、参加会议或从事经济、文化、体育、宗教活动的人数，即出境游客。统计时，按每出境一次统计1人次。

(3)国内旅游人数：指在报告期内在中国（大陆）观光游览、度假、探亲访友、就医疗养、购物、参加会议或从事经济、文化、体育、宗教活动的中国（大陆）居民人数，其出游的目的不是通过所从事的活动谋取报酬。统计时，国内游客按每出游一次统计1人次。

国际旅游(外汇)收入 指入境游客在中国（大陆）境内旅行、游览过程中用于交通、参观游览、住宿、餐饮、购物、娱乐等全部花费。

国内旅游收入 指国内游客在国内旅行、游览过程中用于交通、参观游览、住宿、餐饮、购物、娱乐等全部花费。

星级饭店 指设备、设施、服务符合《旅游饭店星级的划分与评定》（GB/T14308-2003），通过相关旅游管理部门评定，并取得星级饭店称号的饭店（含预备星级饭店）。

EXPLANATORY NOTES ON MAIN STATISTICAL INDICATORS

Total Imports and Exports at Customs refer to the real value of commodities imported and exported across the border of China. They include the actual imports and exports through foreign trade, imported and exported goods under the processing and assembling trades and materials, supplies and gifts as aid given gratis between governments and by the United Nations and other international organizations, and contributions donated by overseas Chinese, compatriots in Hong Kong and Macao and Chinese with foreign citizenship, leasing commodities owned by tenant at the expiration of leasing period, the imported and exported commodities processed with imported materials, commodities trading in border areas, the imported and exported commodities and articles for public use of the Sino-foreign joint ventures, cooperative enterprises and ventures with sole foreign investment. Also included is import or export of samples and advertising goods for which CIF or FOB value are beyond the permitted ceiling (excluding goods of no trading or use value and free commodities for export), imported goods sold in China from bonded warehouses and other imported or exported goods. The indicator of the total imports and exports at customs can be used to observe the total size of external trade in a country. In accordance with the stipulation of the Chinese government, imports are calculated at CIF, while exports are calculated at FOB.

Utilization of Foreign Capitals refers to remittance, equipment and technology financed from abroad, by loans, foreign direct investment and other forms undertaken by the Chinese governments at all levels, by various departments, enterprises and other economic units.

Foreign Direct Investment refers to the investments inside China by foreign enterprises and economic organizations or individuals (including overseas Chinese, compatriots from Hong Kong, Macao and Taiwan, and Chinese enterprises registered abroad), following the relevant policies and laws of China, for the establishment of ventures exclusively with foreign own investment, Sino-foreign joint ventures and cooperative enterprises or for co-operative exploration of resources with enterprises or economic organizations in China. It includes the re- investment of the foreign entrepreneurs with the profits gained from the investment and the funds that enterprises borrow from abroad in the total investment of projects which are approved by the relevant department of the government.

Other Foreign Investment refers to all forms of utilization of foreign capitals other than foreign borrowings and foreign direct investment. It includes the total value of stock shares in foreign currencies issued by enterprises at domestic or foreign stock exchanges (now mainly consisting of H shares issued at Hong Kong Security Market and B shares issued at domestic security markets), rent payable for the imported equipment through international leasing arrangement, cost of imported equipment, technology and materials provided by foreign counterparts in compensation trade and processing and assembly trade.

Overseas Direct Investment refers to enterprises set up or bought by domestic investors in foreign countries and in Hong Kong, Macao and Taiwan, and the economic activities centring on operation and management of those enterprises are under the control of domestic investors.

Overseas Contracted Project refers to projects undertaken by Chinese contractors (project contracting companies) through bidding process. They include: (1) overseas civil engineering construction projects financed by foreign investors; (2) overseas projects financed by the Chinese government through its foreign aid programs; (3) construction projects of Chinese diplomatic missions, trade offices and other institutions stationed abroad; (4) construction projects in China financed by foreign investment; (5) sub-contracted projects to be taken by Chinese contractors through a joint umbrella project with foreign contractor(s); (6) housing development projects. The business income from international contracted projects is the work volume of contracted projects completed during the reference period, expressed in monetary terms, including completed work on projects signed in previous years.

Overseas Labour Services refer to the activities of providing technology and labour services to employers or contractors in the forms of receiving salaries and wages. Labour services providing by contractual joint ventures of Chinese international contracting corporations should be included in the statistics of service co-operation with foreign countries. The business income of labour service cooperation is the income in the form of wages and salaries, overtime pay, bonuses and other remuneration received from the employers during the reference period.

Number of Tourists

(1) Visitor arrivals refer to the number of foreigners, Chinese compatriots from Hong Kong, Macao and Taiwan Chinese (mainland) who come to China (mainland) for sight-seeing, vacation, visiting relatives, medical treatment, shopping, attending conference, or to engage in economic, cultural, sports and religious activities. In compiling statistics, each time of entering China is counted as one person-time. The number of overseas visitor arrivals includes inbound overnight tourists and one-day tourists.

(2) Number of Chinese residents going abroad refer to the number of Chinese (mainland) residents going to other countries, Hong Kong Special Administrative region, Macao Special Administrative region and Taiwan for on official or private purposes, for sight-seeing, vacation, visiting relatives, medical treatment, shopping, attending conference, or to engage in economic, cultural, sports and religious activities. In compiling statistics, each time of leaving is counted as one person-time.

(3) Number of domestic tourists refers to the number Of Chinese (mainland) residents who travel within China (mainland) for sight-seeing, vacation, visiting relatives, medical treatment, shopping, attending conference, or to engage in economic, cultural, sports and religious activities. In compiling statistics, each time of travelling is counted as one person-time.

Foreign Exchange Earnings from International Tourism refer to the total expenditure of foreigners, overseas Chinese, Chinese compatriots from Hong Kong, Macao and Taiwan during their stay in the mainland of China on transportation,sighting, accommodation, food, shopping and entertainment.

Income from Domestic Tourism refer to expenditure of domestic tourists on transportation, sighting, accommodation, food, shopping and entertainment while they travel.

Star-rated Hotels refer to hotels rated with stars as assessed by the relevant tourism authorities according to GB/T14308-2003 standard with reference to their infrastructure, facilities and service levels.

九、服务业

CHAPTER 9
SERVICES

9 服务业 SERVICES

主要统计指标 MAJOR STATISTICAL INDICATORS

2018年服务业税收	Tax of Services	1 770.85	亿元	100 million yuan
比上年增长	Increase Over Last Year	24.2	%	
2018年服务业投资	Investment of Services	3 450.39	亿元	100 million yuan
比上年增长	Increase Over Last Year	6.1	%	
2018年服务业实际使用外资	Actual Use of Foreign Investment by Services	19.78	亿美元	USD 100 million
比上年增长	Increase Over Last Year	29.1	%	
2018年服务业用电量	Services Consumption of Electricity	184.57	亿千瓦时	100 million kwh
比上年增长	Increase Over Last Year	12.3	%	
服务业集聚区	Service Area	98	个	unit
# 省　级	Provincial Level	25	个	unit

表9-1 规模以上服务业法人单位主要指标 (2018年)

单位：万元

项　　目	Item	单位数(个) Number of Enterprises (unit)	固定资产原价 Original Value of Fixed Assets
总　　计	**Total**	**2 645**	**27 725 302**
1. 按地区分	**Grouped by Region**		
市　区	Urban Area	1 459	19 783 732
# 吴江区	Wujiang District	146	1 041 097
常　熟	Changshu	240	1 731 430
张家港	Zhangjiagang	304	1 885 632
昆　山	Kunshan	458	2 345 076
太　仓	Taicang	184	1 979 432
2. 按登记注册类型分	**Grouped by Registration Status**		
国有企业	State-owned Enterprises	39	662 471
集体企业	Collective-owned Enterprises	53	593 844
股份合作企业	Share-holding Cooperative Enterprises	3	34 155
联营企业	Joint Ownership Enterprises	–	–
有限责任公司	Limited Liability Corporations	650	14 908 302
股份有限公司	Share-holding Cooperative Ltd.	97	3 673 600
私营企业	Private Enterprises	1511	2 844 077
其他企业	Other Enterprises	33	86 500
港澳台商投资企业	Enterprises with Investment from HongKong, Macao and Taiwan	93	2 669 722
外商投资企业	Enterprises with Foreign Investment	166	2 252 631
3. 按主要行业分	**Grouped by Sector**		
交通运输、仓储和邮政业	Transportation, Storage and Postal Services	786	12 887 428
道路运输业	Road Transport	367	8 481 882
水上运输业	Water Transport	38	1 689 973
航空运输业	Air Transport	1	933
多式联运和运输代理业	Multimodal Combined Transportation and Transportation Agencies	225	246 903
装卸搬运和仓储业	Loading，Unloading and Storage	135	2 329 059
邮政业	Postal Services	20	138 677
信息传输、软件和信息技术服务业	Information Transmission, Software and IT Services	282	4 872 430
电信、广播电视和卫星传输服务	Telecommunications, Radio and Television and Satellite Transmission Services	14	4 210 017
互联网和相关服务	Internet and Related Services	30	48 422
软件和信息技术服务业	Software and IT Services	238	613 991

MAIN INDICATORS OF CORPORATE UNITS OF ABOVE-SCALE SERVICES (2018)

(10 000 yuan)

本年折旧 Depreciation Charge of the Year	资产总计 Total Assets	负债总计 Total Liabilities	营业收入 Business Revenue	营业成本 Business Cost	所有者权益合计 Total Creditors Equity	税金及附加 Taxes and Extra Charges from Business
1 407 674	**98 464 181**	**55 376 101**	**25 959 236**	**19 070 651**	**43 088 080**	**206 093**
919 707	60 913 268	33 521 756	17 477 337	12 693 423	27 391 512	129 099
45 886	2 966 749	1 448 517	716 297	478 477	1 518 232	5 660
90 654	7 550 058	4 551 293	1 475 918	1 050 943	2 998 765	15 132
152 662	8 486 837	4 460 141	2 378 911	1 909 158	4 026 696	12 923
140 743	17 272 831	10 616 758	3 246 873	2 363 366	6 656 073	33 897
103 908	4 241 187	2 226 153	1 380 197	1 053 760	2 015 034	15 043
29 043	7 943 983	4 710 603	709 029	554 015	3 233 379	7 125
26 354	4 003 098	3 243 701	181 221	117 135	759 397	4 500
1 573	27 873	13 112	8 572	3 919	14 761	202
–	–	–	–	–	–	–
589 447	63 434 101	35 146 020	9 335 883	7 736 964	28 288 081	102 638
215 193	4 587 385	2 342 087	2 989 851	1 518 227	2 245 298	13 098
243 735	10 553 225	6 714 199	9 229 460	7 169 779	3 839 026	43 283
18 308	238 933	191 637	197 987	120 976	47 296	570
166 799	3 956 655	1 561 033	1 629 254	938 378	2 395 622	12 403
117 223	3 718 928	1 453 708	1 677 980	911 258	2 265 220	22 274
503 633	22 344 986	11 787 051	7 203 105	6 202 162	10 557 935	43 734
246 392	15 030 631	8 316 295	2 742 724	2 708 438	6 714 336	14 370
91 452	1 814 790	714 110	478 094	319 213	1 100 680	4 891
66	1 773	843	1 719	1 083	930	20
14 461	1 461 167	795 260	1 948 876	1 704 827	665 907	4 421
144 258	3 793 087	1 830 521	1 329 311	873 031	1 962 565	18 601
7 005	243 539	130 021	702 381	595 571	113 517	1 432
320 362	7 211 100	3 817 288	5 908 233	3 193 144	3 393 812	24 551
243 009	2 158 822	1 441 073	2 206 322	1 096 898	717 749	7 452
7 950	639 825	231 815	489 812	173 268	408 010	1 393
69 403	4 412 452	2 144 399	3 212 099	1 922 978	2 268 053	15 706

表9-1 续表 1

单位：万元

项 目	Item	单位数(个) Number of Enterprises (unit)	固定资产原价 Original Value of Fixed Assets
房地产业	Real Estate	270	1 899 416
物业管理	Property Management	211	632 201
房地产中介服务	Real Estate Services	16	13 004
房地产租赁经营	Real Estate Leasing Businesses	43	1 254 211
其他房地产业	Other Real Estate Industries	–	–
租赁和商务服务业	Leasing and Business Services	493	4 023 283
租赁业	Leasing Industry	20	104 898
商务服务业	Business Services	473	3 918 384
科学研究和技术服务业	Scientific Research and Technical Services	386	1 977 555
研究和试验发展	Research and Experimental Development	60	409 133
专业技术服务业	Professional Technical Services	293	915 384
科技推广和应用服务业	Technology Promotion and Application Services	33	653 038
水利、环境和公共设施管理业	Water, Environment and Public Facilities Management Industry	116	673 600
水利管理业	Water Conservancy	6	151 779
生态保护和环境治理业	Ecological Protection and Environmental Management Industry	14	57 344
公共设施管理业	Public Facilities Management	90	347 986
土地管理业	Land Management Industries	6	116 491
居民服务、修理和其他服务业	Resident Services, Repairs and Other Services	94	144 327
居民服务业	Resident Services	22	37 674
机动车、电子产品和日用产品修理业	Motor Vehicles, Electronics and Household Goods Repair Industry	47	81 988
其他服务业	Other Services	25	24 665
教 育	Education	64	175 615
卫生和社会工作	Health and Social Work	82	573 361
卫 生	Health	78	516 731
社会工作	Social Work	4	56 630
文化、体育和娱乐业	Culture, Sports and Entertainment	72	498 289
新闻和出版业	Press and Publishing	5	53 358
广播、电视、电影和影视录音制作业	Radio, Television, Film and Video Recording Production Industry	34	47 499
文化艺术业	Culture and Arts	10	47 252
体 育	Physical Education	17	258 317
娱乐业	Entertainment	6	91 864

Continued 1

(10 000 yuan)

本年折旧 Depreciation Charge of the Year	资产总计 Total Assets	负债总计 Total Liabilities	营业收入 Business Revenue	营业成本 Business Cost	所有者权益合计 Total Creditors Equity	税金及附加 Taxes and Extra Charges from Business
92 944	9 626 066	6 072 457	1 266 969	891 202	3 553 609	37 338
30 916	2 419 438	1 673 175	925 980	694 854	746 263	12 370
2 016	65 440	40 451	110 486	67 307	24 989	730
60 011	7 141 188	4 358 832	230 503	129 041	2 782 357	24 238
–	–	–	–	–	–	–
233 128	40 701 899	23 629 663	6 296 955	5 206 041	17 072 237	54 608
19 870	294 688	209 727	89 988	73 230	84 960	229
213 259	40 407 212	23 419 935	6 206 967	5 132 811	16 987 277	54 379
128 874	5 542 742	2 443 937	2 833 566	1 791 211	3 098 805	20 332
25 316	1 329 810	591 420	491 108	292 641	738 390	3 693
68 742	2 677 981	1 058 263	1 935 552	1 256 905	1 619 718	10 548
34 817	1 534 951	794 254	406 905	241 665	740 697	6 092
35 656	10 100 751	5 980 480	877 904	708 475	4 120 271	11 296
7 027	393 494	304 145	48 813	26 824	89 349	648
3 562	221 515	102 391	98 368	57 500	119 124	1 293
22 208	4 521 251	2 901 087	374 985	288 190	1 620 164	6 702
2 858	4 964 491	2 672 857	355 737	335 960	2 291 633	2 653
8 856	633 515	306 569	356 792	246 426	326 946	2 141
2 020	197 671	114 980	103 206	55 592	82 691	224
4 675	392 217	172 261	172 477	131 092	219 956	1 438
2 162	43 627	19 328	81 109	59 742	24 299	480
23 404	403 948	295 505	297 822	172 895	108 443	1 323
33 093	723 014	455 852	710 337	492 019	267 162	3 614
30 326	651 216	432 229	698 939	482 095	218 988	3 092
2 768	71 798	23 624	11 398	9 924	48 174	522
27 723	1 176 161	587 300	207 556	167 075	588 861	7 156
3 983	112 871	84 439	32 372	25 693	28 432	359
10 358	135 009	87 311	81 958	63 785	47 698	1 494
2 881	284 105	185 713	27 733	22 893	98 393	1 490
6 528	260 023	120 167	49 794	40 264	139 855	3 541
3 973	384 153	109 669	15 699	14 439	274 484	272

表9-1 续表 2

单位：万元

项　目	Item	销售费用 Cost Related With Sale	管理费用 Managerial Cost
总　计	**Total**	**1 677 477**	**3 294 746**
1. 按地区分	**Grouped by Region**		
市　区	Urban Area	1 313 872	2 275 789
# 吴江区	Wujiang District	126 389	100 976
常　熟	Changshu	57 592	190 633
张家港	Zhangjiagang	85 821	216 749
昆　山	Kunshan	165 127	499 474
太　仓	Taicang	55 064	112 102
2. 按登记注册类型分	**Grouped by Registration Status**		
国有企业	State-owned Enterprises	10 997	115 871
集体企业	Collective-owned Enterprises	7 814	65 584
股份合作企业	Share-holding Cooperative Enterprises	1 324	2 567
联营企业	Joint Ownership Enterprises	–	–
有限责任公司	Limited Liability Corporations	433 518	964 263
股份有限公司	Share-holding Cooperative Ltd.	383 214	336 398
私营企业	Private Enterprises	484 642	1 025 154
其他企业	Other Enterprises	20 346	50 514
港澳台商投资企业	Enterprises with Investment from HongKong, Macao and Taiwan	187 189	220 286
外商投资企业	Enterprises with Foreign Investment	148 433	514 109
3. 按主要行业分	**Grouped by Sector**		
交通运输、仓储和邮政业	Transportation, Storage and Postal Services	236 596	603 256
道路运输业	Road Transport	54 565	219 339
水上运输业	Water Transport	3 817	49 776
航空运输业	Air Transport	–	323
多式联运和运输代理业	Multimodal Combined Transportation and Transportation Agencies	33 818	129 305
装卸搬运和仓储业	Loading，Unloading and Storage	135 680	142 610
邮政业	Postal Services	8 716	61 903
信息传输、软件和信息技术服务业	Information Transmission, Software and IT Services	790 740	850 102
电信、广播电视和卫星传输服务	Telecommunications, Radio And Television and Satellite Transmission Services	308 877	80 192
互联网和相关服务	Internet and Related Services	139 708	142 519
软件和信息技术服务业	Software and IT Services	342 155	627 392

Continued 2

(10 000 yuan)

财务费用 Financing Activities Cost	投资收益 Income from Investment	营业利润 Business Profits	利润总额 Total Profits	所得税费用 Income Tax and Fee	应付职工薪酬 Employee Salary payable	应交增值税 Value Added Tax Payable	从业人员平均人数(人) Average Employment (person)
598 350	**497 143**	**2 547 784**	**2 679 438**	**453 151**	**5 157 517**	**632 492**	**495 325**
373 957	276 042	1 631 725	1 734 305	279 849	3 397 784	432 800	286 186
14 272	920	37 428	37 296	12 946	130 660	18 814	17 313
100 014	3 383	173 645	175 699	45 235	310 337	37 154	38 676
26 459	50 762	227 939	234 660	35 947	365 149	52 690	42 971
69 459	166 280	377 727	389 429	62 835	828 517	88 674	99 724
28 462	677	136 748	145 346	29 286	255 730	21 175	27 768
5 016	5 193	30 563	43 115	7 563	208 009	12 957	12 216
15 602	3 568	121	400	4 079	47 031	5 273	5 162
261	–	299	297	35	1 570	157	135
–	–	–	–	–	–	–	–
442 192	304 856	752 898	823 415	143 949	1 777 911	202 175	153 111
12 079	72 034	789 828	797 301	82 542	416 393	83 544	23 644
64 329	29 059	503 071	537 164	117 798	1 846 834	228 483	240 634
2 218	2 299	6 289	7 348	1 719	88 084	4 074	6 403
35 679	61 884	353 256	356 010	52 863	225 410	44 822	18 850
20 974	18 250	111 458	114 389	42 604	546 275	51 008	35 170
284 919	69 416	587 019	618 854	136 094	1 174 503	114 963	109 306
206 797	27 846	226 443	245 952	60 278	667 181	55 405	63 342
24 561	16 644	99 716	99 017	19 249	67 087	9 622	5 164
24	–	270	341	86	312	165	32
10 525	12 511	79 153	89 055	20 088	147 629	21 422	15 593
41 658	12 416	148 582	152 799	30 897	158 279	26 204	15 555
1 354	–	32 854	31 692	5 496	134 015	2 145	9 620
15 972	89 673	1 153 444	1 172 495	110 526	1 248 550	199 798	82 611
8 384	–	694 599	698 466	60 228	207 761	77 436	8 552
-1 754	29 540	66 012	67 286	12 949	107 014	10 386	4 913
9 342	60 134	392 833	406 744	37 349	933 774	111 976	69 146

表9-1 续表 3

单位：万元

项　　目	Item	销售费用 Cost Related With Sale	管理费用 Managerial Cost
房地产业	Real Estate	68 198	198 894
物业管理	Property Management	42 918	148 707
房地产中介服务	Real Estate Services	18 742	12 798
房地产租赁经营	Real Estate Leasing Businesses	6 538	37 390
其他房地产业	Other Real Estate Industries	–	–
租赁和商务服务业	Leasing and Business Services	294 741	584 439
租赁业	Leasing Industry	6 316	7 799
商务服务业	Business Services	288 426	576 640
科学研究和技术服务业	Scientific Research and Technical Services	121 195	668 148
研究和试验发展	Research and Experimental Development	19 868	122 726
专业技术服务业	Professional Technical Services	77 147	335 129
科技推广和应用服务业	Technology Promotion and Application Services	24 180	210 293
水利、环境和公共设施管理业	Water, Environment and Public Facilities Management Industry	31 898	79 749
水利管理业	Water Conservancy	5 842	4 891
生态保护和环境治理业	Ecological Protection and Environmental Management Industry	2 502	8 024
公共设施管理业	Public Facilities Management	23 554	65 368
土地管理业	Land Management Industries	–	1 467
居民服务、修理和其他服务业	Resident Services, Repairs and Other Services	16 729	72 544
居民服务业	Resident Services	8 149	23 047
机动车、电子产品和日用产品修理业	Motor Vehicles, Electronics and Household Goods Repair Industry	6 400	33 564
其他服务业	Other Services	2 181	15 933
教　育	Education	39 664	71 415
卫生和社会工作	Health and Social Work	48 872	115 831
卫　生	Health	48 592	112 920
社会工作	Social Work	280	2 911
文化、体育和娱乐业	Culture, Sports and Entertainment	28 845	50 368
新闻和出版业	Press and Publishing	2 237	10 212
广播、电视、电影和影视录音制作业	Radio, Television, Film and Video Recording Production Industry	11 185	7 650
文化艺术业	Culture and Arts	2 974	14 747
体　育	Physical Education	6 406	14 675
娱乐业	Entertainment	6 044	3 083

Continued 3

(10 000 yuan)

财务费用 Financing Activities Cost	投资收益 Income from Investment	营业利润 Business Profits	利润总额 Total Profits	所得税费用 Income Tax and Fee	应付职工薪酬 Employee Salary Payable	应交增值税 Value Added Tax Payable	从业人员平均人数(人) Average Employment (Person)
85 367	36 349	57 166	78 386	25 105	468 092	54 352	83 930
15 691	3 745	27 777	48 323	15 627	391 380	38 898	77 581
77	130	11 062	11 085	854	58 403	5 713	5 067
69 600	32 475	18 327	18 977	8 624	18 309	9 741	1 282
–	–	–	–	–	–	–	–
154 322	251 156	337 608	353 478	61 662	885 471	109 116	104 746
932	143	1 409	974	1 256	13 260	3 900	1 778
153 390	251 013	336 199	352 505	60 405	872 211	105 216	102 968
18 826	28 087	261 701	284 380	67 636	782 733	97 821	47 434
3 840	11 643	67 361	72 418	9 191	151 438	13 655	7 109
7 322	14 703	263 803	268 339	50 044	504 794	75 040	35 720
7 665	1 741	-69 463	-56 377	8 400	126 501	9 126	4 605
14 525	5 506	46 699	45 404	14 305	107 122	32 501	18 342
371	–	10 068	10 174	2 624	8 215	2 475	467
3 219	138	26 073	27 387	3 617	10 547	8 343	1 005
13 283	647	-12 299	-3 775	3 517	87 181	9 511	16 823
-2 349	4 721	22 857	11 617	4 547	1 179	12 173	47
511	9 108	27 857	25 829	6 266	87 697	8 416	13 210
17	–	16 311	16 853	3 205	14 933	203	2 092
44	9 039	9 179	9 636	2 349	24 799	5 186	2 875
450	69	2 367	-660	712	47 964	3 027	8 243
5 645	7 160	15 246	17 186	4 483	138 850	7 134	10 311
10 642	692	45 272	46 635	13 316	187 433	128	18 540
10 608	603	46 719	47 765	13 244	181 366	113	17 694
34	89	-1 447	-1 131	72	6 067	15	846
7 621	-5	15 772	36 791	13 759	77 067	8 263	6 895
96	228	-5 970	11 339	–	15 271	3 654	800
1 034	23	-2 301	-1 519	537	15 714	2 110	1 723
6 169	5	-8 743	-7 354	585	11 456	560	697
287	-78	-12 524	-11 894	296	23 879	1 792	2 518
35	-184	45 311	46 219	12 341	10 748	146	1 157

表9-2

全市规模以上服务业营业收入三十强企业(2018年)
TOP 30 ABOVE-SCALE SERVICE ENTERPRISES OF OPERATING INCOME (2018)

序　号 No.	单位名称 Name of Enterprises	地　区 Region	行业类别 Category of Employment
1	苏州程会玩国际旅行社有限公司	工业园区	商务服务业
2	中国移动通信集团江苏有限公司苏州分公司	姑苏区	电信、广播电视和卫星传输服务
3	中国电信股份有限公司苏州分公司	姑苏区	电信、广播电视和卫星传输服务
4	八爪鱼在线旅游发展有限公司	工业园区	商务服务业
5	同程国际旅行社有限公司	工业园区	商务服务业
6	苏州工业园区顺丰速运有限公司	工业园区	邮政业
7	华为数字技术（苏州）有限公司	工业园区	软件和信息技术服务业
8	中国联合网络通信有限公司苏州市分公司	高新区、虎丘区	电信、广播电视和卫星传输服务
9	玖隆钢铁物流有限公司	张家港市	道路运输业
10	同程网络科技股份有限公司	工业园区	互联网和相关服务
11	华住酒店管理有限公司	昆山市	商务服务业
12	中国邮政集团公司苏州市分公司	姑苏区	邮政业
13	苏州高新区国有资产经营公司	高新区、虎丘区	土地管理业
14	苏州创旅天下信息技术有限公司	工业园区	软件和信息技术服务业
15	苏州市华谊商务有限公司	高新区、虎丘区	多式联运和运输代理业
16	江苏沿江高速公路有限公司	常熟市	道路运输业
17	江苏京迅递供应链管理有限公司	太仓市	道路运输业
18	苏州高创特新能源工程有限公司	高新区、虎丘区	专业技术服务业
19	江苏沙钢物流运输管理有限公司	张家港市	多式联运和运输代理业
20	苏州苏嘉杭高速公路有限公司	工业园区	道路运输业
21	万国数据服务有限公司	工业园区	软件和信息技术服务业
22	创发信息科技（苏州）有限公司	工业园区	软件和信息技术服务业
23	苏州九龙医院有限公司	工业园区	卫　生
24	江苏国泰新点软件有限公司	张家港市	软件和信息技术服务业
25	华拓金服数码科技集团有限公司	昆山市	软件和信息技术服务业
26	宝通易捷智能科技(苏州)有限公司	吴江区	装卸搬运和仓储业
27	卡特彼勒（苏州）物流有限公司	工业园区	多式联运和运输代理业
28	苏州热工研究院有限公司	姑苏区	研究和试验发展
29	中移(苏州)软件技术有限公司	高新区、虎丘区	软件和信息技术服务业
30	丰田汽车仓储贸易（常熟）有限公司	常熟市	装卸搬运和仓储业

表9-3

全市规模以上服务业资产三十强企业（2018年）
TOP 30 ABOVE-SCALE SERVICE ENTERPRISES OF ASSETS(2018)

序 号 No.	单位名称 Name of Enterprises	地 区 Region	行业类别 Category of Employment
1	苏州市轨道交通集团有限公司	姑苏区	道路运输业
2	苏州城市建设投资发展有限责任公司	姑苏区	商务服务业
3	昆山国创投资集团有限公司	昆山市	商务服务业
4	江苏省吴中经济技术发展总公司	吴中区	商务服务业
5	苏州高新区国有资产经营公司	高新区、虎丘区	土地管理业
6	昆山高新集团有限公司	昆山市	房地产业
7	张家港保税区张保实业有限公司	张家港市	商务服务业
8	江苏省太仓港港口开发建设投资有限公司	太仓市	公共设施管理业
9	常熟市滨江城市建设经营投资有限责任公司	常熟市	商务服务业
10	华住酒店管理有限公司	昆山市	商务服务业
11	苏州高新区城乡一体化建设发展有限公司	高新区、虎丘区	土地管理业
12	江苏沿江高速公路有限公司	常熟市	道路运输业
13	常熟东南资产经营投资有限公司	常熟市	商务服务业
14	苏州市吴中区胥口镇集体资产经营公司	吴中区	商务服务业
15	中国电信股份有限公司苏州分公司	姑苏区	电信、广播电视和卫星传输服务
16	苏州营财投资集团有限公司	姑苏区	房地产业
17	苏州新时代文体会展集团有限公司	工业园区	商务服务业
18	苏州高新区城市建设投资发展有限公司	高新区、虎丘区	土地管理业
19	昆山阳澄湖文商旅集团有限责任公司	昆山市	房地产业
20	苏州工业园区兆阳资产管理有限公司	工业园区	商务服务业
21	中国移动通信集团江苏有限公司苏州分公司	姑苏区	电信、广播电视和卫星传输服务
22	苏州市甪直集团有限公司	吴中区	商务服务业
23	苏州历史文化名城保护集团有限公司	姑苏区	商务服务业
24	苏州工业园区科技发展有限公司	工业园区	商务服务业
25	苏州创元投资发展（集团）有限公司	姑苏区	商务服务业
26	常熟服装城集团有限公司	常熟市	商务服务业
27	江苏扬子江国际冶金工业园资产经营有限公司	张家港市	商务服务业
28	苏州市吴中资产经营管理有限公司	吴中区	商务服务业
29	中新苏州工业园区创业投资有限公司	工业园区	商务服务业
30	苏州苏嘉杭高速公路有限公司	工业园区	道路运输业

表9-4

全市规模以上服务业利润总额三十强企业 (2018年)
TOP 30 ABOVE-SCALE SERVICE ENTERPRISES OF TOTAL PROFITS(2018)

序　号 No.	单位名称 Name of Enterprises	地　区 Region	行业类别 Category of Employment
1	中国移动通信集团江苏有限公司苏州分公司	姑苏区	电信、广播电视和卫星传输服务
2	中国电信股份有限公司苏州分公司	姑苏区	电信、广播电视和卫星传输服务
3	苏州苏嘉杭高速公路有限公司	工业园区	道路运输业
4	华住酒店管理有限公司	昆山市	商务服务业
5	昆山国创投资集团有限公司	昆山市	商务服务业
6	江苏沿江高速公路有限公司	常熟市	道路运输业
7	中国联合网络通信有限公司苏州市分公司	高新区、虎丘区	电信、广播电视和卫星传输服务
8	苏州高新旅游产业集团有限公司	高新区、虎丘区	娱乐业
9	六和机械投资（中国）有限公司	昆山市	商务服务业
10	同程网络科技股份有限公司	工业园区	互联网和相关服务
11	苏州创旅天下信息技术有限公司	工业园区	软件和信息技术服务业
12	江苏国泰新点软件有限公司	张家港市	软件和信息技术服务业
13	苏州市好屋信息技术有限公司	姑苏区	软件和信息技术服务业
14	张家港保税区张保实业有限公司	张家港市	商务服务业
15	苏州好玩友网络科技有限公司	工业园区	软件和信息技术服务业
16	苏州城市建设投资发展有限责任公司	姑苏区	商务服务业
17	创发信息科技（苏州）有限公司	工业园区	软件和信息技术服务业
18	苏州市科远软件技术开发有限公司	高新区、虎丘区	软件和信息技术服务业
19	苏州UL美华认证有限公司	工业园区	专业技术服务业
20	华为数字技术（苏州）有限公司	工业园区	软件和信息技术服务业
21	苏州电视广告有限公司	姑苏区	商务服务业
22	张家港海力码头有限公司	张家港市	水上运输业
23	苏州汽车客运集团有限公司	姑苏区	道路运输业
24	中新苏州工业园区创业投资有限公司	工业园区	商务服务业
25	苏州创元投资发展（集团）有限公司	姑苏区	商务服务业
26	苏州工业园区顺丰速运有限公司	工业园区	邮政业
27	苏州玩友时代科技股份有限公司	工业园区	软件和信息技术服务业
28	丰田汽车仓储贸易（常熟）有限公司	常熟市	装卸搬运和仓储业
29	苏州九龙医院有限公司	工业园区	卫　生
30	中衡设计集团股份有限公司	工业园区	专业技术服务业

表9-5

服务业集聚区发展情况 (2018年)
DEVELOPMENT OF THE SERVICE AREA(2018)

服务业集聚区名称 Service Area	地　区 Region	入区企业数(家) Enterprises Entered Service Area (households)
全　市(98个)		**97 910**
一、省级服务业集聚区(25个)		**49 792**
张家港保税物流集聚区	张家港市	5 896
江苏化工品交易中心	张家港市	1 948
江苏扬子江冶金物流集聚区	张家港市	1 980
张家港保税港区进口汽车物流园	张家港市	300
张家港玖隆钢铁物流园	张家港市	1 920
中国常熟服装城	常熟市	10 000
常熟国家大学科技园	常熟市	761
天镜湖文化科技产业园	太仓市	172
太仓物流园区	太仓市	936
昆山花桥国际商务城	昆山市	10 563
昆山软件服务业集聚区	昆山市	433
昆山综合保税区保税物流集聚区	昆山市	64
中国东方丝绸市场	吴江区	7 050
吴江汾湖商务服务业集聚区	吴江区	4 122
吴江现代物流集聚区	吴江区	39
吴江丝绸创业设计产业园	吴江区	185
吴中科技园	吴中区	239
吴中区检验检测产业集聚区	吴中区	37
中国珍珠宝石城	相城区	690
阳澄湖数字文化创意产业园	相城区	185
苏州工业园区国际科技服务业集聚区	工业园区	572
苏州工业园区现代物流集聚区	工业园区	359
苏州高新区综合保税区	高新区、虎丘区	253
苏州科技城服务业集聚区	高新区、虎丘区	1 000
苏州高新区人力资源服务产业园	高新区、虎丘区	88

表9-5 续表 1 Continued 1

服务业集聚区名称 Service Area	地 区 Region	入区企业数(家) Enterprises Entered Service Area (households)
二、市级服务业集聚区(73 个)		**48 118**
张家港电子商务产业园	张家港市	105
东沙湖基金小镇	工业园区	406
张家港保税区纺织原料市场	张家港市	1 560
常熟市汽车汽配商贸城	常熟市	2 020
苏州工业园区金鸡湖景区	工业园区	514
南太湖文化产业集聚区	吴江区	50
苏州高新区科技金融服务集聚区	高新区、虎丘区	65
江苏省汾湖高新技术产业开发区科技创业园	吴江区	230
苏州湾黄金湖岸旅游集聚区	吴江区	158
苏州中鲈国际物流科技园	吴江区	145
相城影视产业园	相城区	68
常熟科创园	常熟市	323
苏大科技创新产业园集聚区	姑苏区	659
昆山智谷创意产业园	昆山市	70
苏州湾科技城	吴江区	225
昆山阳澄湖科技园	昆山市	178
苏州留学人员创业园	高新区、虎丘区	350
苏州高铁新城大数据产业园集聚区	相城区	150
昆山高新技术创业服务中心集聚区	昆山市	69
常熟纺织服装创意产业园	常熟市	520
淀山湖镇电子商务物流园	昆山市	38
太仓市科技创业园暨留学人员创业园	太仓市	135
平江路休闲旅游特色街	姑苏区	377
张家港软件（动漫）产业园	张家港市	86

表9-5 续表 2　Continued 2

服务业集聚区名称 Service Area	地　区 Region	入区企业数(家) Enterprises Entered Service Area (households)
苏州2.5产业园	工业园区	140
金枫城市设计产业集聚区	吴中区	470
常熟国际物流园	常熟市	610
苏州市吴中科技创业园	吴中区	249
苏州阳澄湖半岛旅游度假区	工业园区	128
江苏医疗器械科技产业园	高新区、虎丘区	114
苏州市平江科技创业园	姑苏区	54
苏州工业园区云彩创新孵化器集聚区	工业园区	102
传化公路港 苏州物流基地	姑苏区	651
吴江市再生资源回收利用市场	吴江区	234
望亭国际物流园	相城区	95
苏州国家环保高新技术产业园	高新区、虎丘区	192
苏州西部生态休闲文化创意集聚区	高新区、虎丘区	2 546
张家港名贵木材国际交易中心	张家港市	385
太仓市森茂汽车城开发有限公司	太仓市	330
同里古镇文化休闲旅游区	吴江区	2 018
常熟虞山尚湖旅游度假区	常熟市	4 155
苏州市高新区狮山中心商务区	高新区、虎丘区	12 972
苏州小样青年社区	相城区	161
盛泽商务集聚区	吴江区	105
苏州生物产业园服务业集聚区	工业园区	442
名城商务科技金融服务集聚区	姑苏区	309
苏州西交漕湖科技园	相城区	87
江苏吴中出口加工区现代物流集聚区	吴中区	85
太仓软件园	太仓市	85

表9-5 续表 3　Continued 3

服务业集聚区名称 Service Area	地　区 Region	入区企业数(家) Enterprises Entered Service Area (households)
苏州高新区综合保税区	高新区、虎丘区	254
苏州工投科技创业园	姑苏区	168
太仓市生物医药产业园	太仓市	104
常熟市城市综合物流园	常熟市	33
张家港众益危化品物流园区	张家港市	39
昆山商贸城	昆山市	2 100
江苏省太仓高新技术产业开发区中央商务区	太仓市	1 333
金枫路创新创意街区	吴中区	1 600
凯马广场汽车街	吴中区	1 175
博济科技创业园	高新区、虎丘区	115
苏州山塘历史街区	姑苏区	103
苏州盛泽纺织科技创业园	吴江区	90
太仓市天镜湖私募基金创业基地	太仓市	77
千灯现代商贸物流园	昆山市	9
昆山文化创意产业园	昆山市	592
江苏蠡口国际家具城	相城区	3 850
沙家浜江南水乡影视产业园	常熟市	136
张家港沙洲湖科创园	张家港市	91
苏州市粮食批发交易市场	吴中区	250
盛泽丝绸现代物流中心	吴江区	47
月亮湾中央商务区	工业园区	218
吴江科技创业园	吴江区	208
张家港市金港物流中心	张家港市	121
平江新城高端商务集聚区	姑苏区	185

主 要 统 计 指 标 解 释

规模以上服务业法人单位　指年营业收入1000万元及以上，或年末从业人员50人及以上服务业法人单位，包括：交通运输、仓储和邮政业，信息传输、软件和信息技术服务业，租赁和商务服务业，科学研究和技术服务业，水利、环境和公共设施管理业，教育，卫生和社会工作；以及物业管理、房地产中介服务、自有房地产经营活动和其他房地产业等行业；以及年营业收入500万元及以上，或年末从业人员50人及以上服务业法人单位，包括：居民服务、修理和其他服务业，文化、体育和娱乐业。

现代服务业集聚区　指以某一服务产业为主体，相关服务产业相配套，产业特色鲜明，空间相对集中，具有资源集合、产业集群、服务集成功能，现代服务业集聚度达到一定水平的区域。

省级服务业集聚区　指根据《江苏省省级现代服务业集聚区认定和管理暂行办法》，符合省发展改革委《关于加快建设现代服务业集聚区的意见》（苏发改服务发［2007］52号）第三条规定，并满足下列条件的现代服务业产业园区：

(1) 有园区发展规划和产业布局规划，边界清晰、形态突出，目标明确；

(2) 有一定的公共服务支撑体系，能够为入区企业提供投融资、合作交流、人才培训、信息管理、技术创新、知识产权保护、检验检测等公共服务；

(3) 有专门的管理机构，专职管理人员不少于3人，实行统一管理，一站式服务；

(4) 建筑面积10000平方米以上，对通过中心城市主城区改造、工业企业“退二进三”、老建筑保护性开发等利用城市存量资产开发的园区，可适当降低标准；

(5) 经省级以上有关部门批准或经省发展改革委批复园区发展规划，并已列入市级现代服务业集聚区。

不同形态的集聚区还应同时满足下列条件：

中央商务区

(1) 城市功能核心区，主要以金融、保险、证券、商务、商贸等企业为主体，高级酒店、商务设施配套；

(2) 企业总部或地区总部集中，拥有跨国公司或国际性金融机构区域性业务总部，或国内行业百强企业总部；

(3) 交通条件便利，通达性良好。

创意产业园

(1) 有较齐备的基础设施和生产环境；能够为创意企业开展创意研发、设计生产和流通交易等活动提供适宜的硬件环境保障；

(2) 产业特色鲜明，具有符合创意产业生产规律的产业形态，拥有注册创意及相关产业链配套企业20家以上，能够引领相关创意产业的发展；

(3) 拥有一定数量的自主知识产权，原创产品占有一定的市场份额，有良好的品牌影响力。

科技创业园

(1) 具有创业企业发展所需的技术支撑体系及相配套的基础设施，能够为企业提供一定的商务、信息、咨询、技术服务；

(2) 实际运营2年以上，经营状况良好；

(3) 产业特色鲜明，注册科技类企业达20家以上。

软件园

(1) 具有软件产业发展的技术支撑体系及相配套的基础设施和通信网络设施;

(2) 注册软件企业数不少于20家，有一定的产业规模;

(3) 拥育一定比例的自主知识产权，并具备一定的软件出口能力。

现代物流园

(1) 依托港口、空港、站场、道口等交通枢纽或正业开发区，具备良好的基础设施条件和信息服务功能;

(2) 至少拥有三种以上物流功能（仓储、加工、包装、分拣、货代、搬运装卸、配送等），并初步具备金融、保险、税务和后勤服务等基本配套服务;

(3) 注册第三方物流企业10家以上。

产品交易市场

(1) 符合全省统一规划，依托当地特色产业或商品集散能力强的优势，采取有形和无形相结合，主要从事工农业产品、材料及其他重要生产资料的批发;

(2) 具有产品展示、交易结算、仓储运输、质量检测、加工配送等功能和条件，初步具备商品集散、加工、交易、价格形成、信息发布和电子商务等功能;

(3) 年商品成交额处于全省同类市场前5名，覆盖全省、辐射华东地区以至全国家，外向度处于同类市场领先地位。

通过认定的现代服务业产业园区，由省发展改革委授予“江苏省现代服务业集聚区”。

市级服务业集聚区 指根据《苏州市现代服务业集聚区认定暂行办法》，通过苏州市级现代服务业集聚区的申报和认定，获批成为苏州市“现代服务业集聚区”的服务业产业园区。

EXPLANATORY NOTES ON MAIN STATISTICAL INDICATORS

The Corporate Unit of Above-scale Services refers to a corporate unit of the service industry employing 50 people or more, or earning annual revenues of 10 million yuan or above, including: transportation, storage and postal services, information transmission, software and IT services, leasing and business services, scientific research and technical services, water, environment and public facilities management, education, health care and social work, property management, real estate services ,business activities with one's own real estate and other real estate industries and so on; also a corporate unit of the service industry employing 50 people or more, or earning annual revenues of 5 million yuan or above, including: resident services, repairs and other services, culture, sports and entertainment.

The Modern Service Area refers to an area with a service industry as the main and related service industries supporting, with distinctive industrial features and relatively concentrated space, with the functions of resources collection, industrial clusters and service integration, and with a certain level of modern services gathering.

The Provincial Service Area refers to a modern service industrial park that should be in accordance with the "Jiangsu's interim measures of recognizing and managing the provincial modern service area" and in line with Article III of the provincial Development and Reform Commission's "Opinions on speeding up the construction of modern service areas" (Su Development and Reform Services [2007] No. 52), and meets the following conditions:

(1) It has industrial park development planning and layout planning, clear boundaries, prominent forms, and clear objectives;

(2) It has a certain public service support system, and can provide the enterprises in the area with such public services as investment and financing, cooperation and exchange, personnel training, information management, technological innovation, intellectual property protection, and inspection and testing;

(3) It has a special management agency with at least three full-time managers, unified management and one-stop service;

(4) It has a building area of over 10,000 square meters. However, to the parks that develop with the city's existing assets such as the transformation of the main city area of the central city, industrial enterprises "two retreat and three advance", and the protective development of old buildings, it may be appropriate to reduce the standard;

(5) It has its development plan approved by the relevant departments above the provincial level or by the Provincial Development and Reform Commission, and has been included in the municipal modern service area.

Clustering areas of different forms should also meet the following conditions:

Central Business District

(1) The core area of urban functions is an area with finance, insurance, securities, business, commerce and other enterprises as the main, and with luxury hotels and business facilities supporting;

(2) It has centralized corporate headquarters or regional headquarters, regional business headquarters of multinational corporations or international financial institutions, or the headquarters of the top 100 domestic industrial enterprises;

(3) Transportation is convenient and accessibility good.

Creative Industrial Park

(1) It has a more complete infrastructure and production environments, and can provide creative enterprises with appropriate hardware environment for such activities as carrying out innovative research and development, designing production and distribution transactions;

(2) It has distinctive industrial features, has industrial forms in line with the production laws of creative industries, has more than 20 companies with registered creativity and related industrial chain supporting, and can lead the development of related creative industries;

(3) It has a certain number of independent intellectual property rights, and original products occupy a certain market share and a good brand influence.

Technology Park

(1) It has the necessary technical support system for the development of entrepreneurial enterprises and supporting infrastructure, and can provide enterprises with a certain business, information, consulting and technology services;

(2) It has actually operated for more than 2 years, and the operating conditions are good;

(3) It has distinctive industrial features, and the registered tech enterprises amounted to more than 20 .

Software Park

(1) It has a technical support system and supporting infrastructure and communications network facilities for the development of the software industry;

(2) It has at least 20 registered software companies with a certain scale of the industry;

(3) It has and will cultivate a certain proportion of independent intellectual property rights, and has a certain software export capacity.

Modern Logistics Park

(1) It relies on transportation hubs such as ports, airports, stations and crossings or a positive industry development zone, and has good infrastructure conditions and information services;

(2) It has at least three or more logistics functions (storage, processing, packing, sorting, forwarding, handling, distribution, etc.), and initially has the finance, insurance, tax, and logistics support services, and other basic services;

(3) It has registered more than 10 third-party logistics companies.

Products Market

(1) It complies with the province's unified planning, relies on the advantages of local specialties industries or commodity distribution capability, combines the tangible and the intangible, and is mainly engaged in the wholesale of agricultural and industrial products, materials and other important means of production;

(2) It has such functions and conditions as product display, transaction clearing, warehousing and transportation, quality testing, processing and distribution, and initially has such functions as commodity distribution, processing, trade, price formation, information dissemination and e-commerce;

(3) It has the annual commodity turnover among the province's top five similar markets, covering the whole province, and spreading over East China and even the whole country, and its outgoing degrees are in the leading position of similar markets.

The modern service industrial park that has been recognized will be awarded "Jiangsu Modern Service Area" by the provincial Development and Reform Commission.

The Municipal Service Area refers to a service industry park that should be in accordance with the "Suzhou's interim measures of recognizing the municipal service area", has been declared and recognized as a Suzhou's municipal modern service area, and approved as Suzhou's "modern service area".

十、能源消费

CHAPTER 10
CONSUMPTION OF ENERGY

10 能源消费 CONSUMPTION OF ENERGY

主要统计指标 MAJOR STATISTICAL INDICATORS

2018年规模以上工业企业能源消费总量	Total Energy Consumption of Industry Above Designated Size	8 703.65	万吨标准煤	10 000 tons of SCE
# 原　煤	Raw Coal	5 185.34	万吨	10 000 tons
焦　炭	Coke	1 236.82	万吨	10 000 tons
汽　油	Gasoline	6.16	万吨	10 000 tons
柴　油	Diesel Oil	15.16	万吨	10 000 tons
燃料油	Fuel Oil	14.16	万吨	10 000 tons
热　力	Heat	123 701 794	百万千焦	1 million kilo-joule
电　力	Electricity	1 009.64	亿千瓦时	100 million kwh
2018年全社会用电量	Total Consumption of Electricity	1 562.49	亿千瓦时	100 million kwh
比上年增长	Increase Over Last Year	3.9	%	
2018年工业用电量	Industrial Consumption of Electricity	1 227.77	亿千瓦时	100 million kwh
比上年增长	Increase Over Last Year	2.1	%	
2018年第三产业用电量	Tertiary Industry Consumption of Electricity	184.57	亿千瓦时	100 million kwh
比上年增长	Increase Over Last Year	12.3	%	
2018年城乡居民生活用电量	Consumption of Electricity for Non-production Purposes	136.60	亿千瓦时	100 million kwh
比上年增长	Increase Over Last Year	9.7	%	

表10-1 全市规模以上工业企业能源购进、消费及库存量（2018年）

ENERGY PURCHASES，CONSUMPTION AND STOCK OF INDUSTRIAL ENTERPRISES OF WHOLE MUNICIPALITY ABOVE DESIGNATED SIZE(2018)

能源品种		Type of Energy		购进量 Purchases	消费量 Consumption	# 工业生产 Industrial Production	#用于原材料 Raw Materials	年末库存量 Stock (year-end)
能源合计	(吨标准煤)	**Total Energy**	(ton of SCE)	**71 259 537**	**87 036 517**	**86 580 874**	**1 000 950**	**2 585 506**
原　煤	(吨)	Raw Coal	(ton)	51 927 496	51 853 367	51 837 799	820 296	2 184 113
洗精煤		Washing Coal		7 231 813	7 193 988	7 193 988	–	410 512
其他洗煤		Other Washed Coals		337 460	334 401	334 401	–	3 059
煤制品		Coal Products		250 924	244 443	244 443	–	8 373
焦　炭		Coke		7 833 598	12 368 191	12 368 191	–	657 225
其他焦化产品		Other Coking Products		273 055	275 286	275 286	275 286	10 185
焦炉煤气	(万立方米)	Coke Oven Gas	(10 000 cu.m)	–	231 335	231 335	–	–
高炉煤气		Blast-furnace Gas		–	4 316 932	4 316 932	–	–
转炉煤气		Converter Gas		–	268 256	268 256	–	–
发生炉煤气		Furnace Gas		–	–	–	–	–
天然气		Natural Gas		502 593	504 335	501 871	1 139	
液化天然气	(吨)	LNG	(ton)	76 878	76 866	76 382	171	51
汽　油		Gasoline		61 412	61 590	11 162	268	203
煤　油		Kerosene		1 096	1 125	1 121	15	138
柴　油		Diesel Oil		151 638	151 626	100 329	–	6 177
燃料油		Fuel Oil		140 129	141 643	141 480	–	15 523
液化石油气		LPG		10 389	10 438	10 180	1	347
润滑油		Lubricating Oil		2 841	2 825	2 525	136	82
石　蜡		Paraffin wax		226	214	214	57	18
溶剂油		Solvent Oil		656	648	648	3	4
石油焦		Petroleum coke		38	28	28	28	17
石油沥青		Petroleum Asphalt		72	59	59	59	23
其他石油制品		Other Petroleum Products		27 384	27 049	24 161	19 086	1 059
热　力	(百万千焦)	Heat	(1 million kilo-joule)	71 347 180	123 701 794	122 567 101	–	–
电　力	(万千瓦时)	Electricity	(10 000 kwh)	8 430 537	10 096 373	9 916 483	–	–
城市生活垃圾用于燃料	(吨)	City Waste For Fuel	(Ton)	1 534 921	1 511 505	1 511 505	–	–
生物质废料用于燃料		Biomass Waste For Fuel		151 704	148 938	147 823	–	2 535
余热余压	(百万千焦)	Heat and Pressure	(1 million kilo-joule)	6 146	23 014 740	23 014 740	–	–
其他工业废料用于燃料	(吨)	Other Industrial Waste For Fuel	(Ton)	5 588	5 588	5 588	–	–
其他燃料	(吨标准煤)	Other Fuels	(ton of SCE)	17 949	17 971	17 971	–	–

表10-2 市区规模以上工业企业能源购进、消费及库存量 (2018年)

ENERGY PURCHASES, CONSUMPTION AND STOCK OF INDUSTRIAL ENTERPRISES OF URBAN AREA ABOVE DESIGNATED SIZE(2018)

能源品种		Type of Energy		购进量 Purchases	消费量 Consumption	# 工业生产 Industrial Production	#用于原材料 Raw Materials	年末库存量 Stock (year-end)
能源合计	(吨标准煤)	**Total Energy**	(ton of SCE)	**16 850 194**	**17 495 788**	**17 284 349**	**340 897**	**264 850**
原　煤	(吨)	Raw Coal	(ton)	10 147 704	10 046 455	10 042 715	94	312 002
洗精煤		Washing Coal		–	–	–	–	–
其他洗煤		Other Washed Coals		–	–	–	–	–
煤制品		Coal Products		250 924	244 443	244 443	–	8 373
焦　炭		Coke		206 301	232 066	232 066	–	27 543
其他焦化产品		Other Coking Products		273 055	275 286	275 286	275 286	10 185
焦炉煤气	(万立方米)	Coke Oven Gas	(10 000 cu.m)	–	–	–	–	–
高炉煤气		Blast-furnace Gas		–	31 662	31 662	–	–
转炉煤气		Converter Gas		–	–	–	–	–
发生炉煤气		Furnace Gas		–	–	–	–	–
天然气		Natural Gas		315 685	315 437	314 211	1 139	–
液化天然气	(吨)	LNG	(ton)	11 366	11 365	11 172	171	–
汽　油		Gasoline		24 643	24 688	4 606	268	123
煤　油		Kerosene		200	211	208	15	10
柴　油		Diesel Oil		41 285	41 337	21 312	–	685
燃料油		Fuel Oil		47 740	48 484	48 437	–	5 526
液化石油气		LPG		3 393	3 408	3 372	–	34
润滑油		Lubricating Oil		1 320	1 292	1 286	118	54
石　蜡		Paraffin wax		210	197	197	57	17
溶剂油		Solvent Oil		163	162	162	–	3
石油焦		Petroleum coke		–	–	–	–	–
石油沥青		Petroleum Asphalt		–	–	–	–	–
其他石油制品		Other Petroleum Products		19 706	19 371	19 365	19 086	1 059
热　力	(百万千焦)	Heat	(1 million kilo-joule)	29 023 075	37 921 296	37 627 860	–	–
电　力	(万千瓦时)	Electricity	(10 000 kwh)	3 269 132	3 509 067	3 407 696	–	–
城市生活垃圾用于燃料	(吨)	City Waste For Fuel	(Ton)	828 158	828 158	828 158	–	–
生物质废料用于燃料		Biomass Waste For Fuel		45 662	45 746	45 732	–	477
余热余压	(百万千焦)	Heat and Pressure	(1 million kilo-joule)	6 146	1 840 229	1 840 229	–	–
其他工业废料用于燃料	(吨)	Other Industrial Waste For Fuel	(Ton)	5 399	5 399	5 399	–	–
其他燃料	(吨标准煤)	Other Fuels	(ton of SCE)	15 129	15 129	15 129	–	–

表10-3

分地区规模以上工业企业能源消费量（2018年）

能源品种		Type of Energy		全市 Whole Municipality	市区 Urban Area
能源合计	**(吨标准煤)**	**Total Energy**	**(ton of SCE)**	**87 036 517**	**17 495 788**
原　煤	(吨)	Raw Coal	(ton)	51 853 367	10 046 455
洗精煤		Washing Coal		7 193 988	–
其他洗煤		Other Washed Coals		334 401	–
煤制品		Coal Products		244 443	244 443
焦　炭		Coke		12 368 191	232 066
其他焦化产品		Other Coking Products		275 286	275 286
焦炉煤气	(万立方米)	Coke Oven Gas	(10 000 cu.m)	231 335	–
高炉煤气		Blast-furnace Gas		4 316 932	31 662
转炉煤气		Converter Gas		268 256	–
发生炉煤气		Furnace Gas		–	–
天然气		Natural Gas		504 335	315 437
液化天然气	(吨)	LNG	(ton)	76 866	11 365
汽　油		Gasoline		61 590	24 688
煤　油		Kerosene		1 125	211
柴　油		Diesel Oil		151 626	41 337
燃料油		Fuel Oil		141 643	48 484
液化石油气		LPG		10 438	3 408
润滑油		Lubricating Oil		2 825	1 292
石　蜡		Paraffin wax		214	197
溶剂油		Solvent Oil		648	162
石油焦		Petroleum coke		28	–
石油沥青		Petroleum Asphalt		59	–
其他石油制品		Other Petroleum Products		27 049	19 371
热　力	(百万千焦)	Heat	(1 million kilo-joule)	123 701 794	37 921 296
电　力	(万千瓦时)	Electricity	(10 000 kwh)	10 096 373	3 509 067
城市生活垃圾用于燃料	(吨)	City Waste For Fuel	(Ton)	1 511 505	828 158
生物质废料用于燃料		Biomass Waste For Fuel		148 938	45 746
余热余压	(百万千焦)	Heat and Pressure	(1 million kilo-joule)	23 014 740	1 840 229
其他工业废料用于燃料	(吨)	Other Industrial Waste For Fuel	(Ton)	5 588	5 399
其他燃料	(吨标准煤)	Other Fuels	(ton of SCE)	17 971	15 129

ENERGY CONSUMPTION OF INDUSTRIAL ENTERPRISES ABOVE DESIGNATED SIZE BY REGION (2018)

# 吴江区 Wujiang District	常 熟 Changshu	张家港 Zhangjiagang	昆 山 Kunshan	太 仓 Taicang
6 473 934	**15 981 456**	**38 798 327**	**4 372 965**	**10 387 983**
3 377 628	14 958 510	12 822 146	1 422 380	12 603 876
–	–	7 193 988	–	–
–	334 401	–	–	–
243 982	–	–	–	–
116	1 151 491	10 983 419	79	1 136
–	–	–	–	–
–	–	231 335	–	–
–	453 913	3 831 357	–	–
–	28 081	240 175	–	–
–	–	–	–	–
102 749	39 258	80 156	55 263	14 222
5 474	5 315	46 293	13 760	135
4 540	7 847	3 743	16 833	8 478
27	425	144	284	61
10 834	17 426	36 574	37 391	18 897
11 424	28 351	6 417	57 362	1 029
9	297	1 612	4 147	975
699	515	407	583	27
141	–	13	–	4
158	108	68	293	16
–	–	–	–	28
–	–	–	–	59
23	1 815	137	5 672	53
24 674 604	28 486 089	25 089 010	13 502 570	18 702 828
1 469 461	1 453 202	2 746 539	1 548 047	839 518
–	–	288 187	394 950	210
10 600	13 430	31 810	10 042	47 910
187 761	–	21 174 512	–	–
–	–	–	190	–
2	198	–	2 622	22

表10-4

全市规模以上工业企业分行业能源消费量 (2018年)

行　　业	Sector	综合能源消费量 (吨标准煤) Overall Consumption Volume of Energy (ton of SCE)	原　煤 (吨) Raw Coal (ton)
总　　计	**Total**	**54 286 874**	**51 853 367**
有色金属矿采选业	Nonferrous Metals Mining and Dressing	–	–
非金属矿采选业	Nonmetal Minerals Mining and Dressing	2 543	–
农副食品加工业	Farming and Side-line Food Processing Trade	194 712	3 120
食品制造业	Food Production	98 654	–
酒、饮料和精制茶制造业	Wine, Beverage and Refined tea manufacturing	74 011	12 457
烟草制品业	Manufacture of Tobacco	4 009	–
纺织业	Textile Industry	2 869 107	1 447 188
纺织服装、服饰业	Garments and Apparel Industry	83 216	7 569
皮革、毛皮、羽绒及其制品业	Leather, Furs, Down and Related Products	14 843	2 415
木材加工和竹、藤、棕、草制品业	Timber Processing, Bamboo, Cane, Palm Fiber &Straw Products	21 504	–
家具制造业	Furniture Manufacturing	19 995	–
造纸和纸制品业	Papermaking and Paper Products	2 650 071	3 409 318
印刷和记录媒介复制业	Printing and Record Medium Reproduction	115 931	3 416
文教工美体育和娱乐用品制造业	Stationary,Educational,Industrial arts, Sports and Entertainment products	118 023	86 795
石油、煤炭及其他燃料加工业	Oil, Coal and Other Fuel Processing Industries	14 077	4 585
化学原料和化学制品制造业	Raw Chemical Materials and Chemical Products	3 802 775	2 027 885
医药制造业	Medical and Pharmaceutical Products	194 406	209 926
化学纤维制造业	Chemical Fiber	2 054 831	1 162 058
橡胶和塑料制品业	Rubber and Plastic Products	854 637	62 244
非金属矿物制品业	Nonmetal Mineral Products	914 055	152 271
黑色金属冶炼和压延加工业	Smelting and Pressing of Ferrous Metals	18 344 806	3 795 398
有色金属冶炼和压延加工业	Smelting and Pressing of Nonferrous Metals	380 099	300
金属制品业	Metal Products	655 171	1 838
通用设备制造业	Ordinary Machinery	475 362	5 471
专用设备制造业	Equipment for Special Purposes	291 545	–
汽车制造业	Automobile Manufacturing	672 889	–
铁路船舶航空航天和其他运输设备制造业	Railway, Ship, Aerospace and other transportation equipment manufacturing	71 909	50
电气机械和器材制造业	Electric Equipment and Machinery	619 889	3 361
计算机通信和其他电子设备制造业	Computer Telecommunications and Other Electronic Equipment Manufacture	2 494 940	525 872
仪器仪表制造业	Instruments, Meters Machinery	68 907	–
其他制造业	Others Industry	5 393	–
废弃资源综合利用业	Comprehensive Utilization of Waste Resources	45 792	–
金属制品、机械和设备修理业	Metal Products, Machinery and Equipment Repair	1 423	–
电力、热力生产和供应业	Production and Supply of Electric Power and Heat Energy	15 954 028	38 929 831
燃气生产和供应业	Production and Supply of Gas	8 512	–
水的生产和供应业	Production and Supply of Water	94 809	–

注:综合能源消费量=各种能源工业生产消费量合计-能源加工厂转换-能源回收利用。

TOTAL ENERGY CONSUMPTION OF INDUSTRIAL ENTERPRISES ABOVE DESIGNATED SIZE BY SECTOR (2018)

洗精煤 (吨) Washing Coal (ton)	焦 炭 (吨) Coke (ton)	汽 油 (吨) Gasoline (ton)	柴 油 (吨) Diesel Oil (ton)	燃料油 (吨) Fuel Oil (ton)	液化石油气 (吨) Liquefied Petroleum Gas (ton)	热 力 (百万千焦) Heat (1 million kilo-joule)	电 力 (万千瓦时) Electricity (10 000 kwh)
7 193 988	**12 368 191**	**61 590**	**151 626**	**141 643**	**10 438**	**123 701 794**	**10 096 373**
–	–	–	–	–	–	–	–
–	–	18	89	–	–	–	1 607
–	–	188	828	814	33	3 728 956	43 856
–	–	227	477	–	19	657 090	28 718
–	–	62	583	–	–	826 961	23 555
–	–	–	–	–	–	85 466	936
–	–	3 835	3 090	2 257	109	30 197 241	837 600
–	–	2 150	1 500	111	12	600 065	33 128
–	–	453	115	50	–	52 125	6 262
–	–	332	614	5	–	55 518	11 309
–	–	335	381		78	5 035	13 250
–	–	1 287	11 359	43	3 583	31 075 727	510 989
–	–	1 452	1 328	–	–	383 139	64 747
–	–	1 091	503	–	1	737 765	36 583
–	–	100	373	–	–	126 052	3 935
–	–	4 264	8 852	1 738	990	30 785 866	1 088 409
–	–	460	473	–	–	1 589 904	65 924
–	–	1 469	1 839	8 727	–	7 032 131	927 523
–	–	3 486	5 942	875	10	5 130 089	391 247
–	–	1 340	45 792	117 589	329	1 659 785	223 432
7 193 988	12 353 100	1 113	24 016	425	591	365 187	1 638 372
–	115	733	2 002	6 008	35	495 873	148 570
–	134	5 137	6 073	1 767	1 129	682 839	335 210
–	2 058	6 680	5 404	44	871	155 506	316 138
–	–	6 027	5 821	11	301	416 186	194 209
–	–	2 255	3 337	68	1 014	634 415	349 110
–	–	628	686	–	603	1 110	38 444
–	91	5 571	3 434	156	375	427 244	440 943
–	–	8 394	11 320	908	351	5 140 357	1 639 345
–	–	1 323	455	–	–	33 561	42 979
–	–	123	9	–	1	24 500	2 964
–	12 694	114	968	–	–	45 653	18 288
–	–	–	–	–	–	–	1 158
–	–	539	3 724	48	4	157 802	544 507
–	–	305	134	–	–	–	6 300
–	–	97	104	–	–	392 645	66 829

Note: Comprehensive energy consumption= All kinds of energy consumption of industrial production–energy conversion by energy plants-Energy recycling

表10-5 市区规模以上工业企业分行业能源消费量 (2018年)

行业	Sector	综合能源消费量(吨标准煤) Overall Consumption Volume of Energy (ton of SCE)	原煤(吨) Raw Coal (ton)
总计	**Total**	**11 410 986**	**10 046 455**
有色金属矿采选业	Nonferrous Metals Mining and Dressing	–	–
非金属矿采选业	Nonmetal Minerals Mining and Dressing	2 543	–
农副食品加工业	Farming and Side-line Food Processing Trade	21 499	3 120
食品制造业	Food Production	58 921	––
酒、饮料和精制茶制造业	Wine, Beverage and Refined tea manufacturing	41 622	3 473
烟草制品业	Manufacture of Tobacco	–	–
纺织业	Textile Industry	1 747 548	878 738
纺织服装、服饰业	Garments and Apparel Industry	30 821	–
皮革、毛皮、羽绒及其制品业	Leather, Furs, Down and Related Products	3 131	50
木材加工和竹、藤、棕、草制品业	Timber Processing, Bamboo, Cane, Palm Fiber &Straw Products	8 754	–
家具制造业	Furniture Manufacturing	7 823	–
造纸和纸制品业	Papermaking and Paper Products	499 616	620 407
印刷和记录媒介复制业	Printing and Record Medium Reproduction	43 385	3 416
文教工美体育和娱乐用品制造业	Stationary,Educational,Industrial arts, Sports and Entertainment products	9 105	1 897
石油、煤炭及其他燃料加工业	Oil, Coal and Other Fuel Processing Industries	6 653	4 585
化学原料和化学制品制造业	Raw Chemical Materials and Chemical Products	563 912	26 608
医药制造业	Medical and Pharmaceutical Products	88 572	9 100
化学纤维制造业	Chemical Fiber	1 200 861	596 983
橡胶和塑料制品业	Rubber and Plastic Products	244 129	–
非金属矿物制品业	Nonmetal Mineral Products	304 075	72 181
黑色金属冶炼和压延加工业	Smelting and Pressing of Ferrous Metals	322 466	44 135
有色金属冶炼和压延加工业	Smelting and Pressing of Nonferrous Metals	129 323	–
金属制品业	Metal Products	275 034	644
通用设备制造业	Ordinary Machinery	189 714	5 471
专用设备制造业	Equipment for Special Purposes	134 045	–
汽车制造业	Automobile Manufacturing	158 623	–
铁路船舶航空航天和其他运输设备制造业	Railway, Ship, Aerospace and other transportation equipment manufacturing	20 876	–
电气机械和器材制造业	Electric Equipment and Machinery	344 651	3 361
计算机通信和其他电子设备制造业	Computer Telecommunications and Other Electronic Equipment Manufacture	1 063 132	–
仪器仪表制造业	Instruments, Meters Machinery	22 048	–
其他制造业	Others Industry	49	–
废弃资源综合利用业	Comprehensive Utilization of Waste Resources	20 472	–
金属制品、机械和设备修理业	Metal Products, Machinery and Equipment Repair	–	–
电力、热力生产和供应业	Production and Supply of Electric Power and Heat Energy	3 782 472	7 772 288
燃气生产和供应业	Production and Supply of Gas	1 545	–
水的生产和供应业	Production and Supply of Water	63 567	–

ENERGY CONSUMPTION OF INDUSTRIAL ENTERPRISES ABOVE DESIGNATED SIZE BY SECTOR IN URBAN AREA (2018)

洗精煤 (吨) Washing Coal (ton)	焦 炭 (吨) Coke (ton)	汽 油 (吨) Gasoline (ton)	柴 油 (吨) Diesel Oil (ton)	燃料油 (吨) Fuel Oil (ton)	液化石油气 (吨) Liquefied Petroleum Gas (ton)	热 力 (百万千焦) Heat (1 million kilo-joule)	电 力 (万千瓦时) Electricity (10 000 kwh)
–	**232 066**	**24 688**	**41 337**	**48 484**	**3 408**	**37 921 296**	**3 509 067**
–	–	–	–	–	–	–	–
–	–	18	89	–	–	–	1 607
–	–	130	349	512	24	188 413	8 649
–	–	167	250	–	–	238 907	16 099
–	–	27	167	–	–	348 189	17 314
–	–	–	–	–	–	–	–
–	–	1 529	492	866	17	22 783 816	499 213
–	–	905	570	–	–	170 259	13 930
–	–	125	50	39	–	1 516	2 445
–	–	94	217	5	–	–	5 289
–	–	25	143	–	–	–	5 192
–	–	578	2 193	43	2 514	4 640 562	104 803
–	–	739	603	–	–	66 873	23 368
–	–	99	55	–	–	–	4 146
–	–	–	–	–	–	–	1 701
–	–	1 557	1 522	11	–	1 050 527	135 408
–	–	116	110	–	–	877 878	35 739
–	–	1 082	1 284	8 533	–	3 993 513	551 622
–	–	1 220	1 674	50	1	913 351	152 714
–	–	618	19 612	36 651	8	66 217	80 608
–	223 380	56	293	–	–	45 804	58 329
–	115	203	404	23	–	94 020	61 422
–	54	2 189	2 033	1 664	307	130 345	150 237
–	922	3 289	1 422	28	70	65 034	121 684
–	–	2 217	745	6	163	250 145	90 740
–	–	436	987	7	5	216 217	85 271
–	–	25	8	–	–	–	13 944
–	–	2 976	1 312	–	27	331 416	244 639
–	–	3 744	3 171	–	272	942 823	812 647
–	–	304	27	–	–	18 410	17 867
–	–	–	–	–	–	–	40
–	7 594	75	355	–	–	14 080	5 002
–	–	–	–	–	–	–	–
–	–	6	1 153	48	–	157 802	143 396
–	–	128	49	–	–	–	773
–	–	10	–	–	–	315 181	43 229

表10-6

主要工业产品单位产量能耗（2018年）
THE ENERGY CONSUMPTION OF MAJOR INDUSTRIAL PRODUCTS (2018)

项目		Item		数值 Numerical Value
吨纱（线）混合数生产用电量	（千瓦时/吨）	Electricity Consumption Per Ton on Production of Yarn	(kwh/ton)	2 972.9
万米布混合数生产用电量	（千瓦时/万米）	Electricity Consumption Per 10000 Meters Cloth	(kwh/10 000 meters)	9 300.3
万米印染布综合能耗	（千克标准煤/万米）	Comprehensive Energy Consumption Per 10000 Meter Dyed Fabric	(kg of SCE/10 000 meters)	1 656.7
万米丝织品用电量	（千瓦时/万米）	Electricity Consumption Per 10000 Meter Silk Fabric	(kwh/10 000 meters)	4 115.9
万米丝织品综合能耗	（千克标准煤/万米）	Comprehensive Energy Consumption Per 10000 Meter Silk Fabric	(kg of SCE/10 000 meters)	1 343.5
机制纸及纸板耗电	（千瓦时/吨）	Electricity Consumption Per Ton of Machine Finish Paper and Paper Board	(kwh/ton)	649.8
机制纸及纸板综合能耗	（千克标准煤/吨）	Comprehensive Energy Consumption Per Ton of Machine Finish Paper and Paper Board	(kg of SCE/ton)	304.3
吨涤纶用电量（长丝）	（千瓦时/吨）	Electricity Consumption Per Ton Terylene Production (Long Fibre)	(kwh/ton)	760.0
吨涤纶综合能耗（长丝）	（千克标准煤/吨）	Comprehensive Energy Consumption Per Ton Terylene Production (Long Fibre)	(kg of SCE/ton)	183.3
吨水泥综合能耗		Comprehensive Energy Consumption Per Ton Cement Production		4.1
每重量箱平板玻璃综合能耗	（千克标准煤/重量箱）	Comprehensive Energy Consumption Per Weighing Tank of Sheet Glass Production	(kg of SCE/weighing tank)	13.6
吨钢综合能耗	（千克标准煤/吨）	Comprehensive Energy Consumption Per Ton Steel Production	(kg of SCE/ton)	481.3
吨钢耗电	（千瓦时/吨）	Electricity Consumption Per Ton Steel Production	(kwh/ton)	422.3
电厂火力发电标准煤耗	（克标准煤/千瓦时）	Standard Coal Consumption of Thermal Power Generation of Power Plants	(g of SCE/kwh)	277.2
电厂火力供电标准煤耗		Standard Coal Consumption of Thermal Power Supply of Power Plants		289.8
发电厂用电率	（%）	Electricity Consumption of Power Plants	(%)	4.6

表10-7

全市规模以上工业企业用水情况（2018年）
WATER CONSUMPTION OF INDUSTRIAL ENTERPRISES ABOVE DESIGNATED SIZE (2018)

行　　业	Sector	工业取水总量（万立方米）Total Industrial Water (10 000 M^3)	重复用水量（万立方米）Repetitive Water Consumption (10 000 M^3)
总　　计	**Total**	**267 001**	**924 313**
有色金属矿采选业	Nonferrous Metals Mining and Dressing	–	–
非金属矿采选业	Nonmetal Minerals Mining and Dressing	86	33
农副食品加工业	Farming and Side-line Food Processing Trade	467	211
食品制造业	Food Production	732	7
酒、饮料和精制茶制造业	Wine, Beverage and Refined tea manufacturing	816	154
烟草制品业	Manufacture of Tobacco	20	–
纺织业	Textile Industry	15 535	2 508
纺织服装、服饰业	Garments and Apparel Industry	858	66
皮革、毛皮、羽绒及其制品业	Leather, Furs, Down and Related Products	146	5
木材加工及竹、藤、棕、草制品业	Timber Processing, Bamboo, Cane, Palm Fiber &Straw Products	74	1
家具制造业	Furniture Manufacturing	209	1
造纸及纸制品业	Papermaking and Paper Products	7 343	90 039
印刷和记录媒介复制业	Printing and Record Medium Reproduction	358	–
文教工美体育和娱乐用品制造业	Stationary,Educational,Industrial arts, Sports and Entertainment products	649	13
石油、煤炭及其他燃料加工业	Oil, Coal and Other Fuel Processing Industries	27	1
化学原料及化学制品制造业	Raw Chemical Materials and Chemical Products	7 908	99 991
医药制造业	Medical and Pharmaceutical Products	796	3 525
化学纤维制造业	Chemical Fiber	2 035	28 251
橡胶和塑料制品业	Rubber and Plastic Products	1 747	4 574
非金属矿物制品业	Nonmetal Mineral Products	1 556	400
黑色金属冶炼及压延加工业	Smelting and Pressing of Ferrous Metals	13 880	493 553
有色金属冶炼及压延加工业	Smelting and Pressing of Nonferrous Metals	704	613
金属制品业	Metal Products	2 129	176
通用设备制造业	Ordinary Machinery	1 872	378
专用设备制造业	Equipment for Special Purposes	1 530	2 008
汽车制造业	Automobile Manufacturing	1 437	403
铁路船舶航空航天和其他运输设备制造业	Railway, Ship, Aerospace and other transportation equipment manufacturing	315	2
电气机械及器材制造业	Electric Equipment and Machinery	3 080	17 146
计算机通信和其他电子设备制造业	Telecommunications Equipment, Computer and Other Electronic Equipment Manufacture	14 343	27 490
仪器仪表制造业	Instruments, Meters Machinery	282	1 384
其他制造业	Others Industry	59	–
废弃资源综合利用业	Comprehensive Utilization of Waste Resources	72	545
金属制品、机械和设备修理业	Metal Products, Machinery and Equipment Repair	24	–
电力、热力生产和供应业	Production and Supply of Electric Power and Heat Energy	10 354	149 770
燃气生产和供应业	Production and Supply of Gas	28	–
水的生产和供应业	Production and Supply of Water	175 529	1 064

表10-8

部分年份分行业用电情况

ENERGY CONSUMPTION BY SECTOR OF PARTIAL YEARS

单位：万千瓦时 (10 000 kwh)

年份 Year	全社会用电量 Electricity Consumption	全行业用电量 Electricity by Sector	第一产业 Primary Industry	第二产业 Secondary Industry	# 工业 Industry	第三产业 Tertiary Industry	城乡居民生活用电 Electricity Consumption by Urban and Rural Residents
1986	348 398	335 660	47 455	278 290	276 982	9 915	12 738
1987	414 500	398 870	61 251	324 947	323 435	12 672	15 630
1988	465 355	447 053	69 520	356 585	354 553	20 948	18 302
1989	473 882	450 438	68 532	361 120	359 404	20 786	23 444
1990	507 687	479 512	70 821	383 297	381 394	25 394	28 175
1991	576 975	543 672	78 876	438 278	436 385	26 518	33 303
1992	680 698	639 687	91 190	516 370	513 597	32 127	41 011
1993	781 374	730 783	101 470	588 418	581 777	40 895	50 591
1994	892 271	819 691	116 611	649 052	639 885	54 028	72 580
1995	998 485	907 323	131 909	716 671	707 424	58 743	91 162
1996	1 126 972	1 023 750	131 616	825 147	815 410	66 987	103 222
1997	1 233 419	1 119 353	136 434	894 080	884 124	88 839	114 066
1998	1 327 589	1 204 818	132 671	973 282	960 857	98 865	122 771
1999	1 538 193	1 409 790	114 363	1 198 521	1 186 270	96 906	128 403
2000	1 900 439	1 730 448	69 778	1 547 146	1 531 665	113 524	169 991
2001	2 259 217	2 072 342	63 833	1 878 092	1 861 413	130 417	186 875
2002	2 735 800	2 555 864	37 781	2 361 451	2 339 938	156 632	179 936
2003	3 576 083	3 333 262	38 653	3 084 335	3 041 342	210 274	242 821
2004	4 544 696	4 261 961	37 838	3 944 098	3 868 402	280 025	282 735
2005	5 660 372	5 314 255	29 646	4 908 405	4 835 611	376 204	346 117
2006	6 864 926	6 436 636	29 352	5 949 106	5 884 112	458 178	428 290
2007	8 072 735	7 587 350	30 980	7 020 584	6 957 336	535 786	485 385
2008	8 484 230	7 917 897	30 956	7 255 717	7 183 172	631 224	566 333
2009	8 799 436	8 198 015	30 730	7 457 042	7 385 410	710 243	601 421
2010	10 241 031	9 514 098	30 044	8 630 199	8 552 481	853 855	726 933
2011	11 316 316	10 544 566	31 281	9 556 668	9 461 876	956 617	771 750
2012	11 899 281	11 034 355	34 268	9 933 221	9 826 579	1 066 866	864 926
2013	12 632 099	11 640 896	37 996	10 430 709	10 306 099	1 172 191	991 204
2014	12 681 174	11 807 895	36 104	10 574 610	10 441 426	1 197 181	873 279
2015	13 117 154	12 171 484	39 854	10 857 998	10 741 986	1 273 632	945 670
2016	13 825 799	12 743 177	44 976	11 261 852	11 162 958	1 436 349	1 082 622
2017	15 035 283	13 789 850	47 394	12 118 082	12 020 351	1 624 374	1 245 433
2018	15 624 897	14 258 880	30 637	12 382 553	12 277 696	1 845 690	1 366 017

注：2018年电力行业按照最新标准开展行业统计工作，与往年数据不可比，下同。

Note: In 2018, the power industry carried out industry statistics work in accordance with the latest standards, which was incomparable with previous years' data, the same below.

表10-9

部分年份分地区全社会用电情况
TOTAL ELECTRICITY CONSUMPTION BY REGION OF PARTIAL YEARS

单位：万千瓦时 (10 000 kwh)

年份 Year	全市 Whole Municipality	市区 Urban Area	#吴江区 Wujiang District	常熟 Changshu	张家港 Zhangjiagang	昆山 Kunshan	太仓 Taicang
1978	138 808	91 452	12 024	15 924	10 263	11 097	10 072
1979	165 231	108 676	14 743	18 882	12 099	13 169	12 405
1980	205 298	133 206	18 852	24 936	16 812	14 943	15 401
1985	311 110	172 271	29 680	45 483	42 084	24 123	27 149
1990	507 687	261 706	51 440	77 178	79 486	47 193	42 124
1991	576 975	290 322	59 824	86 428	95 583	55 643	48 999
1992	680 698	332 054	72 093	98 870	127 698	64 764	57 312
1993	781 374	377 816	88 287	114 514	153 527	71 894	63 623
1994	892 271	439 174	111 226	126 616	174 599	81 084	70 798
1995	998 485	495 962	124 318	140 406	192 717	92 293	77 107
1996	1 126 972	547 926	138 220	153 003	239 546	104 768	81 729
1997	1 233 419	591 387	153 872	166 149	263 076	123 566	89 241
1998	1 327 589	639 045	164 801	169 582	284 233	143 046	91 683
1999	1 538 193	728 939	177 281	215 680	320 260	170 913	102 401
2000	1 900 439	901 274	236 722	265 272	387 696	219 556	126 641
2001	2 259 217	1 037 898	302 808	314 308	493 471	263 767	149 773
2002	2 735 800	1 240 050	394 185	356 277	614 238	347 936	177 299
2003	3 576 083	1 611 285	544 873	431 064	826 736	477 193	229 805
2004	4 544 696	2 007 707	741 799	538 955	1 060 249	618 148	317 295
2005	5 660 372	2 415 752	894 024	665 584	1 388 054	798 771	389 621
2006	6 864 926	2 868 272	1 057 185	784 605	1 712 749	1 021 111	475 222
2007	8 072 735	3 369 140	1 254 637	922 355	1 967 880	1 231 591	576 003
2008	8 484 230	3 563 320	1 295 607	980 504	2 018 468	1 319 483	602 455
2009	8 799 436	3 647 936	1 351 511	1 064 578	2 143 411	1 322 036	621 475
2010	10 241 031	4 283 235	1 590 285	1 246 016	2 384 474	1 619 135	708 171
2011	11 316 316	4 780 971	1 881 632	1 413 760	2 595 963	1 746 314	779 308
2012	11 899 281	5 140 791	2 103 025	1 473 379	2 655 946	1 819 148	810 017
2013	12 632 099	5 492 795	2 241 800	1 559 753	2 783 828	1 900 279	895 444
2014	12 681 174	5 454 612	2 168 444	1 552 047	2 830 481	1 943 532	900 502
2015	13 117 154	5 679 415	2 294 076	1 623 840	2 899 183	2 004 999	909 717
2016	13 825 799	6 069 996	2 424 055	1 723 339	2 888 066	2 175 123	969 275
2017	15 035 283	6 618 411	2 697 371	1 865 315	3 088 248	2 413 439	1 049 870
2018	15 624 897	6 961 903	2 837 074	1 917 613	3 138 331	2 534 661	1 072 389

表10-10

全社会用电情况 (2018年)

单位：万千瓦时

行　　业	Sector	全　市 Whole Municipality
全社会用电量总计	**Total Electricity Consumption**	**15 624 897**
一、全行业用电合计	**Total Electricity by Sector**	**14 258 880**
按产业分	**Grouped by Industry**	
第一产业	Primary Industry	30 637
第二产业	Secondary Industry	12 382 553
第三产业	Tertiary Industry	1 845 690
按行业分	**Grouped by Sector**	
（一）农、林、牧、渔业	Farming, Forestry, Animal Husbandry and Fishery	47 648
（二）工　业	Industry	12 277 696
采矿业	Mining and Quarrying	2 399
制造业	Manufacturing	11 393 937
1.农副食品加工业	Agricultural and Sideline Food Processing	44 152
2.食品制造业	Food Production	60 798
3.酒、饮料及精制茶制造业	Wine, Beverage and Refined Tea Manufacturing	20 660
4.烟草制品业	Manufacture of Tobacco	803
5.纺织业	Textile Industry	2 432 321
6.纺织服装、服饰业	Garments and Apparel Industry	183 573
7.皮革、毛皮、羽毛及其制品和制鞋业	Leather, Fur, Wool and Shoes Products	50 113
8.木材加工和木、竹、藤、棕、草制品业	Wood Processing, Wood, Bamboo, Rattan and Coir Products Straw Products	39 296
9.家具制造业	Furniture Manufacturing	42 452
10.造纸及纸制品业	Papermaking and Paper Products	210 858
11.印刷业和记录媒介复制业	Printing and Record Duplicating	55 432
12.文教、工美、体育和娱乐用品制造业	Stationary,Educational, Industrial arts, Sports and Entertainment products	36 758
13.石油、煤炭及其他燃料加工业	Oil, Coal and Other Fuel Processing Industries	15 350
14.化学原料和化学制品制造业	Raw Chemical Materials and Chemical Products	783 558
15.医药制造业	Medical and Pharmaceutical Products	89 202
16.化学纤维制造业	Chemical Fiber Manufacturing	400 183
17.橡胶和塑料制品业	Rubber and Plastic Products	621 260
18.非金属矿物制品业	Nonmetal Mineral Products	246 301
19.黑色金属冶炼和压延加工业	Smelting and Pressing of Ferrous Metals	1 432 323

TOTAL ELECTRICITY CONSUMPTION (2018)

(10 000 kwh)

市 区 Urban Area	# 吴江区 Wujiang District	常 熟 Changshu	张家港 Zhangjiagang	昆 山 Kunshan	太 仓 Taicang
6 961 903	**2 837 074**	**1 917 613**	**3 138 331**	**2 534 661**	**1 072 389**
6 235 117	**2 677 773**	**1 752 203**	**3 000 962**	**2 279 734**	**990 864**
14 474	9 763	5 105	1 499	5 583	3 976
5 107 979	2 501 689	1 582 781	2 857 044	1 959 766	874 983
1 112 664	166 321	164 317	142 419	314 385	111 905
21 996	14 960	8 355	3 095	6 570	7 632
5 045 637	2 487 305	1 572 400	2 846 570	1 944 720	868 369
2 066	3	–	242	67	24
4 689 610	2 381 482	1 342 781	2 703 341	1 834 298	823 907
7 223	4 450	3 097	25 478	5 956	2 398
35 218	5 514	2 886	2 881	12 530	7 283
15 895	7 756	1 016	721	2 071	957
–	–	–	–	–	803
1 494 233	1 380 595	283 117	354 512	18 147	282 312
91 896	55 466	34 044	12 232	27 366	18 035
9 299	6 393	10 082	14 989	11 816	3 927
19 096	13 907	5 373	5 470	5 203	4 154
18 642	6 925	5 445	2 461	10 170	5 734
48 172	10 315	75 752	10 377	23 112	53 445
23 965	1 881	2 053	2 369	24 446	2 599
10 599	3 333	4 008	5 692	11 172	5 287
1 181	393	272	2 055	129	11 713
93 184	26 150	152 507	455 756	61 908	20 203
56 219	7 350	10 314	5 805	5 562	11 302
270 191	243 889	56 053	53 808	2 060	18 071
268 921	77 080	56 556	70 093	155 114	70 576
108 518	60 812	17 407	30 625	62 500	27 251
55 335	57	116 288	1 245 993	283	14 424

表10-10 续表

单位：万千瓦时

行　　业	Sector	全　市 Whole Municipality
20.有色金属冶炼和压延加工业	Smelting and Pressing of Nonferrous Metals	62 416
21.金属制品业	Metal Products	785 959
22.通用设备制造业	General Equipment Manufacture	526 035
23.专用设备制造业	Special Purposes Equipment Manufacturing	267 260
24.汽车制造业	Automobile Manufacturing	183 661
25.铁路.船舶.航空航天和其他运输设备制造业	Railway, Ship, Aerospace and Other Transportation Equipment Manufacturing	168 518
26.电气机械和器材制造业	Electric Equipment and Machinery Manufacturing	474 812
27.计算机、通信和其他电子设备制造业	Computer Telecommunications and Other Electronic Equipment Manufacture	1 769 337
28.仪器仪表制造业	Instruments, Meters Machinery	110 442
29.其他制造业	Other Products Manufacture	251 014
30.废弃资源综合利用业	Comprehensive Utilization of Waste Resources	27 429
31.金属制品、机械和设备修理业	Metal Products, Machinery and Equipment Repair	1 661
电力、燃气及水的生产和供应业	Power, Gas and Water Production and Supply	881 360
1.电力、热力的生产和供应业	Production and Supply of Electricity and Thermal Power	744 616
2.燃气生产和供应业	Production and Supply of Gas	14 433
3.水的生产和供应业	Production and Supply of Water	122 311
（三）建筑业	Construction	106 518
（四）交通运输、仓储和邮政业	Transportation, Warehousing and Post	166 981
（五）信息传输、计算机服务和软件业	Information Transmission, Computer Services and Software Industries	90 114
（六）批发和零售业	Wholesale and Retail Trade Services	414 251
（七）住宿和餐饮业	Accommodation and Catering Services	140 674
（八）金融业	Financial Industries	29 307
（九）房地产业	Real Estate	357 828
（十）租赁和商务服务业	Leasing and Business Services	112 598
（十一）公共事业及管理组织	Public Administration and Social Organizations	515 265
教育、文化、体育和娱乐业	Education, Culture, Sports and Entertainment	140 300
卫生和社会工作	Health and Social Work	72 416
二、城乡居民生活用电合计	**Total Electricity Consumption by Urban and Rural Residents**	**1 366 017**
城镇居民	Urban Residents	781 504
乡村居民	Rural Residents	584 513

Continued

(10 000 kwh)

市 区 Urban Area	# 吴江区 Wujiang District	常 熟 Changshu	张家港 Zhangjiagang	昆 山 Kunshan	太 仓 Taicang
17 972	9 050	985	25 573	4 799	13 087
316 474	98 651	159 512	178 127	67 255	64 591
140 793	45 488	71 268	46 336	192 655	74 983
130 782	21 797	36 400	27 238	40 889	31 951
25 091	776	17 481	20 507	111 298	9 284
47 672	9 337	11 900	19 420	72 884	16 642
293 645	114 412	68 220	37 749	52 717	22 481
816 740	158 686	90 123	35 663	808 232	18 579
93 060	1 665	6 335	471	9 182	1 394
173 380	7 600	41 399	2 314	32 251	1 670
6 075	1 700	2 886	8 621	2 585	7 262
139	54	2	5	6	1 509
353 961	105 820	229 619	142 987	110 355	44 438
284 027	82 918	211 191	126 037	90 273	33 088
2 021	258	236	7 124	622	4 430
67 913	22 644	18 192	9 826	19 460	6 920
62 481	14 438	10 383	10 479	15 052	8 123
76 812	10 248	9 655	11 387	48 666	20 461
50 786	6 965	7 955	7 262	18 122	5 989
222 200	43 627	54 390	37 668	77 499	22 494
83 079	16 651	12 637	13 129	23 303	8 526
19 008	2 205	2 903	2 316	2 967	2 113
265 476	26 877	20 057	15 604	47 030	9 661
60 652	4 726	5 809	10 673	27 986	7 478
326 990	49 771	47 659	42 779	67 819	30 018
94 871	9 844	11 036	10 163	18 254	5 976
43 275	6 649	7 703	8 854	8 241	4 343
726 786	**159 301**	**165 410**	**137 369**	**254 927**	**81 525**
524 279	65 933	63 186	59 480	103 088	31 471
202 507	93 368	102 224	77 889	151 839	50 054

主 要 统 计 指 标 解 释

工业企业能源消费量　指工业企业在工业生产活动和非工业生产活动中消费的能源，包括工业生产活动中作为燃料、动力、原料、辅助材料使用的能源，生产工艺中使用的能源，用于能源加工转换的能源；非工业生产活动中使用的能源。具体包括：

1.用于本企业产品生产、工业性作业和其他生产性活动的能源；

2.用于技术更新改造措施、新技术研究和新产品试制以及科学试验等方面的能源；

3.用于经营维修、建筑及设备大修理、机电设备和交通运输工具等方面的能源；

4.用于劳动保护的能源；

5.生产交通运输工具的企业(如造船厂、汽车制造厂)，向成品轮船、汽车中添加动力用油，应算作企业的能源消费，但不作为工业生产消费，应作为非工业生产消费和交通运输工具消费。

6.其他非生产消费的能源。

不包括：

1.由仓库发到车间，但在报告期最后一天没有消费的能源。这部分能源应在办理假退料手续后计入库存量。

2.拨到外单位，委托外单位加工用的能源。

3.调出本单位或借给外单位的能源。

工业生产能源消费量　指工业企业为进行工业生产活动所消费的能源。主要包括：

1.用于本企业产品生产、工业性作业的能源，包括用作原料、材料、燃料、动力的能源；作为能源加工转换企业，还包括用作加工转换的能源(这部分能源不能理解为用作原材料，用作原材料的概念见后面的解释)；

2.产品生产过程中作为辅助材料使用的能源；

3.生产工艺过程使用的能源；

4.新技术研究、新产品试制、科学试验使用的能源；

5.为了工业生产活动而在进行的各种修理过程中使用的能源；

6.生产区内的劳动保护用能等。

非工业生产能源消费量　指在工业企业能源消费中，除“工业生产能源消费”以外的能源消费，即非工业生产用能和工业企业附属的不从事工业生产活动的非独立核算单位用能。比如本企业施工单位进行技术更新改造、维修等过程用能，非生产区的劳动保护用能，科研单位、农场、车队、学校、医院、食堂、托儿所等单位用能。但是必须注意，上述单位如果是独立核算的，其用能既不能包括在“工业企业能源消费”中，亦不能包括在“非工业生产能源消费”中。

生产交通运输工具的企业(如造船厂、汽车制造厂)，向成品轮船、汽车中添加动力用油，应算作企业的非工业生产消费。

能源库存量　指能源使用企业(单位)在报告期的某时间点所拥有的、用于企业(单位)消费或转卖(不包括本企业自己生产的)的各种能源的库存量。

能源使用企业(单位)的能源库存统计范围，是企业购进和调入(加工来料和借入)的、在报告期某一时点尚未消费或转卖、存放在原材料、能源供应仓库(或场地)、车间、工地中的各种能源。

EXPLANATORY NOTES ON MAIN STATISTICAL INDICATORS

Energy Consumption of Industrial Enterprise refers to the energy consumed by an industrial enterprise in its industrial and non-industrial production activities, which includes the energy used as fuel, power, raw materials, and auxiliary materials in its industrial production activities, that used in its production technology, and that used in energy processing and conversion; the energy used in its non-industrial production activities. Specifically it includes:

1. The energy used in the enterprise's production of products, industrial work and other production activities;

2. The energy used for technical renovation measures, new technology research and new product trial production, scientific experiments, and so on;

3. The energy used for operation and maintenance, building and equipment repair, mechanical and electrical equipment, means of transport, and so on;

4. The energy used for labor protection;

5. In enterprises producing means of transport (e.g., shipyards, automobile factories), the power oil added to such finished products as ships and cars should be classified as the energy consumption of the enterprise, and it is not treated as industrial production consumption but should be as non-industrial production consumption and the consumption of means of transport.

6. Other non-production consumption energies.

It does not include:

1. The energy sent from the warehouse to the workshop but not yet consumed in the last day of the reporting period. This part of the energy should be included in the inventory after the false material return formalities.

2. The energy transferred to other units and used for processing by them.

3. The energy brought out of this unit or lent to other units.

Industrial Production Energy Consumption refers to the energy consumed by an industrial enterprise for its industrial production activities. It mainly includes:

1. The energy used by the enterprise for its production and industrial operation, including the energy used as raw materials, materials, fuel and power; in an energy processing and conversion enterprise, it also includes the energy used for processing and conversion (this part of the energy cannot be understood as raw materials, and as to the concept of energy used as a raw material, see the explanation below);

2. The energy used as auxiliary materials during the production of products;

3. The energy used in the process of production;

4. The energy used for new technology research, new product trial production and scientific experiments;

5. The energy used in the process of repairs of all kinds for industrial production activities;

6. The energy used for labor protection in the production area, and so on.

Non-industrial Production Energy Consumption refers to the energy consumption except the "industrial production energy consumption" in the energy consumption of an industrial enterprise, namely, the energy used in its non-industrial production and in its affiliated non-independent accounting units not engaged in industrial production activities. For example, the energy used in the process of technical upgrading, maintenance and so on by the construction units of the enterprise, the energy used for labor protection in the non-production area, and the energy used in scientific research units, farms, car teams, schools, hospitals, canteens, nurseries and other units. But it must be noted that if the above units are independent business accounting units, the energy used by them can neither be included in the "industrial enterprise energy consumption", nor in the "non-industrial production energy consumption".

In enterprises producing means of transport (e.g., shipyards, automobile factories), the power oil added to such finished products as ships and cars should be classified as the non-industrial production energy consumption of the enterprise.

Energy Stocks refers to the inventory of the energies of various kinds owned by an energy-using enterprise (unit) at a certain point in time during the reporting period and used for its consumption or reselling (not including the energy produced by the enterprise itself).

The energy inventory statistics scope of an energy-using enterprise (unit) is the energies of various kinds which the enterprise buys and brings in (processing supplied materials and borrowing), has not yet consumed or resold at a certain point in time during the reporting period, and stores in the warehouses (or sites) for raw materials and energy supply, workshops, and construction sites.

十一、固定资产投资

CHAPTER 11
INVESTMENT IN FIXED ASSETS

11 固定资产投资 INVESTMENT IN FIXED ASSETS

主要统计指标 MAJOR STATISTICAL INDICATORS

2018年固定资产投资额	Investment in Fixed Assets	4 555.70	亿元	100 million yuan
比上年增长	Increase Over Last Year	4.5	%	
2018年工业投资额	Industrial Investment	1 102.42	亿元	100 million yuan
比上年增长	Increase Over Last Year	0.0	%	
2018年第三产业投资额	Tertiary Industry Investment	3 450.39	亿元	100 million yuan
比上年增长	Increase Over Last Year	6.1	%	
2018年房地产开发投资额	Value of Investment in Real Estate Development	2 557.91	亿元	100 million yuan
比上年增长	Increase Over Last Year	10.9	%	
2018年民间投资额	Private Investment	2 949.34	亿元	100 million yuan
比上年增长	Increase Over Last Year	14.0	%	
2018年外资投资额	Enterprises with Foreign Investment	623.14	亿元	100 million yuan
比上年增长	Increase Over Last Year	-11.2	%	

表11-1

历年固定资产投资完成额

单位：万元

年　份 Year	全　市 Whole Municipality	按地区分 Grouped by Region					
		市　区 Urban Area	# 吴江区 Wujiang District	常　熟 Changshu	张家港 Zhangjiagang	昆　山 Kunshan	太　仓 Taicang
1990	553 691	253 932	68 648	105 992	93 632	60 830	39 305
1991	803 288	370 601	103 363	158 605	114 416	90 126	69 540
1992	1 543 906	612 895	135 277	328 248	359 525	140 505	102 733
1993	2 718 565	1 185 428	180 264	429 146	542 526	330 320	231 145
1994	3 076 978	1 356 598	217 474	413 504	580 270	470 065	256 541
1995	3 340 991	1 574 996	211 232	383 553	670 679	479 444	232 319
1996	3 805 873	2 011 104	321 946	442 400	555 130	577 948	219 291
1997	4 051 760	2 172 709	230 727	445 330	601 212	562 505	270 004
1998	4 501 061	2 569 089	264 224	506 488	444 469	573 897	407 118
1999	4 751 365	2 671 338	331 525	531 468	481 840	598 705	468 014
2000	5 164 346	3 027 810	621 844	550 168	543 846	638 316	404 206
2001	5 648 539	3 138 199	703 355	703 995	685 043	683 494	437 808
2002	8 128 145	4 061 464	1 060 739	1 162 638	1 150 731	1 153 000	600 312
2003	14 089 329	7 588 970	1 721 190	1 821 089	1 801 076	1 766 358	1 111 836
2004	15 547 986	8 330 734	1 897 918	1 965 100	1 955 030	1 910 868	1 386 254
2005	18 701 431	9 968 338	2 131 580	2 341 375	2 334 337	2 348 141	1 709 240
2006	21 069 898	11 182 879	2 360 556	2 593 063	2 486 481	2 805 816	2 001 659
2007	23 663 595	12 486 968	2 656 766	2 911 910	2 811 570	3 210 071	2 243 076
2008	26 111 595	13 592 361	2 932 522	3 178 027	3 160 398	3 700 316	2 480 493
2009	29 673 482	15 286 269	3 386 178	3 608 902	3 635 092	4 300 572	2 842 647
2010	36 178 211	18 651 157	4 170 136	4 406 523	4 459 095	5 306 914	3 354 522
2011	45 020 211	23 276 099	5 216 865	5 353 678	5 828 073	6 461 539	4 100 822
2012	52 664 852	26 859 457	6 300 746	6 354 752	7 029 782	7 700 434	4 720 427
2013	60 019 428	31 541 738	7 213 614	7 152 070	7 705 555	8 420 018	5 200 047
2014	62 306 662	34 197 405	7 572 883	6 504 377	7 800 216	8 500 504	5 304 160
2015	61 244 251	34 265 426	7 205 664	6 312 157	7 560 469	8 106 097	5 000 102
2016	56 484 864	31 563 905	6 810 230	5 449 065	7 247 656	7 574 238	4 650 000
2017	56 295 920	31 268 680	6 815 002	5 502 451	7 272 054	7 583 415	4 669 320
2018	45 556 977	26 456 225	5 742 213	4 504 365	3 897 933	7 011 947	3 686 507

注：2018年国家固定资产投资统计方法制度改革，统计方法口径有调整，总量、增速与以往年度不具可比性。

INVESTMENT IN FIXED ASSETS OVER THE YEARS

(10 000 yuan)

按产业分 Grouped by Industry				基础设施投资 Infrastructure Investment	民间投资 Private Investment	外资投资 Foreign Investment
第一产业 Primary Industry	第二产业 Secondary Industry	# 工业 Industry	第三产业 Tertiary Industry			
14 976	3 219 770	3 200 143	1 929 600	1 136 156	2 098 565	1 840 875
24 289	3 521 830	3 400 106	2 102 420	1 242 678	2 979 960	1 775 825
31 168	5 109 445	5 095 013	2 987 532	1 788 191	4 035 864	2 331 114
29 163	8 456 066	8 423 117	5 604 100	4 127 901	6 299 125	4 291 620
30 527	8 714 648	8 695 765	6 802 811	4 175 242	7 824 699	4 464 037
21 525	10 506 332	10 491 501	8 173 574	4 881 033	8 795 983	5 811 660
21 962	11 635 037	11 598 665	9 412 899	4 770 675	10 223 735	6 230 337
36 481	12 186 580	12 062 876	11 440 534	4 556 100	12 061 831	8 107 918
48 021	12 775 782	12 676 938	13 287 792	5 142 200	12 910 914	9 180 967
64 613	13 050 274	12 933 066	16 558 595	6 769 853	15 677 012	7 684 425
83 258	15 648 515	15 548 129	20 446 438	7 322 092	20 399 903	8 125 763
88 022	18 918 951	18 806 853	26 013 238	7 636 059	25 981 532	9 976 988
100 052	21 848 885	21 764 295	30 715 915	7 753 049	29 522 385	10 876 385
67 126	24 343 062	24 312 799	35 609 240	10 305 956	32 591 070	12 225 141
43 160	23 081 032	23 049 631	39 182 470	10 221 487	33 217 850	11 745 885
38 617	22 042 446	22 005 198	39 163 188	10 709 269	32 843 605	11 184 472
9 110	19 873 097	19 822 925	36 602 657	7 380 930	32 379 317	9 989 136
15 069	19 901 460	19 833 405	36 379 391	7 566 125	34 687 605	8 531 708
19 180	11 033 857	11 024 190	34 503 940	4 884 587	29 493 369	6 231 413

Note: In 2018, the national statistical system for fixed assets investment was reformed, the statistical methods adjusted, and the total amount and growth rate not comparable to those of previous years.

表11-2

分地区固定资产投资完成额 (2018年)

单位：万元

项　目	Item	全　市 Whole Municipality	市　区 Urban Area	# 姑苏区 Gusu District
总　计	**Total**	**45 556 977**	**26 456 225**	**2 364 270**
# 基础设施投资	Investment in Infrastructure	4 884 587	3 216 096	33 199
# 民间投资	Private Investment	29 493 369	16 593 217	1 949 209
# 新兴产业投资	Investment in Emerging Industries	9 167 452	4 204 015	7 700
按构成分	**Grouped by Use of Funds**			
建安工程	Construction and Installation Projects	23 464 346	13 165 242	792 920
设备工器具购置	Purchase of Equipment and Instruments	6 603 042	3 100 804	25 826
其他费用	Others	15 489 589	10 190 179	1 545 524
按建设性质分	**Grouped by Type of Construction**			
# 新　建	New Construction	9 130 663	5 899 279	192 353
扩　建	Expansion	5 153 840	2 031 564	63 047
改　建	Reconstruction	3 837 318	1 943 803	17 893
按登记注册类型分	**Grouped by Registration Status**			
内　资	Domestic Funded	38 511 990	22 841 728	2 305 797
# 国　有	State-owed Enterprises	3 748 893	2 271 626	94 252
集　体	Collective-owned Enterprises	288 887	147 477	–
股份合作	Share-holding Cooperative Enterprises	8 996	8 996	1 146
联　营	Joint Ownership Enterprises	22 560	13 746	–
国有独资公司	State Sole Funded Corporations	2 620 460	1 850 954	18 842
其他有限责任公司	Other Limited Liability Corporations	11 106 627	6 273 034	840 615
股份有限公司	Share-holding Corporations Ltd.	1 059 346	827 990	4 125
私　营	Private	19 428 633	11 283 627	1 346 817
港澳台商投资	Enterprises with Investment from HongKong, Macao and Taiwan	2 594 415	1 776 907	58 473
外商投资	Enterprises with Foreign Investment	4 449 727	1 837 090	–
个体经营	Self-employed Individual	845	500	–

INVESTMENT IN FIXED ASSETS BY REGION (2018)

(10 000 yuan)

# 吴中区 Wuzhong District	# 相城区 Xiangcheng District	#高新区、虎丘区 New & Hi-tech Zone, Huqiu District	# 工业园区 Industrial Park	# 吴江区 Wujiang District	常 熟 Changshu	张家港 Zhangjiagang	昆 山 Kunshan	太 仓 Taicang
4 864 918	**3 832 360**	**4 428 260**	**3 889 181**	**5 742 213**	**4 504 365**	**3 897 933**	**7 011 947**	**3 686 507**
453 309	451 606	259 023	332 515	363 581	348 580	297 993	471 907	550 011
3 351 465	2 846 761	2 975 591	1 387 199	4 077 857	3 178 458	3 066 765	4 363 286	2 291 643
444 391	604 004	771 505	1 162 993	1 211 322	1 201 436	1 264 832	1 644 677	852 492
2 532 813	1 889 416	1 925 542	1 982 186	3 064 788	2 199 366	2 121 786	3 916 758	2 061 194
347 118	232 407	454 169	682 315	1 153 972	1 000 261	700 370	1 249 240	552 367
1 984 987	1 710 537	2 048 549	1 224 680	1 523 453	1 304 738	1 075 777	1 845 949	1 072 946
1 195 946	836 275	598 440	1 004 493	979 497	697 059	398 465	1 114 378	1 021 482
189 440	216 336	457 256	323 715	672 297	929 999	905 749	712 171	574 357
255 654	94 070	327 024	321 521	802 422	303 864	465 441	873 552	250 658
4 507 649	3 654 136	3 791 181	2 357 657	4 890 285	3 592 040	3 659 098	5 438 343	2 980 781
622 439	446 058	310 164	374 285	266 769	264 564	337 100	272 950	602 653
54 884	36 004	42 609	–	13 980	17 223	70 510	42 130	11 547
7 850	–	–	–	–	–	–	–	–
2 584	11 162	–	–	–	–	–	–	8 814
67 594	214 930	83 470	134 953	314 070	175 783	50 363	447 031	96 329
1 508 392	478 332	1 569 455	968 161	908 079	841 781	1 512 617	1 725 063	754 132
30 912	204 759	78 042	233 210	116 673	86 112	65 040	48 346	31 858
2 156 767	2 262 891	1 625 180	629 338	3 262 634	2 190 945	1 606 110	2 874 703	1 473 248
251 715	134 899	242 057	540 461	549 302	234 671	28 598	355 250	198 989
105 554	42 825	395 022	991 063	302 626	677 654	210 237	1 218 009	506 737
–	500	–	–	–	–	–	345	–

表11-2 续表

单位：万元

项 目	Item	全 市 Whole Municipality	市 区 Urban Area	# 姑苏区 Gusu District
按产业分	**Grouped by Industry**			
第一产业	Primary Industry	19 180	15 864	–
第二产业	Secondary Industry	11 033 857	4 706 406	–
#工 业	Industry	11 024 190	4 696 739	–
#工业技改投资	Investment in Industrial Technical Reformation	8 548 570	3 852 646	–
#高新技术产业投资	Investment in Hi-tech Manufacturing Industries	4 460 077	2 214 025	–
第三产业	Tertiary Industry	34 503 940	21 733 955	2 364 270
本年新增固定资产	**Newly Increased Fixed Assets this year**	**18 873 835**	**9 594 388**	**766 265**
本年实际到位资金小计	**Actual Funds for Investment**	**62 535 975**	**37 421 529**	**2 641 894**
国家预算内资金	State Budgetary Appropriation	762 972	600 623	16 699
国内贷款	Domestic Loans	12 637 415	8 240 751	429 807
债 券	Bonds	1 347	1 347	–
利用外资	Foreign Investment	681 550	268 092	–
自筹资金	Fundraising	19 435 658	10 749 827	504 058
定金及预收款	Deposit and Advance Receipt	17 396 657	10 544 015	1 222 232
个人按揭贷款	Personal Mortgage Loan	7 675 253	4 679 462	397 934
其他资金来源	Others	3 945 123	2 337 412	71 164
房屋建筑面积(万平方米)	**Floor Space of Buildings** (10 000 sq. m)			
本年施工房屋面积	Floor space of Buildings under Construction	14 191.22	7 181.54	629.53
#住 宅	Residential Buildings	8 370.83	4 179.08	330.09
本年竣工房屋面积	Floor Space of Buildings Completed	2 034.00	981.01	72.75
#住 宅	Residential Building	1 008.91	506.81	28.76

注：新增固定资产和实际到位资金统计口径为规模以上口径（即不包括5000万以下投资项目）。

Continued

(10 000 yuan)

# 吴中区 Wuzhong District	# 相城区 Xiangcheng District	#高新区、虎丘区 New & Hi-tech Zone, Huqiu District	# 工业园区 Industrial Park	# 吴江区 Wujiang District	常 熟 Changshu	张家港 Zhangjiagang	昆 山 Kunshan	太 仓 Taicang
10 280	5 491	93	–	–	–	–	3 316	–
635 119	620 035	773 899	1 022 772	1 621 107	1 767 173	1 291 673	2 046 638	1 221 967
633 619	620 035	765 732	1 022 772	1 621 107	1 767 173	1 291 673	2 046 638	1 221 967
460 173	464 706	594 712	1 004 804	1 308 355	1 333 655	1 039 767	1 592 660	729 842
211 275	261 913	500 346	771 455	469 036	339 725	469 445	1 035 045	401 837
4 219 519	3 206 834	3 654 268	2 866 409	4 121 106	2 737 192	2 606 260	4 961 993	2 464 540
1 267 100	**1 268 435**	**1 929 828**	**2 810 465**	**1 513 095**	**2 950 611**	**1 326 927**	**4 005 284**	**996 625**
6 996 151	**5 521 258**	**6 184 417**	**6 241 479**	**8 717 562**	**4 910 017**	**5 370 451**	**10 552 070**	**4 281 908**
73 524	90 000	67 509	288 030	54 701	124 779	600	7 000	29 970
1 688 866	1 470 763	1 527 557	1 073 553	1 451 705	1 121 427	1 015 063	1 506 441	753 733
1 085	262	–	–	–	–	–	–	–
12 000	261	757	30 973	224 101	189 185	74 431	113 367	36 475
1 270 764	1 813 717	2 321 800	1 838 495	2 490 885	2 231 320	1 405 453	3 016 338	2 032 720
2 403 658	1 119 671	1 271 353	1 634 195	2 892 906	524 225	1 924 042	3 607 335	797 040
1 304 381	515 792	530 853	714 145	1 216 357	319 398	805 579	1 390 909	479 905
241 873	510 792	464 588	662 088	386 907	399 683	145 283	910 680	152 065
1 476.26	967.77	962.54	976.51	2 168.92	1 262.01	1 288.09	3 591.12	868.46
945.30	662.31	594.53	269.72	1 377.13	693.13	958.11	1 947.82	592.69
118.85	97.74	163.34	244.00	284.34	260.89	93.02	634.47	64.60
85.48	57.14	125.08	45.01	165.35	127.07	66.43	278.82	29.78

Note: The statistical caliber of newly added fixed assets and actual in-place funds was that above the scale (ie, excluding investment projects of less than 50 million yuan).

表11-3

分行业固定资产投资完成额 (2018年)

单位：万元

项　　目	Item	全　市 Whole Municipality	市　区 Urban Area	# 姑苏区 Gusu District
总　计	**Total**	**45 556 977**	**26 456 225**	**2 364 270**
按行业分	**Grouped by Sector**			
农、林、牧、渔业	Farming, Forestry, Animal Husbandry and Fishery	19 930	15 864	–
采矿业	Mining and Quarrying	–	–	–
制造业	Manufacturing	10 634 239	4 499 904	–
农副食品加工业	Farm and Sideline Products	20 932	3 934	–
食品制造业	Food Production	71 523	45 922	–
酒、饮料和精制茶制造业	Wine, Beverage and Refined tea manufacturing	19 527	11 307	–
纺织业	Textile Industry	316 564	194 409	–
纺织服装和服饰业	Garments and Apparel Industry	64 068	25 335	–
皮革、毛皮、羽毛(绒)及其制品业	Leather, Fur, Wool and shoes Products	7 812	3 800	–
木材加工和木、竹、藤、棕、草制品业	Wood Processing, Wood, Bamboo, Rattan and Coir Products Straw Products	35 460	21 947	–
家具制造业	Furniture Manufacturing	89 924	72 012	–
造纸和纸制品业	Papermaking and Paper Products	145 856	26 586	–
印刷和记录媒介的复制业	Printing and Record Duplicating	83 131	39 895	–
文教工美和体育娱乐用品制造业	Stationary, Educational, Industrial arts, Sports and Entertainment products	113 770	34 632	–
石油煤炭及其他燃料加工业	Oil, Coal and Other Fuel Processing Industries	51 240	34 925	—
化学原料和化学制品制造业	Raw Chemical Materials and Chemical Products	827 419	98 312	–
医药制造业	Medical and Pharmaceutical Products	176 272	129 397	–
化学纤维制造业	Chemical Fiber Manufacturing	398 686	349 017	–
橡胶和塑料制品业	Rubber and Plastic Products	341 540	108 653	–
非金属矿制品业	Nonmetal Mineral Products	443 786	274 316	–
黑色金属冶炼和压延加工业	Smelting and Pressing of Ferrous Metals	383 605	20 651	–
有色金属冶炼和压延加工业	Smelting and Pressing of Nonferrous Metals	132 148	91 843	–
金属制品业	Metal Products	248 109	93 053	–

INVESTMENT IN FIXED ASSETS BY SECTOR (2018)

(10 000 yuan)

# 吴中区 Wuzhong District	# 相城区 Xiangcheng District	#高新区、虎丘区 New & Hi-tech Zone, Huqiu District	# 工业园区 Industrial Park	# 吴江区 Wujiang District	常 熟 Changshu	张家港 Zhangjiagang	昆 山 Kunshan	太 仓 Taicang
4 864 918	**3 832 360**	**4 428 260**	**3 889 181**	**5 742 213**	**4 504 365**	**3 897 933**	**7 011 947**	**3 686 507**
10 280	5 491	93	–	–	–	–	3 316	750
–	–	–	–	–	–	–	–	–
555 057	616 254	748 739	986 020	1 593 834	1 705 226	1 230 134	2 015 826	1 183 149
–	937	–	618	2 379	5 322	–	11 676	–
–	32 860	–	6 334	6 728	10 328	–	15 273	–
–	–	–	–	11 307	–	–	8 220	–
2 537	193	–	91	191 588	70 129	43 937	1 560	6 529
7 730	6 776	–	–	10 829	18 750	7 990	10 493	1 500
–	–	–	–	3 800	2 100	–	1 912	–
–	315	–	–	21 632	12 563	–	950	–
6 857	–	19 632	–	45 523	4 296	–	5 789	7 827
3 000	9 386	500	6 900	6 800	13 235	2 940	29 581	73 514
1 823	5 634	8 163	15 478	8 797	7 998	800	22 385	12 053
2 425	–	9 626	–	22 581	13 928	23 000	36 246	5 964
–	–	10 300	–	24 625	4 435	–	–	11 880
18 390	22 887	5 000	21 018	31 017	183 920	404 776	35 647	104 764
7 335	4 100	525	107 386	10 051	17 287	2 296	5 493	21 799
10 229	10 678	–	–	328 110	13 129	1 806	2 064	32 670
53 792	6 034	5 585	12 571	30 671	44 533	29 666	111 019	47 669
14 114	74 871	92 667	13 771	78 893	47 178	22 105	25 802	74 385
–	5 000	–	646	15 005	55 231	266 000	9 425	32 298
1 050	61 415	–	413	28 965	1 834	–	35 836	2 635
20 528	14 206	19 242	16 807	22 270	42 941	45 602	31 594	34 919

表11-3

单位：万元

项　　目	Item	全　市 Whole Municipality	市　区 Urban Area	# 姑苏区 Gusu District
通用设备制造业	General Equipment Manufacture	901 033	381 218	-
专用设备制造业	Special Purposes Equipment Manufacturing	737 736	349 564	-
汽车制造业	Automobile Manufacturing	1 319 230	254 547	-
铁路、船舶、航空航天等制造业	Railway, Ship and Aerospace Transportation Equipment Manufacturing	143 359	45 287	-
电气机械和器材制造业	Electric Equipment and Machinery Manufacturing	837 844	521 456	-
计算机、通信和其他电子设备制造业	Computer Telecommunications and Other Electronic Equipment Manufacture	2 371 591	1 159 454	-
仪器仪表制造业	Instruments, Meters Machinery	154 197	73 380	-
其他制造业	Other Products Manufacture	136 903	11 562	-
废弃资源综合利用业	Comprehensive Utilization of Waste Resources	60 974	23 490	-
电力、热力、燃气及水的生产和供应业	Power, Gas and Water Production and Supply	389 951	196 835	-
建筑业	Construction	9 667	9 667	-
批发和零售业	Wholesale and Retail Trade Services	338 092	215 725	7 782
交通运输、仓储和邮政业	Transportation, Logistics and Postal	2 147 134	1 609 129	9 647
住宿和餐饮业	Accommodation and Catering Services	139 981	115 598	8 123
信息传输、软件和信息技术服务业	Information Transmission, Computer Services and Software Industries	354 101	339 769	4 005
金融业	Financial Industries	79 137	68 097	-
房地产业	Real Estate	26 170 227	16 044 481	2 090 977
租赁和商务服务业	Leasing and Business Services	759 141	493 135	68 929
科学研究和技术服务业	Scientific Research and Technical Services	378 308	347 968	36 532
水利、环境和公共设施管理业	Water Conservancy, Environment and Public Facilities Management	2 357 921	1 252 871	24 492
居民服务和其他服务业	Community Service and Other Services	28 037	20 453	2 146
教　育	Education	819 756	537 936	14 653
卫生和社会工作	Health Care and Social Work	232 401	95 090	32 005
文化、体育和娱乐业	Culture, Sports and Entertainment	620 504	564 797	64 089
公共管理社会保障和社会组织	Public Management, Social Security and Social Organizations	78 450	28 906	890

Continued

(10 000 yuan)

# 吴中区 Wuzhong District	# 相城区 Xiangcheng District	#高新区、虎丘区 New & Hi-tech Zone, Huqiu District	# 工业园区 Industrial Park	# 吴江区 Wujiang District	常熟 Changshu	张家港 Zhangjiagang	昆山 Kunshan	太仓 Taicang
149 266	25 186	51 047	55 778	99 941	86 464	11 341	175 046	246 964
50 541	55 331	47 922	135 907	59 863	127 563	66 819	163 967	29 823
41 391	59 697	57 457	54 103	41 899	594 565	114 545	151 355	204 218
–	15 749	1 364	26 517	1 657	11 543	1 576	14 446	70 507
45 586	22 361	131 319	48 531	273 659	101 792	36 411	81 212	96 973
87 271	180 348	269 723	435 416	186 696	107 329	88 169	981 253	35 386
27 348	–	11 566	27 631	6 835	31 192	10 447	23 239	15 939
3 844	–	7 101	104	513	75 641	15 232	21 553	12 915
–	2 290	–	–	21 200	–	34 676	2 790	18
78 562	3 781	16 993	36 752	27 273	61 947	61 539	30 812	38 818
1 500	–	8 167	–	–	–	–	–	–
75 489	12 560	41 291	66 453	12 150	–	27 422	39 936	55 009
–	417 118	11 440	32 883	11 452	150 349	76 872	257 758	53 026
33 181	17 150	–	2 050	55 094	4 279	–	15 904	4 200
10 179	7 848	45 713	28 951	95 158	1 225	7 765	5 342	–
45 700	–	–	8 297	14 100	–	290	10 750	–
3 267 164	2 492 384	2 975 677	1 913 170	3 305 109	2 218 227	2 226 034	3 997 424	1 684 061
190 183	51 823	63 057	48 228	70 915	41 705	7 555	106 754	109 992
30 439	8 614	8 713	246 223	5 287	17 181	7 100	4 099	1 960
374 747	27 359	230 590	273 899	306 899	175 963	168 925	261 929	498 233
5 908	–	–	–	12 399	–	4 190	3 394	–
107 081	92 665	139 453	123 309	60 775	82 695	28 860	152 053	18 212
4 812	1 141	11 646	8 301	37 185	25 150	40 796	64 865	6 500
52 170	78 172	126 688	111 945	131 733	13 923	–	30 984	10 800
22 466	–	–	2 700	2 850	6 495	10 451	10 801	21 797

表11-4

分月固定资产投资完成额(2018年)

单位：万元

项　目	Item	1~2月 From Jan. to Feb.	1~3月 From Jan. to Mar.
固定资产投资	**Investment in Fixed Assets**	**5 439 826**	**10 012 641**
# 亿元以上项目	Projects with More than 100 Million Yuan	1 992 235	3 444 762
# 本年新开工项目	New Projects	371 527	1 223 155
# 基础设施投资	Investment in Infrastructure	460 916	782 306
# 新兴产业投资	Investment in Emerging Industries	641 695	1 444 325
按地区分	**Grouped by Region**		
市　区	Urban Area	3 436 119	6 101 518
# 姑苏区	Gusu District	256 658	518 434
吴中区	Wuzhong District	734 751	1 301 888
相城区	Xiangcheng District	443 017	802 900
高新区、虎丘区	New & Hi-tech Zone , Huqiu District	536 391	998 886
工业园区	Industrial Park	517 771	914 500
吴江区	Wujiang District	818 172	1 350 430
常　熟	Changshu	483 178	968 740
张家港	Zhangjiagang	404 850	778 213
昆　山	Kunshan	805 724	1 485 173
太　仓	Taicang	309 955	678 997
按产业分	**Grouped by Industry**		
第一产业	Primary Industry	5 291	5 691
第二产业	Secondary Industry	993 544	1 938 365
# 工　业	Industry	989 283	1 932 663
# 制造业	Manufacturing	966 252	1 868 809
# 工业技改投资	Investment in Industrial Technical Reformation	645 486	1 296 266
# 高新技术产业投资	Investment in Hi-tech Manufacturing Industries	452 123	818 705
第三产业	Tertiary Industry	4 440 991	8 068 585
按投资主体分	**Grouped by Investment Subjects**		
国有投资	State-owned Investment	1 145 045	1 937 408
民间投资	Private Investment	3 496 707	6 897 432
# 私营个体经济	Value of Investment in Fixed Assets Private and Individuals	1 976 467	4 146 363
外资投资	Foreign Investment	798 074	1 177 801

INVESTMENT IN FIXED ASSETS BY MONTH(2018)

(10 000 yuan)

1~4月 From Jan. to Apr.	1~5月 From Jan. to May	1~6月 From Jan. to Jun.	1~7月 From Jan. to Jul.	1~8月 From Jan. to Aug.	1~9月 From Jan. to Sept.	1~10月 From Jan. to Oct.	1~11月 From Jan. to Nov.	1~12月 From Jan. to Dec.
13 784 916	**18 101 618**	**22 959 738**	**27 088 851**	**30 925 026**	**35 009 369**	**38 328 860**	**42 190 433**	**45 556 977**
4 935 169	6 383 024	8 355 580	9 816 943	11 393 202	13 064 359	14 446 660	16 014 814	17 501 509
2 277 594	3 381 268	4 771 389	6 432 999	8 247 310	10 088 965	11 563 054	13 225 731	14 590 694
1 077 065	1 364 634	1 913 771	2 429 043	2 906 816	3 344 044	3 844 761	4 430 178	4 884 587
2 277 996	3 051 503	3 994 298	4 940 526	5 840 838	6 663 440	7 437 808	8 220 492	9 167 452
8 130 543	10 356 593	13 047 052	15 391 925	17 609 752	19 960 693	21 901 752	24 232 787	26 456 225
667 615	782 392	992 413	1 160 632	1 245 463	1 602 198	1 796 453	2 140 374	2 364 270
1 704 166	2 190 946	2 698 384	3 118 447	3 569 952	3 876 310	4 166 500	4 460 135	4 864 918
1 168 101	1 549 340	2 010 808	2 389 096	2 726 846	3 000 033	3 286 049	3 614 248	3 832 360
1 310 863	1 685 126	2 143 831	2 465 817	2 769 260	3 228 964	3 597 675	4 013 566	4 428 260
1 170 040	1 413 560	1 793 468	2 158 821	2 569 926	2 879 237	3 130 297	3 464 086	3 889 181
1 804 608	2 338 389	2 900 649	3 491 925	4 009 865	4 504 586	4 923 091	5 400 048	5 742 213
1 352 741	1 831 027	2 261 743	2 718 730	3 083 979	3 488 945	3 806 455	4 190 937	4 504 365
1 144 870	1 520 628	2 090 929	2 502 883	2 860 085	3 174 799	3 487 387	3 712 716	3 897 933
2 076 049	2 752 814	3 594 058	4 143 034	4 643 714	5 410 189	5 821 929	6 490 970	7 011 947
1 080 713	1 640 556	1 965 956	2 332 279	2 727 496	2 974 743	3 311 337	3 563 023	3 686 507
6 041	6 501	8 753	10 973	12 474	13 898	15 251	16 949	19 180
2 860 272	3 927 679	5 153 151	6 142 985	7 218 263	8 021 750	8 968 565	10 046 108	11 033 857
2 854 163	3 917 866	514 351	6 137 773	7 212 586	8 014 801	8 960 551	10 037 941	11 024 190
2 764 926	3 805 237	4 989 817	5 948 052	6 973 530	7 751 986	8 657 745	9 702 495	10 634 239
2 027 705	2 768 806	3 652 402	4 461 236	5 292 919	5 913 350	6 771 219	7 636 872	8 548 570
1 188 502	1 583 251	2 068 563	2 455 122	2 850 754	3 219 201	3 584 458	4 019 131	4 460 077
10 918 603	14 167 438	17 797 834	20 934 893	23 694 289	26 973 721	29 345 044	32 127 376	34 503 940
2 722 049	3 456 019	4 567 752	5 463 044	6 610 010	7 568 408	8 418 276	9 429 007	9 832 195
9 386 641	12 342 425	15 587 602	18 173 002	20 146 635	22 731 040	24 738 622	26 944 367	29 493 369
5 708 964	7 545 938	9 471 523	11 210 736	12 437 901	14 268 332	15 522 077	16 964 663	19 429 478
1 676 226	2 303 174	2 804 384	3 452 805	4 168 381	4 709 921	5 171 962	5 817 059	6 231 413

表11-5

分地区新兴产业投资额(2018年)

项　目	Item	全　市 Whole Municipality
在建项目数　(个)	**Construction Projects in Total**　(unit)	**1 581**
新型平板显示	New Flat Panel Displays	84
新材料	New Materials	319
智能电网和物联网	Smart Grid and Internet Of Things	117
高端装备制造	High-End Equipment Manufacturing	640
节能环保	Energy Saving and Environmental Protection	109
新能源	New Energy	87
生物和新医药	Biotechnology and New Medicines	95
软件和集成电路	Software and Integrated Circuit	130
按行业分	**Grouped by sector**	
工业新兴产业	Emerging Industries	1 523
服务业新兴产业	Emerging Service Industries	58
在建项目本年完成投资　(万元)	**Investment in Construction Projects Completed This Year**　(10 000 yuan)	**9 167 452**
新型平板显示	New Flat Panel Displays	860 289
新材料	New Materials	2 112 595
智能电网和物联网	Smart Grid and Internet Of Things	551 325
高端装备制造	High-End Equipment Manufacturing	2 837 313
节能环保	Energy Saving and Environmental Protection	660 021
新能源	New Energy	550 453
生物和新医药	Biotechnology and New Medicines	511 514
软件和集成电路	Software and Integrated Circuit	1 083 942
按行业分	**Grouped by sector**	
工业新兴产业	Emerging Industries	8 687 192
服务业新兴产业	Emerging Service Industries	480 260

INVESTMENT OF EMERGING INDUSTRIES BY REGION(2018)

市 区 Urban Area	# 吴江区 Wujiang District	常 熟 Changshu	张家港 Zhangjiagang	昆 山 Kunshan	太 仓 Taicang
732	**229**	**175**	**182**	**346**	**146**
61	17	7	3	11	2
163	93	34	56	38	28
42	16	9	9	52	5
287	63	85	50	156	62
34	7	5	36	13	21
31	9	22	14	5	15
49	12	10	13	10	13
65	12	3	1	61	–
690	227	173	176	342	142
42	2	2	6	4	4
4 204 015	**1 211 322**	**1 201 436**	**1 264 832**	**1 644 677**	**852 492**
391 142	83 790	33 790	145 072	274 614	15 671
1 021 790	660 755	211 511	460 078	248 513	170 703
164 142	99 881	15 179	75 687	286 147	10 170
1 074 306	188 137	749 841	184 734	430 343	398 089
266 710	73 559	15 602	267 915	19 973	89 821
174 616	50 369	116 637	102 592	18 571	138 037
356 830	29 040	56 476	21 381	46 826	30 001
754 479	25 791	2 400	7 373	319 690	–
3 845 369	1 209 488	1 180 463	1 202 967	1 625 639	832 754
358 646	1 834	20 973	61 865	19 038	19 738

表11-6

民间固定资产投资额 (2018年)

单位：万元

项　目	Item	全　市 Whole Municipality
总　计	**Total**	**29 493 369**
按建设性质分	**Grouped by Type of Construction**	
新　建	New Construction	3 103 531
扩　建	Expansion	2 421 356
改　建	Reconstruction	1 976 977
其　他	Others	21 991 505
按工程构成分	**Grouped by Use of Funds**	
建安工程	Construction and Installation Projects	13 637 315
设备工器具购置	Purchase of Equipment and Instruments	3 372 630
其他费用	Others	12 483 424
按登记注册类型分	**Grouped by Registration Status**	
集体企业	Collective-owned Enterprises	288 887
股份合作企业	Share-holding Cooperative Enterprises	8 996
联营企业	Joint Ownership Enterprises	14 657
有限责任公司	Limited Liability Corporations	7 975 145
股份有限公司	Share-holding Corporations Ltd.	671 863
私营个体经济	Individuals	19 429 478
其　他	Others	227 588
港澳台商投资企业	Enterprises with Investment from HongKong, Macao and Taiwan	283 343
外商投资企业	Enterprises with Foreign Investment	593 412
按产业分	**Grouped by Industry**	
第一产业	Primary Industry	11 087
第二产业	Secondary Industry	6 155 412
#工　业	Industry	6 145 745
第三产业	Tertiary Industry	23 326 870
按行业分	**Grouped by Sector**	
农林牧渔业	Farming, Forestry, Animal Husbandry and Fishery	11 087
采矿业	Mining and Quarrying	–
制造业	Manufacturing	6 000 602
电力、煤气及水的生产和供应业	Power, Gas and Water Production and Supply	145 143

PRIVATE INVESTMENT IN FIXED ASSETS(2018)

(10 000 yuan)

市　区 Urban Area	# 吴江区 Wujiang District	常　熟 Changshu	张家港 Zhangjiagang	昆　山 Kunshan	太　仓 Taicang
16 593 217	**4 077 857**	**3 178 458**	**3 066 765**	**4 363 286**	**2 291 643**
1 784 613	435 411	284 187	176 965	539 981	317 785
890 009	430 090	506 337	579 195	266 045	179 770
925 150	538 160	235 147	393 275	339 455	83 950
12 993 445	2 674 196	2 152 787	1 917 330	3 217 805	1 710 138
7 016 979	1 900 741	1 381 078	1 643 286	2 361 096	1 234 876
1 451 704	792 913	698 204	545 083	465 709	211 930
8 124 534	1 384 203	1 099 176	878 396	1 536 481	844 837
147 477	13 980	17 223	70 510	42 130	11 547
8 996	–	–	–	–	–
5 843	–	–	–	–	8 814
4 106 120	599 245	560 382	1 297 868	1 355 883	654 892
470 436	115 535	81 712	64 748	28 259	26 708
11 284 127	3 262 634	2 190 945	1 606 110	2 875 048	1 473 248
164 278	8 080	15 632	17 358	28 120	2 200
247 464	65 986	3 926	7 091	11 165	13 697
158 476	12 397	308 638	3 080	22 681	100 537
7 771	–	–	–	3 316	–
2 473 161	1 104 787	1 182 236	1 007 291	879 011	613 713
2 463 494	1 104 787	1 182 236	1 007 291	879 011	613 713
14 112 285	2 973 070	1 996 222	2 059 474	3 480 959	1 677 930
7 771	–	–	–	3 316	–
–	–	–	–	–	–
2 424 625	1 096 148	1 160 720	945 752	856 837	612 668
38 869	8 639	21 516	61 539	22 174	1 045

表11-6 续表

单位：万元

项　　目	Item	全　市 Whole Municipality
建筑业	Construction	9 667
批发和零售业	Wholesale and Retail Trade Services	184 848
交通运输、仓储和邮政业	Transportation, Logistics and Postal	82 437
住宿和餐饮业	Accommodation and Catering Services	75 025
信息传输、软件和信息技术服务业	Information Transmission, Software and Information Technology Services	121 303
金融业	Financial Industries	21 400
房地产业	Real Estate	21 278 440
租赁和商务服务业	Leasing and Business Services	412 156
科学研究和技术服务业	Scientific Research and Technical Services	238 168
水利、环境和公共设施管理业	Water Conservancy, Environment and Public Facilities Management	390 697
居民服务和其他服务业	Community Service and Other Services	8 374
教　育	Education	232 982
卫生和社会工作	Health Care and Social Work	70 938
文化、体育和娱乐业	Culture, Sports and Entertainment	185 821
公共管理和社会组织	Public Administration and Social Organizations	24 281
本年资金来源合计	**Total**	**55 620 431**
上年末结余资金	Balance of Last Year	14 266 789
本年资金来源小计	Total Fund for This Year	41 353 642
国家预算内资金	State Budgetary Appropriation	57 221
国内贷款	Domestic Loans	8 787 152
债　券	Bonds	262
利用外资	Foreign Investment	77 365
自筹资金	Fundraising	12 501 912
定金及预收款	Deposit and Advance Receipt	12 449 976
个人按揭贷款	Personal Mortgage Loan	5 608 631
其他资金来源	Others	1 871 123
本年新增固定资产	**Newly Increased Fixed Assets this year**	**10 151 690**
房屋建筑面积 (万平方米)	**Floor Space of Buildings** (10 000 sq.m)	
施工房屋建筑面积	Floor Space of Buildings Under Construction	10 124.62
# 住　宅	Residential Buildings	6 457.46
竣工房屋建筑面积	Floor Space of Buildings Completed	1 338.55
# 住　宅	Residential Building	771.84

Continued

(10 000 yuan)

市 区 Urban Area	# 吴江区 Wujiang District	常 熟 Changshu	张家港 Zhangjiagang	昆 山 Kunshan	太 仓 Taicang
9 667	–	–	–	–	–
119 015	12 150	–	26 700	35 814	3 319
16 513	–	10 000	6 345	32 700	16 879
50 642	27 854	4 279	–	15 904	4 200
109 968	64 909	645	7 765	2 925	–
21 400	7 200	–	–	–	–
12 723 131	2 670 332	1 919 907	1 942 367	3 135 373	1 557 662
260 143	50 550	994	3 355	84 631	63 033
230 659	5 287	–	1 450	4 099	1 960
247 517	113 245	39 429	17 740	74 634	11 377
8 053	5 999	–	321	–	–
136 632	4 426	13 783	16 450	63 917	2 200
17 387	4 600	4 000	36 981	6 070	6 500
149 109	3 668	1 800	–	24 112	10 800
22 116	2 850	1 385	–	780	–
31 481 421	**7 533 336**	**4 325 480**	**5 929 844**	**9 620 505**	**4 263 181**
8 407 992	1 413 101	983 500	1 443 644	2 374 077	1 057 576
23 073 429	6 120 235	3 341 980	4 486 200	7 246 428	3 205 605
56 621	1 821	–	600	–	–
5 532 253	1 391 019	857 991	901 415	858 314	637 179
262	–	–	–	–	–
261	–	63 726	–	–	13 378
6 707 608	1 978 952	1 498 352	1 025 243	1 979 792	1 290 917
6 831 055	1 763 745	404 206	1 680 293	2 832 742	701 680
2 969 839	811 419	262 330	802 602	1 129 005	444 855
975 530	173 279	255 375	76 047	446 575	117 596
4 354 582	**967 331**	**1 985 992**	**972 698**	**2 319 361**	**519 057**
4 703.43	1 518.27	969.83	1 119.80	2 632.88	698.68
2 907.02	992.00	562.91	872.17	1 600.50	514.85
567.33	216.69	170.02	90.05	453.36	57.79
371.50	134.47	76.81	66.43	227.32	29.78

表11-7

建设项目投资完成额 (2018年)

单位：万元

项　　目	Item	全　市 Whole Municipality
总　　计	**Total**	**19 977 875**
按建设性质分	**Grouped by Type of Construction**	
新　建	New Construction	9 130 663
扩　建	Expansion	5 153 840
改　建	Reconstruction	3 837 318
其　他	Others	1 856 054
按工程构成分	**Grouped by Use of Funds**	
建安工程	Construction and Installation Projects	11 650 877
设备工器具购置	Purchase of Equipment and Instruments	6 481 928
其他费用	Others	1 845 070
按登记注册类型分	**Grouped by Registration Status**	
国有企业	State-owed Enterprises	3 493 616
集体企业	Collective-owned Enterprises	267 631
股份合作企业	Share-holding Cooperative Enterprises	8 996
联营企业	Joint Ownership Enterprises	22 560
有限责任公司	Limited Liability Corporations	5 519 355
# 国有独资	State-owned Sole Investment	1 956 718
股份有限公司	Share-holding Corporations Ltd.	645 933
私营个体经济	Individuals	4 549 090
其　他	Others	182 088
港澳台商投资企业	Enterprises with Investment from HongKong, Macao and Taiwan	1 531 995
外商投资企业	Enterprises with Foreign Investment	3 756 611
按行业分	**Grouped by Sector**	
农林牧渔业	Farming, Forestry, Animal Husbandry and Fishery	19 930
采矿业	Mining and Quarrying	–
制造业	Manufacturing	10 634 239
电力、煤气及水的生产和供应业	Power, Gas and Water Production and Supply	389 951
建筑业	Construction	9 667
批发和零售业	Wholesale and Retail Trade Services	338 092
交通运输、仓储和邮政业	Transportation, Logistics and Postal	2 147 134

THE FIXED ASSETS OF CONSTRUCTION PROJECTS INVESTMENT(2018)

(10 000 yuan)

市 区 Urban Area	# 吴江区 Wujiang District	常 熟 Changshu	张家港 Zhangjiagang	昆 山 Kunshan	太 仓 Taicang
10 778 014	**2 526 300**	**2 297 804**	**1 780 887**	**3 041 856**	**2 079 314**
5 899 279	979 497	697 059	398 465	1 114 378	1 021 482
2 031 564	672 297	929 999	905 749	712 171	574 357
1 943 803	802 422	303 864	465 441	873 552	250 658
903 368	72 084	366 882	11 232	341 755	232 817
6 641 204	1 238 709	1 213 695	915 677	1 609 062	1 271 239
3 044 238	1 144 139	986 345	681 800	1 234 170	535 375
1 092 572	143 452	97 764	183 410	198 624	272 700
2 116 749	266 769	264 564	236 700	272 950	602 653
135 121	13 980	17 223	70 510	33 230	11 547
8 996	–	–	–	–	–
13 746	–	–	–	–	8 814
3 248 529	534 125	366 338	803 112	721 907	379 469
1 410 348	87 408	144 509	41 376	273 573	86 912
451 984	93 765	86 111	59 040	16 940	31 858
2 226 949	964 458	660 443	355 332	844 823	461 543
118 778	8 080	15 632	17 358	28 120	2 200
839 486	380 626	209 839	28 598	261 601	192 471
1 617 676	264 497	677 654	210 237	862 285	388 759
15 864	–	–	–	3 316	750
–	–	–	–	–	–
4 499 904	1 593 834	1 705 226	1 230 134	2 015 826	1 183 149
196 835	27 273	61 947	61 539	30 812	38 818
9 667	–	–	–	–	–
215 725	12 150	–	27 422	39 936	55 009
1 609 129	11 452	150 349	76 872	257 758	53 026

表11-7 续表

单位：万元

项　　目	Item	全　市 Whole Municipality
住宿和餐饮业	Accommodation and Catering Services	139 981
信息传输、软件和信息技术服务业	Information Transmission, Software and Information Technology Services	354 101
金融业	Financial Industries	79 137
房地产业	Real Estate	591 125
租赁和商务服务业	Leasing and Business Services	759 141
科学研究和技术服务业	Scientific Research and Technical Services	378 308
水利、环境和公共设施管理业	Water Conservancy, Environment and Public Facilities Management	2 357 921
居民服务和其他服务业	Community Service and Other Services	28 037
教　育	Education	819 756
卫生和社会工作	Health Care and Social Work	232 401
文化、体育和娱乐业	Culture, Sports and Entertainment	620 504
公共管理和社会组织	Public Administration and Social Organizations	78 450
本年资金来源合计	**Total**	**16 187 756**
上年末结余资金	Balance of Last Year	1 715 410
本年资金来源小计	Total Fund for This Year	14 472 346
国家预算内资金	State Budgetary Appropriation	762 972
国内贷款	Domestic Loans	1 840 931
债　券	Bonds	1 347
利用外资	Foreign Investment	665 491
自筹资金	Fundraising	9 557 743
其他资金来源	Others	1 643 862
本年新增固定资产	**Newly Increased Fixed Assets this year**	**8 643 324**
房屋建筑面积 (万平方米)	**Floor Space of Buildings** (10 000 sq.m)	
施工房屋建筑面积	Floor Space of Buildings Under Construction	2 532.70
# 住　宅	Residential Buildings	33.72
竣工房屋建筑面积	Floor Space of Buildings Completed	526.66
# 住　宅	Residential Building	1.71

Continued

(10 000 yuan)

市 区 Urban Area	# 吴江区 Wujiang District	常 熟 Changshu	张家港 Zhangjiagang	昆 山 Kunshan	太 仓 Taicang
115 598	55 094	4 279	–	15 904	4 200
339 769	95 158	1 225	7 765	5 342	–
68 097	14 100	–	290	10 750	–
366 270	89 196	11 666	108 988	27 333	76 868
493 135	70 915	41 705	7 555	106 754	109 992
347 968	5 287	17 181	7 100	4 099	1 960
1 252 871	306 899	175 963	168 925	261 929	498 233
20 453	12 399	–	4 190	3 394	–
537 936	60 775	82 695	28 860	152 053	18 212
95 090	37 185	25 150	40 796	64 865	6 500
564 797	131 733	13 923	–	30 984	10 800
28 906	2 850	6 495	10 451	10 801	21 797
9 466 073	**1 687 103**	**1 671 345**	**1 076 441**	**2 497 990**	**1 475 907**
1 313 934	116 160	94 099	32 525	237 120	37 732
8 152 139	1 570 943	1 577 246	1 043 916	2 260 870	1 438 175
600 623	54 701	124 779	600	7 000	29 970
1 217 299	91 076	148 322	94 513	170 355	210 442
1 347	–	–	–	–	–
268 092	224 101	189 185	74 431	113 367	20 416
5 138 382	1 113 603	1 022 713	803 263	1 473 508	1 119 877
926 396	87 462	92 247	71 109	496 640	57 470
3 611 750	**668 254**	**1 522 730**	**1 026 059**	**1 842 580**	**640 205**
1 162.19	352.85	272.46	119.17	822.75	156.12
18.71	16.98	–	–	14.56	0.44
229.65	80.07	73.79	5.96	187.04	30.21
0.91	–	–	–	0.37	0.44

表11-8

5000万元以上建设项目投资新增固定资产额 (2018年)

单位：万元

项　　目	Item	全　市 Whole Municipality
总　　计	**Total**	**8 643 324**
按建设性质分	**Grouped by Type of Construction**	
新　建	New Construction	3 642 003
扩　建	Expansion	2 882 165
改　建	Reconstruction	1 639 505
其　他	Others	479 651
按登记注册类型分	**Grouped by Registration Status**	
国有企业	State-owed Enterprises	1 559 637
集体企业	Collective-owned Enterprises	119 504
股份合作企业	Share-holding Cooperative Enterprises	–
联营企业	Joint Ownership Enterprises	–
有限责任公司	Limited Liability Corporations	2 295 625
股份有限公司	Share-holding Corporations Ltd.	203 708
私营个体经济	Individuals	1 337 167
其　他	Others	42 822
港澳台商投资企业	Enterprises with Investment from HongKong, Macao and Taiwan	740 706
外商投资企业	Enterprises with Foreign Investment	2 344 155
按产业分	**Grouped by Industry**	
第一产业	Primary Industry	8 000
第二产业	Secondary Industry	5 407 019
#工　业	Industry	5 404 255
第三产业	Tertiary Industry	3 228 305

NEW FIXED ASSETS IN THE INVESTMENT IN CONSTRUCTION PROJECTS OF MORE THAN 50 MILLION YUAN(2018)

(10 000 yuan)

市 区 Urban Area	# 吴江区 Wujiang District	常 熟 Changshu	张家港 Zhangjiagang	昆 山 Kunshan	太 仓 Taicang
3 611 750	**668 254**	**1 522 730**	**1 026 059**	**1 842 580**	**640 205**
2 001 778	192 236	409 576	262 801	726 657	241 191
773 751	279 554	988 797	534 111	315 746	269 760
548 879	186 932	76 374	229 147	713 689	71 416
287 342	9 532	47 983	–	86 488	57 838
954 160	64 186	63 467	192 906	235 050	114 054
35 209	–	–	55 000	24 995	4 300
–	–	–	–	–	–
–	–	–	–	–	–
936 610	84 602	270 752	395 172	527 666	165 425
123 373	8 124	22 330	45 932	3 073	9 000
460 297	195 226	218 202	190 161	375 221	93 286
42 222	–	–	600	–	–
397 749	189 167	261 049	9 019	45 045	27 844
662 130	126 949	686 930	137 269	631 530	226 296
8 000	–	–	–	–	–
1 516 745	481 407	1 351 092	742 774	1 379 399	417 009
1 513 981	481 407	1 351 092	742 774	1 379 399	417 009
2 087 005	186 847	171 638	283 285	463 181	223 196

表11-8 续表

单位：万元

项　目	Item	全　市 Whole Municipality
按行业分	**Grouped by Sector**	
农林牧渔业	Farming, Forestry, Animal Husbandry and Fishery	8 000
采矿业	Mining and Quarrying	–
制造业	Manufacturing	5 079 391
电力、煤气及水的生产和供应业	Power, Gas and Water Production and Supply	324 864
建筑业	Construction	2 764
批发和零售业	Wholesale and Retail Trade Services	83 182
交通运输、仓储和邮政业	Transportation, Logistics and Postal	339 560
住宿和餐饮业	Hoteling and Catering Services	6 752
信息传输、软件和信息技术服务业	Information Transmission, Software and Information Technology Services	67 447
金融业	Financial Industries	63 408
房地产业	Real Estate	172 508
租赁和商务服务业	Leasing and Business Services	502 317
科学研究和技术服务业	Scientific Research and Technical Services	129 195
水利、环境和公共设施管理业	Water Conservancy, Environment and Public Facilities Management	710 854
居民服务和其他服务业	Community Service and Other Services	–
教　育	Education	410 199
卫生和社会工作	Health Care and Social Work	101 498
文化、体育和娱乐业	Culture, Sports and Entertainment	614 224
公共管理和社会组织	Public Administration and Social Organizations	27 161

Continued

(10 000 yuan)

市 区 Urban Area	# 吴江区 Wujiang District	常 熟 Changshu	张家港 Zhangjiagang	昆 山 Kunshan	太 仓 Taicang
8 000	–	–	–	–	–
–	–	–	–	–	–
1 452 950	481 407	1 329 545	742 727	1 173 860	380 309
61 031	–	21 547	47	205 539	36 700
2 764	–	–	–	–	–
48 500	9 000	–	34 682	–	–
122 317	28 710	94 737	641	44 672	77 193
6 752	6 752	–	–	–	–
67 447	77	–	–	–	–
63 408	–	–	–	–	–
115 278	49 296	–	57 230	–	–
364 830	–	–	–	110 793	26 694
116 690	–	–	9 930	2 575	–
276 230	62 714	52 205	116 802	150 608	115 009
–	–	–	–	–	–
254 064	25 000	17 546	18 000	120 589	–
44 048	2 110	7 150	46 000	–	4 300
607 441	3 188	–	–	6 783	–
–	–	–	–	27 161	–

表11-9 重大投资项目情况 (2018年)

项　目	Item	全　市 Whole Municipality
投资项目数 (个)	**Number of Projects** (unit)	
重大投资项目	**Major Investment Projects**	**415**
按内外资分	**Grouped by Domestic and Foreign Capitals**	
5亿元以上内资项目	Domestic Projects of More Than 500 Million Yuan	349
1亿美元以上外资项目	Foreign Projects of More Than $100 Million	66
按行业分	**Grouped by Sector**	
# 工业重大项目	Major Industrial Projects	133
服务业重大项目	Major Service Industry Projects	280
亿元项目	**Projects of More Than 100 Million Yuan**	**1 548**
# 亿元以上工业项目	Industrial Projects of More Than 100 Million Yuan	787
亿元以上服务业项目	Service Industry Projects of More Than 100 Million Yuan	758
亿元以上新开工项目	**New Projects of More Than 100 Million Yuan**	**482**
# 工业新开工项目	New Industrial Projects	298
服务业新开工项目	New Service Industry Projects	184
5亿元以上新开工项目	**New Projects of More Than 500 Million Yuan**	**84**
# 工业新开工项目	New Industrial Projects	39
服务业新开工项目	New Service Industry Projects	45

THE MAJOR PROJECTS INVESTMENT IN FIXED ASSETS (2018)

市　区 Urban Area	# 吴江区 Wujiang District	常　熟 Changshu	张家港 Zhangjiagang	昆　山 Kunshan	太　仓 Taicang
254	**52**	**34**	**31**	**60**	**36**
221	46	22	28	50	28
33	6	12	3	10	8
60	21	16	18	20	19
192	31	18	13	40	17
793	**186**	**173**	**153**	**278**	**151**
323	102	122	92	150	100
467	84	51	61	128	51
247	**49**	**51**	**47**	**82**	**55**
132	36	42	39	50	35
115	13	9	8	32	20
48	**13**	**6**	**11**	**7**	**12**
20	9	3	8	1	7
28	4	3	3	6	5

表11-9 续表

项　　目	Item	全　市 Whole Municipality
本年完成投资额 (万元)	**Investment Completed This Year** (10 000 yuan)	
重大投资项目	**Major Investment Projects**	**10 107 545**
按内外资分	**Grouped by Domestic and Foreign Capitals**	
5亿元以上内资项目	Domestic Projects of More Than 500 Million Yuan	8 070 694
1亿美元以上外资项目	Foreign Projects of More Than $100 Million	2 036 851
按行业分	**Grouped by Sector**	
# 工业重大项目	Major Industrial Projects	3 357 383
服务业重大项目	Major Service Industry Projects	6 736 671
亿元项目	**Projects of More Than 100 Million Yuan**	**17 501 509**
# 亿元以上工业项目	Industrial Projects of More Than 100 Million Yuan	7 827 151
亿元以上服务业项目	Service Industry Projects of More Than 100 Million Yuan	9 652 700
亿元以上新开工项目	**New Projects of More Than 100 Million Yuan**	**5 427 839**
# 工业新开工项目	New Industrial Projects	3 205 352
服务业新开工项目	New Service Industry Projects	2 222 487
5亿元以上新开工项目	**New Projects of More Than 500 Million Yuan**	**2 234 003**
# 工业新开工项目	New Industrial Projects	1 106 587
服务业新开工项目	New Service Industry Projects	1 127 416

Continued

市 区 Urban Area	# 吴江区 Wujiang District	常 熟 Changshu	张家港 Zhangjiagang	昆 山 Kunshan	太 仓 Taicang
6 498 546	**971 481**	**750 094**	**795 378**	**1 090 594**	**972 933**
5 433 617	784 269	300 588	767 898	796 656	771 935
1 064 929	187 212	449 506	27 480	293 938	200 998
1 385 502	442 975	456 595	586 762	471 269	457 255
5 099 553	528 506	293 499	208 616	619 325	515 678
10 151 445	**1 789 573**	**1 669 439**	**1 531 817**	**2 538 818**	**1 609 990**
3 258 149	978 453	1 197 664	1 077 190	1 381 504	912 644
6 871 638	811 120	471 775	454 627	1 157 314	697 346
3 132 110	**702 994**	**409 570**	**670 345**	**741 986**	**473 828**
1 631 321	525 279	342 629	556 733	463 879	210 790
1 500 789	177 715	66 941	113 612	278 107	263 038
1 371 493	**375 469**	**102 485**	**332 502**	**192 233**	**235 290**
658 431	277 218	66 079	250 073	68 202	63 802
713 062	98 251	36 406	82 429	124 031	171 488

表11-10

分地区高技术制造业投资情况（2018年）
INVESTMENT IN HIGH-TECH MANUFACTURING BY REGION (2018)

单位：万元 (10 000yuan)

项　目	Item	在建项目数（个）Construction Projects in Total (unit)	在建项目计划总投资 Planned Total Investment in the Projects Under Construction	在建项目本年完成投资 Investment in Construction Projects Completed This Year
总　计	**Total**	**587**	**14 242 261**	**3 611 075**
按登记注册类型分	**Grouped by Registration Status**			
国　资	State Capital	11	1 273 969	245 074
民　资	Private Investment	303	6 211 493	1 479 913
外　资	Foreign Investment	273	6 756 799	1 886 088
按行业分	**Grouped by sector**			
医药制造业	Medical and Pharmaceutical Products	42	1 023 744	176 272
航空、航天器及设备制造业	Aircraft and Spacecraft and Equipment Manufacturing	7	99 633	26 511
电子及通信设备制造业	Electronic and Communication Equipment Manufacturing	392	10 208 763	2 528 217
计算机及办公设备制造业	Computer and Office Equipment Manufacturing	49	425 961	212 315
医疗仪器设备及仪器仪表制造业	Medical Equipment and Instrument Manufacturing	92	1 563 848	390 399
信息化学品制造业	Information Chemicals Manufacturing	5	920 312	277 361
按地区分	**Grouped by Region**			
市　区	Urban Area	308	6 069 065	1 836 445
姑苏区	Gusu District	–	–	–
吴中区	Wuzhong District	48	558 381	136 564
相城区	Xiangcheng District	31	528 394	213 830
高新区、虎丘区	New & Hi-tech Zone , Huqiu District	46	1 152 554	368 434
工业园区	Industrial Park	104	2 229 428	726 092
吴江区	Wujiang District	79	1 600 308	391 525
常　熟	Changshu	52	912 963	220 173
张家港	Zhangjiagang	27	1 466 430	379 178
昆　山	Kunshan	168	5 294 497	1 072 093
太　仓	Taicang	32	499 306	103 186

表11-11

历年房地产开发投资情况
REAL ESTATE DEVELOPMENT OVER THE YEARS

年 份 Year	投资额(万元) Investment (10 000 yuan)	新增固定资产(万元) Newly Increased Fixed Assets (10 000 yuan)	竣工房屋面积(万平方米) Floor Space of Buildings Completed (10 000 sq.m)	# 住 宅 Residential Housing
1990	16 516	16 049	46.95	40.21
1991	22 578	18 015	44.42	39.15
1992	61 858	32 111	89.12	65.36
1993	336 437	150 033	337.47	282.81
1994	400 268	218 471	378.39	299.81
1995	586 461	364 429	398.24	301.47
1996	501 411	430 700	334.16	250.45
1997	512 313	440 908	354.96	277.46
1998	585 447	541 232	403.23	313.12
1999	601 124	515 846	425.72	349.99
2000	611 792	611 091	444.49	376.30
2001	686 178	701 954	467.24	386.26
2002	1 073 363	829 151	558.05	464.94
2003	1 779 403	1 218 305	825.89	709.15
2004	3 343 245	2 024 119	1 462.78	1 269.29
2005	4 143 333	3 439 283	1 677.29	1 380.58
2006	4 707 472	4 070 670	1 823.12	1 484.16
2007	6 019 565	4 794 361	1 873.29	1 481.42
2008	7 180 805	4 023 663	1 481.24	1 131.91
2009	7 243 408	6 488 907	1 878.68	1 409.81
2010	9 358 018	7 054 660	1 761.08	1 221.53
2011	11 991 278	6 361 455	1 514.52	1 102.41
2012	12 633 597	8 954 225	1 827.56	1 386.17
2013	14 757 684	10 192 954	1 692.51	1 227.53
2014	17 644 440	8 708 742	1 527.19	1 129.36
2015	18 649 472	10 350 854	1 653.14	1 274.57
2016	21 632 440	11 428 378	1 882.07	1 402.80
2017	23 058 238	12 104 994	2 145.62	1 472.03
2018	25 579 102	10 230 511	1 507.34	1 007.20

表11-12

房地产开发投资完成额 (2018年)

单位：万元

项　　目	Item	全　市 Whole Municipality
投资额合计	**Investment**	**25 579 102**
# 住宅投资完成额	Completed Investment Value of Residential Housing	21 115 951
一、按工程构成分	**Grouped by Use of Funds**	
建筑工程	Construction	10 710 773
安装工程	Installation	1 102 696
设备、工器具购置	Purchase of Equipment and Instruments	121 114
其他费用	Others	13 644 519
二、按登记注册类型分	**Grouped by Registration Status**	
国有企业	State-owed Enterprises	255 277
集体企业	Collective-owned Enterprises	21 256
股份合作企业	Share-holding Cooperative Enterprises	–
联营经济	Joint Ventures of State-owned and Collective Enterprises	–
国有独资	State-owned Enterprises	663 742
其他有限责任公司	Limited Liability Corporations	7 543 990
股份有限公司	Share-holding Corporations Ltd.	413 413
私营个体企业	Private and Individuals Enterprises	14 880 388
港澳台商投资企业	Enterprises with Investment from HongKong, Macao and Taiwan	1 062 420
外商投资企业	Enterprises with Foreign Investment	693 116
其　他	Others	45 500
本年资金来源合计	**Total**	**67 611 967**
上年末结余资金	Balance of Last Year	19 548 338
本年资金来源小计	Total Fund for This Year	48 063 629
国家预算内资金	State Budgetary Appropriation	–
国内贷款	Domestic Loans	10 796 484
债　券	Bonds	–
利用外资	Foreign Investment	16 059
自筹资金	Fundraising	9 877 915
定金及预收款	Deposit and Advance Receipt	17 396 657
个人按揭贷款	Personal Mortgage Loan	7 675 253
其他资金来源	Others	2 301 261
本年新增固定资产	**Newly Increased Fixed Assets this year**	**10 230 511**
房屋建筑面积 (万平方米)	**Floor Space of Buildings** (10 000 sq.m)	
施工房屋建筑面积	Floor space of Buildings under Construction	11 658.52
# 住　宅	Residential Buildings	8 337.12
竣工房屋建筑面积	Floor Space of Buildings Completed	1 507.34
# 住　宅	Residential Building	1 007.20

INVESTMENT IN REAL ESTATE DEVELOPMENT (2018)

(10 000 yuan)

市区 Urban Area	# 吴江区 Wujiang District	常熟 Changshu	张家港 Zhangjiagang	昆山 Kunshan	太仓 Taicang
15 678 211	**3 215 913**	**2 206 561**	**2 117 046**	**3 970 091**	**1 607 193**
12 873 663	2 629 602	1 828 564	1 834 123	3 217 994	1 361 607
5 883 947	1 721 585	905 448	1 078 409	2 151 391	691 578
640 091	104 494	80 223	127 700	156 305	98 377
56 566	9 833	13 916	18 570	15 070	16 992
9 097 607	1 380 001	1 206 974	892 367	1 647 325	800 246
154 877	–	–	100 400	–	–
12 356	–	–	–	8 900	–
–	–	–	–	–	–
–	–	–	–	–	–
440 606	226 662	31 274	8 987	173 458	9 417
4 434 853	461 362	619 952	750 881	1 276 729	461 575
376 006	22 908	1	6 000	31 406	–
9 057 178	2 298 176	1 530 502	1 250 778	2 030 225	1 011 705
937 421	168 676	24 832	–	93 649	6 518
219 414	38 129	–	–	355 724	117 978
45 500	–	–	–	–	–
40 826 801	**8 922 441**	**4 934 749**	**5 975 538**	**11 738 575**	**4 136 304**
11 557 411	1 775 822	1 601 978	1 649 003	3 447 375	1 292 571
29 269 390	7 146 619	3 332 771	4 326 535	8 291 200	2 843 733
–	–	–	–	–	–
7 023 452	1 360 629	973 105	920 550	1 336 086	543 291
–	–	–	–	–	–
–	–	–	–	–	16 059
5 611 445	1 377 282	1 208 607	602 190	1 542 830	912 843
10 544 015	2 892 906	524 225	1 924 042	3 607 335	797 040
4 679 462	1 216 357	319 398	805 579	1 390 909	479 905
1 411 016	299 445	307 436	74 174	414 040	94 595
5 982 638	**844 841**	**1 427 881**	**300 868**	**2 162 704**	**356 420**
6 019.35	1 816.07	989.54	1 168.92	2 768.37	712.34
4 160.36	1 360.15	693.13	958.11	1 933.26	592.25
751.36	204.27	187.10	87.06	447.43	34.39
505.91	165.35	127.07	66.43	278.45	29.34

表11-13

房地产开发基本情况（2018年）

项　目		Item		全　市 Whole Municipality
开发企业数	(个)	**Number of Development Enterprises**	(unit)	**1 242**
按资质等级分		**Classified by Qualification**		
一　级		A Qualification		15
二　级		B Qualification		276
三　级		C Qualification		103
四　级		D Qualification		6
暂　定		Provisional		740
其　他		Others		102
从业人员平均人数	(人)	**Number of Employed Persons**	(person)	**31 282**
土地开发及购置	(平方米)	**Land Development and Acquisition**	(sq.m)	
待开发土地面积		Area of Land to be Developed		6 794 480
本年土地购置面积		Acreage of Land Acquired Within the Year		3 510 516
本年土地成交价款	(万元)	Actual Land Price of the Year	(10 000 yuan)	4 298 242
资产及损益情况		**Assets and Expenditure**		
资产总计		Total Assets		181 922 110
负债总计		Total Liabilities		135 663 972
所有者权益		Creditors Equity		46 258 138
实收资本合计		Total Capital Hold		31 781 069
主营业务收入总计		Total from Business Revenue		37 183 096
土地转让收入		Revenue from Land Transfer		981 955
商品房销售收入		Revenue Sale of Housing		35 134 700
房屋出租收入		Income for House Lease		251 365
其他收入		Other Revenue		781 608
主营业务成本		Cost from Major Business		25 470 737
销售费用		Cost Related With Sale		904 187
主营业务税金及附加		Taxes and Extra Charges from Major Business		2 394 038
其他业务利润		Other Business Profits		94 607
管理费用及财务费用		Cost of Management and Financing Activities		1 239 401
投资收益及营业外收入		Benefits of Investment and Non-Business Income		513 811
营业外支出		Non-Business Expenditure		114 516
利润总额		Total Profits		7 191 252
所得税费用		Income Tax Expense		1 173 824
应交增值税		Value Added Tax Payable		1 421 564

BASIC CONDITION OF REAL ESTATE DEVELOPMENT (2018)

市 区 Urban Area	# 吴江区 Wujiang District	常 熟 Changshu	张家港 Zhangjiagang	昆 山 Kunshan	太 仓 Taicang
617	**168**	**129**	**116**	**278**	**102**
10	3	1	2	2	–
148	57	23	23	67	15
53	19	4	11	25	10
3	2	–	1	–	2
340	70	90	70	169	71
63	17	11	9	15	4
17 223	**3 847**	**2 379**	**2 938**	**6 819**	**1 923**
2 670 439	545 319	618 092	360 041	1 984 149	1 161 759
1 348 337	353 615	582 195	987 768	134 932	457 284
2 451 640	412 694	531 565	818 261	213 864	282 912
112 386 665	20 808 511	14 815 589	13 157 081	33 410 025	8 152 751
83 410 533	16 015 271	10 631 390	10 941 129	24 749 518	5 931 403
28 976 133	4 793 239	4 184 199	2 215 952	8 660 506	2 221 348
20 477 335	3 188 492	3 186 016	1 423 897	4 814 510	1 879 313
20 752 904	5 114 543	3 116 785	4 098 656	7 831 248	1 383 504
533 478	350 438	–	257 685	190 793	–
19 636 575	4 543 060	2 972 628	3 814 463	7 336 407	1 374 628
187 930	9 935	13 646	4 754	41 984	3 051
364 706	210 040	128 470	21 754	260 854	5 823
13 894 335	3 435 142	2 387 299	3 235 661	4 909 699	1 043 742
503 471	131 905	42 157	106 534	198 132	53 892
1 424 121	362 412	101 374	120 394	684 158	63 991
29 075	2 166	2 103	12 576	49 186	1 667
657 847	84 904	126 997	181 312	212 117	61 127
314 163	25 731	25 061	78 741	86 363	9 484
42 580	23 558	12 408	11 992	45 260	2 276
4 246 179	1 089 439	485 952	482 547	1 792 300	184 273
707 918	156 693	56 736	48 869	310 367	49 934
838 365	217 661	101 022	111 844	259 759	110 574

表11-13 续表

项　目	Item	全　市 Whole Municipality
房屋施工面积 (平方米)	**Floor Space of Buildings under Construction** (sq. m)	**116 585 158**
住　宅	Residential Buildings	83 371 159
办公楼	Office Buildings	6 257 199
商业营业用房	Commercial Business Premises	11 778 915
其　他	Others	15 177 885
新开工面积	**Floor Space of Starting This Year**	**28 007 595**
住　宅	Residential Buildings	20 717 349
办公楼	Office Buildings	1 059 438
商业营业用房	Commercial Business Premises	2 216 318
其　他	Others	4 014 490
房屋竣工面积	**Floor Space of Buildings Completed**	**15 073 402**
住　宅	Residential Buildings	10 071 966
办公楼	Office Buildings	854 497
商业营业用房	Commercial Business Premises	2 231 854
其　他	Others	1 915 085
商品房销售面积	**Floor Space of Housing Sold**	**19 941 321**
住　宅	Residential Buildings	17 882 978
办公楼	Office Buildings	585 715
商业营业用房	Commercial Business Premises	1 082 849
其　他	Others	389 779
待售面积	**Area Of Land For Sale**	**7 890 252**
住　宅	Residential Buildings	3 209 529
办公楼	Office Buildings	1 415 068
商业营业用房	Commercial Business Premises	2 710 193
其　他	Others	555 462
商品房销售额 (万元)	**Sales of housing** (10 000 yuan)	**31 178 307**
住　宅	Residential Buildings	28 991 872
办公楼	Office Buildings	672 529
商业营业用房	Commercial Business Premises	1 230 523
其　他	Others	283 383

Continued

市　区 Urban Area	# 吴江区 Wujiang District	常　熟 Changshu	张家港 Zhangjiagang	昆　山 Kunshan	太　仓 Taicang
60 193 492	**18 160 698**	**9 895 427**	**11 689 169**	**27 683 689**	**7 123 381**
41 603 624	13 601 479	6 931 336	9 581 071	19 332 609	5 922 519
3 530 694	745 067	531 359	95 549	2 027 800	71 797
6 950 544	1 717 977	1 067 780	1 110 352	2 374 719	275 520
8 108 630	2 096 175	1 364 952	902 197	3 948 561	853 545
12 447 340	**4 535 864**	**4 214 014**	**3 179 045**	**5 051 887**	**3 115 309**
8 864 580	3 859 319	2 964 059	2 711 839	3 613 378	2 563 493
519 356	3 206	173 474	42 377	291 921	32 310
1 282 738	134 427	375 713	90 454	296 301	171 112
1 780 666	538 912	700 768	334 375	850 287	348 394
7 513 579	**2 042 683**	**1 871 027**	**870 587**	**4 474 285**	**343 924**
5 059 068	1 653 474	1 270 720	664 289	2 784 503	293 386
395 919	–	31 198	51 040	337 053	39 287
1 160 177	120 105	253 998	93 520	716 500	7 659
898 415	269 104	315 111	61 738	636 229	3 592
10 188 087	**3 168 492**	**1 693 147**	**2 807 472**	**3 973 971**	**1 278 644**
9 197 108	2 888 758	1 470 527	2 526 049	3 591 374	1 097 920
262 862	41 489	4 267	69 674	187 998	60 914
597 944	191 035	182 115	161 583	129 990	11 217
130 173	47 210	36 238	50 166	64 609	108 593
4 482 304	**1 015 268**	**484 197**	**847 233**	**1 558 602**	**517 916**
1 801 034	354 541	100 122	216 014	801 754	290 605
816 181	37 285	31 082	272 222	259 870	35 713
1 520 007	571 419	336 416	284 841	462 919	106 010
345 082	52 023	16 577	74 156	34 059	85 588
18 226 030	**4 825 899**	**2 017 470**	**3 435 965**	**5 956 688**	**1 542 154**
16 996 474	4 594 280	1 911 029	3 174 267	5 496 436	1 413 666
351 175	42 785	3 043	43 157	227 454	47 700
760 998	166 628	94 029	188 608	170 337	16 551
117 383	22 206	9 369	29 933	62 461	64 237

表11-14

全市房地产开发四大指标十强企业（2018年）

序号 No.	开发企业名称 Name of Development Enterprises	资质等级 Grouped by Grade	地区 Region	经济类型 Ownership
一、完成投资额 Investment				
1	苏州国瑞地产有限公司	暂定二级	吴中区	有限责任公司
2	苏州仁安置业有限公司	暂定二级	姑苏区	有限责任公司
3	苏州聿盛房地产开发有限公司	暂定二级	相城区	有限责任公司
4	苏州金俊房地产开发有限公司	暂定二级	姑苏区	有限责任公司
5	昆山合泰房地产开发有限公司	暂定二级	昆山市	有限责任公司
6	苏州正润房地产开发有限公司	暂定二级	吴中区	有限责任公司
7	苏州安茂置业有限公司	暂定二级	高新区、虎丘区	有限责任公司
8	苏州鲁能广宇置地有限公司	暂定二级	相城区	国有
9	中海发展（苏州）有限公司	一级	工业园区	港澳台商独资
10	昆山融信恺庭房地产开发有限公司	暂定二级	昆山市	有限责任公司
二、房屋施工面积 Floor Space of Buildings under Construction				
1	昆山市阳澄湖房产有限责任公司	二级	昆山市	有限责任公司
2	张家港市悦丰投资开发建设有限公司	二级	张家港市	有限责任公司
3	张家港汇金置业有限公司	暂定二级	张家港市	有限责任公司
4	苏州科技城城乡一体化发展有限公司	暂定二级	高新区、虎丘区	有限责任公司
5	常熟市城市经营投资有限公司	二级	常熟市	国有
6	苏州恒力置业有限公司	二级	吴江区	有限责任公司
7	昆山万科房地产有限公司	暂定二级	昆山市	有限责任公司
8	昆山蔚洲房产开发有限公司	二级	昆山市	有限责任公司
9	苏州市保障性住房建设有限公司	二级	姑苏区	有限责任公司
10	苏州高龙房产发展有限公司	暂定二级	工业园区	中外合资经营

TOP 10 OF REAL ESTATE DEVELOPMENT ENTERPRISES THAT BEST COMPLETED THE FOUR MAJOR INDICATORS (2018)

序 号 No.	开发企业名称 Name of Development Enterprises	资质等级 Grouped by Grade	地 区 Region	经济类型 Ownership
三、房屋竣工面积	**Floor Space of Buildings Completed**			
1	常熟市城市经营投资有限公司	二 级	常熟市	国 有
2	张家港市悦丰投资开发建设有限公司	二 级	张家港市	有限责任公司
3	苏州城投地产发展有限公司	二 级	姑苏区	有限责任公司
4	苏州晶汇置业有限公司	暂定二级	工业园区	与港澳台商合资经营
5	昆山蔚洲房产开发有限公司	二 级	昆山市	有限责任公司
6	昆山万达广场投资有限公司	暂定二级	昆山市	有限责任公司
7	昆山美吉特置业有限公司	暂定二级	昆山市	有限责任公司
8	昆山中南世纪城房地产发展有限公司	暂定二级	昆山市	有限责任公司
9	昆山琨华投资发展有限公司	二 级	昆山市	有限责任公司
10	苏州高新新吴置地有限公司	暂定二级	吴江区	有限责任公司
四、商品房销售面积	**Floor Space of Housing Sold**			
1	苏州市惠民置业投资有限公司	暂定二级	吴中区	有限责任公司
2	张家港市祥盛房地产开发有限公司	暂定二级	张家港市	有限责任公司
3	昆山华地房地产有限公司	暂定二级	昆山市	有限责任公司
4	张家港建丰房地产开发有限公司	暂定二级	张家港市	有限责任公司
5	昆山市阳澄湖房产有限责任公司	二 级	昆山市	有限责任公司
6	张家港城南碧桂园房地产开发有限公司	暂定二级	张家港市	有限责任公司
7	苏州德尔太湖湾地产有限公司	暂定二级	吴中区	有限责任公司
8	苏州聿盛房地产开发有限公司	暂定二级	相城区	有限责任公司
9	苏州华丽家族置业投资有限公司	二 级	吴中区	有限责任公司
10	常熟市城市经营投资有限公司	二 级	常熟市	国 有

表11-15

建成投产的主要建设项目一览 (2018年)
KEY CONSTRUCTION PROJECTS COMPLETED (2018)

项目名称 Name of Projects	开工年月 Start of Construction	全部建成投产年月 Date of Projects Completed and Put into Use	新增生产能力或效益 Newly Increased Production Capacity and Benefit	累计投资总额(万元) Total Increased (10 000 yuan)
姑苏区费家村保障房	2014.09	2018.40	总建筑面积约21.7万平米，共15幢，1624套	110 000
苏州高新区有轨电车二号线工程	2015.03	2018.08	线路全长18.463千米(主线长17.036,支线1.427)；共设置13座站点	260 720
苏州高新区喜年广场	2013.11	2018.12	项目占地面积7.3万平方米，建筑面积22.14万平方米	237 263
苏州石湖景区上方山环境整治与景观提升工程南区项目	2014.01	2018.12	动物展示区3.05万平方米，景观绿化48.6万平方米，规划范围为83.4公顷	130 278
苏州高新区天都大厦	2008.06	2018.12	项目占地面积11.28万平方米，建筑面积33.24万平方米，其办公楼14.35万平方米	114 722
苏州国巨电子AC系列精密片式电阻器及超微型片式陶瓷积电容技改项目	2018.01	2018.12	年产1000亿只AC系列精密片式电阻器及1000亿只超微型片式陶瓷积体电容器	80 949
苏州市吴中区舟山文化创意产业园一期	2015.01	2018.12	建成总占地面积7.43万平方米，建筑面积13.5万平方米	121 000
苏州溪江实业发展有限公司商务金融及酒店用房项目	2014.01	2018.12	总建筑面积12万平米，用地面积2.3万平方米	115 500
苏州市吴中区东太湖路改造	2012.05	2018.03	道路改造全长5400米，新建、改建桥梁5座，道路下穿3处，种植绿化25万平方米	75 000
苏州嘉盛集团年产100万平方米混凝土预制构件项目	2017.02	2018.12	总建筑面积5万平方米，预计年产混凝土预制构件100万平方米	24 500
苏州市吴中度假区2.5产业园项目	2015.05	2018.12	总建筑总占地面积6.53万平方米，建筑面积8.7万平方米	24 400
苏州市相城区朱巷安置小区三期	2013.04	2018.12	总建筑面积67.74万平方米	279 753
苏州市相城区汇萃商业广场	2014.07	2018.06	总建筑面积16.55万平方米	112 143
苏州市相城区卡士酸奶新建年产6万吨发酵乳项目	2017.03	2018.06	年产6万吨发酵乳，总建筑面积5.8万平方米	80 000
苏州市相城区中惠铂尔曼酒店	2016.01	2018.12	总建筑面积18.88万平方米	79 890
苏州市相城区中翔元和市民广场	2013.05	2018.12	总建筑面积7.18万平方米	68 000
苏州市相城区黄桥中学扩建	2016.05	2018.01	总建筑面积3.8万平方米	19 050
苏州市相城区北桥中学扩建	2016.09	2018.04	总建筑面积4.7万平方米	15 000
苏州东方之门	2006.07	2018.06	总建筑面积约45万平方米	788 129
苏州奥林匹克体育中心	2014.04	2018.12	总建筑面积37.4万平方米	573 764
苏州丰隆城市中心	2013.10	2018.04	总建筑面积约41万平方米	374 471
苏州华谊兄弟电影世界	2015.11	2018.07	总建筑面积12.6万平方米，包含五大电影主题区域	220 000
礼来苏州制药扩建厂房	2014.01	2018.10	扩建建筑面积2.8万平方米，新增1条胰岛素灌装生产线	206 260
中国工商银行苏州分行办公楼	2011.05	2018.12	建筑面积4.1万平方米	63 408
苏州园区时尚舞台酒店商业综合项目	2015.04	2018.08	总建筑面积约11万平方米	60 335

表11-15 续表 Continued

项目名称 Name of Projects	开工年月 Start of Construction	全部建成投产年月 Date of Projects Completed and Put into Use	新增生产能力或效益 Newly Increased Production Capacity and Benefit	累计投资总额(万元) Total Increased (10 000 yuan)
吴江经济技术开发区人民医院新建项目	2013.11	2018.12	占地面积117亩，总建筑面积16.5万平方米，床位1000张	132 360
敏华家具总部（吴江）有限公司普通住宅及商业项目	2015.04	2018.12	占地61.5亩，建筑面积22万平方米	98 093
江苏亨通光导新材料有限公司年产光纤预制棒800吨项目	2017.01	2018.03	新增建筑面积7.8万平方米，年产800吨光棒的能力	86 153
吴江佳力高纤有限公司高性能差别化聚酯纤维生主线建设项目	2017.01	2018.12	年产10万吨高性能差别化聚酯纤维	75 268
苏州德亚纺织有限公司功能性涤纶低弹丝项目	2017.03	2018.12	年产15万吨功能性涤纶低弹丝	66 286
吴江易湖仓储项目	2016.04	2018.12	仓储用房总建筑面积9.6万平方米	45 555
常熟市奇瑞捷豹路虎汽车有限公司年产7万辆乘用车改扩建项目	2016.06	2018.12	年产7万辆乘用车	614 912
常熟市城市经营投资有限公司藕渠家园安置房项目	2014.09	2018.05	总建筑面积为30.94万平方米	188 132
常熟市乐歌仓储（常熟）有限公司新建仓储项目	2016.09	2018.11	总建筑面积7.0万平方米	78 377
常熟市常熟宝鸿投资发展有限公司宝鸿商业广场项目	2014.10	2018.12	总建筑面积12.84万平方米	68 000
常熟市世名化工科技有限公司年产5万吨纳米级水性色浆和溶剂色浆项目	2013.12	2018.06	年产5万吨纳米级水性色浆和溶剂色浆	35 752
江苏沙钢集团有限公司冷轧硅钢加工项目	2018.01	2018.09	年加工冷轧硅钢48万吨，新建生产用房5.2万平方米	110 000
张家港利柏特年产840套模撬块设备等项目	2016.06	2018.01	年产840套模撬块设备、7000吨压力容器	70 050
张家港市霍尼韦尔扩建年产4000吨催化剂项目	2016.05	2018.01	年产4000吨烯烃催化剂并副产磷酸钙4000吨等	58 959
张家港通用汽车城建设项目	2017.06	2018.11	建造展厅、仓储、维修车间等建筑面积6万平方米	33 482
江苏华昌（集团）有限公司扩建年产3万吨新戊二醇等产品及配套设施技术项目	2017.01	2018.12	年产3万吨新戊二醇等产品	29 545
友达光电(昆山)有限公司生产设备购置项目	2015.05	2018.12	月加工第6代低温多晶硅薄膜晶体管液晶显示面板6万片	1 105 016
昆山之奇美材料科技有限公司一期生产厂房门卫食堂和化学品仓库等项目	2015.07	2018.12	年产偏光板（膜）1512万米、光学功能膜84万米、光学补偿膜84万米	155 668
昆山市张浦彩印厂超薄膜型金属化合金材料项目	2013.01	2018.12	年产超薄型金属化合金材料12万吨	106 600
世硕电子（昆山）有限公司智能手机制造项目	2017.03	2018.01	年产智能型手机2880万台	78 419
昆山协鑫蓝天天然气分布式能源项目建设	2016.12	2018.12	年发电量7.734亿千万时，年供热量358.475万吉焦	74 484
舍弗勒（中国）有限公司2018年设备工程一期	2018.01	2018.07	引进ZHEB装配线等进口设备193台	54 106
太仓市印溪商务大厦	2015.02	2018.12	总建筑面积约3.8万平方米	35 495
江苏宇兆能源科技有限公司建设太阳能晶体硅电池及电池组件项目	2011.01	2018.11	建设太阳能晶体硅光伏电池生产线8条及电池组件生产线50条	30 005

主 要 统 计 指 标 解 释

全社会固定资产投资 是以货币形式表现的在一定时期内全社会建造和购置固定资产的工作量以及与此有关的费用的总称。该指标是反映固定资产投资规模、结构和发展速度的综合性指标,又是观察工程进度和考核投资效果的重要依据。全社会固定资产投资按登记注册类型可分为国有、集体、个体、联营、股份制、外商、港澳台商、其他等，由建设项目投资和房地产开发投资两部分组成。

建设项目投资 指各种登记注册类型的企业、事业、行政单位及个体户进行的计划总投资(或实际需要总投资)500万元及500万元以上的建设项目投资。

房地产开发投资 指各种登记注册类型的房地产开发公司、商品房建设公司及其他房地产开发法人单位和附属于其他法人单位实际从事房地产开发或经营活动的单位统一开发的包括统代建、拆迁还建的住宅、厂房、仓库、饭店、宾馆、度假村、写字楼、办公楼等房屋建筑物和配套的服务设施，土地开发工程（如道路、给水、排水、供电、供热、通讯、平整场地等基础设施工程）的投资；不包括单纯的土地交易活动。

固定资产投资的资金来源 根据固定资产投资的资金来源不同，分为国家预算内资金、国内贷款、利用外资、自筹资金和其他资金。

(1)国家预算内资金：分为财政拨款和财政安排的贷款两部分。包括中央财政的基本建设基金(分经营性基金和非经营性基金两部分)、专项支出(如煤代油专项等)、收回再贷、贴息资金，财政安排的挖潜改造和新产品试制支出、城建支出、商业部门简易建筑支出、不发达地区发展基金等资金中用于固定资产投资的资金；地方财政中由国家统筹安排的资金等。

(2)国内贷款：指报告期固定资产投资单位向银行及非银行金融机构借入的用于固定资产投资的各种国内借款，包括银行利用自有资金及吸收的存款发放的贷款、上级主管部门拨入的国内贷款、国家专项贷款、地方财政专项资金安排的贷款、国内储备贷款、周转贷款等。

(3)利用外资：指报告期收到的用于固定资产建造和购置的国外资金(包括设备、材料、技术在内)。包括对外借款(外国政府、国际金融组织贷款、出口信贷、外国银行商业贷款、对外发行债券和股票)、外商直接投资及外商其他投资。不包括我国自有外汇资金(国家外汇、地方外汇、留成外汇、调剂外汇和中国银行自有资金发行的外汇贷款等)。计算利用外资时，需要折算成人民币，折算中所使用的外汇汇率按现汇计算，即按使用外汇时的汇率计算。

(4)自筹资金：指固定资产投资单位报告期收到的，由各地区、各部门及企、事业单位筹集用于固定资产投资的预算外资金，包括中央各部门、各级地方和企、事业单位的自筹资金。

(5)其他资金：指在报告期收到的除以上各种资金之外其他用于固定资产投资的资金，包括企业或金融机构通过发行各种债券筹集到的资金、群众集资、个人资金、无偿捐赠的资金及其他单位拨入的资金等。

固定资产投资按国民经济行业分 根据建设项目建成投产后的主要产品或主要用途及社会经济活动性质来确定国民经济行业。一般情况下，一个建设项目或一个企业、事业单位只能属于一种国民经济行业。

固定资产投资按隶属关系分 是按建设单位或企业、事业、行政单位的主管上级机关确定的。

（1）中央：是指中共中央、人大常委会和国务院各部、委、局、总公司以及直属机构直接领导的建设项目和企业、事业、行政单位。这些单位的固定资产投资计划由国务院各部门直接编制和下达，建设中所需物资、主要设备以及建设中的问题都由中央有关部门安排和解决。

（2）地方：是由省（自治区、直辖市）、地区（州、盟、省辖市）、县（旗、县级市）三级政府及业务主管部门直接领导和管理的建设项目、企业、事业、行政单位。地方项目还包括不隶属以上各级政府及主管部门的建设项目和企业、事业单位，如外商投资企业和无主管部门的企业等。

固定资产投资按建设性质分 根据整个建设项目情况来确定。建设项目的性质一般分为新建、扩建、改建和技术改造、迁建、恢复。房地产开发单位、农村投资、城镇工矿区私人建房投资不划分建设性质。

(1)新建：一般指从无到有开始建设的企业、事业和行政单位或建设项目。现有企业、事业、行政单位一般不属于新建。但如有的单位原有基础很小，经过建设后新增的固定资产价值超过该企、事业、行政单位原有固定资产价值(原值)三倍以上的也应作为新建。

(2)扩建：指在厂内或其他地点，为扩大原有产品的生产能力(或效益)或增加新的产品生产能力，而增建主要的生产车间(或主要工程)、分厂、独立的生产线。行政、事业单位在原单位增建业务用房(如学校增建教学用房、医院增建门诊部、病房等)也作为扩建。

现有企、事业单位为扩大原有主要产品生产能力或增加新的产品生产能力，增建一个或几个主要生产车间(或主要工程)、分厂，同时进行一些更新改造工程的，也应作为扩建。

(3)改建和技术改造：指现有企业、事业单位，对原有设施进行技术改造或更新(包括相应配套的辅助性生产、生活福利设施) 的建设项目。现有企业、事业单位为适应市场变化的需要，而改变企业的主要产品种类(如军工企业转产民用品等) 的建设项目，应作为改建。原有产品生产作业线由于各工序(车间)之间能力不平衡，为填平补齐充分发挥原有生产能力而增建不增加本企业主要产品设计能力的车间，也应作为改建。技术改造是指企业、事业单位在现有基础上，用先进的技术代替落后的技术，用先进的工艺和装备代替落后的工艺和装备，以改变企业落后的技术经济面貌，实现以内涵为主的扩大再生产，达到提高产品质量、促进产品更新换代、节约能源、降低消耗、扩大生产规模、全面提高社会经济效益的目的。技术改造具体包括以下内容：机器设备和工具的更新改造；生产工艺改革、节约能源和原材料的改造；厂房建筑和公共设施的改造；劳动条件和生产环境的改造等。

固定资产投资按构成分 固定资产投资活动按其工作内容和实现方式分为建筑安装工程，设备、工具、器具购置，其他费用三个部分。

(1)建筑安装工程(建筑安装工作量)：指各种房屋、建筑物的建造工程和各种设备、装置的安装工程。包括各种房屋建造工程；各种用途设备基础和各种工业窑炉的砌筑工程及金属结构工程；为施工而进行的各种准备工作和临时工程以及完工后的清理工作等；铁路、道路的铺设，矿井的开凿及石油管道的架设等；水利工程；防空地下建筑等特殊工程；列入房屋工程预算内的暖气、卫生、通风、照明、煤气等设备的价值及装设油饰工程；列入建筑工程预算内的各种管道(蒸汽、压缩空气、石油、给排水等管道)、电力、电讯电缆导线等的敷设工程；以及各种机械设备的安装工程；为测定安装工程质量，对设备进行的试运工作；房地产开发单位进行的商品房屋开发建设工程、土地开发工程。

在安装工程中，不包括被安装设备本身的价值。

(2)设备、工具、器具购置：指建设单位或企、事业单位购置或自制的，达到固定资产标准的设备、工具、器具的价值。新建单位及扩建单位的新建车间，按照设计或计划要求购置或自制的全部设备、工具、器具，不论是否达到固定资产标准均计入“设备、工具、器具购置”中。

(3)其他费用：指在固定资产建造和购置过程中发生的，除上述几项内容以外的各种应分摊计入固定资产的费用。

施工项目 指报告期内进行过建筑或安装施工活动的项目。凡是报告期内施过工的建设项目，不论施工时间长短，均作为施工项目统计。施工项目个数可以反映一定时期固定资产投资的实际规模，与同期全部建成投产项目个数相比，可以从建设速度的角度反映固定资产投资的效果。根据建设项目施工活动的不同性质，施工项目又分为：本年正式施工项目、本年收尾项目和以前年度全部停缓建项目。

全部建成投产项目 工业项目指设计文件规定形成生产能力的主体工程及其相应配套的辅助设施全部建成，经负荷试运转，证明具备生产设计规定合格产品的条件，并经过验收鉴定合格或达到竣工验收标准，与生产性工程配套的生活福利设施可以满足近期正常生产的需要，正式移交生产的建设项目。非工业项目指设计文件规定的主体工程和相应的配套工程全部建成，能够发挥设计规定的全部效益，经验收鉴定合格或达到竣工验收标准，正式移交使用的建设项目。

新增生产能力(或工程效益) 指通过固定资产投资活动而增加的设计能力(或工程效益)，该指标是以实物形态表现的反映固定资产投资成果的指标，也是考核投资经济效果的重要依据之一。

新增生产能力(或工程效益)一般有以下几种表现形式：

(1)用产品数量表示，以工程在单位时间内(一般是一年)所能生产的产品数量(即年产量)表示。如原煤开采用万吨/年表示，化学农药用吨 / 年表示，拖拉机制造用台 / 年表示等。某些化工产品由于含量差别较大，按其设计含量计算折合量表示，如硫酸、纯碱、烧碱等。

(2)用单位时间内所能处理的原料数量表示，以工程每天(或小时)所能处理原料的数量表示。如机制糖工程日处理原料吨，食用植物油日处理原料吨，城市污水处理能力用万吨 / 日表示等。

(3)用新增加的主要设备的数量或容量表示，如新增棉布织机、丝织机等台数，毛纺锭等锭数，发电厂新增发电机组容量用千瓦表示等。

(4)用建筑物容积、容量、面积、长度表示，是非工业项目或工程新增效益的一种表现形式。如铁路投产里程、新建公路、水库容量、粮食仓库、学校学生席位、医院病床、有效灌溉面积等。

根据工程的特点，有时需要用两种或两种以上的复合计量单位表示新增生产能力(或工程效益)，如新增内燃机生产能力同时用年产台数、千瓦数表示等。

为了规范新增生产能力(或工程效益)的名称和计算单位，国家统计局制订了《新增生产能力(或工程效益)目录及代码》。各固定资产投资单位在统计新增生产能力(或工程效益)时，必须按目录中规定的名称、计量单位和代码填报。

房屋建筑面积 指房屋建筑物勒脚以上外墙外围的水平截面面积，包括房屋建筑物的有效面积和结构面积。该指标是从实物形态上反映建设规模和建设成果的重要指标之一，也是检查工程形象进度、计算工程造价、分析投资效果、研究施工任务和建筑材料之间平衡情况的重要依据。

住宅建筑面积 指施工和竣工房屋建筑面积中供居住用的房屋建筑面积。

施工面积 指报告期内施工的全部房屋建筑面积。包括本期新开工的面积和上期开工跨入本期继续施工的房屋面积，以及上期已停建在本期恢复施工的房屋面积。本期竣工和本期施工后又停缓建的房屋，其建筑面积仍计入本期房屋施工面积中。

竣工面积 指在报告期内房屋建筑按照设计要求已经全部完工，达到住人和使用条件，经验收鉴定合格(或达到竣工验收标准)，正式移交使用单位的各栋房屋建筑面积的总和。

房屋建筑面积竣工率 指一定时期内房屋竣工面积占同期房屋施工面积的比率。

新增固定资产 指报告期内已经完成建造和购置过程，并已交付生产或使用单位的固定资产价值。该指标是表示固定资产投资成果的价值指标，也是反映建设进度，计算固定资产投资效果的重要指标。

项目建成投产率 指一定时期内全部建成投产项目个数与同期施工项目个数的比率。该指标是从建设单位建设速度的角度反映投资效果的指标。

固定资产交付使用率 指一定时期新增固定资产与同期完成投资额的比率。该指标是反映固定资产动用速度，衡量建设过程中宏观投资效果的综合指标。由于新增固定资产是较长时期内形成的结果，而投资额则是当年完成的，因此，该指标一般适宜于反映较长时期内固定资产的动用情况。

商品房销售面积 指报告期内出售商品房屋的合同总面积(即双方签署的正式买卖合同中所确定的建筑面积)。由现房销售建筑面积和期房销售建筑面积两部分组成。

商品房销售额 指报告期内出售商品房屋的合同总价款(即双方签署的正式买卖合同中所确定的合同总价)。该指标与商品房销售面积同口径，由现房销售额和期房销售额两部分组成。

EXPLANATORY NOTES ON MAIN STATISTICAL INDICATORS

Total Investment in Fixed Assets in the Whole Country refers to the volume of activities in construction and purchases of fixed assets of the whole country and related fees, expressed in monetary terms during the reference period. It is a comprehensive indicator which shows the size, structure and growth of the investment in fixed assets, providing a basis for observing the progress of construction projects and evaluating results of investment. Total investment in fixed assets in the whole country includes, by type of ownership, the investment by State-owned units, collective-owned units, individuals, joint ownership units, share-holding units, as well as investments by entrepreneurs from foreign countries and from Hong Kong, Macao and Taiwan, and by other units, by investment in construction projects and investment in real estate development two parts.

Investment in Construction Projects refers to construction projects involving a total planned (or required) investment of 5 million yuan and over by enterprises of various types of ownership, institutions, administrative units and individuals in urban areas.

Investment in Real Estate Development refers to investment by real estate development companies, commercialized buildings construction companies and other real estate development units of various types of ownership in the construction of buildings, such as residential buildings, factory buildings, warehouses, hotels, guesthouses, holiday villages, office buildings, and the complementary service facilities and land development projects, such as roads, water supply, water drainage, power supply, heating supply, telecommunications, land leveling and other infrastructural projects. It does not include activities in pure land transactions.

Sources of Funds for Investment in Fixed Assets are categorized as funds from the State budget, domestic loans, foreign investment, self-raised funds, and others, depending on the sources of investment.

(1) Fund from the State budget consists of budgetary appropriation and loans from the State budget. More specifically, it includes, from the budget of the central government, capital construction fund (operation fund and non-operational fund), special expenses (e.g. expenses on substituting petroleum with coal), loans from repayment, discount fund, expenses on innovation and trial production of new products, expenses on urban construction, expenses on temporary construction from business departments, development fund for less developed areas, as well as local budgetary fund transferred from the central budget.

(2) Domestic loans refer to loans of various forms borrowed by investing units from banks and non-bank financial institutions during the reference period for the purpose of investment in fixed assets, including loans issued by banks from their self-owned funds and deposit, loans appropriated by higher authorities, special loans by government, loans arranged by local government from special funds, domestic reserve loan, and working loan.

(3) Foreign investment refers to foreign funds received during the reference period for the construction and purchase of investment in fixed assets (covering equipment, materials and technology), including foreign borrowings (loans from foreign governments and international financial institutions, export credit, commercial loans from foreign banks, issue of bonds and stocks overseas), foreign direct investment and other foreign investments. Excluded from this category is capital in foreign exchanges owned by China (foreign exchanges owned by the central and local governments, foreign exchanges retained by enterprises, foreign exchanges by enterprises through the regulating mechanism, loans in foreign exchanges issued by the Bank of China with its own fund, etc.). In calculating the utilization of foreign capital, foreign currencies are converted into Chinese Renminbi applying the current exchange rate when the foreign capitals are actually used.

(4) Self-raised funds refer to extra-budgetary funds for investment in fixed assets received during the reference period by investing units from central government ministries, local governments, enterprises and institutions, including their self-raised funds.

(5) Others refer to funds for investment in fixed assets received from sources other than those listed above, including capital raised through issuing bonds by enterprises or financial institutions, funds raised from individuals and through donations, and funds transferred from other units.

Investment in Fixed Assets by Sector The classification of construction projects by sector is determined by the major products or the purpose of the projects when they are put into production or use, and by the nature of their social economic activities. In general, one project or one enterprise or institution can only be classified into one sector.

Investment in Fixed Assets by Jurisdiction of Management refers to the classification of investment by the competent authorities under which investment is made by construction units, enterprises, institutions or administrative units.

(1) Central investment refers to the investment in projects or by enterprises, institutions or administrative units which are under the direct leadership and management of the State Council and of the national commissions, ministries, agencies and State-owned large corporations. Various ministries and departments of the State Council prepare and implement plans for investment in fixed assets by those departments, and arrange and ensure the supply of materials and key equipment required for the projects.

(2) Local investment refers to the investment in projects or by enterprises, institutions or administrative units which are under the direct leadership and management of departments under the provincial, prefecture and county governments. Also included are projects by foreign-invested enterprises and enterprises without competent managing authorities.

Investment in Fixed Assets by Type of Construction Construction projects in general can be classified, by the type of construction, into new construction, expansion, reconstruction and technical transformation, moving and restoration. However, investment by type of construction is not applied to investment by real-estate development units, investment in rural areas and private investment in housing construction in urban areas and in industrial and mining areas.

(1) New construction in general refers to construction projects, which start from scratch, of enterprises, institutions, administrative agencies. Construction in existing enterprises, institutions or agencies is generally not considered as new construction. In case the size of the existing unit is quite small, and the value of newly added fixed assets is more than three times of the original value, the expansion will be considered as new construction.

(2) Expansion refers to construction of new major production workshop, branch factory or independent production line within a factory or in other locations, for the purpose of increasing the production capacity (or improving efficiency) or adding new production capacity. Newly constructed accommodation for the operation of institutions and administrative organizations (such as newly constructed buildings for teaching in schools, buildings for clinics or wards in hospitals, etc.) are also classified as expansion.

Also included in expansion are investments by existing enterprises or institutions in building major production line(s) or branch factory(ies) along with some work on innovation, for the purpose of expanding the production capacity of original products or producing new products.

(3) Reconstruction and technical transformation refers to construction projects by existing enterprises or institutions in innovation or technical transformation of the old facilities (including auxiliary production equipment and welfare facilities). Also considered as reconstruction is the construction of new workshops by the existing enterprises or institutions to change the variety of products to meet the market demand (such as the production of civil products by defence industries), or to bring the designed production capacity into full play through a more balanced production process on production lines. Technical transformation refers to replacement of old technology or equipment by new technology or equipment, in order to expand the reproduction through improvement of technology contents in production, to improve product quality, to promote new products, to save energy, to reduce consumption, to expand the production scale and to improve overall social-economic efficiency. Contents of technical transformation include: updating of machinery, equipment and tools; reforming production process by using energy or materials saving technology; construction of factory workshops and transformation of public facilities; improvement of working conditions and environment, etc.

Investment in Fixed Assets by Structure By their contents and the mode of implementation, investment activities are classified into 3 categories, i.e. construction and installation, purchase of equipment and instrument, and other expenses.

(1) Construction and installation (work volume of construction and installation) refers to the construction of houses and buildings and the installation of various kinds of equipment and instruments. They include construction of houses; equipment foundations, industrial kilns and stoves, and metal structure work; preparation works and temporary works for project construction, and clearing up works post project construction; pavement of railways and roads, drilling of mines and putting up of oil pipes; construction of water conservancy; construction of underground air-raid shelters and construction of other special projects; value of equipment for heating, sanitation, ventilation, lighting, gas, painting, etc. that are covered by the budget of housing projects; laying out of various pipelines (for steam, compressed air, petroleum, tap water and sewage) and wiring and cabling for electric power and for communications; installation of various machinery and equipment; testing operation for pre-testing the quality of installation projects, and land and other development work conducted by real estate developers for commercialized housing. The value of equipment installed is itself not included in the value of installation projects.

(2) Purchase of equipment and instruments refers to the total value of equipment, tools, and instruments purchased or self-produced which come up to the cut-off point for fixed assets by the construction units or investing enterprises or institutions. Equipment, tools and instruments purchased or self-produced for new workshops by newly established or expanded units are categorized as "purchase of equipment and instruments" no matter whether they come up to the cut-off point for fixed assets.

(3) Other expenses refer to expenses arising during the construction or purchase of fixed assets other than those mentioned

above.

Projects under Construction refer to projects with construction and installation activities undertaken in the reference period. All projects that have construction activities undertaken during the reference period are reported as projects under construction irrespective of the length of construction work. The number of projects under construction can reflect the actual size of investment in fixed assets during a given period, and when compared with the number of projects completed and put into use during the same period, it demonstrates the results of investment in fixed assets from the angle of the speed of the construction. Depending on the nature of construction activities, projects under construction can also be classified into projects beginning construction in current year, winding-up projects in current year and stopped or suspended projects in previous years (with resumption of work in current year).

Projects Completed and Put into Use Industrial projects refer to the major projects and anxilliary facilities having been completed in accordance with the design documents, resulting in forming production capacity and having checked and accepted after relevant tests, while the living and welfare facilities having been completed and being capable of ensuring normal production. Non-industrial projects refer to the major projects and anxilliary facilities which have been completed in accordance with the design documents ; have been checked, accepted after relevant examination; and have been formally delivered for use.

Newly Increased Production Capacity (or Project Efficiency) refers to the increase in design capacity (or project efficiency) through investment in fixed assets, which reflects the accomplishment of investment in fixed assets in physical form and serves as an important basis for evaluating the economic efficiency of investment.

The newly increased production capacity (project efficiency) are usually expressed in one of the following forms:

(1) volume of output of products, i.e. the volume of output that the project can produce during a given period (usually a year). For instance, the capacity in coal mining is expressed in 10,000 tons/year, the capacity in producing chemical pesticides expressed in ton/year, the capacity in producing tractors in tractor/year, etc. For some chemical products where the effective contents differ significantly, the production capacity is expressed as the designed effective content equivalent, such as in the case of sulphuric acid, soda ash, caustic soda, etc;

(2) volume of raw materials processed per unit of time, i.e. the volume of raw materials that could be processed by the project per day (or per hour), such as tons of materials processed per day by a sugar refining project or edible vegetable oil project, or tons of urban sewage processed per day, etc;

(3) number or capacity of major equipment increased, such as number of cotton or silk looms increased, wool spindles increased, or capacity (in kilowatts) of power generators increased, etc;

(4) physical measures (volume, capacity, area, and length) of construction, which is typical for non-industrial projects, for instance, the length of railways put into operation, the length of highways, the capacity of reservoirs, the capacity of warehouses, the floor space of housing projects, capacity for new students in schools or beds in hospitals, areas under new irrigation project, etc.

The special features of projects may sometimes call for the combined use of two or more measurements to reflect the increase in production capacity (or project efficiency); for instance, the new capacity for the production of internal combustion engines is expressed in sets per year and kilowatts per year simultaneously.

To standardize the nomenclature and unit of measurement for newly increased production capacity (or project efficiency), the National Bureau of Statistics has developed the *Nomenclature and Codes for New Production Capacity (Project Efficiency)*. All reporting units with investment activities are required to follow these two nomenclatures in reporting statistics on new production capacity (project efficiency).

Floor Space of Buildings under Construction refers to the total floor space of the horizontal section of outer walls above the plinth of the building, including the effective area and the area occupied by the structure. This indicator is one of the important indicators in physical terms to reflect the scale and accomplishment of the construction industry and also an important basis for monitoring the progress, calculating the cost, analyzing the efficiency and studying the supply of building materials in relation to the construction projects.

Floor Space of Residential Buildings refers to the floor space of the residential buildings among the total space of buildings under construction or completed.

Floor Space under Construction refers to total floor space of all buildings under construction during the reference period, including floor space of newly started buildings during the reference period, floor space of construction extended from the previous period to the current period, and floor space of construction suspended during the previous period and resumed in the current period. Floor space of construction completed in the current period, and floor space of construction started and then suspended in the current period are also included in the floor space under construction of the current year.

Floor Space Completed refers to the floor space of all buildings completed in the reference period, which have been appraised and accepted (or come up to the designed standards) and have been transferred to owner units.

Completion Rate of Floor Space of Buildings refers to the ratio of the floor space of buildings completed in a certain period of time to the floor space of buildings under construction in the same period.

Newly Increased Fixed Assets refer to the newly increased value of fixed assets, constructed or purchased, that have been transferred to the investors. This is an indicator that demonstrates the results of investment in fixed assets in monetary terms, and an important indicator to reflect the speed of construction and to calculate the efficiency of investment.

Rate of Construction Projects Completed and Put into Use refers to the ratio of the number of construction projects completed and put into use in a certain period of time to the number of projects under construction in the same period. This reflects the investment efficiency from the perspective of the speed of projects construction.

Rate of Projects of Fixed Assets Completed and Put into Operation refers to the ratio of the newly increased fixed assets to the total investment made in the same period. This is a comprehensive indicator reflecting the speed of the employment of fixed assets and the investment efficiency at the macro-level. As the newly increase fixed assets is the result of a long period while the investment is completed in the current year, this indicator is expected to be used to reflect the employment of fixed assets over a long period of time.

Area of Commercialized Housing Sold refers to total contracted area of commercialized housing (i.e. area of floor space as designated in the formal contracts signed by both sides) during the reference time. It constitutes floor space of completed housing and floor space of future housing.

Value of Commercialized Housing Sold refers to the total contracted value (i.e. value of sales/purchase for selling/purchase of commercialized housing as designated in the contract signed by both sides) during the reference time. This indicator has the same coverage as the area of commercialized housing sold, which constitutes floor space of completed housing and floor space of housing yet to be completed.

十二、企业调查

CHAPTER 12
ENTERPRISES SURVEY

12 企业调查
ENTERPRISES SURVEY

主要统计指标
MAJOR STATISTICAL INDICATORS

2018年末总部经济企业数	Number of Corporate Headquarters	312	个	unit
2018年总部经济企业营业收入	Business Income of Corporate Headquarters	16 875.72	亿元	100 million yuan
比上年增长	Increase Over Last Year	9.3	%	
2018年总部经济企业利润总额	Total Profits of Corporate Headquarters	1 184.08	亿元	100 million yuan
比上年增长	Increase Over Last Year	6.1	%	
2018年末总部企业数	Number of Corporate Headquarters	164	个	unit
2018年总部企业营业收入	Business Income of Corporate Headquarters	12 561.66	亿元	100 million yuan
2018年总部企业利润总额	Total Profits of Corporate Headquarters	827.53	亿元	100 million yuan
2018年末上市公司数	Number of Listing Corporation	135	个	unit
2018年上市公司营业收入	Business Income of Listing Corporation	4 881.37	亿元	100 million yuan
2018年上市公司利润总额	Total Profits of Listing Corporation	301.42	亿元	100 million yuan
2018年跨国公司地区性总部和功能性机构数	The number of regional headquarters and functional agencies of multinational corporations	115	个	unit
2018年跨国公司地区性总部和功能性机构营业收入	The operating income of regional headquarters and functional agencies of multinational corporations	4 064.04	亿元	100 million yuan
2018年跨国公司地区性总部和功能性机构利润总额	The total profit of regional headquarters and functional agencies of multinational corporations	331.95	亿元	100 million yuan

表12-1

总部经济主要经济指标 (2018年)

单位：万元

项　　目	Item	单位数 (个) Number of Units (unit)	年末资产总计 Total Assets at the End of Year
总部经济	**Corporate Headquarters**	**312**	**256 603 842**
按企业类型分	**Classified by Enterprise Type**		
# 总部企业	Corporate Headquarters	164	195 050 907
# 上市公司	Listing Corporation	135	114 643 815
# 跨国公司地区性总部和功能性机构	Regional Headquarters and Functional Agencies of Multinational Corporations	115	36 580 171
# 地标性企业	Landmark Enterprises	47	88 588 872
按母公司控股情况分	**Classified by Number Shares Held by Parent Companies**		
国有控股	Stately Majority Share Holding	17	48 621 925
集体控股	Collectively Majority Share Holding	8	21 975 040
私人控股	Privately Majority Share Holding	114	128 402 503
港澳台商控股	Majority Share Holding by Investors from Hong Kong, Macau and Taiwan	51	17 860 431
外商控股	Majority Share Holding by Foreign Investors	103	31 700 938
其　他	Others	19	8 043 005
按总部经济主营行业分	**Classified by Main Field of Operation**		
工　业	Industry	184	118 142 506
建筑业	Construction	10	3 216 803
批发和零售业	Wholesale and Retail Sale Trades	29	25 869 125
交通运输、仓储和邮政业	Transportation, Logistics and Postal	11	1 830 499
住宿和餐饮业	Accommodation and Catering Services	1	71 309
信息传输、软件和信息技术服务业	Information Transmission, Software and Information Technology Services	16	2 795 557
金融业	Financial Industries	13	83 829 260
房地产业	Real Estate	3	64 618
租赁和商务服务业	Leasing and Business Services	25	16 148 081
科学研究和技术服务业	Scientific Research and Technical Services	20	4 636 084

MAIN ECONOMIC INDICATORS ON CORPORATE HEADQUARTERS(2018)

(10 000 yuan)

流动资产合计 Circulating Funds	#存 货 Inventory	#应收票据及应收账款 Bills Receivable and Accounts Receivable	年末负债总计 Total Liabilities at the End of Year	银行借款 Bank Loans	所有者权益合计 Total Creditors Equity	营业收入 Business Revenue
124 079 725	**26 903 131**	**29 793 888**	**175 656 403**	**24 706 622**	**80 947 439**	**168 757 214**
92 393 509	19 982 152	21 263 100	139 365 688	17 845 417	55 685 219	125 616 618
57 351 234	14 791 763	13 484 073	77 880 017	8 754 195	36 763 798	48 813 706
23 176 364	4 424 456	7 575 245	20 319 584	3 426 312	16 260 587	40 640 375
46 805 103	10 455 858	12 726 113	52 581 929	11 794 705	36 006 943	82 917 467
20 249 487	1 315 529	2 575 349	40 352 620	1 436 071	8 269 305	13 596 841
7 590 042	1 992 802	269 133	18 317 920	216 584	3 657 120	2 607 412
59 311 352	16 949 326	15 256 146	86 100 241	17 004 905	42 302 262	92 603 225
12 338 679	2 029 944	3 357 138	9 654 814	1 991 988	8 205 617	19 147 218
19 620 293	4 004 315	7 074 374	17 136 210	3 451 987	14 564 728	34 451 426
4 969 872	611 215	1 261 748	4 094 598	605 087	3 948 407	6 351 092
64 207 705	13 540 469	18 263 255	66 006 059	16 737 948	52 136 447	103 036 077
2 725 463	615 946	1 148 624	2 370 150	386 616	846 653	3 601 931
16 773 779	3 496 243	5 138 726	17 097 491	5 222 318	8 771 634	41 244 595
1 004 279	136 151	378 057	969 396	276 136	861 103	1 963 693
23 684	1 869	1 074	35 691	4 500	35 618	246 048
1 922 397	111 592	580 805	1 454 149	145 670	1 341 408	4 085 082
24 068 603	5 745 357	139 259	75 379 115	640 945	8 450 145	2 992 035
58 347	265	10 503	24 983	1 000	39 635	134 586
11 114 681	3 130 645	3 450 709	9 896 167	911 378	6 251 914	9 195 656
2 180 787	124 594	682 876	2 423 202	380 111	2 212 882	2 257 511

表12-1 续表 1

单位：万元

项　　目	Item	出口交货值 Delivery Value for Export
总部经济	**Corporate Headquarters**	**21 286 281**
按企业类型分	**Classified by Enterprise Type**	
# 总部企业	Corporate Headquarters	15 000 644
# 上市公司	Listing Corporation	10 117 354
# 跨国公司地区性总部和功能性机构	Regional Headquarters and Functional Agencies of Multinational Corporations	8 570 617
# 地标性企业	Landmark Enterprises	10 432 861
按母公司控股情况分	**Classified by Number Shares Held by Parent Companies**	
国有控股	Stately Majority Share Holding	3 365 445
集体控股	Collectively Majority Share Holding	98 155
私人控股	Privately Majority Share Holding	7 049 507
港澳台商控股	Majority Share Holding by Investors from Hong Kong, Macau and Taiwan	3 437 454
外商控股	Majority Share Holding by Foreign Investors	6 830 988
其　他	Others	504 732
按总部经济主营行业分	**Classified by Main Field of Operation**	
工　业	Industry	16 391 391
建筑业	Construction	18 324
批发和零售业	Wholesale and Retail Sale Trades	3 943 043
交通运输、仓储和邮政业	Transportation, Logistics and Postal	–
住宿和餐饮业	Accommodation and Catering Services	–
信息传输、软件和信息技术服务业	Information Transmission, Software and Information Technology Services	61 672
金融业	Financial Industries	–
房地产业	Real Estate	–
租赁和商务服务业	Leasing and Business Services	871 851
科学研究和技术服务业	Scientific Research and Technical Services	–

Continued 1

(10 000 yuan)

营业成本 Business costs	销售费用 Cost Related With Sale	管理费用 Managerial Cost	财务费用 Financing Activities Cost	# 利息费用 Interest Expenses	税金及附加 Business Tax and Surcharges	投资收益 Investment Income
138 514 597	**7 135 190**	**6 601 760**	**1 947 086**	**1 930 931**	**865 460**	**1 980 206**
105 675 035	3 782 937	4 410 744	1 437 179	1 440 344	555 058	1 593 761
38 864 042	2 214 573	2 023 961	731 265	728 649	297 650	686 287
30 554 685	3 223 634	2 812 084	281 057	303 404	204 693	303 710
69 788 073	2 216 636	1 898 984	1 156 440	1 206 911	411 688	603 429
11 916 710	414 826	860 539	112 460	83 413	53 034	893 421
1 616 928	257 658	82 582	23 813	31 472	76 291	32 126
79 164 458	1 951 443	2 149 734	1 337 180	1 257 740	456 721	664 448
14 109 037	1 595 393	1 541 538	86 514	138 703	104 493	190 569
26 683 122	2 466 358	1 703 259	284 745	288 613	147 644	196 510
5 024 342	449 512	264 108	102 374	130 990	27 277	3 132
85 000 249	4 061 019	2 801 191	1 298 047	1 429 489	516 825	695 568
3 243 687	18 819	123 522	17 971	26 408	7 151	3 655
34 152 623	2 130 824	2 047 913	418 032	249 809	146 597	209 078
1 781 286	17 930	62 871	25 084	19 898	5 983	4 296
123 610	63 204	22 547	155	239	90	–
3 277 911	226 141	147 395	24 390	33 627	5 337	24 750
1 815 895	44 776	675 164	2 499	532	21 333	846 695
114 851	2 684	7 545	-8	113	713	–
7 158 434	526 576	487 893	110 309	107 480	144 970	111 306
1 846 051	43 217	225 719	50 607	63 336	16 461	84 858

表12-1 续表 2

单位：万元

项　目	Item	利润总额 Total Profits
总部经济	**Corporate Headquarters**	**11 840 830**
按企业类型分	**Classified by Enterprise Type**	
# 总部企业	Corporate Headquarters	8 275 264
# 上市公司	Listing Corporation	3 014 216
# 跨国公司地区性总部和功能性机构	Regional Headquarters and Functional Agencies of Multinational Corporations	3 319 487
# 地标性企业	Landmark Enterprises	6 264 192
按母公司控股情况分	**Classified by Number Shares Held by Parent Companies**	
国有控股	Stately Majority Share Holding	815 893
集体控股	Collectively Majority Share Holding	444 252
私人控股	Privately Majority Share Holding	5 931 656
港澳台商控股	Majority Share Holding by Investors from Hong Kong, Macau and Taiwan	1 539 614
外商控股	Majority Share Holding by Foreign Investors	2 925 622
其　他	Others	183 793
按总部经济主营行业分	**Classified by Main Field of Operation**	
工　业	Industry	7 278 248
建筑业	Construction	134 621
批发和零售业	Wholesale and Retail Sale Trades	2 564 339
交通运输、仓储和邮政业	Transportation, Logistics and Postal	65 951
住宿和餐饮业	Accommodation and Catering Services	36 647
信息传输、软件和信息技术服务业	Information Transmission, Software and Information Technology Services	243 560
金融业	Financial Industries	705 470
房地产业	Real Estate	10 871
租赁和商务服务业	Leasing and Business Services	855 290
科学研究和技术服务业	Scientific Research and Technical Services	-54 167

Continued 2

(10 000 yuan)

所得税费用 Income Tax Expenses	应交增值税 Added Value Tax Payable	研发费用 Research and Development Expenses	平均用工人数(人) Annual Average Employees (person)	#技术(研究)开发人数 Number of Technical (Research) Developers	应付职工薪酬 Employee Compensation Payable	#科研人员工资及福利 Researcher's Salary and Benefits
2 542 293	**2 992 633**	**2 275 875**	**765 862**	**64 762**	**9 473 181**	**1 087 745**
1 784 142	2 053 119	1 325 887	494 873	44 760	6 635 634	703 574
660 614	581 700	1 141 999	338 649	35 898	3 911 086	451 330
759 442	1 119 648	637 137	202 145	16 076	3 222 479	318 193
1 263 549	1 291 855	987 130	287 130	26 533	3 215 160	464 251
146 514	120 626	60 658	39 223	2 016	866 133	36 869
105 764	63 058	15 723	14 367	377	218 385	6 135
1 270 039	1 494 671	1 169 120	375 031	38 484	4 112 421	601 215
372 823	512 638	417 004	145 969	8 673	1 713 264	160 803
616 156	730 510	493 041	152 048	11 443	2 092 875	233 591
30 997	71 130	120 329	39 224	3 769	470 103	49 132
1 509 297	1 790 852	1 698 779	495 763	44 839	4 882 445	828 021
27 228	52 283	44 833	21 607	1 603	267 260	33 280
622 137	698 024	63 432	94 613	4 070	1 882 423	19 399
16 710	12 716	12 622	10 315	206	64 370	2 357
9 046	–	–	16 643	–	53 049	–
29 443	38 032	164 051	23 125	6 888	319 740	103 746
105 054	115 534	2 234	19 522	132	654 462	2 734
3 418	5 932	–	6 843	–	57 252	–
193 305	206 785	99 088	52 454	3 115	785 321	45 983
26 655	72 475	190 836	24 977	3 909	506 859	52 225

表12-2

总部企业主要经济指标 (2018年)

单位：万元

项　目	Item	单位数（个）Number of Units (unit)	年末资产总计 Total Assets at the End of Year
总部企业	**Corporate Headquarters**	**164**	**195 050 907**
按母公司控股情况分	**Classified by Number Shares Held by Parent Companies**		
国有控股	Stately Majority Share Holding	13	45 218 807
集体控股	Collectively Majority Share Holding	5	20 470 936
私人控股	Privately Majority Share Holding	71	95 255 723
港澳台商控股	Majority Share Holding by Investors from Hong Kong, Macau and Taiwan	27	11 935 319
外商控股	Majority Share Holding by Foreign Investors	36	15 756 606
其　他	Others	12	6 413 516
按总部企业主营行业分	**Classified by Main Field of Operation**		
工　业	Industry	75	82 292 790
# 纺织业	Textile Industry	2	1 027 138
化学纤维制造业	Chemical Fiber Manufacturing	2	16 584 730
黑色金属冶炼和压延加工业	Smelting and Pressing of Ferrous Metals	2	26 262 630
电气机械和器材制造业	Electric Equipment and Machinery Manufacturing	11	10 185 567
建筑业	Construction	12	6 933 245
批发和零售业	Wholesale and Retail Sale Trades	22	22 268 341
交通运输、仓储和邮政业	Transportation, Logistics and Postal	10	1 672 415
住宿和餐饮业	Accommodation and Catering Trade	1	71 309
信息传输、软件和信息技术服务业	Information Transmission, Software and Information Technology Services	11	1 641 809
金融业	Financial Industries	9	72 400 792
# 货币金融服务	Monetary and financial services	6	62 433 139
# 资本市场服务	Capital Market Services	1	8 420 908
房地产业	Real Estate	4	64 618
租赁和商务服务业	Leasing and Business Services	11	4 220 111
# 商务服务业	Business Services	11	4 220 111
科学研究和技术服务业	Scientific Research and Technical Services	9	3 485 477

MAIN ECONOMIC INDICATORS ON CORPORATE HEADQUARTERS (2018)

(10 000 yuan)

流动资产合计 Circulating Funds	#存 货 Inventory	#应收票据及应收账款 Bills Receivable and Accounts Receivable	年末负债总计 Total Liabilities at the End of Year	银行借款 Bank Loans	所有者权益合计 Total Creditors Equity	营业收入 Business Revenue
92 393 509	**19 982 152**	**21 263 100**	**139 365 688**	**17 845 417**	**55 685 219**	**125 616 618**
17 831 751	834 820	1 692 421	38 443 654	1 264 621	6 775 153	10 884 664
5 474 198	484 376	322 057	17 181 039	66 763	3 289 897	7 430 207
45 506 126	14 814 583	10 173 649	64 720 880	13 922 704	30 534 843	74 370 325
8 511 109	1 340 495	2 516 577	6 661 510	894 738	5 273 809	14 236 954
10 680 004	1 993 347	4 939 131	9 053 173	1 481 672	6 703 433	14 520 576
4 390 321	514 531	1 619 265	3 305 432	214 919	3 108 084	4 173 892
41 537 077	9 672 347	11 357 493	48 012 522	10 413 872	34 280 268	71 563 417
557 715	261 542	53 656	447 605	159 705	579 533	2 441 655
5 465 876	2 194 323	872 030	12 439 225	3 045 751	4 145 505	9 955 150
11 205 953	2 466 676	1 514 531	14 168 719	2 317 346	12 093 911	30 302 532
6 245 283	1 254 992	1 899 502	6 060 931	1 465 631	4 124 636	7 135 701
6 002 363	634 278	3 714 343	4 623 202	488 081	2 310 043	6 411 745
14 731 196	3 055 117	4 509 230	15 266 975	5 192 318	7 001 366	35 342 298
987 906	136 027	371 206	900 013	266 436	772 402	1 923 535
23 684	1 869	1 074	35 691	4 500	35 618	246 048
1 202 981	9 129	395 470	904 315	110 837	737 494	3 429 978
24 038 096	5 745 357	139 178	65 021 644	637 945	7 379 148	2 688 432
16 956 789	5 745 357	125 235	57 379 655	599 601	5 053 484	2 260 576
6 803 181	–	12 947	6 378 309	38 344	2 042 599	222 480
58 347	265	10 503	24 983	1 000	39 635	134 586
1 971 863	622 978	130 377	2 757 982	396 546	1 462 129	1 900 468
1 971 863	622 978	130 377	2 757 982	396 546	1 462 129	1 900 468
1 839 996	104 785	634 226	1 818 361	333 882	1 667 116	1 976 111

表12-2 续表 1

单位：万元

项　　目	Item	出口交货值 Delivery Value for Export
总部企业	**Corporate Headquarters**	**15 000 644**
按母公司控股情况分	**Classified by Number Shares Held by Parent Companies**	
国有控股	Stately Majority Share Holding	2 822 084
集体控股	Collectively Majority Share Holding	629 529
私人控股	Privately Majority Share Holding	5 650 388
港澳台商控股	Majority Share Holding by Investors from Hong Kong, Macau and Taiwan	1 400 238
外商控股	Majority Share Holding by Foreign Investors	4 212 130
其　他	Others	286 275
按总部企业主营行业分	**Classified by Main Field of Operation**	
工　业	Industry	10 989 480
# 纺织业	Textile Industry	100 878
化学纤维制造业	Chemical Fiber Manufacturing	328 316
黑色金属冶炼和压延加工业	Smelting and Pressing of Ferrous Metals	2 751 374
电气机械和器材制造业	Electric Equipment and Machinery Manufacturing	1 266 917
建筑业	Construction	18 324
批发和零售业	Wholesale and Retail Sale Trades	3 924 226
交通运输、仓储和邮政业	Transportation, Logistics and Postal	–
住宿和餐饮业	Accommodation and Catering Trade	–
信息传输、软件和信息技术服务业	Information Transmission, Software and Information Technology Services	61 672
金融业	Financial Industries	–
# 货币金融服务	Monetary and financial services	–
# 资本市场服务	Capital Market Services	–
房地产业	Real Estate	–
租赁和商务服务业	Leasing and Business Services	6 942
# 商务服务业	Business Services	6 942
科学研究和技术服务业	Scientific Research and Technical Services	–

Continued 1

(10 000 yuan)

营业成本 Business costs	销售费用 Cost Related With Sale	管理费用 Managerial Cost	财务费用 Financing Activities Cost	# 利息费用 Interest Expenses	税金及附加 Business Tax and Surcharges	投资收益 Investment Income
105 675 035	**3 782 937**	**4 410 744**	**1 437 179**	**1 440 344**	**555 058**	**1 593 761**
9 775 621	278 756	670 690	86 516	65 588	29 406	873 410
6 240 070	62 424	113 629	53 184	77 209	23 679	43 417
64 470 495	1 196 934	1 538 473	1 058 718	1 015 619	346 116	445 469
10 349 147	1 139 036	1 298 072	52 830	82 559	79 352	150 245
11 851 444	671 009	526 470	132 759	118 982	55 041	75 470
2 988 258	434 778	263 410	53 172	80 387	21 464	5 750
60 293 480	1 650 078	1 672 481	925 446	1 041 601	341 251	385 698
2 346 956	16 821	13 854	21 977	21 377	5 922	11 908
9 015 464	66 930	105 111	164 322	260 282	42 281	32 816
25 569 479	254 067	440 815	321 693	332 133	152 607	152 780
5 878 767	324 500	226 967	192 854	138 875	32 571	122 254
5 527 895	88 045	216 267	26 278	36 953	16 674	14 055
30 265 816	1 581 938	1 363 442	384 641	245 481	116 190	166 571
1 757 456	17 670	59 112	21 886	16 612	5 276	3 480
123 610	63 204	22 547	155	239	90	–
2 862 036	195 089	126 497	3 083	9 585	3 533	18 913
1 601 019	43 340	669 672	2 042	94	21 313	839 028
1 301 636	11 992	424 243	2 039	87	17 544	562 832
102 639	–	193 297	–	–	3 475	197 988
114 851	2 684	7 545	-8	113	713	–
1 430 936	118 190	116 407	36 157	39 927	37 676	83 209
1 430 936	118 190	116 407	36 157	39 927	37 676	83 209
1 697 936	22 699	156 774	37 499	49 739	12 342	82 807

表12-2 续表 2

单位：万元

项　目	Item	利润总额 Total Profits
总部企业	**Corporate Headquarters**	**8 275 264**
按母公司控股情况分	**Classified by Number Shares Held by Parent Companies**	
国有控股	Stately Majority Share Holding	607 140
集体控股	Collectively Majority Share Holding	752 824
私人控股	Privately Majority Share Holding	4 306 398
港澳台商控股	Majority Share Holding by Investors from Hong Kong, Macau and Taiwan	1 268 563
外商控股	Majority Share Holding by Foreign Investors	1 179 916
其　他	Others	160 423
按总部企业主营行业分	**Classified by Main Field of Operation**	
工　业	Industry	4 943 053
# 纺织业	Textile Industry	42 087
化学纤维制造业	Chemical Fiber Manufacturing	512 906
黑色金属冶炼和压延加工业	Smelting and Pressing of Ferrous Metals	3 148 333
电气机械和器材制造业	Electric Equipment and Machinery Manufacturing	216 951
建筑业	Construction	407 543
批发和零售业	Wholesale and Retail Sale Trades	1 782 250
交通运输、仓储和邮政业	Transportation, Logistics and Postal	57 121
住宿和餐饮业	Accommodation and Catering Trade	36 647
信息传输、软件和信息技术服务业	Information Transmission, Software and Information Technology Services	143 122
金融业	Financial Industries	616 559
# 货币金融服务	Monetary and financial services	593 752
# 资本市场服务	Capital Market Services	37 605
房地产业	Real Estate	10 871
租赁和商务服务业	Leasing and Business Services	266 014
# 商务服务业	Business Services	266 014
科学研究和技术服务业	Scientific Research and Technical Services	12 084

Continued 2

(10 000 yuan)

所得税费用 Income Tax Expenses	应交增值税 Added Value Tax Payable	研发费用 Research and Development Expenses	平均用工人数(人) Annual Average Employees (person)	#技术(研究)开发人数 Number of Technical (Research) Developers	应付职工薪酬 Employee Compensation Payable	#科研人员工资及福利 Researcher's Salary and Benefits
1 784 142	**2 053 119**	**1 325 887**	**494 873**	**44 760**	**6 635 634**	**703 574**
114 707	116 203	38 611	22 984	1 738	678 910	32 928
145 296	102 126	1 097	18 242	516	233 567	5 505
966 719	1 047 804	813 910	254 092	30 095	2 889 025	464 745
286 044	427 236	218 382	80 929	4 961	1 409 564	87 510
237 582	285 494	181 573	87 004	5 584	1 082 020	87 851
33 794	74 256	72 314	31 622	1 866	342 548	25 035
1 063 232	1 211 756	926 524	271 486	28 702	2 822 392	519 919
9 697	12 428	12 767	10 773	576	61 118	8 750
100 604	134 061	84 862	21 133	2 610	182 649	29 250
631 320	628 535	159 441	42 067	3 743	437 774	143 907
47 649	64 017	173 005	30 773	4 024	372 979	77 453
66 257	116 716	126 909	41 184	4 225	577 081	61 216
425 354	444 176	62 914	83 408	4 042	1 676 649	19 051
14 399	12 259	12 622	9 820	206	63 673	2 357
9 046	–	–	16 643	–	53 049	–
19 910	27 067	105 896	19 820	4 303	247 186	63 810
101 126	107 023	2 234	17 171	132	579 405	2 734
97 495	71 437	2 234	12 557	92	419 624	1 702
2 863	33 986	–	2 740	40	120 505	1 032
3 418	5 932	–	6 843	–	57 252	–
62 019	63 841	2 315	7 749	154	133 097	1 804
62 019	63 841	2 315	7 749	154	133 097	1 804
19 381	64 349	86 473	20 749	2 996	425 850	32 683

表12-3

上市公司主要经济指标 (2018年)

单位：万元

项　　目	Item	单位数（个） Number of Units (unit)	年末资产总计 Total Assets at the End of Year
上市公司	**Listing Company**	**135**	**114 643 815**
按上市公司控股情况分	**Classified by Number Shares Held by Listing Companies**		
国有控股	Stately Majority Share Holding	5	11 558 511
集体控股	Collectively Majority Share Holding	6	21 643 657
私人控股	Privately Majority Share Holding	74	57 817 840
港澳台商控股	Majority Share Holding by Investors from Hong Kong, Macau and Taiwan	20	4 603 076
外商控股	Majority Share Holding by Foreign Investors	22	13 203 627
其　他	Others	8	5 817 104
按上市公司主营行业分	**Classified by Main Field of Operation**		
工　业	Industry	105	49 332 445
#化学原料和化学制品制造业	Raw Chemical Materials and Chemical Products	11	2 643 884
金属制品业	Metal Products	7	3 167 823
电气机械和器材制造业	Electric Equipment and Machinery Manufacturing	14	10 068 486
计算机、通信和其他电子设备制造业	Computer Telecommunications and Other Electronic Equipment Manufacture	23	12 650 943
建筑业	Construction	2	3 729 529
批发和零售业	Wholesale and Retail Sale Trades	3	5 619 997
交通运输、仓储和邮政业	Transportation, Logistics and Postal	3	612 775
信息传输、软件和信息技术服务业	Information Transmission, Software and Information Technology Services	4	1 194 921
金融业	Financial Industries	6	48 296 930
#资本市场服务	Capital Market Services	1	8 420 908
租赁和商务服务业	Leasing and Business Services	4	4 510 248
科学研究和技术服务业	Scientific Research and Technical Services	8	1 346 970

MAIN ECONOMIC INDICATORS ON LISTING CORPORATION (2018)

(10 000 yuan)

流动资产合计 Circulating Funds	#存 货 Inventory	#应收票据及应收账款 Bills Receivable and Accounts Receivable	年末负债总计 Total Liabilities at the End of Year	银行借款 Bank Loans	所有者权益合计 Total Creditors Equity	营业收入 Business Revenue
57 351 234	**14 791 763**	**13 484 073**	**77 880 017**	**8 754 195**	**36 763 798**	**48 813 706**
9 105 130	405 019	718 106	7 941 221	311 514	3 617 290	4 465 949
7 344 977	1 929 993	200 303	18 096 435	199 084	3 547 222	2 017 934
25 716 336	9 817 253	6 973 846	38 920 029	5 486 494	18 897 811	23 396 151
3 110 014	773 956	1 127 878	2 222 315	556 826	2 380 761	4 358 965
8 835 920	1 516 900	3 611 625	8 087 590	1 748 215	5 116 037	12 002 472
3 238 857	348 642	852 315	2 612 427	452 062	3 204 677	2 572 235
28 677 806	5 860 650	9 385 599	24 917 839	7 525 920	24 414 606	33 565 150
1 303 774	191 154	539 871	1 272 277	602 773	1 371 607	1 738 927
1 893 398	449 720	825 584	1 626 419	593 410	1 541 404	2 470 552
6 119 198	1 179 352	2 436 217	5 518 863	1 287 809	4 549 623	5 722 274
7 193 739	1 053 491	2 601 365	6 474 539	1 688 561	6 176 404	6 811 645
3 184 419	22 228	2 461 746	2 255 502	124 551	1 474 027	2 747 385
3 994 301	1 161 070	934 381	3 790 800	764 469	1 829 197	6 280 917
202 734	4 862	95 379	296 378	90 911	316 397	232 952
709 301	603	126 544	441 466	3 500	753 455	2 652 220
16 481 824	5 746 990	123 931	42 787 846	65 207	5 509 084	1 554 747
6 803 181	–	12 947	6 378 309	38 344	2 042 599	222 480
3 469 957	1 943 575	133 165	2 738 010	95 292	1 772 238	1 319 561
630 892	51 785	223 328	652 176	84 345	694 794	460 774

表12-3 续表 1

单位：万元

项　　目	Item	出口交货值 Delivery Value for Export
上市公司	**Listing Company**	**10 117 354**
按上市公司控股情况分	**Classified by Number Shares Held by Listing Companies**	
国有控股	Stately Majority Share Holding	3 314 407
集体控股	Collectively Majority Share Holding	98 155
私人控股	Privately Majority Share Holding	3 716 239
港澳台商控股	Majority Share Holding by Investors from Hong Kong, Macau and Taiwan	979 374
外商控股	Majority Share Holding by Foreign Investors	1 605 258
其　他	Others	403 921
按上市公司主营行业分	**Classified by Main Field of Operation**	
工　业	Industry	5 948 798
#化学原料和化学制品制造业	Raw Chemical Materials and Chemical Products	294 948
金属制品业	Metal Products	514 548
电气机械和器材制造业	Electric Equipment and Machinery Manufacturing	1 330 820
计算机、通信和其他电子设备制造业	Computer Telecommunications and Other Electronic Equipment Manufacture	2 503 881
建筑业	Construction	–
批发和零售业	Wholesale and Retail Sale Trades	4 106 762
交通运输、仓储和邮政业	Transportation, Logistics and Postal	–
信息传输、软件和信息技术服务业	Information Transmission, Software and Information Technology Services	–
金融业	Financial Industries	–
#资本市场服务	Capital Market Services	–
租赁和商务服务业	Leasing and Business Services	61 794
科学研究和技术服务业	Scientific Research and Technical Services	–

Continued 1

(10 000 yuan)

营业成本 Business costs	销售费用 Cost Related With Sale	管理费用 Managerial Cost	财务费用 Financing Activities Cost	# 利息费用 Interest Expenses	税金及附加 Business Tax and Surcharges	投资收益 Investment Income
38 864 042	**2 214 573**	**2 023 961**	**731 265**	**728 649**	**297 650**	**686 287**
3 769 257	213 175	307 145	33 058	18 226	13 901	279 120
1 075 561	240 726	65 518	23 692	29 174	75 414	31 047
18 508 969	982 971	1 030 874	433 278	403 352	130 548	276 973
3 514 025	275 459	170 700	24 721	32 730	18 717	8 143
10 166 143	310 744	321 082	160 931	158 836	42 027	63 344
1 830 087	191 498	128 642	55 585	86 331	17 043	27 660
27 061 669	1 578 336	1 196 945	557 086	582 859	185 416	274 954
1 395 180	79 051	83 795	27 252	28 148	10 269	13 293
2 152 267	74 879	81 912	37 530	43 792	11 727	- 4 033
4 492 579	326 393	242 742	147 771	138 238	39 334	102 039
5 284 300	224 428	268 704	142 737	180 243	41 272	17 485
2 217 745	69 602	100 335	8 568	10 767	9 418	10 220
5 185 805	366 019	200 472	103 191	64 128	16 080	114 114
166 146	7 381	30 819	9 303	10 295	1 950	4 186
2 243 439	126 557	78 882	17 094	18 987	2 141	25 624
724 375	–	305 935	-23	–	10 165	258 526
102 639	–	193 297	–	–	3 475	197 988
980 434	39 430	52 768	24 006	29 061	68 452	-4 884
284 429	27 248	57 805	12 040	12 552	4 028	3 547

表12-3 续表 2

单位：万元

项　目	Item	利润总额 Total Profits
上市公司	**Listing Company**	**3 014 216**
按上市公司控股情况分	**Classified by Number Shares Held by Listing Companies**	
国有控股	Stately Majority Share Holding	286 144
集体控股	Collectively Majority Share Holding	429 365
私人控股	Privately Majority Share Holding	1 149 060
港澳台商控股	Majority Share Holding by Investors from Hong Kong, Macau and Taiwan	154 499
外商控股	Majority Share Holding by Foreign Investors	865 143
其　他	Others	130 005
按上市公司主营行业分	**Classified by Main Field of Operation**	
工　业	Industry	1 577 222
#化学原料和化学制品制造业	Raw Chemical Materials and Chemical Products	98 920
金属制品业	Metal Products	-49 995
电气机械和器材制造业	Electric Equipment and Machinery Manufacturing	224 426
计算机、通信和其他电子设备制造业	Computer Telecommunications and Other Electronic Equipment Manufacture	268 122
建筑业	Construction	262 505
批发和零售业	Wholesale and Retail Sale Trades	452 242
交通运输、仓储和邮政业	Transportation, Logistics and Postal	17 883
信息传输、软件和信息技术服务业	Information Transmission, Software and Information Technology Services	155 860
金融业	Financial Industries	412 743
#资本市场服务	Capital Market Services	37 605
租赁和商务服务业	Leasing and Business Services	171 915
科学研究和技术服务业	Scientific Research and Technical Services	-36 154

Continued 2

(10 000 yuan)

所得税费用 Income Tax Expenses	应交增值税 Added Value Tax Payable	研发费用 Research and Development Expenses	平均用工人数(人) Annual Average Employees (person)	#技术(研究)开发人数 Number of Technical (Research) Developers	应付职工薪酬 Employee Compensation Payable	#科研人员工资及福利 Researcher's Salary and Benefits
660 614	**581 700**	**1 141 999**	**338 649**	**35 898**	**3 911 086**	**451 330**
54 205	44 419	23 139	21 179	878	239 408	4 839
101 932	53 372	15 575	11 259	319	198 892	6 012
296 199	313 295	604 845	192 674	22 790	2 082 714	291 697
42 784	49 240	221 452	42 890	3 966	423 529	63 949
143 230	96 897	190 531	52 914	5 852	702 142	57 594
22 264	24 477	86 457	17 733	2 093	264 401	27 239
387 205	359 674	836 797	255 037	27 288	2 508 474	360 752
17 311	23 035	39 117	12 709	1 409	156 780	18 671
9 972	-5 891	55 726	22 308	1 866	223 312	25 550
37 483	63 889	174 652	47 585	4 547	410 280	63 564
55 072	78 109	308 676	69 613	9 969	828 061	148 938
38 537	64 356	80 378	19 843	2 776	349 295	26 654
94 944	20 147	35 580	28 810	943	272 340	5 566
3 239	2 816	3 446	4 539	116	12 675	1 445
23 344	18 041	47 545	4 747	2 290	120 326	24 104
55 381	65 376	2 234	11 720	114	431 595	2 377
2 863	33 986	–	2 740	40	120 505	1 032
49 561	36 066	16 983	5 911	675	74 379	2 441
8 403	15 224	119 036	8 042	1 696	142 002	27 991

表12-4 跨国公司地区性总部和功能性机构主要经济指标（2018年）

单位：万元

项　　目	Item	单位数（个）Number of Units (unit)	年末资产总计 Total Assets at the End of Year
跨国公司地区性总部和功能性机构	**Regional Headquarters and Functional Agencies of Multinational Corporations**	**115**	**36 580 171**
按母公司控股情况分	**Classified by Number Shares Held by Parent Companies**		
私人控股	Privately Majority Share Holding	1	114 589
港澳台商控股	Majority Share Holding by Investors from Hong Kong, Macau and Taiwan	32	12 327 175
外商控股	Majority Share Holding by Foreign Investors	79	22 899 344
其　他	Others	3	1 239 063
按跨国公司地区性总部和功能性机构主营行业分	**According to the Main Industries of Regional Headquarters and Functional Agencies of Multinational Corporations**		
工　业	Industry	65	18 148 778
# 化学原料和化学制品制造业	Raw Chemical Materials and Chemical Products	8	1 076 141
黑色金属冶炼和压延加工业	Smelting and Pressing of Ferrous Metals	1	694 640
电气机械和器材制造业	Electric Equipment and Machinery Manufacturing	4	1 197 455
计算机、通信和其他电子设备制造业	Computer Telecommunications and Other Electronic Equipment Manufacture	16	4 955 600
批发和零售业	Wholesale and Retail Sale Trades	20	12 498 419
信息传输、软件和信息技术服务业	Information Transmission, Software and Information Technology Services	3	381 643
金融业	Financial Industries	4	678 368
租赁和商务服务业	Leasing and Business Services	14	2 093 678
科学研究和技术服务业	Scientific Research and Technical Services	9	2 779 285

REGIONAL HEADQUARTERS AND FUNCTIONAL AGENCIES OF MULTINATIONAL CORPORATIONS(2018)

(10 000 yuan)

流动资产合计 Circulating Funds	#存 货 Inventory	#应收票据及应收账款 Bills Receivable and Accounts Receivable	年末负债总计 Total Liabilities at the End of Year	银行借款 Bank Loans	所有者权益合计 Total Creditors Equity	营业收入 Business Revenue
23 176 364	**4 424 456**	**7 575 245**	**20 319 584**	**3 426 312**	**16 260 587**	**40 640 375**
46 164	704	13 690	43 645	–	70 944	52 014
8 388 710	1 221 483	2 520 184	6 866 382	993 550	5 460 793	14 881 324
13 842 523	3 068 227	4 839 970	12 627 478	2 371 429	10 271 866	24 163 528
898 967	134 042	201 401	782 079	61 333	456 984	1 543 509
12 279 507	2 021 536	4 706 500	9 688 582	1 662 708	8 460 196	19 937 898
775 633	156 943	354 981	454 241	70 495	621 900	1 418 101
348 988	143 923	72 162	287 177	136 250	407 463	1 854 911
768 893	57 072	154 752	539 073	3 122	658 382	657 335
3 750 779	665 913	1 763 874	2 535 577	437 925	2 420 023	6 560 236
8 029 207	2 018 691	2 193 508	7 624 887	1 136 149	4 873 532	17 320 770
349 959	102 127	94 042	301 499	31 333	80 144	240 657
436 241	–	10 505	552 867	285 511	125 501	65 906
891 761	209 423	224 397	619 729	112 248	1 473 949	1 534 410
1 189 689	72 679	346 293	1 532 020	198 363	1 247 265	1 540 734

表12-4 续表 1

单位：万元

项　　目	Item	出口交货值 Delivery Value for Export
跨国公司地区性总部和功能性机构	**Regional Headquarters and Functional Agencies of Multinational Corporations**	**8 570 617**
按母公司控股情况分	**Classified by Number Shares Held by Parent Companies**	
私人控股	Privately Majority Share Holding	–
港澳台商控股	Majority Share Holding by Investors from Hong Kong, Macau and Taiwan	2 505 240
外商控股	Majority Share Holding by Foreign Investors	6 046 560
其　他	Others	18 817
按跨国公司地区性总部和功能性机构主营行业分	**According to the Main Industries of Regional Headquarters and Functional Agencies of Multinational Corporations**	
工　业	Industry	7 111 061
# 化学原料和化学制品制造业	Raw Chemical Materials and Chemical Products	245 018
黑色金属冶炼和压延加工业	Smelting and Pressing of Ferrous Metals	181 910
电气机械和器材制造业	Electric Equipment and Machinery Manufacturing	104 348
计算机、通信和其他电子设备制造业	Computer Telecommunications and Other Electronic Equipment Manufacture	5 013 318
批发和零售业	Wholesale and Retail Sale Trades	970 317
信息传输、软件和信息技术服务业	Information Transmission, Software and Information Technology Services	–
金融业	Financial Industries	–
租赁和商务服务业	Leasing and Business Services	489 239
科学研究和技术服务业	Scientific Research and Technical Services	–

Continued 1

(10 000 yuan)

营业成本 Business costs	销售费用 Cost Related With Sale	管理费用 Managerial Cost	财务费用 Financing Activities Cost	# 利息费用 Interest Expenses	税金及附加 Business Tax and Surcharges	投资收益 Investment Income
30 554 685	**3 223 634**	**2 812 084**	**281 057**	**303 404**	**204 693**	**303 710**
38 178	82	4 783	-798	34	228	653
11 059 935	1 119 574	1 306 820	46 468	81 130	82 155	161 696
18 013 608	2 082 779	1 487 629	204 276	191 177	120 354	149 028
1 442 964	21 199	12 852	31 111	31 063	1 956	-7 667
15 664 498	1 464 801	818 201	69 142	140 140	96 295	61 554
999 434	196 452	75 308	5 422	5 622	8 752	592
1 757 574	292	14 113	-74	6 806	4 101	1 317
484 125	66 455	17 832	19 556	23 291	3 840	5 029
5 924 692	57 594	129 451	-24 074	14 738	18 476	1 047
12 099 225	1 526 282	1 767 920	162 977	100 049	86 656	96 829
166 223	11 824	8 368	3 800	5 158	797	308
21 865	13 428	9 630	2 496	525	235	7 200
1 196 949	193 338	76 692	4 747	8 011	9 944	57 017
1 405 925	13 961	131 273	37 895	49 521	10 766	80 802

表12-4 续表 2

单位：万元

项　　目	Item	利润总额 Total Profits
跨国公司地区性总部和功能性机构	**Regional Headquarters and Functional Agencies of Multinational Corporations**	**3 319 487**
按母公司控股情况分	**Classified by Number Shares Held by Parent Companies**	
私人控股	Privately Majority Share Holding	9 195
港澳台商控股	Majority Share Holding by Investors from Hong Kong, Macau and Taiwan	1 229 189
外商控股	Majority Share Holding by Foreign Investors	2 079 098
其　他	Others	2 005
按跨国公司地区性总部和功能性机构主营行业分	**According to the Main Industries of Regional Headquarters and Functional Agencies of Multinational Corporations**	
工　业	Industry	1 428 120
# 化学原料和化学制品制造业	Raw Chemical Materials and Chemical Products	122 999
黑色金属冶炼和压延加工业	Smelting and Pressing of Ferrous Metals	12 546
电气机械和器材制造业	Electric Equipment and Machinery Manufacturing	34 821
计算机、通信和其他电子设备制造业	Computer Telecommunications and Other Electronic Equipment Manufacture	348 754
批发和零售业	Wholesale and Retail Sale Trades	1 815 761
信息传输、软件和信息技术服务业	Information Transmission, Software and Information Technology Services	-6 558
金融业	Financial Industries	21 406
租赁和商务服务业	Leasing and Business Services	119 168
科学研究和技术服务业	Scientific Research and Technical Services	-58 410

Continued 2

(10 000 yuan)

所得税费用 Income Tax Expenses	应交增值税 Added Value Tax Payable	研发费用 Research and Development Expenses	平均用工人数(人) Annual Average Employees (person)	#技术(研究)开发人数 Number of Technical (Research) Developers	应付职工薪酬 Employee Compensation Payable	#科研人员工资及福利 Researcher's Salary and Benefits
759 442	**1 119 648**	**637 137**	**202 145**	**16 076**	**3 222 479**	**318 193**
1 169	–	2 079	801	347	13 369	929
285 295	433 954	246 733	92 607	6 042	1 437 944	113 887
472 501	680 618	373 793	107 299	8 786	1 737 212	196 111
477	5 076	14 532	1 438	901	33 954	7 266
264 632	442 336	487 885	127 942	11 296	1 490 501	259 237
28 594	51 266	11 374	4 366	411	74 454	13 336
579	8 779	66 332	1 895	195	39 341	3 968
3 123	88 251	29 634	4 239	580	88 459	39 036
68 080	21 244	120 720	56 421	4 068	478 054	49 506
450 902	568 387	32 953	46 838	1 009	1 331 051	4 365
1 307	5 179	52 015	2 712	2 428	59 419	36 330
4 681	1 323	–	873	18	16 580	357
26 530	51 951	2 075	9 774	298	137 134	3 224
11 390	50 472	62 209	14 006	1 027	187 794	14 680

表12-5

总部经济营业收入50强（2018年）
TOP 50 HEADQUARTER ECONOMY OF THE MAJOR BUSINESS REVENUE (2018)

序号 No.	企业名称 Name of Enterprises	所在地区 Location	序号 No.	企业名称 Name of Enterprises	所在地区 Location
1	江苏沙钢集团有限公司	张家港市	26	苏州胜利精密制造科技股份有限公司	高新区、虎丘区
2	盛虹控股集团有限公司	吴江区	27	纬创资通（昆山）有限公司	昆山市
3	恒力集团有限公司	吴江区	28	江苏中利集团股份有限公司	常熟市
4	江苏永钢集团有限公司	张家港市	29	江苏沙钢股份有限公司	张家港市
5	东华能源股份有限公司	张家港市	30	玖隆钢铁物流有限公司	张家港市
6	通鼎集团有限公司	吴江区	31	保利协鑫（苏州）新能源有限公司	工业园区
7	江苏国泰国际集团有限公司	张家港市	32	中亿丰建设集团股份有限公司	相城区
8	江苏国泰国际集团国贸股份有限公司	张家港市	33	江苏吴中集团有限公司	吴中区
9	耐克体育（中国）有限公司	太仓市	34	苏州裕景泰贸易有限公司	张家港市
10	阿迪达斯体育（中国）有限公司	工业园区	35	华润苏州礼安医药有限公司	工业园区
11	永鼎集团有限公司	吴江区	36	恩斯克投资有限公司	昆山市
12	三一重机有限公司	昆山市	37	香塘集团有限公司	太仓市
13	苏州金螳螂企业（集团）有限公司	工业园区	38	唯品会（昆山）电子商务有限公司	昆山市
14	苏州金螳螂建筑装饰股份有限公司	工业园区	39	波司登股份有限公司	常熟市
15	阿特斯阳光电力集团有限公司	高新区、虎丘区	40	金红叶纸业集团有限公司	工业园区
16	华芳集团有限公司	张家港市	41	波司登国际控股有限公司	常熟市
17	昆山润华商业有限公司	昆山市	42	苏州银行股份有限公司	工业园区
18	苏州同程网络科技有限公司	工业园区	43	江苏荣成环保科技股份有限公司	昆山市
19	苏州创元投资发展（集团）有限公司	姑苏区	44	康得新复合材料集团股份有限公司	张家港市
20	紫光数码（苏州）集团有限公司	相城区	45	伟创力电子技术（苏州）有限公司	工业园区
21	苏州东山精密制造股份有限公司	吴中区	46	瑞仪光电（苏州）有限公司	吴江区
22	通力电梯有限公司	昆山市	47	陶氏（张家港）投资有限公司	张家港市
23	常熟市龙腾特种钢有限公司	常熟市	48	昆山丘钛微电子科技有限公司	昆山市
24	浦项（张家港）不锈钢股份有限公司	张家港市	49	江苏隆力奇集团有限公司	常熟市
25	江苏东方盛虹股份有限公司	吴江区	50	江苏骏马集团有限责任公司	张家港市

表12-6

总部经济利润总额50强（2018年）
TOP 50 HEADQUARTER ECONOMY OF THE TOTAL PROFITS (2018)

序号 No.	企业名称 Name of Enterprises	所在地区 Location	序号 No.	企业名称 Name of Enterprises	所在地区 Location
1	江苏沙钢集团有限公司	张家港市	26	永鼎集团有限公司	吴江区
2	阿迪达斯体育(中国)有限公司	工业园区	27	陶氏(张家港)投资有限公司	张家港市
3	耐克体育(中国)有限公司	太仓市	28	南极电商股份有限公司	吴江区
4	江苏永钢集团有限公司	张家港市	29	恩斯克投资有限公司	昆山市
5	恒力集团有限公司	吴江区	30	江苏吴中集团有限公司	吴中区
6	盛虹控股集团有限公司	吴江区	31	康宝莱(中国)保健品有限公司	工业园区
7	三一重机有限公司	昆山市	32	正新橡胶(中国)有限公司	昆山市
8	江苏沙钢股份有限公司	张家港市	33	江苏吴江农村商业银行股份有限公司	吴江区
9	通鼎集团有限公司	吴江区	34	苏州东山精密制造股份有限公司	吴中区
10	通力电梯有限公司	昆山市	35	江苏张家港农村商业银行股份有限公司	张家港市
11	苏州金螳螂企业(集团)有限公司	工业园区	36	华住酒店管理有限公司	昆山市
12	苏州金螳螂建筑装饰股份有限公司	工业园区	37	威富服饰(中国)有限公司	昆山市
13	苏州银行股份有限公司	工业园区	38	住友橡胶（中国）有限公司	常熟市
14	阿特斯阳光电力集团有限公司	高新区、虎丘区	39	常熟开关制造有限公司	常熟市
15	江苏国泰国际集团有限公司	张家港市	40	艾默生环境优化技术(苏州)有限公司	工业园区
16	江苏国泰国际集团国贸股份有限公司	张家港市	41	常熟三爱富中昊化工新材料有限公司	常熟市
17	江苏常熟农村商业银行股份有限公司	常熟市	42	沪士电子股份有限公司	昆山市
18	波司登股份有限公司	常熟市	43	苏州安洁科技股份有限公司	吴中区
19	波司登国际控股有限公司	常熟市	44	通鼎互联信息股份有限公司	吴江区
20	苏州新区高新技术产业股份有限公司	高新区、虎丘区	45	卫材(中国)投资有限公司	工业园区
21	东华能源股份有限公司	张家港市	46	江苏亨通光电股份有限公司	吴江区
22	国巨电子(中国)有限公司	高新区、虎丘区	47	科沃斯机器人股份有限公司	吴中区
23	苏州创元投资发展(集团)有限公司	姑苏区	48	卫材(中国)药业有限公司	工业园区
24	常熟市龙腾特种钢有限公司	常熟市	49	天顺风能(苏州)股份有限公司	太仓市
25	江苏东方盛虹股份有限公司	吴江区	50	长江润发医药股份有限公司	张家港市

表12-7

总部经济资产50强（2018年）
TOP 50 HEADQUARTER ECONOMY OF THE TOTAL ASSETS (2018)

序 号 No.	企业名称 Name of Enterprises	所在地区 Location	序 号 No.	企业名称 Name of Enterprises	所在地区 Location
1	苏州银行股份有限公司	工业园区	26	江苏东方盛虹股份有限公司	吴江区
2	江苏沙钢集团有限公司	张家港市	27	江苏国泰国际集团国贸股份有限公司	张家港市
3	江苏常熟农村商业银行股份有限公司	常熟市	28	亨通集团有限公司	吴江区
4	恒力集团有限公司	吴江区	29	阿迪达斯体育（中国）有限公司	工业园区
5	江苏吴江农村商业银行股份有限公司	吴江区	30	江苏吴中集团有限公司	吴中区
6	江苏张家港农村商业银行股份有限公司	张家港市	31	江苏亨通光电股份有限公司	吴江区
7	盛虹控股集团有限公司	吴江区	32	耐克体育（中国）有限公司	太仓市
8	东吴证券股份有限公司	工业园区	33	苏州胜利精密制造科技股份有限公司	高新区、虎丘区
9	江苏太仓农村商业银行股份有限公司	太仓市	34	通力电梯有限公司	昆山市
10	苏州金螳螂企业（集团）有限公司	工业园区	35	永鼎集团有限公司	吴江区
11	苏州新区高新技术产业股份有限公司	高新区、虎丘区	36	波司登国际控股有限公司	常熟市
12	康得新复合材料集团股份有限公司	张家港市	37	东吴人寿保险股份有限公司	高新区、虎丘区
13	苏州金螳螂建筑装饰股份有限公司	工业园区	38	华住酒店管理有限公司	昆山市
14	阿特斯阳光电力集团有限公司	高新区、虎丘区	39	苏州天沃科技股份有限公司	张家港市
15	江苏永钢集团有限公司	张家港市	40	天顺风能（苏州）股份有限公司	太仓市
16	苏州东山精密制造股份有限公司	吴中区	41	江苏荣成环保科技股份有限公司	昆山市
17	金红叶纸业集团有限公司	工业园区	42	常熟市龙腾特种钢有限公司	常熟市
18	东华能源股份有限公司	张家港市	43	澳洋集团有限公司	张家港市
19	苏州创元投资发展（集团）有限公司	姑苏区	44	江苏沙钢股份有限公司	张家港市
20	江苏中利集团股份有限公司	常熟市	45	通鼎互联信息股份有限公司	吴江区
21	江苏国泰国际集团有限公司	张家港市	46	波司登羽绒服装有限公司	常熟市
22	三一重机有限公司	昆山市	47	华芳集团有限公司	张家港
23	波司登股份有限公司	常熟市	48	正新橡胶（中国）有限公司	昆山市
24	通鼎集团有限公司	吴江区	49	江苏骏马集团有限责任公司	张家港市
25	保利协鑫（苏州）新能源有限公司	工业园区	50	苏州安洁科技股份有限公司	吴中区

表12-8

制造业采购经理指数（2018年）
THE MANUFACTURING PURCHASING MANAGERS INDEX (2018)

月　份	制造业采购经理指数 The Manufacturing Purchasing Managers Index	分项指数 Partial Index				
		生产指数 The Production Index	新订单指数 The New Orders Index	原材料库存指数 Raw Materials Inventory Index	从业人员指数 Practitioners Index	供应商配送时间指数 The Supplier Delivery Time Index
1	52.8	55.3	54.4	52.0	50.0	49.8
2	50.0	49.5	49.9	50.6	48.5	53.0
3	52.3	54.2	53.2	52.0	50.6	50.1
4	52.5	55.0	53.3	52.1	50.2	50.3
5	52.6	55.8	52.7	51.7	50.8	50.4
6	52.3	54.7	54.0	49.8	48.9	51.4
7	51.4	52.9	53.5	48.4	48.6	50.8
8	51.9	52.4	53.7	50.8	49.0	52.2
9	51.9	53.5	54.0	48.3	48.1	52.3
10	49.6	50.3	51.0	47.0	47.6	50.0
11	48.5	49.1	49.6	45.6	46.5	49.9
12	46.5	48.3	47.3	43.5	44.2	46.7

表12-9

非制造业采购经理指数（2018年）
NON THE MANUFACTURING PURCHASING MANAGERS INDEX (2018)

月　份	非制造业采购经理指数 Non Manufacturing Purchasing Managers Index	分项指数 Partial Index			
		商务活动指数 Business Activity Index	新订单指数 The New Orders Index	从业人员指数 Practitioners Index	供应商配送时间指数 The Supplier Delivery Time Index
1	50.1	51.6	49.2	49.7	49.7
2	51.2	51.9	51.8	49.2	51.0
3	49.3	48.9	49.0	50.4	49.6
4	49.5	50.7	49.5	48.1	48.7
5	48.9	50.0	48.7	48.2	48.4
6	48.4	48.4	48.4	47.6	49.8
7	49.9	50.7	50.2	48.6	49.2
8	50.9	52.0	51.5	49.7	49.0
9	50.4	52.0	50.5	49.6	48.3
10	48.6	49.8	47.5	49.2	48.4
11	48.8	49.9	48.5	47.7	49.0
12	47.1	47.6	47.5	45.5	47.4

主 要 统 计 指 标 解 释

总部企业 其统计范围是2018年末苏州市总部经济发展领导小组认定的总部企业。

上市公司 其统计范围是 2018 年末在境内外证券交易所上市的，并在苏州注册的企业。

跨国公司地区总部和功能性机构 其统计范围是省商务厅认定的江苏省八批次苏州范围内跨国公司地区总部和功能性机构。跨国公司地区总部是指注册地在境外的跨国公司设立的履行跨省以上区域范围管理和服务职能的总部类型的外商投资企业，从公司形式上可分为投资性公司和非投资性公司两类。跨国公司功能性机构是指注册地在境外的跨国公司设立的履行跨省以上区域范围的研发、资金管理、采购、销售、物流、支持服务等运营功能的外商投资企业。

采购经理指数（简称PMI） 是宏观经济先行监测指标，是经济景气监测的重要指标和反映经济增长和衰退的晴雨表。PMI指数体系无论对于政府部门、金融机构、投资公司，还是企业来说，在经济预测和商业分析方面都有重要的意义，是政府部门调控、金融机构与投资公司决策的重要依据，也是企业及时判断行业供应及整体走势，更好地进行决策的依据。PMI是一个综合指数，由5个扩散指数（分类指数）加权计算而成。5个分类指数及其权数是依据其对经济的先行影响程度确定的。具体包括：1.新订单指数；2.生产量指数；3.从业人员指数；4.供应商配送时间指数；5.原材料库存指数。PMI是国际上通行的宏观经济监测指标体系之一，通常以50作为经济强弱的分界点，PMI高于50时，反映经济扩张；低于50，则反映经济衰退。

EXPLANATORY NOTES ON MAIN STATISTICAL INDICATORS

Corporate headquarters the statistical range is the corporate headquarters which were recognized by Suzhou Headquarters Economic Development Leading Group at the end of 2018.

Public Enlisted Company the statistics include those enterprises registered in Suzhou and enlisted in domestic and overseas at the end of 2018.

Regional Headquarters and Functional Agencies of Multinational Corporations the statistical scope of regional headquarters and functional agencies of multinational corporations is the regional headquarters and functional agencies of multinational corporations in Suzhou within the eight batches of Jiangsu Province identified by the Provincial Department of Commerce. The regional headquarters of a multinational corporation refer to the headquarters-type foreign-invested enterprise established by transnational corporations registered outside the country that performs trans-provincial regional management and service functions. They can be divided into two types: investment companies and non-investment companies. The functional agency of a multinational corporation refers to a foreign-invested enterprise established by a multinational corporation registered outside the country that performs the trans-provincial regional functions of research and development, capital management, procurement, sales, logistics, support services, etc..

Purchasing Managers Index (PMI for short) is the first monitoring indicators of the macro-economy, an important indicator of economic monitoring and a barometer reflecting economic growth and decline. The PMI index system is of important significance both for government departments, financial institutions, investment companies, and for enterprises, in terms of economic forecasts and business analysis. It is an important basis for the regulation of government departments, and for the decision-making of financial institutions and investment companies. It is also a basis for enterprises to make timely judgment of the industry supply and the overall trend, and to make better decisions. PMI is a composite index that is weighted by five diffusion indices (classification indices). The five sub-indexes and their weights are based on the degree of their prior economic impact. Specifically they include: 1. new order index; 2. production index; 3. employees index; 4. supplier delivery time index; 5. raw material inventory index. PMI is one of the systems of macro-economic monitoring indicators internationally accepted, usually with 50 as the cut-off point of an economic strength, PMI above 50, reflecting the economic expansion; less than 50, reflecting the recession.

十三、财政 金融 保险

CHAPTER 13
FINANCE, BANKING AND INSURANCE

13 财政 金融 保险
FINANCE, BANKING AND INSURANCE

主 要 统 计 指 标
MAJOR STATISTICAL INDICATORS

2018年一般公共预算收入	General Public Budget Revenue	2 119.99	亿元	100 million yuan
比上年增长	Increase Over Last Year	11.1	%	
2018年一般公共预算支出	General Public Budget Expenditure	1 952.71	亿元	100 million yuan
比上年增长	Increase Over Last Year	10.2	%	
2018年末金融机构人民币存款余额	Deposits of National Banking System at Year-end	28 560.45	亿元	100 million yuan
比上年末增长	Increase Over Last Year	7.9	%	
2018年末住户存款余额	Deposits of Households	9 168.45	亿元	100 million yuan
比上年末增长	Increase Over Last Year	12.3	%	
2018年末金融机构人民币贷款余额	Balance of Loans of National Banking System at Year-end	26 546.23	亿元	100 million yuan
比上年末增长	Increase Over Last Year	10.7	%	

表13-1

历年一般公共预算收入

单位：万元

年 份 Year	全 市 Whole Municipality	市 区 Urban Area	# 姑苏区 Gusu District	# 吴中区 Wuzhong District	# 相城区 Xiangcheng District
1998	450 672	235 316			
1999	549 832	291 332			
2000	803 864	445 455			
2001	1 088 083	578 465			
2002	1 237 382	661 452			
2003	1 704 977	904 360			
2004	2 195 667	1 142 030			
2005	3 167 841	1 607 909			
2006	4 002 284	2 030 997			
2007	5 418 177	2 739 597			
2008	6 689 063	3 289 067	312 575	448 005	245 002
2009	7 451 800	3 701 670	358 062	500 147	276 126
2010	9 005 527	4 512 708	415 027	600 365	370 555
2011	11 008 808	5 504 360	459 040	723 733	462 093
2012	12 043 336	6 161 435	516 813	854 051	534 253
2013	13 310 254	6 946 083	568 927	1 005 303	604 168
2014	14 438 174	7 636 194	580 347	1 108 974	658 219
2015	15 607 575	8 295 463	592 122	1 211 348	700 451
2016	17 300 398	9 198 240	500 024	1 344 255	801 092
2017	19 081 002	10 129 103	510 098	1 439 304	900 031
2018	21 199 931	11 325 636	622 970	1 606 135	1 085 033

GENERAL PUBLIC BUDGET REVENUE OVER THE YEARS

(10 000 yuan)

#高新区、虎丘区 New & Hi-tech Zone, Huqiu District	# 工业园区 Industrial Park	# 吴江区 Wujiang District	常　熟 Changshu	张家港 Zhangjiagang	昆　山 Kunshan	太　仓 Taicang
		34 966	77 365	64 941	43 437	29 613
		42 259	94 065	76 646	53 144	34 645
		56 143	118 919	100 605	90 389	48 496
		84 198	144 216	179 545	125 967	59 890
		98 906	163 360	180 060	164 104	68 406
		148 022	223 860	246 102	241 717	88 938
		182 188	300 598	316 380	315 368	121 291
		249 298	370 725	483 838	516 168	189 201
		350 788	430 845	610 858	653 718	275 866
		480 957	600 630	839 800	865 562	372 588
461 894	950 818	601 600	701 528	1 039 800	1 156 868	501 800
510 828	1 075 009	702 000	780 778	1 050 018	1 331 331	588 003
571 002	1 331 800	902 828	1 000 864	1 160 618	1 631 331	700 006
710 317	1 643 008	1 128 772	1 225 011	1 423 188	2 002 188	854 061
820 365	1 850 006	1 193 202	1 281 504	1 496 131	2 202 750	901 516
918 659	2 069 017	1 295 133	1 385 809	1 541 828	2 435 188	1 001 346
1 001 818	2 302 623	1 373 583	1 474 042	1 626 618	2 636 593	1 064 727
1 100 035	2 572 026	1 473 908	1 576 969	1 742 188	2 847 589	1 145 366
1 298 028	2 881 030	1 652 525	1 735 805	1 900 019	3 189 188	1 277 146
1 430 017	3 178 080	1 835 198	1 918 107	2 100 088	3 525 088	1 408 616
1 590 009	3 500 188	2 029 000	2 110 591	2 334 288	3 878 858	1 550 558

表13-2

历年一般公共预算支出

单位：万元

年 份 Year	全 市 Whole Municipality	市 区 Urban Area	# 姑苏区 Gusu District	# 吴中区 Wuzhong District	# 相城区 Xiangcheng District
1998	459 927	247 165			
1999	565 065	304 851			
2000	781 116	438 872			
2001	1 103 617	604 354			
2002	1 363 942	747 019			
2003	1 835 976	1 027 454			
2004	2 331 312	1 252 319			
2005	3 352 789	1 823 140			
2006	3 861 990	2 064 381			
2007	4 969 424	2 576 611			
2008	6 223 668	3 197 262	175 898	420 005	205 203
2009	6 867 778	3 510 161	208 304	436 123	236 090
2010	8 256 650	4 116 504	230 838	544 865	297 428
2011	10 026 263	4 997 507	260 756	636 183	367 459
2012	11 134 678	5 609 766	289 417	687 561	394 320
2013	12 126 837	6 255 136	321 082	806 896	488 777
2014	13 048 293	6 933 722	445 164	825 465	506 625
2015	15 271 682	8 361 405	523 762	971 168	561 042
2016	16 171 070	8 887 164	517 421	1 080 376	564 166
2017	17 714 698	9 924 965	477 815	1 168 325	678 902
2018	19 527 090	11 065 155	494 493	1 417 359	741 405

GENERAL PUBLIC BUDGET EXPENDITURE OVER THE YEARS

(10 000 yuan)

#高新区、虎丘区 New & Hi-tech Zone, Huqiu District	# 工业园区 Industrial Park	# 吴江区 Wujiang District	常熟 Changshu	张家港 Zhangjiagang	昆山 Kunshan	太仓 Taicang
		34 257	75 706	63 863	44 667	28 526
		40 565	87 996	75 883	59 954	36 381
		53 291	102 686	101 276	91 126	47 156
		74 599	139 945	177 519	124 218	57 581
		106 271	171 273	196 867	171 093	77 690
		154 202	204 747	264 175	235 768	103 832
		191 322	272 511	337 245	329 541	139 696
		254 902	408 625	476 269	442 380	202 375
		308 308	420 980	556 075	562 293	258 261
		420 502	537 613	787 004	718 040	350 156
290 678	793 043	530 858	643 676	942 317	968 965	471 448
328 888	812 842	638 326	678 286	988 444	1 143 625	547 262
376 541	868 508	840 293	953 904	1 140 706	1 387 647	657 889
460 207	1 036 479	1 080 593	1 150 183	1 327 723	1 745 761	805 089
571 670	1 236 508	1 088 494	1 282 681	1 429 162	1 951 473	861 596
605 648	1 286 635	1 229 246	1 280 824	1 450 240	2 217 013	923 624
726 092	1 594 909	1 262 843	1 380 187	1 527 799	2 229 762	976 823
834 748	1 956 694	1 378 659	1 552 550	1 713 442	2 553 588	1 090 697
845 480	1 840 485	1 592 870	1 587 404	1 848 059	2 690 029	1 158 414
934 526	2 090 271	1 743 596	1 658 019	1 936 161	2 930 442	1 265 111
1 143 891	2 106 544	1 930 641	1 831 208	2 119 909	3 184 901	1 325 917

表13-3

财 政 收 入 (2018年)

单位：万元

指　　标	Item	全　市 Whole Municipality
上划中央收入	**Revenue of Central Government**	**16 389 109**
增值税 (50%)	Value-added Tax (50%)	8 228 193
消费税	Consumption Tax	344 666
企业所得税 (60%)	Enterprise's Income Tax (60%)	5 890 276
个人所得税 (60%)	Individual Income Tax (60%)	1 925 974
一般公共预算收入	**Public Finance Budget Revenue**	**21 199 931**
# 税收收入	Tax Revenue	19 295 407
1. 增值税 (50%)	Value-added Tax (50%)	8 180 520
2. 营业税	Business Tax	46 324
3. 企业所得税 (40%)	Enterprise's Income Tax (40%)	3 926 851
4. 个人所得税 (40%)	Individual Income Tax (40%)	1 283 985
5. 资源税	Resources Tax	73
6. 城市维护建设税	Tax on Urban Construction and Maintenance	1 180 186
7. 房产税	Tax on Real Estates	932 685
8. 印花税	Stamp Tax	259 778
9. 城镇土地使用税	Tax on Use of Urban Land	381 445
10.土地增值税	Land Value Added Tax	1 147 710
11.车船使用税和牌照税	Tax on the Use of Vehicles and Ships	127 064
12.耕地占用税	Tax on the Occupancy of Cultivated Land	72 751
13.契　税	Contract Tax	1 719 163
14.专项收入	Expert Project Income	1 014 246
15.行政性收费收入	Income From Administrative Fees	274 117
16.罚没收入	Penalty and Confiscatory Income	155 521
17.国有资源(资产)有偿使用收入	Revenues of Compensation for Use of State-owned Resources (Assets)	368 054
18.其他收入	Other Income	129 458
政府性基金收入	**Government Fund's Income**	**16 909 879**
国有资本经营收入	**State-owned Assets Profit**	**171 606**
附：土地基金收入	**Land Fund Income**	**16 442 958**
社保基金收入	**Social Security Fund's Income**	**12 320 758**

FINANCIAL REVENUE (2018)

(10 000 yuan)

市 区 Urban Area	# 吴江区 Wujiang District	常 熟 Changshu	张家港 Zhangjiagang	昆 山 Kunshan	太 仓 Taicang
8 708 976	**1 428 115**	**1 684 987**	**1 860 525**	**2 917 417**	**1 217 204**
4 206 832	745 494	794 312	999 973	1 581 033	646 043
182 163	4 111	127 484	3 848	11 085	20 086
3 155 417	532 101	577 217	683 124	1 019 531	454 987
1 164 564	146 409	185 974	173 580	305 768	96 088
11 325 636	**2 029 000**	**2 110 591**	**2 334 288**	**3 878 858**	**1 550 558**
10 396 907	1 835 998	1 843 172	2 099 997	3 560 096	1 395 235
4 167 653	741 579	793 195	995 401	1 578 921	645 350
37 833	3 915	1 116	4 571	2 111	693
2 103 611	354 734	384 812	455 416	679 687	303 325
776 377	97 606	123 983	115 720	203 846	64 059
73	–	–	–	–	–
634 231	114 685	107 009	123 203	225 344	90 399
510 374	90 524	98 757	81 153	181 078	61 323
127 180	27 804	24 747	42 591	46 541	18 719
176 800	60 379	45 808	45 180	72 286	41 371
562 889	141 345	75 523	100 539	349 341	59 418
69 677	15 216	17 461	15 913	15 992	8 021
35 264	18 085	2 943	16 405	5 653	12 486
1 187 083	166 179	160 853	85 910	197 352	87 965
512 561	95 857	104 495	118 579	200 976	77 635
128 059	56 674	31 012	59 667	35 502	19 877
81 173	25 829	15 583	18 801	30 024	9 940
133 983	8 734	108 342	35 074	51 172	39 483
80 815	9 855	14 952	20 165	3 032	10 494
10 316 163	**1 702 031**	**1 941 497**	**1 901 869**	**1 306 247**	**1 444 103**
141 621	**14 305**	**11 192**	**5 828**	**7 559**	**5 406**
10 116 747	**1 656 457**	**1 876 506**	**1 834 983**	**1 218 284**	**1 396 438**
7 105 925	**1 083 839**	**1 504 696**	**974 635**	**2 089 194**	**646 308**

表13-4

财 政 支 出 (2018年)

单位：万元

指 标	Item	全 市 Whole Municipality
一般公共预算支出	**Public Finance Budget Expenditure**	**19 527 090**
1. 一般公共服务支出	General Public Services Spending	1 869 266
2. 国防支出	Expenditure on National Defense	32 013
3. 公共安全支出	Public Safety Spending	1 503 563
4. 教育支出	Expenditure for Operating Expenses of Education	3 129 530
5. 科学技术支出	Science and Technology Spending	1 522 777
6. 文化体育与传媒支出	Culture, Sports and the Media	488 845
7. 社会保障与就业支出	Social Security and Employment	1 854 606
8. 医疗卫生与计划生育支出	Expenditure for Medicine and Public Health	1 128 882
9. 节能环保支出	Energy Saving and Environmental Protection Spending	578 667
10. 城乡社区支出	Urban and Rural Community Affairs Spending	3 778 974
11. 农林水支出	Agricultural, Forestry and Water Affairs Spending	1 081 020
12. 交通运输支出	Transportation Spending	649 632
13. 资源勘探信息等支出	Resource Exploring, Mining, Power, Information and Other Matters	520 904
14. 商业服务业等支出	Expenditure for Affairs of Commerce and Services	260 626
15. 金融支出	Financial Supervision Expenditures	30 560
16. 住房保障支出	Housing Security Expenditure	630 727
17. 其他支出	Other Expenditure	466 498
政府性基金支出	**Fund Expenditure**	**17 382 713**
国有资金经营支出	**State-owned Assets Expenditure**	**110 358**
附：土地基金支出	**Land Fund Expenditures**	**16 604 292**
社保基金支出	**Social Insurance Funds Spending**	**9 385 583**

FINANCIAL EXPENDITURE (2018)

(10 000 yuan)

市 区 Urban Area	# 吴江区 Wujiang District	常 熟 Changshu	张家港 Zhangjiagang	昆 山 Kunshan	太 仓 Taicang
11 065 155	**1 930 641**	**1 831 208**	**2 119 909**	**3 184 901**	**1 325 917**
1 087 494	204 060	200 044	185 976	268 234	127 518
26 445	18	433	4 361	765	9
888 771	153 586	161 872	113 595	242 092	97 233
1 676 496	309 077	353 352	336 026	537 698	225 958
790 959	110 466	196 100	129 778	304 800	101 140
356 198	20 372	28 106	35 310	47 010	22 221
885 978	192 140	181 710	197 043	466 866	123 009
665 381	184 935	104 402	125 578	165 362	68 159
329 953	72 229	66 958	82 770	59 069	39 917
2 223 673	293 512	161 575	496 371	667 500	229 855
480 195	180 642	130 453	171 604	195 086	103 682
388 806	40 811	107 398	69 793	55 681	27 954
400 463	27 945	28 050	7 511	49 517	35 363
139 784	26 301	36 930	17 035	52 170	14 707
19 768	324	5 273	1 810	3 555	154
465 890	67 140	4 005	98 307	6 882	55 643
238 901	47 083	64 547	47 041	62 614	53 395
10 516 032	**1 719 575**	**2 154 706**	**1 788 463**	**1 481 104**	**1 442 408**
92 061	**12 311**	**6 729**	**3 779**	**5 559**	**2 230**
10 122 569	**1 633 039**	**2 056 132**	**1 686 292**	**1 358 558**	**1 380 741**
4 839 366	**873 118**	**1 516 675**	**1 044 281**	**1 351 891**	**633 370**

表13-5

历年末金融机构人民币存贷款余额
RMB SAVINGS DEPOSITS AND LOANS BALANCES OF BANK OVER THE YEARS

单位：万元 (10 000 yuan)

年 份 Year	存款余额 Deposits Balance	# 非金融企业存款 Deposits of Non-financial Enterprises	# 住户存款 Deposits of Households	贷款余额 Loans Balance	# 短期贷款 Short-term Loans	# 中长期贷款 Medium-term & Long-term Loans
1949	156			42		
1952	2 628			1 129		
1957	10 086			14 829		
1962	15 282			43 349		
1970	46 648		6 594	55 652		
1975	58 822		12 166	107 202		
1978	73 712		17 650	154 512		
1980	156 817		36 420	211 885		
1985	375 702		148 233	530 070		
1990	1 321 970		733 332	1 340 967		
1995	5 666 541		2 964 938	4 240 689		
2000	14 770 111	6 733 142	8 036 969	9 705 954	7 932 854	1 083 065
2001	17 316 246	7 946 830	9 369 416	10 598 232	7 180 674	2 092 396
2002	22 320 343	10 677 086	11 643 257	14 909 634	9 628 354	3 566 462
2003	31 497 894	16 792 849	14 705 045	23 592 819	13 182 488	7 852 521
2004	38 145 281	21 022 535	17 122 746	29 157 370	13 238 438	12 332 891
2005	47 300 532	26 705 335	20 595 197	34 783 428	14 500 920	16 102 524
2006	57 979 732	33 705 530	24 274 202	44 297 084	19 137 227	20 910 608
2007	70 688 313	44 754 186	25 934 127	53 438 723	23 500 261	27 119 966
2008	83 407 921	50 034 758	33 373 163	63 018 052	25 972 919	32 042 110
2009	109 502 460	69 961 663	39 540 797	85 053 331	29 919 426	49 617 005
2010	135 703 495	89 147 878	46 555 617	101 331 459	36 213 284	62 210 323
2011	151 807 837	93 011 695	50 785 927	118 738 914	46 491 697	68 747 120
2012	176 634 972	107 584 791	57 877 466	136 268 590	57 167 975	75 039 745
2013	200 375 764	121 140 828	64 083 214	154 952 420	64 243 243	85 633 724
2014老口径	214 281 958	131 009 027	67 534 428	172 479 352	65 043 131	99 991 516
2014新口径	217 551 680	88 486 421	70 226 320			
2015	236 590 970	96 762 241	73 580 383	192 001 015	66 332 289	114 026 353
2016	258 642 564	103 976 434	79 138 477	219 244 382	64 904 030	139 918 079
2017	264 675 936	102 081 735	81 664 372	239 866 220	71 247 882	159 507 657
2018	285 604 469	107 778 780	91 684 488	265 462 298	76 168 054	176 798 368

注：2014年老口径及以前年份，住户存款为城乡居民人民币储蓄存款余额口径，非金融企业存款为单位存款口径。2014年新口径及以后调整为住户存款口径和非金融企业存款。下同。

Note: 2014 year old caliber and previous years, the scope of household deposits was amount of saving deposits in urban and rural areas, the scope of non-financial enterprises deposits was the unit deposit caliber. 2014 new caliber and later adjusted to the scope of the household deposits and non-financial enterprises deposits. The same below.

表13-6

历年末分地区住户存款余额
RMB SAVINGS DEPOSITS OF URBAN HOUSEHOLDS OVER THE YEARS BY REGION

单位：万元 (10 000 yuan)

年 份 Year	全 市 Whole Municipality	市 区 Urban Area	# 吴江区 Wujiang District	常 熟 Changshu	张家港 Zhangjiagang	昆 山 Kunshan	太 仓 Taicang
1952				146		73	77
1957		346	346	237		243	125
1962		206	206	479		272	343
1965	6 474	3 430	253	1 393	389	517	745
1970	6 594	3 248	366	1 372	628	401	945
1975	12 166	6 483	734	2 510	1 290	594	1 289
1978	17 650	9 195	966	3 502	1 927	1 151	1 875
1980	36 420	18 145	2 394	7 302	3 859	3 238	3 876
1985	148 233	70 885	12 565	28 046	21 082	11 861	16 359
1990	733 332	347 646	59 407	145 781	105 913	63 927	70 065
1995	2 964 938	1 321 069	240 825	575 609	511 887	301 570	254 803
2000	8 036 969	3 679 369	779 731	1 688 509	1 280 208	764 219	624 664
2001	9 369 416	4 377 810	915 158	1 920 292	1 447 239	923 303	700 772
2002	11 643 257	5 636 011	1 131 190	2 342 284	1 719 504	1 138 562	806 896
2003	14 705 045	7 461 035	1 497 336	2 791 462	1 989 168	1 488 977	974 403
2004	17 122 746	8 672 455	1 747 441	3 187 039	2 285 995	1 827 811	1 149 446
2005	20 595 197	10 582 414	2 231 149	3 790 046	2 668 182	2 229 722	1 324 832
2006	24 274 202	12 646 581	2 715 870	4 207 394	3 162 974	2 740 382	1 516 871
2007	25 934 127	13 413 765	2 861 672	4 404 905	3 385 526	3 126 929	1 603 002
2008	33 373 163	17 243 013	3 648 183	5 545 651	4 393 591	4 148 668	2 042 241
2009	39 540 797	20 485 695	4 414 443	6 522 628	5 208 800	4 921 289	2 402 385
2010	46 555 617	23 992 753	5 155 580	7 563 039	5 970 374	6 092 794	2 936 656
2011	50 785 927	25 914 766	5 556 569	8 120 828	6 656 161	6 840 035	3 254 137
2012	57 877 466	29 695 083	6 349 442	9 071 807	7 467 598	7 871 313	3 771 664
2013	64 083 214	32 856 112	7 009 079	9 874 241	8 330 538	8 814 077	4 208 246
2014老口径	67 534 428	34 328 749	7 387 036	10 219 900	8 770 608	9 709 029	4 506 142
2014新口径	70 226 320	36 315 257	7 745 463	10 499 016	9 051 169	9 800 530	4 560 348
2015	73 580 383	37 621 561	8 079 506	11 046 000	9 587 678	10 460 263	4 864 881
2016	79 138 477	40 250 001	8 711 252	11 927 531	10 182 254	11 551 279	5 227 413
2017	81 664 372	41 505 981	9 249 541	12 253 697	10 272 831	12 185 389	5 446 474
2018	91 684 488	47 639 244	10 454 738	13 417 989	11 133 659	13 560 468	5 933 127

表13-7 金融机构人民币信贷收支情况（2018年末）

单位：万元

指　标	Item	全　市 Whole Municipality
年末金融机构人民币存款余额	**Deposits Balance of National Banking System by Year End**	**285 604 469**
# 住户存款	Deposits of Households	91 684 488
活期存款	Demand Deposits	36 648 967
定期及其他存款	Time & Other Deposits	55 035 521
非金融企业存款	Deposits of Non-financial Enterprises	107 778 780
活期存款	Demand Deposits	41 252 603
定期及其他存款	Time & Other Deposits	66 526 177
广义政府存款	Fiscal Deposit	72 611 019
年末金融机构人民币贷款余额	**Loans Balance of National Banking System by Year End**	**265 462 298**
境内贷款	Domestic Loans	265 162 930
# 住户贷款	Loans to Households	99 223 375
短期贷款	Short-term Loans	13 150 244
中长期贷款	Mid & Long-term Loans	86 073 131
非金融企业及机关团体贷款	Loans to Non-financial Enterprises and Government Departments & Organizations	165 919 554
# 短期贷款	Short-term Loans	63 017 810
中长期贷款	Mid & Long-term Loans	90 725 237
票据融资	Paper Financing	10 584 435
境外贷款	Overseas Loans	299 368

RMB CREDIT FUNDS BALANCE OF FINANCIAL INSTITUTIONS (END OF 2018)

(10 000 yuan)

市　区 Urban Area	# 吴江区 Wujiang District	常　熟 Changshu	张家港 Zhangjiagang	昆　山 Kunshan	太　仓 Taicang
171 009 791	**27 399 945**	**30 566 388**	**28 101 976**	**40 649 893**	**15 276 421**
47 639 244	10 454 738	13 417 989	11 133 659	13 560 468	5 933 127
19 690 162	4 373 850	4 856 239	3 624 149	6 261 682	2 216 736
27 949 083	6 080 887	8 561 750	7 509 511	7 298 786	3 716 391
67 004 411	11 014 340	10 352 815	11 131 607	13 549 232	5 740 715
25 732 378	4 348 604	3 730 609	3 770 404	5 888 625	2 130 587
41 272 033	6 665 736	6 622 206	7 361 203	7 660 607	3 610 129
45 299 330	5 656 821	6 087 839	5 189 281	12 535 280	3 499 289
170 840 564	**26 424 780**	**24 440 621**	**23 240 111**	**32 080 114**	**14 860 888**
170 638 626	26 401 521	24 437 099	23 225 847	32 004 764	14 856 593
63 219 937	8 865 401	7 660 532	6 801 862	16 906 533	4 634 511
8 028 640	1 092 521	1 850 536	1 040 782	1 589 958	640 329
55 191 298	7 772 880	5 809 997	5 761 080	15 316 575	3 994 182
107 418 689	17 536 119	16 776 567	16 423 985	15 098 231	10 202 082
35 309 087	10 341 120	7 787 480	8 800 215	6 393 693	4 727 335
63 138 836	6 734 005	8 129 971	6 551 062	7 972 107	4 933 261
7 424 382	458 115	858 090	1 065 120	731 273	505 569
201 938	23 259	3 521	14 264	75 350	4 294

表13-8 金融机构本外币信贷收支情况（2018年末）

单位：万元

指　　标	Item	全　市 Whole Municipality
年末金融机构本外币存款余额	**Deposits Balance of National Banking System by Year End**	**305 233 686**
# 住户存款	Deposits of Households	93 095 170
活期存款	Demand Deposits	37 381 168
定期及其他存款	Time & Other Deposits	55 714 002
非金融企业存款	Deposits of Non-financial Enterprises	125 156 574
活期存款	Demand Deposits	47 760 130
定期及其他存款	Time & Other Deposits	77 396 443
广义政府存款	Fiscal Deposit	73 019 549
年末金融机构本外币贷款余额	**Loans Balance of National Banking System by Year End**	**274 409 404**
境内贷款	Domestic Loans	273 859 142
# 住户贷款	Loans to Households	99 229 363
短期贷款	Short-term Loans	13 156 232
中长期贷款	Mid & Long-term Loans	86 073 131
非金融企业及机关团体贷款	Loans to Non-financial Enterprises and Government Departments & Organizations	174 609 779
# 短期贷款	Short-term Loans	70 852 107
中长期贷款	Mid & Long-term Loans	91 564 352
票据融资	Paper Financing	10 584 494
境外贷款	Overseas Loans	550 262

RMB AND FOREIGN CURRENCY CREDIT FUNDS BALANCE OF FINANCIAL INSTITUTIONS (END OF 2018)

(10 000 yuan)

市 区 Urban Area	# 吴江区 Wujiang District	常 熟 Changshu	张家港 Zhangjiagang	昆 山 Kunshan	太 仓 Taicang
180 701 232	**29 129 654**	**32 795 792**	**29 287 228**	**46 749 381**	**15 700 053**
48 617 360	10 539 669	13 553 311	11 247 487	13 689 105	5 987 907
20 209 656	4 414 426	4 911 497	3 680 109	6 334 888	2 245 018
28 407 704	6 125 242	8 641 814	7 567 377	7 354 217	3 742 889
74 953 797	12 654 959	12 426 684	12 184 013	19 489 275	6 102 806
29 207 944	4 759 879	4 335 085	4 515 906	7 290 451	2 410 745
45 745 853	7 895 080	8 091 599	7 668 106	12 198 824	3 692 061
45 692 930	5 656 835	6 088 048	5 189 313	12 549 777	3 499 481
175 791 987	**27 308 445**	**25 521 430**	**23 688 491**	**34 413 966**	**14 993 528**
175 403 067	27 265 225	25 464 095	23 670 359	34 332 387	14 989 234
63 223 423	8 865 876	7 661 234	6 802 663	16 907 204	4 634 839
8 032 125	1 092 996	1 851 238	1 041 583	1 590 629	640 657
55 191 298	7 772 880	5 809 997	5 761 080	15 316 575	3 994 182
112 179 645	18 399 349	17 802 861	16 867 696	17 425 183	10 334 395
39 436 424	11 192 055	8 813 176	9 222 373	8 538 633	4 841 501
63 756 271	6 746 300	8 130 509	6 572 046	8 154 119	4 951 407
7 424 382	458 115	858 149	1 065 120	731 273	505 569
388 920	43 221	57 336	18 132	81 579	4 294

表13-9

金融机构人民币法定存款利率
OFFICIAL INTEREST RATES OF DEPOSITS OF FINANCIAL INSTITUTIONS

单位:年利率 % (% p.a.)

调整时间 Adjustment Time	活 期 Demand	定 期 Time					
		3个月 3 Months	6个月 6 Months	1年 1 Year	2年 2 Years	3年 3 Years	5年 5 Years
1990.04.15	2.88	6.30	7.74	10.08	10.98	11.88	13.68
1990.08.21	2.16	4.32	6.48	8.64	9.36	10.08	11.52
1991.04.21	1.80	3.24	5.40	7.56	7.92	8.28	9.00
1993.05.15	2.16	4.86	7.20	9.18	9.90	10.80	12.06
1993.07.11	3.15	6.66	9.00	10.98	11.70	12.24	13.86
1996.05.01	2.97	4.86	7.20	9.18	9.90	10.80	12.06
1996.08.23	1.98	3.33	5.40	7.47	7.92	8.28	9.00
1997.10.23	1.71	2.88	4.14	5.67	5.94	6.21	6.66
1998.03.25	1.71	2.88	4.14	5.22	5.58	6.21	6.66
1998.07.01	1.44	2.79	3.96	4.77	4.86	4.95	5.22
1998.12.07	1.44	2.79	3.33	3.78	3.96	4.14	4.50
1999.06.10	0.99	1.98	2.16	2.25	2.43	2.70	2.88
2002.02.21	0.72	1.71	1.89	1.98	2.25	2.52	2.79
2004.10.29	0.72	1.71	2.07	2.25	2.70	3.24	3.60
2006.08.19	0.72	1.80	2.25	2.52	3.06	3.69	4.14
2007.03.18	0.72	1.98	2.43	2.79	3.33	3.96	4.41
2007.05.19	0.72	2.07	2.61	3.06	3.69	4.41	4.95
2007.07.21	0.81	2.34	2.88	3.33	3.96	4.68	5.22
2007.08.22	0.81	2.61	3.15	3.60	4.23	4.95	5.49
2007.09.15	0.81	2.88	3.42	3.87	4.50	5.22	5.76
2007.12.21	0.72	3.33	3.78	4.14	4.68	5.40	5.85
2008.10.09	0.72	3.15	3.51	3.87	4.41	5.13	5.58
2008.10.30	0.72	2.88	3.24	3.60	4.14	4.77	5.13
2008.11.27	0.36	1.98	2.25	2.52	3.06	3.60	3.87
2008.12.23	0.36	1.71	1.98	2.25	2.79	3.33	3.60
2010.10.20	0.36	1.91	2.20	2.50	3.25	3.85	4.20
2010.12.26	0.36	2.25	2.50	2.75	3.55	4.15	4.55
2011.02.09	0.40	2.60	2.80	3.00	3.90	4.50	5.00
2011.04.06	0.50	2.85	3.05	3.25	4.15	4.75	5.25
2011.07.07	0.50	3.10	3.30	3.50	4.40	5.00	5.50
2012.06.08	0.40	2.85	3.05	3.25	4.10	4.65	5.10
2012.07.06	0.35	2.60	2.80	3.00	3.75	4.25	4.75
2014.11.22	0.35	2.35	2.55	2.75	3.35	4.00	
2015.03.01	0.35	2.10	2.30	2.50	3.10	3.75	
2015.05.11	0.35	1.85	2.05	2.25	2.85	3.50	
2015.06.28	0.35	1.60	1.80	2.00	2.60	3.25	
2015.08.26	0.35	1.35	1.55	1.75	2.35	3.00	
2015.10.24	0.35	1.10	1.30	1.50	2.10	2.75	

注：自2014年11月22日起，人民银行不再公布金融机构人民币五年期定期存款基准利率。
Note: Since November 22, 2014, People's Bank of China stoped publishing five years benchmark deposit rate on a regular basis of financial institutions.

表13-10

金融机构人民币法定贷款利率
OFFICIAL INTEREST RATES OF LOANS OF FINANCIAL INSTITUTIONS

单位:年利率 % (% p.a.)

调整时间 Adjustment Time	6个月 6 Months	1年 1 Year	1至3年(含) 1-3 Years (include 3 years)	3至5年(含) 3-5 Years (include 5 years)	5年以上 Above 5 Years
1991.04.21	8.10	8.64	9.00	9.54	9.72
1993.05.15	8.82	9.36	10.80	12.06	12.24
1993.07.11	9.00	10.98	12.24	13.86	14.04
1995.01.01	9.00	10.98	12.96	14.58	14.76
1995.07.01	10.08	12.06	13.50	15.12	15.30
1996.05.01	9.72	10.98	13.14	14.94	15.12
1996.08.23	9.18	10.08	10.98	11.70	12.42
1997.10.23	7.65	8.64	9.36	9.90	10.53
1998.03.25	7.02	7.92	9.00	9.72	10.35
1998.07.01	6.57	6.93	7.11	7.65	8.01
1998.12.07	6.12	6.39	6.66	7.20	7.56
1999.06.10	5.58	5.85	5.94	6.03	6.21
2002.02.21	5.04	5.31	5.49	5.58	5.76
2004.10.29	5.22	5.58	5.76	5.85	6.12
2006.04.28	5.40	5.85	6.03	6.12	6.39
2006.08.19	5.58	6.12	6.30	6.48	6.84
2007.03.18	5.67	6.39	6.57	6.75	7.11
2007.05.19	5.85	6.57	6.75	6.93	7.20
2007.07.21	6.03	6.84	7.02	7.20	7.38
2007.08.22	6.21	7.02	7.20	7.38	7.56
2007.09.15	6.48	7.29	7.47	7.65	7.83
2007.12.21	6.57	7.47	7.56	7.74	7.83
2008.09.16	6.21	7.20	7.29	7.56	7.74
2008.10.09	6.12	6.93	7.02	7.29	7.47
2008.10.30	6.03	6.66	6.75	7.02	7.20
2008.11.27	5.04	5.58	5.67	5.94	6.12
2008.12.23	4.86	5.31	5.40	5.76	5.94
2010.10.20	5.10	5.56	5.60	5.96	6.14
2010.12.26	5.35	5.81	5.85	6.22	6.40
2011.02.09	5.60	6.06	6.10	6.45	6.60
2011.04.06	5.85	6.31	6.40	6.65	6.80
2011.07.07	6.10	6.56	6.65	6.90	7.05
2012.06.08	5.85	6.31	6.40	6.65	6.80
2012.07.06	5.60	6.00	6.15	6.40	6.55
2014.11.22	1年(含)以内：5.60		1-5年(含)：6.00		6.15
2015.03.01	1年(含)以内：5.35		1-5年(含)：5.75		5.90
2015.05.11	1年(含)以内：5.10		1-5年(含)：5.50		5.65
2015.06.28	1年(含)以内：4.85		1-5年(含)：5.25		5.40
2015.08.26	1年(含)以内：4.60		1-5年(含)：5.00		5.15
2015.10.24	1年(含)以内：4.35		1-5年(含)：4.75		4.90

注：自2014年11月22日起，金融机构人民币贷款基准利率期限档次简并为一年以内（含一年）、一至五年（含五年）和五年以上三个档次。
Note:Since November 22, 2014, financial institutions RMB loan benchmark interest rates merge into three grades, within a year (including one year), one to five years (including five years) and more than five years .

表13-11

保险业务情况 (2018年)

单位：万元

指　标	Item	全　市 Whole Municipality
一、财产险承保额	**Insurance Value of Property Insurance**	**2 556 248 890**
# 企业财产险	Enterprise Property Insurance	380 408 655
机动车辆险	Motor Vehicle Insurance	433 253 430
货物运输险	Freight Transport Insurance	156 887 786
家庭财产险	Family Property Insurance	49 792 231
二、保费收入	**Premiums**	**6 297 057**
1.财产险	Property Insurance	2 084 359
# 企业财产险	Enterprise Property Insurance	159 045
机动车辆险	Motor Vehicle Insurance	1 470 247
货物运输险	Freight Transport Insurance	31 292
家庭财产险	Family Property Insurance	19 449
2.人身险	Life Insurance	4 212 698
# 寿　险	Life Insurance	3 234 299
三、当年赔款和给付	**Indemnity Expenditure and Payment of the Year**	**1 813 029**
1.财产险	Property Insurance	1 195 501
# 企业财产险	Enterprise Property Insurance	67 017
机动车辆险	Motor Vehicle Insurance	930 280
货物运输险	Freight Transport Insurance	10 532
家庭财产险	Family Property Insurance	6 628
2.人身险	Life Insurance	617 528
# 寿　险	Life Insurance	401 947

CONDITIONS OF INSURANCE BUSINESS (2018)

(10 000 yuan)

市 区 Urban Area	# 吴江区 Wujiang District	常 熟 Changshu	张家港 Zhangjiagang	昆 山 Kunshan	太 仓 Taicang
2 018 590 831	**94 627 951**	**152 061 355**	**108 840 954**	**202 606 866**	**74 148 884**
285 798 280	18 290 565	23 952 159	26 962 572	26 451 522	17 244 121
327 397 703	26 014 063	35 134 294	27 571 707	27 398 550	15 751 176
126 328 058	7 495 066	9 090 205	10 213 329	4 661 045	6 595 150
32 287 668	2 614 547	2 777 929	4 142 185	8 261 886	2 322 564
4 047 771	**446 930**	**563 308**	**613 559**	**801 058**	**271 361**
1 280 377	187 802	212 647	188 730	287 329	115 276
108 697	9 632	17 233	11 228	13 272	8 616
837 687	147 797	165 179	149 890	229 449	88 041
23 089	1 604	2 225	2 306	1 973	1 699
14 104	1 448	1 436	799	2 226	884
2 767 394	259 127	350 661	424 829	513 730	156 085
2 141 006	205 319	282 321	334 636	348 807	127 529
1 109 991	**138 239**	**192 795**	**183 156**	**229 101**	**97 986**
715 594	98 990	131 778	120 322	159 505	68 303
47 845	3 792	6 871	3 378	3 749	5 173
545 762	86 079	104 651	94 364	130 667	54 835
8 499	560	383	1 040	418	193
4 620	510	818	278	613	298
394 398	39 249	61 017	62 834	69 596	29 683
228 614	28 730	51 070	48 575	48 832	24 856

表13-12

外资金融机构及代表处一览表
LIST OF FOREIGN FINANCIAL LNSTITUTIONS AND REPRESENTATIVE OFFICES

机构(代表处)名称 Name of Institutions	所属国家(地区) Representative Offices	所在地区 Location	批准日期 Date of Approval
三井住友银行(中国)有限公司苏州分行	日　本	高新区、虎丘区	2009年04月07日
汇丰银行(中国)有限公司苏州分行	中国香港	工业园区	2007年03月29日
渣打银行(中国)有限公司苏州分行	英　国	工业园区	2007年03月29日
星展银行(中国)有限公司苏州分行	新加坡	工业园区	2007年05月24日
日本池田泉州银行股份有限公司苏州代表处	日　本	吴中区	2006年08月02日
友利银行(中国)有限公司苏州分行	韩　国	工业园区	2007年10月30日
企业银行(中国)有限公司苏州分行	韩　国	工业园区	2009年06月10日
东亚银行(中国)有限公司苏州分行	中国香港	工业园区	2010年03月15日
国民银行(中国)有限公司苏州分行	韩　国	工业园区	2012年12月04日
瑞穗银行(中国)有限公司苏州分行	日　本	工业园区	2010年08月25日
合作金库商业银行股份有限公司苏州分行	中国台湾	工业园区	2010年12月17日
富邦华一银行有限公司苏州分行	中国台湾	工业园区	2011年06月24日
摩根大通银行(中国)有限公司苏州分行	美　国	工业园区	2012年05月18日
兆丰国际商业银行股份有限公司苏州分行	中国台湾	工业园区	2012年06月15日
三菱日联银行(中国)有限公司苏州分行	日　本	工业园区	2014年05月04日
南洋商业银行(中国)有限公司苏州分行	中国香港	工业园区	2014年06月09日
华侨永亨银行(中国)有限公司苏州分行	新加坡	工业园区	2014年10月09日
大华银行(中国)有限公司苏州分行	新加坡	工业园区	2015年02月16日
彰银商业银行有限公司昆山分行	中国台湾	昆山市	2018年09月20日

表13-13

外资保险公司及代表处一览表
LIST OF FOREIGN INSURANCE COMPANIES AND REPRESENTATIVE OFFICES

机构(代表处)名称 Name of Institutions	所属国家(地区) Representative Offices	所在地区 Location	批准日期 Date of Approval
史带财产保险股份有限公司苏州分公司	美　国	工业园区	2001年09月28日
中信保诚人寿苏州营销服务部	英　国	工业园区	2005年04月21日
北大方正人寿苏州中心支公司	日　本	姑苏区	2006年12月19日
安盛天平财产保险股份有限公司苏州中心支公司	法　国	工业园区	2006年12月20日
陆家嘴国泰人寿江苏分公司苏州营销服务部	中国台湾	工业园区	2007年11月09日
中德安联人寿江苏分公司苏州营销服务部	德　国	高新区、虎丘区	2007年12月26日
华泰人寿苏州中心支公司	美　国	工业园区	2008年03月28日
恒安标准人寿江苏分公司苏州中心支公司	英　国	工业园区	2008年05月26日
友邦保险苏州中心支公司	中国香港	工业园区	2008年05月29日
三星财产(中国)苏州分公司	韩　国	工业园区	2008年07月10日
工银安盛人寿保险有限公司苏州中心支公司	法　国	姑苏区	2008年12月02日
中美联泰大都会人寿保险有限公司苏州支公司	美　国	工业园区	2010年03月05日
日本财险(中国)江苏分公司	日　本	工业园区	2010年06月10日
长生人寿江苏分公司苏州营销服务部	日　本	吴中区	2010年07月21日
乐爱金苏州营销服务部	韩　国	工业园区	2011年01月04日
三井住友海上火灾保险(中国)江苏分公司苏州营销服务部	日　本	工业园区	2011年05月20日
东京海上日动(中国)江苏分公司	日　本	工业园区	2011年07月19日
国泰产险江苏分公司苏州营销服务部	中国台湾	姑苏区	2011年07月21日
中意人寿江苏省分公司苏州中心支公司	意大利	姑苏区	2011年08月02日
中宏人寿保险有限公司江苏分公司苏州中心支公司	中国香港	姑苏区	2011年08月03日
交银康联苏州市中心支公司	澳大利亚	工业园区	2012年04月10日
瑞泰人寿苏州中心支公司	英　国	工业园区	2013年05月07日
美亚保险江苏分公司苏州营业部	美　国	工业园区	2014年10月13日
招商信诺人寿保险有限公司江苏省苏州分公司	美　国	工业园区	2016年07月28日
平安健康保险股份有限公司苏州分公司	南　非	工业园区	2018年01月16日
中银三星人寿保险有限公司苏州中心支公司	韩　国	工业园区	2018年09月28日
德华安顾人寿保险有限公司苏州中心支公司	德　国	工业园区	2018年12月29日

表13-14 分地区养老、医疗、失业、工伤、生育及居民养老保险人数（2018年末）
NUMBER OF PEOPLE PARTICIPATING IN PENSION, MEDICAL, UNEMPLOYMENT, WORK INJURY, MATERNITY AND RESIDENT INSURANCE BY REGION(END OF 2018)

单位：人 (person)

地　区	Region	基本养老保险参保人数 Number of People Covered by Endowment Insurance	基本医疗保险参保人数 Number of People Covered by Medical Insurance		
			在职职工参保人数 Fully Employed Staff and Workers	退休人员参保人数 Number of Retired People	
全　市	**Whole Municipality**	**5 758 290**	**7 370 769**	**5 826 329**	**1 544 440**
市　区	**Urban Area**	**2 932 407**	**3 697 628**	**3 023 360**	**674 268**
本　级	The Level	825 819	1 188 448	864 112	324 336
吴中区	Wuzhong District	431 704	556 884	453 867	103 017
相城区	Xiangcheng District	262 278	317 170	276 658	40 512
工业园区	Industrial Park	824 819	876 405	837 736	38 669
吴江区	Wujiang District	587 787	758 721	590 987	167 734
县级市	**Cities at County Level**	**2 825 883**	**3 673 141**	**2 802 969**	**870 172**
常　熟	Changshu	624 708	907 208	608 681	298 527
张家港	Zhangjiagang	511 485	742 834	537 343	205 491
昆　山	Kunshan	1 338 725	1 511 479	1 297 752	213 727
太　仓	Taicang	350 965	511 620	359 193	152 427

表13-14 续表 Continued

单位：人 (person)

地　区	Region	失业保险参保人数 Number of People Covered by Unemployment Insurance	工伤保险参保人数 Number of People Covered by Work Injury Insurance	生育保险参保人数 Number of People Covered by Childbirth Insurance	居民养老保险参保人数 Rural Number of People Covered by Endowment Insurance
全　市	**Whole Municipality**	**5 050 209**	**5 122 263**	**5 291 255**	**478 525**
市　区	**Urban Area**	**2 667 173**	**2 701 186**	**2 872 109**	**258 776**
本　级	The Level	763 674	775 690	853 507	21 610
吴中区	Wuzhong District	378 403	382 606	447 957	20 309
相城区	Xiangcheng District	235 529	237 620	274 477	61 546
工业园区	Industrial Park	805 214	810 200	801 100	34 282
吴江区	Wujiang District	484 353	495 070	495 068	121 029
县级市	**Cities at County Level**	**2 383 036**	**2 421 077**	**2 419 146**	**219 749**
常　熟	Changshu	474 215	491 950	490 649	88 465
张家港	Zhangjiagang	431 743	438 550	437 931	73 898
昆　山	Kunshan	1 172 248	1 180 983	1 180 994	30 823
太　仓	Taicang	304 830	309 594	309 572	26 563

注：本级数据为姑苏区和高新区、虎丘区的合计数。
Note: The level data is the totals of Gusu District, Suzhou New District and Huqiu (Tiger Hill) District.

表13-15 分地区养老、医疗、失业、工伤、生育及居民养老保险基金收入(2018年) FUND INCOME OF PENSION, MEDICAL, UNEMPLOYMENT, WORK INJURY, MATERNITY AND RESIDENT INSURANCE BY REGION(2018)

单位：万元 (10 000 yuan)

地 区	Region	基本养老保险基金收入 Fund's Income Covered by Endowment Insurance	基本医疗保险基金收入 Fund's Income Covered by Medical Insurance	失业保险基金收入 Fund's Income Covered by Unemployment Insurance
全 市	**Whole Municipality**	**6 116 859**	**2 383 333**	**234 229**
市 区	**Urban Area**	**3 719 226**	**1 320 301**	**147 158**
本 级	The Level	1 201 614	521 056	49 633
吴中区	Wuzhong District	485 588	190 320	16 315
相城区	Xiangcheng District	299 183	107 756	9 701
工业园区	Industrial Park	1 189 519	284 566	54 496
吴江区	Wujiang District	543 322	216 603	17 013
县级市	**Cities at County Level**	**2 397 633**	**1 063 032**	**87 071**
常 熟	Changshu	543 024	248 502	19 348
张家港	Zhangjiagang	466 106	220 287	16 764
昆 山	Kunshan	1 061 129	448 712	38 844
太 仓	Taicang	327 374	145 531	12 116

表13-15 续表 Continued

单位：万元 (10 000 yuan)

地 区	Region	工伤保险基金收入 Fund's Income Covered by Work Injury Insurance	生育保险基金收入 Fund's Income Covered by Childbirth Insurance	居民养老保险基金收入 Fund's Income Covered by Endowment Insurance
全 市	**Whole Municipality**	**224 419**	**196 319**	**228 946**
市 区	**Urban Area**	**83 231**	**124 169**	**100 072**
本 级	The Level	16 104	41 683	12 507
吴中区	Wuzhong District	7 521	14 100	12 583
相城区	Xiangcheng District	7 798	8 348	13 292
工业园区	Industrial Park	26 099	44 378	5 364
吴江区	Wujiang District	25 709	15 660	56 326
县级市	**Cities at County Level**	**141 188**	**72 150**	**128 874**
常 熟	Changshu	25 765	16 985	56 125
张家港	Zhangjiagang	39 532	13 517	32 582
昆 山	Kunshan	56 568	31 955	26 190
太 仓	Taicang	19 323	9 693	13 977

注:本级数据为姑苏区和高新区、虎丘区的合计数。
Note: The level data is the totals of Gusu District, Suzhou New District and Huqiu (Tiger Hill) District.

主 要 统 计 指 标 解 释

中央财政收入和地方财政收入 指按现行分税制财政体制划分的中央本级收入和地方本级收入。1994年实行分税制财政体制以后，属于中央财政的收入包括关税、海关代征消费税和增值税，消费税，中央企业所得税，地方银行和外资银行及非银行金融企业所得税，铁道部门、各银行总行、各保险总公司等集中缴纳的营业税、利润和城市维护建设税，车辆购置税，船舶吨税，增值税的75%部分，证券交易税(印花税)94%部分，个人所得税中的利息所得税，利息所得税之外的个人所得税中央分享的部分，海洋石油资源税。属于地方财政的收入包括营业税，地方企业所得税，利息所得税之外的个人所得税地方分享的部分，城镇土地使用税，固定资产投资方向调节税，城镇维护建设税，房产税，车船使用税，印花税，屠宰税，农牧业税，农业特产税，耕地占用税，契税，土地增值税、国有土地有偿使用收入，增值税25%部分，证券交易税(印花税)6%部分和除海洋石油资源税以外的其他资源税。

中央财政支出和地方财政支出 指根据政府在经济和社会活动中的不同职责，划分中央和地方政府的责权，按照政府的责权划分确定的支出。中央财政支出包括国防支出，武装警察部队支出，中央级行政管理费和各项事业费，重点建设支出以及中央政府调整国民经济结构、协调地区发展、实施宏观调控的支出。地方财政支出主要包括地方行政管理和各项事业费，地方统筹的基本建设、技术改造支出，支援农村生产支出，城市维护和建设经费，价格补贴支出等。

存款 指企业、机关、团体或居民根据资金必须收回的原则，把货币资金存入银行或其他信贷机构保管并取得一定利息的一种信用活动形式。根据存款对象或性质的不同可划分为住户存款、非金融企业存款、政府存款、非银行业金融机构存款等科目。它是银行信贷资金的主要来源。

贷款 指银行或其他信贷机构根据资金必须归还的原则，按一定利率，为企业、个人等提供资金的一种信用活动形式。我国银行贷款分为短期贷款、中长期贷款、融资租赁、票据融资、各项垫款、境外贷款等。

保险公司 在中国境内的、经过保险监督管理部门批准设立，并依法登记注册的各类商业保险公司。

保险金额 指保险人承担赔偿或者给付保险金责任的最高限额。

保费 指投保人为取得保险人在约定范围内所承担赔偿责任而支付给保险人的费用。

赔款 指保险人根据保险合同的规定，向被保险人支付的赔偿保险责任损失的金额。

给付 包括死伤医疗给付和满期给付。死伤医疗给付是指保险人根据人寿保险及长期健康保险合同的规定，因被保险人在保险期内发生保险责任范围内的保险事故支付给被保险人(或受益人)的金额。满期给付是指被保险人生存期满，保险人按人寿保险合同规定支付给被保险人的满期保险金额。

基本养老保险（参保）职工人数 指报告期末按照国家法律、法规和有关政策规定参加基本养老保险并在社保经办机构已建立缴费记录档案的职工人数，包括中断缴费但未终止养老保险关系的职工人数，不包括只登记未建立缴费记录档案的人数。

基本医疗保险参保人数 指报告期末按国家有关规定参加基本医疗保险的人数。包括参加保险的职工人数和退休人员人数。

失业保险参保人数 指报告期末按照国家法律、法规和有关政策规定参加了失业保险的城镇企业事业单位的职工及地方政府规定参加失业保险的其他人员的人数。

工伤保险参加保险人数 指报告期末依据国家有关规定参加工伤保险的职工人数。

生育保险参保人数 指报告期末依据有关规定参加生育保险的职工人数。

居民养老保险参保人数 指报告期末，参加城乡居民养老保险（在经办机构参保登记并已建立缴费记录以及制度实施当年已经年满60周岁并在经办机构参保登记）的总人数（不包括已经办理注销登记手续的人数）。

EXPLANATORY NOTES ON MAIN STATISTICAL INDICATORS

Revenue of the Central Government and Revenue of the Local Governments refer to the revenue of the Central Government and that of the local governments as defined by the decentralized taxation system starting from 1994. In accordance with this system, the revenue of the Central Government includes tariff, consumption tax and value added tax levied by the Customs, consumption tax, income tax of the enterprises subordinate to the Central Government, income taxes of local banks, foreign-funded banks and non-bank financial institutions, business tax and profits of railways, head offices of banks, head office of insurance company, which are handed over to the government in a centralized way, tax on city maintenance and construction, tax on purchasing motor vehicles, tonnage tax of ships, 75% of the value added tax, 94% of the tax on stock dealing (stamp tax), interest income tax in the personal income tax, that proportion of the personal income tax (other that interest income tax) to be shared by the Central Government, and tax on ocean petroleum resources. The revenue of the local governments includes business tax, income tax of the enterprises subordinate to the local government, that proportion of the personal income tax (other that interest income tax) to be shared by the Central Government, tax on the use of urban land, tax on the adjustment of investment in fixed assets, tax on town maintenance and construction, tax on real estates, tax on the use of vehicles and ships, stamp tax, slaughter tax, tax on agriculture and animal husbandry, tax on special agricultural products, tax on the occupancy of cultivated land, contract tax, value-added tax on land, income from charges on use of State-owned land, 25% of the value added tax, 6% of the tax on stock dealing (stamp tax) and tax on resources other than the tax on ocean petroleum resources.

Expenditure of the Central Government and Expenditure of the Local Governments according to the different functions of the Central Government and local governments in economic and social activities, the rights of affairs administration are demarcated between those of the Central Government and those of local governments; and the classification of the expenditure between the Central Government and local governments are made on the basis of the classification of the rights of affairs administration between them. The expenditure of the Central Government includes the expenditure for national defence, expenditure for armed police forces, the administrative expenses and various operating expenses at the level of Central Government, expenditure for key projects and the expenditure of the Central Government for adjusting the national economic structure; coordinating the development among different regions; and exercising macro-economic regulation and control. The expenditure of the local governments includes mainly the administrative expenses and various operating expenses at the level of local governments, the expenditure for capital construction and technological innovation with the funds raised by the local government, expenditure for supporting rural production, expenditure for city maintenance and construction and expenditure for price subsidies, etc.

Deposit is a form of credit by which enterprises, institutions, organizations or households can put money into banks and other credit institutions for safekeeping and interest earning under the principle of free withdrawal. According to different depositors, deposits are divided into household deposits, non financial enterprise deposits, government deposits, non banking financial institutions deposits. Deposits are major sources of the credit funds of banks.

Loan is a form of credit by which banks and other credit institutions provide funds at certain interest rate to enterprises and individuals in the light of the principle of unconditional repayment. Loans from Chinese banks include short-term loan, medium-term and long-term loans, financial lease, bill financing, various money advanced, foreign loans.

Insurance Companies refer to commercial insurance companies of various forms registered by law and established in China with the approval of insurance regulatory agencies.

Amount Insured refers to the maximum that the insurant will get for the claim of the case insured.

Premium is the fee paid by the insurant to the insurer to obtain the obligation of compensation from the insurance within the agreed terms.

Settled Claim is the compensation paid by the insurer to the insurant in accordance with the insurance contract.

Payment includes payment for death, injury or medical treatment and payment at maturity. Payment for death, injury or medical treatment refers to the money paid to the insurant (or the beneficiary) in accordance with the life or health insurance contract when the insurant encounters accidents within the insured period covered in the contract. Payment at maturity refers to the payment to the insurant in accordance with the life insurance contract at the end of the insured period.

Number of People Covered by Endowment Insurance refers to staff and workers participating in the basic pension insurance programme according to national laws, regulations and related policies at the end of the reference period, who have already had payment records in social security management agencies, including those who have interrupt payment without terminating the insurance programme. Those who have registered in the programme but with no payment records are not included.

Number of People Covered by Medical Insurance refers to people participating in the basic medical care insurance programme according to related regulations as at the end of reference period, including number of staff and workers and retirees participating in this insurance programme.

Number of People Covered by Unemployment Insurance refers to staff and workers in urban enterprises or institutions who have participated in the unemployment insurance programme according to relevant policies and regulations, and other people who have participated according to local government regulations, as at the end of reference period.

Number of People Covered by Labor Injury Work Injury Insurance refers to staff and workers who have participated in the work injury insurance programme according to relevant national regulations.

Number of People Covered by Insurance refers to staff and workers who have participated in the maternity insurance programme according to relevant regulation at the end of the reporting period.

Number of Residents Participating in Pension Insurance refers to the total number (not including the number of the residents who have already gone through the deregistration procedures) of the urban and rural residents participating in pension insurance (residents who have been registered to participate in pension insurance at the agency and have established payment records and in the year of the implementation of the system are 60 years of age or older and have been registered to participate in pension insurance at the agency) at the end of the reporting period.

十四、物价指数

CHAPTER 14
PRICE INDICES

14 物价指数 PRICE INDICES

主要统计指标 MAJOR STATISTICAL INDICATORS

(以上年价格为100 The Price of Preceding Year is Taken as 100)

2018年市区居民消费价格总指数	General Consumer Price Index of Urban Residents	102.6
食品烟酒类价格指数	General Price Index of Food, Cigarette and Wine in Urban Area	102.2
衣着类价格指数	General Price Index of Clothing in Urban Area	105.0
居住类价格指数	General Price Index of Residence in Urban Area	102.9
生活用品及服务价格指数	General Price Index of Life Articles and Service in Urban Area	103.5
交通和通信类价格指数	General Price Index of Transportation and Communication in Urban Area	101.6
教育文化和娱乐价格指数	General Price Index of Education, Cultural and Recreation in Urban Area	103.1
医疗保健价格指数	General Price Index of Medical Service in Urban Area	100.8
其他用品和服务价格指数	General Price Index of Other Articles and Service in Urban Area	102.5
2018年市区商品零售价格总指数	General Retail Price Index in Urban Area	102.5

表14-1

市区居民消费价格指数及商品零售价格指数
RESIDENTS CONSUMER PRICE INDICES AND RETAIL PRICE INDICES OF COMMODITIES

(2018年以下列各年价格为100　The Price of Following Years is Taken as 100 in 2018)

年 份 Year	居民消费价格总指数 General Residents Consumer Price Index	# 食 品 Food	# 衣 着 Clothing	# 居 住 Inhabitation	# 服务项目 Services	商品零售价格总指数 General Retail Price Index
1978	–	–	–	–	–	548.7
1980	–	–	–	–	–	515.7
1985	630.7	1071.4	533.2	–	1223.9	427.3
1986	592.1	985.6	515.7	–	1138.5	401.5
1987	532.5	848.1	471.8	–	1102.2	359.1
1988	434.0	666.8	368.0	–	1021.5	289.9
1989	371.6	593.3	303.3	–	814.5	249.7
1990	357.6	573.8	283.9	–	726.7	241.9
1991	330.0	507.7	263.3	–	688.8	222.5
1992	299.3	455.3	249.1	–	530.2	205.7
1993	243.4	367.8	216.8	445.1	379.3	169.4
1994	197.2	279.5	172.5	406.1	318.2	138.2
1995	167.1	228.6	143.5	323.0	268.3	122.0
1996	150.6	208.9	133.8	232.3	235.8	114.8
1997	149.7	213.1	131.7	208.4	201.7	116.7
1998	151.2	220.4	140.8	188.1	189.6	120.4
1999	152.4	231.1	143.6	176.1	168.3	124.8
2000	152.6	234.7	144.2	166.3	159.7	126.8
2001	153.4	241.8	147.9	161.0	147.0	129.2
2002	152.7	238.2	151.7	161.6	141.6	129.8
2003	151.5	230.9	149.3	160.1	138.0	130.4
2004	144.3	207.0	145.6	150.9	130.8	128.3
2005	140.9	198.0	143.9	142.4	126.3	126.9
2006	138.7	191.5	142.1	135.4	125.0	125.8
2007	133.1	172.9	138.7	128.0	123.7	122.6
2008	126.4	150.5	136.0	124.9	122.9	117.0
2009	126.7	147.1	130.0	128.2	123.6	119.0
2010	122.6	138.8	132.5	123.6	119.9	115.4
2011	116.6	121.1	127.5	119.9	119.3	110.2
2012	113.4	115.3	122.1	116.8	117.4	108.2
2013	111.2	110.6	120.5	114.3	115.7	106.9
2014	108.9	107.9	114.8	111.4	113.0	105.1
2015	107.2	105.4	111.1	109.2	109.6	104.6
2016	104.4	99.9	108.9	107.4	105.3	104.1
2017	102.6	102.1	105.0	102.9	102.5	102.5

注:本章市区数据不包含吴江区。　Note: The data of urban area in this chapter does not include Wujiang District.

表14-2

市区居民消费价格指数及商品零售价格指数
RESIDENTS CONSUMER PRICE INDICES AND RETAIL PRICE INDICES OF COMMODITIES

(各年以上年价格为100 The Price of Preceding Year is Taken as 100)

年份 Year	居民消费价格总指数 General Residents Consumer Price Index	#食品 Food	#衣着 Clothing	#居住 Inhabitation	#服务项目 Services	商品零售价格总指数 General Retail Price Index
1979	-	-	-	-	-	102.1
1980	-	-	-	-	-	104.2
1985	111.9	117.4	101.9	-	109.8	112.1
1986	106.5	108.7	103.4	-	107.5	106.4
1987	111.2	116.2	109.3	-	103.3	111.8
1988	122.7	127.2	128.2	-	107.9	123.9
1989	116.8	112.4	121.3	-	125.4	116.1
1990	103.9	103.4	106.9	-	112.1	103.2
1991	108.4	113.0	107.8	-	105.5	108.7
1992	110.2	111.5	105.7	-	129.9	108.2
1993	123.0	123.8	114.9	-	139.8	121.4
1994	123.4	131.6	125.7	109.6	119.2	122.6
1995	118.0	122.3	120.2	125.7	118.6	113.3
1996	111.0	109.4	107.2	139.1	113.8	106.2
1997	100.6	98.0	101.6	111.4	116.9	98.4
1998	99.0	96.7	93.6	110.8	106.4	97.0
1999	99.2	95.4	97.8	106.9	112.6	96.4
2000	99.9	98.4	99.8	105.8	105.4	98.5
2001	99.5	97.1	97.5	103.3	108.7	98.1
2002	100.4	101.5	97.5	99.7	103.8	99.5
2003	100.8	103.2	101.6	100.9	102.6	99.5
2004	105.0	111.6	102.5	106.1	105.4	101.7
2005	102.4	104.5	101.2	106.0	103.6	101.1
2006	101.6	103.4	101.3	105.1	101.1	100.9
2007	104.2	110.7	102.4	105.8	101.0	102.6
2008	105.3	114.9	102.0	102.5	100.7	104.8
2009	99.8	102.3	104.6	97.4	99.4	98.3
2010	103.4	106.0	98.1	103.7	103.1	103.1
2011	105.1	114.6	104.0	103.1	100.5	104.7
2012	102.7	105.1	104.4	102.7	101.6	101.9
2013	102.1	104.2	101.3	102.2	101.5	101.2
2014	102.1	102.5	105.0	102.6	102.4	101.7
2015	101.6	102.4	103.3	102.0	103.1	100.4
2016	102.7	105.5	102.0	101.7	104.1	100.5
2017	101.7	97.8	103.7	104.3	102.7	101.5
2018	102.6	102.1	105.0	102.9	102.5	102.5

表14-3

市区居民消费价格指数
RESIDENTS CONSUMER PRICE INDICES

(以上年价格为100 The Price of Preceding Year is taken as 100)

项　目	Item	2017年	2018年
居民消费价格总指数	**General Residents Consumer Price Index**	**101.7**	**102.6**
服务项目价格指数	**Price Index of Service**	**102.7**	**102.5**
消费品价格指数	**Price Index of Consumer Goods**	**101.0**	**102.7**
一、食品烟酒	**Food, Cigarette and Wine**	**99.5**	**102.2**
1.食　品	Food	97.8	102.1
(1)粮　食	Grain	101.9	101.6
(2)薯　类	Tubers	91.2	105.2
(3)豆　类	Beans	99.6	100.0
(4)食用油	Edible Oil	97.6	102.2
(5)菜	Vegetables	90.2	105.3
#鲜　菜	Fresh Vegetables	89.3	105.8
(6)畜肉类	Livestock Meat	96.9	98.2
(7)禽肉类	Poultry Meat	101.0	104.8
(8)水产品	Aquatic Products	99.1	100.1
(9)蛋　类	Eggs	97.0	110.5
(10)奶　类	Dairy	103.6	102.6
(11)干鲜瓜果	Dried and Fresh Melons and Fruits	97.9	103.9
#鲜瓜果	Fresh Fruits	97.7	105.5
(12)糖果糕点类	Confectionery	101.9	102.4
#食　糖	Sugar	113.5	93.0
(13)调味品	Flavoring	112.5	102.3
(14)其他食品类	Other Food	99.9	105.5
2.茶及饮料	Tea and Beverage	102.5	105.4
3.烟　酒	Cigarette and Wine	102.7	103.1
4.在外餐饮	Foods Consumed not at Home	102.0	101.5
二、衣　着	**Clothing**	**103.7**	**105.0**
1.服　装	Garments	103.8	104.4
#男式服装	Man’s Garments	103.3	100.3
女式服装	Women’s Garments	105.0	104.6
儿童服装	Children’s Garments	101.0	114.0

表14-3 续表 Continued

项　　目	Item	2017年	2018年
2.服装材料	Garments Material	100.6	101.7
3.其他衣着及配件	Other Clothing and Accessories	102.8	100.7
4.衣着加工服务费	Tailoring Service	103.5	122.9
5.鞋　类	Footwear	103.6	106.5
三、居　住	**Residence**	**104.3**	**102.9**
1.租赁房房租	House Rent	103.6	102.4
2.住房保养维修及管理	Housing Maintenance and Management	112.1	110.0
3.水电燃料	Light, Water and Fuel	101.1	100.6
4.自有住房	Own Housing	103.7	102.0
四、生活用品及服务	**Life Articles and Service**	**104.0**	**103.5**
1.家具及室内装饰品	Furniture and Interior Decorations	100.8	104.0
# 家　具	Furniture	101.1	104.6
2.家用器具	Household Appliances	103.4	100.9
3.家用纺织品	Household Textiles	103.2	99.7
4.家庭日用杂品	Daily Use Household Articles	103.7	105.2
5.个人护理用品	Personal Care Products	102.8	102.3
6.家庭服务	Household Service	112.4	109.5
五、交通和通信	**Transportation and Communication**	**100.9**	**101.6**
1.交　通	Transportation	100.9	103.2
2.通　信	Communication	100.8	97.8
六、教育文化和娱乐	**Education Cultural and Recreation**	**100.4**	**103.1**
1.教　育	Education	103.0	102.6
2.文化娱乐	Cultural and Recreational Articles	97.7	103.7
七、医疗保健	**Medical Service**	**101.2**	**100.8**
1.药品及医疗器具	Drugs and Medical Devices	103.7	102.4
2.医疗服务	Medical Service	100.0	100.0
八、其他用品及服务	**Other Articles and Service**	**103.4**	**102.5**
1.其他用品类	Other Articles	101.9	100.7
2.其他服务类	Other Service	104.5	103.8

表14-4

市区商品零售价格指数

RETAIL PRICE INDICES OF COMMODITIES

(以上年价格为100 The Price of Preceding Year is taken as 100)

项　　目	Item	2017年	2018年
商品零售价格总指数	**General Retail Price Index**	**101.5**	**102.5**
一、食　品	**Food**	**98.8**	**102.0**
1.粮　食	Grain	101.9	101.7
2.薯　类	Tubers	91.2	105.2
3.豆　类	Beans	99.8	100.1
4.食用油	Edible Oil	97.6	102.2
5.菜	Vegetables	90.0	105.4
6.畜肉类	Livestock Meat	96.9	98.1
7.禽肉类	Poultry Meat	101.0	104.7
8.水产品	Aquatic Products	99.1	100.1
9.蛋　类	Eggs	97.0	110.5
10.奶　类	Dairy	103.6	102.7
11.干鲜瓜果	Dried and Fresh Melons and Fruits	97.9	103.8
12.糖果糕点类	Confectionery	101.8	102.4
13.调味品	Flavoring	111.2	102.2
14.其他食品类	Other Food	99.9	105.5
15.在外餐饮	Foods Consumed not at Home	102.0	101.5
二、饮料、烟酒	**Beverage, Tobacco and Liquor**	**102.5**	**103.3**
1.茶及饮料	Tea and Beverage	102.3	105.6
2.烟　草	Cigarette	100.5	100.7
3.酒　类	Wine	106.9	107.4
三、服装、鞋帽	**Garments, Shoes and Hats**	**103.7**	**104.7**
1.服　装	Garments	103.8	104.3
2.鞋帽袜	Footwear and Hats	103.3	106.0
3.其他衣着配件	Other Clothing and Accessories	112.7	99.8
四、纺织品	**Textiles**	**103.2**	**99.5**
1.服装材料	Garments Material	100.6	101.7
2.床上用品	Bed Articles	103.6	99.2
五、家用电器及音像器材	**Household Electric Appliances and Sound-video Equipment**	**101.2**	**100.4**
1.家庭设备	Household Facilities and Articles	103.2	100.9
2.文娱用耐用消费品	Durable Consumer Goods for Recreational Use	97.6	99.4

表14-4 续表 Continued

项　　目	Item	2017年	2018年
3.专业音像器材	Sound-video Equipment	100.5	100.8
六、文化办公用品	**Culture and Office Articles**	**99.5**	**103.0**
七、日用品	**Articles for Daily Use**	**102.5**	**103.9**
1.日用百货	Daily Consumer Goods	100.9	102.6
2.厨具餐具茶具	Kitchenware, Tableware, Tea Set	99.5	106.4
3.清洗用品	Washing Articles	108.4	106.1
4.其他日用品	Others Articles for Daily Use	101.4	101.3
八、体育娱乐用品	**Sports and Recreational Goods**	**100.2**	**102.6**
1. 体育户外用品	Sports and Outdoor Goods	96.9	101.8
2. 娱乐用品	Recreational Goods	101.6	102.9
九、交通、通信用品	**Transportation and Communication**	**98.3**	**97.8**
1. 交通运输机械	Transportation Machines	97.6	97.7
2. 通讯器材	Communication Apparatus	102.4	98.4
十、家　具	**Furniture**	**101.1**	**104.6**
十一、化妆品	**Cosmetics**	**102.9**	**101.3**
十二、金银饰品	**Jewelry**	**103.2**	**100.5**
十三、中西药品及医疗保健用品	**Chinese and Western Medicines and Medical Care Articles**	**103.7**	**102.7**
1.医疗卫生器具	Medical Appliances	100.0	99.7
2.中　药	Traditional Chinese Medicine	103.3	107.0
3.西　药	Western Medicine	100.3	102.9
4.保健器具及用品	Health Articles	109.2	100.3
十四、书报杂志及电子出版物	**Newspapers, Magazines and Electronic Publication**	**100.8**	**107.8**
1.教材及参考书	Teaching Materials and Reference Books	102.2	108.2
2.书报杂志	Newspapers and Magazines	100.0	107.2
3.计算机办公软件	Office Software	98.9	109.2
十五、燃　料	**Fuels**	**106.9**	**109.6**
1. 煤炭及制品	Coal and Coal Products	110.4	103.2
2. 石油及制品	Petroleum and Petroleum Products	106.6	110.2
十六、建筑材料及五金电料	**Building Materials and Metal Hardware**	**106.4**	**105.5**
1. 建筑装璜材料	Building Decoration Materials	105.7	106.9
2. 五金水暖	Hardware Plumbing	108.6	100.9

表14-5

分月市区居民消费价格指数及商品零售价格指数

(2018年以上年同期价格为100)

项　　目	Item	全　年 Annual Total	1月 Jan.	2月 Feb.	3月 Mar.
居民消费价格总指数	**Urban General Consumer Price Index**	**102.6**	**101.9**	**102.8**	**102.1**
1.食品烟酒	Food, Tobacco and Alcohol	102.2	101.2	104.0	102.4
2.衣　着	Clothing	105.0	103.3	103.3	104.2
3.居　住	Residence	102.9	103.7	102.9	103.2
4.生活用品及服务	Life Articles and Service	103.5	104.5	103.8	103.7
5.交通和通信	Transportation and Communication	101.6	100.6	100.3	99.6
6.教育文化和娱乐	Education Cultural and Recreation	103.1	100.6	103.4	101.9
7.医疗保健	Medical Service	100.8	100.1	100.3	100.0
8.其他用品及服务	Other Articles and Service	102.5	101.8	101.9	101.4
商品零售价格总指数	**Urban General Retail Price Index**	**102.5**	**101.5**	**101.7**	**101.1**
1.食　品	Food	102.0	100.7	104.3	102.1
2.饮料、烟酒	Beverages, Tobacco and Liquor	103.3	103.0	102.7	103.5
3.服装、鞋帽	Garments , Shoes and Hats	104.7	103.1	103.0	103.8
4.纺织品	Textiles	99.5	101.8	100.9	100.4
5.家用电器及音像器材	Household Electric Appliances and Sound-video Equipment	100.4	101.1	98.9	99.0
6.文化办公用品	Culture and Office Articles	103.0	101.1	102.0	100.4
7.日用品	Articles for Daily Use	103.9	103.3	104.2	102.6
8.体育娱乐用品	Sports and Recreational Goods	102.6	100.2	99.9	100.6
9.交通、通信用品	Transportation and Communication	97.8	97.8	96.8	96.7
10.家　具	Furniture	104.6	102.2	102.5	103.9
11.化妆品	Cosmetics	101.3	101.2	100.7	104.1
12.金银珠宝	Jewelry	100.5	101.0	99.2	99.3
13.中西药品及医疗保健用品	Chinese and Western Medicines and Medical Care Articles	102.7	100.5	101.2	100.3
14.书报杂志及电子出版物	Newspapers, Magazines and Electronic Publication	107.8	103.0	103.0	104.7
15.燃　料	Fuels	109.6	104.7	104.7	103.1
16.建筑材料及五金电料	Building Materials and Metal Hardware	105.5	108.9	107.2	105.2

CONSUMER PRICE INDICES AND RETAIL PRICE INDICES OF COMMODITIES BY MONTH

(The Price of 2018 Takes the Price of Preceding Year as 100)

4月 Apr.	5月 May	6月 Jun.	7月 Jul.	8月 Aug.	9月 Sept.	10月 Oct.	11月 Nov.	12月 Dec.
102.3	**102.3**	**102.8**	**102.8**	**102.8**	**103.1**	**103.1**	**102.9**	**102.3**
101.4	101.0	101.8	101.5	101.3	103.0	103.2	102.8	102.9
105.5	105.8	106.8	104.7	104.8	104.8	105.8	105.1	105.6
103.3	102.6	102.6	102.8	103.3	103.5	102.3	102.6	102.2
101.9	102.8	103.6	103.6	104.5	104.1	103.0	103.0	103.6
100.9	101.7	102.8	104.1	102.2	102.8	103.5	101.7	98.6
103.1	103.6	103.5	103.9	104.6	102.9	103.8	104.1	102.3
100.0	100.3	101.1	100.9	101.1	101.0	101.2	101.4	101.9
103.0	102.4	101.2	102.9	102.7	102.7	101.8	103.5	104.9
101.2	**101.7**	**102.8**	**103.0**	**103.1**	**103.8**	**103.9**	**103.4**	**102.7**
101.0	100.6	101.6	101.1	100.8	103.1	103.1	102.6	102.8
103.6	103.2	102.9	103.3	103.6	102.9	103.7	103.7	103.6
105.1	105.5	106.5	104.3	104.5	104.5	105.5	104.8	105.6
98.5	99.0	99.0	99.0	99.0	99.0	99.0	99.7	98.8
99.7	98.0	101.3	102.1	102.8	101.4	100.7	100.3	100.1
100.1	101.8	102.0	102.0	103.2	104.4	106.1	106.9	106.4
100.5	104.0	102.6	103.4	106.1	109.4	104.2	102.7	103.6
102.3	103.0	103.2	103.5	102.6	103.7	104.2	101.4	106.5
96.7	96.7	97.7	98.4	98.1	98.2	98.6	99.1	99.2
106.6	105.4	104.2	104.2	104.3	104.6	104.7	105.9	106.7
100.0	98.7	99.0	100.0	101.1	98.9	104.2	103.2	104.4
99.5	101.2	99.8	100.4	102.1	99.0	97.7	103.0	103.8
100.1	101.4	103.9	103.1	103.6	103.3	104.1	104.8	106.2
104.7	104.7	105.0	112.1	112.2	110.6	110.6	111.5	111.3
106.2	109.7	112.5	115.5	113.6	116.4	117.5	110.8	101.6
105.2	105.4	105.6	105.4	105.4	105.9	104.4	105.3	102.6

表14-6

主要食品年平均价格
MAJOR FOOD AVERAGE PRICE

单位：元/千克 (yuan/kg)

商品名称	Item	代表规格品	Standard and Rate	2017年	2018年
大　米	Rice	袋装东北大米	Bagged Northeast rice	6.58	6.59
面　粉	Flour	特一粉	Special class	5.81	6.16
小　米	Millet	一　级	First class	14.31	14.23
黄　豆	Soybeans	一　级	First class	8.63	8.41
绿　豆	Mung beans	一　级	First class	13.03	13.17
花生油　(元/升)	Peanut oil (yuan/L)	瓶装5升　鲁花压榨	Luhuayazha (5l. a bottle)	25.53	25.46
调和油　(元/升)	Blend oil (yuan/L)	瓶装5升　金龙鱼	Jinlongyu (5l. a bottle)	11.90	12.34
动物油	Animal oil	猪板油　一级	Lard　(first class)	21.54	19.81
猪　肉	Pork	后　腿	Hind legs	30.03	28.32
鸡	Chickens	活草母鸡	Live grass hens	31.19	33.63
蛋	Eggs	洋鸡蛋	Plant-feeding eggs	8.06	9.57
鲫　鱼	Crucian carp	尾重350克左右	About 350 grams a fish	24.70	22.71
带　鱼	Hairtail fish	尾重250克左右	About 250 grams a fish	46.93	45.51
大白菜	Chinese cabbages	一　级	First class	3.94	4.15
菠　菜	Spinach	一　级	First class	9.76	10.12
青　菜	Greens	一　级	First class	6.67	7.51
黄　瓜	Cucumbers	一　级	First class	7.65	8.50
番　茄	Tomatoes	一　级	First class	9.67	9.87
黄豆芽	Soybean sprouts	一　级	First class	6.10	6.38
生　姜	Ginger	一　级	First class	13.13	12.70
青　蒜	Garlic	一　级	First class	12.04	10.83
苹　果	Apples	红富士　一级	Red Fuji (first class)	13.24	13.41
香　蕉	Bananas	国　产　一级	Home-grown (first class)	6.93	8.47
西　瓜	Watermelons	普　通　一级	Ordinary (first class)	7.85	8.60

主 要 统 计 指 标 解 释

居民消费价格指数 是反映一定时期内城乡居民所购买的生活消费品价格和服务项目价格变动趋势和程度的相对数，是对城市居民消费价格指数和农村居民消费价格指数进行综合汇总计算的结果。该指数可以观察和分析消费品的零售价格和服务项目价格变动对城乡居民实际生活费支出的影响程度。

商品零售价格指数 是反映一定时期内城乡商品零售价格变动趋势和程度的相对数。商品零售价格的变动直接影响到城乡居民的生活支出和国家的财政收入，影响居民购买力和市场供需的平衡，影响到消费与积累的比例关系。因此，该指数可以从一个侧面对上述经济活动进行观察和分析。

代表规格品 居民消费价格指数要根据市场上的实际商品价格来计算，市场上的商品和服务项目数量繁多，在编制价格指数时不可能也没有必要把全部商品都纳入指数计算。因此，要选择一部分有代表性的商品和服务来代表全部的商品和服务，也就是从众多的不同的产地、规格、等级、牌号、花色的商品中抽选一部分，又称为规格品。

EXPLANATORY NOTES ON MAIN STATISTICAL INDICATORS

Consumer Price Indices reflect the trend and degree of changes in prices of consumer goods and services purchased by urban and rural households during a given period. They are obtained by combining the Urban Consumer Price Indices and the Rural Consumer Price Indices. The Indices enable the observation and analysis of the degree of impact of the changes in the prices of retailed goods and services on the actual living expenses of urban and rural residents.

Retail Price Indices reflect the trend and degree of change in retail prices of commodities during a given period. The change in retail prices of commodities directly affect the living expenses of urban and rural residents, government revenue, purchasing power of residents and the equilibrium of market supply and demand, and the ratio of consumption to accumulation. Therefore, the retail price indices are useful from an oblique perspective for observing and analyzing the changes of the above economic activities.

Representative specification items The consumer price index is calculated according to the actual price of the product on the market. However, there is a vast amount of goods and services on the market, and in the preparation of the price index it is neither possible nor necessary to include all the goods in the index calculation. Therefore, it is necessary to select a representative part of the goods and services to represent all the goods and services, that is, to select a part from the many commodities of different places of origin, sizes, grades, trademarks, and colors, also known as specification items.

十五、人民生活

CHAPTER 15
PEOPLE 'S LIVELIHOOD

15 人民生活 PEOPLE'S LIVELIHOOD

主要统计指标 MAJOR STATISTICAL INDICATORS

2018年全体常住居民人均可支配收入	Per Capita Disposable Income of the Resident Population	55 476	元	yuan
比上年增长	Increase Over Last Year	8.3	%	
2018年全体常住居民人均消费支出	Per Capita Consumer Spending of the Resident Population	33 327	元	yuan
比上年增长	Increase Over Last Year	6.8	%	
2018年城镇常住居民人均可支配收入	Per Capita Disposable Income of the Urban Residents	63 481	元	yuan
比上年增长	Increase Over Last Year (by the same caliber)	8.0	%	
2018年城镇常住居民人均消费支出	Per Capita Consumer Spending of the Urban Residents	37 403	元	yuan
比上年增长	Increase Over Last Year (by the same caliber)	6.5	%	
2018年农村常住居民人均可支配收入	Per Capita Disposable Income of the Rural Residents	32 420	元	yuan
比上年增长	Increase Over Last Year (by the same caliber)	8.1	%	
2018年农村常住居民人均消费支出	Per Capita Consumer Spending of the Rural Residents	21 587	元	yuan
比上年增长	Increase Over Last Year (by the same caliber)	6.4	%	

表15-1

居民家庭人均收入和消费支出 (1985-2018年)
PER CAPITA DISPOSABLE INCOME AND CONSUMPTION EXPENDITURE OF THE RESIDENTS (1985-2018)

单位：元 (yuan)

年 份 Year	全体常住居民人均可支配收入 Per Capita Disposable Income of the Resident Population	全体常住居民人均消费支出 Per Capita Consumer Spending of the Resident Population	城镇常住居民人均可支配收入 Per Capita Disposable Income of the Urban Resident	城镇常住居民人均消费支出 Per Capita Consumer Spending of the Urban Residents	农村常住居民人均可支配收入 Per Capita Disposable Income of the Rural Residents	农村常住居民人均消费支出 Per Capita Consumer Spending of the Rural Residents
1985			918	787	739	661
1989			1 865	1 619	1 470	1 281
1990			2 150	1 805	1 664	1 415
1991			2 427	2 187	1 731	1 527
1992			2 788	2 199	2 001	1 722
1993			3 695	3 416	2 558	1 893
1994			4 885	4 027	3 457	2 676
1995			5 790	4 877	4 444	3 414
1996			6 591	5 264	5 088	3 804
1997			7 479	5 955	5 219	4 014
1998			7 812	6 289	5 347	3 958
1999			8 406	6 545	5 308	3 785
2000			9 274	7 027	5 462	4 073
2001			10 515	7 270	5 796	4 127
2002			10 617	7 682	6 140	4 229
2003			12 361	9 272	6 681	4 641
2004			14 451	9 783	7 503	5 436
2005			16 276	11 163	8 393	6 143
2006			18 532	12 472	9 278	6 811
2007			21 260	13 959	10 475	7 623
2008			23 867	15 183	11 785	8 443
2009			26 320	16 402	12 969	9 354
2010			29 219	17 879	14 657	10 397
2011			33 243	21 046	17 226	12 485
2012			37 531	23 092	19 396	14 381
2013			41 143	25 197	21 578	16 251
2014	39 780	24 920	46 677	28 973	23 560	15 390
2015	42 987	26 847	50 390	31 136	25 580	16 761
2016	46 595	28 983	54 341	33 305	27 691	18 820
2017	51 208	31 202	58 806	35 104	29 977	20 298
2018	55 476	33 327	63 481	37 403	32 420	21 587

注：2014年起公布城乡住户调查一体化改革后的新口径数据。2013年及以前，城镇居民收支为不包含吴江区的市区居民收支；农村居民人均可支配收入为全市农民人均纯收入。2017年收入、支出数据根据国家统计局统一计算方法进行了重新审定。

Note: Starting from 2014, the new caliber data is announced by the reform of urban-and-rural integration of the household survey ; in 2013 and the previous years , the urban residents' income and expenditure did not include those of the urban residents of Wujiang District.; Per capita disposable income of the rural residents is the per capita net income of the farmers of the city. The 2017 income and expenditure data were re-examined according to the unified calculation method of the National Bureau of Statistics.

表15-2

调查户和调查人口基本情况（2018年）
BASIC INFORMATION ON THE HOUSEHOLDS AND THE POPULATION OF THE SURVEY (2018)

指　标	Item	全体常住居民 All The Residents	城镇常住居民 Urban Residents	农村常住居民 Rural Residents
一、调查户数　（户）	**Number of Households of Survey （household）**	**1 790**	**1 370**	**420**
二、期末家庭常住成员基本情况	**Basic Information of Family Members**			
（一）户均常住人口　（人）	Average Number of Residents Per Household (person)	3.35	3.29	3.58
（二）性别比例　（%）	Sex Ratio （%）	100.0	100.0	100.0
男　性	Male	49.2	49.1	49.6
女　性	Female	50.8	50.9	50.4
（三）15岁及以上常住成员受教育程度比例	Proportion of Level of Education of Residents of 15 Years Old and Above	100.0	100.0	100.0
未上过学	Uneducated	5.2	4.4	7.5
小　学	Primary School	24.1	21.3	32.3
初　中	Junior Secondary School	30.0	29.3	32.1
高　中	Senior Secondary School	15.0	16.2	11.5
大学专科	Junior College	12.9	14.3	8.9
大学本科	Undergraduate College	12.0	13.6	7.3
研究生	Graduate College	0.8	1.0	0.3
三、常住家庭成员就业情况	**Information on Employment of Family Members**			
（一）户均常住从业人数　（人）	Number of Employees Per Household （person）	1.9	1.8	2.1
（二）就业状况比例　（%）	Employment Ratio （%）	100.0	100.0	100.0
雇　主	Employers	2.4	2.5	2.2
公职人员	Public Officials	1.4	1.7	0.6
事业单位人员	Institution Employees	5.9	6.5	4.1
国有企业雇员	State-owned Enterprise Employees	2.2	2.7	0.9
其他雇员	Other Employees	79.1	79.1	79.1
农业自营	Agricultural Self-employed	2.5	1.0	6.8
非农自营	Non-agricultural Self-employed	6.5	6.5	6.4
（三）主要从事行业比例	Ratio of Industries Mainly Engaged in	100.0	100.0	100.0
第一产业	Primary Industry	3.8	2.0	8.8
第二产业	Secondary Industry	47.8	46.1	52.6
第三产业	Tertiary Industry	48.5	51.9	38.7

表15-3

居民人均可支配收入(2018年)
PER CAPITA DISPOSABLE INCOME OF THE RESIDENTS (2018)

单位：元 (yuan)

指　　标	Item	全体常住居民 All The Residents	城镇常住居民 Urban Residents	农村常住居民 Rural Residents
人均可支配收入	**Per Capita Disposable Income**	**55 476.40**	**63 481.37**	**32 419.73**
一、工资性收入	**Wage Income**	**34 948.41**	**40 412.20**	**19 211.07**
(一)工　资	Wages	33 087.99	38 157.84	18 410.54
(二)实物福利	Physical Benefits	327.06	345.29	250.68
(三)其　他	Others	1 533.36	1 909.07	549.85
二、经营净收入	**Net Operating Income**	**5 275.21**	**5 010.75**	**6 036.92**
(一)第一产业净收入	Net Income of the Primary Industry	555.67	246.83	1 398.98
(二)第二产业净收入	Net income of the Secondary Industry	662.74	525.65	1 040.49
(三)第三产业净收入	Net Income of the Tertiary Industry	4 056.80	4 238.27	3 597.45
三、财产净收入	**Property Net Income**	**9 028.49**	**10 991.84**	**3 373.45**
# 利息净收入	Net Interest Income	198.10	299.44	-177.52
红利收入	Dividend Income	429.37	471.19	382.98
出租房屋净收入	Net Income of Renting Houses	2 818.55	3 108.71	2 446.69
四、转移净收入	**Transfer Net Income**	**6 224.30**	**7 066.57**	**3 798.29**

注：转移净收入=转移性收入-转移性支出。
Note: Transfer net income = Transfer income - Transfer expenditure

表15-3 续表 Continued

单位：元 (yuan)

指　　标	Item	全体常住居民 All The Residents	城镇常住居民 Urban Residents	农村常住居民 Rural Residents
(一)转移性收入	Transfer Income	9 027.76	10 935.69	4 736.44
养老金或离退休金	Pensions or Retirement Pensions	7 870.42	9 533.58	4 129.45
社会救济和补助	Social Relief and Subsidies	60.54	55.63	51.69
现金政策性惠农补贴	Cash Policy Subsidies that Benefit Farmers	18.20	8.36	24.95
政策性生活补贴	Policy-oriented Living Allowances	23.87	33.12	7.79
报销医疗费	Reimbursement of Medical Expenses	592.12	705.18	324.25
外出从业人员寄回带回收入	Income Sent Back or Brought Back Home by Employees Working in Other Places	74.74	112.07	14.96
赡养收入	Maintenance Income	162.66	215.77	64.25
其他经常转移收入	Other Frequent Transfer Incomes	200.43	245.77	101.80
从政府和组织得到的实物产品和服务折价	Physical Products and Discounts on Services Received from Governments and Organizations	24.78	26.21	17.28
(二)转移性支出	Transfer Expenditure	2 803.46	3 869.12	938.15
个人所得税	Individual Income Tax	368.38	574.76	48.57
社会保障支出	The Expenditure of Social Security	2 176.49	2 902.71	842.18
外来从业人员寄给家人的支出	Spending Sent Home by Employees from Other Places	22.66	18.18	22.32
赡养支出	Maintenance Expenses	145.12	229.26	15.95
其他经常转移支出	Other Frequent Transfer Expenses	90.81	144.20	9.13

15-4

居民人均消费支出(2018年)
PER CAPITA CONSUMPTION EXPENDITYRE OF THE RESIDENTS (2018)

单位：元 (yuan)

指　　标	Item	全体常住居民 All The Residents	城镇常住居民 Urban Residents	农村常住居民 Rural Residents
居民生活消费支出	**Consumer Expenditure of the Residents**	**33 327.28**	**37 403.42**	**21 586.78**
一、食品烟酒	**Food, Alcoholic Drinks and Tobacco**	**8 384.67**	**9 405.89**	**5 443.26**
食　品	Food	4 988.51	5 567.41	3 301.96
烟　酒	Alcoholic Drinks and Tobacco	1 006.28	1 009.65	916.97
饮　料	Beverages	195.81	220.31	125.68
饮食服务	Catering Services	2 194.08	2 608.52	1 098.65
二、衣　着	**Clothing**	**1 874.88**	**2 119.80**	**1 169.46**
衣　类	Clothes	1 538.42	1 747.90	937.72
鞋　类	Footwear	336.46	371.89	231.74
三、居　住	**Residence**	**8 263.21**	**9 306.44**	**5 258.40**
# 租赁房房租	Rent for Renting Houses	204.40	266.72	41.44
住房维修及管理	Housing Maintenance and Management	674.60	676.07	632.43
水电燃料及其他	Water, Electricity, Fuel and Others	839.15	872.26	710.77
四、生活用品及服务	**Daily Necessities and Services**	**1 775.56**	**1 965.32**	**1 229.01**
家具及室内装饰品	Furniture and Interior Decoration	339.19	371.76	244.90
家用器具	Household Appliances	432.17	481.68	290.00

15-4 续表 Continued

单位：元 (yuan)

指 标	Item	全体常住居民 All The Residents	城镇常住居民 Urban Residents	农村常住居民 Rural Residents
家用纺织品	Home Textiles	121.20	136.50	77.45
家庭日用杂品	Household Sundries	411.66	432.31	349.06
个人用品	Personal Articles	375.58	427.18	228.49
家庭服务	Family Services	95.76	115.89	39.11
五、交通通信	**Transportation and Communication**	**5 564.35**	**6 152.76**	**3 869.56**
交 通	Transportation	4 405.21	4 871.40	3 062.55
通 信	Communication	1 159.14	1 281.36	807.01
六、教育文化娱乐	**Education, Culture and Entertainment**	**4 900.45**	**5 702.84**	**2 589.35**
教 育	Education	2 426.33	2 852.78	1 205.93
文化娱乐	Culture and Entertainment	2 474.13	2 850.05	1 383.42
七、医疗保健	**Healthcare**	**1 704.54**	**1 775.69**	**1 499.59**
医疗器具及药品	Medical Equipment and Medicines	385.80	422.10	292.36
医疗服务	Medical Services	1 318.74	1 353.59	1 207.23
八、其他用品及服务	**Other Supplies and Services**	**859.61**	**974.69**	**528.15**
其他用品	Other Supplies	516.35	563.96	377.24
其他服务	Other Services	343.26	410.73	150.91
附：通过互联网购买的商品和服务	**Appendix: Goods and Services Purchased Over the Internet**	**5.04**	**5.65**	**3.20**

表15-5

全体常住居民家庭基本情况(2018年)
(按收入等级分)

项　　目	Item	总平均 Average
一、家庭成员情况	**Basic Situation of Households**	
（一）调查户数　（户）	Number of Households Surveyed　(household)	1 790
（二）平均每户家庭常住人口　（人）	Average Household Size　(person)	3.35
# 从业人员	Average Number of Employees per Household	1.90
（三）平均每一从业者负担人数(包括从业者本人)	Number of Persons Supported by Each Employee (including the employee himself or herself)	1.77
二、家庭收支情况	**Family Income and Expenditure**	
（一）人均可支配收入　（元）	Per Capita Disposable Income　(yuan)	55 476
工资性收入	Wage Income	34 948
经营净收入	Net Operating Income	5 275
财产净收入	Property Net Income	9 028
转移净收入	Transfer Net Income	6 224
（二）人均消费支出	Per Capita Annual Living Expenditure	33 327
食品烟酒	Food, Alcoholic Drinks and Tobacco	8 385
衣　着	Clothing	1 875
居　住	Residence	8 263
生活用品及服务	Household Facilities, Articles and Services	1 776
交通通信	Medicine and Medical Services	5 564
教育文化娱乐	Transport, Post and Communication Services	4 900
医疗保健	Education, Cultural and Recreation Services	1 705
其他用品和服务	Miscellaneous Commodities and Services	860

BASIC INTORMATION OF ALL RESIDENT HOUSEHOLDS (2018)
(DIVIDED BY INCOME LEVEL)

20%	20%	20%	20%	20%
低收入户 Low Income House-holds	中低收入户 Lower Middle Income House-holds	中等收入户 Middle Income House-holds	中高收入户 Upper Middle Income House-holds	高收入户 High Income House-holds
358	358	358	358	358
3.75	3.77	3.41	3.21	2.64
1.74	2.17	1.97	1.97	1.65
2.15	1.74	1.73	1.63	1.60
24 307	37 231	48 386	64 119	124 506
16 033	24 261	31 582	42 224	72 602
1 436	1 348	3 458	4 295	19 892
2 872	5 409	7 305	10 210	23 743
3 966	6 213	6 040	7 390	8 268
19 617	24 479	30 012	36 878	65 427
5 746	7 092	8 223	9 795	12 473
977	1 227	1 547	2 162	4 152
5 047	6 045	7 545	9 181	15 816
886	1 236	1 658	1 909	3 800
2 911	4 150	4 727	6 155	11 721
2 394	2 958	4 128	5 041	12 067
1 354	1 355	1 518	1 689	2 964
302	415	665	947	2 433

表15-6

城镇常住居民家庭基本情况(2018年)
(按收入等级分)

项　　目		Item		总平均 Average
一、家庭成员情况		**Basic Situation of Households**		
（一）调查户数	(户)	Number of Households Surveyed	(household)	1 370
（二）平均每户家庭常住人口	(人)	Average Household Size	(person)	3.29
# 从业人员		Average Number of Employees per Household		1.84
（三）平均每一从业者负担人数(包括从业者本人)		Number of Persons Supported by Each Employee (including the employee himself or herself)		1.79
二、家庭收支情况		**Family Income and Expenditure**		
（一）人均可支配收入	(元)	Per Capita Disposable Income	(yuan)	63 481
工资性收入		Wage Income		40 412
经营净收入		Net operating Income		5 011
财产净收入		Property net Income		10 992
转移净收入		Transfer net Income		7 067
（二）人均消费支出		Per Capita Annual Living Expenditure		37 403
食品烟酒		Food, Alcoholic Drinks and Tobacco		9 406
衣　着		Clothing		2 120
居　住		Residence		9 306
生活用品及服务		Household Facilities, Articles and Services		1 965
交通通信		Medicine and Medical Services		6 153
教育文化娱乐		Transport, Post and Communication Services		5 703
医疗保健		Education, Cultural and Recreation Services		1 776
其他用品和服务		Miscellaneous Commodities and Services		975

THE BASIC SITUATION OF THE URBAN RESIDENT FAMILIES(2018)
(DIVIDED BY INCOME LEVEL)

20% 低收入户 Low Income House-holds	20% 中低收入户 Lower Middle Income House-holds	20% 中等收入户 Middle Income House-holds	20% 中高收入户 Upper Middle Income House-holds	20% 高收入户 High Income House-holds
274	274	274	274	274
3.82	3.61	3.26	3.10	2.64
1.81	2.03	1.88	1.84	1.63
2.11	1.78	1.73	1.68	1.61
28 819	43 587	55 486	72 843	139 797
18 794	27 705	37 281	46 833	85 444
1 321	1 266	3 641	3 592	18 843
4 710	7 598	8 526	12 483	26 029
3 993	7 018	6 038	9 936	9 481
21 449	27 889	32 984	42 219	73 338
6 484	8 080	9 470	10 935	13 576
1 098	1 374	1 791	2 385	4 715
5 327	7 173	8 445	10 701	17 417
1 091	1 357	1 681	2 226	4 109
3 359	4 256	4 642	7 153	13 486
2 549	3 789	4 623	6 015	13 858
1 225	1 349	1 577	1 752	3 430
314	510	755	1 053	2 748

表15-7

农村常住居民家庭基本情况(2018年)
(按收入等级分)

项　　目	Item	总平均 Average
一、家庭成员情况	**Basic Situation of Households**	
（一）调查户数 (户)	Number of Households Surveyed (household)	420
（二）平均每户家庭常住人口 (人)	Average Household Size (person)	3.58
# 从业人员	Average Number of Employees per Household	2.09
（三）平均每一从业者负担人数(包括从业者本人)	Number of Persons Supported by Each Employee (including the employee himself or herself)	1.71
二、家庭收支情况	**Family Income and Expenditure**	
（一）人均可支配收入 (元)	Per Capita Disposable Income (yuan)	32 420
工资性收入	Wage Income	19 211
经营净收入	Net operating Income	6 037
财产净收入	Property Net Income	3 373
转移净收入	Transfer Net Income	3 798
（二）人均消费支出	Per Capita Annual Living Expenditure	21 587
食品烟酒	Food, Alcoholic Drinks and Tobacco	5 443
衣　着	Clothing	1 169
居　住	Residence	5 258
生活用品及服务	Household Facilities, Articles and Services	1 229
交通通信	Medicine and Medical Services	3 870
教育文化娱乐	Transport, Post and Communication Services	2 589
医疗保健	Education, Cultural and Recreation Services	1 500
其他用品和服务	Miscellaneous Commodities and Services	528

THE BASIC SITUATION OF THE RURAL RESIDENT FAMILIES(2018)
(DIVIDED BY INCOME LEVEL)

20%	20%	20%	20%	20%
低收入户 Low Income House-holds	中低收入户 Lower Middle Income House-holds	中等收入户 Middle Income House-holds	中高收入户 Upper Middle Income House-holds	高收入户 High Income House-holds
84	84	84	84	84
3.47	3.80	3.92	3.57	3.13
1.51	2.06	2.51	2.23	2.15
2.29	1.85	1.56	1.60	1.45
14 543	21 973	27 800	35 867	66 728
9 051	16 150	19 905	22 771	29 246
1 608	1 467	2 004	4 419	23 368
1 086	1 312	2 025	4 473	8 842
2 799	3 044	3 866	4 204	5 272
16 382	17 480	18 412	24 132	33 404
3 998	5 058	5 126	5 242	8 136
684	967	1 024	1 224	2 072
4 388	4 537	4 827	4 792	8 167
698	828	1 106	1 602	2 033
3 000	2 254	2 708	6 177	5 618
1 818	2 149	2 160	2 724	4 360
1 476	1 387	1 154	1 659	1 912
319	299	307	711	1 106

表15-8

居民家庭现住房情况(2018年末)
THE HOUSING SITUATION OF THE RESIDENT FAMILIES (END OF 2018)

指标	Item	全体常住居民 All The Residents	城镇常住居民 Urban Residents	农村常住居民 Rural Residents
一、居民人均住房建筑面积 (平方米)	**Per Capita Housing Construction Area** (square meter)	**51.3**	**45.8**	**67.5**
二、居民家庭现住房构成 (%)	**Housing for the Residents Households** (%)			
(一)按主要建筑材料分的住房比例	Proportion of Number of Households According to Main Building Materials	100.0	100.0	100.0
# 钢筋混凝土	Reinforced Concrete	60.7	70.1	30.2
砖混材料	Brick and Concrete Material	35.8	28.1	60.7
砖瓦砖木	Brick, Tile and Timber	3.4	1.7	9.0
(二)按房屋来源分的住房比例	Proportion of Number of Households According to The Source of Housing	100.0	100.0	100.0
# 租赁住房	Rental Housing	6.0	7.7	0.7
自建住房	Self-built Housing	44.7	28.7	96.9
购买商品房	Purchased Commercial Housing	30.6	39.6	1.2
购买房改住房	Purchased Housing-reform Housing	3.6	4.7	-
购买保障性住房	Purchased Affordable Housing	0.1	0.1	-
拆迁安置房	Removal and Resettlement Housing	13.7	18.0	-
(三)住房外道路为硬化路面的户比例	Proportion of Number of Households with Roads of Hardened Pavement Outside Their Housing	99.7	99.8	99.5

表15-9

每百户居民家庭耐用消费品拥有量(2018年末)
THE OWNERSHIP OF DURABLE CONSUMER GOODS PER ONE-HUNDRED HOUSEHOLDS (END OF 2018)

指　　标		Item		全体常住居民 All The Residents	城镇常住居民 Urban Residents	农村常住居民 Rural Residents
家用汽车	(辆)	Home Car	(car)	78.6	82.4	66.0
摩托车		Motorcycle		7.3	5.0	14.8
电冰箱(柜)	(台)	Refrigerator	(unit)	108.7	107.1	113.8
洗衣机		Washing Machine		105.1	104.3	107.6
热水器		Water Heater		114.4	113.9	116.0
# 太阳能热水器		Solar Water Heater		38.0	30.9	61.2
空　调		Air Conditioner		275.4	275.2	276.2
彩色电视机		Color TV Set		203.3	196.8	224.5
照相机		Camera		27.2	29.1	20.7
计算机		Computer		89.9	93.9	76.7
# 接入互联网的计算机		Computer Access to the Internet		81.7	85.2	70.5
中高档乐器	(架)	Middle- and High-grade Musical Instrument	(unit)	9.1	10.1	5.5
固定电话	(部)	Fixed Telephone	(unit)	44.4	43.8	46.4
移动电话		Mobile Phone		271.8	270.0	277.6
# 接入互联网的移动电话		Mobile Phone Access to the Internet		217.0	224.5	192.9

表15-10

分地区全体常住居民收支情况(2018年)

指　　标	Item	全　市 Whole Municipality
一、家庭成员情况	**Basic Situation of Households**	
（一）调查户数　(户)	Number of Households Surveyed　(household)	1 790
（二）平均每户家庭常住人口　(人)	Average Household Size　(person)	3.35
# 从业人员	Average Number of Employees per Household	1.90
（三）平均每一从业者负担人数(包括从业者本人)	Number of Persons Supported by Each Employee (including the employee himself or herself)	1.77
二、家庭收支情况	**Family Income and Expenditure**	
（一）人均可支配收入　(元)	Per Capita Disposable Income　(yuan)	55 476
工资性收入	Wage Income	34 948
经营净收入	Net operating Income	5 275
财产净收入	Property Net Income	9 028
转移净收入	Transfer Net Income	6 224
（二）人均消费支出	Per Capita Annual Living Expenditure	33 327
食品烟酒	Food, Alcoholic Drinks and Tobacco	8 385
衣　着	Clothing	1 875
居　住	Residence	8 263
生活用品及服务	Household Facilities, Articles and Services	1 776
交通通信	Medicine and Medical Services	5 564
教育文化娱乐	Transport, Post and Communication Services	4 900
医疗保健	Education, Cultural and Recreation Services	1 705
其他用品和服务	Miscellaneous Commodities and Services	860

THE INCOME AND EXPENDITURE OF ALL THE RESIDENTS IN THE REGION (2018)

市 区 Urban Area	# 吴江区 Wujiang District	常 熟 Changshu	张家港 Zhangjiagang	昆 山 Kunshan	太 仓 Taicang
990	200	200	200	200	200
3.44	3.45	3.38	3.15	3.03	3.45
1.94	2.06	2.08	1.63	1.71	1.97
1.77	1.67	1.63	1.93	1.78	1.76
57 077	52 969	53 296	53 456	55 081	52 538
35 704	35 265	34 115	33 892	35 868	34 564
5 374	6 708	6 577	6 496	4 694	5 724
9 450	5 577	5 709	6 201	8 085	6 334
6 549	5 419	6 895	6 866	6 434	5 916
34 409	33 295	31 979	30 816	32 248	32 034
9 117	9 146	8 771	8 687	8 896	9 427
1 825	3 121	1 838	1 827	2 010	1 848
9 313	5 463	6 988	6 003	7 135	6 762
1 659	1 592	1 520	1 640	1 742	1 802
5 749	6 864	4 987	6 061	5 174	5 291
4 457	4 979	5 065	4 543	5 116	4 810
1 449	1 342	1 783	1 330	1 389	1 294
838	788	1 027	726	785	801

表15-11

分地区城镇常住居民收支情况(2018年)

指　　标	Item	全　市 Whole Municipality
一、家庭成员情况	**Basic Situation of Households**	
（一）调查户数　(户)	Number of Households Surveyed　(household)	1 370
（二）平均每户家庭常住人口　(人)	Average Household Size　(person)	3.29
# 从业人员	Average Number of Employees per Household	1.84
（三）平均每一从业者负担人数(包括从业者本人)	Number of Persons Supported by Each Employee (including the employee himself or herself)	1.79
二、家庭收支情况	**Family Income and Expenditure**	
（一）人均可支配收入　(元)	Per Capita Disposable Income　(yuan)	63 481
工资性收入	Wage Income	40 412
经营净收入	Net operating Income	5 011
财产净收入	Property Net Income	10 992
转移净收入	Transfer Net Income	7 067
（二）人均消费支出	Per Capita Annual Living Expenditure	37 403
食品烟酒	Food, Alcoholic Drinks and Tobacco	9 406
衣　着	Clothing	2 120
居　住	Residence	9 306
生活用品及服务	Household Facilities, Articles and Services	1 965
交通通信	Medicine and Medical Services	6 153
教育文化娱乐	Transport, Post and Communication Services	5 703
医疗保健	Education, Cultural and Recreation Services	1 776
其他用品和服务	Miscellaneous Commodities and Services	975

THE INCOME AND EXPENDITURE OF ALL THE URBAN IN THE REGION (2018)

市 区 Urban Area	# 吴江区 Wujiang District	常 熟 Changshu	张家港 Zhangjiagang	昆 山 Kunshan	太 仓 Taicang
820	120	130	130	150	140
3.35	3.48	3.42	3.20	3.03	3.16
1.86	2.03	2.15	1.63	1.67	1.80
1.80	1.72	1.59	1.96	1.81	1.76
63 237	63 425	63 712	64 055	63 926	63 076
39 826	43 734	40 736	41 831	42 097	42 162
5 167	5 411	6 709	6 477	4 504	5 481
10 816	6 968	7 633	7 642	9 912	8 301
7 429	7 312	8 634	8 104	7 413	7 132
37 602	39 752	35 848	35 491	36 396	37 187
9 919	10 747	9 867	10 029	9 947	10 841
1 980	3 932	2 150	2 094	2 273	2 167
10 211	6 630	7 714	6 776	8 279	8 083
1 812	1 873	1 729	1 833	1 905	2 066
6 327	8 155	5 456	7 405	5 817	6 061
4 951	5 931	5 785	5 246	5 844	5 570
1 512	1 526	1 944	1 269	1 475	1 398
892	958	1 203	839	856	1 001

表15-12 分地区农村常住居民收支情况(2018年)

指　　标		Item		全　市 Whole Municipality
一、家庭成员情况		**Basic Situation of Households**		
（一）调查户数	(户)	Number of Households Surveyed	(household)	420
（二）平均每户家庭常住人口	(人)	Average Household Size	(person)	3.58
# 从业人员		Average Number of Employees per Household		2.09
（三）平均每一从业者负担人数(包括从业者本人)		Number of Persons Supported by Each Employee (including the employee himself or herself)		1.71
二、家庭收支情况		**Family Income and Expenditure**		
（一）人均可支配收入	(元)	Per Capita Disposable Income	(yuan)	32 420
工资性收入		Wage Income		19 211
经营净收入		Net operating Income		6 037
财产净收入		Property net Income		3 373
转移净收入		Transfer net Income		3 798
（二）人均消费支出		Per Capita Annual Living Expenditure		21 587
食品烟酒		Food, Alcoholic Drinks and Tobacco		5 443
衣　着		Clothing		1 169
居　住		Residence		5 258
生活用品及服务		Household Facilities, Articles and Services		1 229
交通通信		Medicine and Medical Services		3 870
教育文化娱乐		Transport, Post and Communication Services		2 589
医疗保健		Education, Cultural and Recreation Services		1 500
其他用品和服务		Miscellaneous Commodities and Services		528

THE INCOME AND EXPENDITURE OF ALL THE RURAL IN THE REGION (2018)

市 区 Urban Area	# 吴江区 Wujiang District	常 熟 Changshu	张家港 Zhangjiagang	昆 山 Kunshan	太 仓 Taicang
170	80	70	70	50	60
3.88	3.40	3.31	3.04	3.04	4.12
2.35	2.11	1.93	1.63	1.80	2.35
1.65	1.61	1.72	1.87	1.69	1.75
32 139	32 194	32 820	32 664	32 916	32 458
19 018	18 437	21 100	18 318	20 257	20 085
6 212	9 286	6 318	6 533	5 171	6 187
3 922	2 814	1 926	3 375	3 506	2 587
2 987	1 657	3 476	4 438	3 982	3 600
21 481	20 467	24 374	21 645	21 851	22 216
5 874	5 967	6 618	6 055	6 261	6 731
1 198	1 511	1 224	1 303	1 352	1 240
5 682	3 145	5 560	4 485	4 268	4 245
1 039	1 033	1 108	1 261	1 335	1 300
3 413	4 298	4 067	3 422	3 562	3 823
2 460	3 087	3 651	3 163	3 293	3 361
1 194	976	1 467	1 451	1 172	1 095
621	450	681	504	608	420

主 要 统 计 指 标 解 释

调查户　依照《中华人民共和国统计法》规定，开展住户收支与生活状况调查的住户为调查户。住户调查对象为中华人民共和国境内的住户，既包括城镇住户，也包括农村住户；既包括以家庭形式居住的户，也包括以集体形式居住的户。无论户口性质和户口登记地，中国公民均以住户为单位，在常住地参加本调查。

可支配收入　指调查户在调查期内获得的、可用于最终消费支出和储蓄的总和，即调查户可以用来自由支配的收入。可支配收入既包括现金收入，也包括实物收入。按照收入的来源，可支配收入包含四项，分别为：工资性收入、经营净收入、财产净收入和转移净收入。计算公式为：

可支配收入 ＝工资性收入 ＋经营净收入 ＋财产净收入 ＋ 转移净收入

工资性收入　指就业人员通过各种途径得到的全部劳动报酬和各种福利，包括受雇于单位或个人、从事各种自由职业、兼职和零星劳动得到的全部劳动报酬和福利。

经营净收入　指住户或住户成员从事生产经营活动所获得的净收入，是全部经营收入中扣除经营费用、生产性固定资产折旧和生产税之后得到的净收入。

财产净收入　指住户或住户成员将其所拥有的金融资产、住房等非金融资产和自然资源交由其他机构单位、住户或个人支配而获得的回报并扣除相关的费用之后得到的净收入。财产净收入包括利息净收入、红利收入、储蓄性保险净收益、转让承包土地经营权租金净收入、出租房屋净收入、出租其他资产净收入和自有住房折算净租金等。但转让资产所有权的溢价所得计入“非收入所得”，不包含在财产净收入中。

转移性收入　指国家、单位、社会团体对住户的各种经常性转移支付和住户之间的经常性收入转移。 包括政府、非行政事业单位、社会团体对居民转移的养老金或退休金、社会救济和补助、惠农补贴、政策性生活补贴、救灾款、经常性捐赠和赔偿以及报销医疗费等；住户之间的赡养收入、经常性捐赠和赔偿以及农村地区（村委会）在外（含国外）工作的本住户非常住成员寄回带回的收入等。转移性收入不包括住户之间的实物馈赠。

转移性支出 指调查户对国家、单位、住户或个人的经常性或义务性转移支付。包括缴纳的税款、各项社会保障支出、赡养支出、经常性捐赠和赔偿支出以及其他经常转移支出等。

转移净收入　计算公式为：转移净收入=转移性收入-转移性支出

消费支出　指调查户在调查期内用于满足家庭日常生活消费需要的全部支出，包括用于消费品的支出和用于服务性消费的支出。根据用途不同，消费支出可划分为食品烟酒、衣着、居住、生活用品及服务、交通通信、教育文化娱乐、医疗保健、其他用品及服务八大类。根据来源不同，消费支出可划分为现金消费支出、实物消费支出（含自产自用、来自单位、来自政府和其他社会组织）。

EXPLANATORY NOTES ON MAIN STATISTICAL INDICATORS

Households of the Survey In accordance with the provisions of 《The Statistical Law of the People's Republic of China》, the households whose income and expenditure and living conditions are to be surveyed are households of the survey.The households of the survey are the households within the People's Republic of China, including both urban and rural households, and households living both in the form of a family and in the form of collective housing. Regardless of the nature of registered residence and the place where residence is registered, the Chinese citizens take the household as the unit, and take part in the survey.

Disposable Income It refers to the sum total of the income which is obtained by the household in the survey period, and can be used for final consumer spending and savings, namely, the income which the household can freely dispose of. Disposable income includes both cash and physical income. According to the sources of income, disposable income includes four incomes, and they are respectively wage income, net operating income, property net income and transfer net income.

Disposable income = wage income + net operating income + property net income + transfer net income.

Wage Income It refers to the total remuneration and benefits which the employed person gets through a variety of ways, including the total remuneration and benefits which the person gets by being employed to units or individuals, and engaged in vaious freelance, part-time work and sporadic labor.

Net Operating Income It refers to the net income which the household or household members get by being engaged in production and business activities, and is the net income of the total operating income after the deduction of operating expenses, the depreciation of fixed assets for production and production tax.

Property Net Income It refers to the net income which a household or household member obtains in return when they have their own financial assets, housing and other non-financial assets and natural resources administrated by other institutional units, households or individuals and after the deduction of the related expenses. Property net income includes net interest income, dividend income, savings insurance net income, rent net income from the transfer of land contracted management right, rental housing net income, rental other assets net income and converted net rent for one's own houses. However, the premium income of the transfer of property rights is included in the "non income", which is not included in the property net income.

Transfer Income It refers to the various regular transfer payments which the state, units and social groups give to households and frequent transfer of income between households. It includes pensions or retirement pensions, social benefits or subsidies, subsidies benefiting farmers, policy-oriented living allowances, relief funds, regular donations and compensations and reimbursement of medical expenses, etc. which the government, the non-administrative institutions, social groups transfer to residents; the maintenance income between residents, the regular donations and compensations, and the income sent back or brought back by the non-resident members of the household from the rural areas (village committees) working in other places (including foreign countries). The transfer income does not include the physical gifts between households.

Transfer Expenditure It refers to the payment which the household of the survey recurrently or compulsorily transfers to the state, units, households or individuals. It includes the payment of taxes, social security expenses, maintenance expenses, recurrent expenses for donations and compensations and other recurrent transfer spendings.

Transfer Net Income The formula of calculation is: transfer net income = transfer income - transfer expenditure.

Consumer spending It refers to all the expenditures which the household of the survey spends to meet all consumption needs of family life in the survey period, including spending on consumer goods and service consumption. Depending on the use, consumption expenditure can be divided into the eight categories of food, alcoholic drinks and tobacco, clothing, housing, articles for daily use and services, transportation and communications, education, culture and entertainment, healthcare, and other supplies and services. According to different sources, consumption expenditure can be divided into cash consumer spending and physical consumption expenditure (including production of one's own use, from the unit, from the government and other social organizations).

十六、科　技

CHAPTER 16
SCIENCE AND TECHNOLOGY

16 科 技 SCIENCE AND TECHNOLOGY

主要统计指标 MAJOR STATISTICAL INDICATORS

2018年高新技术企业数	Number of High & New Tech Enterprises	5 416	个	unit
2018年发明专利申请数	Invention Patent Applications	50 116	件	unit
比上年增长	Increase Over Last Year	9.5	%	
2018年发明专利授权数	Invention Patents Warrants	10 845	件	unit
比上年增长	Increase Over Last Year	-6.7	%	
2018年末专业技术人员数	Number of Scientific & Technical Personnel	1 917 801	人	person
比上年增长	Increase Over Last Year	10.1	%	
2018年末高级职称专业技术人员数	Number of Scientific & Technical Personnel with Senior Professional Titles	98 787	人	person
比上年增长	Increase Over Last Year	7.9	%	

表16-1

部分年份科研机构和人员情况
RESEARCH INSTITUTIONS AND PERSONNEL OF PARTIAL YEARS

项　目	Item	2013年	2014年	2015年	2016年	2017年	2018年
机构数　(个)	**Number of Institutions　(unit)**						
全　市	**Whole Municipality**	**80**	**80**	**78**	**80**	**155**	**155**
市　区	Urban Area	62	62	60	60	97	94
# 吴江区	Wujiang District	2	2	2	3	5	6
常　熟	Changshu	7	7	6	6	26	26
张家港	Zhangjiagang	4	4	5	6	15	15
昆　山	Kunshan	5	5	5	5	11	12
太　仓	Taicang	2	2	2	3	6	8
职工人数　(人)	**Number of Staff & Workers　(person)**						
全　市	**Whole Municipality**	**9 715**	**9 687**	**9 678**	**8 876**	**9 836**	**11 008**
市　区	Urban Area	8 421	8 672	8 800	8 056	8 421	9 412
#吴江区	Wujiang District	17	17	15	152	230	259
常　熟	Changshu	143	133	109	127	513	418
张家港	Zhangjiagang	410	223	281	319	260	289
昆　山	Kunshan	608	528	397	317	496	588
太　仓	Taicang	133	131	91	57	146	301
专业技术人员数 (人)	**Number of Scientific and Technical Personnel (person)**						
全　市	**Whole Municipality**	**6 265**	**6 306**	**6 100**	**7 188**	**7 468**	**8 557**
市　区	Urban Area	5 100	5 438	5 301	6 496	6 468	7 460
# 吴江区	Wujiang District	14	14	13	152	170	185
常　熟	Changshu	126	122	103	113	331	254
张家港	Zhangjiagang	352	197	255	263	167	195
昆　山	Kunshan	592	462	368	262	380	484
太　仓	Taicang	95	87	73	54	122	164

注：本表反映的是当年科技部门纳入调查的科学研究与技术服务机构和人员情况。

Note: This table reflects the scientific research and technical service institutions and personnel involved in the survey by the science and technology department.

表16-2

部分年份分地区专利申请情况
PATENT APPLICATIONS EXAMINED BY REGION OF PARTIAL YEARS

单位：件 (unit)

地 区	Region	1995年	2000年	2010年	2013年	2014年	2015年	2016年	2017年	2018年
全 市	**Whole Municipality**	**773**	**2 021**	**77 194**	**141 076**	**103 249**	**98 704**	**106 700**	**113 694**	**135 862**
# 市 区	Urban Area	478	731	38 361	68 537	51 393	61 738	64 855	67 108	83 746
# 吴江区	Wujiang District	82	58	19 469	23 828	12 010	12 295	10 438	11 456	16 785
常 熟	Changshu	98	205	12 812	13 079	12 246	6 324	6 571	6 914	8 037
张家港	Zhangjiagang	105	221	7 147	15 735	13 232	9 964	8 889	8 933	10 958
昆 山	Kunshan	22	787	14 923	34 053	18 302	14 229	18 159	20 961	24 685
太 仓	Taicang	70	77	3 951	9 672	8 076	6 449	8 226	9 778	8 399

表16-3

部分年份分地区专利授权情况
PATENT GRANTED BY REGION OF PARTIAL YEARS

单位：件 (unit)

地 区	Region	1995年	2000年	2010年	2013年	2014年	2015年	2016年	2017年	2018年
全 市	**Whole Municipality**	**415**	**1 922**	**46 109**	**81 665**	**54 709**	**62 263**	**53 528**	**53 223**	**75 837**
# 市 区	Urban Area	244	599	25 466	38 966	26 418	38 387	32 823	31 705	44 913
# 吴江区	Wujiang District	35	38	14 698	17 438	6 998	11 878	5 872	5 492	9 005
常 熟	Changshu	81	159	4 242	13 070	3 990	3 267	3 078	3 088	4 373
张家港	Zhangjiagang	27	136	3 049	8 011	10 086	6 791	4 162	4 413	5 658
昆 山	Kunshan	30	972	10 750	15 439	9 867	10 947	9 833	10 854	16 703
太 仓	Taicang	33	56	2 602	6 179	4 348	2 871	3 632	3 163	4 182

表16-4

部分年份专利申请和授权分类情况
PATENT APPLICATIONS EXAMINED AND GRANTED BY TYPE OF PARTIAL YEARS

单位：件 (unit)

年份 Year	申请 Applications Examined	发明 Inventions	实用新型 Utility Models	外观 Designs	授权 Applications Granted	发明 Inventions	实用新型 Utility Models	外观 Designs
1995	773	47	405	321	415	41	252	122
2000	2 021	224	927	870	1 922	32	1 076	814
2005	6 780	988	2 349	3 443	3 315	148	1 496	1 671
2006	12 874	2 002	2 841	8 031	4 855	180	2 075	2 600
2007	33 752	4 666	4 106	24 980	9 157	292	2 948	5 917
2008	48 558	5 371	6 209	36 978	18 270	645	4 217	13 408
2009	61 336	8 281	8 972	44 083	39 288	1 030	5 585	32 673
2010	77 194	12 935	12 833	51 426	46 109	1 370	10 541	34 198
2011	102 164	21 765	19 428	60 971	77 281	2 492	14 220	60 569
2012	139 965	31 984	28 778	79 203	98 276	4 309	21 577	72 390
2013	141 076	44 477	36 235	60 364	81 665	4 413	30 082	47 170
2014	103 249	40 842	35 432	26 975	54 709	5 264	32 012	17 433
2015	98 704	43 241	42 760	12 703	62 263	10 488	35 901	15 874
2016	106 700	47 429	51 866	7 405	53 528	13 267	34 656	5 605
2017	113 694	45 768	60 357	7 569	53 223	11 618	36 566	5 039
2018	135 862	50 116	77 633	8 113	75 837	10 845	58 262	6 730

表16-5

分地区专利申请和授权分类情况 (2018年)
PATENT APPLICATIONS EXAMINED AND GRANTED BY TYPE AND REGION (2018)

单位：件 (unit)

地区	Region	申请 Applications Examined	发明 Inventions	实用新型 Utility Models	外观 Designs	授权 Applications Granted	发明 Inventions	实用新型 Utility Models	外观 Designs
全　市	**Whole Municipality**	**135 862**	**50 116**	**77 633**	**8 113**	**75 837**	**10 845**	**58 262**	**6 730**
# 市　区	Urban Area	83 746	31 727	46 770	5 249	44 913	6 512	34 213	4 188
# 吴江区	Wujiang District	16 785	5 920	10 021	844	9 005	1 031	7 256	718
常　熟	Changshu	8 037	2 998	4 488	551	4 373	602	3 342	429
张家港	Zhangjiagang	10 958	4 858	5 575	525	5 658	983	4 183	492
昆　山	Kunshan	24 685	6 468	16 784	1 433	16 703	2 000	13 414	1 289
太　仓	Taicang	8 399	4 060	3 984	355	4 182	748	3 103	331

表16-6

部分年份科技成果情况
SCIENTIFIC AND TECHNOLOGICAL ACHIEVMENTS OF PARTIAL YEARS

单位：项 (item)

年 份 Year	年末高新技术企业(个) Number of High & New Tech Enterprisesat Year-end (unit)		科技进步奖 Scientific and Technological Progress Prizes	
		# 当年认定 Certified In this Year	江苏省 Jiangsu Province	国 家 Nation
1995	102	38	50	–
2000	346	68	32	–
2005	706	103	8	3
2006	844	162	13	–
2007	1 430	599	11	1
2008	1 246	361	19	2
2009	680	319	15	3
2010	975	297	17	4
2011	1 345	430	16	4
2012	1 864	588	33	3
2013	2 416	623	26	3
2014	2 950	910	23	3
2015	3 478	712	21	1
2016	4 133	1 521	28	4
2017	4 464	1 568	28	4
2018	5 416	2 331	46	4

注：从2009年开始是按照国家高新技术企业新标准认定办法认定的企业数。
Note: Since 2009 it has been the number of enterprises identified in accordance with the National High-tech Enterprise New Standards Recognition Method.

表16-7

分地区科技创新载体情况 (2018年末)
CARRIER OF SCIENTIFIC AND TECHNOLOGICAL INNOVATION BY REGION (END OF 2018)

单位：个 (unit)

地 区 Region	高新技术企业 Number of High & New Tech Enterprises	# 当年认定 Certified In this Year	省级以上研发机构 Research And Development Institutions at or above the Provincial Level		
			工程技术研究中心 Engineering Technology Centers	企业技术中心 Enterprise Technology Centers	工程中心(实验室) Engineering Centers (Laboratories)
全 市 Whole Municipality	**5 416**	**2 331**	**732**	**505**	**90**
# 市 区 Urban Area	2 962	1 255	363	262	58
# 吴江区 Wujiang District	488	199	57	78	13
常 熟 Changshu	436	198	84	56	9
张家港 Zhangjiagang	458	184	109	51	7
昆 山 Kunshan	1 211	535	133	96	9
太 仓 Taicang	349	159	42	40	7

表16-8 规模以上工业科技活动企业与机构数（2018年末）

THE NUMBER OF ABOVE-SCALE ENTERPRISES AND INSTITUTIONS WITH INDUSTRIAL SCIENTIFIC AND TECHNOLOGICAL ACTIVITIES (END OF 2018)

单位：个 (unit)

项目	Item	企业数 Number of Enterprises	# 有R&D活动企业数 Number of Enterprises With R&D Activities	# 有科技机构企业数 The Number of Enterprises with Scientific Institutions
总计	**Total**	**10 393**	**4 501**	**4 786**
一、按地区分	**Grouped by Region**			
市区	**Urban Area**	**4 721**	**2 108**	**2 255**
姑苏区	Gusu District	13	5	4
吴中区	Wuzhong District	903	419	451
相城区	Xiangcheng District	742	329	322
高新区、虎丘区	New & Hi-tech Zone , Huqiu District	743	406	403
工业园区	Industrial Park	794	448	448
吴江区	Wujiang District	1 526	501	627
县级市	**Cities at County Level**	**5 672**	**2 393**	**2 531**
常熟市	Changshu	1 373	476	468
张家港市	Zhangjiagang	1 197	512	523
昆山市	Kunshan	2 100	986	1 071
太仓市	Taicang	1 002	419	469
二、按企业规模分	**By Size of Enterprises**			
大型	Large	372	312	344
中型	Medium-sized	1 512	1 266	1 441
小型	Small	8 105	2 884	2 959
微型	Micro	404	39	42
三、按登记注册类型分	**Grouped by Registration Status**			
内资企业	**Domestic Funded Enterprises**	**6 336**	**2 716**	**2 837**
国有企业	State-owned Enterprises	2	1	1
集体企业	Collective-owned Enterprises	9	–	–
股份合作企业	Share-holding Cooperative Enterprises	15	7	6
联营企业	Joint Ownership Enterprises	2	2	2
有限责任公司	Limited Liability Corporations	640	360	374
股份有限公司	Share-holding Corporations Ltd.	269	230	238
私营企业	Private Enterprises	5 399	2 116	2 216
其他企业	Other Enterprises	–	–	–
港澳台商投资企业	**Enterprises with Investment from HongKong, Macao and Taiwan**	**1 157**	**544**	**590**
外商投资企业	**Enterprises with Foreign Investment**	**2 900**	**1 241**	**1 359**
四、按国民经济行业大类分	**Grouped by Sector**			
采矿业	**Mining and Quarrying**	**1**	**1**	**1**
有色金属矿采选业	Nonferrous Metals Mining and Processing	-	–	–
非金属矿采选业	Nonmetal Minerals Mining and Dressing	1	1	1

表16-8 续表 Continued

单位：个 (unit)

项　　目	Item	企业数 Number of Enterprises	# 有R&D活动企业数 Number of Enterprises With R&D Activities	# 有科技机构企业数 The Number of Enterprises with Scientific Institutions
制造业	**Manufacturing**	**10 293**	**4 476**	**4 759**
农副食品加工业	Food Processing	53	19	20
食品制造业	Food Production	58	26	28
酒、饮料和精制茶制造业	Wine, Beverage and Refined tea manufacturing	20	8	8
烟草制造业	Manufacture of Tobacco	1	1	–
纺织业	Textile Industry	1 260	268	309
纺织服装、服饰业	Garments and Apparel Industry	352	109	115
皮革、毛皮、羽毛及其制品和制鞋业	Leather, Fur, Wool and Shoes Products	51	14	15
木材加工和木、竹、藤、棕、草制品业	Wood Processing, Wood, Bamboo, Rattan and Coir Products Straw Products	50	10	10
家具制造业	Furniture Manufacturing	76	23	30
造纸和纸制品业	Papermaking and Paper Products	174	51	59
印刷和记录媒介复制业	Printing and Record Medium Reproduction	158	41	49
文教、工美、体育和娱乐用品制造业	Stationary,Educational,Industrial arts, Sports and Entertainment products	123	44	52
石油、煤炭及其他燃料加工业	Oil, Coal and Other Fuel Processing Industries	23	10	9
化学原料和化学制品制造业	Raw Chemical Materials and Chemical Products	565	264	264
医药制造业	Medical and Pharmaceutical Products	105	75	77
化学纤维制造业	Chemical Fiber	339	78	89
橡胶和塑料制品业	Rubber and Plastic Products	794	310	315
非金属矿物制品业	Nonmetal Mineral Products	337	108	114
黑色金属冶炼和压延加工业	Smelting and Pressing of Ferrous Metals	139	53	51
有色金属冶炼和压延加工业	Smelting and Pressing of Nonferrous Metals	242	69	76
金属制品业	Metal Products	823	315	336
通用设备制造业	General Equipment Manufacture	1 049	568	587
专用设备制造业	For Special Purposes Equipment Manufacturing	759	436	446
汽车制造业	Automobile Manufacturing	519	291	300
铁路、船舶、航空航天和其他运输设备制造业	Railway, Ship, Aerospace and other transportation equipment manufacturing	116	52	59
电气机械和器材制造业	Electric Equipment and Machinery	749	427	446
计算机、通信和其他电子设备制造业	Computer Telecommunications and Other Electronic Equipment Manufacture	1 105	663	753
仪器仪表制造业	Instruments, Meters Machinery	199	128	128
其他制造业	Other Products Manufacture	20	6	6
废弃资源综合利用业	Comprehensive Utilization of Waste Resources	30	8	7
金属制品、机械和设备修理业	Metal Products, Machinery and Equipment Repair	4	1	1
电力、热力、燃气及水生产和供应业	**Production and Supply of Electricity, Gas and Water**	**99**	**24**	**26**
电力、热力生产和供应业	Production and Supply of Electricity and Thermal Power	43	11	11
燃气生产和供应业	Production and Supply of Gas	27	4	6
水的生产和供应业	Production and Supply of Water	29	9	9

表16-9 规模以上工业企业科技活动人员情况 (2018年末)

NUMBER OF PERSONS ENGAGED IN SCIENTIFIC & TECHNOLOGICAL ACTIVTIES OF ABOVE-SCALE INDUSTRIAL ENTERPRISES (END OF 2018)

单位：人 (person)

项　　目	Item	研究与试验发展人员 Research and Development Personnel	# 参加项目人员 Present Item Personnel	企业办科技机构人员 Personnel in Science & Technology Institutions Run by Enterprises
总　计	**Total**	**185 622**	**174 862**	**193 436**
一、按地区分	**Grouped by Region**			
市　区	**Urban Area**	**92 498**	**87 537**	**97 477**
姑苏区	Gusu District	103	99	102
吴中区	Wuzhong District	13 205	12 474	14 005
相城区	Xiangcheng District	11 348	10 675	12 398
高新区、虎丘区	New & Hi-tech Zone , Huqiu District	21 087	20 001	17 482
工业园区	Industrial Park	26 808	25 474	30 560
吴江区	Wujiang District	19 947	18 814	22 930
县级市	**Cities at County Level**	**93 124**	**87 325**	**95 959**
常熟市	Changshu	16 772	15 792	15 324
张家港市	Zhangjiagang	17 606	16 644	12 263
昆山市	Kunshan	46 302	43 199	56 055
太仓市	Taicang	12 444	11 690	12 317
二、按企业规模分	**By Size of Enterprises**			
大　型	Large	66 489	63 523	71 055
中　型	Medium-sized	60 037	56 112	63 691
小　型	Small	58 693	54 843	58 429
微　型	Micro	403	384	261
三、按登记注册类型分	**Grouped by Registration Status**			
内资企业	**Domestic Funded Enterprises**	**94 024**	**88 403**	**92 612**
国有企业	State-owned Enterprises	56	50	22
集体企业	Collective-owned Enterprises	–	–	–
股份合作企业	Share-holding Cooperative Enterprises	223	214	199
联营企业	Joint Ownership Enterprises	43	42	44
有限责任公司	Limited Liability Corporations	19 044	18 063	18 387
股份有限公司	Share-holding Corporations Ltd.	15 194	14 089	15 897
私营企业	Private Enterprises	59 464	55 945	58 063
其他企业	Other Enterprises	–	–	–
港澳台商投资企业	**Enterprises with Investment from HongKong, Macao and Taiwan**	**27 870**	**26 372**	**32 546**
外商投资企业	**Enterprises with Foreign Investment**	**63 728**	**60 087**	**68 278**
四、按国民经济行业大类分	**Grouped by Sector**			
采矿业	**Mining and Quarrying**	**69**	**68**	**68**
有色金属矿采选业	Nonferrous Metals Mining and Processing	–	–	–
非金属矿采选业	Nonmetal Minerals Mining and Dressing	69	68	68

表16-9 续表 Continued

单位：人 (person)

项 目	Item	研究与试验发展人员 Research and Development Personnel	# 参加项目人员 Present Item Personnel	企业办科技机构人员 Personnel in Science & Technology Institutions Run by Enterprises
制造业	**Manufacturing**	**185 088**	**174 372**	**192 922**
农副食品加工业	Food Processing	410	375	381
食品制造业	Food Production	643	618	568
酒、饮料和精制茶制造业	Wine, Beverage and Refined tea manufacturing	326	294	140
烟草制造业	Manufacture of Tobacco	20	14	-
纺织业	Textile Industry	6 363	5 946	5 144
纺织服装、服饰业	Garments and Apparel Industry	2 551	2 445	2 024
皮革、毛皮、羽毛及其制品和制鞋业	Leather, Fur, Wool and Shoes Products	213	196	185
木材加工和木、竹、藤、棕、草制品业	Wood Processing, Wood, Bamboo, Rattan and Coir Products Straw Products	244	231	277
家具制造业	Furniture Manufacturing	602	538	756
造纸和纸制品业	Papermaking and Paper Products	2 377	2 282	2 704
印刷和记录媒介复制业	Printing and Record Medium Reproduction	1 767	1 629	1 886
文教、工美、体育和娱乐用品制造业	Stationary,Educational,Industrial arts, Sports and Entertainment products	2 014	1 876	1 850
石油、煤炭及其他燃料加工业	Oil, Coal and Other Fuel Processing Industries	158	152	165
化学原料和化学制品制造业	Raw Chemical Materials and Chemical Products	7 616	7 115	7 265
医药制造业	Medical and Pharmaceutical Products	2 356	2 153	2 850
化学纤维制造业	Chemical Fiber	5 433	5 232	3 827
橡胶和塑料制品业	Rubber and Plastic Products	9 960	9 459	9 534
非金属矿物制品业	Nonmetal Mineral Products	2 633	2 469	3 027
黑色金属冶炼和压延加工业	Smelting and Pressing of Ferrous Metals	3 669	3 577	1 711
有色金属冶炼和压延加工业	Smelting and Pressing of Nonferrous Metals	2 344	2 147	2 300
金属制品业	Metal Products	8 673	8 121	8 646
通用设备制造业	General Equipment Manufacture	20 204	19 154	21 898
专用设备制造业	For Special Purposes Equipment Manufacturing	14 235	13 381	16 167
汽车制造业	Automobile Manufacturing	13 273	12 386	14 618
铁路、船舶、航空航天和其他运输设备制造业	Railway, Ship, Aerospace and other transportation equipment manufacturing	1 634	1 484	2 110
电气机械和器材制造业	Electric Equipment and Machinery	15 988	14 926	17 658
计算机、通信和其他电子设备制造业	Computer Telecommunications and Other Electronic Equipment Manufacture	52 065	49 330	58 127
仪器仪表制造业	Instruments, Meters Machinery	7 011	6 563	6 853
其他制造业	Other Products Manufacture	77	77	66
废弃资源综合利用业	Comprehensive Utilization of Waste Resources	217	193	176
金属制品、机械和设备修理业	Metal Products, Machinery and Equipment Repair	12	9	9
电力、热力、燃气及水生产和供应业	**Production and Supply of Electricity, Gas and Water**	**465**	**422**	**446**
电力、热力生产和供应业	Production and Supply of Electricity and Thermal Power	181	170	149
燃气生产和供应业	Production and Supply of Gas	43	41	87
水的生产和供应业	Production and Supply of Water	241	211	210

表16-10

规模以上工业企业科技活动经费支出情况（2018年）
THE EXPENDITURE OF SCIENTIFIC AND TECHNOLOGICAL ACTIVITIES OF ABOVE-SCALE INDUSTRIAL ENTERPRISES (2018)

单位：万元 (10 000 yuan)

项　目	Item	R&D经费内部支出合计 Internal Expenditures on Research and Development	# 政府资金 Government Funds	# 企业资金 Enterprises Funds	# 境外资金 Abroad Funds
总　计	**Total**	**5 180 492**	**51 981**	**5 048 464**	**53 931**
一、按地区分	**Grouped by Region**				
市　区	**Urban Area**	**2 262 833**	**26 115**	**2 195 022**	**28 517**
姑苏区	Gusu District	1 400	54	1 347	–
吴中区	Wuzhong District	276 203	2 606	273 404	193
相城区	Xiangcheng District	230 202	1 596	226 596	818
高新区、虎丘区	New & Hi-tech Zone , Huqiu District	494 663	3 958	482 686	7 509
工业园区	Industrial Park	780 862	8 420	749 493	16 544
吴江区	Wujiang District	479 502	9 481	461 496	3 453
县级市	**Cities at County Level**	**2 917 659**	**25 867**	**2 853 442**	**25 414**
常熟市	Changshu	652 815	8 656	622 619	11 463
张家港市	Zhangjiagang	755 515	6 079	739 467	8 199
昆山市	Kunshan	1 169 071	7 403	1 156 202	4 494
太仓市	Taicang	340 258	3 729	335 153	1 259
二、按企业规模分	**By Size of Enterprises**				
大　型	Large	2 317 881	16 452	2 262 770	32 120
中　型	Medium-sized	1 519 186	19 609	1 471 194	13 233
小　型	Small	1 335 879	15 826	1 307 259	8 402
微　型	Micro	7 546	94	7 240	176
三、按登记注册类型分	**Grouped by Registration Status**				
内资企业	**Domestic Funded Enterprises**	**2 597 798**	**35 704**	**2 533 626**	**16 842**
国有企业	State-owned Enterprises	2 000	–	2 000	–
集体企业	Collective-owned Enterprises	–	–	–	–
股份合作企业	Share-holding Cooperative Enterprises	16 737	28	16 709	–
联营企业	Joint Ownership Enterprises	1 356	–	1 356	–
有限责任公司	Limited Liability Corporations	590 727	9 075	577 689	3 427
股份有限公司	Share-holding Corporations Ltd.	472 530	12 630	453 457	6 363
私营企业	Private Enterprises	1 514 449	13 970	1 482 415	7 052
其他企业	Other Enterprises	–	–	–	–
港澳台商投资企业	**Enterprises with Investment from HongKong, Macao and Taiwan**	**802 320**	**5 521**	**787 358**	**7 509**
外商投资企业	**Enterprises with Foreign Investment**	**1 780 374**	**10 756**	**1 727 480**	**29 580**
四、按国民经济行业大类分	**Grouped by Sector**				
采矿业	**Mining and Quarrying**	**1 093**	**22**	**1 070**	**–**
有色金属矿采选业	Nonferrous Metals Mining and Processing	–	–	–	–
非金属矿采选业	Nonmetal Minerals Mining and Dressing	1 093	22	1 070	–

表16-10 续表 Continued

单位：万元 (10 000 yuan)

项 目	Item	R&D经费内部支出合计 Internal Expenditures on Research and Development	# 政府资金 Government Funds	# 企业资金 Enterprises Funds	# 境外资金 Abroad Funds
制造业	**Manufacturing**	**5 165 321**	**51 896**	**5 033 397**	**53 912**
农副食品加工业	Food Processing	13 487	82	13 405	–
食品制造业	Food Production	16 299	15	16 148	136
酒、饮料和精制茶制造业	Wine, Beverage and Refined tea manufacturing	5 649	–	5 648	1
烟草制造业	Manufacture of Tobacco	286	–	286	–
纺织业	Textile Industry	129 575	1 386	126 980	671
纺织服装、服饰业	Garments and Apparel Industry	40 132	257	39 483	201
皮革、毛皮、羽毛及其制品和制鞋业	Leather, Fur, Wool and Shoes Products	3 541	–	3 416	54
木材加工和木、竹、藤、棕、草制品业	Wood Processing, Wood, Bamboo, Rattan and Coir Products Straw Products	3 648	39	2 954	–
家具制造业	Furniture Manufacturing	9 428	32	9 389	8
造纸和纸制品业	Papermaking and Paper Products	108 759	65	108 578	57
印刷和记录媒介复制业	Printing and Record Medium Reproduction	43 435	41	43 394	–
文教、工美、体育和娱乐用品制造业	Stationary,Educational,Industrial arts, Sports and Entertainment products	32 697	1 060	31 057	292
石油、煤炭及其他燃料加工业	Oil, Coal and Other Fuel Processing Industries	3 336	5	3 298	33
化学原料和化学制品制造业	Raw Chemical Materials and Chemical Products	316 435	6 404	300 816	4 774
医药制造业	Medical and Pharmaceutical Products	73 726	1 172	69 987	2 436
化学纤维制造业	Chemical Fiber	201 876	1 424	192 481	2 390
橡胶和塑料制品业	Rubber and Plastic Products	234 892	949	232 189	675
非金属矿物制品业	Nonmetal Mineral Products	56 387	593	55 172	295
黑色金属冶炼和压延加工业	Smelting and Pressing of Ferrous Metals	261 147	3 031	257 804	149
有色金属冶炼和压延加工业	Smelting and Pressing of Nonferrous Metals	72 025	324	71 622	79
金属制品业	Metal Products	187 543	1 512	185 436	373
通用设备制造业	General Equipment Manufacture	468 254	5 862	457 006	3 848
专用设备制造业	For Special Purposes Equipment Manufacturing	373 442	4 168	367 101	2 049
汽车制造业	Automobile Manufacturing	394 153	808	382 723	9 400
铁路、船舶、航空航天和其他运输设备制造业	Railway, Ship, Aerospace and other transportation equipment manufacturing	44 328	164	43 859	107
电气机械和器材制造业	Electric Equipment and Machinery	554 595	10 716	539 013	3 512
计算机、通信和其他电子设备制造业	Computer Telecommunications and Other Electronic Equipment Manufacture	1 346 250	9 012	1 309 405	20 320
仪器仪表制造业	Instruments, Meters Machinery	165 528	2 721	160 337	2 053
其他制造业	Other Products Manufacture	1 913	–	1 913	–
废弃资源综合利用业	Comprehensive Utilization of Waste Resources	2 439	54	2 385	–
金属制品、机械和设备修理业	Metal Products, Machinery and Equipment Repair	114	–	114	–
电力、热力、燃气及水生产和供应业	**Production and Supply of Electricity, Gas and Water**	**14 079**	**63**	**13 997**	**19**
电力、热力生产和供应业	Production and Supply of Electricity and Thermal Power	8 532	17	8 515	–
燃气生产和供应业	Production and Supply of Gas	1 188	–	1 188	–
水的生产和供应业	Production and Supply of Water	4 359	46	4 293	19

表16-11

规模以上工业企业自主知识产权情况（2018年）
THE INDEPENDENT INTELLECTUAL PROPERTY RIGHTS OF ABOVE-SCALE INDUSTRIAL ENTERPRISES (2018)

单位：件 (unit)

项　　目	Item	专利申请数 Patents Submitted for Examination	# 发明专利 Invention	年末拥有发明专利数 Owning Inventive Patent by Year End
总　计	**Total**	**42 150**	**14 721**	**59 612**
一、按地区分	**Grouped by Region**			
市　区	**Urban Area**	**21 090**	**6 946**	**29 956**
姑苏区	Gusu District	18	1	24
吴中区	Wuzhong District	4 143	1 155	3 704
相城区	Xiangcheng District	3 613	871	4 486
高新区、虎丘区	New & Hi-tech Zone , Huqiu District	4 335	1 696	5 384
工业园区	Industrial Park	3 900	1 451	8 834
吴江区	Wujiang District	5 081	1 772	7 524
县级市	**Cities at County Level**	**21 060**	**7 775**	**29 656**
常熟市	Changshu	3 490	1 293	4 471
张家港市	Zhangjiagang	3 783	1 654	5 369
昆山市	Kunshan	11 216	4 065	16 573
太仓市	Taicang	2 571	763	3 243
二、按企业规模分	**By Size of Enterprises**			
大　型	Large	9 867	4 616	14 839
中　型	Medium-sized	10 686	3 771	16 025
小　型	Small	21 326	6 222	28 505
微　型	Micro	271	112	243
三、按登记注册类型分	**Grouped by Registration Status**			
内资企业	**Domestic Funded Enterprises**	**27 700**	**9 880**	**34 578**
国有企业	State-owned Enterprises	–	–	–
集体企业	Collective-owned Enterprises	–	–	–
股份合作企业	Share-holding Cooperative Enterprises	30	4	28
联营企业	Joint Ownership Enterprises	19	7	26
有限责任公司	Limited Liability Corporations	4 960	2 322	5 528
股份有限公司	Share-holding Corporations Ltd.	4 214	1 910	7 338
私营企业	Private Enterprises	18 477	5 637	21 658
其他企业	Other Enterprises	–	–	–
港澳台商投资企业	**Enterprises with Investment from HongKong, Macao and Taiwan**	**5 171**	**1 843**	**8 266**
外商投资企业	**Enterprises with Foreign Investment**	**9 279**	**2 998**	**16 768**
四、按国民经济行业大类分	**Grouped by Sector**			
采矿业	**Mining and Quarrying**	**2**	**2**	**15**
有色金属矿采选业	Nonferrous Metals Mining and Processing	–	–	–
非金属矿采选业	Nonmetal Minerals Mining and Dressing	2	2	15

表16-11 续表 Continued

单位：件 (unit)

项 目	Item	专利申请数 Patents Submitted for Examination	# 发明专利 Invention	年末拥有发明专利数 Owning Inventive Patent by Year End
制造业	**Manufacturing**	**41 988**	**14 688**	**59 423**
农副食品加工业	Food Processing	56	8	119
食品制造业	Food Production	41	28	65
酒、饮料和精制茶制造业	Wine, Beverage and Refined tea manufacturing	12	4	10
烟草制造业	Manufacture of Tobacco	8	6	8
纺织业	Textile Industry	1 056	306	1 191
纺织服装、服饰业	Garments and Apparel Industry	145	56	293
皮革、毛皮、羽毛及其制品和制鞋业	Leather, Fur, Wool and Shoes Products	–	–	10
木材加工和木、竹、藤、棕、草制品业	Wood Processing, Wood, Bamboo, Rattan and Coir Products Straw Products	48	17	155
家具制造业	Furniture Manufacturing	390	101	630
造纸和纸制品业	Papermaking and Paper Products	443	141	664
印刷和记录媒介复制业	Printing and Record Medium Reproduction	306	80	335
文教、工美、体育和娱乐用品制造业	Stationary,Educational,Industrial arts, Sports and Entertainment products	792	145	866
石油、煤炭及其他燃料加工业	Oil, Coal and Other Fuel Processing Industries	32	17	32
化学原料和化学制品制造业	Raw Chemical Materials and Chemical Products	2 012	1 096	2 392
医药制造业	Medical and Pharmaceutical Products	335	193	677
化学纤维制造业	Chemical Fiber	526	213	735
橡胶和塑料制品业	Rubber and Plastic Products	2 487	754	2 915
非金属矿物制品业	Nonmetal Mineral Products	799	265	1 065
黑色金属冶炼和压延加工业	Smelting and Pressing of Ferrous Metals	474	243	705
有色金属冶炼和压延加工业	Smelting and Pressing of Nonferrous Metals	411	93	706
金属制品业	Metal Products	2 509	652	3 166
通用设备制造业	General Equipment Manufacture	5 389	1 593	7 181
专用设备制造业	For Special Purposes Equipment Manufacturing	4 835	1 640	8 251
汽车制造业	Automobile Manufacturing	2 559	748	3 328
铁路、船舶、航空航天和其他运输设备制造业	Railway, Ship, Aerospace and other transportation equipment manufacturing	380	132	797
电气机械和器材制造业	Electric Equipment and Machinery	5 222	1 548	7 604
计算机、通信和其他电子设备制造业	Computer Telecommunications and Other Electronic Equipment Manufacture	8 753	3 957	13 495
仪器仪表制造业	Instruments, Meters Machinery	1 870	622	1 958
其他制造业	Other Products Manufacture	33	10	20
废弃资源综合利用业	Comprehensive Utilization of Waste Resources	65	20	50
金属制品、机械和设备修理业	Metal Products, Machinery and Equipment Repair	–	–	–
电力、热力、燃气及水生产和供应业	**Production and Supply of Electricity, Gas and Water**	**160**	**31**	**174**
电力、热力生产和供应业	Production and Supply of Electricity and Thermal Power	79	20	66
燃气生产和供应业	Production and Supply of Gas	26	3	3
水的生产和供应业	Production and Supply of Water	55	8	105

表16-12

部分年份专业技术人员
SCIENTIFIC AND TECHNICAL PERSONNEL OF PARTIAL YEARS

单位：人 (person)

项 目	Item	2014年	2015年	2016年	2017年	2018年
总 计	**Total**	**1 366 119**	**1 496 406**	**1 634 233**	**1 742 622**	**1 917 801**
# 高级职称人员	Personnel with Senior Professional Titles	65 108	74 493	84 236	91 583	98 787
中级职称人员	Personnel with Medium Professional Titles	338 951	371 186	390 474	409 191	439 455
总计中：市 区	Urban Area	663 804	736 746	816 804	866 259	982 444
# 吴江区	Wujiang District	173 201	187 374	188 649	214 330	228 791
常 熟	Changshu	189 601	208 754	223 184	238 451	253 510
张家港	Zhangjiagang	191 598	210 668	231 686	248 895	268 785
昆 山	Kunshan	225 909	236 400	250 875	269 203	287 571
太 仓	Taicang	95 207	103 838	111 684	119 814	125 491

表16-13

分经济类型专业技术人员 (2018年末)
SCIENTIFIC AND TECHNICAL PERSONNEL BY SECTOR (END OF 2018)

单位：人 (person)

类 型	Sector	总 计 Total	按职称分 Grouped by Professional Titles		按学历分 Grouped by Educational Level		
			# 高级职称 Senior Professional Titles	#中级职称 Medium Professional Titles	#研究生 Postgraduates	#大学本科 University and College	#大学专科 Specialized Institutions of Higher Education
总 计	**Total**	**1 917 801**	**98 787**	**439 455**	**120 883**	**750 158**	**786 430**
全民事业	Institutions Owned by the Whole People	123 659	23 190	57 903	12 641	94 417	13 045
国有企业	State-owned Enterprises	17 182	1 365	3 575	1 233	9 101	4 233
部省属	Province and State Council Department Owned Enterprises	41 292	7 031	10 786	11 785	22 484	5 619
外资及港澳台资企业	Enterprises with Foreign Investment or Investment from Hongkong, Macao and Taiwan	878 245	29 613	209 222	53 365	307 574	384 132
民营企业	Enterprises of Private Ownership	857 423	37 588	157 969	41 859	316 582	379 401

表16-14

分地区专业技术人员（2018年末）
NUMBER OF SCIENTIFIC AND TECHNICAL PERSONNEL BY REGION (END OF 2018)

单位：人　　(person)

地　区	Region	总　计 Total	# 女　性 Female	按职称分 Grouped by Professional Titles # 高级职称人员 Personnel with Senior Professional Titles	# 中级职称人员 Personnel with Medium Professional Titles	# 初级职称人员 Personnel with Junior Professional Titles
全　市	**Whole Municipality**	**1 917 801**	**686 257**	**98 787**	**439 455**	**775 603**
市　区	Urban Area	982 444	334 994	54 419	250 662	386 622
# 吴江区	Wujiang District	228 791	105 823	8 264	25 141	39 360
常　熟	Changshu	253 510	77 580	12 972	43 687	93 858
张家港	Zhangjiagang	268 785	103 727	13 961	61 062	141 079
昆　山	Kunshan	287 571	124 454	12 570	55 381	98 825
太　仓	Taicang	125 491	45 502	4 865	28 663	55 219

表16-14 续表　Continued

单位：人　　(person)

地　区	Region	按学历分 Grouped by Educational Level 研究生 Postgraduates	大学本科 University and College	大学专科 Specialized Institutions of Higher Education	中　专 Specialized Secondary School	高中以下 Senior Middle School and below
全　市	**Whole Municipality**	**120 883**	**750 158**	**786 430**	**181 785**	**78 545**
市　区	Urban Area	86 905	400 645	377 020	78 233	39 641
# 吴江区	Wujiang District	8 894	87 159	87 549	34 834	10 355
常　熟	Changshu	8 637	98 815	129 384	11 980	4 694
张家港	Zhangjiagang	11 027	97 016	102 430	44 905	13 407
昆　山	Kunshan	8 513	110 683	129 596	26 341	12 438
太　仓	Taicang	5 801	42 999	48 000	20 326	8 365

主要统计指标解释

专利 是专利权的简称，是对发明人的发明创造经审查合格后，由专利局依据专利法授予发明人和设计人对该项发明创造享有的专有权。包括发明、实用新型和外观设计。反映拥有自主知识产权的科技和设计成果情况。

发明（专利） 指对产品、方法或者其改进所提出的新的技术方案。是国际通行的反映拥有自主知识产权技术的核心指标。

实用新型（专利） 指对产品的形状、构造或者其结合所提出的适于实用的新的技术方案。反映具有一定技术含量的技术成果情况。

外观设计（专利） 指对产品的形状、图案、色彩或者其结合所作出的富有美感并适于工业上应用的新设计。反映拥有自主知识产权的外观设计成果情况。

专业技术人员 指从事专业技术工作的人员以及从事专业技术管理工作且已在1983年以前评定了专业技术职称或在1984年以后聘任了专业技术职务的人员。

专业技术人员具体指工程技术人员、农业技术人员、科研人员(自然科学研究、社会科学研究及实验技术人员)、卫生技术人员、教学人员(含高等院校、中等专业学校、技工学校、中学、小学)、民用航空飞行技术人员、船舶技术人员、经济人员、会计人员、统计人员、翻译人员、图书资料、档案、文博人员、新闻、出版人员、律师、公证人员、广播电视播音人员、工艺美术人员、体育人员、艺术人员及政工人员。

专业技术管理人员具体指企业、事业单位的领导；企业、事业单位下设的职能机构、企业的生产车间和辅助车间(或附属辅助生产单位)中从事生产、技术、经济管理和政治工作人员。

按照公务员管理或参照公务员管理的人员不统计为专业技术人员。

EXPLANATORY NOTES ON MAIN STATISTICAL INDICATORS

Patent is an abbreviation for the patent right and refers to the exclusive right of ownership by the inventors or designers for the creation or inventions, given from the patent offices after due process of assessment and approval in accordance with the Patent Law. Patents are granted for inventions, utility models and designs. This indicator reflects the achievements of S&T and design with independent intellectual property.

Patented Inventions refer to new technical proposals to the products or methods or their modifications. This is universal core indicator reflecting the technologies with independent intellectual property.

Patented Utility Models refer to the practical and new technical proposals on the shape and structure of the product or the combination of both. This indicator reflects the condition of technological results with certain technical content.

Designs refer to the aesthetics and industrially applicable new designs for the shape, pattern and colour of the product, or their combinations. This indicator reflects the appearance design achievements with independent intellectual property.

Professional Personnel refers to the persons who are engaged in special professional work or in professional management who got the titles of a professional post before 1983 or who were appointed to professional positions since 1984.

Professional personnel specifically refers to engineering professionals, agricultural professionals, scientific research professionals (natural science researchers, social science researchers and laboratory technicians), health professionals, teaching professionals (including institutions of higher education, specialized secondary schools, technical schools, regular secondary schools, and primary schools), civil aviation professionals, nautical professionals, economic professionals, accounting professionals, statistical professionals, interpretation professionals, library professionals, archives professionals, professionals of culture, arts and cultural relics, newsman and publishing professionals, lawyers, notary professionals, radio and television announcers, industrial arts professionals, sports professionals, artists and political professionals.

Professional management personnel specifically refers to the managers of enterprises and institutions, the personnel engaged in the management of production, technical, economic management and political aspects in the functional departments under the enterprise and institution, production workshops and accessorial workshops (or accessorial production units) under the enterprises.

Professional personnel do not include personnel under or managed according to the system of civil servants.

十七、教育　文化

CHAPTER 17
EDUCATION AND CULTURE

17 教育　文化 EDUCATION AND CULTURE

主要统计指标 MAJOR STATISTICAL INDICATORS

2018年各类学校数	Number of Schools of Various Types	799	所	unit
普通高等学校数	Number of Institutions of Higher Education	26	所	unit
中等职业教育学校	Secondary Vocational Education Schools	25	所	unit
技工学校	Technical Schools	12	所	unit
普通中学	Regular Secondary Schools	304	所	unit
小　学	Primary Schools	420	所	unit
特殊教育学校	Special Education Schools	12	所	unit
2018年在校学生数	Number of Students Enrollment	1 464 171	人	person
普通高等学校	Institutions of Higher Education	235 649	人	person
中等职业教育学校	Secondary Vocational Education Schools	58 880	人	person
技工学校	Technical Schools	26 381	人	person
普通中学	Regular Secondary Schools	360 488	人	person
小　学	Primary Schools	781 274	人	person
特殊教育学校	Special Education Schools	1 499	人	person
2018年毕业生数	Graduates	286 112	人	person
2018年招生数	New Student Enrollment	390 483	人	person
2018年幼儿园数	Number of Kindergartens	821	所	unit
2018年幼儿园在园幼儿数	Number of Enrollment in Kindergartens	352 735	人	person
2018年末艺术表演团体	Number of Art Troupes (Year-end)	17	个	unit
2018年末公共图书馆	Number of Public Libraries (Year-end)	11	个	unit
2018年末博物馆	Number of Museums (Year-end)	46	个	unit

表17-1

历年各类学校及幼儿园数
NUMBER OF SCHOOLS OF ALL TYPES AND KINDERGARTENS OVER THE YEARS

单位：所 (unit)

年份 Year	各类学校总计 Total	普通高等学校 Institutions of Higher Education	中等职业教育学校 Secondary Vocational Education Schools	技工学校 Technical Schools	普通中学 Regular Secondary Schools	小学 Primary Schools	特殊教育学校 Special Education Schools	幼儿园 Kindergartens
1949	1 694	2	14		60	1 617	1	
1952	3 272	2	17		67	3 185	1	
1957	3 373	2	14		94	3 262	1	
1962	3 685	4	13	1	164	3 502	1	
1965	4 472	4	143	1	136	4 187	1	
1970	5 445	4	1	1	519	4 919	1	
1975	4 986	4	6	2	606	4 365	3	
1978	4 392	4	7	6	544	3 828	3	
1980	4 103	5	19	9	523	3 543	3	
1985	3 788	10	48	13	544	3 169	3	
1990	3 276	9	58	17	424	2 757	10	
1995	2 471	8	71	18	302	2 061	10	
1996	2 234	8	73	20	288	1 834	10	
1997	2 018	7	72	21	278	1 628	11	
1998	1 740	7	72	21	262	1 366	11	
1999	1 542	7	78	21	260	1 164	11	
2000	1 352	7	69	20	264	980	11	
2001	1 151	8	66	19	270	776	11	
2002	1 047	9	62	18	268	678	11	
2003	902	12	41	17	270	550	11	
2004	832	13	39	11	268	488	12	
2005	802	16	40	12	270	452	12	347
2006	745	17	41	13	265	397	12	357
2007	681	18	33	14	260	344	12	368
2008	677	18	34	15	261	337	12	389
2009	668	19	33	13	257	334	12	385
2010	652	20	34	12	257	317	12	411
2011	646	20	34	11	263	306	12	444
2012	632	20	33	11	261	294	13	465
2013	639	21	30	10	261	304	13	509
2014	733	21	30	10	276	383	13	555
2015	744	21	29	10	283	387	14	731
2016	754	22	27	10	292	391	12	754
2017	771	26	26	10	297	400	12	766
2018	799	26	25	12	304	420	12	821

注：1.1980年至2004年的学校相关资料中包含1所工读学校数据（下同）。2.2014年起，外来工子弟学校学生学籍计入普通中小学，普通中小学相关数据包含外来工子弟学校（下同）。3.由于教育改革，2017年起高等院校二级学院独立计算学校数。

Note:1.From 1980 to2004, the total number of schools including a reform school. 2.Starting from 2014, the student status of schools for the children of migrant workers is included in the students' enrollment of ordinary primary and secondary schools, and the related data of ordinary primary and secondary schools contains that of schools for the children of migrant workers. (Same below) 3.Due to educational reforms, the secondary colleges of colleges and universities independently counted the number of colleges since 2017.

表17-2

历年在校学生数
STUDENT ENROLLMENT OVER THE YEARS

单位：人 (person)

年 份 Year	各类学校在校学生总计 Total	普通高等学校 Institutions of Higher Education	中等职业教育学校 Secondary Vocational Education Schools	技工学校 Technical Schools	普通中学 Regular Secondary Schools	小 学 Primary Schools	特殊教育学校 Special Education Schools	幼儿园在园幼儿数 Number of Enrollment in Kindergartens
1949	167 633	847	2 443		15 121	149 148	74	
1952	339 287	2 349	8 616		34 028	294 220	74	
1957	415 729	3 251	7 738		55 497	349 164	79	
1962	436 498	5 772	1 896	344	58 585	369 788	113	
1965	560 023	2 579	12 070	515	62 397	482 322	140	
1970	839 053	37			171 242	667 632	142	
1975	956 704	3 922	1 309	540	215 023	735 619	291	
1978	968 070	6 502	2 748	1 181	327 561	629 614	464	
1980	812 756	8 819	5 231	1 757	228 618	567 858	460	
1985	706 893	12 443	19 802	3 244	235 600	435 340	445	
1990	711 333	16 280	25 293	5 866	217 284	445 627	951	
1995	789 526	23 182	57 999	10 844	270 832	422 643	3 993	
1996	822 296	25 749	63 162	13 228	260 130	455 903	4 071	
1997	833 785	29 031	67 844	15 174	233 225	484 903	3 537	
1998	845 618	32 375	73 606	16 442	230 019	488 831	4 312	
1999	860 296	39 341	68 594	14 347	263 133	470 812	4 025	
2000	876 897	47 701	60 185	12 346	304 661	448 363	3 605	
2001	900 019	61 165	58 273	12 783	335 136	429 066	3 552	
2002	918 446	69 614	69 588	15 297	360 305	400 183	3 389	
2003	939 800	80 523	84 731	22 118	367 460	381 542	3 361	
2004	936 782	94 960	93 708	21 206	358 882	364 951	3 060	
2005	956 948	113 090	115 541	27 215	338 222	359 930	2 950	141 666
2006	941 320	130 622	102 737	28 875	324 690	351 549	2 847	149 387
2007	948 683	152 389	93 656	31 119	314 089	354 569	2 861	158 521
2008	961 934	166 828	94 661	33 018	300 886	363 807	2 734	174 886
2009	960 812	187 678	81 493	32 627	285 990	370 224	2 800	183 467
2010	958 474	187 829	74 828	32 158	272 541	388 353	2 765	197 889
2011	972 642	188 750	71 409	29 371	265 442	414 972	2 698	209 965
2012	989 146	192 206	64 706	27 244	261 788	440 400	2 802	229 746
2013	1 026 996	201 926	57 936	25 069	266 943	472 418	2 704	248 006
2014	1 179 769	209 479	57 606	24 173	279 557	606 251	2 703	273 769
2015	1 243 728	214 816	59 227	23 743	292 521	650 730	2 691	300 936
2016	1 310 358	219 347	61 202	23 593	309 824	693 657	2 735	324 380
2017	1 375 638	222 838	61 061	23 861	334 417	730 617	2 844	339 332
2018	1 464 171	235 649	58 880	26 381	360 488	781 274	1 499	352 735

注：2018年特殊教育学校在校学生数剔除了义务教育随班就读人数与送教上门人数。

Note : In 2018, the number of students in special education schools excluded the number of compulsory education students attending classes and that of students receiving education at home.

表17-3

历年毕业生数
NUMBER OF GRADUATES OVER THE YEARS

单位：人 (person)

年 份 Year	各类学校毕业生数总计 Total	普通高等学校 Institutions of Higher Education	中等职业教育学校 Secondary Vocational Education Schools	技工学校 Technical Schools	普通中学 Regular Secondary Schools	小 学 Primary Schools	特殊教育学校 Special Education Schools
1949	12 766	126	802		3 919	7 919	
1952	21 973	140	920		4 936	15 972	5
1957	46 371	890	2 300		12 572	30 609	
1962	55 127	1 416	879	29	20 200	32 595	8
1965	50 427	1 280	401	131	15 828	32 780	7
1970	135 095	528			46 969	87 585	13
1975	180 176	501	850	368	76 247	102 189	21
1978	262 706	1 757	83	422	152 832	107 604	8
1980	184 353	1 260	614	571	90 439	91 414	55
1985	140 384	2 386	5 829	758	65 943	65 410	54
1990	141 461	4 965	8 787	1 814	55 259	70 574	57
1995	181 891	7 246	12 214	2 239	83 993	76 053	134
1996	155 056	6 817	14 666	2 730	78 902	51 737	165
1997	166 338	6 791	18 346	4 231	92 661	43 866	373
1998	189 452	6 612	21 549	4 853	91 013	65 061	312
1999	184 905	7 926	18 739	4 861	69 435	83 525	379
2000	192 596	9 094	21 331	5 818	67 780	88 191	311
2001	213 613	9 551	22 390	4 965	88 808	87 317	533
2002	223 826	11 544	16 179	3 807	103 193	88 466	591
2003	217 663	15 187	12 434	3 014	109 347	76 964	645
2004	231 199	18 756	17 295	4 302	117 878	72 349	571
2005	247 087	22 498	21 257	6 965	126 944	68 878	545
2006	235 206	23 236	22 050	5 953	115 345	68 092	530
2007	236 025	30 335	23 937	7 532	108 974	64 845	402
2008	238 243	39 717	21 950	8 104	107 089	60 936	447
2009	234 727	40 995	23 992	7 387	102 375	59 494	484
2010	241 924	54 009	22 825	8 403	98 078	58 109	500
2011	231 498	55 176	18 098	9 539	90 001	58 206	478
2012	224 189	49 652	17 726	8 651	86 898	60 769	493
2013	226 286	49 441	19 761	8 467	84 580	63 533	504
2014	229 653	53 211	19 708	6 305	83 958	65 982	489
2015	250 341	57 243	18 659	5 901	87 906	80 085	547
2016	268 560	59 274	17 681	9 031	92 143	89 873	558
2017	290 286	67 237	18 549	9 053	95 199	99 724	524
2018	286 112	59 071	19 874	8 243	98 649	100 096	179

注：2018年特殊教育学校毕业生数剔除了义务教育随班就读人数与送教上门人数。

Note: In 2018, the number of graduates of special education schools excluded the number of compulsory education students attending classes and that of students receiving education at home.

表17-4

历年专任教师数
NUMBER OF FULL-TIME TEACHERS OVER THE YEARS

单位：人 (person)

年 份 Year	各类学校专任教师总计 Total	普通高等学校 Institutions of Higher Education	中等职业教育学校 Secondary Vocational Education Schools	技工学校 Technical Schools	普通中学 Regular Secondary Schools	小 学 Primary Schools	特殊教育学校 Special Education Schools	幼儿园专任教师数 Number of Full-time eachers in Kindergartens
1949	6 285	86	321	-	780	5 090	8	
1952	10 573	270	485	-	1 280	8 530	8	
1957	12 636	513	723	-	1 876	9 516	8	
1962	17 518	797	261	51	3 194	13 201	14	
1965	19 512	880	571	46	3 289	14 706	20	
1970		789	86	48		20 823	21	
1975	35 441	886	154	98	9 820	24 434	49	
1978	40 127	1 288	264	161	15 217	23 134	63	
1980	35 978	1 375	591	167	12 570	21 209	62	
1985	36 103	2 358	1 432	435	12 833	18 962	77	
1990	40 145	2 927	2 164	656	14 584	19 609	192	
1995	44 140	2 793	3 367	1 220	16 585	19 896	265	
1996	45 800	2 691	3 869	1 225	17 017	20 698	273	
1997	45 824	2 775	3 847	1 365	17 026	20 543	247	
1998	46 459	2 821	4 143	1 184	17 109	20 895	285	
1999	47 072	2 877	3 881	1 179	17 644	21 232	238	
2000	47 908	3 127	3 543	824	19 023	21 122	245	
2001	49 736	3 461	3 324	957	20 548	21 181	236	
2002	51 125	3 769	3 529	806	21 870	20 893	238	
2003	53 125	4 408	3 750	655	23 366	20 671	249	
2004	54 324	5 435	3 024	552	24 220	20 821	248	
2005	56 371	6 428	4 040	545	24 268	20 851	239	4 963
2006	58 189	7 138	4 423	1 153	24 323	20 909	243	5 480
2007	59 898	7 762	4 563	1 351	24 614	21 353	255	6 045
2008	61 704	8 498	4 739	1 351	24 868	21 969	279	6 988
2009	62 881	8 787	4 626	1 237	25 270	22 668	293	7 611
2010	65 174	10 104	4 680	1 411	25 295	23 375	309	8 658
2011	66 265	9 832	4 697	1 350	25 558	24 555	273	9 702
2012	68 404	10 392	4 830	1 310	25 916	25 656	300	11 082
2013	69 739	10 704	4 988	1 310	25 792	26 619	326	11 967
2014	76 340	11 316	5 070	1 296	26 337	31 985	336	13 436
2015	79 114	11 647	5 107	1 257	26 772	33 969	362	14 800
2016	82 015	11 706	4 956	1 484	27 726	35 770	373	16 087
2017	86 054	12 074	5 166	1 173	29 023	38 240	378	18 199
2018	92 496	12 491	5 246	1 181	31 301	41 868	409	20 340

表17-5

分地区各类学校基本情况 (2018年)

项　目	Item	全　市 Whole Municipality
学校数 (所)	**Number of Schools** (unit)	**799**
普通高等学校	Institutions of Higher Education	26
中等职业教育学校	Secondary Vocational Education Schools	25
技工学校	Technical Schools	12
普通中学	Regular Secondary Schools	304
# 高　中	Senior	73
小　学	Primary Schools	420
特殊教育学校	Special Education Schools	12
招生数 (人)	**New Student Enrollment** (person)	**390 483**
普通高等学校	Institutions of Higher Education	77 789
中等职业教育学校	Secondary Vocational Education Schools	19 248
技工学校	Technical Schools	8 157
普通中学	Regular Secondary Schools	128 206
# 高　中	Senior	36 804
小　学	Primary Schools	156 857
特殊教育学校	Special Education Schools	226
在校学生数 (人)	**Student Enrollment** (person)	**1464 171**
普通高等学校	Institutions of Higher Education	235 649
中等职业教育学校	Secondary Vocational Education Schools	58 880
技工学校	Technical Schools	26 381
普通中学	Regular Secondary Schools	360 488
# 高　中	Senior	98 064
小　学	Primary Schools	781 274
特殊教育学校	Special Education Schools	1 499

注：特殊教育学校招生数、在校学生数、毕业生数均剔除了义务教育随班就读人数与送教上门人数。

BASIC CONDITION OF SCHOOLS BY REGION (2018)

市 区 Urban Area	# 吴江区 Wujiang District	常 熟 Changshu	张家港 Zhangjiagang	昆 山 Kunshan	太 仓 Taicang
418	**98**	**114**	**89**	**117**	**61**
17	–	1	2	5	1
13	2	3	4	4	1
9	–	1	1	1	–
155	41	46	43	41	19
44	9	8	9	8	4
216	54	62	38	65	39
8	1	1	1	1	1
226 492	**37 576**	**41 004**	**40 680**	**61 561**	**20 746**
58 193	–	5 478	3 778	8 369	1 971
9 928	1 887	2 906	2 446	2 943	1 025
6 693	–	69	967	428	–
65 966	16 017	16 580	16 666	20 774	8 220
18 810	4 875	5 597	4 757	5 448	2 192
85 567	19 663	15 945	16 809	29 034	9 502
145	9	26	14	13	28
828 399	**148 851**	**159 398**	**157 133**	**237 881**	**81 360**
174 494	–	20 238	11 173	24 017	5 727
31 471	5 675	8 164	8 104	7 944	3 197
23 363	–	485	2 105	428	–
183 959	45 611	48 249	47 422	57 391	23 467
50 202	13 276	14 464	12 945	14 352	6 101
414 193	97 389	82 121	88 113	147 975	48 872
919	176	141	216	126	97

Note: The number of enrolled students in special education schools, that of students in the school and that of graduates all excluded the number of compulsory education students attending classes and that of students receiving education at home.

表17-5 续表

项　目	Item	全　市 Whole Municipality
毕业生数 (人)	**Graduates** (person)	**286 112**
普通高等学校	Institutions of Higher Education	59 071
中等职业教育学校	Secondary Vocational Education Schools	19 874
技工学校	Technical Schools	8 243
普通中学	Regular Secondary Schools	98 649
#高　中	Senior	27 365
小　学	Primary Schools	100 096
特殊教育学校	Special Education Schools	179
教职工数 (人)	**Staff and Teachers** (person)	**106 342**
普通高等学校	Institutions of Higher Education	18 763
中等职业教育学校	Secondary Vocational Education Schools	5 812
技工学校	Technical Schools	1 548
普通中学	Regular Secondary Schools	37 466
小　学	Primary Schools	42 273
特殊教育学校	Special Education Schools	480
专任教师数 (人)	**Number of Full-time Teachers** (person)	**92 496**
普通高等学校	Institutions of Higher Education	12 491
中等职业教育学校	Secondary Vocational Education Schools	5 246
技工学校	Technical Schools	1 181
普通中学	Regular Secondary Schools	31 301
#高　中	Senior	9 978
小　学	Primary Schools	41 868
特殊教育学校	Special Education Schools	409

Continued

市 区 Urban Area	# 吴江区 Wujiang District	常 熟 Changshu	张家港 Zhangjiagang	昆 山 Kunshan	太 仓 Taicang
162 031	**27 372**	**34 164**	**31 865**	**42 558**	**15 494**
44 021	–	4 435	2 318	6 917	1 380
10 582	1 946	2 488	3 063	2 564	1 177
7 212	–	305	726	–	–
49 369	12 646	14 243	13 331	15 172	6 534
13 897	3 750	4 074	3 782	3 821	1 791
50 718	12 744	12 684	12 416	17 888	6 390
129	36	9	11	17	13
61 704	**9 903**	**12 544**	**11 567**	**15 126**	**5 401**
14 528	–	1 377	647	1 882	329
2 674	450	1 040	1 083	730	285
1 109	–	135	275	29	–
21 421	4 253	4 994	4 364	4 528	2 159
21 650	5 166	4 944	5 151	7 920	2 608
322	34	54	47	37	20
52 728	**9 172**	**10 998**	**10 604**	**13 091**	**5 075**
9 468	–	1 088	429	1 262	244
2 398	435	950	997	632	269
777	–	109	272	23	–
17 352	3 948	3 947	3 889	4 136	1 977
5 605	1 260	1 287	1 352	1 137	597
22 453	4 758	4 867	4 974	7 008	2 566
280	31	37	43	30	19

表17-6

普通高等学校基本情况（2018年）
CONDITIONS OF INSTITUTIONS OF HIGHER EDUCATION (2018)

单位：人 (person)

学校名称	Schools	毕业生数 Graduates	招生数 New Student Enrollment	在校学生数 Student Enrollment	专任教师数 Number of Full-time Teachers
总　计	**Total**	**59 071**	**77 789**	**235 649**	**12 491**
# 研究生	Postgraduates	3 966	5 725	15 589	-
苏州大学	Soochow University	9 511	11 482	41 884	3 194
苏州科技大学	Suzhou University Of Science And Technology	4 438	5 446	18 938	1 191
常熟理工学院	Changshu Institute Of Technology	4 435	5 478	20 238	1 088
西交利物浦大学	Xi'An Jiaotong-Liverpool University	1 998	3 826	13 702	745
昆山杜克大学	Duke Kunshan University	82	360	426	47
苏州工艺美术职业技术学院	Suzhou Art & Design Technology Institute	1 602	1 846	5 178	290
苏州农业职业技术学院	Suzhou Polytechnic Institute Of Agriculture	2 816	3 183	8 982	438
苏州经贸职业技术学院	Suzhou Institute Of Trade & Commerce	2 774	6 880	10 354	325
苏州卫生职业技术学院	Suzhou Vocational Health College	3 282	3 450	9 890	405
苏州市职业大学	Suzhou Vocational University	3 947	4 808	13 504	793
苏州市工业职业技术学院	Suzhou Vocational Institute Of Industrial Technology	2 288	2 630	7 973	379
沙洲职业工学院	Shazhou Professional Institute Of Technology	1 000	1 950	4 442	226
苏州健雄职业技术学院	Suzhou Chien-Shiung Institute Of Technology	1 380	1 971	5 727	244
苏州工业园区服务外包职业学院	Suzhou Industrial Park Institute Of Services Outsourcing	1 556	1 979	5 373	205
苏州工业园区职业技术学院	Suzhou Industrial Park Institute Of Vocational Technology	1 554	2 273	5 411	223
硅湖职业技术学院	Silicon Lake College	1 189	2 320	5 015	299
苏州托普信息职业技术学院	Suzhou Top Institute Of Information Technology	1 438	1 428	4 254	160
昆山登云科技职业学院	Kunshan Dengyun College Of Science And Technologe	2 206	1 631	5 867	218
苏州百年职业学院	Suzhou Centential College	57	832	1 379	76
苏州高博软件技术职业学院	Global Institute Of Software Technology	1 611	1 766	5 099	230
苏州信息职业技术学院	Suzhou College Of Information Technology	1 571	1 675	4 868	195
苏州幼儿师范高等专科学校	Suzhou Early Childhood Education College	475	739	1 729	129
*苏州大学文正学院	Wenzheng College Of Soochow University	2 934	3 290	11 607	349
*苏州大学应用技术学院	Applied Technology College Of Soochou University	2 002	2 630	8 455	538
*苏州科技大学天平学院	Tianping College Of Suzhou University Of Science And Technology	1 607	2 088	8 623	301
*江苏科技大学苏州理工学院	Suzhou Institute Of Technology,Jiangsu University Of Science And Technology	1 318	1 828	6 731	203

注：带“*”号的学院为二级学院。 Note: The college With "*" is secondary colleges.

表17-7

成人高等教育基本情况（2018年）
BASIC STATISTICS OF ADULT HIGHER EDUCATION (2018)

单位：人 (person)

学校名称	Schools	毕业生数 Graduates	招生数 New Student Enrollment	在校学生数 Student Enrollment
成人高等教育	**Adult Education**	**12 391**	**19 430**	**36 143**
苏州大学	Soochow University	4 052	4 044	9 237
苏州科技大学	Suzhou University Of Science And Technology	1 999	3 702	6 758
常熟理工学院	Changshu Institute Of Technology	1 747	1 618	4 785
苏州工艺美术职业技术学院	Suzhou Art & Design Technology Institute	102	25	138
苏州农业职业技术学院	Suzhou Polytechnic Institute Of Agriculture	650	1 018	1 952
苏州经贸职业技术学院	Suzhou Institute Of Trade & Commerce	45	399	468
苏州市职业大学	Suzhou Vocational University	1 435	2 908	4 754
苏州市工业职业技术学院	Suzhou Vocational Institute Of Industrial Technology	444	261	631
沙洲职业工学院	Shazhou Professional Institute Of Technology	691	970	1 731
苏州健雄职业技术学院	Suzhou Chien-Shiung Institute Of Technology	679	1 732	2 319
苏州工业园区职业技术学院	Suzhou Industrial Park Institute Of Vocational Technology	449	1 084	1 553
硅湖职业技术学院	Silicon Lake College	98	16	164
苏州托普信息职业技术学院	Suzhou Top Institute Of Information Technology	–	1 504	1 504
苏州高博软件技术职业学院	Global Institute Of Software Technology	–	149	149

注：成人高等教育学生不含自学考试学生。 Note: Adult education students do not include the self-examination students.

表17-8

幼儿园基本情况 (2018年)
BASIC CONDITION OF KINDERGARTENS (2018)

单位：人 (person)

地 区	Region	园数 (所) Number of Kindergartens (unit)	招生数 Number of Newly Enrolled in Kindergartens	在园幼儿数 Number of Enrollment in Kindergartens	专任教师 Number of Full-time Teachers
全 市	**Whole Municipality**	**821**	**128 453**	**352 735**	**20 340**
市 区	Urban Area	480	69 068	188 595	11 416
# 吴江区	Wujiang District	101	11 843	35 231	1 649
常 熟	Changshu	88	12 907	37 925	2 088
张家港	Zhangjiagang	69	17 676	46 100	2 110
昆 山	Kunshan	142	22 978	63 131	3 724
太 仓	Taicang	42	5 824	16 984	1 002

表17-9

专任教师合格率 (2018年)
RATE OF QUALIFIED FULL-TIME TEACHERS (2018)

单位：% (%)

地 区	Region	专任教师合格率 Rate of Qualified Full-time Teachers in Secondary and Primary Schools				
		高 中 Senior Secondary Schools	初 中 Junior Secondary Schools	中等职业学校 Specialized Secondary Schools	小 学 Primary Schools	幼儿园 Kindergartens
全 市	**Whole Municipality**	**99.77**	**99.95**	**98.51**	**99.99**	**99.96**
市 区	Urban Area	99.71	99.95	98.67	100.00	100.00
# 吴江区	Wujiang District	99.52	99.89	100.00	99.98	100.00
常 熟	Changshu	100.00	100.00	98.84	100.00	100.00
张家港	Zhangjiagang	99.70	100.00	98.19	99.96	100.00
昆 山	Kunshan	99.91	99.93	97.31	100.00	99.76
太 仓	Taicang	99.66	99.86	100.00	100.00	100.00

表17-10

各类学校师资配备情况 (2018年)
TEACHING STAFF SITUATION OF ALL TYPES OF SCHOOLS (2018)

单位：人 (person)

地 区	Region	普通中学 Regular Secondary Schools					中等职业教育 Specialized Secondary Schools	
		每一教职工负担学生数 Every staff of average number of students	高中 Senior Secondary Schools		初中 Junior Secondary Schools			
			每班教师数 Teachers per class	每一教师负担学生数 Every burden on Teachers' number	每班教师数 Teachers per class	每一教师负担学生数 Every burden on Teachers' number	每一教职工负担学生数 Every staff of average number of students	每一教师负担学生数 Every burden on Teachers' number
全 市	**Whole Municipality**	**9.62**	**4.43**	**9.83**	**3.58**	**12.31**	**10.13**	**11.22**
市 区	Urban Area	8.59	4.52	8.96	3.70	11.39	11.77	13.12
# 吴江区	Wujiang District	10.72	4.06	10.54	3.62	12.03	12.61	13.05
常 熟	Changshu	9.66	4.55	11.24	3.62	12.70	7.85	8.59
张家港	Zhangjiagang	10.87	4.83	9.57	3.46	13.59	7.48	8.13
昆 山	Kunshan	12.67	3.73	12.62	3.30	14.35	10.88	12.57
太 仓	Taicang	10.87	4.12	10.22	3.46	12.58	11.22	11.88

表17-10 续表 Continued

单位：人 (person)

地 区	Region	小 学 Primary Schools			幼儿园 Kindergartens		
		每一教职工负担学生数 Every staff of average number of students	每班教师数 Teachers per class	每一教师负担学生数 Every burden on Teachers' number	每一教职工负担学生数 Every staff of average number of students	每班教师数 Teachers per class	每一教师负担学生数 Every burden on Teachers' number
全 市	**Whole Municipality**	**18.48**	**2.44**	**18.66**	**10.10**	**1.98**	**17.34**
市 区	Urban Area	19.13	2.43	18.45	9.40	1.98	16.52
# 吴江区	Wujiang District	18.85	2.19	20.47	15.72	1.59	21.37
常 熟	Changshu	16.61	2.58	16.87	9.53	1.95	18.16
张家港	Zhangjiagang	17.11	2.62	17.71	18.24	1.79	21.85
昆 山	Kunshan	18.68	2.33	21.12	8.69	2.10	16.95
太 仓	Taicang	18.74	2.36	19.05	15.33	2.04	16.95

注：表中市区数据含市直属学校和代管学校。
Note:The urban data in the table contains the schools directly under the city supervision and those hosted by the city authorities.

表17-11

部分年份文化事业基本情况
BASIC STATISTICS ON CULTURAL UNDERTAKINGS OF PARTIAL YEARS

项目		Item		2014年	2015年	2016年	2017年	2018年
机构数	(个)	**Number of Institutions**	(unit)					
艺术事业		Art		13	13	13	14	14
文物事业		Historical Relics		51	53	53	55	59
图书馆事业		Libraries		11	11	11	11	11
群众文化事业		Mass Cultural		109	109	109	100	101
艺术教育事业		Art Education		2	2	2	2	2
其他文化事业		Others		13	12	12	12	12
职工人数	(人)	**Number of Staff and Workers**	(person)					
艺术事业		Art		368	364	427	400	377
文物事业		Historical Relics		871	869	913	957	967
图书馆事业		Libraries		526	559	667	658	644
群众文化事业		Mass Cultural		1 127	1 182	1 319	1 196	1 230
艺术教育事业		Art Education		58	56	55	55	52
其他文化事业		Others		98	154	158	149	147
主要文化活动		**Main Culture Activities**						
艺术表演团体演出场次	(千场次)	Number of Art Performance Troupes' Performers	(1 000 show-times)	15.9	15.3	16.3	18.0	16.4
博物馆参观人数	(千人次)	Number of Visitor to Museums	(1 000 person-times)	5 721	7 940	9 185	9 582	10 371
书刊文献外借人次		Person-times of Borrowers of Books, Magazines and Documents		7 607	8 240	9 067	6 771	8 967
书刊文献外借册次	(千册次)	Number of Books, Magazines and Documents Borrowed by the Readers	(1 000 volume-times)	15 286	15 493	16 092	14 815	17 645

表17-12

艺术表演团体基本情况 (2018年)
BASIC STATISTICS ON ART TROUPES (2018)

地 区	Region	机构数(个) Number of Institutions (unit)	从业人员(人) Employed Persons (person)	演出场次(场次) Number of Performances (show-time)	观众人次(千人次) Number of Spectators (1 000 person-times)	公用房屋建筑面积(平方米) Floor Space of Public Buildings (sq.m)
全 市	**Whole Municipality**	**17**	**577**	**16 394**	**3 971**	**46 067**
市 区	Urban Area	10	397	7 319	1 912	14 544
# 吴江区	Wujiang District	2	9	760	78	–
常 熟	Changshu	2	62	2 555	318	2 171
张家港	Zhangjiagang	2	58	6 290	1 676	10 480
昆 山	Kunshan	3	60	230	65	18 872
太 仓	Taicang	–	–	–	–	–

表17-13

艺术表演场馆基本情况 (2018年)
BASIC SITUATION OF PERFORMING ARTS VENUES (2018)

地 区	Region	机构数(个) Number of Institutions (unit)	从业人员(人) Employed Persons (person)	座席数(个) Seating Capacity (set)	演(映)出场次(场次) Number of Performances (show-time)	观众人次(千人次) Number of Spectators (1 000 person-times)	公用房屋建筑面积(平方米) Floor Space of Public Buildings (sq.m)
全 市	**Whole Municipality**	**11**	**245**	**13 286**	**100 305**	**2 070**	**95 462**
市 区	Urban Area	5	82	4 161	35 936	852	12 117
# 吴江区	Wujiang District	2	37	2 345	18 874	483	9 731
常 熟	Changshu	3	58	3 484	240	203	57 931
张家港	Zhangjiagang	–	–	–	–	–	–
昆 山	Kunshan	3	105	5 641	64 129	1 015	25 414
太 仓	Taicang	–	–	–	–	–	–

表17-14

文化馆、文化站及文物保护基本情况（2018年）

指　　标		Item		全　市 Whole Municipality
文化馆		**Cultural Centers**		
机构数	(个)	Number of Institutions	(unit)	11
从业人员	(人)	Employed Persons	(person)	309
举办展览个数	(个)	Number of Exhibitions	(unit)	174
组织文艺活动次数	(次)	Art Performances and Story-Telling Sessions	(time)	2 618
举办训练班班次		Number of Training Courses		1 661
举办训练班培训人次	(人次)	Number of People Trained in Training Courses	(person-time)	78 864
公用房屋建筑面积	(平方米)	Floor Space of Public Buildings	(sq.m)	132 772
# 业务用房		Space for Business		111 714
群众业余文艺团队	(个)	Masses' Amateur Arts Teams	(unit)	973
文化站		**Cultural Stations**		
机构数	(个)	Number of Institutions	(unit)	90
从业人员	(人)	Employed Persons	(person)	921
举办展览个数	(个)	Number of Exhibitions	(unit)	858
组织文艺活动次数	(次)	Art Performances and Story-Telling Sessions	(time)	10 485
藏　书	(册)	Collection of Books	(volume)	4 875 431
举办训练班班次	(次)	Number of Training Courses	(time)	4 977
举办训练班培训人次	(人次)	Number of People Trained in Training Courses	(person-time)	320 694
公用房屋建筑面积	(平方米)	Floor Space of Public Buildings	(sq.m)	871 989
# 文化活动用房		Space for Cultural Activities		655 998
村（社区）文化室个数	(个)	Number of Culture Rooms	(unit)	1 702
文物保护		**Historical Relics Preservation**		
机构数	(个)	Number of Institutions	(unit)	11
从业人员	(人)	Employed Persons	(person)	110
文物藏品	(件)	Number of Collections	(piece)	12 840
公用房屋建筑面积	(平方米)	Floor Space of Public Buildings	(sq.m)	9 599
# 展览用房		Space for Exhibitions		4 152

BASIC SITUATION OF CULTURAL CENTERS, CULTURAL STATIONS AND HISTORICAL RELICS PRESERVATION (2018)

市 区 Urban Area	# 吴江区 Wujiang District	常 熟 Changshu	张家港 Zhangjiagang	昆 山 Kunshan	太 仓 Taicang
7	1	1	1	1	1
138	14	63	66	22	20
127	12	18	7	12	10
1 526	456	180	365	270	277
940	48	120	232	134	235
25 134	9 173	1 500	14 800	13 400	24 030
82 444	7 600	10 000	7 600	6 726	26 002
67 193	7 600	7 800	5 000	5 719	26 002
118	–	15	100	708	32
54	8	10	8	11	7
485	87	86	72	231	47
476	67	84	96	160	42
4 843	792	844	1 112	2 950	736
1 774 547	576 681	900 195	1 274 443	767 629	158 617
2 634	75	665	315	1 077	286
164 161	6 373	17 908	48 003	69 642	20 980
390 437	139 659	67 354	217 007	161 855	35 336
220 794	36 325	53 455	217 007	132 809	31 933
763	246	231	263	332	113
7	3	2	1	1	–
93	6	5	5	7	–
7 011	1	463	–	5 366	–
6 549	112	2 500	–	550	–
2 981	–	1 171	–	–	–

表17-15

博物馆及公共图书馆基本情况 (2018年)

指　　标		Item		全　市 Whole Municipality
博物馆		**Museums**		
机构数	(个)	Number of Institutions	(unit)	46
从业人员	(人)	Employed Persons	(person)	814
藏　品	(件、套)	Number of Collections	(piece)	146 221
# 一级品		Grade One		277
二级品		Grade Two		1 481
参观人次	(千人次)	Number of Visitors	(1000 person-times)	10 371
公用房屋建筑面积	(平方米)	Floor Space of Public Buildings	(sq.m)	195 376
# 展览用房		Space for Exhibitions		102 971
公共图书馆		**Public Libraries**		
机构数	(个)	Number of Institutions	(unit)	11
从业人员	(人)	Employed Persons	(person)	644
总藏量	(册、件)	Total Collections	(volume)	32 143 599
# 电子图书		E-book		8 408 942
图　书		Books Published		22 361 331
古　籍		Ancient Books		454 839
报　刊		Newspapers and Magazines		463 056
累计发放有效借书证数	(个)	Grand Total Number of Valid Library Cards Released	(unit)	9 741 792
书刊文献外借人次	(人次)	Number of Borrowers of Books, Magazines and Documents	(person-time)	8 966 643
书刊文献外借册次	(册次)	Number of Books, Magazines and Documents Borrowed by the Readers	(volume-time)	17 645 165
为读者举办各种活动	(次)	Various Activities Held for Readers	(time)	1 693
参加人数	(人次)	Number of Visitors	(person-time)	480 526
公用房屋建筑面积	(平方米)	Floor Space of Public Buildings	(sq.m)	200 261
# 书　库		Stock Rooms		13 207
阅览室		Reading Rooms		69 337
阅览室座席数	(个)	Seating Capacity of Reading Rooms	(set)	11 846
# 少儿阅览室座席数		Seating Capacity of Children's Reading Rooms		3 241

BASIC STATISTICS ON MUSEUMS AND PUBLIC LIBRARIES (2018)

市 区 Urban Area	# 吴江区 Wujiang District	常 熟 Changshu	张家港 Zhangjiagang	昆 山 Kunshan	太 仓 Taicang
29	2	6	1	3	7
492	49	171	48	38	65
111 372	28 678	23 696	5 035	3 556	2 562
240	10	22	1	–	14
1 167	17	293	8	–	13
5 918	203	3 097	121	307	928
121 986	6 515	29 596	12 060	5 043	26 691
56 891	4 262	15 533	8 000	4 252	18 295
7	1	1	1	1	1
373	55	44	101	69	57
21 733 853	5 512 517	2 755 943	3 050 994	3 225 657	1 377 152
7 213 462	3 109 000	87 300	645 887	386 192	76 101
13 668 752	2 305 384	2 377 718	2 304 679	2 825 218	1 184 964
247 809	72 839	205 065	104	168	1 693
229 410	13 221	77 905	65 643	6 360	83 738
7 263 549	116 097	1 419 695	236 681	314 251	507 616
6 288 516	211 791	646 769	929 646	505 917	595 795
11 253 900	1 105 735	1 395 249	2 277 049	1 716 260	1 002 707
1 133	106	217	173	68	102
277 470	28 363	101 146	50 085	14 400	37 425
120 858	16 000	13 188	27 500	18 600	20 115
6 116	775	2 191	4 200	250	450
45 930	4 000	3 300	6 200	8 000	5 907
7 589	1 069	525	2 046	962	724
1 372	176	200	1 241	207	221

表17-16

广播节目播出情况 (2018年)
BROADCASTING BROADCAST SITUATION (2018)

单位：小时 (hours)

地　　区	Region	全年公共广播节目播出时间合计 The Whole year's Public Radio Program Broadcast Time	# 新闻资讯类 News and Information	# 专题服务类 Feature Services	# 综艺益智类 Variety Puzzles	合计中：自制节目 In Total：Self-made Program
全　市	**Whole Municipality**	**60 309**	**9 033**	**20 993**	**17 356**	**49 264**
市　区	Urban Area	34 770	4 001	11 814	10 127	31 337
# 吴江区	Wujiang District	6 205	800	3 770	1 030	4 014
常　熟	Changshu	6 753	1 004	3 650	1 095	5 566
张家港	Zhangjiagang	6 646	2 321	2 610	1 518	4 526
昆　山	Kunshan	6 300	820	901	2 061	4 550
太　仓	Taicang	5 840	887	2 018	2 555	3 285

表17-17

电视节目播出情况(2018年)
TV BROADCAST SITUATION (2018)

单位：小时 (hours)

地　　区	Region	全年公共电视节目播出时间合计 The Whole year's Public TV Program Broadcast Time	# 新闻资讯类 News and Information	# 专题服务类 Feature Services	# 影视剧类 Film and Television Drama	合计中：自制节目 In Total：Self-made Program
全　市	**Whole Municipality**	**57 952**	**9 549**	**8 590**	**28 310**	**35 203**
市　区	Urban Area	36 009	5 012	6 634	18 757	26 566
# 吴江区	Wujiang District	6 205	923	1 602	2 737	2 903
常　熟	Changshu	6 899	763	507	3 624	3 075
张家港	Zhangjiagang	5 388	1 621	815	1 649	2 366
昆　山	Kunshan	3 690	340	105	2 175	790
太　仓	Taicang	5 966	1 813	529	2 105	2 406

表17-18

广播节目制作情况(2018年)
BROADCASTING PROGRAMMING SITUATION (2018)

单位：小时 (hours)

地 区	Region	全年制作广播节目时间 Annual Production of Broadcasting Programs	# 新闻资讯类 News and Information	# 专题服务类 Feature Services	# 综艺益智类 Variety Puzzles	# 广告类 Advertisements
全 市	**Whole Municipality**	**40 791**	**5 960**	**15 639**	**10 473**	**1 540**
市 区	Urban Area	26 749	3 366	8 697	7 735	635
# 吴江区	Wujiang District	2 271	558	1 595	58	60
常 熟	Changshu	3 468	913	2 190	360	4
张家港	Zhangjiagang	3 811	1 133	2 190	365	120
昆 山	Kunshan	2 550	365	545	–	780
太 仓	Taicang	4 213	183	2 017	2 013	1

表17-19

电视节目制作情况 (2018年)
TV PROGRAMMING SITUATION (2018)

单位：小时 (hours)

地 区	Region	全年制作电视节目时间 Annual Production of TV Programs	# 新闻资讯类 News and Information	# 专题服务类 Feature Services	# 综艺益智类 Variety Puzzles	# 广告类 Advertisements
全 市	**Whole Municipality**	**15 939**	**5 202**	**4 078**	**2 032**	**2 633**
市 区	Urban Area	12 080	4 114	3 704	1 856	826
# 吴江区	Wujiang District	804	287	239	–	208
常 熟	Changshu	1 764	216	65	13	1 363
张家港	Zhangjiagang	747	326	230	60	130
昆 山	Kunshan	920	288	36	8	288
太 仓	Taicang	428	258	43	95	26

主 要 统 计 指 标 解 释

普通高等学校 指按照国家规定的设置标准和审批程序批准举办的，通过全国普通高等学校统一招生考试，招收高中毕业生为主要培养对象，实施高等教育的全日制大学、独立设置的学院和高等专科学校、高等职业学校和其他机构。

大学、独立设置的学院主要实施本科层次以上教育，高等专科学校、高等职业学校实施专科层次教育，其他机构是承担国家普通招生计划任务不计校数的机构。包括普通高等学校分校和批准筹建的普通高等学校等。

文化事业机构 指从事专业文化工作和为专业文化工作服务的独立建制的单位。不包括这些单位另外举办独立核算的其他机构和各部门的业余文化组织。该指标主要反映文化事业机构发展规模水平。

艺术表演团体 指由文化部门主办或实行行业管理（经文化行政部门审批或已申报登记并领取相关许可证），专门从事表演艺术等活动的各类专业艺术表演团体，含民间职业剧团。不包括群众业余文艺表演团体。

艺术表演观众人数(人次) 指售票、包场演出或民族地区免费演出的艺术表演观众人次数，不包括彩排审查和内部观摩演出的观看人次数。该指标主要反映全国观看专业艺术表演团体演出的效益规模。

EXPLANATORY NOTES ON MAIN STATISTICAL INDICATORS

Regular Institutions of Higher Learning refer to educational establishments set up according to the government evaluation and approval procedures, enrolling graduates from senior secondary schools and providing higher education courses and training for senior professionals. They include full-time universities, colleges, institutions of higher professional education, institutions of higher vocational education and others.

Universities and colleges primarily provide undergraduate courses; institutions of higher professional education and institutions of higher vocational education primarily provide professional trainings; and others refer to educational establishments, which are responsible for enrolling higher education students under the State Plan but not enumerated in the total number of schools, including: branch schools of universities and colleges, and universities and colleges that have been approved and under plan for construction.

Cultural Institutions refer to units which have their own organizational system and independent accounting system and specialize in cultural work or service cultural work. They do not include other establishments run by these units with separate accounting system and amateur cultural groups established by various departments. The statistics reflect the scale and level of development of institutions engaged in cultural undertakings.

Arts Performance Troupes refer to the various professional performing arts groups, which sponsored by the cultural sectors or guided by the cultural society (approved by the cultural administration authority, or registered and permitted with the relative certificate), including non-governmental troupes. The mass amateur arts performance troupes are not included.

Number of Audience at Art Performance refers to the number of spectators at commercial shows, privately organized shows or free shows given in ethnic minority areas, and does not include the number of spectators at rehearsals and internal viewings. This indicator mainly reflects the scale and effects of viewing of performances given by professional art troupes across the country.

十八、卫生 体育

CHAPTER 18
PUBLIC HEALTH AND SPORTS

18 卫生 体育 PUBLIC HEALTH AND SPORTS

主要统计指标 MAJOR STATISTICAL INDICATORS

2018年末卫生机构数	Number of Health Institutions	3 380	个	unit
2018年末卫生机构床位数	Number of Beds in Health Institutions	68 921	张	unit
2018年末卫生技术人员	Number of Medical Technical Personnel	85 188	人	person
# 医生数	Doctors	32 852	人	person
注册护士数	Professional Nurses	37 584	人	person
2018年末按常住人口计算:	Calculated by Resident Population:			
每万人拥有卫生机构床位数	Number of Beds in Health Institutions Per 10 000 Persons	64.28	张	unit
每万人拥有医院床位数	Number of Hospital Beds Per 10 000 Persons	54.12	张	unit
每万人拥有卫生技术人员	Number of Medical Technical Personnel Per 10 000 Persons	79.45	人	person
每万人拥有医生数	Number of Doctors Per 10 000 Persons	30.64	人	person
每万人拥有注册护士数	Number of Professional Nurses Per 10 000 Persons	35.05	人	person
2018年发展二级以上等级裁判员	Newly-added Number of Referees of Grade II and Above	190	人	person
2018年发展二级以上等级运动员	Newly-added Number of Sportsmen of Grade II and Above	181	人	person

表18-1

历年卫生事业基本情况
BASIC STATISTICS ON PUBLIC HEALTH OVER THE YEARS

年 份 Year	机构数 (所) Institutions (unit)	#医 院、 卫生院 Hospitals	#诊所、卫生所、医务室、社区卫生服务站 Clinics	床位数 (张) Number of Beds (unit)	人员数 (人) Number of Persons (person)	#卫生技术人员 Medical Technical Personnel
1949	27	12	7	778	3 270	3 100
1952	238	16	163	1 372	4 908	3 256
1957	447	16	410	2 655	7 773	6 037
1962	683	155	457	6 727	9 582	7 831
1965	823	170	549	7 661	10 891	8 862
1970	675	169	496	9 001	9 338	7 593
1975	806	194	581	13 759	14 202	11 174
1978	971	204	714	14 470	16 465	12 902
1980	1 125	207	864	13 720	18 752	14 514
1985	1 544	203	1 280	15 064	24 921	19 343
1990	1 537	207	1 256	18 424	29 545	22 253
1995	1 486	210	1 197	19 535	33 076	25 326
1996	1 485	212	1 196	19 489	33 321	25 835
1997	1 433	212	1 143	19 747	32 669	25 070
1998	1 440	212	1 147	19 486	32 855	25 233
1999	1 466	209	1 175	19 293	30 303	25 550
2000	1 319	197	1 045	19 504	31 793	24 881
2001	1 254	191	986	19 791	31 559	24 706
2002	1 463	213	1 187	19 978	31 601	24 535
2003	1 450	199	1 152	20 631	33 958	27 805
2004	1 715	207	1 392	21 662	34 970	29 069
2005	1 945	197	1 582	26 185	38 736	32 049
2006	2 285	205	1 902	28 872	43 954	36 951
2007	2 314	214	1 901	31 261	46 952	38 091
2008	2 344	233	1 876	33 631	50 810	40 336
2009	2 524	234	2 041	37 235	53 869	43 232
2010	2 675	216	2 152	39 204	56 910	46 507
2011	2 858	242	2 292	42 972	63 409	50 866
2012	2 992	251	2 380	46 070	70 449	57 168
2013	3 007	263	2 363	51 663	74 661	61 051
2014	3 063	263	2 353	55 218	78 811	64 281
2015	3 121	271	2 418	59 304	83 997	68 179
2016	3 175	283	2 387	63 241	89 276	72 166
2017	3 160	286	2 392	66 640	98 921	79 623
2018	3 380	302	2 537	68 921	106 591	85 188

表18-2

部分年份分地区卫生事业基本情况
BASIC STATISTICS ON PUBLIC HEALTH BY REGION OF PARTIAL YEARS

项　　目	Item	2013年	2014年	2015年	2016年	2017年	2018年
机构数 (所)	**Institutions** (unit)	**3 007**	**3 063**	**3 121**	**3 175**	**3 160**	**3 380**
市　区	Urban Area	1 488	1 489	1 500	1 514	1 545	1 636
# 吴江区	Wujiang District	385	394	403	419	420	430
常　熟	Changshu	446	455	468	481	483	493
张家港	Zhangjiagang	405	418	422	429	417	425
昆　山	Kunshan	445	474	493	504	470	558
太　仓	Taicang	223	227	238	247	245	268
床位数 (张)	**Beds** (unit)	**51 663**	**55 218**	**59 304**	**63 241**	**66 640**	**68 921**
市　区	Urban Area	27 654	29 701	32 495	34 757	37 304	39 111
# 吴江区	Wujiang District	5 255	5 317	5 700	5 723	5 921	6 276
常　熟	Changshu	6 868	7 052	7 346	7 882	8 247	8 497
张家港	Zhangjiagang	7 878	8 588	9 093	9 601	9 841	9 721
昆　山	Kunshan	5 966	6 300	6 640	7 148	7 225	7 522
太　仓	Taicang	3 297	3 577	3 730	3 853	4 023	4 070
卫生技术人员 (人)	**Medical Technical Personnel** (person)	**61 051**	**64 281**	**68 179**	**72 166**	**79 623**	**85 188**
市　区	Urban Area	31 551	33 044	35 771	38 174	44 393	48 061
# 吴江区	Wujiang District	6 174	6 357	6 578	6 917	7 226	7 829
常　熟	Changshu	7 887	8 278	8 569	9 114	9 508	9 984
张家港	Zhangjiagang	7 937	8 441	8 910	9 288	9 559	9 753
昆　山	Kunshan	9 804	10 375	10 626	11 070	11 616	12 601
太　仓	Taicang	3 872	4 143	4 303	4 520	4 547	4 789
医生数 (人)	**Doctors** (person)	**24 296**	**25 352**	**26 197**	**27 667**	**30 259**	**32 852**
市　区	Urban Area	12 168	12 717	13 174	13 929	16 141	17 762
# 吴江区	Wujiang District	2 521	2 536	2 547	2 547	2 677	2 933
常　熟	Changshu	3 350	3 495	3 570	3 834	3 944	4 202
张家港	Zhangjiagang	3 278	3 331	3 599	3 814	3 857	3 914
昆　山	Kunshan	3 959	4 194	4 218	4 312	4 519	5 027
太　仓	Taicang	1 541	1 615	1 636	1 778	1 798	1 947

表18-3 分地区卫生机构、人员及床位数 (2018年末)

指　标	Item	全　市 Whole Municipality
卫生机构数 (个)	**Number of Health Institutions (unit)**	**3 380**
医　院	Hospitals	206
社区卫生服务中心	Neighborhood Medical Service Station	76
卫生院	Rural Township Hospitals	96
门诊部	Clinics	385
急救中心（站）	First Aide Center	4
采供血机构	Blood Collection and Supply Center	7
妇幼保健院（所、站）	Hospitals for Maternity and Child Care	8
专科疾病防治院	Disease Control Center	4
疾病预防控制中心	Disease Prevention Center	11
卫生监督所	Medical Supervision Station	9
医学在职培训机构	On-the-Job Medical Training	2
健康教育所（站、中心）	Health Education Station	4
诊所、卫生所、医务室、社区卫生服务站	Clinic, Medical Station, Medical Office and Neighborhood Medical Station	2 537
其他卫生机构	Other Health Care Institutions	31
卫生机构人员数 (人)	**Number of Persons Engaged in Health Institution (person)**	**106 591**
# 卫生技术人员	Medical Technical Personnel	85 188
医　生	Doctors	32 852
执业医师	Professional medical worker	30 109
执业助理医师	Professional assistant medical worker	2 743
注册护士	Professional nurse	37 584
药师（士）	Apothecary and Assistant Pharmacist	4 734
技师（士）	Technician	4 295
其　他	Others	5 723
# 私营卫生机构人员数	Number of Medical Staff in Privately Owned Medical Institutions	27 658
# 医　生	Doctors	6 930
卫生机构床位数 (张)	**Number of Beds in Health Institutions (unit)**	**68 921**
医　院	Hospitals	58 022
# 综合医院	General Hospitals	30 714
中医医院	Hospitals of Chinese Medicine	5 067
专科医院	Disease Control and Prevention Station	8 505
卫生院	Rural Township Hospitals	8 604
专科疾病防治院	Disease Prevention Academy	20
其　他	Others	2 275

NUMBER OF HEALTH INSTITUTIONS, PERSONS ENGAGED AND BEDS BY REGION (END OF 2018)

市 区 Urban Area	# 吴江区 Wujiang District	常 熟 Changshu	张家港 Zhangjiagang	昆 山 Kunshan	太 仓 Taicang
1 636	**430**	**493**	**425**	**558**	**268**
107	13	24	36	27	12
52	5	8	–	12	4
31	17	24	16	9	16
119	35	56	18	142	50
1	–	1	–	1	1
2	1	2	1	1	1
4	1	1	1	1	1
4	2	–	–	–	–
7	1	1	1	1	1
5	1	1	1	1	1
1	–	–	1	–	–
1	1	1	–	1	1
1 279	348	372	349	359	178
23	5	2	1	3	2
60 611	**8 944**	**12 513**	**11 673**	**15 753**	**6 041**
48 061	7 829	9 984	9 753	12 601	4 789
17 762	2 933	4 202	3 914	5 027	1 947
16 593	2 643	3 731	3 393	4 734	1 658
1 169	290	471	521	293	289
22 003	3 287	4 066	4 168	5 388	1 959
2 596	457	620	527	699	292
2 323	404	465	499	719	289
3 377	748	631	645	768	302
15 335	1 326	2 227	4 188	4 454	1 454
3 498	414	631	1 147	1 290	364
39 111	**6 276**	**8 497**	**9 721**	**7 522**	**4 070**
35 250	5 207	6 618	7 904	5 380	2 870
17 687	3 312	3 404	5 607	2 597	1 419
1 443	377	991	846	1 087	700
5 514	280	669	806	935	581
2 107	931	1 684	1 817	1 951	1 045
20	–	–	–	–	–
1 734	138	195	–	191	155

表18-4

卫生机构诊疗基本情况 (2018年)

BASIC STATISTICS OF MEDICAL INSTITUTIONS ON PATIENTS TREATING (2018)

地区或类别	Region and Type	诊疗总人次 (万人次) Total Number of Patients Treated (10 000 person-times)	#门诊 Out-patients	入院人数 (人) Hospital Admissions (person)	病床使用率 (%) Utilization Rate of Beds (%)	病床周转次数 Bed Turnover
总 计	**Total**	**9 907.43**	**8 835.35**	**1 931 024**	**84.66**	**29.30**
一、按地区分	**Grouped by Region**					
市 区	Urban Area	5 220.44	4 684.83	1 014 292	84.66	29.30
# 吴江区	Wujiang District	876.77	786.96	156 012	78.00	25.09
常 熟	Changshu	1 374.50	1 221.47	266 798	87.80	32.91
张家港	Zhangjiagang	1 091.85	984.76	313 733	87.53	33.05
昆 山	Kunshan	1 651.51	1 432.14	222 187	78.74	31.17
太 仓	Taicang	569.13	512.13	114 014	79.82	28.13
二、按类别分	**Grouped by Type of Hospital**					
1. 医 院	Hospitals	4 702.96	4 140.35	1 594 065	87.42	28.74
# 综合医院	General Hospitals	3 249.34	2 869.49	1 163 976	90.32	38.88
中医医院	Hospitals of Chinese Medicine	741.05	638.55	197 284	94.99	40.33
专科医院	Disease Control and Prevention Station	567.01	510.87	158 778	84.15	20.26
儿童医院	Children's Hospital	231.47	199.55	63 892	84.28	47.31
传染病院	Hospitals for Infectious Diseases	27.11	24.50	9 802	86.64	19.37
精神病院	Mental Hospitals	91.75	82.40	16 498	96.80	5.67
口腔医院	Stomata logical Hospitals	85.74	85.35	–	–	–
耳鼻喉科医院	Otolaryngology Hospitals	14.08	13.65	8 777	66.03	49.98
其他专科医院	Other Specialized Hospitals	116.86	105.42	59 809	72.51	21.04
2. 社区卫生服务中心	Community Medical Service Station	1 915.01	1 743.00	44 866	50.99	21.76
3. 卫生院	Rural Township Hospitals	1 871.63	1 606.85	292 093	74.80	34.84
4. 门诊部	Outpatient Department	301.15	259.70	–	–	–
5. 妇幼保健院（所、站）	Hospitals for Maternity and Child Care	40.21	39.86	–	–	–
6. 专科疾病防治院	Disease Prevention Academy	3.96	3.96	–	–	–
7. 其 他	Others	1 072.51	1 041.63	–	–	–

注：床位周转次数是指在一定时期内每张床位的病人出院人数，其公式：床位周转次数=出院人数/平均开放床位数。

Note: The bed turnover refers to the number of patients per bed discharged from hospital within a certain period of time, and the formula is: bed turnover times = number of discharged patients / average number of open beds.

表18-5

全市前十位疾病死因及比重（2018年）
DEATH RATE OF 10 MAJOR DISEASES IN WHOLE MUNICIPALITY (2018)

位次 NO.	死因	Cause of Death	占全部死因比重(%) As % of Total Deaths
	总计	**Total**	**94.09**
1	恶性肿瘤	Malignant Tumor	29.46
2	脑血管病	Cerebrovascular Disease	19.77
3	心脏病	Heart Trouble	11.60
4	呼吸系统疾病	Respiratory Disease	11.32
5	损伤和中毒	Trauma and Toxicosis	9.12
6	内分泌、营养和代谢疾病	Endocrine, Nutrition and Metabolic Diseases	5.17
7	神经系统疾病	Nervous System Diseases	3.18
8	消化系统疾病	Digestive Disease	2.21
9	精神和行为障碍	Mental and Behavioral Disorders	1.15
10	泌尿生殖系统疾病	Urinary Disease	1.11

表18-6

体育系统从业人员（2018年）
SPORTS SYSTEM EMPLOYEES (2018)

单位：人 (person)

人员分类	Category of Personnel	总计 Total	#体育行政机关 Sports Administration	#运动项目管理部门 Sports Management	#训练单位 Training Units	#体育场馆 Stadiums and Gyms
总计	**Total**	**870**	**118**	**196**	**123**	**62**
公务员	Orderly	118	113	–	–	–
教练员	Coaches	154	–	14	82	53
运动员	Athletes	156	–	156	–	–
科研人员	Scientific and Technical Personnel	10	–	–	–	–
管理人员	Administrative Staff	238	–	14	34	–
其他	Others	194	5	12	7	9

表18-7

运动员获奖牌情况（2018年）
ATHLETES' AWARD-WINNING (2018)

单位：枚 (unit)

项 目	Item	总 计 Total	金 牌 Gold Medal	银 牌 Silver Medal	铜 牌 Bronze Medal
合 计	**Total**	**28**	**7**	**14**	**7**
世界比赛	World Competition	2	–	2	–
亚洲比赛	Asian Competition	7	1	6	–
全国比赛	National Competition	19	6	6	7

表18-8

发展等级运动员、裁判员及社会体育指导员认证人数
NUMBER OF CERTIFIED LEVEL ATHLETES, REFEREES AND COMMUNITY PHYSICAL EDUCATION INSTRUCTORS RECRUITED

单位：人 (person)

项 目	Item	2014年	2015年	2016年	2017年	2018年
年内发展二级以上等级运动员	**Newly-added Number of Sportsmen of Grade II and Above**	**169**	**115**	**130**	**128**	**181**
运动健将	Master of Sports	–	–	–	–	–
一 级	First Grade	–	–	–	–	–
二 级	Second Grade	169	115	130	128	181
年内发展二级以上等级裁判员	**Newly-added Number of Referees of Grade II and Above**	**522**	**374**	**441**	**288**	**190**
国家(际)级	National (International) Referees	–	–	–	–	–
一 级	First Grade	–	–	–	–	–
二 级	Second Grade	522	374	441	288	190
年末社会体育指导员认证总人数	**Total Number of Certified Community Physical Education Instructors by the End of the Year**	**29 829**	**32 838**	**35 705**	**38 405**	**43 051**

表18-9

体育彩票
SPORT LOTTERY

项 目	Item	2017年	2018年
体育彩票销售网点 (个)	**Number of Computer Sport Lottery Sold** (unit)	**2 072**	**1 802**
体育彩票销售金额 (万元)	**Circulation of Sport Lottery** (10 000 yuan)	**450 784**	**573 155**
电脑彩票	Computer Lottery	416 803	549 097
即开型彩票	Instant Lottery	33 981	24 058
体育彩票公益基金提取额	**Public Welfare Funds Drawn form Sport Lottery**	**38 959**	**49 316**
电脑彩票	Computer Lottery	35 901	47 151
即开型彩票	Instant Lottery	3 058	2 165

主 要 统 计 指 标 解 释

卫生机构 包括医疗机构、疾病预防控制中心(防疫站)、采供血机构、卫生监督及监测(检验)机构、医学科研和在职培训机构、健康教育所等。

医疗机构 包括医院、社区卫生服务中心(站)、疗养院、卫生院、门诊部、诊所(卫生所、医务室)、妇幼保健院(所、站)、专科疾病防治院(所、站)、急救中心(站)和临床检验中心。医疗机构分为非赢利性医疗机构和赢利性医疗机构。

医院 包括综合医院、中医医院、中西医结合医院、民族医院、各类专科医院和护理院。

卫生技术人员 指卫生机构中医生、护理人员 、药剂人员、检验人员等卫生技术人员。

医生 指在医疗、预防保健机构工作且取得《执业医师证书》的执业医师和执业助理医师。

等级运动员人数 指经考核正式批准授予等级运动员称号的人数。运动员等级分为国际级运动健将、运动健将、一级运动员、二级运动员、三级运动员、少年级运动员。

等级裁判员人数 指经考核正式批准授予等级裁判员称号的人数。裁判员等级分为国际裁判、国家级裁判、一级裁判、二级裁判、三级裁判。

EXPLANATORY NOTES ON MAIN STATISTICAL INDICATORS

Health Care Institutions include: medical institutions, disease prevention and control centres (epidemic prevention stations), blood gathering and supplying institutions, health supervision and inspection (check up) institutions, medicinal scientific research and on-job training institutions, health education centres and so on.

Medical Organizations include: hospitals, health service centres (stations) in communities, sanatoria, health centres, out-patient clinics, clinics (health stations and infirmaries), maternity and child care agencies (centres and stations), special disease prevention and curing agencies (centres and stations), first aid centres (stations) and clinical inspection centres. Medical organizations are grouped by two types: profit-making and non-profit-making medical organizations.

Hospitals include: polyclinics, traditional Chinese medical hospitals, hospitals integrating traditional Chinese therapeutics and western therapeutics, ethnic hospitals, various specialist hospitals and nursing homes.

Medical Technical Personnel refers to doctors, nurses, pharmacists and laboratory technicians working in medical institutions.

Doctors refer to certified physicians and certified assistant physicians with certifications working in medical and health care and prevention agencies.

Number of Athletes in Grades refers to the number of athletes who have been given titles through examination. The titles of athletes include international masters of sports, masters of sports, first-grade, second-grade and third-grade sportsmen and young athletes.

Number of Referees in Grades refers to the number of referees who have been given titles after examination. They are classified as international referees, national referees and referees of the first, second and third grades.

十九、民政　司法

CHAPTER 19
CIVIL ADMINISTRATION, JUDICIARY

19 民政 司法 CIVIL ADMINISTRATION, JUDICIARY

主要统计指标 MAJOR STATISTICAL INDICATORS

2018年末社会福利院数	Number of Social Welfare Homes	9	个	unit
2018年末社会福利医院数	Number of Social Welfare Hospitals	2	个	unit
2018年末养老机构数	Number of Old-age Care Institutions	206	个	unit
2018年末社会福利院床位数	Number of Beds in Social Welfare Homes	5 012	张	unit
2018年末社会福利医院床位数	Number of Beds in Social Welfare Hospitals	528	张	unit
2018年末机构养老床位数	Number of Beds in Old-age Care Institutions	60 804	张	unit
2018年末律师事务所	Number of Law Offices	323	所	unit
2018年末专职律师数	Number of Full-time Lawyers	4 140	人	person
2018年末人民调解委员会数	Number of People's Mediation Committees	4 221	个	unit
2018年调解纠纷总数	Number of Disputes Mediated	137 145	起	case

表19-1

部分年份民政事业基本情况

指　　标		Item		1990年	1995年	2000年	2005年
社会福利院		**Social Welfare Homes**					
院　数	(个)	Number of Homes	(unit)	6	6	6	10
职工人数	(人)	Number of Staff and Workers	(person)	268	331	410	817
床位数	(张)	Number of Beds	(unit)	845	970	1 315	2 964
在院人数	(人)	Number of Persons Housed	(person)	561	732	971	1 879
社会福利医院		**Social Welfare Hospitals**					
院　数	(个)	Number of Hospitals	(unit)	5	4	4	2
职工人数	(人)	Number of Staff and Workers	(person)	282	302	302	192
床位数	(张)	Number of Beds	(unit)	524	554	694	560
在院人数	(人)	Number of Persons Housed	(person)	399	405	690	469
养老机构		**Old-age Care Institutions**					
院　数	(个)	Number of Homes	(unit)	169	183	181	144
职工人数	(人)	Number of Staff and Workers	(person)	921	1 022	938	1 470
床位数	(张)	Number of Beds	(unit)	4 135	5 005	5 400	10 125
在院人数	(人)	Number of Persons Housed	(person)	3 133	3 326	3 391	6 716

BASIC STATISTICS ON CIVIL ADMINISTRATION OF PARTIAL YEARS

2010年	2012年	2013年	2014年	2015年	2016年	2017年	2018年
10	10	9	9	9	9	10	9
904	949	950	946	949	939	1 125	904
3 164	3 659	4 199	4 199	4 199	4 199	4 632	5 012
2 297	2 299	2 217	2 172	2 170	2 118	2 627	2 159
2	2	2	2	2	2	2	2
238	253	243	231	234	230	202	201
560	560	580	580	580	580	528	528
555	565	528	509	511	507	475	380
162	205	213	221	234	226	224	206
2 325	4 677	4 837	4 330	4 453	4 882	10 781	10 092
25 455	46 223	51 840	57 915	64 014	65 301	67 323	60 804
16 035	24 327	24 751	28 062	28 173	28 850	31 080	27 811

表19-2

分地区民政事业基本情况 (2018年末)
BASIC STATISTICS ON CIVIL ADMINISTRATION BY REGION (END OF 2018)

地　　区	Region	院　数 (个) Number of Homes (unit)	职工人数 (人) Number of Staff and Workers (person)	床位数 (张) Number of Beds (unit)	在院人数 (人) Number of Persons Housed (person)
社会福利院	**Social Welfare Homes**				
全　　市	**Whole Municipality**	**9**	**904**	**5 012**	**2 159**
市　区	Urban Area	6	488	2 372	1 258
# 吴江区	Wujiang District	1	43	480	85
常　熟	Changshu	1	48	90	47
张家港	Zhangjiagang	1	255	650	650
昆　山	Kunshan	1	113	1 900	204
太　仓	Taicang	–	–	–	–
社会福利医院	**Social Welfare Hospitals**				
全　　市	**Whole Municipality**	**2**	**201**	**528**	**380**
市　区	Urban Area	1	160	450	337
# 吴江区	Wujiang District	–	–	–	–
常　熟	Changshu	–	–	–	–
张家港	Zhangjiagang	1	41	78	43
昆　山	Kunshan	–	–	–	–
太　仓	Taicang	–	–	–	–
养老机构	**Old-age Care Institutions**				
全　　市	**Whole Municipality**	**206**	**10 092**	**60 804**	**27 811**
市　区	Urban Area	116	6 458	31 442	11 445
# 吴江区	Wujiang District	27	891	7 299	2 582
常　熟	Changshu	28	1 131	7 830	4 720
张家港	Zhangjiagang	24	727	9 063	5 184
昆　山	Kunshan	18	914	7 471	3 867
太　仓	Taicang	20	862	4 998	2 595

表19-3

部分年份社会保障相关待遇标准
THE TREATMENT STANDARDS RELATED TO SOCIAL SECURITY OF PARTIAL YEARS

单位：元/月 (yuan/month)

年 份 Year	职工最低工资标准 Minimum Wage Standard for Employees	失业保险金最低标准 Minimum Standard of Unemployment Insurance Benefits	城市最低生活保障标准 Standards of Subsistence Allowances for Urban Residents	农村最低生活保障标准 Standards of Subsistence Allowances for Rural Residents	企业退休人员基本养老金最低标准 Minimum Standards of Basic Pensions for Enterprise Retirees
1995	210	80			
1996	240	120	180		
1997	280	144	180		
1998	280	168	180	100	
1999	320	168	200	100	
2000	390	220	200	100	
2001	430	220	200	100	
2002	460	220	220	100	
2003	540	220	260	120	
2004	620	260	260	130	
2005	690	260	300	180	
2006	750	300	300	180	
2007年1月	750	320	300	180	
2007年7月	850	400	320	200	
2008	850	400	350	230	
2009	850	500	380	260	
2010	960	500	420	340	
2011年1月	960	650	450	400	
2011年7月	1 140	650	500	500	
2012	1 370	650	570	570	650
2013	1 530	741	630	630	750
2014	1 680	820	700	700	800
2015	1 680	910	750	750	860
2016	1 820	975	810	810	910
2017	1 940	1 053	875	875	980
2018	2 020	1 138	945	945	980

表19-4

社会救助情况 (2018年)
SOCIAL ASSISTANCE (2018)

地 区	Region	社会救助总人数(人) Total Number of people Who Received Social Assistance (person)	城市低保 Subsistence Allowances For Urban		农村低保 Subsistence Allowances For Rural Residents	
			人数(人) Number of People (person)	资金(万元) Fund (10 000 yuan)	人数(人) Number of People (person)	资金(万元) Fund (10 000 yuan)
全 市	**Whole Municipality**	**59 340**	**8 882**	**9 714**	**12 572**	**12 002**
市 区	Urban Area	32 010	6 664	7 259	5 762	5 093
# 吴江区	Wujiang District	10 506	589	658	4 157	3 766
常 熟	Changshu	8 404	257	289	2 510	2 476
张家港	Zhangjiagang	9 596	870	949	2 789	2 913
昆 山	Kunshan	5 422	700	764	782	794
太 仓	Taicang	3 908	391	453	729	726

表19-4 续表 Continued

地 区	Region	特困供养 Support For Those With Special Hardships		低保边缘 On the Margin of Subsistence Allowances		残疾人生活补贴 Living Allowances For The Disabled	
		人数(人) Number of People (person)	资金(万元) Fund (10 000 yuan)	人数(人) Number of People (person)	资金(万元) Fund (10 000 yuan)	人数(人) Number of People (person)	资金(万元) Fund (10 000 yuan)
全 市	**Whole Municipality**	**2 826**	**3 315**	**11 056**	**8 711**	**24 004**	**20 244**
市 区	Urban Area	1 258	1 268	7 316	5 232	11 010	9 394
# 吴江区	Wujiang District	379	443	1 174	1 077	4 207	3 326
常 熟	Changshu	517	718	585	578	4 535	3 622
张家港	Zhangjiagang	427	608	889	801	4 621	3 783
昆 山	Kunshan	494	548	1 389	1 195	2 057	1 892
太 仓	Taicang	130	173	877	905	1 781	1 552

表19-5

社会组织情况（2018年末）
SITUATION OF SOCIAL ORGANIZATIONS (END OF 2018)

单位：个 (unit)

地　区	Region	社会组织数 Number of Social Organizations	社会团体 Social Groups	民办非企业 Private Non-Enterprises	基金会 Foundation
全　市	**Whole Municipality**	**9 472**	**3 315**	**6 100**	**57**
市　区	Urban Area	4 907	1 772	3 089	46
# 吴江区	Wujiang District	622	321	300	1
常　熟	Changshu	1 626	397	1 228	1
张家港	Zhangjiagang	987	489	497	1
昆　山	Kunshan	1 074	442	624	8
太　仓	Taicang	878	215	662	1

表19-6

社区服务平台建设情况（2018年末）
CONSTRUCTION OF COMMUNITY SERVICE PLATFORMS (END OF 2018)

地　区	Region	服务平台达标个数(个) Number of Community Service Platforms Up To The Standard (unit)		办公活动用房平均面积(平方米) Average Area of Community Offices And Activity Rooms (sq.m)		工作者人数(人) Number of Community Workers (person)	
		区(市)级社区 District-(City-) Level Community	镇(街)级社区 Town-(Street-) Level Community	城市社区 Urban Community	农村社区 Rural Community	城市社区 Urban Communities	农村社区 Rural Communities
全　市	**Whole Municipality**	**9**	**104**	**1 400**	**1 600**	**10 928**	**10 217**
市　区	Urban Area	5	57	1 506	1 204	6 477	4 305
# 吴江区	Wujiang District	1	8	1 710	1 541	436	2 016
常　熟	Changshu	1	14	1 120	1 260	597	2 160
张家港	Zhangjiagang	1	10	1 500	1 970	1 335	2 062
昆　山	Kunshan	1	15	1 480	1 409	1 944	1 030
太　仓	Taicang	1	8	1 247	1 586	575	660

表19-7

部分年份律师、公证工作情况
STATISTICS ON LAWYERS AND NOTARIZATION OF PARTIAL YEARS

指　　标		Item		2014年	2015年	2016年	2017年	2018年
律师工作情况		**Lawyers**						
律师事务所	(所)	Number of Law Offices	(unit)	224	242	268	310	323
律师事务所人员	(人)	Personnel of Law Offices	(person)	2 706	3 048	3 435	3 809	4 513
# 女律师		Female		748	900	1 061	1 304	1 542
# 专职律师		Full-time Lawyers		2 667	2 963	3 346	3 763	4 140
兼职律师		Part-time Lawyers		39	41	46	46	45
担任法律顾问	(家)	Number of Units with Permanent Legal Advisors	(unit)	12 713	12 445	13 976	14 912	16 475
刑事诉讼辩护及代理	(件)	Defender and Agent of Criminal Cases	(case)	5 396	4 372	6 347	7 786	9 465
民事案件诉讼代理		Agent of Civil Cases		46 819	47 940	68 502	75 470	89 954
经济案件诉讼代理		Agent of Economic Cases		–	–	–	–	–
非诉讼法律事务		Agent of Non-litigious Legal Affairs		4 814	4 565	5 644	6 551	7 370
涉外及涉港澳台		Agent of Foreign-related, Hong Kong, Macao & Taiwan Legal Affairs		–	–	–	–	–
经济案件索回赔欠款	(万元)	Debt and Indemnity Claimed in Economic Cases	(10 000 yuan)	–	–	–	–	–
公证工作情况		**Notarization**						
公证处	(所)	Number of Notary Offices	(unit)	11	11	11	11	11
公证处人员	(人)	Notarial Personnel	(person)	175	199	218	210	216
# 公证员		Notaries		71	83	82	85	93
办理公证总数	(件)	Number of Notarial Documents Issued	(case)	128 556	152 252	188 224	153 851	122 876
# 国内公证数		Number of Domestic Notarization Cases		91 791	113 388	147 503	113 827	83 471
涉外及涉港澳台		Foreign-related, Hong Kong, Macao & Taiwan Legal Affairs		36 765	38 864	40 721	40 024	39 405

表19-8

部分年份人民调解基层司法工作情况
STATISTICS ON PEOPLE'S MEDIATION AND BASIC-LEVEL JUDICIAL WORK OF PARTIAL YEARS

指　　标		Item		2014年	2015年	2016年	2017年	2018年
人民调解委员会	(个)	Number of People's Mediation Committees	(unit)	7 253	8 064	8 288	4 514	4 221
调委会人员数	(人)	Number of Mediators	(person)	29 474	26 066	28 578	12 707	13 625
调解纠纷总数	(起)	Number of Disputes Mediated	(case)	99 686	108 915	116 695	118 363	137 145
# 婚姻家庭		Marriage and family		2 577	2 673	2 844	3 098	3 656
邻里纠纷		Neighbor Disputes		4 170	3 698	4 436	3 995	6 128
调解纠纷成功数		Number of Disputes Successful Mediated		99 534	108 686	116 301	118 058	136 623
防止民间纠纷引起自杀	(件)	Prevention of Suicide Due to Civil Disputes	(case)	126	1	–	–	–
	(人)		(person)	124	4	–	–	–
防止民间纠纷转化为刑事案件	(件)	Prevention of Civil Disputes from Turning into Criminal Cases	(case)	41	10	6	22	–
	(人)		(person)	175	108	71	94	–
宣讲法律	(场)	Lectures on Law	(time)	4 600	4 556	4 185	3 401	4 854
受教育人数	(万人次)	Number of Persons Receiving Law Education	(10 000 person-times)	94	92	101	106	153
为基层政府提供司法建议	(条)	Providing Legal Advice for Local Governments	(piece)	30	94	129	269	1 208
协助基层政府处理社会矛盾纠纷	(件)	Helping Local Government on Social Conflicts	(case)	1 063	1 232	1 312	998	3 223
代理诉讼事务		Service as legal representative		8 687	7 753	6 593	6 127	7 543
代理非诉讼事务		Service not as legal representative		3 010	2 026	2 195	1 197	1 039
担任法律顾问	(家)	Number of Units with Legal Advisors	(unit)	2 915	1 404	1 771	1 832	2 408

表19-9

分地区律师、公证工作情况 (2018年)

指　标		Item		全　市 Whole Municipality
律师工作情况		**Lawyers**		
律师事务所	(所)	Number of Law Offices	(unit)	323
律师事务所人员	(人)	Personnel of Law Offices	(person)	4 513
# 女律师		Female		1 542
# 专职律师		Full-time Lawyers		4 140
兼职律师		Part-time Lawyers		45
公益法律服务件数	(件)	Number of Public Interest Legal Service Cases	(case)	63 332
担任法律顾问	(家)	Number of Units with Permanent Legal Advisors	(unit)	16 475
刑事诉讼辩护及代理	(件)	Defender and Agent of Criminal Cases	(case)	9 465
民事案件诉讼代理		Agent of Civil Cases		89 954
非诉讼法律事务		Agent of Non-litigious Legal Affairs		7 370
公证工作情况		**Notarization**		
公证处	(所)	Number of Notary Offices	(unit)	11
公证处人员	(人)	Notarial Personnel	(person)	216
# 公证员		Notaries		93
办理公证总数	(件)	Number of Notarial Documents Issued	(case)	122 876
# 国内公证数		Number of Domestic Notarization Cases		83 471
涉外及涉港澳台		Foreign-related, Hong Kong, Macao & Taiwan Legal Affairs		39 405

STATISTICS ON LAWYERS AND NOTARIZATION BY REGION (2018)

市 区 Urban Area	# 吴江区 Wujiang District	常 熟 Changshu	张家港 Zhangjiagang	昆 山 Kunshan	太 仓 Taicang
224	15	15	14	55	15
3 305	222	238	291	540	139
1 191	61	70	85	163	33
2 981	208	227	265	530	137
43	–	2	–	–	–
42 499	5 502	2 108	8 944	8 424	1 357
10 063	874	1 386	1 090	2 748	1 188
6 155	498	1 040	522	1 422	326
56 127	4 667	7 080	6 889	16 270	3 588
6 043	177	173	101	870	183
6	1	1	1	2	1
141	17	19	20	24	12
60	7	7	11	11	4
74 483	7 673	18 144	8 634	15 848	5 767
48 406	4 897	14 773	5 416	10 711	4 165
26 077	2 776	3 371	3 218	5 137	1 602

表19-10

分地区人民调解基层司法工作情况 (2018年)

指　　标		Item		全　市 Whole Municipality
人民调解委员会	(个)	Number of People's Mediation Committees	(unit)	4 221
调委会人员数	(人)	Number of Mediators	(person)	13 625
调解纠纷总数	(起)	Number of Disputes Mediated	(case)	137 145
# 婚姻家庭		Marriage and family		3 656
邻里纠纷		Neighbor Disputes		6 128
调解纠纷成功数		Number of Disputes Successful Mediated		136 623
防止民间纠纷引起自杀	(件)	Prevention of Suicide Due to Civil Disputes	(case)	-
	(人)		(person)	-
防止民间纠纷转化为刑事案件	(件)	Prevention of Civil Disputes from Turning into Criminal Cases	(case)	-
	(人)		(person)	-
宣讲法律	(场)	Lectures on Law	(time)	4 854
受教育人数	(万人次)	Number of Persons Receiving Law Education	(10 000 person-times)	153
为基层政府提供司法建议	(条)	Providing Legal Advice for Local Governments	(piece)	1 208
协助基层政府处理社会矛盾纠纷	(件)	Helping Local Government on Social Conflicts	(case)	3 223
代理诉讼事务		Service as legal representative		7 543
代理非诉讼事务		Service not as legal representative		1 039
担任法律顾问	(家)	Number of Units with Legal Advisors	(unit)	2 408

STATISTICS ON PEOPLE'S MEDIATION AND BASIC-LEVEL JUDICIAL WORK BY REGION (2018)

市 区 Urban Area	# 吴江区 Wujiang District	常 熟 Changshu	张家港 Zhangjiagang	昆 山 Kunshan	太 仓 Taicang
2 080	557	765	350	818	208
7 914	1 771	2 311	1 307	1 508	585
82 995	8 192	18 216	14 005	17 364	4 565
1 381	137	378	1 105	564	228
1 855	43	2 022	668	1 432	151
82 484	8 160	18 213	14 005	17 356	4 565
–	–	–	–	–	–
–	–	–	–	–	–
–	–	–	–	–	–
–	–	–	–	–	–
2 574	172	312	984	559	425
53	8	7	40	40	13
1 065	30	28	45	39	31
1 991	97	72	973	127	60
3 564	1 003	729	1 810	788	652
506	123	13	441	6	73
802	311	318	741	241	306

表19-11

道路、船舶交通事故及火灾情况（2018年）
STATISTICS ON HIGHWAY，WATERWAY TRAFFIC ACCIDENTS AND FIRES (2018)

地　区	Region	事故数（起）Number of Traffic Accidents (case)	死　亡（人）Number of Deaths (person)	伤　人（人）Number of Injuries (person)	损失折款(万元) Losses Converted into Cash (10 000 yuan)
道路交通事故	**Road Accidents**				
全　市	**Whole Municipality**	**2 993**	**588**	**2 877**	**2 389**
高速公路	Thruway	67	59	58	1 014
城市快速路	Urban Expressway	14	6	15	29
市　区	Urban Area	1 171	196	1 140	456
# 吴江区	Wujiang District	770	80	783	220
常　熟	Changshu	550	110	510	334
张家港	Zhangjiagang	670	85	692	352
昆　山	Kunshan	198	74	157	80
太　仓	Taicang	323	58	305	124
船舶交通事故	**Waterway Accidents**				
全　市	**Whole Municipality**	**3**	**1**	**–**	**4**
市　区	Urban Area	3	1	–	4
# 吴江区	Wujiang District	1	1	–	–
常　熟	Changshu	–	–	–	–
张家港	Zhangjiagang	–	–	–	–
昆　山	Kunshan	–	–	–	–
太　仓	Taicang	–	–	–	–
火　灾	**Fires**				
全　市	**Whole Municipality**	**1 873**	**21**	**21**	**5 235**
市　区	Urban Area	792	13	10	2 669
# 吴江区	Wujiang District	123	4	6	1 746
常　熟	Changshu	426	6	4	875
张家港	Zhangjiagang	206	1	–	742
昆　山	Kunshan	297	1	7	512
太　仓	Taicang	152	–	–	436

主 要 统 计 指 标 解 释

社会福利事业单位 指集中收养社会孤老、残、幼的机构，包括由民政部门管理的社会福利院、儿童福利院、精神病人福利院和城镇集体举办的福利院及农村集体举办的敬老院以及优抚医院和具有收养能力的社区服务中心等。该指标主要反映我国社会福利性单位的投入水平。

社会福利事业单位收养人数 包括民政部门管理和城镇、农村集体举办的社会福利事业单位中收养的老人、少年儿童、缺乏生活自理能力的残疾人员和精神病人。该指标主要反映收养性社会福利单位的收养能力。

城市居民最低生活保障人数 指在报告期末共同生活的家庭成员人均收入低于当地最低生活保障标准，且家庭财产状况符合相关规定的城镇居民，并已发放补助经费的人数。

农村居民最低生活保障人数 指报告期末共同生活的家庭成员人均收入低于当地最低生活保障标准，得到当地政府给予最低生活保障待遇的农业人口家庭人数。

五保户 指无劳动能力、无生活来源、又无法定赡养、抚养、扶养义务人，或者其法定赡养、抚养、扶养义务人无赡养、抚养、扶养能力的老年、残疾或者未满16岁的村民。

律师 指依法取得律师执业证书，担任法律顾问，民事(刑事、行政)案件代理人、刑事案件辩护人、办理非诉讼业务，解答法律询问，代写法律事务文书等，为社会提供法律服务的人员。

公证人员 指在公证处工作的人员总称，包括公证处主任、副主任、公证员、公证员助理(助理公证员)和其他从事辅助性工作的人员。

公证文书 指公证处根据当事人申请，依照事实和法律，按照法定程序制作的，具有法律效力的司法证明文书。根据公证书用途和使用地，公证书分为国内公证书、国内经济公证书、涉外民事公证书、涉外经济公证书四类。

调解员 指在人民调解委员会担负调解民间纠纷工作的人员，包括调解委员会的委员和调解小组的调解员。该指标主要反映从事人民调解工作的人员数量。

调解民间纠纷 指调解委员会按照法律规定，根据自愿原则，用说服教育的方法调解民间发生的有关民事权利和义务争执的件数，包括调解成功数和调解未成功数。该指标主要反映人民调解委员会的工作量。

EXPLANATORY NOTES ON MAIN STATISTICAL INDICATORS

Social Welfare Institutions refer to institutions taking care of old people without children, handicapped people and orphans. They include social welfare institutions run by civil affairs departments, children welfare institutions, social welfare institutions for mental patients, collective-owned old people's homes in rural areas, convalescent homes and community service centers with the capacity of receiving those people. This indicator reflects the input in social welfare institutions.

Number of People Accommodated by Social Welfare Institutions refers to the number of old people, children, totally dependent handicapped people and mental patients Accommodated by social welfare institutions run by civil affairs departments and those run by collective units in urban and rural areas. This indicator reflects the capacity of social welfare institutions.

Number of Urban Residents Entitled to Minimum Living Allowances refers to the number of those urban residents whose average family income is below a minimum local standard, and status of family property meets the relevant regulation, and have received subsidies by the end of the reporting period.

Number of Rural Residents Entitled to Minimum Living Allowances refers to the number of those rural residents whose average family income is below a minimum local standard, and receiving the minimum living allowances from the local government by the end of the reporting period.

Households Enjoying Five Guarantees refers to the elderly, disabled or under the age of 16 villagers, without working capacity, without the source of life, and without legal supporter, upbringing persons, brought up persons, or legal supporter, upbringing persons, brought up persons can not support, upbringing, bring up.

Lawyers are certified legal workers according to law, and who are employed by legal counselling firms to act as legal advisers; agents in criminal or civil lawsuits; and defenders in criminal lawsuits; or to handle non-litigious legal affairs, to advise on matters of law or to write legal papers for others and provide service to the public.

Notary Personnel refers to people working for notary offices including: directors, deputy directors, notaries, assistant notaries and other people providing assistance.

Notary Documents refer to the judicial notary documents drawn up at the request of the interested party and are in accordance with facts and the law and following certain legal proceedings. According to usage and locality, notary documents are divided into the following 4 types: domestic notary documents, domestic economic notary documents, foreign-related civil notary documents and foreign-related economic notary documents.

Mediators refer to workers on people's mediation committees responsible for mediating in civil disputes and cases of slight infraction of the law. They include members of the mediation committees and mediators of mediation groups. This indicator reflects the number of people engaged in mediation.

Mediation of Civil Disputes refers to number of cases made by mediation committees in mediating in civil disputes concerning civil rights and duties through persuasion and education in accordance with the provisions of law on a voluntary basis, so as to solve disputes by helping the parties involved come to an agreement and understanding, including those unsuccessful ones. This indicator reflects the workload of the mediation committees.

二十、城市建设 环境保护

CHAPTER 20
URBAN CONSTRUCTION AND ENVIRONMENTAL PROTECTION

20 城市建设　环境保护
URBAN CONSTRUCTION AND ENVIRONMENTAL PROTECTION

主要统计指标
MAJOR STATISTICAL INDICATORS

2018年市区建成区面积	Build up Area of Urban District	475.88	平方公里	sq.km
2018年市区人均城市道路面积	Per Capita Roads Area of Urban District	31.49	平方米	sq.m
2018年市区人均公园绿地面积	Per Capita Park Green Space of Urban District	13.01	平方米	sq.m
2018年市区建成区绿化覆盖率	Coverage Rate of Green Areas in Developed Areas of Urban District	41.44	%	
2018年市区污水处理率	Treatment Rate of Urban District	95.11	%	
2018年市区供水总量	Total Water Supply of Urban District	78 082	万立方米	10 000 cu.m
2018年市区天然气供气总量	Total Natural Gas Supply of Urban District	103 299	万立方米	10 000 cu.m
2018年市区公共汽车客运量	Number of Passengers Carried by Bus of Urban District	55 576	万人次	10 000 person-times
2018年市区轨道交通客运量	Number of Passengers Carried by Urban Rail Transit	32 805	万人次	10 000 person-times

表20-1

分地区城市设施水平 (2018年)
URBAN FACILITY CONDITION BY REGION (2018)

地　区	Region	人均日生活用水量(升) Per Capita Daily Consumption of Tap Water for Residential Use (liter)	人均城市道路面积(平方米) Per Capita Area of Roads (sq.m)	人均公园绿地面积(平方米) Per Capita Park Green Areas (sq.m)	建成区绿化覆盖率(%) Coverage Rate of Green Areas in Developed Areas (%)	污水处理率(%) Treatment Rate of Sewage (%)
全　市	**Whole Municipality**	**274.98**	**30.54**	**13.72**	**42.27**	**95.79**
市　区	Urban Area	285.08	31.49	13.01	41.44	95.11
# 吴江区	Wujiang District	142.68	29.40	11.60	38.43	98.85
常　熟	Changshu	277.14	33.78	20.13	45.88	95.99
张家港	Zhangjiagang	205.34	28.09	14.90	41.20	96.00
昆　山	Kunshan	319.99	24.09	12.95	44.95	98.29
太　仓	Taicang	154.77	28.89	12.72	40.55	95.08

表20-2

分地区城市市政设施情况 (2018年末)
URBAN CIVIL FACILITIES BY REGION (END OF 2018)

地　区	Region	实有道路长度(公里) Length of Roads (km)	实有道路面积(万平方米) Area of Roads (10 000 sq.m)	路灯数(盏) Number of Street Lights (unit)	桥梁数(座) Number of Bridges (unit)	排水管道长度(公里) Length of Drainage Pipelines (km)
全　市	**Whole Municipality**	**9 994**	**15 891**	**642 484**	**3 882**	**15 676**
市　区	Urban Area	7 350	11 250	440 850	2 946	11 105
# 吴江区	Wujiang District	768	1 938	66 893	467	2 379
常　熟	Changshu	726	1 474	59 705	339	1 786
张家港	Zhangjiagang	702	1 079	40 105	126	957
昆　山	Kunshan	802	1 271	44 915	209	970
太　仓	Taicang	413	818	56 909	262	858

表20-3

分地区城市建设用地（2018年末）
LAND USE OF URBAN CONSTRUCTION BY REGION (END OF 2018)

单位：平方公里 (sq.km)

地　区	Region	建成区面积 Build up Area	城市建设用地面积 Urban Construction Areas	居住用地 Residential	公共管理与服务用地 Public Administration and Service Land	商业服务业设施用地 Land to be used for Business Services Facilities
全　市	**Whole Municipality**	**756.20**	**731.89**	**223.73**	**46.47**	**56.77**
市　区	Urban Area	475.88	474.38	137.31	32.09	34.71
# 吴江区	Wujiang District	106.20	104.84	29.72	7.96	4.43
常　熟	Changshu	98.00	89.71	34.99	3.85	13.21
张家港	Zhangjiagang	58.65	48.49	18.56	4.30	3.64
昆　山	Kunshan	72.00	67.64	22.34	5.00	2.38
太　仓	Taicang	51.67	51.67	10.53	1.23	2.83

表20-3　续 表　　Continued

单位：平方公里 (sq.km)

地　区	Region	工业用地 Industrial	物流仓储用地 The land to be used for logistics warehouses	道路与交通设施用地 Land to be used for Road and Traffic Facilities	公用设施用地 Public Administration Land	绿地与广场用地 Land to be Used for Green and Squares
全　市	**Whole Municipality**	**170.73**	**12.41**	**104.25**	**17.01**	**100.52**
市　区	Urban Area	129.06	8.08	67.75	9.39	55.99
# 吴江区	Wujiang District	39.91	0.83	12.85	1.72	7.42
常　熟	Changshu	13.84	1.27	14.77	1.71	6.07
张家港	Zhangjiagang	2.21	0.23	9.01	0.53	10.01
昆　山	Kunshan	15.26	1.69	7.79	4.23	8.95
太　仓	Taicang	10.36	1.14	4.93	1.15	19.50

表20-4

分地区城市供水情况 (2018年)
URBAN WATER SUPPLY BY REGION (2018)

地　区	Region	综合生产能力 (万立方米/日) General Production Capacity (10 000 cu.m/day)	全年供水总量 (万立方米) Total Annual Volume of Water Supply (10 000 cu.m)			供水管道长度 (公里) Length of Water Supply Pipelines (km)
				#生产运营用水量 For Productive Use	#居民家庭用水量 For Residential Use	
全　市	**Whole Municipality**	**792.32**	**114 613**	**49 263**	**34 814**	**17 064**
市　区	Urban Area	414.86	78 082	33 259	23 815	9 410
# 吴江区	Wujiang District	134.86	16 111	11 275	2 756	1 601
常　熟	Changshu	87.50	10 590	4 247	3 056	2 976
张家港	Zhangjiagang	65.00	4 708	1 224	1 553	1 009
昆　山	Kunshan	150.00	17 056	8 779	4 947	3 281
太　仓	Taicang	74.96	4 176	1 754	1 443	389

表20-5

分地区城市天然气供气情况 (2018年)
URBAN NATURAL GAS SUPPLY BY REGION (2018)

地　区	Region	供气总量 (万立方米) Total Gas Supply (10 000 cu.m)		用气户数(户) Total Number of Residents with Access to Gas (household)		供气管道长度 (公里) Total Length of Gas Pipelines (km)
			# 家庭用量 Consumption for Residential Use		# 家庭用户 Residential Households	
全　市	**Whole Municipality**	**292 732**	**45 098**	**2 204 426**	**2 191 549**	**18 328**
市　区	Urban Area	103 299	20 473	1 036 775	1 031 392	9 301
# 吴江区	Wujiang District	35 115	2 644	132 416	132 358	912
常　熟	Changshu	58 598	3 275	271 476	267 683	2 401
张家港	Zhangjiagang	45 688	4 569	196 035	194 819	1 639
昆　山	Kunshan	63 797	12 516	509 066	507 211	3 542
太　仓	Taicang	21 350	4 264	191 074	190 444	1 445

表20-6

分地区城市液化石油气供气情况（2018年）
URBAN LIQUEFIED PETROLEUM GAS SUPPLY BY REGION (2018)

地 区	Region	供气总量（吨）Total Gas Supply (ton)	# 家庭用量 Consumption for Residential Use	用气户数(户) Total Number of Residents with Access to Gas (household)	# 家庭用户 Residential Households
全 市	**Whole Municipality**	**193 351**	**106 536**	**388 741**	**359 421**
市 区	Urban Area	85 125	53 173	194 032	192 632
# 吴江区	Wujiang District	15 838	15 838	51 050	51 050
常 熟	Changshu	30 497	25 503	49 183	45 219
张家港	Zhangjiagang	36 617	6 954	64 235	63 104
昆 山	Kunshan	35 054	17 986	69 600	47 876
太 仓	Taicang	6 059	2 919	11 691	10 590

表20-7

分地区城市园林绿化情况（2018年末）
URBAN PARKS，GARDENS & GREEN AREAS BY REGION (END OF 2018)

单位：公顷 (hectare)

地 区	Region	绿化覆盖面积 Coverage Space of Green Areas	# 建成区 Build up Area	绿地面积 Total Area of Green Areas	# 建成区 Build up Area	公园绿地面积 Total Area of Park Green Areas
全 市	**Whole Municipality**	**41 909**	**31 967**	**35 604**	**29 152**	**7 141**
市 区	Urban Area	27 729	19 722	22 518	17 837	4 646
# 吴江区	Wujiang District	10 197	4 081	6 933	3 966	764
常 熟	Changshu	4 858	4 497	4 555	4 187	879
张家港	Zhangjiagang	2 438	2 416	2 212	2 194	572
昆 山	Kunshan	3 861	3 236	3 509	2 984	683
太 仓	Taicang	3 024	2 095	2 811	1 950	360

表20-8

分地区城市清洁卫生情况 (2018年)
URBAN ENVIRONMENT SANITATION BY REGION (2018)

地 区	Region	生活垃圾清运量 (万吨) Volume of Residential Garbage Disposed (10 000 tons)	生活垃圾无害化处理量 (万吨) Volume of No Harm Disposal of Garbage (10 000 tons)	公共厕所(座) Number of Public Lavatories (unit)
全 市	**Whole Municipality**	**325.56**	**325.56**	**2 229**
市 区	Urban Area	247.84	247.84	979
# 吴江区	Wujiang District	43.01	43.01	141
常 熟	Changshu	19.76	19.76	817
张家港	Zhangjiagang	15.36	15.36	208
昆 山	Kunshan	32.85	32.85	138
太 仓	Taicang	9.76	9.76	87

表20-9

分地区城市污水处理情况 (2018年)
URBAN SEWAGE TREATMENT BY REGION (2018)

地 区	Region	污水处理厂 (座) Sewage Treatment Plants (spots)	污水处理厂处理能力 (万立方米/日) Treatment Capacity of Sewage Treatment Plants (10 000 cubic meters / day)	污水处理总量 (万立方米) Total Volume of Sewage Treatment (10 000 cubic meters)	#污水处理厂处理量 Disposal Capacity of Sewage Treatment Plants
全 市	**Whole Municipality**	**43**	**291.1**	**91 811**	**87 032**
市 区	Urban Area	25	195.3	60 325	59 092
# 吴江区	Wujiang District	4	40.8	11 664	11 263
常 熟	Changshu	6	29.7	8 263	7 027
张家港	Zhangjiagang	4	14.5	3 604	3 604
昆 山	Kunshan	5	36.6	16 664	14 354
太 仓	Taicang	3	15.0	2 955	2 955

表20-10

分地区保障性安居工程建设情况（2018年）
THE CONSTRUCTION SITUATION OF LOW-INCOME HOUSING PROJECTS BY REGIONS (2018)

单位：套 (set)

地区	Region	全市 Whole Municipality	市区 Urban Area	# 吴江区 Wujiang District	常熟 Changshu	张家港 Zhang-jiagang	昆山 Kunshan	太仓 Taicang
一、开工情况	**Work Situation**	**21 205**	**9 817**	**1 015**	**2 992**	**3 420**	**3 535**	**1 441**
公共租赁住房（含廉租住房）	Public Rental Housing (Including Low-rent Housing)	–	–	–	–	–	–	–
经济适用住房	Economically Applicable Housing	–	–	–	–	–	–	–
限价商品住房	Commercial Housing at Limited Prices	–	–	–	–	–	–	–
棚户区改造	The Transformation of Shanty Towns	21 205	9 817	1 015	2 992	3 420	3 535	1 441
二、基本建成情况	**Basic Completion Situation**	**27 196**	11 124	317	4 373	2 834	8 001	864
公共租赁住房（含廉租住房）	Public Rental Housing (Including Low-rent Housing)	–	–	–	–	–	–	–
经济适用住房	Economically Applicable Housing	–	–	–	–	–	–	–
限价商品住房	Commercial Housing at Limited Prices	–	–	–	–	–	–	–
棚户区改造	The Transformation of Shanty Towns	27 196	11 124	317	4 373	2 834	8 001	864

表20-11

市区轨道交通情况（2018年）
URBAN RAIL TRANSIT (2018)

指标	Item	地铁 Metro	有轨电车 Tram
运营车辆 (辆)	The Number of Operating Vehicles (coach)	608	207
运营线路 (条)	Number of Routes (line)	3	2
营运线路总长度 (公里)	Total Length of Light Rail Transit Operating Routes (km)	120.66	28.94
客运量 (万人次)	Number of Passengers Carried by Light Rail (10 000 person-times)	32 414	391
运营里程 (万列公里)	Operating Mileage (10 000 km/ train)	1 446	230
年末从业人员 (人)	Year-end Number of Staff and Workers (person)	6 535	384
# 驾驶员	Light Rail Driver	643	146
运营收入 (万元)	Operation Revenues (10 000 yuan)	55 585	465

表20-12

分地区城市公共交通情况(2018年)

指　　标		Item		全　市 Whole Municipality
公共汽车		**Bus Routes**		
运营车辆	(辆)	Operating Bus	(coach)	8 780
运营线路条数	(条)	Number of Routes	(line)	827
营运线路总长度	(公里)	Length of Bus Routes	(km)	14 658
客运量	(万人次)	Number of Passengers Carried by Bus	(10 000 person-times)	85 420
# 使用IC卡的客运量		The passenger traffic using the IC card		38 598
运营里程	(万公里)	Length of Bus Operating	(10 000 kms)	53 105
年末从业人员	(人)	Year-end Number of Staff and Workers	(person)	18 223
# 驾驶员		Bus Driver		13 318
出租车		**Taxis**		
运营车辆	(辆)	Operating Vehicles	(coach)	9 018
载客车次	(万车次)	Number of Carryings	(10 000 times)	6 801
客运量	(万人次)	Number of Passengers Carried by Taxi	(10 000 person-times)	13 541
运营里程	(万公里)	Length of Bus Operating	(10 000 kms)	88 036
# 载客里程		Transport Lengths of Passengers		48 730
年末从业人员	(人)	Year-end Number of Staff and Workers	(person)	15 996
# 驾驶员		Taxi Driver		15 529
公共自行车		**Public Bicycle**		
租赁点	(个)	Public Bicycle Rental Point	(unit)	4 999
累计投入车辆	(辆)	A Total Investment of Public Bicycle	(coach)	122 712

THE PUBLIC TRANSPORTATINN IN CITIES BY REGION (2018)

市 区 Urban Area	# 吴江区 Wujiang District	常 熟 Changshu	张家港 Zhangjiagang	昆 山 Kunshan	太 仓 Taicang
5 838	607	659	474	1 606	203
446	53	42	46	249	44
8 289	801	745	1 094	3 692	838
55 576	5 512	6 192	4 777	14 674	4 202
21 849	2 659	3 829	1 037	8 480	3 403
33 066	4 059	3 942	3 790	9 377	2 930
11 374	1 442	1 126	789	4 400	534
8 879	1 194	925	711	2 407	396
5 638	835	759	557	1 606	458
4 152	734	1 009	602	609	430
8 420	1 584	2 017	1 331	913	860
58 864	7 983	8 670	6 770	8 383	5 349
33 732	4 092	4 263	3 266	4 610	2 859
9 842	1 145	1 468	1 087	2 792	807
9 532	1 085	1 443	1 064	2 713	777
2 513	486	651	341	1 063	431
60 132	10 890	18 300	6 625	32 055	5 600

表20-13

分地区环境保护情况（2018年）

指　　标		Item		全　市 Whole Municipality
工业废水排放量	（万吨）	Volume of Industrial Wastewater Discharged	(10 000 tons)	39 730
工业废水处理量		Volume of Treated Industrial Wastewater		103 057
工业废气排放总量	（亿立方米）	Total Volume of Industrial Waste Gas Emission	(100 million cu.m)	21 844
工业二氧化硫产生量	（吨）	Volume of Sulphur Dioxide Produced	(ton)	631 879
工业二氧化硫排放量		Volume of Sulphur Dioxide Emission		61 674
工业化学需氧量产生量		Industrial Volume of COD Produced		366 222
工业化学需氧量排放量		Industrial Volume of COD Emission		23 045
工业氨氮产生量		Industrial Volume of Ammonia Nitrogen Produced		22 179
工业氨氮排放量		Industrial Volume of Ammonia Nitrogen Emission		1 537
工业氮氧化物产生量		Industrial Volume of Nitrogen Oxides Produced		275 941
工业氮氧化物排放量		Industrial Volume of Nitrogen Oxides Emission		92 404
工业烟（粉）尘产生量		Volume of Industrial Smoke (Powder) Dust Produced		6 275 697
工业烟（粉）尘排放量		Volume of Industrial Smoke (Powder) Dust Emission		39 669
一般工业固体废物产生量	（万吨）	Volume of Industrial Solid Wastes Produced	(10 000 tons)	2 780
一般工业固体废物处置量		Volume of Industrial Solid Wastes Treated		159
一般工业固体废物综合利用量		Volume of Industrial Solid Wastes Utilized in a Comprehensive Way		2 621
环境污染治理本年投资总额	(万元)	Investment For Environmental Pollution Abatement in 2018	(10 000 yuan)	2 580 179
空气质量优良天数比例	(%)	Proportion of Days with Good Air Quality	(%)	77.4
工业锅炉	(台)	Industrial Boilers	(unit)	1 329
	(蒸吨)		(ton vapor)	75 374
工业炉窑	(台)	Industrial Furnaces & Kilns	(unit)	656

ENVIRONMENTAL PROTECTION BY REGION (2018)

市 区 Urban Area	# 吴江区 Wujiang District	常 熟 Changshu	张家港 Zhangjiagang	昆 山 Kunshan	太 仓 Taicang
19 685	9 545	7 057	5 749	3 660	3 580
24 455	10 222	7 108	62 385	5 223	3 885
3 567	666	2 644	12 858	1 640	1 136
141 044	34 950	188 239	163 710	31 591	107 296
12 024	5 139	11 504	24 945	1 563	11 639
129 366	72 727	114 630	26 792	14 631	80 803
12 048	5 990	4 041	2 617	1 605	2 733
4 414	2 235	1 794	1 009	649	14 313
750	325	288	164	112	222
82 166	20 080	52 235	67 030	21 176	53 334
25 031	7 192	19 601	28 710	5 652	13 409
1 719 507	527 561	1 481 560	1 423 102	197 364	1 454 165
5 705	2 042	8 305	20 715	1 107	3 837
451	95	385	1 627	84	233
59	32	21	38	28	14
392	62	364	1 589	57	219
1 147 586	345 391	347 961	263 527	606 414	214 691
73.7	74.5	83.6	78.1	77.5	76.7
628	199	244	119	236	102
20 044	6 774	21 570	14 384	2 348	17 028
201	11	113	184	144	14

主 要 统 计 指 标 解 释

供水综合生产能力 指按供水设施取水、净化、送水、出厂输水干管等环节设计能力计算的综合生产能力。包括在原设计能力的基础上，经挖、革、改增加的生产能力。计算时，以四个环节中最薄弱的环节为主确定能力。

年末供水管道长度 指从送水泵至用户水表之间所有管道的长度。不包括新安装尚未使用、水厂内以及用户建筑物内的管道。

全年供水总量 指报告期供水企业(单位)供出的全部水量。包括有效供水量和漏损水量。

生活用水量 包括公共服务用水和居民家庭用水。公共服务用水指为城市社会公共生活服务的用水。包括行政事业单位、部队营区和公共设施服务、社会服务业、批发零售贸易业、旅馆饮食业以及其他公共服务业等单位的用水。居民家庭用水指城市范围内所有居民家庭的日常生活用水。包括城市居民、农民家庭、公共供水站用水。

用水普及率 指城市用水人口数与城市人口总数的比率。计算公式：

$$用水普及率=\frac{城市用水人口数}{城市人口总数}\times 100\%$$

供气管道长度 指报告期末从气源厂压缩机的出口或门站出口至各类用户引入管之间的全部已经通气投入使用的管道长度。不包括煤气生产厂、输配站、液化气储存站、灌瓶站、储配站、气化站、混气站、供应站等厂(站)内的管道。

全年供气总量 指全年燃气企业(单位)向用户供应的燃气数量。包括销售量和损失量。

燃气普及率 指报告期末使用燃气的城市人口数与城市人口总数的比率。计算公式为：

$$燃气普及率=\frac{城市用气人口数}{城市人口总数}\times 100\%$$

年末道路长度 指年末道路长度和与道路相通的桥梁、隧道的长度，按车行道中心线计算。在统计时只统计路面宽度在3.5米(含3.5米)以上的各种铺装道路，包括开放型工业区和住宅区道路在内。

城市桥梁 指为跨越天然或人工障碍物而修建的构筑物。包括跨河桥、立交桥、人行天桥以及人行地下通道等。按使用年限分为永久性桥和半永久性桥。

城市排水管道长度 指所有排水总管、干管、支管、检查井及连接井进出口等长度之和。

城市污水日处理能力 指污水处理厂(或污水处理装置)每昼夜处理污水量的设计能力。

年末运营车数 指年末城市用于公共交通运营业务的全部车辆数。新购、新制和调入的运营车辆，自投入之日起开始计算；调出、报废和调作他用的运营车辆，自上级主管机关批准之日起不再计入。

园林绿地面积 指报告期末用作园林和绿化的各种绿地面积。包括公园绿地、生产绿地、防护绿地、单位附属绿地、防护绿地、生产绿地、道路绿地和风景林地面积。

公园绿地 城市中向公众开放的以游憩为主要功能，有一定的游憩设施和服务设施，同时兼有健全生态、美化景观，防灾减灾等综合作用的绿化用地。包括综合公园，社区公园、专类公园、带状公园和街旁绿地。其中综合公园、专类公园和带状公园面积之和为公园面积。

工业废水排放量 指经过企业厂区所有排放口排到企业外部的工业废水量。包括生产废水、外排的直接冷却水、超标排放的矿井地下水和与工业废水混排的厂区生活污水，不包括外排的间接冷却水(清污不分流的间接冷却水应计算在内)。

工业废水排放达标量 指报告期内废水中各项污染物指标都达到国家或地方排放标准的外排工业废水量，包括未经处理外排达标的，经废水处理设施处理后达标排放的，以及经污水处理厂处理后达标排放的。

工业废水排放达标率 指工业废水排放达标量占工业废水排放量的百分率，计算公式为：

$$\text{工业废水排放达标率}=\frac{\text{工业废水排放达标量}}{\text{工业废水排放量}}\times 100\%$$

生活污水排放量 指城镇居民每年排放的生活污水。用人均系数法测算。测算公式为：

$$\begin{matrix}\text{生活污水}\\\text{排放量}\end{matrix}=\begin{matrix}\text{城镇生活污水}\\\text{排放系数}\end{matrix}\times\begin{matrix}\text{市镇非}\\\text{农业人口}\end{matrix}\times 365$$

工业废气排放量 指报告期内企业厂区内燃料燃烧和生产工艺过程中产生的各种排入大气的含有污染物的气体的总量，以标准状态(273K，101325Pa)计算。测算公式为：

$$\begin{matrix}\text{工业废气}\\\text{排放量}\end{matrix}=\begin{matrix}\text{燃料燃烧过程}\\\text{中废气排放量}\end{matrix}+\begin{matrix}\text{生产工艺过程}\\\text{中废气排放量}\end{matrix}$$

工业二氧化硫（SO_2）排放量 指报告期内企业在燃料燃烧和生产工艺过程中排入大气的SO_2总量，计算公式为：

$$\begin{matrix}\text{工业}SO_2\\\text{排放量}\end{matrix}=\begin{matrix}\text{燃料燃烧过程}\\\text{中}SO_2\text{排放量}\end{matrix}+\begin{matrix}\text{生产工艺过程}\\\text{中}SO_2\text{排放量}\end{matrix}$$

工业烟尘排放量 指企业厂区内燃料燃烧过程中产生的烟气中夹带的颗粒物排放量。

工业粉尘排放量 指企业在生产工艺过程中排放的能在空气中悬浮一定时间的固体颗粒物排放量。如钢铁企业的耐火材料粉尘、焦化企业的筛焦系统粉尘、烧结机的粉尘、石灰窑的粉尘、建材企业的水泥粉尘等。不包括电厂排入大气的烟尘。

工业固体废物产生量 指报告期内企业在生产过程中产生的固体状、半固体状和高浓度液体状废弃物的总量，包括危险废物、冶炼废渣、粉煤灰、炉渣、煤矸石、尾矿、放射性废物和其他废物等；不包括矿山开采的剥离废石和掘进废石(煤矸石和呈酸性或碱性的废石除外)。酸性或碱性废石指采掘的废石其流经水、雨淋水的pH值小于4或pH值大于10.5者。

工业固体废物综合利用量 指报告期内企业通过回收、加工、循环、交换等方式，从固体废物中提取或者使其转化为可以利用的资源、能源和其他原材料的固体废物量(包括当年利用往年的工业固体废物贮存量)，如用作农业肥料、生产建筑材料、筑路等。综合利用量由原产生固体废物的单位统计。

工业固体废物综合利用率 指工业固体废物综合利用量占工业固体废物产生量(包括综合利用往年贮存量)的百分率。计算公式为：

$$\begin{matrix}\text{工业固体废物}\\\text{综合利用率}\end{matrix}=\frac{\begin{matrix}\text{工业固体废物}\\\text{综合利用率}\end{matrix}}{\begin{matrix}\text{工业固体废物产生量}+\\\text{综合利用往年贮存量}\end{matrix}}\times 100\%$$

工业固体废物处置量 指报告期内企业将固体废物焚烧或者最终置于符合环境保护规定要求的场所，并不再回取的工业固体废物量(包括当年处置往年的工业固体废物贮存量)。处置方式有填埋(其中危险废物应安全填埋)、焚烧、专业贮存场(库)封场处理、深层灌注、回填矿井及海洋处置(经海洋管理部门同意投海处置)等。

工业固体废物排放量 指报告期内企业将所产生的固体废物排到固体废物污染防治设施、场所以外的数量，不包括矿山开采的剥离废石和掘进废石(煤矸石和呈酸性或碱性的废石除外)。

空气质量良好以上（API）天数 API即空气污染指数，是Air Pollution Index的英文缩写，就是将常规监测的几种空气污染物浓度简化成为单一的概念性指数值形式，并分级表征空气污染程度和空气质量状况，适合于表示城市的短期空气质量状况和变化趋势。API分级计算参考的标准是老的环境空气质量标准（GB3095-1996），评价的污染物仅为SO_2、NO_2和PM_{10}等三项。

空气质量良好以上（AQI）天数 AQI是定量描述空气质量状况的无量纲指数，是Air Quality Index的英文缩写。AQI分级计算参考的标准是新的环境空气质量标准（GB3095-2012），参与评价的污染物为SO_2、NO_2、PM_{10}、$PM_{2.5}$、O_3、CO等六项 。

EXPLANATORY NOTES ON MAIN STATISTICAL INDICATORS

Production Capacity of Water Supply refers to the designed overall production capacity of water facilities, covering the four segments of water collection, purification, conveyance, and outflow through trunk pipelines. Increased capacity through transformation and innovation projects is included as well. The capacity is determined mainly on the weakest of the above-mentioned four segments.

Length of Water Supply Pipelines at the Year-end refers to the total length of all the pipelines between the water pumps and the user water meters, excluding pipelines newly installed but not used yet, pipeline in the water factory,and pipeline in the user's buildings.

Annual Volume of Water Supply refers to the total volume of water supplied by water-works (units) during the reference period, including both the effective water supply and loss during the water supply.

Consumption of Water for Residential Use refers to water consumption of households for daily life and water consumption of public service facilities. The latter refers to water consumption for urban public services, including the consumption of government agencies and public institutions, military barracks, public facilities, wholesale and retail outlets, restaurants, hotels, and other units providing public services. Household water consumption refers to consumption of water for daily life of all households within the boundary of cities, including households of urban residents and farmers, and public water supply stations.

Coverage Rate of Urban Population with Access to Tap Water refers to the ratio of the urban population with access to tap water to the total urban population. The formula is:

$$\text{Coverage of urban population with access to tap water} = \frac{\text{Urban population with access to tap water}}{\text{Urban population}} \times 100\%$$

Length of Gas Pipelines refers to the total length of pipelines in use between the outlet of the compressor of gas-work or outlet of gas stations and the leading pipe of users, excluding pipelines within gasworks, delivery stations, LPG storage stations, refilling stations, gas-mixing stations and supply stations.

Volume of Gas Supply refers to the total volume of gas provided to users by gas-producing enterprises (units) in a year, including the volume sold and the volume lost.

Coverage Rate of Urban Population with Access to Gas refers to the ratio of the urban population with access to gas to the total urban population at the end of the reference period. The formula is:

$$\text{Coverage rate of urban population with access to gas} = \frac{\text{Urban population with access to gas}}{\text{Urban population}} \times 100\%$$

Length of Paved Roads at Year-end refers to the length of roads with paved surface including bridges and tunnels connected with roads by the end of the year. Length of the roads is measured by the central lines for vehicles for paved roads with a width of 3.5 meters and over, including roads in open-ended factory compounds and residential quarters.

Urban Bridges refer to bridges built to cross over natural or man-made barriers, including bridges over rivers, overpasses for traffic and for pedestrians, underpasses for pedestrians, etc. Both permanent and semi-permanent bridges are included.

Length of Urban Sewage Pipes refers to the total length of general drainage, trunks, branch and inspection wells, connection wells, inlets and outlets, etc.

Daily Disposal Capacity of Urban Sewage refers to the designed 24-hour capacity of sewage disposal by the sewage treatment works or facilities.

Number of Vehicles under Operation at Year-end refers to the total number of vehicles under operation by public transport enterprises (units) at the end of the year, based on the records of operational vehicles by the enterprises (units).

Area of Gardens and Green Areas refers to the total area occupied for green projects at the end of the reference period, including park green land, residential area green land, subsidiary green land of the units, protection green land, production green land, roadside green land and scenic forest land.

Park Green Area refers to green areas open to the public for amusement and rest with the facilities of amusement, rest and services. Its function includes perfecting ecology, beautifying landscape, and preventing and reducing disaster. Park green areas include comprehensive park, community park, topic park, belt-shaped park and green area nearby street. Total areas of comprehensive park, topic park and belt-shaped is the area of park.

Waste Water Discharged by Industry refers to the volume of waste water discharged by industrial enterprises through all their outlets, including waste water from production process, directly cooled water, groundwater from mining wells which does not meet discharge standards and sewage from households mixed with waste water produced by industrial activities, but excluding indirectly cooled water discharged (It should be included if the discharge is not separated from waste water).

Industrial Waste Water Meeting Discharge Standards refers to volume of industrial waste water discharge which, with or without treatment, reaches national or local standards with regard to all pollutants.

Ratio of Industrial Waste Water Meeting Discharge Standards refers to percentage of industrial waste water meeting discharge standards over total industrial waste water discharge. It is calculated as:

$$\begin{array}{c}\text{Ratio of industrial waste water}\\\text{meeting discharge standards}\end{array}=\frac{\begin{array}{c}\text{industrial waste water}\\\text{meeting discharge standards}\end{array}}{\begin{array}{c}\text{total industrial waste}\\\text{water discharge}\end{array}}$$

Urban Non-industrial Waste Water Discharge refers to annual discharge of non-industrial waste water by urban households. It is estimated by per capita coefficient using the formula:

$$\begin{array}{c}\text{Urban non - industrial}\\\text{waste water discharge}\end{array}=\begin{array}{c}\text{urban non - industrial waste}\\\text{water discharge coefficient}\end{array}\times\begin{array}{c}\text{urban non - agricultural}\\\text{population}\end{array}\times 365$$

Industrial Waste Air Emission refers to the discharge into atmosphere of waste air containing pollutants generated from fuel burning and production processes in enterprises within a given period of time. It is calculated at standard status (273K, 101325Pa) as:

$$\begin{array}{c}\text{Industrial waste}\\\text{air emission}\end{array}=\begin{array}{c}\text{emission through}\\\text{fuel burning}\end{array}+\begin{array}{c}\text{emission through}\\\text{production process}\end{array}$$

SO_2 Emission through Industrial Activities refers to volume of sulphur dioxide emission from fuel burning and production process by enterprises during a given period of time. It is calculated as:

$$\begin{array}{l}SO_2\text{ emission}\\\text{through industrial}\\\text{activities}\end{array}=\begin{array}{c}SO_2\text{ emission from}\\\text{fuel burning}\end{array}+\begin{array}{c}SO_2\text{ emission from}\\\text{production process}\end{array}$$

Industrial Soot Emission refers to the volume of soot in smoke emitted in the process of fuel burning in the premises of enterprises.

Industrial Dust Emission refers to volume of dust emitted by production process of enterprises and suspended in the air for a given period of time, including dust from refractory material of iron and steel works, dust from coke-screening systems and sintering machines of coke plants, dust from lime kilns and dust from cement production in building material enterprises, but excluding soot and dust emitted from power plants.

Industrial Solid Wastes Produced refers to total volume of solid, semi-solid and high concentration liquid residues produced by industrial enterprises from production process in a given period of time, including hazardous wastes, slag, coal ash, gangue, tailings, radioactive residues and other wastes, but excluding stones stripped or dug out in mining - gangue and acid or alkaline stones not included (a stone is acid or alkaline according to the pH value of the water being below 4 or above 10.5 when the stone is in, or soaked by water).

Industrial Solid Wastes Utilized refers to volume of solid wastes from which useful materials can be extracted or which can be converted into usable resources, energy or other materials by means of reclamation, processing, recycling and exchange (including utilizing in the year the stocks of industrial solid wastes of the previous year). Examples of such utilizations include fertilizers, building materials and road materials. The information shall be collected by the producing units of the wastes.

Rate of Utilization of Industrial Solid Wastes refers to the percentage of industrial solid wastes utilized over industrial solid wastes produced (including stocks of the previous years). It is calculated as:

$$\text{Rate of utilization of industrial solid wastes} = \frac{\text{volume of industrial solid wastes utilized}}{\text{industrial solid wastes produced + stock of previous years}} \times 100\%$$

Industrial Solid Wastes Disposed refers to the quantity of industrial solid wastes which are burnt or placed ultimately in the sites meeting the requirements for environmental protection and not salvaged or recycled (including disposition in the year of those wastes of previous years). The disposition includes landfill (Safe landfills should be conducted for hazardous wastes), incineration, containment spaces, deep underground disposal, backfill in mining pits and disposal at sea.

Industrial Solid Wastes Discharged refers to the volume of industrial solid wastes discharged by producing enterprises to disposal facilities or to other sites. The wastes exclude stones stripped or dug from mining (gangue and acid or alkaline waste stones not included).

The Above-good Air Quality (API) Days API, i.e. the air pollution index, is the abbreviation of Air Pollution Index. API is to simplify the several air pollutant concentrations routinely monitored into a single form of conceptual index value, and to classify and characterize air pollution and air quality, suitable for representing the short-term air quality status and trends of the city. The standard to which the calculation of API grade refers is (GB3095-1996), and the pollutants to be evaluated are only the three -- SO_2, NO_2 and PM_{10}.

The Above-good Air Quality (AQI) Days AQI is the dimensionless index of a quantitative description of the air quality status and is the abbreviation of Air Quality Index. The standard to which the calculation of AQI grade refers is the new ambient air quality standard (GB3095-2012), and the pollutants to be evaluated are only the six -- SO_2, NO_2, PM_{10}, $PM_{2.5}$, O_3 and CO.

二十一、城市比较

CHAPTER 21
CITIES COMPARE

21 城市比较 CITIES COMPARE

全国副省级城市

CITIES UNDER PROVINCIAL LEVELS

哈尔滨	长 春	沈 阳	大 连	青 岛	西 安	成 都	济 南
Haerbin	Changchun	Shenyang	Dalian	Qingdao	Xi'an	Chengdu	Jinan
南 京	武 汉	杭 州	宁 波	厦 门	广 州	深 圳	
Nanjing	Wuhan	Hangzhou	Ningbo	Xiamen	Guangzhou	Shenzhen	

全国首批沿海开放城市

FIRST BATCH OF OPEN COASTAL CITIES

大 连	秦皇岛	天 津	烟 台	青 岛	连云港	南 通
Dalian	Qinhuangdao	Tianjin	Yantai	Qingdao	Lianyungang	Nantong
上 海	宁 波	温 州	福 州	广 州	湛 江	北 海
Shanghai	Ningbo	Wenzhou	Fuzhou	Guangzhou	Zhanjiang	Beihai

全国首批历史文化名城

FIRST BATCH OF HISTORICAL AND CULTURAL CITIES

北 京	承 德	大 同	南 京	苏 州	扬 州
Beijing	Chengde	Datong	Nanjing	Suzhou	Yangzhou
杭 州	绍 兴	泉 州	景德镇	曲 阜	洛 阳
Hangzhou	Shaoxing	Quanzhou	Jingdezhen	Qufu	Luoyang
开 封	江 陵	长 沙	广 州	桂 林	成 都
Kaifeng	Jiangling	Changsha	Guangzhou	Guilin	Chengdu
遵 义	昆 明	大 理	拉 萨	西 安	延 安
Zunyi	Kunming	Dali	Lasa	Xi'an	Yanan

表21-1

全国部分大中城市主要经济指标 (2018年)

单位：亿元

城　市	City	地区生产总值 Gross Domestic Product	第一产业 Primary Industry	第二产业 Secondary Industry	第三产业 Tertiary Industry	社会消费品零售总额 Total Retail Sales of Consumer Goods	一般公共预算收入 General Public Finance Budget Revenue	进出口总额 Total Imports and Exports
苏　州	**Suzhou**	**18 597.47**	**213.99**	**8 933.28**	**9 450.20**	**5 746.90**	**2 119.99**	**23 375.60**
南　京	Nanjing	12 820.40	273.42	4 721.61	7 825.37	5 832.46	1 470.02	4 317.20
无　锡	Wuxi	11 438.62	125.07	5 464.01	5 849.54	3 672.70	1 012.28	6 161.83
常　州	Changzhou	7 050.27	156.25	3 263.29	3 630.73	2 613.19	560.33	2 266.40
上　海	Shanghai	32 679.87	104.37	9 732.54	22 842.96	12 668.69	7 108.15	34 009.93
杭　州	Hangzhou	13 509.15	305.51	4 571.93	8 631.71	5 715.33	1 825.06	5 245.28
宁　波	Ningbo	10 745.46	305.96	5 507.53	4 931.97	4 154.93	1 379.66	8 576.29
武　汉	Wuhan	14 847.29	362.00	6 377.75	8 107.54	6 843.90	1 528.70	2 146.00
重　庆	Chongqing	20 363.19	1 378.27	8 328.79	10 656.13		2 265.52	5 222.62
南　昌	Nanchang	5 274.67	190.68	2 660.92	2 423.07	2 131.63	461.75	787.55
成　都	Chengdu	15 342.77	522.59	6 516.19	8 303.99	6 801.80	1 424.20	4 983.20
长　沙	Changsha	11 003.41	318.73	4 660.19	6 024.49	4 765.04	879.71	1 283.34
合　肥	Hefei	7 822.90	277.60	3 612.30	3 933.10	2 976.74	712.49	2 030.61
昆　明	Kunming	5 206.90	222.16	2 038.02	2 946.71	2 787.41	595.63	131.20亿美元
嘉　兴	Jiaxing	4 871.98	115.03	2 624.49	2 132.46	1 938.59	518.55	2 821.20
湖　州	Huzhou	2 719.10	127.70	1 273.60	1 317.80	1 297.24	287.10	885.13
广　州	Guangzhou	22 859.35	223.44	6 234.07	16 401.84	9 256.19	1 632.30	9 810.15
深　圳	Shenzhen	24 221.98	22.09	9 961.95	14 237.94	6 168.87	3 538.41	29 983.74
青　岛	Qingdao	12 001.50	386.90	4 850.60	6 764.00	4 842.50	1 231.90	5 321.20
大　连	Dalian	7 668.48	442.70	3 241.58	3 984.20	3 880.05	703.98	4 701.41
北　京	Beijing	30 320.00	118.70	5 647.70	24 553.60	11 747.68	5 785.90	27 182.48
天　津	Tianjin	18 809.64	172.71	7 609.81	11 027.12		2 106.19	8 077.01
济　南	Jinan	7 856.56	272.42	2 829.31	4 754.83	4 404.50	752.80	825.00
沈　阳	Shenyang	6 292.40	260.10	2 376.60	3 655.70	4 051.20	720.60	984.30
厦　门	Xiamen	4 791.41	24.40	1 980.16	2 786.85	1 542.42	754.53	6 002.05
郑　州	Zhengzhou	10 143.32	147.05	4 450.74	5 545.53	4 268.09	1 152.05	4 105.00

MAJOR ECONOMIC INDICATORS OF MAIN LARGE AND MEDIUM-SIZED CITIES (2018)

(100 million yuan)

#出口总额 Total Exports	实际使用外资(亿美元) Amount of Foreign Capital Actually Used (USD 100 million)	全社会用电量(亿千瓦时) Electricity Consumption of the Whole Society (100 million kwh)	# 工 业 Industry	金融机构本外币存款余额 Deposits Balance of National Banking System	金融机构本外币贷款余额 Loans Balance of National Banking System	城镇居民人均可支配收入（元） Per Capita Disposable Income of Town Residents (yuan)	农村居民人均可支配收入(元) Per Capita Net Income of Rural Residents (yuan)	市区居民消费价格总指数(%) General Consumer Price Index(%)
13 656.91	**45.25**	**1 562.49**	**1 227.77**	**30 523.37**	**27 440.94**	**63 481**	**32 420**	**102.6**
2 500.68	38.53	606.40	331.27	34 524.86	29 065.66	59 308	25 263	102.4
3 743.68	37.15	732.81	551.49	16 056.79	12 102.76	56 989	30 787	102.3
1 652.94	24.22	489.72	373.05	10 090.05	7 564.83	54 000	28 014	102.2
13 666.85	173.00	1 566.66	780.21	121 112.33	73 272.35	68 034	30 375	101.6
3 417.11	68.27	796.96	446.09	39 810.50	36 598.30	61 172	33 193	102.3
5 550.65	43.20	775.30	571.70	19 150.00	19 935.90	60 134	33 633	102.2
1 272.70	109.27	580.34	279.67	26 331.62	28 270.77	47 359	22 652	101.9
3 395.28	32.50	1 114.47	653.67	36 887.34	32 247.75	34 889	13 781	102.0
451.67	34.89	230.00	116.85	10 733.08	12 124.64	40 844	17 866	102.3
2 746.90	76.30	637.41	289.68	37 826.00	32 637.00	42 128	22 135	101.4
823.15	57.80	363.69	148.87	18 633.60	18 360.89	50 792	29 714	102.0
1 203.46	32.30	344.83	172.03	15 677.27	14 196.54	41 484	20 389	102.0
37.63亿美元	8.50	337.44		13 787.49	16 667.97	42 988	14 895	101.7
2 017.33	31.40	522.06	415.56	8 298.46	6 863.38	57 437	34 279	102.3
770.98	12.71	274.80	203.50	4 589.40	3 886.20	54 393	31 767	102.2
5 607.58	66.11	936.90	435.16	54 788.09	40 749.32	59 982	26 020	102.4
16 274.69	82.03	917.23	490.77	72 250.36	52 539.79	57 543	–	102.8
3 172.20	86.90	432.00	238.00	16 121.30	16 098.00	50 817	20 820	102.1
1 889.60	26.78	369.30	232.80	13 999.10	12 006.20	43 550	18 103	103.0
4 878.54	167.40	1 142.40	307.30	157 092.20	70 483.70	67 990	–	102.5
3 207.16	48.50	861.44		30 983.17	34 084.90	42 976	23 065	102.0
519.30	178.20亿元	284.40	121.50	17 060.10	16 059.90	50 146	17 924	102.6
342.10	14.30	357.40	172.30	17 746.20	14 911.60	44 054	16 530	103.0
3 338.51	107.31亿元	269.59	135.65	10 995.00	10 554.05	54 401	18 842	101.8
2 577.14	42.11	560.30	297.50	22 710.55	22 055.67	39 042	21 652	102.4

表21-2

全省各设区市主要经济指标 (2018年)

城 市	City	土地面积 (平方公里) Area of Land (sq.km)	年末户籍人口 (万人) Year-end Household Population (10 000 persons)	年末常住人口 (万人) Year-end Resident Population (10 000 persons)	城镇人口比重(%) Proportion of Urban Population(%)	地区生产总值 (亿元) Gross Domestic Product (100 million yuan)	第一产业 Primary Industry
南京市	Nanjing City	6 587	696.94	843.62	82.5	12 820.40	273.42
无锡市	Wuxi City	4 627	497.21	657.45	76.3	11 438.62	125.07
徐州市	Xuzhou City	11 765	1 044.77	880.20	65.1	6 755.23	631.39
常州市	Changzhou City	4 372	382.20	472.86	72.5	7 050.27	156.25
苏州市	**Suzhou City**	**8 657**	**703.55**	**1 072.17**	**76.1**	**18 597.47**	**213.99**
南通市	Nantong City	10 549	762.52	731.00	67.1	8 427.00	397.77
连云港市	Lianyungang City	7 615	534.34	452.00	62.6	2 771.70	325.57
淮安市	Huaian City	10 030	561.33	492.50	62.4	3 601.25	358.70
盐城市	Yancheng City	16 931	824.73	720.00	64.0	5 487.08	573.40
扬州市	Yangzhou City	6 591	458.83	453.10	67.1	5 466.17	273.34
镇江市	Zhenjiang City	3 840	270.78	319.64	71.2	4 050.00	138.40
泰州市	Taizhou City	5 787	503.39	463.57	66.0	5 107.63	280.05
宿迁市	Suqian City	8 524	591.26	492.59	60.0	2 750.72	300.84

MAJOR ECONOMIC INDICATORS OF THE MUNICIPALITY OF JIANGSU PROVINCE (2018)

第二产业 Secondary Industry	第三产业 Tertiary Industry	按常住人口计算人均地区生产总值(元) Resident Population Per-capita GDP (yuan)	农林牧渔业总产值(亿元) Gross Output Value of Farming,Forestry,Animal Husbandry and Fishery (100 million yuan)	粮食产量(万吨) Total of Grain (10 000 tons)	油料产量(万吨) Total of Oil-bearing Crops (10 000 tons)	肉类产量(万吨) Total of Meat (10 000 tons)
4 721.61	7 825.37	152 886	489.47	106.92	3.34	4.86
5 464.01	5 849.54	174 270	226.19	56.80	0.48	2.00
2 812.02	3 311.82	76 915	1 211.96	484.48	12.32	69.90
3 263.29	3 630.73	149 277	293.80	78.15	1.57	8.28
8 933.28	**9 450.20**	**173 765**	**410.09**	**87.92**	**0.59**	**3.85**
3 947.88	4 081.35	115 320	761.23	336.90	20.89	45.61
1 207.39	1 238.74	61 332	636.65	364.03	8.35	22.85
1 508.11	1 734.44	73 204	662.58	482.26	5.57	24.05
2 436.45	2 477.23	75 987	1 183.89	704.31	13.10	73.80
2 623.24	2 569.59	120 944	514.02	287.36	3.88	16.07
1 976.60	1 935.00	126 906	245.94	107.30	3.25	6.80
2 434.01	2 393.57	109 988	484.36	287.11	8.73	23.88
1 279.54	1 170.34	55 906	559.37	401.02	3.96	27.99

表21-2 续表 1

城 市	City	水产品产量(万吨) Total of Aquatic Products(10 000 tons)	规模以上工业企业(亿元) Industrial Enterprises Above Designated Size (100 million yuan)			
			资产总计 Total Assets	主营业务收入 Major Business Revenue	主营业务成本 Major Business Cost	利润总额 Total Profits
南京市	Nanjing City	16.60	12 632.89	11 945.91	9 645.12	894.96
无锡市	Wuxi City	12.23	17 028.44	16 576.71	14 194.75	1 204.94
徐州市	Xuzhou City	16.87	6 216.03	5 030.28	4 095.55	292.71
常州市	Changzhou City	14.01	9 670.52	11 394.03	9 810.25	726.26
苏州市	**Suzhou City**	**19.56**	**32 223.44**	**34 108.40**	**29 295.28**	**2 094.05**
南通市	Nantong City	81.13	9 812.43	14 029.55	12 023.81	1 165.55
连云港市	Lianyungang City	72.85	3 481.03	2 493.70	1 814.33	230.47
淮安市	Huaian City	26.10	2 597.38	3 866.77	3 268.32	213.40
盐城市	Yancheng City	119.75	5 150.22	5 815.97	5 070.18	298.31
扬州市	Yangzhou City	39.61	4 898.00	6 803.15	5 896.95	424.88
镇江市	Zhenjiang City	9.57	5 019.13	4 162.10	3 570.02	233.36
泰州市	Taizhou City	38.92	5 948.08	6 979.70	5 636.39	455.51
宿迁市	Suqian City	26.16	2 470.17	2 188.65	1 743.46	271.83

Continued 1

房地产开发投资(亿元) Value of Investment in Real Estate Development(100 million yuan)	# 住 宅 Residential Buildings	全社会用电量(亿千瓦时) Electricity Consumption of the Whole Society (100 million kwh)	# 工 业 Industry	社会消费品零售总额(亿元) Total Retail Sales of Consumer Goods (100 million yuan)	进出口总额(亿美元) Total Imports and Exports (USD 100 million)	# 出 口 Exports	实际使用外资(亿美元) Foreign Capital Actually Utilized (USD 100 million)
2 354.17	1 574.64	606.40	331.27	5 832.46	654.91	378.79	38.53
1 314.86	1 004.57	732.81	551.49	3 672.70	934.44	567.81	36.91
716.43	585.31	352.05	219.91	3 102.00	117.44	97.08	18.98
595.89	460.05	489.72	373.05	2 613.19	343.86	250.72	24.22
2 557.91	**2 111.60**	**1 562.49**	**1 227.77**	**5 746.90**	**3 541.14**	**2 068.31**	**45.25**
759.52	540.05	433.31	295.86	3 088.77	385.91	254.53	25.81
341.52	283.64	178.51	106.52	1 121.31	95.47	41.59	6.03
312.02	226.69	186.59	115.97	1 239.66	50.10	33.67	11.82
454.94	360.56	320.93	212.54	1 778.74	95.49	60.31	9.13
620.98	455.87	248.99	165.64	1 557.03	119.93	85.42	12.20
355.99	281.22	255.24	183.42	1 360.92	118.39	79.80	8.68
345.07	275.37	286.14	205.74	1 282.87	147.30	95.31	15.07
253.04	206.61	192.05	123.84	833.82	36.01	27.17	3.77

表21-2 续表 2

城 市	City	一般公共预算收入(亿元) General Public Budget Revenue (100 million yuan)	一般公共预算支出(亿元) General Public Budget Expenditure (100 million yuan)	金融机构人民币存款余额(亿元) RMB Deposits Balance of National Banking System (100 million yuan)	# 住户存款 Deposits of Households	金融机构人民币贷款余额(亿元) RMB Loans Balance of National Banking System (100 million yuan)
南京市	Nanjing City	1 470.02	1 532.72	33 740.63	6 914.84	28 402.34
无锡市	Wuxi City	1 012.28	1 055.94	15 568.68	5 511.59	11 971.55
徐州市	Xuzhou City	526.21	880.86	7 107.39	3 604.84	4 912.47
常州市	Changzhou City	560.33	594.82	9 798.55	3 841.90	7 533.42
苏州市	**Suzhou City**	**2 119.99**	**1 952.71**	**28 560.45**	**9 168.45**	**26 546.23**
南通市	Nantong City	606.19	877.18	12 001.61	6 287.26	8 811.69
连云港市	Lianyungang City	234.31	419.57	3 218.79	1 420.02	2 921.36
淮安市	Huaian City	247.27	486.77	3 638.01	1 605.25	3 303.44
盐城市	Yancheng City	381.00	840.08	6 177.28	3 171.33	4 887.74
扬州市	Yangzhou City	340.03	563.39	5 997.55	2 860.65	4 630.51
镇江市	Zhenjiang City	301.50	408.41	5 042.97	2 161.07	4 450.60
泰州市	Taizhou City	357.15	532.36	6 119.38	2 876.63	4 784.04
宿迁市	Suqian City	206.20	433.54	2 746.69	1 344.78	2 563.61

Continued 2

全体常住居民人均可支配收入(元) Per Capita Disposable Income of the Resident Population (yuan)	全体常住居民人均消费支出(元) Per Capita Living Expenditure for Consumption of the Resident Population (yuan)	城镇常住居民人均可支配收入(元) Per Capita Disposable Income of Town Residents (yuan)	城镇常住居民人均消费支出(元) Per Capita Living Expenditure for Consumption of Town Residents (yuan)	农村常住居民人均可支配收入(元) Per Capita Net Income of Rural (yuan)	农村常住居民人均消费支出(元) Per Capital Living Expenditure of Rural (yuan)	市区居民消费价格总指数(%) General Consumer Price Index(%)
52 916	30 706	59 308	33 537	25 263	18 457	102.0
50 373	31 593	56 989	35 016	30 787	21 460	102.3
27 385	16 818	33 586	19 463	18 206	12 902	102.3
45 933	26 863	54 000	30 351	28 014	19 116	102.2
55 476	**33 327**	**63 481**	**37 403**	**32 420**	**21 587**	**102.6**
37 071	23 379	46 321	28 259	22 369	15 624	102.3
25 864	16 649	32 749	20 445	16 607	11 545	102.3
27 696	15 634	35 828	19 015	17 058	11 210	102.1
29 488	17 580	35 896	19 731	20 357	14 515	101.9
34 076	20 683	41 999	23 718	21 457	15 848	102.2
40 883	24 359	48 903	27 278	24 687	18 463	102.0
34 642	21 560	43 452	25 488	21 219	15 576	102.0
22 918	14 350	28 281	17 255	16 639	10 948	102.1

表21-3

全省分县(市)主要经济指标(2018年)

市县名称	City and County	年末户籍人口(万人) Year-end Household Population (10 000 persons)	地区生产总值(亿元) Gross Domestic Product (100 million yuan)	第一产业 Primary Industry	第二产业 Secondary Industry	第三产业 Tertiary Industry
无锡市	**Wuxi**					
江阴市	Jiangyin City	125.95	3 806.18	36.98	2 071.91	1 697.29
宜兴市	Yixing City	108.13	1 713.28	50.61	890.31	772.36
徐州市	**Xuzhou**					
丰　县	Feng County	121.48	460.14	86.85	182.69	190.60
沛　县	Pei County	129.81	762.62	104.11	332.87	325.64
睢宁县	Suining County	144.10	577.30	96.40	235.56	245.34
新沂市	Xinyi City	113.21	653.32	73.82	261.91	317.59
邳州市	Pizhou City	194.36	920.66	132.32	364.44	423.90
常州市	**Changzhou**					
溧阳市	Liyang City	79.04	935.51	51.06	453.97	430.48
苏州市	**Suzhou**					
常熟市	Changshu City	106.80	2 400.23	39.90	1 230.01	1 130.32
张家港市	Zhangjiagang City	92.94	2 720.18	30.63	1 423.68	1 265.87
昆山市	Kunshan City	90.32	3 832.06	31.62	2 074.53	1 725.91
太仓市	Taicang City	49.40	1 330.72	34.98	675.47	620.27
南通市	**Nantong**					
如东县	Rudong County	102.08	952.29	75.22	439.13	437.94
启东市	Qidong City	111.04	1 063.33	72.04	505.34	485.95
如皋市	Rugao City	141.97	1 120.48	69.39	534.36	516.73
海门市	Haimen City	99.59	1 249.00	58.80	609.51	580.69
海安市	Haian City	92.73	993.00	61.41	467.40	464.19
连云港市	**LianyunGang**					
东海县	Donghai County	124.62	494.42	73.46	207.78	213.18
灌云县	Guanyun County	103.74	375.00	69.15	159.06	146.79
灌南县	Guannan County	81.92	352.99	57.24	162.12	133.63

MAIN ECONOMIC INDICATORS OF COUNTRIES (CITIES) OF THE PROVINCE (2018)

粮食产量 (万吨) Total of Grain (10 000 tons)	一般公共 预算收入(亿元) General Public Budget Revenue (100 million yuan)	社会消费品零售 总额(亿元) Total Retail Sales of Consumer Goods (100 million yuan)	工业用电量 (亿千瓦时) Electricity Consumption of Industry (100 million kwh)	出口总额 (亿美元) Total Exports (USD 100 million)	实际使用外资 (亿美元) Foreign Capital Actually Utilized (USD 100 million)	农村常住居民人均 可支配收入(元) Per Capita Net Income of Rural (yuan)
13.06	254.04	949.29	240.84	142.64	9.51	33 136
37.71	120.01	667.27	78.00	34.33	4.63	27 860
55.18	28.10	180.78	13.38	3.73	0.80	16 725
63.12	56.21	294.46	27.97	6.52	1.94	18 799
93.74	41.74	215.32	9.79	6.78	1.37	16 546
70.44	52.38	209.48	23.78	11.09	2.72	17 325
80.69	58.78	303.56	14.42	14.41	2.34	18 207
45.57	66.29	356.82	79.13	9.98	3.01	25 908
22.96	211.06	824.92	157.24	172.98	4.87	32 820
22.60	233.43	605.87	284.66	175.18	3.95	32 664
9.25	387.89	1 021.77	194.47	580.52	7.27	32 916
13.19	155.06	338.44	86.84	67.31	4.40	32 458
97.92	57.55	377.66	43.27	20.63	3.01	20 387
32.10	72.31	376.94	22.61	23.09	3.08	23 687
67.26	70.01	404.27	40.32	30.26	4.57	20 166
24.62	71.01	399.36	29.44	26.78	3.26	24 654
61.85	61.71	324.93	39.40	15.31	3.38	21 473
116.32	23.00	211.88	14.33	3.89	0.99	17 291
86.87	22.33	143.49	5.00	1.84	0.21	15 493
63.59	22.50	112.08	20.07	1.48	0.83	14 826

表21-3 续表

市县名称	City and County	年末户籍人口 (万人) Year-end Household Population (10 000 persons)	地区生产总值 (亿元) Gross Domestic Product (100 million yuan)	第一产业 Primary Industry	第二产业 Secondary Industry	第三产业 Tertiary Industry
淮安市	**Huaian**					
涟水县	Lianshui County	113.28	476.27	62.39	183.93	229.95
盱眙县	Xuyi County	79.82	441.34	59.39	173.78	208.17
金湖县	Jinhu County	34.90	296.29	37.04	111.51	147.74
盐城市	**Yancheng**					
响水县	Xiangshui County	62.36	349.86	42.82	173.91	133.13
滨海县	Binhai County	122.57	475.42	63.45	193.75	218.22
阜宁县	Funing County	112.28	482.83	58.88	210.42	213.53
射阳县	Sheyang County	95.18	536.61	87.67	196.71	252.23
建湖县	Jianhu County	78.42	561.68	50.17	238.93	272.58
东台市	Dongtai City	109.81	878.68	99.03	356.12	423.53
扬州市	**Yangzhou**					
宝应县	Baoying County	88.76	630.46	71.79	282.24	276.43
仪征市	Yizheng City	56.03	673.94	23.84	347.49	302.61
高邮市	Gaoyou City	80.82	669.02	77.71	291.33	299.98
镇江市	**Zhenjiang**					
丹阳市	Danyang City	80.63	1 250.25	48.56	631.07	570.62
扬中市	Yangzhong City	28.25	542.00	18.36	273.24	250.40
句容市	Jurong City	58.90	571.10	46.41	264.19	260.50
泰州市	**Taizhou**					
兴化市	Xinghua City	155.67	905.13	124.85	339.92	440.36
靖江市	Jingjiang City	65.88	1 002.05	24.44	492.51	485.10
泰兴市	Taixing City	117.88	1 050.34	60.42	490.63	499.29
宿迁市	**Suqian**					
沭阳县	Shuyang County	198.28	825.45	97.35	373.98	354.11
泗阳县	Siyang County	106.79	479.22	61.22	236.25	181.75
泗洪县	Sihong County	109.58	478.95	69.99	203.20	205.76

Continued

粮食产量 (万吨) Total of Grain (10 000 tons)	一般公共预算收入(亿元) General Public Budget Revenue (100 million yuan)	社会消费品零售总额(亿元) Total Retail Sales of Consumer Goods (100 million yuan)	工业用电量 (亿千瓦时) Electricity Consumption of Industry (100 million kwh)	出口总额 (亿美元) Total Exports (USD 100 million)	实际使用外资 (亿美元) Foreign Capital Actually Utilized (USD 100 million)	农村常住居民人均可支配收入(元) Per Capita Net Income of Rural (yuan)
93.25	21.50	143.48	9.26	2.97	1.30	15 939
103.82	18.01	134.41	10.23	1.40	1.24	17 206
56.48	22.03	104.44	8.37	5.17	1.35	18 718
60.17	25.35	77.69	38.84	6.01	0.58	17 020
96.46	28.94	130.93	18.60	4.70	0.55	17 746
94.26	27.70	134.70	15.82	3.13	0.35	18 282
112.61	26.36	190.02	14.47	2.73	0.61	19 653
71.50	28.32	157.14	14.59	3.69	0.38	20 184
100.05	56.70	290.10	28.77	8.68	0.90	23 317
86.88	27.59	181.72	13.63	8.83	0.70	20 119
27.49	50.92	129.57	37.57	6.56	1.40	20 688
84.88	36.80	191.15	29.11	4.48	0.93	20 140
46.13	61.40	358.74	65.88	27.83	1.62	25 633
7.86	32.77	166.52	12.85	6.23	1.03	28 199
29.30	50.00	167.54	16.99	6.00	1.10	22 313
126.79	39.41	203.63	51.65	7.04	1.12	20 066
29.05	56.22	204.07	30.28	20.11	0.90	23 220
63.17	74.51	237.05	52.07	31.35	3.69	21 268
127.12	47.00	233.54	35.19	7.04	0.92	16 877
62.69	25.46	119.00	17.02	4.69	0.56	16 648
113.53	26.03	124.67	12.20	1.71	0.56	16 274

中国统计出版社有限公司最新图书简目

(仅供参考,以实际出版为准)

统计资料

中国统计年鉴　中国统计摘要　中国第三产业统计年鉴
中国第三次全国农业普查综合资料　国际统计年鉴　金砖国家联合统计手册
中国-东盟国家统计手册　中国农村统计年鉴　中国县域统计年鉴
中国农产品价格调查年鉴　中国城市统计年鉴　中国价格统计年鉴
中国贸易外经统计年鉴　中国零售和餐饮连锁企业统计年鉴　中国商品交易市场统计年鉴
大中型批发零售和住宿餐饮企业统计年鉴　中国住户调查年鉴　中国工业统计年鉴
中国环境统计年鉴　中国能源统计年鉴　中国建筑业统计年鉴
中国房地产统计年鉴　中国固定资产投资统计年鉴　中国对外直接投资统计公报
中国人口和就业统计年鉴　中国劳动统计年鉴　中国社会统计年鉴
中国科技统计年鉴　中国高技术产业统计年鉴　全国企业创新调查年鉴
中国文化及相关产业统计年鉴　2018年时间利用调查资料　中国妇女儿童状况统计资料
中国基本单位统计年鉴　中国教育统计年鉴　中国教育经费统计年鉴
中国民族统计年鉴　中国残疾人事业统计年鉴　长江经济带发展统计年鉴

省级综合统计年鉴系列

北京 天津 河北 山西 内蒙古 辽宁 吉林 黑龙江 上海 江苏 浙江 安徽 福建 江西 山东 河南 湖北 湖南 广东 广西 海南 重庆 四川 贵州 云南 西藏 陕西 甘肃 青海 宁夏 新疆 新疆生产建设兵团

市(县)级综合统计年鉴系列

滨海新区 石家庄 唐山 邯郸 保定 沧州 邢台 廊坊 承德 衡水 秦皇岛 张家口 太原 大同 阳泉 长治 晋城 朔州 晋中 运城 忻州 临汾 吕梁 呼和浩特 鄂尔多斯 包头 沈阳 大连 长春 延吉 四平 白山 通化 哈尔滨 齐齐哈尔 黑龙江垦区 上海浦东新区 南京 无锡 徐州 常州 苏州 南通 连云港 淮安 盐城 扬州 镇江 泰州 宿迁 江阴 丹阳 海门 张家港 杭州 宁波 温州 嘉兴 湖州 绍兴 金华 衢州 舟山 台州 丽水 合肥 安庆 福州 厦门 宁德 漳州 龙岩 莆田 泉州 三明 南平 南昌 九江 上饶 新余 抚州 赣州 景德镇 济南 青岛 潍坊 枣庄 潍坊 聊城 郑州 洛阳 平顶山 三门峡 南阳 商丘 信阳 济源 汝州 武汉 十堰 荆州 宜昌 荆门 咸宁 黄冈 长沙 鹰潭 广州 深圳 惠州 东莞 汕尾 湛江 肇庆 南宁 柳州 桂林 贵港 梧州 来宾 河池 防城港 海口 三亚 儋州 成都 内江 贵阳 黔南 毕节 昆明 文山 德宏 西安 延安 安康 铜川 汉中 商洛 银川 兰州 庆阳 乌鲁木齐 昌吉 阿勒泰 兵团一师、二师、三师、四师、六师、七师、八师、十师、十三师、十四师

调查年鉴系列

天津 内蒙古 上海 河南 湖北 湖南 广东 广西 重庆 四川 云南 甘肃 宁夏 南宁 贵港 昆明

统计方法应用/实用手册

Python数据分析基础（第二版）　医用多元统计分析（第三版）　中华生物统计用表
中国国民经济核算体系（2016）基础知识　国民经济核算初级教程　医学统计学手册
全国统计专业技术资格考试系列考试用书：统计业务知识（第四版修订版）　统计业务知识学习指导与习题
全国统计专业技术资格考试系列考试用书：统计相关知识（第四版）　统计相关知识学习指导与习题

统计通俗读物/统计科普图书

领导干部统计知识问答　《防范和惩治统计造假、弄虚作假督察工作规定》辅导读本
统计新媒体运营指南　统计公文知识问答　理解国民账户　中国古代统计史简编

重点图书

新中国70年　第三次全国农业普查农作物面积遥感测量图集　中国第四次经济普查年鉴
新编英汉汉英统计大词典　中国国民经济核算体系2016　国民经济行业分类注释
挑大学选专业2019—考研择校指南　挑大学选专业2019—高考志愿填报指南　中华医学统计百科全书